Baseball's Business: The Winter Meetings
Volume 2
1958-2016

Edited by Steve Weingarden and Bill Nowlin

Associate editors Marshall Adesman and Len Levin

Society for American Baseball Research, Inc.
Phoenix, AZ

Baseball's Business: The Winter Meetings
Volume 2 - 1958-2016
Edited by Steve Weingarden and Bill Nowlin
Associate Editors: Marshall Adesman and Len Levin

Copyright © 2017 Society for American Baseball Research, Inc.
All rights reserved. Reproduction in whole or in part without permission is prohibited.

ISBN 978-1-943816-63-7
(Ebook ISBN 978-1-943816-62-0)

Cover and book design: Gilly Rosenthol

Cover artwork: Courtesy of Minor League Baseball

Society for American Baseball Research
Cronkite School at ASU
555 N. Central Ave. #416
Phoenix, AZ 85004
Phone: (602) 496-1460
Web: www.sabr.org
Facebook: Society for American Baseball Research
Twitter: @SABR

Baseball's Business: The Winter Meetings

Volume 2 - 1958–2016

With a special section on Negro Leagues business meetings

	Introduction by Steve Weingarden	1
1958	THE LAST WORD IN UTTER FUTILITY — Mike Lynch	3
1959	WINDS OF CHANGE — David M. Kritzler and Alan P. Henry	9
1960	THE MISSOURI COMPROMISE — David M. Kritzler and Alan P. Henry	17
1961	THE METS, THE COLT .45s, AND DEBATING THE RETURN OF THE SPITBALL — Christopher Matthews	27
1962	ADDITION BY SUBTRACTION — Chris Jones	31
1963	NO LITTLE LEAGUE BATS ALLOWED — Chris Jones	36
1964	COMMISSIONER'S POWERS, FREE-AGENT DRAFT, & ALL-STAR VOTING — Donald G. Frank	41
1965	EXIT THE SPORTSWRITER AND ENTER THE GENERAL — Andy Bokser	45
1966	TOMORROW NEVER KNOWS — Jason Myers	51
1967	EXPANSION, INEVITABLY — Mark Armour	58
1968	DOWN GOES ECKERT — Mark Armour	63
1969	REORGANIZATION TALK — Mark Armour	68
1970	KUHN THWARTED — Mark Armour	73
1971	THE SWAP MEET — Mark Armour	78
1972	CALM BETWEEN STORMS — Mark Armour	82
1973	MANAGERIAL CONFUSION, RON SANTO REACTS, & THE PADRES' DILEMMA — Donald G. Frank	86
1974	DÉTENTE BEORE THE STORM — Clayton Trutor	92
1975	THE THREAT OF FREE AGENCY AND THE RETURN OF THE MASTER SHOWMAN — Gregory H. Wolf	96
1976	CHANGING DEMOGRAPHICS AND BROADCAST CHALLENGES — Gregory H. Wolf	105
1977	SO MUCH PROMISE, BUT WAIT TILL NEXT YEAR — Steve Cardullo	115
1978	FIGURING OUT FREE AGENCY — Dan Levitt	122

1979	FIRST CHANCE AT A NEW POST-FREE-AGENCY CBA — Dan Levitt	135
1980	FUTURE HALL OF FAMERS IN THE SPOTLIGHT — Kent Henderson and Paul Hensler	141
1981	THE POST-STRIKE INTRIGUE OF KUHN, SMITH, AND TEMPLETON — Paul Hensler	148
1982	DISPIRITED AND ARGUMENTATIVE — Dan Levitt	155
1983	THE END OF THE BOWIE KUHN ERA — Michael Huber	161
1984	SUPERSTATIONARY — Ross E. Davies	166
1985	FREE-AGENT FREEZEOUT: COLLUSION I — Jeff Barto	175
1986	A RIGGED MARKET: COLLUSION II — Jeff Barto	183
1987	CHANGING TIMES: COLLUSION III — Bob Whelan	191
1988	RANGERS MAKE HUGE SPLASH — Steve West	195
1989	MINOR MOVES MAKE MAJOR IMPACTS — Mark S. Sternman	202
1990	THEY ALMOST DIDN'T HAPPEN — John Burbridge	209
1991	VINCENT EXPRESSES CONCERN FOR SMALL MARKET CLUBS; MINORS CHOOSE A NEW LEADER — Tim Rask	214
1992	THE CIRCUS COMES TO TOWN — Rodger A. Payne	219
1993	A COOLING HOT STOVE AND BOILING TEMPERS — Abigail Miskowiec	224
1994	YEAR-ROUND LABOR NEGOTIATONS RESOLVE STRIKE — Abigail Miskowiec	233
1995	INTERLEAGUE PLAY: INNOVATION OR ABOMINATION? — Paul D. Brown	240
1996	THE YEAR THAT BROUGHT LABOR PEACE — Chip Greene	243
1997	MINOR-LEAGUE CHANGES, MAJOR-LEAGUE IMPACT — Jessica Frank	249
1998	TEMPERS FLARE, CONTRACTS EXPLODE — Jessica Frank	264
1999	ALL ABOUT JUNIOR — Steve West	278
2000	SHOW ME THE MONEY — Steve West	285
2001	ALL QUIET ON THE CHARLES — Clayton Trutor	292
2002	RETURN TO NASHVILLE — Jerry Swenson	295
2003	BACK IN THE BAYOU — Jerry Swenson	301
2004	IT'S ALL A GAMBLE — Hawkins DuBois	306
2005	A LOT OF ACTION IN DALLAS — Robert K. Whelan	315
2006	A BARRY ACTIVE MEETING — Jason C. Long	321

Year	Title	Page
2007	THE PROMISE AND CURSE OF TECHNOLOGY — Paul D. Brown	328
2008	CLOUDS OVER THE GAME — John Bauer	334
2009	CHANGES HERE, CHANGES THERE, CHANGES EVERYWHERE: A BLOCKBUSTER, AN OOPS, A SUCCESSION, AND MAGIC TRICKS BY OWNERS — Steve Weingarden	342
2010	BASEBALL'S MOVERS AND SHAKERS CONVENE IN THE SUNSHINE STATE — Andy Bokser	347
2011	BREAKING THE BUDGET IN THE OFFSEASON — Chad Hagan	354
2012	LAYING GROUNDWORK — Darren Munk	358
2013	IT ALL HAPPENED THE WEEK BEFORE — Luca Rossi	361
2014	A NEW DAWN RISING — Tom Cuggino	366
2015	THE MUSIC CITY PLAYS GRACIOUS HOST TO BASEBALL'S WINTER MEETINGS FOR THE SEVENTH TIME — Wayne G. McDonnell, Jr.	373
2016	HAS A NEW DIAMOND AGE BEGUN FOR BASEBALL? — Charles H. Martin	381

SPECIAL SECTION ON THE NEGRO LEAGUES BUSINESS MEETINGS

THE BUSINESS MEETINGS OF NEGRO LEAGUE BASEBALL — 1933-1962 — Duke Goldman..........390

CONTRIBUTORS..........459

INTRODUCTION

IT'S BEEN ABOUT A YEAR SINCE WE published Volume 1, *Baseball's Business: The Winter Meetings*. I gave copies of Volume 1 to friends who are interested in baseball. Since giving out copies of the book, I have been surprised by how many text messages that I've received in return, with one friend or another commenting that he or she was reading a portion of the book and the fascination with what they learned. Each text amazes me, considering that none of these friends, to my knowledge, are devoted historians. Really, that's what it's about … knowledge. In Volume 1, we seemingly tapped into a topic that rarely enters the mind of most baseball fans, and we researched that topic in a way that created an appealing story. Plenty of well-described characters. Plenty of plot twists. Somehow, we stumbled upon a part of history rife with previously-untold suspense, anticipation, uncertainty, and heightened anxiety. While I wish I could say this accomplishment was due to our careful planning, instead I can only say that, hopefully, Volume 2 continues to deliver delight to readers.

I know that Volume 2 elicited much more emotional torment from me, possibly because the years represented are mostly within my own lifetime, and I remember many of these stories from when the events originally occurred. My visceral reactions could be intense at times. Reading chapter after chapter about de facto commissioners, owners, executives, and general managers saying that they couldn't attend the meetings, and deflecting the blame for that decision on loathsome player agents or on the untenable labor agreements that oppressed the game, or any other force-majeure. I often had to take a break, because I was worn down from the excuses, and wanted the return of the winter meetings as a landmark event, so common in Volume 1.

I'm pretty sure I suffered periods of baseball anhedonia, as well as misery. For example, I'm trying to forgive, but it's hard when there wasn't just Collusion I … but also Collusion II … and Collusion III … and denial that any collusion ever transpired.

I'm decidedly-impressed with the authors who wrote chapters that followed the 1994 strike. I could argue that the winter meetings, as we understood their essence, changed with the strike (as well as with changes in media technology). Coverage was different. Researching post-strike years required different approaches than researching previous chapters.

I will tell you there were some inset stories that I left alone. As mentions of these events came up during a chapter, I started towards pursuit of expanding on these important anecdotes, but soon realized the complexities were too much to give justice to the context within the framework of this book. It's astounding to me that after nearly 1,000 pages, vast amounts remain untold from the business side. We've only scratched the surface of the winter meetings.

Even with a survey level approach to the book, I think we covered nearly all the seven deadly sins. Volume 2 has envy, gluttony, greed, pride, sloth, and wrath. I don't think we get into the specifics of lust in Volume 2, so that's our missed sin. Maybe we'll get that one in Volume 3!

Actually, a Volume 3, indeed, is in the works. I'm looking forward to reading that book, as it delivers a prequel to Volume 1. Coverage in the book I'm referring to as Volume 3 covers the business meetings (not always winter) that took place in the 19th century, allowing SABR to extend this important story for you. In composing Volumes 1 and 2, there have been many times where I've wished that I had information regarding what came before a particular year we covered. Without that critical information about the past, we assume more risk when we define the identity of baseball. For that reason—as well as the confusing concept when discussing history that the past helps us understand the present, which is really the past (e.g., events of 1876 help us understand the machinations of 1901, when we study 1901 in the year 2000, in order to better understand our current context)—I'm ready to read Volume 3. Yes, an analogy here is someone reading an abundance of meeting minutes, and then becoming highly-excited over finding more meeting minutes to read. I realize how silly this sounds when I say it out loud. That's why I'm writing it on this page, instead. I'm highly-excited in anticipation of Volume 3.

It's remarkable to me that we've covered the number of years that we have, and that an entire separate volume is in process. Even then, there is more to cover around baseball meetings. As part of that coverage, we've been fortunate enough, in Volume 1 to include Jim Overmyer's article on the Eastern Colored League Winter Meetings, and in this volume, to include Duke Goldman's essential work, *The Business Meetings of Negro League Baseball: 1933-1962*. If I had to guess, I would say that even Duke was surprised by the amount of research he unearthed on the topic. That's part of the fun of research. One discovery leads to another, and missing elements of the story begin to weave together in a more meaningful way than previously was possible. New details allow for at least the opportunity to correct old errors. Deserving characters begin to receive attention not provided to them in the past. Stories from one universe on a topic connect better to stories from a different universe on the topic. It's sense-making; in this case related to baseball.

As a reminder to form, each chapter is designed to begin with a high-level overview of that year's winter meetings. More detail regarding the plans and decisions of the minor leagues and the major leagues follows. Finally, player transactions are recounted. The aforementioned three building blocks are contained within each chapter. However, an individual chapter also reflects the methods each author applied in order to tell the needed story in the manner most appropriate to the year and to his or her own writing style. As available and appropriate, sidebars are also included with chapters.

As we reach the milestone of publishing Volume 2, a thank you goes out to each author who completed or attempted the daunting task of writing about a set of meetings within a particular year. This was an unusual assignment, compared to writing about a specific individual. I believe it also was a worthwhile and rewarding endeavor. I know I've observed the growth of several of our writers, whether it was through technique realizations from draft to draft, or through first publication opportunity and associated recognition. It's been a pleasure for me. A special callout is proper for my co-editor and associate editors. We were sticklers when it came to providing supporting evidence, and we were gatekeepers on ensuring that content was sensible, consistent, and hopefully well-written. Considering the amount of writing contained within both volumes, I'm sure, we weren't perfect, but I know how much effort my colleagues contributed. Without Bill Nowlin, Marshall Adesman, and Len Levin there would not be a Volume 1 or Volume 2.

Once again, our team has exhausted our efforts to pull this book together for you. Our team is at your service through the following pages and stories. We are appreciative of your interest in sharing in the allure of baseball history from the business side.

Enjoy,
Steve Weingarden
October 2017

— 1958 —
THE LAST WORD IN UTTER FUTILITY

By Mike Lynch

ORGANIZED BASEBALL'S 1958 WINTER Meetings were held in Washington from December 1 to 4, with the major leagues headquartered at the Statler Hilton Hotel and the minors at the Mayflower Hotel, both within walking distance of the White House. As usual, there were many items on the table to be discussed and voted on, including two major issues that would impact major-league baseball in the near future.

The players fired a loud salvo at the owners and demanded that their salaries to be calculated based on 20 percent of gross revenue, a stipulation that had Jesse Outlar, sports editor of the *Atlanta Constitution*, claiming that baseball "has declared war against itself."[1] Some magnates laughed it off, including one unnamed owner who expressed his facetious desire to see the 20 percent deal adopted.

"We'll just give them meal money during the season; no salary at all," he gloated. "Then, at the end of the year, just toss the 20 percent take into a room. I want to be there to see those players divide the money. That would be the greatest fight in history."[2] Most, however, were resentful and could see the writing on the wall, that the players were "moving closer and closer to a union."[3]

One owner, Tom Yawkey of the Boston Red Sox, who was also vice president of the American League, earned loud applause from his peers when he denounced the ultimatum. The players had initially requested 25 percent of TV revenue before shifting gears and demanding 20 percent of all gross revenue. Yawkey was apoplectic and threatened to walk away from baseball after 25 years at Boston's helm, citing the fact that only once or twice since he purchased the Red Sox in 1933 had he cut a player's salary.[4]

"I've put a lot of money into this game," Yawkey declared. "I did it voluntarily. I never asked the players to share my losses.... Over the years, more ballplayers have been overpaid than underpaid."[5] The players cited large bonuses given to untested kids as their reasoning for demanding a larger piece of the pie. "If there is so much money around," they reasoned, "why can't we get more of it?"[6]

But dissension wasn't present only at the major-league level. The International League's players threatened to strike if the Triple-A circuit didn't establish a pension for them. At a cost of $293,000 a year, $256,000 (87 percent) of which would come from the league while the players would contribute the remaining $37,000 (13 percent), league President Frank Shaughnessy told the players that the league "could not see its way clear to meet the tremendous financial obstacles that formed roadblocks to a pension system."[7]

The other major issue on the table was major-league expansion, led by representatives from Houston and New York. With more than 9 million residents, Texas was the largest state without a major-league baseball team, and Houston was the largest city. George Kirksey, executive secretary of the Houston Sports Association, was hoping the group could purchase an existing team and made a $5 million offer for the Cleveland Indians, the highest price ever proffered for a team at the time.[8]

The offer was rejected and Houston filed applications with both the National and American Leagues in hopes that one of them would expand. New York, still reeling from the loss of the Dodgers and Giants (who moved to Los Angeles and San Francisco, respectively, after the 1957 season), was also itching to get back into the National League. William Shea, a lawyer and native New Yorker, tried to persuade the Pittsburgh

Pirates, Philadelphia Phillies, and Cincinnati Reds to relocate to New York but was rebuffed by all three.

When he was told by National League President Warren Giles that no team would move to New York in the immediate future, Shea, along with legendary baseball executive Branch Rickey and New York Mayor Robert Wagner, hatched a plan to form a third major league—the Continental League—to begin play in 1961.[9]

St. Louis Cardinals president August A. Busch Jr. was in favor of a 10-team National League and offered to lease or sell Houston's Busch Stadium, home of the Houston Buffaloes of the Double-A Texas League, to the Houston Sports Association if it was awarded a major-league team. Busch had put the Buffaloes up for sale in November and subsequently sold the franchise to former Cardinals All-Star shortstop Marty Marion, but retained ownership of the stadium.[10]

About Houston's attempt to achieve major-league status, Busch said he'd "offer the highest degree of cooperation," and would do "everything possible to help" as long as it was best for the city and Organized Baseball.[11] Busch Stadium seated only 11,500 spectators but plans to expand its capacity to 23,000 were already in place and it was expected to be ready for the 1959 season. The park's renovation was to include new restrooms and concession booths, additional parking, and new lights, if necessary.

Of course, Busch Stadium was to be a temporary solution until a new venue could be built, and Houston was out in front of that problem, having garnered the votes needed by Harris County voters to secure a $20 million bond for the construction of a stadium.[12] The Harris County Board of Park Commissioners was studying "population growth, traffic flow, accessibility from all directions, drainage and acreage for a parking lot capable of holding 20,000 cars," and had 13 different locations in mind.[13]

The stadium issue in New York, on the other hand, was one that had Dodgers vice president Buzzie Bavasi accusing Shea and Wagner of "putting the cart before the horse." Bavasi was all for putting an NL team in Gotham, but opposed the idea of a new team sharing Yankee Stadium with the Yankees. "I shudder at the thought of trying to buck the Yankees in their own park with a new club that has no tradition or fan following," Bavasi said.[14]

Many were in favor of putting an NL team in New York, including Yankees co-owners Del Webb and Dan Topping, and general manager George Weiss, but they thought Shea and Wagner were going about it the wrong way. Weiss called the thought of an outlaw league "so silly it doesn't call for any consideration whatsoever," and Webb was even more critical, stating, "The scheme outlined … is the most ridiculous thing of its kind within my experience as a baseball man."[15]

Commissioner Ford Frick expressed a desire to see two leagues of 12 split into East and West divisions, but was miffed that Shea and Wagner failed to notify him of their plans and wondered how they'd pull off their impossible plot. Still, the thought of expansion was intriguing for some, including Cubs owner Philip K. Wrigley and Milwaukee Braves president Joe Cairnes, and Bavasi thought it might happen as early as 1960.[16]

Longtime AL President Will Harridge, who'd served in that capacity for 27 years and had been working for the AL since 1911, announced his resignation in a special meeting on December 3, citing the players' demands, the pressure of expansion and the threat of a third major league as his reasons for stepping down. He opposed a 10-team league, insisting the junior circuit was better off with eight, and didn't want to go through what he'd experienced in 1914-1915 when a third league, the Federal League, "almost wrecked baseball."[17]

"I feel that the American League should have the opportunity of bringing in a younger and more energetic man to handle the problems confronting it," the 77-year-old Harridge announced.[18]

Warren Giles, on the other hand, who'd been NL president for only seven years, was awarded a new five-year contract shortly after Harridge made his surprising announcement. NL magnates canceled the last year of Giles' four-year deal and renewed his contract for five years at a higher salary.[19]

Perhaps emboldened by his new deal, Giles proposed an idea that appeared to be radical but had been adopted by teams in the past, and the league prexy hoped it would become standard across all of baseball. In 1939, when Giles was general manager of the Cincinnati Reds, he assigned numbers to his players based on the position they played. The manager, coaches, and catchers wore single digits; infielders wore numbers from 10-19; outfielders from 20-29; and pitchers from 30 on up.

Opponents of the idea cited Stan Musial and Elston Howard as examples of why the numbering system idea could be shot down. After spending his first four years in the majors in the outfield Musial began playing first base in 1946 and bounced between first and the outfield for the next 15 years. Sportswriter Earl Lawson wondered if Musial would be expected to switch uniforms from his familiar number 6 to a number from 20 to 29 when he played the outfield.

About Howard, who played outfield, catcher, and first base for the Yankees, Lawson jokingly suggested that he and his three uniforms might be too expensive to keep around.[20] He concluded that the numbering system could prove to be complicated and subject to ridicule. The numbering system was one of 30 proposed amendments. Others included interleague trades, the bonus rule and unrestricted draft, the sacrifice-fly rule, and Federal League records.

The majors approved a rule that would suspend traditional waivers from November 21 to December 15 each year to allow for trades between leagues without requiring players to be waived out of their respective leagues.[21]

Since the elimination of the old bonus rule at the 1957 Winter Meetings, teams had shelled out approximately $6 million for high-school and college prospects, and even the wealthier teams agreed that new restrictions were needed. In order to curtail large bonuses given out to unproven youngsters, one proposal called for players signed as free agents to be subject to an unrestricted draft after one year of service, the logic being that teams would be reluctant to hand out large bonuses if they knew a player might be lost to another team after only a year. A Frick-appointed committee also reduced the amounts teams would be required to pay to draft players, making the draft more attractive. After a $25,000 price tag was established for players drafted by a major-league club in 1957, the price was reduced to $15,000. The Triple-A price was set at $7,500, Double-A at $6,000, Single-A at $4,000, and Class B and C at $3,000.[22]

Ed Costello of the *Boston Herald* suggested a graduated bonus plan that would give teams more time to pay their bonus babies and force those players to earn the money. Under Costello's plan, a $50,000 bonus would be distributed depending on which level of ball a player was slated to begin his career. A player starting in Single A would be awarded $20,000 up front and paid the minor-league minimum salary. Each time the player advanced to the next level, he'd receive another $10,000. Players who eventually earned a major-league roster spot would receive the entire $50,000 bonus over time, while those who didn't make it would receive only a portion of the promised bonus.[23] "Such an arrangement would make the young fellow work hard to improve himself," Costello wrote, "or out he goes with only the bonus money he earned."[24]

Because the $15,000 price tag had yet to be approved prior to the 1958 draft, 12 players were selected at a cost of $300,000 on December 1, including two who went on to have productive careers or played important roles for their teams. Journeyman first baseman Rocky Nelson was selected by the Pittsburgh Pirates, one of six teams he'd played for from 1949 to 1956, and would prove to be an invaluable platoon man and pinch-hitter from 1959 to 1961, capping off his '60 campaign with a two-run homer in the first inning of Game Seven of the World Series against the Yankees.

The Chicago White Sox selected 21-year-old right-handed pitcher Claude Raymond from the American Association's Wichita club, the Triple-A affiliate of the Milwaukee Braves, and though he would only appear in three games for the White Sox before being released and returned to the Braves, Raymond went on to have a solid 12-year career.[25]

The minor-league draft, held on December 2, was in stark contrast to the '57 draft that saw 44 players selected, mostly due to steep prices, bonuses, and prior salary commitments. Only 18 players were chosen at a cost of $84,500, the lowest number of draftees since World War II. The Los Angeles Dodgers estimated that they'd already invested $800,000 in salary and bonuses in more than 100 players, half of whom were expected to make their professional debuts in 1959.[26]

Other transactions included a trade between the Cleveland Indians and Boston Red Sox that saw 21-year-old center fielder Gary Geiger and veteran slugger Vic Wertz go from Cleveland to Boston on December 2 for eccentric Gold Glove center fielder Jimmy Piersall, one of the best defensive outfielders in the game. Cleveland also dealt second baseman and former batting champion Bobby Avila to the Baltimore Orioles for right-handed minor-league pitcher Russ Heman and $30,000.

On December 3 the Philadelphia Phillies acquired young infielder Ruben Amaro from the Cardinals for outfielder and future World Series stud Chuck Essegian, and sent right-handed pitcher Jack Sanford to the Giants for right-handed pitcher Ruben Gomez and catcher Valmy Thomas; while the Pirates traded left-handed relief pitcher Luis Arroyo to the Reds for minor-league outfielder Nino Escalera. The next day the Cardinals sent outfielder Wally Moon and righty hurler Phil Paine to the Dodgers for outfielder Gino Cimoli, and the Yankees signed right-handed pitcher Jim Bouton as an amateur free agent.

The Sanford trade had sportswriter Dick Young speculating that the Phillies must have known something about the former Rookie of the Year that forced them to trade him.[27] Sanford had gone 19-8 with a 3.08 ERA and league-leading 188 strikeouts in 1957, but followed that up with a disappointing 1958 campaign. The *Boston Globe* reported that the Phillies were desperate for a catcher and although Thomas was a weak hitter, he had a strong arm and was very good behind the plate. And despite an inconsistent track record, Gomez was considered a front-line starter.[28]

Records and rules were also discussed during the convention. Minor-league writers and scorers proposed a rule change that would give a batter credit for a sacrifice fly even if the ball was caught in foul territory. Section 10.08 of the rule book gave credit for a sacrifice fly only if a fair ball was caught and a run scored, but the writers wanted the Rules Committee to eliminate the word "fair" and award a sacrifice fly for all balls caught that produced a run.[29]

Meanwhile the Records Committee of the Baseball Writers' Association of America struggled with the idea of including Federal League records and statistics in baseball's record books. For years there was a divide between those who thought the records should count and those who ignored them on the grounds that the Federal League was not of "big league caliber."[30]

One concern was how to recognize records of stars like Eddie Plank, Three Finger Brown, Joe Tinker, and Ed Reulbach. Plank had won 284 games for the Philadelphia Athletics from 1901 to 1914 before jumping to the St. Louis Terriers of the FL in 1915, for whom he went 21-11. He rejoined the AL in 1916 and went 21-21 for the St. Louis Browns to end his career with a record of 326-194. With 305 wins in the AL, the southpaw was a Hall of Famer regardless, but the Records Committee wondered which win total the Hall of Fame should reflect on his plaque.[31]

The Records Committee also tasked itself with completing Ty Cobb's RBI total, Walter Johnson's won-lost record, and Lou Gehrig's home-run total. RBIs weren't officially adopted until 1920, but Hall of Fame historian Ernie Lanigan had been keeping track of them since 1907, and only had to pore through Detroit newspapers to find Cobb's RBIs from 1905 and 1906. At the time, Cobb was credited with 1,901 runs batted in, third all-time behind Babe Ruth and Gehrig.[32]

Unlike the 1957 Winter Meetings that saw controversy over the writers' choice of Mickey Mantle over Ted Williams in MVP voting, no one quibbled with their selections in 1958, although one writer, Ed McAuley of the *Cleveland News*, questioned why there was an MVP Award for each league but only one Cy Young Award for both leagues.[33]

Yankees right-hander Bob Turley led the Cy Young voting and narrowly defeated National Leaguers Warren Spahn, Lew Burdette, and Bob Friend. He also finished second to Boston outfielder Jackie Jensen in the MVP balloting.

Newspapermen and baseball officials had mixed opinions when all was said and done. The *New York*

Times's John Drebinger described the sessions as attaining the "last word in utter futility," having produced "more expansive talk, more intensive plotting and scheming and accomplished less" than any of the previous winter meetings.[34] According to him, the only unanimous vote was the owners' refusal to meet the players' demands for 20 percent of the gross revenue, a decision that earned the approval of at least one player who realized his team used 27 percent of its gross revenue for payroll, and he'd be forced to take a pay cut if the 20 percent demand had been approved.[35]

Drebinger also claimed the legislation that was passed was "more or less of a negative sort," calling the one-year draft rule "virtually worthless" because of all the amendments attached to it, and citing the "inconsequential deals" made by big-league clubs. He credited Phil Wrigley, head of the National League's realignment committee, with being forthright enough to realize the question of expansion was beyond Organized Baseball's scope, and that a group that included an outside research agency was necessary. "They may even find out how to pitch to Ernie Banks or Hank Aaron," he joked.[36]

Bob Addie of the Washington Post was not only in favor of the interleague trade period that ran from November 21 to December 15, but he called the passage of the rule "a long time coming," and hoped that some day interleague play would eventually become a reality.[37] It finally did in 1997.

NOTES

1 *Atlanta Constitution*, December 4, 1958.
2 Ibid.
3 *The Sporting News*, December 10, 1958: 5.
4 Ibid.
5 Ibid.
6 *The Sporting News*, December 10, 1958: 6.
7 Ibid.
8 *The Sporting News*, November 26, 1958: 3. One prominent member of the Houston Sports Association was Kenneth Stanley "Bud" Adams Jr., who used his wealth to help form the American Football League in 1959. The league began play in 1960 and Adams's Houston Oilers won the first two league championships before the AFL merged with the NFL in 1970. At the time of his death in 2013, Adams's 409 wins as an owner were the most among all current NFL owners.
9 The Continental League was to put teams in New York, Houston, Minneapolis-St. Paul, Toronto, Denver, Atlanta, Dallas-Fort Worth, and Buffalo. Although the Continental League never got off the ground, all but Buffalo would eventually get a major-league team in future expansions, including New York and Houston, which joined the National League in 1962.
10 *The Sporting News*, November 26, 1958: 3.
11 Ibid.
12 *The Sporting News*, November 26, 1958: 4.
13 *The Sporting News*, November 26, 1958: 3.
14 *The Sporting News*, November 26, 1958: 5. When the New York Mets joined the National League in 1962, they used the Polo Grounds in 1962-1963 before moving into Shea Stadium in 1964. It's interesting to note that the Yankees shared the Polo Grounds with the New York Giants from 1911 to 1922, before Yankee Stadium was built, then shared Shea Stadium with the Mets in 1974-1975 while Yankee Stadium was being renovated. So it's not impossible to believe the Yankees would have allowed the Mets to call Yankee Stadium home in 1962-1963.
15 Ibid.
16 Ibid.
17 *The Sporting News*, December 10, 1958: 5.
18 Ibid. Hall of Fame shortstop Joe Cronin, who had been serving as the Red Sox' general manager since 1948, succeeded Harridge in January 1959.
19 Ibid.
20 *The Sporting News*, November 26, 1958: 4.
21 *Chicago Tribune*, December 4, 1958.
22 *The Sporting News*, December 3, 1958: 11.
23 *The Sporting News*, November 26, 1958: 12.
24 Ibid.
25 Claude Raymond was named to the National League All-Star team in 1966, and from 1961 to 1971 he was one of seven NL pitchers to record at least 80 saves.
26 *The Sporting News*, December 10, 1958: 12.
27 *The Sporting News*, December 10, 1958: 25.
28 *Boston Globe*, December 4, 1958. The Giants easily got the better of the Jack Sanford trade that netted the Phillies Ruben Gomez and Valmy Thomas. Sanford won 80 games for the Giants from 1959 to 1963, including 24 for the pennant-winning 1962 squad, before numbness in his hand effectively ended his days as a start-

ing pitcher. Over that same period, he paced the Giants in wins, innings, starts, and strikeouts. Gomez went only 3-11 for the Phillies with a horrible 5.78 ERA before being sent back to the minors in 1961 at the age of 33. Thomas spent only one year in Philadelphia and batted an anemic .200. He also committed a career-worst seven errors, but threw out 46 percent of would-be base thieves.

29 *The Sporting News*, December 10, 1958: 15.

30 Ibid.

31 Ibid. Plank was inducted into the Hall of Fame by the Old Timers Committee in 1946. His plaque at the Hall of Fame Museum in Cooperstown, New York, simply mentions that he's "one of few pitchers to win more than 300 games in big leagues." Brown won 239 games, including 31 in the Federal League, and his Hall of Fame plaque reflects that. Reulbach won 182 games, including 21 in the FL, but he's not in the Hall of Fame. Tinker's plaque doesn't mention his stats, just who he played for and the fact that he was a shortstop on four pennant winners.

32 As of this writing, Baseball-Reference.com credits Cobb with 1,933 RBIs; the sixth edition of Total Baseball, the official encyclopedia of Major League Baseball, credits him with 1,937, and Retrosheet.org has him with 1,944. Walter Johnson's won-lost record is listed as 417-279 in all three of the above; Lou Gehrig's home-run total is listed as 493 in all three of the above.

33 *The Sporting News*, November 26, 1958: 10. From 1956 to 1966 only one Cy Young Award was given out. It wasn't until 1967 that the Baseball Writers Association of America awarded a Cy Young trophy to a pitcher from each league.

34 *New York Times*, December 6, 1958.

35 Ibid.

36 Ibid.

37 *Washington Post*, December 6, 1958.

— 1959 —
WINDS OF CHANGE

By David M. Kritzler and Alan P. Henry

AS THE 1959 WINTER MEETINGS APproached, both the nation and baseball were on a roll.

For America, the postwar economy was firing on all cylinders. The Space Race against the Soviet Union was on, and a burly, proud nation was confident of ultimate victory. Television ratings toppers like *Father Knows Best* reflected a culture that honored idyllic family life and wholesome middle-class values.

Major-league baseball was on a roll, too, burnishing its reputation as the national pastime. Steadily recovering from a decade-long attendance lag, it attracted 19,199,419 million fans in 1959.[1]

But while the nation's love affair with major-league baseball was once again heating up, the owners of the major- and minor-league franchises converging on South Florida for their annual gatherings knew they had a range of problematic issues ahead of them. The majors were trying to figure out how to expand and control costs. The minors were trying to figure out how to simply survive. And both were attempting to manage their futures within a swirl of shifting demographic, sociological, political, lifestyle, and economic factors.

One new reality was television. Simply put, television was changing how the public watched baseball, and as such was a cause both for the implosion of minor-league attendance and the growing popularity of major-league baseball.

When the All-Star Game in Chicago's Comiskey Park was televised for the first time on July 11, 1950, there were 9.7 million television sets in America.[2] By 1959, the same year an early version of instant replay was introduced, the number of television sets in use had swelled to over 67 million.[3] Regional broadcasts had expanded quickly into weekend national broadcasts, so if you could find a television, you could see major-league baseball. A total of 13 of the 16 teams televised 669 games.[4] By the end of the decade, there were more TV sets in America than combined sales of baseball tickets. And for the first time in the history of professional baseball, more people were watching major-league rather than minor-league baseball.

In the 1949 season, 448 teams in 59 minor leagues, both all-time highs, attracted 39,782,717 fans, a record that stood for 54 years. By 1959 only 21 leagues and 148 teams remained, and attendance had dropped to 12,171,848, a decrease of 69 percent! Not only did attendance dry up, but radio revenue did as well, as local fans could now see on televised major-league games the players they had watched in the minors.[5]

At various points along the way, major-league owners had rejected pleas from the minor-league owners to protect minor-league provinces from escalating air-wave intrusion by the majors. Instead, the big-league owners "proved quite willing to sacrifice their minor league dependencies on the twin altars of cost control and television profits."[6]

A nation on the move was also changing and challenging Organized Baseball.

National League franchise expansion into California, along with television viewer habits, had already degraded the minor leagues there. But the majors were feeling the pinch as well. The nation's population had more than doubled, from 76 million to 179 million, since 1901, but the majors still had 16 teams, and most were in cities east of the Mississippi River. The migration of fans from the cities to the suburbs had resulted in attendance issues at some urban ballparks. But the migration of people from the aging industrialized urban centers in the East to points south and west, thanks in part to the relativelynew phenomenon of home air-conditioning, was eliminating fans altogether and creating new untapped markets.

Those factors would help explain why, deep into a stretch of peace and national prosperity, and with television already making up almost 20 percent of ballclub revenues, major-league owners were casting their expansionist eyes toward booming cities like Houston, Fort Worth, Dallas, and Atlanta.[7] The Minneapolis-St. Paul metropolitan area was also on the radar.

Meanwhile, New York City Mayor Robert Wagner was aggressively mounting attempts to replace one of the two franchises the city had lost when the Giants moved to San Francisco and the Dodgers moved to Los Angeles after the 1957 season. New York attorney and power broker William Shea, tapped by Wagner to make it happen, had failed in his attempts to relocate franchises from Cincinnati, Philadelphia, and Pittsburgh. In what was an open secret, Shea and his compatriots then began planning the creation of a Continental League that would eventually compete for talent with the American and National Leagues.[8]

On May 21, 1958, Commissioner Ford Frick and the baseball owners met in Columbus, Ohio, and agreed on conditions that must be met for a rival league to gain their endorsement as a legitimate major league.[9]

On July 27 the new league was formally announced, with teams in Denver, Houston, Minneapolis-St. Paul, New York City, and Toronto. Legendary executive Branch Rickey resigned as president of the Pittsburgh Pirates and was named president of the league on August 18.[10] "By trial and error it developed that the only way to provide major-league baseball for an increasing number communities on this continent was to form a new major league. There was no other way," Shea said at the announcement.[11]

Adding to its assault on baseball's established order, Rickey proposed that the clubs would pool and share their television revenue so that no one club could have an unfair advantage, as the New York Yankees had at the time.[12]

Owners in each city had agreed to pay $50,000 to the league and committed to a capital investment of $2.5 million, not including stadium costs. A minimum seating capacity of 35,000 was established by the league for the venues in which its teams would play.[13]

While it was likely that the American and National Leagues did not want to share expansion with a third league, major-league owners also understood that they ran the risk of congressional involvement that could jeopardize their exemption from the Sherman Antitrust Act. But court precedents did not discourage Rickey and his allies.

A bill that targeted baseball's organizational structure was introduced in February 1959 by Senator Estes Kefauver (D-Tennessee). The bill specifically denied the Sherman exemption to any baseball team that controlled more than 40 players at one time, and it was motivated by the belief that the large number of players under contract to major-league teams prevented the creation of new independent major leagues.[14]

Rickey and Shea did not necessarily want the exemption overturned, but as the owners pushed back against the Continental League, "[T]hey began contemplating the possibility of establishing the league without baseball's blessing and support."[15]

In a July 1959 hearing before the Senate Antitrust and Monopoly Subcommittee, Commissioner Frick assured members that he would be as helpful as possible to the new league's backers, while Sen. Kefauver warned the major-league owners that Congress was closely monitoring the "attitudes of Organized Baseball" toward the Continental League in an effort to prevent any antitrust issues.[16] Ultimately, none of Kefauver's proposals passed either house of Congress.

This was the testy atmosphere as the Winter Meetings began.

The meetings were actually a series of two meetings and conventions at two locations. First came the National Association of Professional Baseball Leagues (NAPBL), the umbrella organization for the minor leagues. Their 58th annual convention took place from November 30 to December 3 at the Vinoy Park Hotel in St. Petersburg, Florida. While its attendees primarily represented minor-league teams, the major-league owners and general managers were also there as members. The convention was, in fact, called to order by Commissioner Frick.

The major-league winter meetings followed, on December 7 to 10 at the Fontainebleau hotel in Miami Beach. Joe Cronin, the American League president, and Warren Giles, the National League president, were collectively more powerful than the commissioner and drove the agenda. The commissioner served as the spokesman.

Leading up to the major-league meetings, Frick had essentially ordered the National and American Leagues to make known their own plans for expansion, and the National League announced on the first day that it really had no plans to expand. "There is not sufficient sentiment at the present time to consider the expansion of the National League," said Giles.[17]

The American League, which had announced some exploration of expansion, deliberated on the same day and came up with no conclusions. Some American League representatives reportedly pressed for an expansion program but could not muster enough votes.[18]

That afternoon Rickey arrived and warned that without expansion, "baseball may die in the 1960s." First, he said, owners had continued to alienate fans by not updating ballparks and refusing to have better parking. But he also opined that "baseball was no longer national," though that could be remedied; at least 32 cities, he said, "can and should play" in an expanded league.[19]

The next day, December 8, Rickey brought to center stage at a press conference some of the proposed Continental League's big-gun owners. Representing New York was Dwight Davis Jr., whose father had funded tennis's Davis Cup. Representing Houston was Texaco heir Craig Cullinan. Representing Denver was Bob Howsam, owner of the minor-league Denver Bears and loaded with powerful political connections through his father-in-law, former Colorado Governor and US Senator Edwin C. Johnson. (Johnson had also been president of the Western League.) Representing Toronto was media mogul Jack Kent Cooke. From Minneapolis, there was businessman Wheelock Whitney Jr. Attorney William Shea was also in attendance.

The Continental League is "as inevitable as tomorrow, but not as imminent," Rickey said.[20] Inevitable, he explained, because five cities had already signed on to begin the season in 1961. And then he announced that Atlanta had signed on as the sixth city, and that Dallas, Montreal, and Buffalo were considering it. Still, he said, potential entrants were holding back to see what American League President Cronin's expansion plans were, in hopes they might be added there instead. In fact, Cronin's "purposeful indecisiveness" had already caused one group to waver. Before ending the press conference, Rickey took a swipe at the major-league establishment, calling major-league baseball "a monopoly that calls itself a national pastime."[21]

When Cronin finally spoke, he said the National League's decision not to expand also killed the AL's plan to add a ninth team. "We kicked around the idea of going to nine without the National League, but it would be impossible unless we had an inter-league schedule. One of the nine clubs would be idle every day," Cronin said.[22]

A frustrated Rickey quickly responded.

"We have just begun to fight. If we go down, they will write an epitaph that they did their best and died trying," he told *Washington Post* sports columnist Shirley Povich after the meetings.[23] But Povich added his own interpretation of events, writing in his *Sporting News* column of December 16, 1959, "Informed baseball men, not those attempting to organize the Continental League as a third major, are now convinced that the fledging circuit will never get off the ground, or even muster eight teams for a takeoff attempt. The Continental League people came away from the winter meetings at Miami Beach with even more problems than they took to that convention. They got a green light of a sort from the entrenched leagues, but it was tinged with so much red that the Continental is newly aware of the peril of proceeding."[24]

On December 22 Rickey went to Dallas, where he announced that city would be the seventh team in the Continental League, and that an eighth team would be named shortly.[25]

While the issue of expansion was a major one at the meetings, it had plenty of company.

High on the agenda were continued attempts by the owners to save themselves from paying large bonuses to amateur prospects.

After World War II, as interest in the game increased and the number of minor-league teams grew, intense competition for players forced teams to offer signing bonuses to top players. For the next 20 years, major-league officials worked to mitigate the problem.[26]

The majors were investing so much money into a few "bonus babies" that it consumed their budgets for development that would have gone into underwriting the lower-level minor-league teams they would have otherwise supported.

In 1947 the major-league owners implemented bonus rules, which were restrictions aimed at reducing player salaries, as well as keeping wealthier teams from monopolizing the player market.[27] The rules were repealed in 1950, reinstated in 1953, and repealed again in 1957.

In short order, spending on bonuses picked up again. Examples of supersized bonuses in 1957 included catcher-outfielder Bob "Hawk" Taylor ($112,000), outfielder John DeMerit ($100,000), right-handed pitcher Jay Hook ($65,000), and right-handed pitcher Von McDaniel ($50,000).[28]

At the 1958 winter meetings, the owners had amended Rule 5 with the addition of the first-year player draft. The new wrinkle, seen as a measure to control costs, added to the existing major- and minor-league Rule 5 drafts. For $15,000, a major-league team, drafting in reverse order of the past season's finish, could draft any first year pro player not protected on a team's 40-man major-league roster. If the drafted player was due a bonus, the original team still was on the hook for those dollars. Owners hoped this would minimize teams paying bonuses to players they might not only lose but would continue to have to pay. But they added the caveat that the drafting team had to keep the player in the majors for the entire season or give him back to his original team for $7,500.

Only one player was taken in this draft, left-handed pitcher Mike Lee of the San Francisco Giants. The Cleveland Indians scooped him up but wound up only pitching him for a total of nine innings. Teams just did not want to burn a precious roster spot on an unproven player.

While the first-year player draft was a flop at the major-league level, 13 other players were picked under the regular selection rule for $25,000 apiece. Of the 13, seven had been in the majors before, among them right-hander Don Lee, catcher Darrell Johnson, infielder Joe Amalfitano, and first baseman Steve Bilko.[29]

At the 1959 Winter Meetings, some executives proposed a formal draft of amateur talent, but the idea was five years head of its time and was defeated.[30]

Over the opposition of Commissioner Frick, the major-league owners had, during their summer meeting, approved interleague trading from November 21 to December 15, which overlapped the winter meetings. For the first time, players could move from one league to the other without having to first clear waivers in their own league.

Speaking during the winter meetings, National League President Giles expressed disappointment that the trades were allowed, calling it "bad business, and that goes especially for the clubs of the National League. We have spent years building up the prestige of our individual leagues, both American and National. But it's especially stupid of us in the National League to sabotage our own prestige at this time, because we happen to be the stronger league in recent years."[31]

In the first interleague trade, on November 21, the NL Chicago Cubs sent first baseman Jim Marshall and right-handed pitcher Dave Hillman to the AL Boston Red Sox in exchange for first baseman Dick Gernert.

On November 30 the San Francisco Giants took advantage of the trading window to bolster their pitching staff by sending Gold Glove-winning outfielder Jackie Brandt, along with right-handed pitcher Gordon Jones and catcher Roger McCardell, to Baltimore in exchange for workhorse right-handed pitcher Billy Loes, who once claimed to lose a grounder in the sun during a World Series game, and southpaw Billy O'Dell, a two-time All-Star.

On December 9, the Pittsburgh Pirates were also active in the interleague market, sending right-handed pitcher Dick Hall and minor-league shortstop Ken Hamlin to Kansas City for catcher-third baseman Hal Smith, whom they planned to platoon with catcher Smoky Burgess.

But the blockbuster trade of the season occurred on December 11, when the New York Yankees traded a quartet of productive veterans — All-Star outfielder Hank Bauer, right-hander Don Larsen, first baseman-outfielder Norm Siebern, and first baseman Marv Throneberry — to the Kansas City Athletics for infielder Joe DeMaestri, first baseman Kent Hadley, and outfielder Roger Maris, who would be named the American League MVP the next two seasons, as well as hit a record 61 home runs in 1961. "I thought Roger Maris was the one guy we needed. He was a complete player who could field, throw and run," Whitey Ford later said.[32]

At its 58th annual convention, the National Association of Professional Baseball Leagues, led by its president, George Trautman, since 1947, once again faced challenging headwinds.

Growing concern related to attracting new talent and protecting investments in players already under contract was reflected in proposals offered for consideration at the convention. "The source of talent is in the minors and with the National Association dwindling from 59 leagues in 1949 to 21 in 1959, it's no secret that the field is getting pretty thin," said veteran Detroit scout Joe Mathis.[33]

Of the 28 items on the docket, 19 were directly or indirectly related to talent issues, centered on a plan to set up a free-agent draft and an unrestricted draft among all minor leagues, attempts to amend the present first-year draft or replace it with another bonus rule, and efforts to establish a minimum salary in the minors.[34]

For their part, the major-league owners knew full well that many minor-league franchises were on life support, in part because they knew that the majors' desire to televise more and more of its games meant minor-league markets and profits were certain to be further squeezed. The major-league owners also knew that the more they were forced to spend on player salaries and amateur prospects, the less money was available to prop up a sagging player-development system. Once vibrant and self-sustaining, the minor leagues by 1959 were dependent on major-league subsidies for survival. At the same time, the major-league owners also knew their dreams of expansion into cities like Denver, Minneapolis, Atlanta, Toronto, and Houston could further impact the viability of the sport's feeder system.

Under the headline "Minors Defeat Free-Agent Draft Motion, Vote for Modified Version of First-Year Player Selections," Clifford Kachline described in *The Sporting News* some of the National Association's actions. "Organized Ball isn't ready for a free-agent draft or unrestricted selection of minor league players, but when major and minor loop officials came out of the legislative sessions of the 58th annual National Association convention … there remained considerable doubt as what the majority actually wanted to do in the way of legislation to curb the bonus rule. Defeating a proposal to restore a bonus rule, the minors voted to continue a first-year player draft on a modified basis."[35]

On other issues, in addition to rejecting a bonus rule, a draft of free-agent talent, and unrestricted selection, they also voted against setting up a college-player rule, but agreed to make a professional career more enticing by setting up minimum salary limits for each classification in the minors.[36] Set at $500 a month for Triple A, $400 for Double A, $350 for A, $300 for B, $275 for C, and $250 for D, it was praised by National League President Giles.

"The biggest problem in baseball today is not television, but getting more boys to play baseball professionally," *The Sporting News* opined. "This is one of the most constructive proposals presented in the National Association in years." Since the new salary scale applied only to the minors, no vote was necessary by the major leagues.[37]

A week later, the major-league owners adopted all but two of nine measures approved by the National Association convention, including an amended first-year draft under which clubs selecting such players would be permitted to option them out the same as any other player. Under the amended first-year draft as adopted by the majors and minors, a uniform price of $12,000 replaced a sliding scale, which had started at $15,000 for the majors, $7,500 for Triple A, and down to $3,000 for B and C clubs.[38]

Voted down by the National League and approved by the American League was a proposal to give clubs in Triple A, Double A, and A the same privileges as lower-class teams to sign six players each after July 1 for service the following year without counting in the under-control limit. With two leagues divided, Commissioner Frick cast a deciding "no" vote. Also defeated were proposals involving allotment of World Series tickets.[39]

But the major-league owners also came through for the minors in a big way.

Understanding that their own future was linked to the ability of the minor leagues to stock their parent clubs with talent, and that they needed to quell any minor-league rumblings concerning antitrust issues, the owners voted unanimously on December 7 to approve the second-year continuation of the Player Development Fund for 1960.

A total of $847,000 was donated, including $65,000 for promotional purposes, with the rest to be distributed by formula to each minor-league franchise that would agree not to sue Major League Baseball for "alleged invasion of territory by television and monopoly of player talent."[40]

The allocation was to be as follows: Triple-A teams, $22,500; Southern Association teams, $12,500; Texas League, $9,000; Mexican League, $5,000. In the lower leagues the amounts were: Class A, $7,500 for teams with limited tie-ups with major-league teams and $5,000 with a general working agreement; Class B, $4,000 for all teams; Class C, $3,500; and Class D, $3,000.[41]

Responding to the vote, Commissioner Frick said: "This program proved a great boon to the minor-league people the past year and I am most happy that the owners saw fit to renew it. There is no doubt but that the player development fund has helped many leagues and clubs to survive."[42]

It's always a bit surprising when 16 strong-willed owners can do anything unanimously, and the vote reinforced the belief in some quarters that the purpose was simply to mollify the minors while they executed their own expansion. Nonetheless, National Association President Trautman called the vote to renew the fund by the major-league owners a "very generous act" and "concrete evidence of their interest in the minors," and predicted that because of it, for the "first time in 10 years, the National Association probably will not lose a single league."[43]

Previously, at the National Association meetings, major-league owners also stepped up in a concrete way to aid their struggling farm-team system by rescuing several of its tottering franchises. After the 1959 season, the Cardinals, Tigers, and Cubs had dropped their teams from the American Association, and with the additional loss of Omaha and Fort Worth, it left the Triple-A league with only seven franchises. League President Ed Doherty came to the meeting looking for help, and got it when the Washington Senators, Kansas City A's, and Philadelphia Phillies agreed to work with Charleston (West Virginia), Dallas, and Indianapolis, respectively. In the Southern League, where there were two dropouts after the season, the Dodgers stepped in to keep the Atlanta franchise alive and the Senators took on Chattanooga. Further, the Braves and Cardinals offered the prospect of future help by attempting to line up additional working agreements for the struggling Pioneer League.[44] (The White Sox, Reds, Dodgers, and Giants would all come into the league in 1960.)

"We've been through some rough times, but maybe we're just getting squared away," said Trautman.[45]

Indeed, with talk of expansion and new television revenues in the air, there was a feeling in some quarters that an era of "harmony" between owners and players was at hand.

"Trade and legislative action notwithstanding, the most important product of the winter meetings at the Hotel Fontainebleau may be the new era of harmony ushered in by the player representatives and major league officials," *The Sporting News* wrote.[46] "Relations between the owners and players have never been better in the history of baseball," echoed Charles Segar, secretary-treasurer of the major leagues.[47]

BASEBALL'S BUSINESS: THE WINTER MEETINGS

That sense was a far cry from a year earlier, when Commissioner Frick had rejected the players' request for a salary scale based on 20 percent of team revenue. "Since then, a more realistic attitude has developed in the player ranks," *The Sporting News* said.[48]

More good feelings were in evidence at the player-management meeting December 6 at Indian Creek Country Club. The player representatives, led by the NL's Robin Roberts and the AL's Harvey Kuenn, asked for improved clubhouses in Philadelphia and Chicago in the National League and stadium improvements at Chicago's Comiskey Park and Washington. They also asked that the leagues standardize the height of the bullpen pitching mounds, and the owners promised to address that issue. The players also won approval on three other proposals regarding night games on getaway days, and guidelines to reschedule postponed games. Also, meal money for players on the road was standardized at $10 a day, where previously it was as little at $7.[49] The representatives also introduced to the major-league chieftains their new legal adviser, Circuit Court Judge Robert C. Cannon, the son of Wisconsin Congressman Raymond J. Cannon, who was the lawyer for some of the Chicago Black Sox and had attempted to unionize the players during the 1920 season.[50]

Of course, it wasn't all sweetness and light. Smack in the midst of the winter meetings, the owners were greeted with a page-one banner headline in the December 9 issue of *The Sporting News* that certainly had to have drawn their attention. "Fading Stars Face '60 Salary Slashes," it read, with the subheadline "Stan, Splinter Big Names on '59 Skid List."[51]

Indeed, the major-league owners were so focused on controlling current player salaries and costs that even future Hall of Famers still in their prime received salary cuts going into the 1960 season after their 1959 performance slid. The Giants were set to move into Candlestick Park and vastly increase revenue, yet Willie Mays's salary was cut as were those of Mickey Mantle and Richie Ashburn.

In 1959 the average National League salary was $16,997, up 23 percent from $13,772 in 1954. In both leagues, the 18 lowest paid players earned $7,000. The middle 117 made from $10,000 to $24,999, and two made $75,000 or more.[52]

"Where is the player payroll rise going to stop? How much higher can we go?" said Yankees general manager George Weiss? He said the club owners were not opposed to increased salaries as long as they were justified by revenues.[53]

At the same time, the reality in 1959 was that any player who complained or made a big salary was the potential subject of trade talk. And multiyear contracts and no-trade clauses were beyond imagination. "Players at all levels of Organized Baseball could do little about owner miserliness since the industry refused to implement any formal system of pay mediation or arbitration," wrote baseball scholar Robert Burk.[54] In the absence of outside arbitration processes, "team general managers exercised unilateral economic power over their charges," Burk wrote. "For most of the 1950s and early 1960s, baseball players remained largely nameless, replaceable links in their industry's chain."[55]

To be sure, one of the small links in that chain weakened in 1959. That was the year Chicago White Sox owner Bill Veeck broke with tradition and placed the surnames of his players on the backs of their jerseys.

The year 1959 also saw the falling of the last official color barrier in the major leagues. Under pressure from the National Association for the Advancement of Colored People and the Massachusetts Commission Against Discrimination, the Red Sox recalled Elijah "Pumpsie" Green from their Minneapolis farm team, and on July 21, 1959, he became the first black player in team history as the Red Sox became the last team to integrate.

NOTES

1. ballparksofbaseball.com/1950-59attendance.htm.
2. ethw.org/Technological_Innovations_in_Sports_Broadcasting.
3. pix11.com/2012/11/17/the-history-of-wpix/.
4. Jonathan Fraser Light, *The Cultural Encyclopedia of Baseball* (Jefferson, North Carolina: McFarland & Co., 2005), 928.
5. Leonard Koppett, *Koppett's Concise History of Major League Baseball* (Philadelphia: Temple University Press, 1998), 263.
6. Robert Burk, *Much More Than a Game* (Chapel Hill, North Carolina: University of North Carolina Press, 2001), 109.
7. Light, 928.
8. Sullivan, 141.
9. Ibid.
10. Ibid.
11. Sullivan, 142.
12. Michael Shapiro, "Memorabilia From the What If Drawer," *New York Times*, January 22, 2009. nytimes.com/2009/07/23/sports/baseball/23league.html? R=0.
13. Fran Zimniuch, *Baseball's New Frontier* (Lincoln: University of Nebraska Press, 2013), 32-33.
14. J. Gordon Hylton, "Why Baseball's Antitrust Exemption Still Survives," *Marquette Sports Law Review*, Volume 9, Issue 2, Spring 1999, Article 11, 401, 402.
15. Shapiro.
16. "Third Major League Under Senate's Eye/Continental League Founder to Testify In Congressional Quiz," *Palm Springs (California) Desert Sun*, July 31, 1959: 1. See also baseball-almanac.com/yearly/yr1959a.shtml.
17. *The Sporting News*, December 16, 1959: 5.
18. Bill Morales, *Farewell to the Last Golden Age of Baseball* (Jefferson, North Carolina: McFarland & Co., 2011), 4.
19. Morales, 7.
20. Ibid.
21. Morales, 8.
22. *The Sporting News*, December 16, 1959: 5.
23. Shirley Povich, *The Sporting News*, December 16, 1959: 10.
24. Ibid.
25. Morales, 10.
26. Allan Simpson, baseballamerica.com/today/2005draft/050604bonus.html, June 4, 2005.
27. Paul D. Staudohar, Franklin Lowenthal, and Anthony K. Lima, "The Evolution of Baseball's Amateur Draft," *NINE: A Journal of Baseball History and Culture*, 15.1, 2006: 27.
28. baseball-almanac.com/players/baseball_signing_bonus.shtml.
29. *The Sporting News*, December 9, 1959, 11.
30. Cliff Blau, "The Real First-Year Player Draft," *Baseball Research Journal*, Summer 2010: sabr.org/research/real-first-year-player-draft.
31. *The Sporting News*, December 2, 1959: 2.
32. Tom Clavin and Danny Peary, *Roger Maris: Baseball's Reluctant Hero* (New York: Touchstone, 2011), quoted in thescore.com/mlb/news/906624.
33. *The Sporting News*, December 2, 1959: 1.
34. *The Sporting News*, December 2, 1959: 2.
35. *The Sporting News*, December 9, 1959: 5.
36. Ibid.
37. *The Sporting News*, December 9, 1959: 6.
38. *The Sporting News*, December 16, 1959: 6.
39. Ibid.
40. *The Sporting News*, December 16, 1959: 1.
41. Ibid.
42. Ibid.
43. Ibid.
44. *The Sporting News*, December 9, 1959: 7.
45. Ibid.
46. *The Sporting News*, December 16, 1959: 2.
47. Ibid.
48. Ibid.
49. *The Sporting News*, December 16, 1959: 6.
50. baseball-almanac.com/yearly/yr1959a.shtml.
51. *The Sporting News*, December 9, 1959: 1.
52. roadsidephotos.sabr.org/baseball/1957-63sals.htm\1/14.
53. *The Sporting News*, January 14, 1959: 2.
54. Burk, 114, 115.
55. Burk, 115.

— 1960 —
THE MISSOURI COMPROMISE

By David M. Kritzler and Alan P. Henry

ON NOVEMBER 8, 1960, JOHN F. Kennedy was elected president, ushering in an era of political comity and refreshed vision. Not to be outdone, the major-league owners were busily ushering in their own visionary plans, culminating in the historic Winter Meetings of 1960.

On December 7, the final day of the meetings at the Park Plaza Hotel in St. Louis, a protracted battle between the National League and American League over expansion was resolved in a deal quickly tagged "The Missouri Compromise."[1]

"In a smoke-filled room 26 floors above the street, the little band of willful men who own baseball was making living, throbbing history," summarized columnist Red Smith, who further characterized the atmosphere as "electric with ennui."[2]

Under the agreement, announced by Commissioner Ford Frick after days of prickly negotiations, the American League was given permission to expand into Los Angeles in 1961, with the National League moving back into New York in 1962. The American League team was to play its home games in 1961 at Wrigley Field, home of the former Los Angeles Angels of Pacific Coast League. After one year, the new Angels major-league team would move into the Dodgers' soon-to-be-completed Chavez Ravine Stadium for the 1962 season, signing a four-year pact to lease the park, with a subsequent three-year option.[3]

The agreement meant both leagues would operate with 10 teams. In the American League the Angels would join a new Washington Senators franchise; the former Senators team was to move to Minneapolis-St. Paul and become the Twins. In the National League the two new teams were the New York Mets and the Houston Colt .45s. The agreement also saw the two leagues set up a formula to guide the future of major-league expansion after meeting Commissioner Frick's call for a plan "we can live by."[4]

The critical vote amending major-league Rule 1 (c), governing the addition of new clubs, was unanimously approved after Los Angeles Dodgers owner Walter F. O'Malley withdrew his objection.[5] Frick said the amendment would permit one league to expand into the other league's cities with a three-quarters approval vote by the owners, rather than the 100 percent vote previously required.[6]

Frick was praised in numerous quarters for his part in making the deal happen. "The commissioner steered a straight course," O'Malley said. "If he had lost his sense of direction, we would have ended up in an awful mess."[7] Bob Burnes, writing in *The Sporting News*, echoed O'Malley's sentiment. "Frick's determination to make the leagues settle the issue between themselves was a credit to the commissioner's judgment."[8]

Like many battles between powerful forces, the road to productive peace was a rocky one, characterized by high-stakes brinksmanship, fluid alliances, and naked self-interest. Or, as baseball historians Eric Thompson and Andy McCue characterized it, "the path to expansion for both leagues was a combination of new markets and old politics."[9] And though technically the major-league portion of the Winter Meetings was only three days long, those days could more accurately be described as having been the final days of a months-long series of meetings and developments that were to change baseball forever.

Prologue to Expansion

Broadly, this group of men, typically characterized as hidebound by tradition, were actually riding the leading edge of an expansion wave that was to sweep across America over the next decade. As the

Winter Meetings began, there were 51 teams among the four major professional sports (baseball, football, basketball, and hockey), including nine new teams that had joined the ranks of pro football months earlier. By 1969, there were 87.[10]

The owners were also riding a wave of public infatuation with major-league baseball — one that poet Walt Whitman acutely characterized in 1889 as capturing "the snap, go, fling of the American atmosphere."[11] Underscoring the point, when the Gallup Organization asked Americans in 1960 to name their favorite spectator sport, 34 percent chose baseball, more than football and basketball combined.[12] And then, to put an exclamation point on it all, the public was treated to what in some quarters has been called the greatest World Series finish of all time: Pittsburgh Pirates second baseman Bill Mazeroski's seventh-game, ninth-inning, Series-winning crushing of a fastball from New York Yankees pitcher Ralph Terry over the left-field fence.

The major-league owners' challenge, then, was to maintain that populist edge. In their view, that meant somehow dispatching the fledgling Continental League, which was fighting to become a viable entity and was therefore competition to baseball's established order.

Continental League President Branch Rickey realized early on that congressional approval of a bill proposed by Senator Estes Kefauver (D-Tennessee), designed to bust baseball's reserve clause, would exert the kind of political pressure necessary to help force major-league owners to cooperate. Predictably, at hearings before Senator Kefauver's Anti-Trust and Monopoly subcommittee on May 19 and 20, Commissioner Frick called the bill "preposterous and vicious," while National League President Warren Giles said it would "do great harm to a great game."[13] On June 28 a test vote on a related measure indicated that the Kefauver bill had only 41 votes, and the bill was withdrawn.[14]

On July 18 the National League voted to expand from eight teams to 10, provided that the Continental League, some of whose teams would play in the same cities as existing major-league franchises, disband.[15]

Then, realizing that 41 votes in the Senate against their position meant that the status quo regarding the reserve clause might not hold much longer, and sensing that expansion was now inevitable, the major-league owners invited the owners from the Continental League to a meeting in Chicago on August 2.[16] "The Continental League comes to Chicago with their hats in their hand. We know we have no control over what is to happen," said Continental League representative William Shea.[17]

At the meeting, led by New York Yankees owner Del Webb and Los Angeles Dodgers owner O'Malley, the major-league owners announced plans to outflank the Continental League by adding up to four new franchises no later than 1962 and four more in the future.[18] In short order, sensing they'd been offered as good a deal as they were going to get, "Rickey and his people gathered in a side room, and when the door was shut, they let out a great shout of victory."[19] The Continental League, some of its prospective owners suddenly dreaming of having their own American or National League franchise, was effectively dead.

Now, the major-league owners were left to fight among themselves over the details of how to turn their expansion dream into reality.

On October 11, the day after Del Webb, chairman of the American League's expansion committee, had made overtures toward expanding into Houston, O'Malley announced that the Houston Continental League group had applied for membership in the National League.[20] Six days later, on October 17, the National League owners met in New York, where they officially approved franchises for Houston and New York, to begin play in 1962.[21] The New York group was headed by heiress and philanthropist Joan Whitney Payson, and the Houston group was headed by oil fortune heir Craig Cullinan, both of whom were owners previously aligned with the Continental League.

Commissioner Frick said he believed the American League would soon go to 10 teams and that Los Angeles might be one of them. He added: "I don't believe either league should be permitted to have exclusive control of cities the size of New York, Los

Angeles, or Chicago, and I will so vote, if it comes to that point."[22] Asked if he would approve an American League move to Los Angeles, O'Malley said: "I don't think that would be smart of them to do that, although I would not oppose it. I believe that eventually they will go to the coast, but there are other fine cities, San Diego and Seattle."[23] Not to be outdone, that day American League President Joe Cronin called for the league to meet in executive session in New York the following week to further discuss expansion plans.[24]

On October 26 American League leaders met at the Savoy Hilton Hotel in New York, where they voted to expand to 10 teams and to one-up the National League by beginning play in 1961. They authorized Calvin Griffith to move his team "lock, stock and batboy" from Washington to Minneapolis-St. Paul, and approved a new franchise for the capital.[25] They also sanctioned a 10th franchise in Los Angeles and said baseball would have its first 162-game schedule.[26] At the meeting, the move garnered the minimum six votes needed for Griffith to move to Minnesota, with Detroit and Cleveland voting against him.[27]

Cronin called the expansion plan "the most forward-looking and progressive program in baseball history,"[28] while also adding, "We've let the National League get too far out ahead of our league."[29] But in their haste to act, observed baseball historians Andy McCue and Eric Thompson, "these teams had no general managers, no managers, no players, no ticket-sales department, and a spring training that would begin in four months."[30]

The league's drive to move into the Los Angeles market was motivated by Dan Topping, co-owner of the Yankees, when it became apparent that the National League was aiming for New York, *The Sporting News*' Joe King reported. In August Topping had asked Commissioner Frick "to affirm a stand that Los Angeles as well as New York was open territory. Frick obliged, and promised that he would vote to that effect should there be a tie between the leagues in the matter."[31]

O'Malley reacted that the move "would wreak havoc," and said he had a right to the territory he had established, having (among other things) paid damages to the Pacific Coast League and being in the process of building a new park in Chavez Ravine.[32]

William Shea was equally irate, calling the American League's expansion plan "one of the lowest blows below the belt in the history of the sport."[33] National League President Giles was more diplomatic, saying: "I think the National League can do a more practical job by waiting until 1962 for our expansion."[34]

But the American League owners were not in a compromising or waiting mood. Columnist Shirley Povich reported after the vote that the American League owners were mad at the National League owners "over what they considered a double cross."[35] Cronin had reportedly talked about the National League as "the opposition we've got to lick."[36] And Webb said the two leagues were supposed to act in concert but the National League had not: "They pulled a fast one on us before the World Series and held a hurry up meeting to take in New York and Houston. This was O'Malley's doing. ... He knew we had our eyes on Houston and then they held this hush hush meeting to grab off Houston. I understand they got together and decide on this while riding on a plane to Pittsburgh for the Series."[37]

On November 9 Frick, after considering objections from O'Malley about a possible American League move to Los Angeles, announced that under Rule 1 (c) of the Major League Rules, the American League could not place a second team in Los Angeles without the unanimous consent of the owners.[38]

On November 17, again meeting at the Savoy, the American League leaders met to award the new Washington franchise to Gen. Elwood "Pete" Quesada and his group over syndicates headed by Admiral John Bergen of New York and Edward Bennett Williams of Washington. Nicknamed The Pilot's General, Quesada had developed many of the principles of tactical air-ground warfare that led to Allied air superiority in Europe, and in the Normandy invasion was noted for flying Gen. Dwight Eisenhower "piggy back" in a two-seater plane to the front lines. At Eisenhower's urging, he took the job as the first head of the Federal Aviation Agency in 1958, serving until 1961. Quesada was also a frequent presence at Griffith Stadium, where he often sat with the team's owner, Calvin Griffith.[39]

At the meeting, American League owners also devised a system for stocking the new teams in Washington and Los Angeles, with each of the eight existing teams losing seven men to the new members. And they agreed on a course of action to amend Rule 1 (c) to allow for a new team to enter a city that already had one. Concurrently, Commissioner Frick was involved in shuttle meetings with representatives from both leagues.[40]

On November 18 Cronin indicated that the American League was prepared to negotiate terms for entry into Los Angeles with O'Malley.[41] On November 22 O'Malley, Giles, National League lawyer Lou Carroll, and Frick met with Cronin, Webb, Topping, Griffith, and John Fetzer of the Detroit Tigers. O'Malley held his ground, and said he would demand strict adherence to Rule 1 (c).[42]

Later that day, American League leaders and Cronin did another about-face. They would attempt to operate in 1961 with nine teams: Washington in the American League and either New York or Houston in the National League, and there would be interleague play, if the National League would also expand to nine teams and begin play in 1961. O'Malley was favorably inclined, but the other National League owners were opposed, preferring an "orderly solution."[43]

The logjam began to disintegrate in New York on November 30, when Frick met with Cronin, Giles, Carroll, and American League attorney Ben Fiery. The resulting settlement eliminated the nine-club idea, rejected interleague play and made possible the American League's entry into Los Angeles in 1961.[44] Amendments were drafted to change to Rule 1 (c). Among the proposed changes, any major-league city with more than 2.4 million people could now be invaded by a rival without the consent of the other league. Only New York, Los Angeles, and Chicago fit that description.[45]

Frick expressed particular concern that any changes to Rule 1 (c) be "solid enough that we can live with and by it. We have to set up a permanent rule to guide not only American League expansion in 1961 by major expansion in 1962 and further major action around 1965, to go to twelve clubs."[46]

In advance of the coming Winter Meetings, *The Sporting News* issued a stern challenge to the major-league owners: "Prosperity or Chaos: Time for Decision" was the headline over the lead editorial of the November 30 issue. "When they open their meeting in St. Louis next week, the major leagues will stand at the cross-roads. … [T]he club owners must choose the roads that lead to prosperity or stumble onto those which detour to chaos. Seldom in its history has Organized Ball needed so urgently the wisdom, the patience, the courage and the unselfishness which must be combined if it is to solve its problems in the long-term interests of millions of fans, as well as of leagues, clubs, officials, and players more directly involved."[47]

Further, the "Bible of Baseball" took the owners to task for their failure to more quickly address antitrust issues, plot orderly expansion plans, and mitigate the damage they were inflicting on the health of the minor leagues. "To do these things, of course, would have required thinking far beyond provincial attitudes and well outside the counting rooms," they editorialized. "We're sorry to say not too many club owners were dedicated to this sort of thinking. Before this situation worsens … [i]t's high time to consider not what's good for any individual or league or any other just, but limited interest. It's time to consider what is good for baseball."[48]

The Winter Meetings Begin

On December 5, the opening day of the winter meetings in St. Louis, National League President Giles told a newsman it had killed the nine-club proposal. "It is not subject to reconsideration. This is final," Giles said.[49] Cronin said the National League had advised the American League that the rejection was based on the lack of stadium facilities in Houston and because indemnities to the American Association had not been satisfied in that city.[50] "Earlier yesterday, the National League had suggested that the expansion problem could be resolved if Elwood (Pete) Quesada withdrew from the picture in Washington. That was not going to happen, as Quesada addressed the American League owners and won their unanimous reaffirmation."[51]

Cronin offered that if the National League would reconsider a nine-team league, the Yankees would withdraw any claims for indemnification or damage and would open the New York territory to the National League. Cronin warned that if the National League refused to cooperate, the American League would move swiftly into Los Angeles. The proposal was relayed to the National League, which did not reconvene, but reiterated its opposition to the nine-team idea.[52]

On December 6, as both leagues met separately, a bold move on the multi-front, high-stakes chessboard was made by O'Malley, who told the Associated Press that he was willing to permit the American League to operate with a 10th club in Los Angeles in 1961 under certain conditions, which he declined to elaborate.[53]

The American League brought in, for screening purposes, the soon-to-be new owners of the Los Angeles Angels, headed by Gene Autry, the legendary "Singing Cowboy" and business tycoon, and Bob Reynolds, a two-time All-American football star from Stanford, successful investor, and civic leader in Southern California. Autry later huddled with O'Malley, then Frick. O'Malley and the league presidents then met with Frick.[54]

That evening, the American League owners called in the press to meet "the owners of the new Los Angeles club." *St. Louis Post-Dispatch* sports columnist Bob Broeg wrote of the pair: "The American League will have difficulty in Los Angeles, whether it moves to the Pacific Coast this year or next, because the Dodgers are formidable and so are the obstacles. But the franchise is in sound financial hands, the hands of sportsmen."[55]

It appeared that difficulties had been cleared and both leagues adjourned until the next morning. But the unofficial meetings were far from over. "The real job of bringing both sides together was accomplished between 9 o'clock Tuesday night and 4 o'clock Wednesday morning in (Pirates owner John) Galbreath's suite," reported Bob Burnes. "Autry and O'Malley were there. Frick was in and out and two representatives of each league attended."[56] By the next afternoon, the "Missouri Compromise" had been hatched and approved. Or, as the *St. Louis Post-Dispatch*'s Neal Russo put it, "O'Malley finally yielded, all the way to the bank," as agreements were reached, among others, indemnifying the Dodgers.[57]

Red Smith described the moment of victory: "The Commissioner cast a tender glance down the room toward the Dodgers' O'Malley, who had wanted to keep Los Angeles for himself. … When it came O'Malley's turn to talk he sat on the edge of the table. His cigar was short, his metaphors long and pre-mixed. He said he was proud of baseball 'which has probably solved one of the most difficult problems in 20 years.'"[58] Welcoming Autry and Reynolds into the ownership club, "his tones were warm. His words cuddly." And then came O'Malley's final flourish: "Baseball is crossing bridges, and sometimes we stumble a lot but if we sit around long enough we seem to get sense."[59]

In short order, with only eight days left until the expansion draft, the Autry group quickly hired former Braves manager Fred Haney as general manager and former Giants manager Bill Rigney as field manager. And in a gesture of goodwill, as part of negotiations over the rival league's entry into Los Angeles, Dodgers owner O'Malley ordered his staff to turn to over to Autry all Dodgers scouting reports on minor leaguers.[60]

Of course, it wasn't all sunshine.

Senator Kefauver complimented the majors but warned that "some other steps must be taken looking forward toward an unrestricted draft" or baseball would run the risk of congressional action. "Now that the big-league owners have faced up to their responsibilities to the public," the senator said, "I am hopeful they now will squarely deal with the problem of player control."[61]

Upset by the roadblocks thrown up by the National League owners that had delayed their expansion to 10 teams, American League owners struck back. Using a procedural technicality, they sidetracked a proposal designed to permit clubs like Houston and New York to set up farm systems immediately, a year in advance of their impending bows. The measure was tabled at a joint meeting on December 7, even though the

National Association and the National League had already passed it. "This is a serious blow to us," said Charlie Hurth, general manager of the fledgling New York team. "We were prepared to announce immediately the signing of three working agreements and possibly arrange a fourth. Unless a rule of this type is adopted, it's virtually impossible for us to sign players, since we wouldn't be able to protect them from the draft next fall."[62]

And while O'Malley praised the Autry group, pointing out that they were respecting the rights of the tenants other than the Dodgers to use the Los Angeles Coliseum, columnist Melvin Durslag suggested that O'Malley had gained some measure of revenge when he "managed to consign the American Leaguers to an obsolete concrete shack called Wrigley Field," with its limited parking, narrow area streets, no washrooms on the upper deck, minor-league level power alleys, and 21,030 seating capacity.[63] Further, the terms of the Angels' four-year lease called for an annual rental of $200,000 or 7.5 percent of revenues, whichever was higher, plus all of the parking and concession revenues and maintenance costs.[64]

There was also a dustup on December 5 when American League owners granted conditional approval for the sale of the Kansas City club to a local group, and its continuation in the league through 1961. The problem arose because there had been no other bidders, and the league expected that the co-executrix of the 52 percent majority share would sign off. That's when Chicago insurance tycoon Charles O. Finley entered the fray and offered more money. He won a subsequent bidding war and on December 19 the league gave official consent to the transfer.[65]

Major-league baseball's historic decision to expand was easily the biggest story to come out of the Winter Meetings, and the move deservedly grabbed the public's attention. But seemingly cast to the side were the continuing struggles of the minor leagues and their increasingly problematic relationship with their parent clubs. Indeed, "grave concern" for the future viability of the leagues was palpable.[66]

The National Association of Professional Baseball Leagues, the minor-league umbrella organization, held its 59th annual convention from November 28 to December 1 at the Kentucky Hotel in Louisville.

Lester Biederman, who covered the Pittsburgh Pirates for the *Pittsburgh Press* for 31 years, wrote that the meetings "represent a touching drama to those who really understand what is taking place. There is no convention like this one held anywhere." Some, he said, come to do business, others to catch up with old friends "and talk of the days when they were in the spotlight." And others come looking for work. "The man you feel sorry for is the manager just released or the coach who was caught in a crossfire and needs work badly. … If he isn't lucky here his last year's salary may have to do for the next 12 months when he can hit the trail for the next minor league meeting."[67]

For its part, *The Sporting News*, in an editorial, outlined a gloomy state of affairs regarding the minor leagues and issued a somber challenge:

"The major leagues, in agreeing to expand, necessarily invaded some minor league territory. This in itself puts an additional burden on the majors. They not only must build strong franchises in new cities, they also must do everything possible to keep the remaining minor league sector alive. Without the minors, the majors have no lifelines. In recent years, there has been so much agitation for major league franchises that interest has deteriorated in minor league ball. … Poor facilities and availability of major league radio and television have further weakened the minors. … Despite all the pump priming, minor league attendance continued to dwindle to the point that revelation of the figures has been delayed. … The burden will rest with the major leagues."[68]

Never mind the old saying "No one grows up playing baseball pretending that they're pitching or hitting Triple-A." *The Sporting News* editorial board aggressively emphasized the critical importance of the minor leagues. Under the headline "Note to Big Spenders—Don't Forget Minors," it wrote: "Expansion … demonstrates clearly that there is no shortage of fresh money to be poured from the top." The minors must be "encouraged and promoted if the great sport is to be maintained as a precious institution. It would be most shortsighted to sprinkle millions among the grown crop of the majors, then to neglect to spread some financial fertilizer in the lower acres on which a large degree of the future of the game depends."[69]

But in fact, the major leagues did appear to be ignoring the plight of the minor leagues, some of which faced an uncertain future without new working agreements so they could continue to operate as eight-team leagues.

As the winter meetings took place, only the Pacific Coast League was sure to have eight teams going forward, and then only after going to Honolulu to replace Sacramento. The International League also had to leave the mainland, replacing Miami with San Juan, but still lacked an eighth team, and Montreal no longer had a working agreement or major league tie-up. The American Association was faced with the knowledge that it was going to lose teams in Minneapolis, St. Paul, and Houston due to the big-league expansion. Deeper into the minors, the situation was even worse. The Southern Association was on life support. The Double-A Texas League had only six teams. The Mexican League, also classified as a Double-A circuit, decided it was not going to get help from the majors and so would develop its own players.[70]

Throughout the minor leagues there was frustration over the lack of assistance from the major leagues, including one minor-league executive who unsuccessfully made the rounds in Louisville and St. Louis seeking sponsorship by one major-league club for a team on his circuit.[71]

"If the majors wanted to build better ball clubs in their expanded program, they could have accomplished it by turning over the money to the minors for development of players," said another minor-league owner.[72]

Still, after the NAPBL announced that Jim Burris had been named president of the American Association, replacing Ed Doherty, who resigned to become general manager of the new Washington club, the 38-year-old former league secretary sounded a note of optimism. "I know that there'll be tough days ahead. However, I believe that when the major leagues finally settle their expansion problems, they will be more cognizant of the need for strong upper-classification leagues."[73]

In addition to announcing Burris's promotion, the minor-league leaders named former Eastern League President Tommy Richardson president of the International League. He replaced Frank "Shag" Shaughnessy, who retired for health reasons after serving as president of the league since 1936. Shaughnessy invented a playoff system known as the Shaughnessy playoffs. Without those playoffs, "the minor leagues would not have been able to survive the critical years," *The Sporting News* wrote in a sendoff editorial. But most significantly, they said, Shaughnessy was a "firm believer in the theory that baseball was popular because people understood it. He refused to let the rulebook be cluttered with amendments and changes."[74]

Encircled by major-league owners squabbling about the where and when of expansion, the NAPBL attendees added to the uncertainty by voting down five measures offered by their own members that proposed increasing monetary assistance from the major leagues.

"Pressure from the parent club organizations and hopes that the majors would extend the player development fund were believed to have prompted the turndowns," wrote Clifford Kachline.[75] Among the financial measures defeated was a radio-television amendment that sought to prohibit the major leagues from permitting broadcasts of their games from stations within 100 miles of a minor-league park. By contrast, a proposal by the Los Angeles Dodgers to cut spring-training costs for the major leagues was approved.[76]

"To use a trite but true expression, 'confusion reigned supreme,'" wrote *The Sporting News*' editor, Oscar Kahan in describing the four-day convention. "Principally because of the expansion problems of the National League and the American League, it was almost impossible for the minors to complete their plans here until the majors settled their difficulties." There was general agreement among the attendees that this year their meeting should have been held after the majors; instead, Kahan summarized, "Most minor leagues with problems left here with no solutions."[77]

There was some forward movement, however, as a number of proposals approved by the minor leagues were ratified a week later by the major-league owners. Among them was the player-development fund, which the major-league owners committed to support at the previous year's level of slightly more than $800,000, and with the same distribution formula.[78]

A "historic first" was established when both the minor-league and major-league meetings approved a college rule that prohibited Organized Baseball from signing college players during the school year. Players could, however, be signed during their summer vacation period.[79]

Everett Barnes, Colgate University baseball coach and chairman of the NCAA Coaches Association, spoke in favor of the measure before the minor-league executives on November 29.[80] Cleveland Indians pitching hero Bob Feller also weighed in, saying professional baseball must turn more to colleges for future prospects. "Today, at least some college education is imperative—the more the better," Feller said.[81]

The Sporting News supported the vote, saying, "[G]ood relations should be maintained with the colleges. They may become a vital necessity in the game if the minor leagues, the sources of talent, keep evaporating."[82]

Also approved was an amendment to permit the major leagues to option players with less than two seasons of professional experience below the Class B level. It was designed to enable big-league clubs to send first-year players who were called up after their rookie season to Class C or D teams the next year in cases where they weren't considered ready for a higher classification.[83]

On the first day of the NAPBL meetings, the annual series of player drafts kicked off. The draft was made in three phases: the draft of players eligible because of their length of time in the minors; first-year players; and a special draft for the Washington team. With a flair for the dramatic, Commissioner Frick announced, "The authorized representative of the Washington club of the American League will now select his draft choices."[84] General manager Ed Doherty announced that the team was claiming right-handed pitchers Ray Semproch from Spokane and John Gabler from Richmond, both at the $25,000 draft price.

All told, 11 major-league teams took 23 players from minor-league rosters at a cost of $497,000, compared with 14 players drafted at a total cost of $325,000 in 1959. The new draftees were made up of 12 pitchers, 7 catchers, 3 infielders, and 1 outfielder. Seventeen of the selections were picked under the normal draft rule at $25,000 apiece. Six first-year players were purchased for $12,000 each after rules were modified to allow a team to send a first-year player to the minors on option.[85]

The minor-league clubs also showed an increase in activity, taking 36 players for $327,000, versus 26 players for $167,000 the previous year.[86]

A simmering feud between Frick and Chicago White Sox owner Bill Veeck added a bit of drama to the draft. Veeck thought he had cleared the decks for a fifth pick with a trade made earlier in the day, but Frick vetoed it, saying his roster had been frozen at 36 on November 7, the same as every other American League club. "This is a violation of the freeze order. You are doing this just to embarrass me, and I don't embarrass easily," snapped Frick. Veeck's indignant response: "Did he freeze the National League rosters? Why, no. This is strictly a unilateral rule. The National League can draft, but we can't. He's strictly a National League commissioner."[87]

On the interleague front, the biggest swap occurred on December 3, when the San Francisco Giants swapped a two-time 20-game winner, Johnny Antonelli, and outfielder Willie Kirkland to the Cleveland Indians for eight-time All-Star and 1959 AL batting champion Harvey Kuenn. Giants manager Alvin Dark said of Kuenn, who sported a .313 lifetime batting average: "Hitters come in all types, and I like to have any kind of a good hitter on my side." Experienced southpaw Antonelli said he would have quit San Francisco if he had not been traded. And "Kirkland is younger than Kuenn and has much more power" and was a better outfielder, said Indians general manager Frank Lane.[88]

Kuenn had been the American League player representative. After the trade, he was replaced by Johnny Temple as the Cleveland Indians player rep and by

BASEBALL'S BUSINESS: THE WINTER MEETINGS

Gene Woodling of the Baltimore Orioles as player representative for all the American League players.[89]

After the Winter Meetings, the American League held its expansion draft on December 14 in Boston, to fill the rosters of the Los Angeles Angels and the Washington Senators. Each existing American League club had to make available for the draft seven players who had been on their active roster as of August 31, 1960, and eight others from their 40-man roster. The expansion clubs paid $75,000 for each of the 28 players they drafted, with a maximum of seven players drafted from each existing club, not including minor-league selections. They were required to take at least 10 pitchers, 2 catchers, 6 infielders, and 4 outfielders. The clubs also had the option of drafting one nonroster player for $25,000 from each established franchise.

Looking back over the last two months of the year, "some credit is due to the American League for what was accomplished in 50 days," wrote baseball historian Eric Thompson. "Between October 26, 1960, when the American League expansion was announced, and December 14, 1960, when the expansion draft took place, the following obstacles were overcome: 1. Ownership for the two new franchises was established. 2. Stadium issues in Los Angeles were settled. 3. New policies for future expansion were established. 4. A method of player distribution, convoluted and mishandled as it was, was established. 5. A 162-game schedule was developed."[90]

NOTES

1 Neal Russo, *St. Louis Post-Dispatch*, December 8, 1960: E1.

2 Red Smith, *St. Louis Post-Dispatch*, December 8, 1960: E-63.

3 Bob Burnes, "Expansion Accord Hailed as Guidepost," *The Sporting News*, December 14, 1960: 2.

4 Ibid., 1

5 *St. Louis Post-Dispatch*, December 7, 1960: E1.

6 Ibid.

7 Burnes, *The Sporting News*, December 14, 1960: 8.

8 Ibid.

9 Andy McCue and Eric Thompson, "Epic Mis-management 101: The American League Expansion for 1961," *The National Pastime*, 2011: 1.

10 Leonard Koppett, *Koppett's Concise History of Major League Baseball* (New York: Carroll & Graf Publishers, 1998), 291.

11 The Walt Whitman Archive, at whitmanarchive.org/criticism/disciples/traubel/WWWiC/4/med.00004.77.html.

12 gallup.com/poll/1696/baseball.aspx.

13 Lee Lowenfish, *Branch Rickey, Baseball's Ferocious Gentleman* (Lincoln: University of Nebraska Press, 2007), 569.

14 Ibid.

15 amazinavenue.com/2013/7/18/4534192/new-york-mets-history-july-18-nl-approves-expansion-1960.

16 Frank P. Jozsa, *Major League Baseball Expansions and Relocations, A History 1876-2008* (Jefferson, North Carolina: McFarland & Co, 2009), 63.

17 Edward Prell, *Chicago Tribune*, August 2, 1960: Section 4, page 1.

18 Lowenfish, 574.

19 Michael Shapiro, "Memorabilia From the What If Drawer," *New York Times*, July 22, 2009.

20 McCue and Thompson, 3.

21 *New York Daily News*, October 18, 1960, nydailynews.com/sports/baseball/mets/mets-born-nl-votes-return-gotham-62-article-1.2144369.

22 Ibid.

23 Ibid.

24 Associated Press, *Asbury Park Press*, October 18, 1960: 22.

25 United Press International, *Simpson's Leader-Times* (Kittanning, Pennsylvania), October 27, 1960: 11.

26 Michael Shapiro, *Bottom of the Ninth* (New York: Henry Holt & Co., 2009), 263.

27 Bob Addie, *The Sporting News*, November 2, 1970: 7.

28 *The Sporting News*, November 2, 1960: 4.

29 Mark Armour, *Joe Cronin* (Lincoln: University of Nebraska Press, 2010), 266.

30 McCue and Thompson.

31 Joe King, *The Sporting News*, November 2, 1960: 4.

32 *Simpson's Leader-Times*, October 27, 1960: 11; Armour, 267.

33 *Simpson's Leader-Times*, October 27, 1960: 11.

34 Ibid.

35 Shirley Povich, *The Sporting News*, November 2, 1960: 4.

36 *The Sporting News*, November 2, 1960: 4.

37 Shirley Povich, *The Sporting News*, November 2, 1960: 4.

38 Dan Daniel, *The Sporting News*, November 23, 1960: 11.

39 Shirley Povich, *The Sporting News*, November 23, 1960: 11.

40 Dan Daniel, *The Sporting News*, November 23, 1960: 11.

41 Ibid.

42 Dan Daniel, *The Sporting News*, November 30, 1960: 2.

43 Ibid.

44 Dan Daniel, *The Sporting News*, December 7, 1960: 1.

45 Bob Burnes, *The Sporting News*, December 14, 1960: 2.

46 Dan Daniel, *The Sporting News*, December 7, 1960: 6.

47 *The Sporting News*, November 30, 1960: 12.

48 Ibid.

49 Bob Burnes, *The Sporting News*, December 14, 1960: 1.

50 United Press International, *Rochester* (New York) *Democrat and Chronicle*, December 6, 1960: 33.

51 Ibid.

52 Bob Burnes, *The Sporting News*, December 14, 1960: 1.

53 Associated Press, *Kansas City Times*, December 7, 1960: 22.

54 *The Sporting News*, December 14, 1960: 2.

55 *St. Louis Post-Dispatch*, December 7, 1960: 58.

56 Bob Burnes, *The Sporting News*, December 14, 1960: 8.

57 *St. Louis Post Dispatch*, December 8, 1960: E1.

58 *St. Louis Post-Dispatch*, December 8, 1960: E2.

59 Ibid.

60 McCue and Thompson.

61 *The Sporting News*, December 14, 1960: 7.

62 Clifford Kachline, *The Sporting News*, December 14, 1960: 8.

63 *The Sporting News*, December 14, 1960: 7.

64 Shapiro, *Bottom of the Ninth*, 272.

65 David Jordan, *The A's: A Baseball History* (Jefferson, North Carolina: McFarland & Co., 2014), 95.

66 Eric Thompson, *Baseball's Lost Tradition* (Lighthouse Publishing of the Carolinas, 2012).

67 *Pittsburgh Press*, December 1, 1960: 53.

68 *The Sporting News*, November 2, 1960: 12.

69 *The Sporting News*, December 14, 1960: 10. The "no one grows up" quotation comes from Joe Feinstein, *Where Nobody Knows Your Name* (New York: Doubleday, 2004), inside front flap of the dust jacket. It is in quotes, attributed to "Chris Schwinlen, Triple-A pitcher."

70 Bob Burnes, *The Sporting News*, December 21, 1960: 1.

71 *The Sporting News*, December 14, 1960: 10.

72 *The Sporting News*, December 21, 1960: 1.

73 Johnny Carrico, *The Sporting News*, December 7, 1960: 7.

74 *The Sporting News*, December 14, 1960: 10.

75 Clifford Kachline, *The Sporting News*, December 7, 1960: 11.

76 Ibid.

77 *The Sporting News*, December 7, 1960: 9.

78 *The Sporting News*, December 14, 1960: 8.

79 Ibid.

80 *The Sporting News*, December 7, 1960: 16.

81 *The Sporting News*, November 16, 1960: 4.

82 *The Sporting News*, December 14, 1960: 10.

83 *The Sporting News*, December 14, 1960: 8.

84 *The Sporting News*, December 7, 1960: 6.

85 *The Sporting News*, December 7, 1960: 14.

86 Ibid.

87 *The Sporting News*, December 7, 1960: 8.

88 *The Sporting News*, December 14, 1960: 9.

89 *The Sporting News*, December 14, 1960: 4.

90 Eric Thompson, *Baseball's Lost Tradition*.

1961

THE METS, THE COLT .45S, AND DEBATING THE RETURN OF THE SPITBALL

By Christopher Matthews

Introduction and Context

IN THE WINTER OF 1961, BASEBALL FANS were gearing up for an expansion of the National League—newcomers named the New York Mets and Houston Colt .45's would play their inaugural season in 1962. Baseball writers around the country, however, were more thrilled by the return of Casey Stengel, hired to manage the Mets. The quotable Stengel was returning from a forced one-year retirement from the game, and in the winter of 1961 the newspapers were once again filled with his colorful pronouncements on such subjects as the possible return of the spitball.[1]

Adding teams in Houston and New York, a year after the American League moved into Los Angeles and Washington (with the shift of the previous D.C. team to Minneapolis), was the backdrop to the winter meetings in Miami in 1961. But the owners had more to deal with than inviting two new members to join their club. The aforementioned spitball was also an issue which was placed on the table and subsequently received plenty of press coverage. After a ban since 1920, a movement to bring back the spitball seemingly came out of nowhere, but received some high-profile support from luminaries like Stengel.[2]

Another more chronic issue that needed addressing was the explosion in the size of signing bonuses being given to first-year players. Commissioner Ford C. Frick was intent on enacting a new bonus rule that would alleviate this problem. There had been no regulations on the books restricting bonuses to unproven talent since 1957, and with the commissioner and most owners united in their desire to create a system that would keep large bonuses in check, this matter was a top priority for Frick in the winter of 1961.[3]

The meetings were also notable for showing signs of a nascent labor movement. It would be several years before the reserve clause was formally challenged, but issues dealt with in the winter of 1961 foreshadowed some of the monumental changes the players union would bring to the game, primarily the contract battle waged by New York Yankees star Roger Maris in the winter after his record-setting season of 1961.[4] Ownership would also address the issue of holding two All-Star Games, a practice that had been in place since the 1959 season in order to finance the players pension fund.[5] The owners were opposed to this, and the disagreement on how to take care of former major leaguers showed the beginnings of a rift between players and management that would grow much wider in years to come.

Player Movement

San Francisco fans were able to breathe a sigh of relief that their team wasn't successful in its attempt to trade its part-time, 23-year-old first baseman, Willie McCovey.[6] McCovey had burst onto the scene two years earlier, hitting .354/.429/.656 in 52 games and being selected the National League Rookie of the Year, but he battled shoulder injuries in the following years and found his career stagnating.[7] The Giants shopped him at the winter meetings in 1961, hoping to trade him to the St. Louis Cardinals for light-hitting second baseman Julian Javier.[8] The trade didn't happen, however, and McCovey went on to post a 154 OPS+ in 1962. He followed that performance by leading the league in home runs in 1963 with 44 on his way to a spot in the Baseball Hall of Fame.[9]

The big player in the trade market that winter was the Chicago White Sox, making two deals in an effort to get younger and shore up their defense.[10] The South Siders dealt 39-year-old outfielder Minnie Miñoso to St. Louis for first baseman-outfielder Joe Cunningham.[11] The White Sox bought low on Cunningham, who bounced back from two down seasons to post a 127 OPS+ in 1962.[12] The team also traded an aging slugger, first baseman Roy Sievers, to the Philadelphia Phillies for infielder Charlie Smith and pitcher John Buzhardt.[13] Though one can question Philadelphia's strategy of trading for a star on the wrong side of 34 when it was rebuilding, the deal proved to be a success for the Phillies. Sievers had a few more productive years, while neither Smith nor Buzhardt ever panned out.

Rule Changes

Though the genesis of the spitball legalization movement is unknown, it was submitted to the rules committee by the White Sox and supported by both Commissioner Frick and the president of the American League, Joe Cronin.[14] The main arguments for removing the ban were that it was a difficult rule to enforce and that it would help keep ballooning home-run totals in check. There was also the idea that it would cause hitters to focus more on making contact, thereby bringing back a brand of "small ball" that had been lost in favor of home runs.[15]

The issue was deliberated by the rules committee, chaired by James Gallagher, a former Chicago Cubs business manager and director of the Phillies scouting department.[16] The committee could have removed the ban on the spitter with a simple majority vote, regardless of what the owners thought of the measure.[17] However, Gallagher made it known that he would bring the rule to a vote only if he saw an overwhelming number either for or against it. "I feel that on such an

More of a Huddle Than a Meeting

Reportedly, Commissioner Frick, the two league presidents, and 20 club presidents conducted their business at the joint meeting in seven minutes.*

*"New Bonus System Cuts Majors' Spending for Big Talent," *Minneapolis Star Tribune*, December 3, 1961: 60.

important change the vote should be at least 7 to 2," Gallagher told the *Chicago Tribune*.[18]

Despite the high-profile support and considerable fanfare in the media, the spitball was voted down 8-1 in the rules committee.[19] The committee was made up of the supervisors of the American and National League umpires, one American League executive, two National League executives, and three representatives from the minor leagues. The only member of the committee to vote in favor of the spitball was Cal Hubbard, supervisor of American League umpires.[20]

The major change adopted at the meetings was the passing of Frick's new regulation on bonuses for first-year players. The old rule, which had been in place from 1953 to 1957, stipulated that a player who signed a bonus over a certain amount was required to remain on a team's major-league roster for two full calendar years, or else be placed on the waiver wire and possibly lost to the signing club. The rule was intended to prevent teams from spending big bucks on unproven players and then stashing them interminably in their farm systems.[21] In reality, it led to teams using up bench space for kids who couldn't cut it in the big leagues, and stirred animosity among veterans whose salaries were dwarfed by the bonuses given to these youngsters. It also brought on scorn from the fans and press. Players like Harmon Killebrew and Sandy Koufax (and a host of players who never panned out) were derisively called "bonus babies."[22] Also, the rule wasn't entirely enforceable. Teams came up with ways to pay the players under the table, or they would put their new signees on the disabled list for cooked-up injuries.²³ On top of this, the rule failed to stem the rising tide of bonuses, so it was abandoned in 1957.

Commissioner Frick was determined, however, to keep these bonuses in check. It was estimated that since the old rule was repealed, teams had shelled out over $6 million annually for bonuses for this young, unproven talent.²⁴ Frick proposed a slight variation on the old rule: A team could option only one first-year player to the minors; all others would have to be kept on the major-league roster or pass through waivers before being sent down. The price to claim the player on waivers was $8,000, regardless of how much bonus money the player had received.²⁵ Theoretically, then, a team would have a heavy incentive not to sign more than one first-year player for more than this amount.

Frick's new rule was passed unanimously in the American League and by 7-3 in the National League, with the big-market Dodgers, Giants, and Mets opposing it.²⁶ As it turned out, there were too many loopholes in the rule, and its failure in part led to the creation of the player draft in 1965.

Finally, it was also decided at the meetings that 1962 would be the final year of holding two All-Star Games. For several years the leagues had played two midseason games in an effort to keep the players' pension fund above water.²⁷ But opposition from the owners of American League teams would bring back the practice of playing just one All-Star Game and force the players in subsequent years to find new ways to keep their fund solvent.

Ford Frick on Overhauling the Minors

"This new bonus rule is the first step. I think we have taken the most forward steps that baseball has made in 15 years. This rule may have some bugs in it but they will be worked out. What I like best about it is that it is self-enforceable. There is no limit. Anybody can pay $100,000 but they may lose the boy in the draft."*

*"Majors Pass New Type Bonus Rule," *Eugene (Oregon) Guard,* December 3, 1961: 14.

Conclusion

On its face, the winter meetings of 1961 weren't that revolutionary. There were no blockbuster trades, the movement to bring back the spitball was shot down, and a new rule to curb first-year player bonuses was enacted, but it was really just a variation on a theme that had been played around with since the end of World War II. Looking back, however, one can see how the major changes of the 1960s and beyond were presaged by the 1961 meetings. The players' pension plan was broke, and having two All-Star Games was an attempt by the players to get a bigger piece of the pie. Rebuffed by the owners, they would be forced to use more confrontational tactics to get their share of baseball's profits. Though Commissioner Frick was very confident in the efficacy of his new bonus rule, it proved to be a failure, directly leading to the Rule 4 (free-agent) Draft, now a staple and a major event of every modern baseball season.

NOTES

1. "Stengel Backs Return of Spitball as Assist for His Met Pitchers," *New York Times,* November 24, 1961: 49.
2. "Rules Group Acts Today on Spitball," *Chicago Tribune,* November 26, 1961: C6.
3. baseballamerica.com/today/2005draft/050604bonus.html.
4. "Yankees Maris Seeks Reward for '61 Showing; Still Can't Come to Terms," *Chicago Daily Defender,* January 25, 1962: 27.
5. mlb.sbnation.com/2011/7/7/2264638/all-star-game-major-league-baseball.
6. "Baseball Rules Committee Votes, 8 to 1, to Retain Ban on Spitball Pitches," *New York Times,* November 27, 1961: 40.
7. Ibid.
8. Ibid.
9. baseball-reference.com/players/m/mccovwi01.shtml.
10. "Sox Trade Sievers for 2 Phillies," *Chicago Tribune,* November 29, 1961: C1.
11. Ibid.
12. baseball-reference.com/players/c/cunnijo01.shtml.
13. "Sox Trade Sievers."
14. "To Spit or Not ..." *Los Angeles Times,* November 26, 1961: L2; "Rules Group Acts Today on Spitball," *Chicago Tribune,* November 26, 1961: C6.
15. "To Spit or Not ..."
16. "Rules Group Acts Today on Spitball."
17. Ibid.
18. Ibid.
19. "Baseball Rules Committee."
20. Ibid.
21. hardballtimes.com/main/article/cash-in-the-cradle-the-bonus-babies/.
22. Ibid.
23. Ibid.
24. "Frick Hails Move to Halt Wild Bonus Bidding," *New York Times,* November 8, 1961: 46.
25. "New Bonus Rule Is Likely at Baseball Meetings," *New York Times,* November 26, 1961: S2.
26. "New 'Bonus Rule' Voted by Majors," *New York Times,* December 3, 1961: S1.
27. Ibid.

— 1962 —
ADDITION BY SUBTRACTION

By Chris Jones

ROCHESTER, NEW YORK, PLAYED host to the 1962 baseball winter meetings, which saw discussion of issues including the pace of play, player travel, and a healthy amount of player movement. The largest issue on the agenda, however, concerned the reorganization of the minor-league system.

Minor League Overhaul

The most extensive action taken during the winter meetings involved a reorganization of what some considered the "rapidly deteriorating minor league structure."[1] Minor-league attendance had declined each year since 1949, going from a high of more than 41 million that year to just over 10 million in 1962.[2] The proposed plan to overhaul the system, known as the "Player Development Plan," provided for a reclassification and realignment of the minor-league system in exchange for monetary support by the major-league clubs.[3]

Specifically, the proposed plan called for reducing the then-current six classifications to three—AAA, AA, and A—with each big-league club (except for the four newest ones, the Mets, Colt .45's, Angels, and Senators) underwriting five minor-league teams. The major-league clubs would further "provide the bulk of players and managers, pay all expenses and salaries over a stipulated amount ($800 monthly in AAA, $150 in AA, and $50 in A[4]), and reimburse the minors for all losses." The major-league clubs would in turn have the right to purchase players from their affiliated clubs for a fixed price.[5]

One of the primary points of contention involving the plan was that "the major-league clubs had decided to extend working agreements to only 20 Triple-A entries for the 1963 season. Unfortunately, there were 22 clubs in the three top circuits—eight in the International, eight in the Coast, and six in the Association."[6] This led to what was described as a "jungle-like atmosphere" at the minor-league convention held from November 26-29, 1962, as the minor-league clubs fought for their survival. *The Sporting News* further described the heated nature of the discussions:

> Any schoolboy knows that eight plus six plus six equals 20 and that ten plus ten equals 20, but eight plus eight plus six equals 22. Yet inability to come to grips with this simple arithmetic created a chaotic condition without compare at the National Association convention here, November 26-29.[7]

In the end, "it took the entire four days of the confab and the combined efforts of major and minor league officials to figure out finally what takes what to make twenty."[8] In sum, the International League and the Pacific Coast League absorbed the American Association and became two 10-club leagues. The teams that had previously constituted the American Association were divided, with Dallas-Fort Worth, Oklahoma City, and Denver heading to the Pacific Coast League and Little Rock[9] and Indianapolis moving to the International League.[10] The International League initially rejected the merger, but a resolution was reached upon the major league's agreement to absorb additional travel costs.[11] Following the minor leagues' agreement to the player development program, it was officially adopted by major-league owners.[12]

The two casualties of the merger were Vancouver of the Pacific Coast League and Omaha of the American Association.[13] While the surviving Triple-A clubs undoubtedly breathed a sigh of relief, fear of additional contraction remained: "This is just like death row," said one baseball official, "with many minor league clubs and their backers waiting to see who is next to be tapped to walk that last mile."[14]

Attempt to Shorten Games

The American and National Leagues each voted in their opening sessions to put new restrictions on pitchers in an effort to shorten "those marathon ball games that frequently run 3 hours and more." Specifically, the leagues focused on warm-up pitches, mound visits, and the on-deck circle.

The National League voted to limit pitchers to five warm-ups per inning instead of the usual eight. The American League also limited pitchers to five warm-up pitches per inning, save for the first 30 days of the season, when the usual eight pitchers would be permitted.

In addition, both leagues agreed that a pitcher awaiting his turn as the next batter must do so from the on-deck circle. Previously, the batter following the pitcher would "keep the on-deck spot warm while the pitcher rests on the bench until he has to bat." The American League went even further and required catchers to remove all protective gear while waiting in the on-deck circle.[15]

Finally, the National League decided that a manager could visit the mound only once per inning. A second mound visit would result in the mandatory removal of the pitcher. The American League already had an even more restrictive rule in place, mandating that a manager could go to the mound to talk to the same pitcher only once in the entire game.[16]

Players' Complaints

Players voiced a number of complaints during the meetings over issues ranging from travel to ballpark lavatories.

With respect to travel, players wanted direct flights from city to city. National League player representative Bob Friend of the Pirates reported that "one team stopped three times from one city to another last season and later made a four-stop trip, both on commercial planes, to save money."[17]

Additional player requests included:

- Eliminating any day-night, two-admission games except in cases of emergency or long-standing tradition, such as the Memorial Day games in Minneapolis and St. Paul.
- An increase in the minimum salary from $7,000 to $8,000.
- Inclusion of the official scorer's name in the program along with those of the umpires.
- A ban on exhibition games with minor-league teams during the season.
- Better mounds in the Yankee Stadium bullpens, and better backgrounds in the visiting bullpens at Yankee Stadium and Fenway Park.
- The installation of phones connecting the bullpen to the dugout in all big-league ballparks.
- More lights in the Houston ballpark and better bullpen lavatory conditions.[18]

No official action was taken with respect to any of these issues.

1963 All Star Game

Players agreed to a proposal from 20 National and American league owners returning the All-Star Game to a one-game format. Under the deal, the owners would give the players 95 percent of the gate, TV, and radio receipts in exchange for returning to a single game.[19] Players had demanded a two-game format since 1959.

Of primary concern to the players was the amount of money allocated to the player pension fund; the loss of a second game reportedly would cost the fund $50,000 per year. Previously, 60 percent of all receipts for the two games were put into the pension fund, totaling an aggregate of $450,000. The higher percentage of receipts for a single game helped to offset the loss of the second game, and would yield an estimated $395,000.[20]

Major-league baseball awarded the 1963 All-Star Game to Cleveland, departing from the procedure that would have awarded the game to a National League city. The change guaranteed the 1964 game to the New York Mets to coincide with crowds in town for the World's Fair.[21]

Yankees Send Skowron to Dodgers

Perhaps the most noteworthy player transaction to be consummated during the winter meetings was the Yankees' trade of their longtime slugger, first baseman Bill Skowron, to the Los Angeles Dodgers in exchange for veteran right-handed pitcher Stan Williams. In Williams, the Yankees acquired "the pitcher they so badly needed last season and couldn't get," and one whom some considered "one of the finest pitchers" on a Dodgers staff consisting of names like Koufax, Drysdale, and Podres.[22] Williams's final appearance with the Dodgers was walking in the winning run during the 1962 National League playoff against the San Francisco Giants.[23]

The Dodgers' acquisition of Skowron, on the other hand, was immediately second-guessed, with the general reaction being, "What does a team with so much talent need Skowron for?" It was rumored that the Dodgers would use Skowron in an additional trade with the Kansas City Athletics for sought-after second baseman Jerry Lumpe, but team officials quickly shot down such speculation.[24] Before being sent to the West Coast, Skowron was rumored to be on his way to Boston. The Yankees reportedly asked for either Bill Monbouquette or Gene Conley in the deal, however, but the Red Sox were not interested in parting with either All-Star right-hander.[25]

Major and Minor League Drafts

Records were set in the major- and minor-league drafts when a total of 116 players were selected. As Edward Prell wrote in the *Chicago Tribune*, "(i)n the first 'game,' the majors selected 56 players at a cost of $696,000." The old record had been set just the year before, in Louisville, when the major-league clubs selected 35 players for $680,000. The minor leagues at the Triple-A, Double-A, A, and B levels spent a collective $483,000 on 60 players. The Orioles were deemed the "biggest losers" in the draft process, as "(18) of their chattels were claimed at the various levels."[26]

Additional Player Transactions:

- The first trade of the Winter Meetings saw the Cleveland Indians send third baseman-outfielder Bubba Phillips to the Detroit Tigers for rookie pitchers Ron Nischwitz (a lefty) and right-hander Gordon Seyfried.[27]
- The Detroit Tigers pulled off a second trade within eight hours of acquiring Phillips when they obtained catcher Gus Triandos and outfielder Whitey Herzog from the Baltimore Orioles for catcher Dick Brown.[28]
- The Red Sox and Houston Colt .45's traded premium hitters; Boston obtained Roman Mejias, an outfielder coming off a 24-home-run season, for infielder Pete Runnels, the American League batting champion in 1960 and 1962.[29]
- The Cincinnati Reds acquired journeyman infielder Harry Bright from the Washington Senators for first baseman Rogelio Alvarez.[30]
- The Cleveland Indians sent right-handed pitcher Frank Funk, outfielder Don Dillard, and a player to be named later (outfielder Ty Cline) to the Milwaukee Braves for first baseman Joe Adcock and left-handed pitcher Jack Curtis.[31]
- The New York Mets purchased right-handed pitcher Wynn Hawkins from the Cleveland Indians for $25,000. Hawkins had spent much of the 1962 season in the Army, but managed to pitch on the weekends in Jacksonville.[32]
- The Philadelphia Phillies acquired infielder Cookie Rojas from Cincinnati in exchange for Jim Owens, a "28-year-old right-hander whose problems outweighed his promise."[33] Owens reportedly had "jumped the club on more than one occasion and was suspended by the club during spring training of 1960 after he and some teammates were fined for staying out after curfew."[34] Phillies general manager John Quinn said that "Owens simply outlived his usefulness for us" and that "it was either make any deal we could for him or sell him for what we could get."[35]
- The Detroit Tigers traded third baseman Steve Boros to the Chicago Cubs for right-handed pitcher Bob Anderson. Boros had hit .270 in his

rookie year and had been named the Most Valuable Player of the American Association in 1960.[36]
- The Houston Colt .45's traded first baseman Norm Larker to the Milwaukee Braves for two minor leaguers, right-handed pitcher Connie Grob and outfielder Jim Bolger. Houston also acquired pitcher Don Nottebart from the Milwaukee Braves in a cash transaction.[37] The Colt .45's also acquired left-handed pitcher Dick Lemay and outfielder (and future pinch-hitter supreme) Manny Mota for second baseman Joe Amalfitano.[38]
- The Mets traded right-handed pitcher Bob Miller to the Dodgers for second baseman Larry Burright and first baseman Tim Harkness. The Mets purchased right-handed pitcher Howard Reed from the Dodgers in a separate cash transaction.[39]

Miscellaneous Notes

- The National League re-elected President Warren Giles for another four-year term.[40]
- The American and National Leagues agreed that no further expansion would occur without "full discussions between both leagues in a joint executive session."[41]
- The major leagues voted against a proposal that would have allowed for interleague trading each June. Commissioner Frick also opposed the proposal, stating that "when you start trading like that in the middle of the season you leave yourself open to considerable criticism," as "you might even find pennant contenders in one league getting help from low-ranked clubs in the other league and that doesn't make sense."[42]

NOTES

1 "Minors to Be Overhauled With Big League Money," *Hartford Courant*, November 25, 1962: 4C1.
2 "Int-AA Merger Bid Pinpoints Plunge by Minors Since 1949," *The Sporting News*, December 1, 1962: 4.
3 "Minors Doomed Unless Majors Act," *The Sporting News*, December 8, 1962: 1-2.
4 "Two Clubs Added to International," *New York Times*, November 30, 1962: 37.
5 "Minors to be Overhauled."
6 "Minors Doomed Unless Majors Act."
7 "22 Clubs, Only 20 Tieups, Add Up to Headache," *The Sporting News*, December 8, 1962: 2.
8 Ibid.
9 Little Rock was an expansion team that effectively replaced Louisville, which dissolved following the 1962 season.
10 "Majors to Foot Bill for Revamped Minors," *Los Angeles Times*, November 30, 1962: B1.
11 "Two Clubs Added to International."
12 "Cleveland Awarded 1963 All-Star Game," *Washington Post and Times Herald*, December 2, 1962: C4.
13 "3 Top Minor Leagues Re-Organized," *Washington Post and Times Herald*, November 30, 1962: B9.
14 "Minors Doomed Unless Majors Act."
15 "Major Leagues Take Steps to Shorten Games," *Los Angeles Times*, December 1, 1962: A3.
16 "Majors Move to Speed Game by Pitching Rule Change," *New York Times*, December 1, 1962: 43.
17 "Players Toss Travel Gripes at Owners," *The Sporting News*, December 1, 1962: 1.
18 Ibid.
19 "Major League Baseball Returns to One All-Star Game for 1963," *Chicago Tribune*, November 30, 1962: C1.
20 Ibid.
21 "Cleveland Awarded 1963 All-Star Game."
22 "Yanks Trade Skowron," *Boston Globe*, November 27, 1962: 22.
23 "Nats Send Bright to Cincinnati; Skowron Traded for Stan Williams," *Washington Post and Times Herald*, November 27, 1962: A17.
24 "Yanks Trade Skowron."
25 "Yanks Trade Skowron": 24.
26 Edward Prell, "Major and Minor Leagues Draft 116 for $1,178,000," *Chicago Tribune*, November 27, 1962: 3, 1.
27 "Indians Trade Phillips to Tigers for Pitchers," *Hartford Courant*, November 26, 1962: 18.
28 "Boston Acquires Mejias from Houston for Runnels," *Chicago Tribune*, November 26, 1962: C1.
29 Ibid.
30 "Yanks Trade Skowron."
31 "Indians Get Adcock in 5-Player Swap," *Boston Globe*, November 28, 1962: 34.

32 "Mets Purchase Hawkins, Hurler," *New York Times*, November 28, 1962: 47.

33 "Mets Buy Pitcher Hawkins From Indians," *Hartford Courant*, November 2, 1962: 21.

34 Ibid.

35 Ibid.

36 "Steve Boros, Joe Adcock Highlight Major Trades," *Los Angeles Times*, November 28, 1962: B1.

37 "Majors Move to Speed Game by Pitching Rule Change."

38 Ibid.

39 "Mets Trade Bob Miller to Dodgers," *Washington Post and Times Herald*, December 2, 1962: C8.

40 "Major Leagues Take Steps to Shorten Games."

41 "Cleveland Awarded 1963 All-Star Game."

42 Ibid.

— 1963 —
NO LITTLE LEAGUE BATS ALLOWED

By Chris Jones

THE 1963 BASEBALL WINTER MEETings were alive with discussion of important issues, including the permissible size of catcher's mitts and the color of baseball bats. The clubs also made time to once again reconfigure the minor-league structure and adopt an amendment designed to assist the player-development efforts of expansion teams. The minor leagues kicked off the meetings in San Diego December 1 to 4; then they moved up the coast to Los Angeles for the major-league meetings, December 5 to 7.[1]

National Association Elects New President

The National Association (the minor leagues) elected Phil Piton, described as "one of baseball's most dedicated servants," as its new president.[2] Piton succeeded George M. Trautman, who had died in June.[3] Piton had spent 32 years in baseball, including time as secretary to baseball's first commissioner, Kenesaw M. Landis and, for the last 17 years, as Trautman's top assistant. Piton was elected for a five-year term at $30,000 per year.[4] Upon his election Piton foresaw the need for more minor leagues in the future:

> Future major-league expansion will create a need for more minors. How to accomplish this (expanding the minor-league structure) is the burning question, but I must disagree with those who say we don't need more leagues.[5]

Amendment to First-Year Player Rule

The primary piece of legislation passed at the majors' meetings was aimed at aiding the four expansion clubs. The amendment permitted the Mets, Colts, Senators, and Angels to "farm out four additional first-year players next spring without the risk of losing them on waivers or having them count against the player roster during the regular season."[6]

The Houston Colts proposed the amendment, and had plenty at stake—they had 10 first-year players on their roster. Before it passed, Mets representative Johnny Murphy, the former major-league pitcher, explained the importance of the amendment:

> For instance, we now have six first-year players on our roster. If this amendment passes we'd be able to send down five with only one counting against our player limit. Without the amendment we either would have to keep four of those five sitting on the bench next year or risk losing them on waivers. And just how could anyone expect a young club to develop under such a handicap?[7]

All other teams, however, had to continue to abide by the existing first-year rule:

> They can option out only one first-year player on the roster, and he must count against the player limit. The rest must be retained or, if farmed out, can be claimed for the $8,000 waiver price.[8]

All-Star Game Voting

A proposal to return voting on All-Star Game players to the fans was also discussed. Fans had previously been permitted to select the starting players, which "worked satisfactorily until 1957, when Cincinnati fans, whipped up by partisan fervor, cast about 500,000 ballots and for a time threatened to place eight members of the Reds in the starting lineup of the N.L. team."[9] Ultimately, the Reds ended up with five starters on the team that year, and as a result the selection of the team was turned over to the players.

That arrangement, however, also proved to be less than ideal, as fans seemed to lose interest in the contest, and because "players have often been inclined to cast their ballots for established stars, without regard for their season's record, while passing over performers who are having outstanding years."[10] The players, "who have a vital stake in the All-Star Game because it helps finance their pension fund," lobbied to return the vote to the fans as well.[11] In fact, "the player representatives of the 20 clubs disclosed they had agreed to ask Commissioner Ford Frick to restore the voting privilege to the fans 'in order to engender more interest in the game.'"[12]

Proposals for how to conduct fan voting were debated, but no resolution was reached. Ultimately the issue was given over to a four-member committee to explore the issue and submit recommendations to Commissioner Frick.[13]

Oversized Catcher's Mitts and "Colorful" Bats Outlawed

The Official Playing Rules Committee was busy in San Diego, outlawing the use of a controversial piece of equipment—the oversized catcher's mitt. It had been "designed to give baffled receivers a better chance to handle the erratic deliveries of knuckleball pitchers."[14] The rules committee barred catcher's mitts with a circumference of more than 34 inches, beginning with the 1964 season.[15] Charley Segar, the former sportswriter who was chairman of the committee, denied that the rule was aimed at knuckleball pitchers:

> "It is not aimed at any pitcher or any club. No names were mentioned in our discussion. The present rule sets a limitation on the size of the fielder's glove and the first baseman's mitt, but not on the catcher's mitt. We felt it should be included."[16]

The move was not made without dissent, perhaps most vocally from Kansas City Athletics owner Charlie Finley and Houston general manager Paul Richards. Finley vehemently disagreed with the ruling and the apparent failure of the committee to seek outside input. He said the committee's decision displayed "complete disregard for the opinions of managers, general managers, and owners."[17] Richards, a former catcher who had designed the first oversized mitt in 1960 to assist in catching knuckleball pitchers,[18] voiced concern over the inferior level of play that might result:

> "I don't think fans are interested in seeing a catcher get a broken finger or seeing a pitch sailing by him that lets a base-runner grab an extra base. It's like playing a shortstop who can't field grounders."[19]

There was also a movement to introduce the use of green bats, but it was summarily shot down. Rules committee chairman Segar commented that while "green bats, red bats or any other may be all right with the Little Leagues … colored bats will not be approved by the Official Playing Rules Committee."[20]

Pacific Coast/International League Reshuffling

For the second consecutive winter meetings, a reorganization of the minor-league structure was deemed to be in order. This time, the Pacific Coast League agreed to absorb Little Rock and Indianapolis from the International League and expand to 12 teams, allowing the International League to contract to eight teams.[21]

A primary driver of the reorganization was travel costs. Four International League clubs adamantly refused to go along with a 10-team arrangement in 1964 unless the majors renewed a travel subsidy (that) amounted to $78,000 last season."[22] The other six clubs voted to continue with the 10-team setup, but fell short of the seven votes needed.[23]

The International League reportedly had actually been willing to expand to 12 teams—without any travel subsidy—if the additions were Oklahoma City and Dallas. This plan went nowhere when Houston balked at moving its Oklahoma City farm club to another league. Roy Hofheinz, owner of the Colts, stated that the Oklahoma City club "started in the American Association in 1962 and then switched to the Coast league a year ago" and that "we don't want to have to start out in another league [in 1964]."[24]

The final hurdle to the new arrangement was cleared when Commissioner Frick brokered a swap of Triple-A clubs between the St. Louis Cardinals and Cleveland Indians. The Cardinals were the only club lacking a Triple-A team and Portland was the only Triple-A club needing a major-league tie-up—which seemed to make a match until the Cardinals resisted re-affiliating with Portland, with whom they had worked in 1961. So Frick, "acting as a conciliator," got the Indians to switch working agreements with the Cardinals, turning over their Jacksonville team to the Cardinals in exchange for Portland.[25] Frick commented that "we have been up to our ears in the Triple-A realignment and requested the change in order to get things finalized."[26]

The resulting arrangement still left something to be desired, as it stretched the Pacific Coast League from Indianapolis to Hawaii. Someone observed that "Indianapolis is closer to Paris than Hawaii."[27] Frick simply commented that it was "not the ideal solution, but the best possible under the circumstances."[28]

New Rookie Leagues / Mexican League Expansion

Two new rookie leagues were organized to operate as part of the National Association beginning in 1964. One of the leagues, the Pioneer League, was set to include Idaho Falls, Twin Falls, Pocatello, and Caldwell, all in Idaho. "We're cognizant of the fact that this rookie league may not have a long life in these cities," said Jack Schwarz, farm director for the New York Giants.[29] Schwarz explained that "this is simply a caretaker action for the day when Organized Baseball needs these cities" and that "when an opportunity for a full-season league there develops, it will replace the rookie league."[30] The second league, yet to be named, was expected to operate in Sarasota and Bradenton, Florida, and consist of six to eight clubs.[31]

In addition, the two circuits operating in Mexico, the Mexican League and the Mexican Center League, announced their expansion. The Mexican League added a franchise in Guadalajara to increase to eight teams, while the Mexican Center League expanded to six teams. Also, the Southwest and Tabasco Leagues, also operating in Mexico but outside of Organized Baseball, planned to combine to form a third league.[32]

Major- and Minor-League Drafts

A total of 63 players were selected during the major-league draft on December 2, 1963, up from 56 selections in the 1962 draft. The amount spent on the drafted players fell slightly, from $695,000 in 1962 to $691,000 in 1963. Fifty-two of the players drafted were first-year players.[33] One innovation in the way the draft was conducted "was the use of portable microphones to amplify the voices of the club representatives announcing their selections."[34]

In contrast, the minor-league phase of the draft contracted dramatically from the previous year. Only 35 players were selected, down from 60 in the 1962 draft, "when the revised first-year player rule was responsible for ballooning the total."[35] Also, "a decrease in the ranks of minor leagues as well as in new signings … contributed to the decline in selections."[36]

Miscellaneous Notes

- A request by the players to have the active roster increased from 25 to 26 was voted down.[37]
- Two proposals submitted by Kansas City Athletics owner Charles O. Finley—that the World Series begin on a weekend and be followed by three night games—were tabled. A third Finley proposal, that the regular season start on a Saturday, was voted down.[38]
- The minors' annual meetings paused to pay remembrance to the late President John F. Kennedy and George M. Trautman, former president of the National Association. A moment of silence was held to honor Kennedy, and a tribute to Trautman was read to delegates.[39]

Player Transactions

- Before the meetings, the Kansas City Athletics made two trades. The club sent infielder Jerry Lumpe and right-handed pitchers Dave Wickersham and Ed Rakow to the Tigers for outfielder Rocky Colavito, right-handed pitcher Bob Anderson, and $50,000.[40] The Athletics also sent first baseman-outfielder Norm Siebern to the Orioles for first baseman Jim Gentile and $25,000.[41]

- The Los Angeles Angels traded slugging outfielder Leon Wagner to the Cleveland Indians for right-handed pitcher Barry Latman and a player to be named later (first baseman Joe Adcock.)[42] While Wagner was coming off two straight All-Star Game appearances and a 26-home-run season, Angels general manager Fred Haney said that "we must tailor our club for pitching and speed, rather than power."[43]

- The New York Mets purchased catcher-outfielder Hawk Taylor from the Milwaukee Braves for what was believed to be around $30,000. The sale was conditional upon Taylor, who had suffered a broken left shoulder during the 1963 season, establishing his health in the spring. Taylor's most significant impact on baseball may well have been on a team he never played for. Taylor signed with Milwaukee in 1957 for $100,000 after the Braves topped a $90,000 offer made by the Brooklyn Dodgers. Exasperated by being outbid, Dodgers owner Walter O'Malley stated, "This is it. With the revenue we draw in Ebbets Field we simply cannot compete with the wealthier clubs. We'll have to go elsewhere." The Dodgers moved to Los Angeles in 1958.[44]

- The San Francisco Giants sent outfielder Felipe Alou, catcher Ed Bailey, and left-handed pitcher Billy Hoeft to Milwaukee in exchange for catcher Del Crandall, right-handed pitcher Bob Shaw, left-hander Bob Hendley, and a player to be named later (who turned out to be infielder Ernie Bowman). "We gave up one good player [Alou] to get two good pitchers," said Giants manager Al Dark.[45] Even after the trade the Giants still planned on having an Alou in their lineup in the person of Felipe's brother Jesus. "Jesus will hit around .275 and we won't lose anything defensively in the outfield," said Dark.[46]

- The Baltimore Orioles traded outfielder-third baseman Al Smith to the Cleveland Indians for power-hitting outfielder Willie Kirkland.[47]

- In what was arguably the biggest deal of the meetings, the Detroit Tigers sent right-handed pitcher Jim Bunning and catcher Gus Triandos to the Philadelphia Phillies for outfielder Don Demeter and right-handed pitcher Jack Hamilton. Bunning was the Tigers' longtime ace, a five-time All-Star and already the author of 118 major-league victories. A future Hall of Famer (as well as congressman and US senator), Bunning was attending the meetings as the Tigers' player representative, and commented that he was "tickled to death that I've been traded."[48]

- The Dodgers sold first baseman Bill Skowron to the Washington Senators for $25,000. The longtime Yankee had been surprisingly sent to the Dodgers during the 1962 Winter Meetings and responded with his poorest season to date, managing only four home runs, 19 RBIs, and a .203 batting average in 89 games during the '62 season.[49] He would, however, rebound for the Senators and White Sox in 1964 and 1965.

Looking Forward

The 1964 Winter Meetings were awarded to San Antonio, Texas; the minors had last met there in 1911.[50] San Antonio beat out a long list of cities, including Mexico City; Portsmouth, Virginia; Columbus, Ohio; Rochester and Syracuse in New York, and five cities in Florida: Miami, Tampa, Fort Lauderdale, Sarasota, and Daytona Beach. A pitch was even made by Honolulu, which proposed arranging for charter planes to fly in delegates so that airfares would be more reasonable. Such a trip was still deemed to be too expensive.

NOTES

1. "Baseball Bigwigs Face Busy Week," *Los Angeles Times*, December 1, 1963: 16.
2. "'Minors Must Expand,' Says New Boss Piton," *The Sporting News*, December 14, 1963: 11.
3. "Rule Change Aids 4 New Ball Clubs," *New York Times*, December 5, 1963: 76.
4. "Large Catcher's Glove Ruled Out of Baseball," *Los Angeles Times*, December 5, 1963: B2.
5. "Minors Must Expand."
6. "Skowron Purchased by Senators; Indians Send Adcock to Angels," *New York Times*, December 7, 1963: 44.
7. "Expansion Teams to Get Relief if Draft Rule Change Is Passed," *New York Times*, December 4, 1963: 77.
8. "Skowron Purchased by Senators."
9. "Tub Thumpers Beat Drums to Give Star Game Back to Fans, *The Sporting News*, December 14, 1963: 2.
10. Ibid.
11. "Players to Ask Frick to Let Fans Name All-Star Teams," *The Sporting News*, December 14, 1963: 2.
12. Ibid.
13. "Tub Thumpers Beat Drums."
14. "New Rule Bars King-Sized Mitt Backstops Used," *The Sporting News*, December 14, 1963: 2.
15. Ibid.
16. Ibid.
17. "Mitt Rule 'Foolish,' Finley Cries," *Washington Post*, December 6, 1963: B2.
18. Future Hall of Famer Hoyt Wilhelm, an acknowledged master of the knuckleball, pitched for the Baltimore Orioles when Richards managed them.
19. "Tigers Send Bunning and Triandos to Phillies for Demeter and Hamilton," *New York Times*, December 6, 1963: 56.
20. "Rules Chief Segar Says No to Plans for 'Colorful' Bats," *The Sporting News*, December 14, 1963: 2.
21. "PCL Expands to 12 Clubs—Int Cut to Eight," *The Sporting News*, December 14, 1963: 7.
22. Ibid.
23. Ibid.
24. Ibid.
25. Ibid.
26. Ibid.
27. Ibid.
28. Ibid.
29. "Plans Laid for Two New Rookie Loops," *The Sporting News*, December 14, 1963: 8.
30. Ibid. The Pioneer remains a rookie league, and Idaho Falls has been a member every season since its inception.
31. Ibid.
32. "2 Mexican Loops Expanding; Ramirez Plans Third Circuit," *The Sporting News*, December 14, 1963: 8.
33. "63 Players Go in Grab Bag; 52 First-Year Kids Selected," *The Sporting News*, December 14, 1963: 9.
34. Ibid.
35. "Minors Draft Only 35 Players, Down From 60 Picks in 1962," *The Sporting News*, December 14, 1963: 10.
36. Ibid.
37. "Skowron Purchased by Senators."
38. Ibid.
39. "Kennedy, Trautman Saluted by Delegates," *The Sporting News*, December 14, 1963: 7.
40. "Sox, Cubs Set to Open Shop in Major Market," *Chicago Tribune*, December 1, 1963: D3; "Majors' Rookie Rule Expected to Change," *Washington Post and Times Herald*," December 1, 1963: C6.
41. "Sox, Cubs Set to Open Shop."
42. "Skowron Purchased by Senators."
43. "Angels send Leon Wagner to Indians for Latman," *Chicago Tribune*, December 3, 1963: C1.
44. "Mets get Taylor in Separate Deal," *New York Times*, December 3, 1963: 71.
45. "Braves Get F. Alou, Bailey, 2 Others," *Chicago Tribune*, December 4, 1963: C1.
46. Ibid.
47. "Al Smith Returns to Cleveland," *Chicago Tribune*, December 5, 1963: H1.
48. "Tigers Send Bunning and Triandos to Phillies for Demeter and Hamilton."
49. "Skowron Purchased by Senators"
50. "San Antonio, Host in 1911, to Be Site of Meeting in '64," *The Sporting News*, December 14, 1963: 6.

— 1964 —
COMMISSIONER'S POWERS, FREE-AGENT DRAFT, & ALL-STAR VOTING

By Donald G. Frank

Introduction and Context

MAJOR-LEAGUE BASEBALL'S 1964 Winter Meetings were conducted in Houston, Texas, from November 30 to December 4, 1964. This was a time when there were 20 teams in the majors, 10 in each league.

Several issues or topics dominated these meetings. The commissioner's powers had been reduced after A.B. "Happy" Chandler succeeded Kenesaw Mountain Landis in 1945; those powers were restored at these meetings. A players' proposal to return the All-Star vote to the fans was supported by the owners, but Commissioner Ford C. Frick was hesitant, probably remembering the Cincinnati ballot stuffing of 1957. As a result, a committee was appointed to study this issue. An amateur free-agent draft was discussed and supported. Players were to be drafted in an orderly process, beginning with the teams at the bottom of the standings. An umpire development program was approved. Commissioner Frick expressed words of caution in relation to expansion. He also discussed CBS's purchase of the New York Yankees, including its implications for baseball. And finally, several trades were completed.

The Business Side

Dramatic increases in the powers of the commissioner were ratified as the owners formally restored the powers that made Judge Kenesaw Mountain Landis the undisputed czar of baseball for more than 20 years. Specifically, two changes were approved. They restored the commissioner's right to veto any action by the owners that he construed as detrimental to baseball. (This right had been stripped from the commissioner after Landis died in 1944.) Also, they granted the commissioner immunity from legal actions if the owners disagreed with him. The vote on the proposal was 9 to 1 in each league, with Bill DeWitt of the Cincinnati Reds and Charles Finley of the Kansas City Athletics reportedly the only votes against it. The changes were advocated by Commissioner Frick, who had succeeded Chandler in 1951.[1]

After five of the nine National League starters in the 1957 All-Star Game played for the Cincinnati Reds as a result of a "razzle-dazzle promotion" in Cincinnati, the players were asked by the commissioner to select the starting lineup for the All-Star Game, with the managers filling out the remainder of the rosters. After the 1964 season, the players proposed that the All-Star voting be returned to the fans, and this idea was supported by the owners. Commissioner Frick, however, did not agree, so he created a committee to study the possibility, using a "card system" to tabulate the fans' votes for the All Stars, with an "electronic computer" determining the final results. This committee was composed of Frick, Judge Robert Cannon, the players' legal adviser, and Bill Giles, the public relations director of the Houston Colt .45's.[2]

It had long been recognized that qualified umpires needed to be recruited, trained, and developed for baseball and, as a result, the umpire development program was recommended and approved, with Edward S. Doherty, assistant to the commissioner, placed in charge of the program. Frick, who viewed this as particularly important, declared that the program was intended "to get more kids interested in umpiring and to make it worth their while by paying minor league umpires more."[3]

Reflecting on expansion to cities on the West Coast, Frick recommended that future expansion be done "be carried out through orderly procedures." As a result of Frick's comments, the 20 teams voted that "any expansion plan entertained by one league or one club must be explained fully to the other league before new territory could be charted."[4]

Frick was questioned on the sale of the New York Yankees to CBS, viewed as controversial by some of the owners. "Because of tax problems and high costs," he asserted, "you are going to see more ownership of teams by corporations before you see less." He indicated that problems stemming from the deal needed to be handled by the American League, not the commissioner's office. (He noted that this was not the first time a broadcast network had purchased a baseball team, pointing to the Fetzer Broadcasting Company acquisition of the Detroit Tigers several years earlier.[5])

The day after the minor leagues adopted a free-agent draft similar to professional football's draft of collegiate players, the major leagues voted to follow this action. Known as the First-Year Player Draft or Rule 4 Draft, it was applicable to "amateur baseball players," including those in high schools, colleges, and other nonprofessional leagues or organizations. Beginning in June 1965, big-league teams would hold three yearly drafts: in January for midyear high-school graduates; in June for spring high-school and college graduates; and in September for players in the American Legion program and other amateur leagues. As in football's draft, the teams at the bottom of the standings would select first. Viewed as "socialistic" by some officials, the free-agent draft was opposed vigorously by the St. Louis Cardinals, Los Angeles Dodgers, New York Mets, and New York Yankees. But only the Cardinals voted against its implementation.[6]

A National League recommendation to let the four expansion teams—the Angels, Astros, Mets, and Senators—option two first-year players to the minors without the fear of exposing them to the draft was debated. Under a one-year grant, the four clubs had been allowed to send out four first-year players in the 1964 season.[7] The proposal was passed by the National League, but the American League vote ended in a 5-5 tie. With the leagues split, Commissioner Frick cast the deciding vote and, "siding with the status quo, vetoed the idea."[8]

A proposal to allow interleague trading from the World Series to December 15 was also defeated, meaning "The present free-for-all period is Nov. 20 to Dec, 15, and it will remain that way."[9]

Player Movement

An abnormally high number of player trades were made, including one that had a major impact on the 1965 season. The Los Angeles Dodgers traded Frank Howard, an outfielder noted for prodigious home runs, to the Washington Senators. The Dodgers sent the 27-year-old Howard, the 1959 National League Rookie of the Year, pitchers Phil Ortega and Pete Richert, and third baseman Ken McMullen to the Senators for southpaw pitcher Claude Osteen and infielder John Kennedy. In 1964, Howard had batted .226 with 26 home runs and 69 RBIs. Right-hander Ortega had posted a 7-9 record with a 4.00 ERA, including three shutouts and one save as he divided his time between the rotation and the bullpen. Richert, 24 (as was Ortega) and considered to be a promising lefty, was 2-3 in 1964, with a 4.15 ERA and one shutout in eight games after being recalled from the minors. In 1964, the 22-year-old McMullen found himself stuck behind Dodgers legend Junior Gilliam and riding the minor-league shuttle. He played in just 24 games in LA, batting .209 with one home run. The Senators were looking for youthful talent and got it, especially with Howard and McMullen. Howard became one of the most feared sluggers in baseball, twice leading the American League in home runs, while McMullen became a solid everyday performer at third. Ortega had three good years in Washington, while Richert, after two-plus years in the Senators' rotation, was traded to Baltimore and became part of the vaunted bullpen that helped the Orioles win three straight AL pennants.[10]

For their part, the Dodgers were willing to sacrifice all this youthful talent in order to solidify their starting rotation behind Sandy Koufax and Don Drysdale, and they succeeded with the 24-year-old Osteen. The southpaw was 15-13 in 1964, including 13 complete games, with a 3.33 ERA for a Senators team that had lost 106 games. He would eventually win nearly 200 games in the majors, most of them with the Dodgers, and helped them win two pennants and the 1965 World Series title; he was also selected to three All-Star teams. In 1964 Kennedy had batted .230 with 7 home runs and 35 runs batted in, and that proved to be his best career mark.[11]

The Los Angeles Angels traded left-hander Bo Belinsky to the Philadelphia Phillies for Rudy May, another southpaw, and Costen Shockley, a first baseman. Belinsky had a 9-8 mark in 1964 with a 2.86 ERA, but had been suspended since August 14 as a result of an altercation with a writer. Belinsky had gained fame in 1962 when, as a rookie, he pitched a no-hitter for the Angels, but he would win only seven more games in the majors. May, 20 at the time of the deal, pitched in the majors from 1965 to 1983 and posted a career record of 152-156, with a 3.46 ERA. Shockley, 22, hit 36 home runs in the Pacific Coast League in 1964 and was considered to be a top prospect, but wound up playing just 51 games in the majors.[12]

The Cleveland Indians traded first baseman Bob Chance and infielder Woodie Held to the Washington Senators for Chuck Hinton, an All-Star outfielder. In 1964 Chance had batted .279 with 14 home runs and 75 RBIs, but never again approached those numbers. Held, a major leaguer since 1957, had batted .236 in 1964 with 18 home runs and 49 RBIs. Hinton was an All-Star in 1964, a year in which he had batted .274 with 11 home runs and 53 runs batted in.[13]

The Philadelphia Phillies, who had just missed making a trip to the World Series in 1964, traded left-hander Dennis Bennett to the Boston Red Sox for first baseman Dick Stuart. Bennett's record in 1964 was 12-14 with a 3.68 ERA. Bennett, 25, was viewed as one of the aces of the Phillies, but they felt they needed more offense at first base. In 1964, Stuart, a controversial slugger, had batted .279 with 33 home runs and 114 RBIs. In his two years with the Red Sox, Stuart had hit 75 home runs and driven in 232 runs. The trade returned Stuart to the National League, where he had hit 117 home runs for the Pittsburgh Pirates in five seasons before his relocation to Fenway Park. Pinky Higgins, general manager of the Red Sox, welcomed Bennett. "This deal has been thoroughly discussed since the World Series," Higgins said. "Despite losing Stuart's power, the Red Sox feel Bennett can be the best left-hander the club has had since Mel Parnell retired." Gene Mauch, the manager of the Phillies, rolled out the red carpet for Stuart, too. "We now have as tough a one-two-three punch as any club in the league." Stuart did hit 28 home runs for the Phillies in 1965, but they shipped him to the New York Mets before the 1966 season and the poor-fielding "Dr. Strangeglove" played only two more seasons in the majors. Bennett also did not live up to expectations. He won only 13 games in 2½ seasons in Boston, spent three months with the Mets in 1967 and two months with the Angels in 1968 before calling it a career.[14]

There were several other deals of some note. The Cincinnati Reds traded infielder Cesar Tovar to the Minnesota Twins for left-hander Gerry Arrigo. Tovar went on to make a name for himself as a supersub, picking up MVP votes in five consecutive seasons. The Los Angeles Angels traded catcher Jack Hiatt to the San Francisco Giants for Jose Cardenal, who proved to be a valuable outfielder for eight teams over the next 18 seasons. The Chicago White Sox traded pitcher Ray Herbert, a 20-game winner in 1962, and outfielder-first baseman Jeoff Long to the Philadelphia Phillies for outfielder Danny Cater and shortstop Lee Elia, who later managed the Cubs and Phillies. The New York Mets traded pitcher Tracy Stallard—the man who gave up Roger Maris's 61st home run—and infielder Elio Chacon to the St. Louis Cardinals for outfielder Johnny Lewis and left-hander Gordie Richardson. The Cardinals also swapped pitcher Roger Craig, who had just helped them win the World Series, plus outfielder Charlie James to Cincinnati for pitcher Bob Purkey. The Cubs and White Sox participated in an all-Chicago trade. The Cubs swapped catcher Jimmie Schaffer, who had batted .205 in 1964 with two home runs and nine runs batted in, to the White Sox for left-hander Frank Baumann, who had led the league in ERA in 1960 but had only a 0-3 record in 1964 with a 6.19 ERA.[15]

Several players were also purchased outright at the meetings; most notably the New York Mets picked up Warren Spahn from the Milwaukee Braves. The winningest left-hander in history, Spahn was almost 44 and would win only seven more games in his Hall of Fame career. The St. Louis Cardinals purchased outfielder-first baseman John "Tito" Francona from the Cleveland Indians. Francona's son, Terry, was later manager of two World Series champions in Boston. And there was one other transaction featuring a name that would become familiar in future years. In the minor-league draft, the Cubs picked up third baseman Bobby Cox from the Los Angeles Dodgers' Double-A team in Albuquerque. Cox played only two seasons in the majors, with the Yankees, but as a manager he won 2,504 games, five pennants, and the 1995 World Series on his way to the Hall of Fame.[16]

Summary

Baseball's 1964 Winter Meetings were active as well as relevant. In particular, the commissioner's powers were restored, effective immediately. As a result, the commissioner's ability to deal effectively with complex issues was improved dramatically. An amateur free-agent draft and the umpire development program were implemented. All-Star Game voting was discussed and a committee was selected to study the issues. The commissioner discussed expansion as well as the purchase of the New York Yankees by a corporate entity.

NOTES

1. Joseph Durso, "Big Leagues Vote Free-Agent Draft, Restoration of Commissioner's Power," *New York Times*, December 4, 1964: 48; Clifford Kachline, "Club Owners Vote Absolute Power to Baseball's Boss," *The Sporting News*, December 19, 1964: 6; "Majors' Official Vote Restores Commissioner's Broad Powers," *New York Times*, December 5, 1964: 36.

2. Clifford Kachline, "All-Star Vote May Be Given Back to Fans," *The Sporting News*, December 12, 1964: 7; "Return of All-Star Vote to Fans to Be Studied," *New York Times*, December 3, 1964: 64.

3. "Majors' Official Vote Restores Commissioner's Broad Powers."

4. Ibid.

5. Ibid.

6. Joseph Durso, "Baseball's Minors Follow Pro Football Pattern in Backing Free-Agent Draft," *New York Times*, December 3, 1964: 64; Joseph Durso, "Big Leagues Vote Free-Agent Draft, Restoration of Commissioner's Power," *New York Times*, December 4, 1964: 48; Clifford Kachline, "First Free-Agent Draft Scheduled for June 1: Selections Held 3 Times Per Year," *The Sporting News*, December 19, 1964: 2; Clifford Kachline, "Frick Lauds 'Great Progress Program': Free-Agent Draft Approval Applauded as Key Decision," *The Sporting News*, December 19, 1964: 2; Clifford Kachline, "Minors Given Added Benefits; Vote 'Yes' on Free-Agent Draft," *The Sporting News*, December 12, 1974: 9; Clifford Kachline, "Path Cleared for Draft of Free Agents," *The Sporting News*, November 21, 1964: 4; C.C. Johnson Spink, "Free-Agent Draft Legal—Antitrust Expert," *The Sporting News*, December 12, 1964: 4; "Suddenly the Future Looks Brighter" (editorial), *The Sporting News*, November 21, 1964: 16.

7. "Majors' Official Vote Restores Commissioner's Broad Powers."

8. Clifford Kachline, "Majors Veto Aid Pitch for Expansion Clubs," *The Sporting News*, December 19, 1964: 7.

9. "Majors' Official Vote."

10. Joseph Durso, "Washington Gives Osteen, Kennedy," *New York Times*, December 5, 1964: 36; Edgar Munzel, "Hurlers, Catchers Hot Interloop Swap Items," *The Sporting News*, December 26, 1964: 2.

11. Ibid.

12. Ibid.

13. Joseph Durso, "Minor Leagues to Vote Today on Changes in Baseball Draft," *New York Times*, December 2, 1964: 61.

14. Joseph Durso, "Red Sox Send Stuart to Phils for Bennett, a Left-Hander," *New York Times* November 30, 1964: 46; "Hurlers, Catchers Hot Interloop Swap Items."

15. "Hurlers, Catchers Hot Interloop Swap Items"; "Convention Transactions," *The Sporting News*, December 12, 1964: 8.

16. Oscar Kahan, "Majors Run Up $572,000 Tab to Draft 63," *The Sporting News*, December 12, 1964: 5-6; "Hurlers, Catchers Hot Interloop Swap Items"; Dick Young, "Casey Once Told Spahn He Didn't Have It," *The Sporting News*, December 12, 1964: 14.

— 1965 —
EXIT THE SPORTSWRITER AND ENTER THE GENERAL

By Andy Bokser

THE 1965 WINTER MEETINGS TOOK place in Florida, with meeting venues in both Miami and Fort Lauderdale. It was the finale of an exciting year that marked the first free-agent draft (limited to players who were United States residents); the sudden end of the four-decade New York Yankees dynasty; the opening of baseball's first indoor ballpark, the air-conditioned Houston Astrodome (frequently called the Eighth Wonder of the World); a thrilling seven-game World Series victory by the Los Angeles Dodgers over the Minnesota Twins; the ongoing court battles involving major-league baseball and the cities of Milwaukee and Atlanta for the location of the Braves franchise; and the beginning of the reign of the fourth commissioner of baseball.

The meetings commenced on November 29 in Fort Lauderdale at the Galt Ocean Mile Hotel, with outgoing Commissioner Ford Frick ending his term. Both the meetings and Frick's term ended on December 3, 1965, under the leadership of the new commissioner, retired Air Force Lieutenant General William Dale Eckert, at the Fontainebleau Hotel in Miami.[1]

In August 1964 Frick had announced he would retire at the end of his term on September 21, 1965. Subsequently he agreed to continue through the conclusion of the 1965 Winter Meetings.

Ford Christopher Frick had replaced Albert Benjamin "Happy" Chandler as baseball's third commissioner in 1951. He had worked as a sportswriter for the *New York American* and the *Evening Journal*. He had also been Babe Ruth's ghostwriter. In 1934, at the age of 39, he became the National League president, replacing the ailing John A. Heydler.[2]

During Frick's tenure, he was credited with helping some teams, among them Brooklyn and Boston, avoid filing for bankruptcy.[3] He also was noted for his strong stand on integrating major-league baseball when, as league president, he was advised that many players were contemplating striking in protest against Jackie Robinson when he was brought up to the majors by the Dodgers in 1947. He warned the players, "If you do this ... you are through, and I don't care if it wrecks the league for 10 years. You cannot do this because this is America."[4]

In an interview during the Meetings, Frick said he was content with his decision to step down, but sometimes wondered whether he would be happy with that choice.[5]

After Frick's retirement announcement, major-league baseball embarked on a search for his successor. Sixteen of the 20 clubs submitted nominations, and baseball initially sifted through 156 candidates (reportedly including former Vice President Richard Nixon, former Supreme Court Justice Byron "Whizzer" White, New York City Mayor Robert Wagner, American League President Joe Cronin, Baltimore Orioles President and general manager Lee McPhail, and San Francisco Giants owner Chub Feeney).[6]

Detroit Tigers owner John Fetzer and Pirates owner John Galbreath served as a screening committee.[7] The original list was pared to 50, and then to 15 finalists by the team owners, who eventually selected the relatively unknown General William D. Eckert. His selection was a surprise to baseball outsiders and caused sportswriter Larry Fox to quip, "They've hired the unknown soldier."[8] Eckert was elected to a seven-year term at an annual salary of $65,000. The owners also added a position of administrative assistant and gave the job to Lee MacPhail (who later became general manager of the Yankees, president of the American League, and eventually an inductee into the Baseball Hall of Fame).[9] It was reported that Eckert's appointment was met with second-guessing largely around the proposition that he was not a "baseball man."[10]

In an interview before the start of his term, Eckert said that he was "no czar," but that if he lacked the authority to take a certain action, he "would ask for legislative changes to give it to me." He said he had no definite plans at that point on how he would address subjects like expansion, interleague play, and franchise relocations, and wanted to take into account the views of other people in major-league baseball. While he expressed satisfaction with having Lee MacPhail as his administrator, the retired three-star general said he was less pleased with baseball's plan to give him five assistants. He was concerned about having more people than he needed.[11] He said he didn't know who provided his name to baseball's search committee.

General Eckert was the former commander of the 452nd Bomb Group in Europe and won several medals, including the Distinguished Flying Cross. He had retired from the Air Force in 1961 after a heart attack. While his term started on November 18, and he attended the Winter Meetings, he considered his start day to be December 15.[12] He advised the media that he would not become a puppet, exclaiming, "Nobody tied any strings on me, so there aren't any to pull."[13] He said he had not even attended a baseball game in the decades before his appointment.

Electing a baseball outsider like Eckert was attributed to the owners' wish to redefine the role of the commissioner. He would be less a czar-like figure like Kenesaw Mountain Landis and more of a coordinator, overseeing a committee of executives with deputies for public relations, broadcasting, player affairs, and amateur baseball. It was thought that having a "baseball man" was not a priority.[14] Not all of the opinions on Eckert expressed by the media or others were negative. He did make a favorable first impression on some people.[15] It was hoped that Eckert would be able to maintain and grow baseball's share of the entertainment dollar in an increasingly competitive market with football, stock-car racing, and other sports.[16]

Eckert's time at the helm proved to be far shorter than the seven years he was given in 1965. Many of the owners who were not looking for a baseball man in 1965 apparently changed their minds, and after a meeting with the owners at the 1968 Winter Meetings, he announced that he had submitted his resignation. His last official day as baseball's fourth commissioner was February 4, 1969.[17]

The 1965 meetings also signaled the last year of the Milwaukee Braves who, after moving from Boston to Milwaukee in 1953, announced that they would be moving again, to Atlanta. The issue quickly moved onto the legal playing field, and while the drama of the Braves' future city was being played out in the courts, a group of businessmen from Milwaukee, led by a car dealer named Bud Selig, tried to lobby baseball for an expansion team in Milwaukee. The Braves' move to Atlanta would be the first time in more than 60 years that baseball abandoned a city for greener pastures—when teams left Boston, St. Louis, Philadelphia, and New York in the 1950s, each city still had another major-league franchise in town. The Milwaukee group had petitioned both leagues for a new team. While they fought for an expansion team, the group was reported to have believed that a refusal would bolster their claim that baseball was violating the nation's antitrust laws by improperly operating as a monopoly.[18]

While the battle in the courts and in Milwaukee and Atlanta raged, the American League listened to lobbying groups—one trying to keep the team in Wisconsin, the other working on getting an expansion franchise. Although the American League "listened informally" to groups seeking to keep the Braves in Milwaukee, to avoid accusations of collusion, no one mentioned the topic during the leagues' joint meeting.[19] The Selig group claimed that their push for a team was not related to the pending litigation.[20]

The National League rejected the proposals by Milwaukee County and the Milwaukee Brewers Baseball Club, Inc. for an expansion team in Milwaukee, as well as a request by the North Texas Baseball Club for a team in Dallas/Fort Worth. Among the reasons offered for rejecting the requests were that the applicants had no farm systems, players, or radio/TV contracts, and could not be ready to field a team in 1966.[21] The NL estimated that expansion was about five years away. Among the cities seeking franchises were San Diego, Toronto, Seattle, and Oakland,[22] all of which were eventually awarded major-league franchises.

One of the first orders of business of the Winter Meetings was the major-league Rule 5 draft, on November 29. The major-league teams drafted 17 players for the $25,000 fee; the Orioles choice of right-handed pitcher Moe Drabowsky paid off in their 1966 World Series win with his historic relief pitching against the Dodgers.

The major-league teams selected only six minor leaguers for the reduced pricetag of $8,000. In addition to Drabowsky, other players of some note who were selected included the Cardinals' drafting of left-handed pitcher Joe Hoerner, and the Pirates' selection of former Mets catcher Jesse Gonder. The Astros drafted a future star in first baseman Nate Colbert.[23]

Hopes that a flurry of big-name players would be involved in trades were perhaps whetted by the Cardinals' two pre-meetings swaps. Just days after the Dodgers won Game Seven of the World Series, St. Louis sent third baseman Ken Boyer, a seven-time All-Star and the National League's Most Valuable Player just the year before, to the Mets for third baseman Charlie Smith and left-handed pitcher Al Jackson. A week later, they sent five-time All-Star first baseman Bill White, five-time All-Star shortstop Dick Groat (the 1960 MVP in the National League), and catcher Bob Uecker to the Phillies for outfielder Alex Johnson, two-time All-Star right-hander Art Mahaffey, and catcher Pat Corrales.[24] Rumors abounded of yet another blockbuster deal. The Cincinnati Reds were reportedly looking to trade star outfielder Frank Robinson. This did not come to pass during the Winter Meetings,[25] but shortly after the meetings ended, the 1961 National League MVP was shipped to the Baltimore Orioles for right-hander Milt Pappas, right-handed relief pitcher Jack Baldschun, and outfielder Dick Simpson.

Nevertheless, no major deals were completed during the meetings,[26] though some smaller swaps were announced. The Mets sent outfielder Joe Christopher to the Red Sox for shortstop Eddie Bressoud. The Phillies and Yankees swapped infielders, with Ruben Amaro moving to New York in exchange for Phil Linz.

The Giants were involved in a pair of deals that had future significance. They obtained right-handed relief pitcher Lindy McDaniel and outfielder Don Landrum from the Cubs for right-handed starting pitcher Bill Hands and catcher Randy Hundley. They also swapped outfielder Matty Alou and a player to be named later to the Pirates for utilityman Ossie Virgil and left-handed pitcher Joe Gibbon.[27] Hands and Hundley would become cornerstones in the resurgence of the Cubs, while Alou would become a consistent .300 hitter, a two-time All-Star, and the 1966 NL batting champion.

In some of the financial decisions made during the meetings, the American and National Leagues increased their umpires' minimum salaries from $7,000 to $9,500 a year, and increased the league contributions to the pension for their men in blue, while limiting the umpires' contribution to the pension to $350 per year. The minimum age for the arbiters' retirement was reduced from 60 to 55. In an effort to curb on-the-field fraternization between players, the leagues increased the fines for a first offense from $5 to $50, and for a second offense from $10 to $100.[28]

The major leagues also increased their contribution to the minor leagues for their expenses, committing to paying all costs above $600 per month for each player as well as all salaries and expenses for training, transportation, and the manager. Previously the minor leagues were responsible for the first $700 of costs for each player.[29] In another policy change, the American League voted to pay each visiting team 20 percent of the gross receipts from ticket sales and other admissions including service and exchange charges (less taxes). This was an increase over the prior practice of paying the visiting teams 20 cents for each bleacher and special admission and 30 cents for other admissions.[30]

> ### Atlanta or Milwaukee? Newly or Outdated National?
>
> Shortly after the 1965 winter meetings, the hearings surrounding the move of the Braves from Milwaukee to Atlanta continued, with the state of Wisconsin asking that the Braves make preliminary arrangements to play in Milwaukee, if later ordered to do so by the court. Here were some statements made during the hearings.
>
> *"We were mindful, your honor, that in all the southeast area of this land there has been no major league baseball and we have taken it there. We're mindful that there has been sadness in Milwaukee about that. We think we have performed the greatest duty for our land. We think we have created a truly National League."*
>
> Bowie Kuhn, attorney for the National League (and successor to Eckert as commissioner).
>
> *"I don't consider his theories of operations the best. He hasn't kept up with the times."*
>
> Bill Veeck, former major league owner, testifying about his acquaintance with National League President Warren Giles.
>
> 1   "Says Braves' Transfer Created 'A Truly NL,'" *Appleton* (Wisconsin) *Post-Crescent*, December 23, 1965: 11.
> 2   "Milwaukee Could Field Team for Three Million," *Eau Claire* (Wisconsin) *Daily Telegram*, December 23, 1965: 9.

At a meeting of the teams' player representatives and the owners, the players asked that night games be limited during spring training for health reasons and the owners consented. The players also asked that all player fines be turned over to the Fred Hutchinson Cancer Fund, which was in memory of the late Reds manager, instead of having them go to leagues' coffers.[31] Subsequent articles mentioning the fund do not indicate that the players' proposal was adopted by the owners.[32]

The retirement of longtime manager Casey Stengel was prominent in the news during the Winter Meetings. After the 75-year-old Stengel broke his hip and was forced to quit managing the New York Mets, there was a movement to make him eligible for the Hall of Fame during the next voting cycle. The Baseball Writers Association of America petitioned the Hall of Fame to waive the requirement that a player or manager be retired for five years before becoming eligible for selection to the Hall. George M. Weiss, who worked with Stengel with the Mets and Yankees, said, "Let him smell the flowers now." Lee McPhail, the new assistant to Commissioner Eckert, said, "I am for it 100 percent."[33]

While there was resistance to the suggestion of waiving the waiting period, it had been permitted in the cases of Connie Mack and Lou Gehrig.[34] While Stengel was not elected to the Hall of Fame along with Ted Williams by the baseball writers, he was voted in a few weeks later by the Committee on Veterans as a result of a rule change that permitted executives, umpires and managers over 65 to be elected six months after they retired. Stengel's election came exactly six months after his retirement.[35]

The major leagues awarded the 1967 All-Star Game to the California Angels, whose new Anaheim Stadium was to open in 1966. The National League gave its president, Warren Giles, a two-year extension to 1968, the relatively short term given with the assumption that the 69-year-old might be contemplating retirement.[36] The American League re-elected Red Sox owner Tom Yawkey vice president of the league and named Gabe Paul, president and general manager of the Cleveland Indians, to the Major League Executive Council. Commissioner Eckert decided to retain

Charley Segar as the secretary-treasurer of baseball, a position he had held since Ford Frick became commissioner in 1951.[37]

On December 3, the major leagues ended their meeting with a 40-minute joint meeting at which they reduced the minimum time a player needed to remain on the disabled list from 30 days to 15 days. The rehabbing player would be permitted to work out with his team. The changes were urged by Yankees general manager Ralph Houk, among others. Houk cited Roger Maris as a player who had benefited from improved modern medical treatments, and said that in such cases the longer period of forced inactivity was unnecessary. The leagues decided to hold their 1966 winter meetings in Pittsburgh; the 1966 minor-league winter meetings would take place in Columbus, Ohio.

A rule change aimed at speeding up games, permitted a manager or coach to come to the mound to speak to their pitcher only once per batter. Two trips to the mound would still be permitted during an inning, but they would have to be for different hitters.[38]

One idea that did not garner much press notice at the meetings but may have contributed to the major leagues' decision to split into two divisions in each league in 1969 was discussed. Lee MacPhail and Gabe Paul thought that splitting the American League into two divisions could be implemented within three years, and they advocated only one additional team making the playoffs. (Both frowned on the National Hockey League and National Basketball Association system of multiple teams participating in the postseason.) But the National League was not interested in the concept, since it had a brighter financial outlook than the American League and therefore not the same motivation to increase fan interest.[39]

The Winter Meetings of 1965 ended with a new baseball commissioner, some minor tinkering, and an apparently optimistic outlook for the 1966 season.

NOTES

1. "The Time and Place," *The Sporting News*, December 4, 1965.
2. "Eckert, Astrodome, Braves in '65 Spotlight," *Sporting News Official Baseball Guide for 1966*.
3. Mlb.com/mlb/history/mlb_history_people.jsp?.story=com_bio_.
4. Red Smith, "Views of Sport," *Philadelphia Inquirer*, September 22, 1951.
5. Milton Richman, "Last Hurrah for Frick," *Daily World* (Opelousas, Louisiana), December 5, 1965.
6. "Eckert, Astrodome, Braves in '65 Spotlight,"
7. Ibid.
8. Jack Zanger, *Major League Baseball—1966* (New York: Pocket Books, 1966), 214.
9. Richard Goldstein, "Lee MacPhail, Executive Who Led American League, Dies at 95," *New York Times*, November 9, 2012.
10. Leonard Koppett, "The New Commissioner," *New York Times*, December 5, 1965.
11. Barney Kremenko, "New Boss Says He'll Get View of Others, Then Act," *The Sporting News*, December 4, 1965.
12. Ibid.
13. Associated Press, "Will Not Become Puppet, Declares New Baseball Boss," *Wilmington* (Delaware) *News Journal*, December 1, 1965.
14. Brian McKenna, "William Eckert," sabr.org/bioproj/person/4691515d.
15. United Press International, "Baseball World in Look at New Boss," *Odessa* (Texas) *American*, December 5, 1965.
16. Chester L. Smith, "Baseball Gets Different Type in Gen. Eckert," *Pittsburgh Press*, December 2, 1965.
17. McKenna, "William Eckert."
18. Joe McGuff, "N.L. Shuns Milwaukee," *Kansas City Times*, December 3, 1965.
19. Leonard Koppett, "Frick Steps Down as Baseball Head," *New York Times*, December 4, 1965.
20. "American League Rejects Milwaukee Bid," *Eau Claire* (Wisconsin) *Daily Telegram*, December 4, 1965.
21. Associated Press, "N.L. Rejects Milwaukee's Bid for 1966," *Chicago Tribune* December 3, 1965.
22. McGuff, "N.L. Shuns Milwaukee."
23. Dick Kaegel, "Majors Pass Up First Year Players in Draft," *The Sporting News*, December 11, 1965.
24. *Sporting News Official Baseball Guide for 1966*.
25. James Enright, "Why Reds Traded Robinson," *Baseball Digest*, February 1966.
26. Associated Press, "Business Is Slow at Trade Mart as Baseball Convention Comes to End," *San Antonio Express and News*, December 4, 1965.
27. *Sporting News Official Baseball Guide for 1966*. Other sources, including Baseball-Reference.com and the *Sporting News Baseball Register*, do not identify the "player to be named later." They report only that Alou went from the Giants to the Pirates.
28. David M. Moffit, Associated Press, "Umps Get Pay Raise," *Eau Claire* (Wisconsin) *Daily Telegram*, December 4, 1965.
29. Leonard Koppett, "Frick Steps Down as Baseball Head."
30. United Press International, "Giles to Head NL Three More Years," *Pittsburgh Press*, December 2, 1965.
31. Joseph Durso, "Coast Team Ends Pitching Search," *New York Times*, December 2, 1965.
32. C.C. Johnson Spink, "We Believe," *The Sporting News*, February 1, 1969.
33. Joseph Durso, "Stengel Is Backed for Hall of Fame," *New York Times*, December 3, 1965.
34. Ibid.
35. "Williams, Stengel Named to Hall of Fame," *Sporting News Official Baseball Guide for 1966*.
36. Associated Press, "N.L. Rejects Milwaukee's Bid for 1966," *Chicago Tribune*, December 3, 1965; United Press International, "Giles to Head NL Three More Years," *Pittsburgh Press* December 2, 1965
37. Associated Press, "N.L. Rejects Milwaukee's Bid for 1966"; "Eckert, Astrodome, Braves in "65 Spotlight."
38. Associated Press, "Umps Get $$ Increase," *Orlando Sentinel*, December 3, 1965.
39. Bob August, "A.L. Studies Two-Division Alignment," *Baseball Digest*, February 1966.

— 1966 —
TOMORROW NEVER KNOWS

By Jason Myers

ON AUGUST 29, 1966, THE BEATLES played what would be their final live concert ever at Candlestick Park, home of the San Francisco Giants. The event provided much enjoyment for the concertgoers as the band, still wearing matching suits and their moptop hair styles, played a set list of hits and other music they had recorded over the previous four years. In reality, if the fans had actually heard the music over their own screaming, they might have realized that the concert did not offer as much enjoyment as it seemed at the time. With the hindsight of history, though, we can see that signs of the pending change of the Beatles were present at the time. When the Fab Four would emerge the next year with "Sgt. Pepper's Lonely Hearts Club Band," they signaled that they, their music, and the world around them had changed.[1]

In some ways, the Beatles' final concert in 1966 offers a useful analogy for examining Organized Baseball's Winter Meetings a few months later. At the time, it was an event that *The Sporting News* described in glowing terms: "Few meetings in the nearly 100-year history of Organized Baseball have brought smiles of satisfaction to the faces of as many persons as did the majors' December 1-2 confabs."[2] But in retrospect, the sessions offered only a little entertainment in the form of player transactions, which drew heavily from some of baseball's greatest hits (i.e., players) from 1962 to 1964. The 1966 Winter Meetings were perhaps most meaningful on the business side, where some developments would help lay the groundwork for how baseball and the business around it would change.

"I Still Believe in Yesterday": Player Transactions During the 1966 Winter Meetings

The most significant player transaction after the 1966 World Series was the unexpected retirement of Sandy Koufax, the dominant southpaw who had won three Cy Young Awards and an MVP trophy in four years. He was not, however, the only retiring player whose career traced back to baseball's Golden Age. Infielder Junior Gilliam also retired from the Dodgers; he, along with Koufax, had played continuously with the team since their days in Brooklyn. Robin Roberts, the hard-throwing right-hander who had won 20 or more games for six consecutive seasons (1950-55) and one of the last remaining active players from the 1950 Philadelphia Phillies' famed Whiz Kids, also called it a career.

Despite being the reigning National League champions, the Los Angeles Dodgers started reshaping their roster in the wake of Koufax's retirement, so that by the end of the Winter Meetings, the Dodgers' roster contained only 27 players who had been with the team during spring training.[3] The most notable trade during the Winter Meetings involved the Dodgers, who moved shortstop and team captain Maury Wills, the 1962 National League Most Valuable Player and a five-time All-Star (including in 1966), in an attempt to get younger. Although some observers speculated that Wills was traded in retaliation for his prematurely leaving a postseason exhibition trip by the Dodgers to Japan, LA officials proclaimed that they saw an opportunity to move the 34-year-old Wills, coming off a season with knee issues, to the Pirates to get two younger infielders—Bob Bailey (age 24) and Gene Michael (27).[4] Despite the Dodgers' hopes at the time, neither Bailey nor Michael ended up doing much while in a Dodgers uniform, nor did either stay in LA for long; Michael was sold to the Yankees after the 1967 season and Bailey was purchased by the brand-new Montreal Expos after the 1968 campaign.

For the Pirates, trading for Wills represented an "all-in" movement as Pittsburgh's general manager Joe Brown proclaimed, "We're shooting for the pennant in 1967 and decided not to worry about the future as much as the present."[5] Having won 92 games in 1966, just three games behind the Dodgers, Pittsburgh was seen as the early favorite for 1967. But unfortunately for the Pirates and their fans, they fell well short of those expectations, finishing 1967 in sixth place with an 81-81 record. Wills, for his part, performed respectably in his two seasons with Pittsburgh, accumulating WAR scores of 4.3 and 3.5 in 1967 and 1968 respectively.[6] Before the 1969 season, though, Pittsburgh lost Wills to the Expos in the expansion draft, where he became a teammate of none other than Bob Bailey.[7]

The Dodgers also reshaped their roster in a trade involving a pair of two-time All-Stars. They sent outfielder Tommy Davis and utilityman Derrell Griffith (who would not play in another major-league game after the trade), to the New York Mets for second baseman Ron Hunt and outfielder Jim Hickman. Although Davis was only 27 years old, he had not played at a high level since his All-Star 1962-1963 seasons, when he led the league in hitting (both years) and in RBIs (1962). Hunt, on the other hand, was two years younger than Davis and had just come off an All-Star season in 1966, after previously appearing in the 1964 All-Star Game. Davis (2.7 WAR) and Hunt (2.0 WAR) performed serviceably for the Mets and Dodgers respectively in 1967. However, neither would return to All-Star levels in their career. That distinction belonged to the 29-year-old Jim Hickman, though not with LA. After appearing in only 65 games for the Dodgers in 1967, Hickman was traded to the Cubs the next offseason and subsequently delivered the game-winning hit in the 1970 All-Star Game, a play more famously known for Pete Rose steamrolling Ray Fosse at home plate to score the winning run.

The Winter Meetings also saw 1964 Cy Young Award winner Dean Chance move from the Angels to the Twins. The right-hander's 1966 performance had dropped off significantly from his award-winning season (12-17 in '66 with a league-high 114 walks, albeit with a solid 3.08 ERA and 2.2 WAR). In what turned out to be the largest trade of the meetings in terms of the number of players moved, Chance and a player to be named later (infielder Jackie Hernandez) went to Minnesota in exchange for right-hander Pete Cimino, outfielder Jimmie Hall, and first baseman Don Mincher. Chance benefited from the change of scenery and had two strong seasons for Minnesota before starting to decline. In 1967, in fact, Chance was named an All-Star, won 20 games, and was the AL's premier workhorse, leading the league in games started, complete games, and innings pitched. He followed up his 5.8 WAR 1967 season with a 6.1 WAR in 1968.

The Angels may have hoped that Jimmie Hall would similarly benefit by donning a new uniform. Third in the 1963 Rookie of the Year balloting, Hall had been an All-Star in 1964 and 1965, but his production dropped in 1966 as reflected in his WAR score of 1.0 for the season. Hall's performance did not improve in 1967 (WAR = 1.4), though, and partway through the 1968 season the Angels traded him to Cleveland. Don Mincher, on the other hand, rewarded the Angels with the best year of his career with 25 home runs, 76 RBIs, and a 4.3 WAR. Mincher's production fell off the next season and the Angels lost him in the expansion draft before the 1969 season to the Seattle Pilots, for whom Mincher is the answer to a trivia question: Who is the only Pilot to ever appear in the All-Star Game?[8]

One other more prominent trade completed during the Winter Meetings saw the Yankees send longtime infielder Clete Boyer to the Braves for outfielder Bill Robinson and right-hander Chi Chi Olivo, although the then-38-year-old Olivo did not appear in a major-league game after the trade. Boyer had been manning the left side of the Yankees infield as their primary third baseman since 1960 and had just completed his age-29 season. He put together a solid 26-homer, 96-RBI season for the Braves in 1967 and would finish his career with the team in 1971, including winning his only career Gold Glove in 1969. Robinson was five years younger than Boyer and was able to play all three outfield positions, but as a Yankee he had three undistinguished seasons; he finally blossomed as a hitter with the Phillies and Pirates.

Other trades during the 1966 Winter Meetings were more limited in scope and impact. After receiving the knuckleballing left-hander Wilbur Wood earlier in the offseason, the Chicago White Sox sent Juan Pizarro, an All-Star in 1963 and 1964, to the Pirates to complete the trade, which added to the Pirates' dreams of a 1967 pennant. Pizarro did not recapture his past level of success, and he lasted just a season and a half in Pittsburgh. Washington sent center fielder Don Lock to the Philadelphia Phillies for left-hander Darold Knowles, who served as the Senators' All-Star Game representative in 1969 and later became a key member of the Oakland A's powerful bullpen. Washington also sent 34-year-old right-handed reliever Ron Kline, coming off a 23-save season after leading the American League with 29 saves in 1965, to Minnesota for five-time All-Star right-handed pitcher Camilo Pascual and infielder Bernie Allen. Finally, the Cubs traded catcher Chris Krug and right-hander Wayne Schurr for to the Angels for two utilitymen, Mike White and Donald Furnald, with only Krug seeing any major-league action after the trade (eight games with the Padres in 1969).

Ted Abernathy, who led the National League in saves in 1965, also changed teams during the 1966 Winter Meetings. Abernathy, however, was picked up by the Reds in the Rule 5 draft. Abernathy certainly was not the typical draftee found in the Rule 5 process, which is usually filled with minor-league or low-level major-league talent. By the end of the 1966 season, Abernathy was a 33-year-old, eight-year veteran coming off a -0.9 WAR year split between the Cubs and Braves. He rebounded nicely for Cincinnati in 1967, once again leading the league in saves (28) and compiling a 6.2 WAR score.

Another high-profile Rule 5 pick was southpaw Bo Belinsky. In 1962 Belinsky threw the first no-hitter in Los Angeles/California Angels history in just the fourth decision of his career, and instantly became a highly recognized Southern California playboy. Thereafter, Belinsky's on-the-field performance varied between slightly above average to below average, but his off-the-field notoriety would continue, to the point of leading to what may have been the best quotation to come out of the Winter Meetings after the Astros selected him in the Rule 5 draft. As reported by Dick Young in *The Sporting News*, "Somebody mentioned that Houston isn't exactly the swingingest city in baseball, and that Bo Belinsky might have trouble finding romance there. 'Don't worry,' said Bob Lemon. 'He'd find it in a monastery.'"[9]

The Kansas City Athletics selected left-hander Dave Roberts from the Pittsburgh organization after he led the Southern League in ERA, complete games, and shutouts while compiling a 14-5 record for the Pirates' affiliate in Asheville, North Carolina. This pick is notable for two reasons. First, Kansas City returned Roberts to the Pirates before the 1967 season started. Second, although Roberts did not make his major-league debut until 1969, he went on to have a 13-year career with a career WAR of 22.2, the highest for any player selected in the Rule 5 draft at the 1966 meetings. In fact, Roberts and Abernathy were the only Rule 5 draftees that year whose career WAR, accrued after the draft, reached double digits.

The story was similar for the minor-league draft. Of the 53 players selected, only one turned in a notable major-league career. The Mets picked up a 19-year-old infielder out of the Red Sox organization. He would switch to the outfield but, after just 67 games in New York, was traded to the Kansas City Royals. Starting in 1970, though, Amos Otis blossomed into a five-time All-Star, a Gold Glove winner, and one of the finest defensive center fielders of his generation who would finish with a career WAR of 42.6.

Looking at the set list for that final Beatles concert, one sees that only one song was recorded, released and reached number-one hit in 1966, "Paperback Writer." The rest of the songs they performed drew from the band's successes between 1963 and 1965, with the most appropriate song to describe the players who switched teams during the 1966 Winter Meetings being "Yesterday." Like that final concert set list, the key players moved during the meetings had their greatest successes between 1962 and 1965—an MVP, a Cy Young Award winner, league leaders in notable statistical categories, and multiple All-Star Game appearances — although 1966 All-Star Ron Hunt may be comparable to "Paperback Writer." These players' performance all had declined since their top seasons a few years earlier, with the acquiring teams hoping to recapture at least some of the players' former stellar play.

Another aspect of the Beatles' Candlestick Park concert was the absence of songs that hinted at the greatness of their future music. As *Rolling Stone* magazine highlighted,

> "Much of their recent work was enhanced by backing musicians and innovative studio techniques, making it simply too challenging to perform given the technical limitations of a live setting. In fact, the Beatles would never play a single track off of their latest album, *Revolver*, released just days before they kicked off their dates."[10]

The player transactions, too, did not reflect any future greatness. Any forthcoming successes would occur either several years after the 1966 Winter Meetings (e.g., Amos Otis's career or Jim Hickman's 1970 season) or were relatively short-lived (the 1967 seasons of Dean Chance and Ted Abernathy). In sum, the player transactions were not particularly forward-looking in purpose, but instead geared to Joe Brown's approach of worrying about the present and not the future.

"Let me tell you how it will be. There's one for you, nineteen for me.": The Business of Baseball During the 1966 Winter Meetings

The 1966 Winter Meetings were in many ways more memorable for their business decisions, which made more of an impact on what happens on the field than most of the player transactions.

One of the most significant matters addressed during the meeting was the adoption of what was referred to as the "four-year college rule." Prior to the rule, college-age players could be drafted and signed during the summers after their sophomore and junior seasons. The four-year college rule, made effective as of January 1, 1967, prohibited the drafting or signing of any college baseball player until after the final game of his senior year, subject to four exceptions involving players who (a) turned 21 before August 1 of their senior year, (b) completed their athletic eligibility, (c) had their school drop them due to scholastic reasons, or (d) quit school and remained out for 120 days.[11] These exceptions left open the possibility that a player, most notably a 21-year-old, could still be drafted after his junior year.

The rule was the product of a working committee of major-league representatives (Chub Feeney of the Giants, John Quinn of the Phillies, Ed Short of the White Sox, and Dan Topping Jr. of the Yankees) and college athletic interests (including the NCAA president, the Big Ten commissioner, and representatives of smaller athletic conferences, college baseball coaches, and athletic directors). Danny Litwhiler, Michigan State University coach, noted, "College coaches owe a vote of thanks to the college-pro committee for work on the rule. College ball will become a much better training and screening facility for professional baseball."[12] Not all in Organized Baseball shared such an assessment, however. For example, the Orioles' Harry Dalton believed that players who do not "enter O.B. until they are 22 seldom make good in the majors."[13] Nevertheless, the measure passed the National League by a 9-1 vote and was approved 6-3 in the American League. In the end, Commissioner William Eckert summed up the measure by citing the benefits to Organized Baseball "of working with the educational institutions and developing players in the summer college programs."[14]

In an effort to bolster the economic well-being of the minor leagues, the major leagues adopted a proposal raised by Walter O'Malley, owner of the Dodgers, under which each major-league team would pay a $5,000 cash subsidy to its Triple-A affiliate, $3,000 to its Double-A affiliate, and $1,500 to its Single-A affiliate at the end of the 1967 season. The most notable aspect of the measure, though, was the manner of its passage. The National League approved the proposal unanimously, but the American League voted it down 6-4. Commissioner Eckert, reversing his position on a similar vote the year before, broke the tie between the leagues by supporting the proposal.

Organized Baseball took a number of steps during the Winter Meetings to support player development and baseball generally. For example, major-league owners approved a series of payments to college baseball summer leagues ($80,000), American Legion ($60,000), boys' baseball programs ($50,000), Association of Professional Ball Players ($50,000), Mexican Youth Clinics ($8,000), American Baseball Congress ($7,500), Hall of Fame ($5,000), National Junior College Athletic Association ($5,000), National Association of Intercollegiate Athletics ($5,000), and a study of high-school baseball ($25,000). This $295,500 in 1966 dollars would be the equivalent of a $2.2 million investment in the future of the game a half-century later. Similarly, the leagues approved continuation of their umpire development program. The leagues also tentatively approved Mexico City to host the 1967 winter meetings, following an appeal to do so by National Association President Phil Piton. Mexico City beat out Orlando, Fort Lauderdale, Tampa, Jacksonville, and San Diego as possible sites, and the drive behind the bid was, in the words of Mexican League President Antonio Ramirez, "to show what baseball means to another country."[15]

The Winter Meetings also saw some rules and other changes affecting or reflecting what happens on the field. The National and American Leagues standardized two rules that had previously been different in the two loops. In one, pitchers were required to have their foot touching the rubber when receiving signals from the catcher, while in the other, managers would be permitted to make a second visit to a pitcher in an inning before being required to remove the pitcher from the game.[16] In terms of roster moves, the required minimum time on the disabled list was extended from 15 to 21 days.[17] The rules for determining a batting champion were changed as well: A player who did not have enough plate appearances to qualify for the batting championship could become eligible by adding sufficient at-bats to allow the batter to reach the minimum number of plate appearances.[18] And in the matter of designating awards, the Baseball Writers' Association of America decided to honor a pitcher in each league with a Cy Young Award, changing the previous system under which a single award was granted for both leagues.[19]

The owners created a new business venture by forming the Major League Baseball Promotions Corp. (MLBPC). Following the lead of football's National Football League Properties, MLBPC was designed to promote the nationwide distribution of baseball novelties. From this seemingly small-scale origin, MLBPC would later become Major League Baseball Properties, Inc. and, "with limited exceptions, the exclusive worldwide agent for licensing the use of all names, logos, trademarks, service marks, trade dress, and other intellectual property owned or controlled by the MLB Clubs, MLB's Office of the Commissioner, and MLBP, on retail products."[20]

But perhaps the most significant action taken in Pittsburgh regarding the business of baseball—as seen both at the time and in historical perspective—was the agreement between major-league owners and the Major League Baseball Players Association regarding the players' pension system. The prior system, which was set to expire March 31, 1967, was funded by a combination of players, coaches, managers, and trainers, each of whom paid in $2 for every day he was in the majors ($344 annual maximum), and owners, who contributed 60 percent of the World Series radio and television receipts and 95 percent of the total revenue from the All-Star Game. The owners' contribution had been averaging between $2.6 million and $2.7 million annually over the previous five years.

The new agreement reached in 1966, which extended the term to 1969, increased the owners' contribution to $4.1 million annually. The availability of these additional funds stemmed from a new radio and television broadcasting contract signed with NBC and Gillette, covering the 1967 and 1968 World Series and All-Star Games. The new pension plan would produce a very tangible result for pension recipients, with benefits expected to double for retirees starting at the age of 50. In addition, the new plan called for a slate of additional benefits to players, managers, coaches, and trainers, including increased life-insurance coverage; increased aid to widows; increased assistance to permanently disabled recipients; and additional health-care benefits. The required player contribution to the pension plan ceased as part of the agreement, and instead, players were given the right to make an optional contribution that would be used to fund the expenses of the Players Association.[21] With a 99 percent contribution rate among players, coupled with the hiring of Dick Moss as the union's general counsel (announced during the Winter Meetings) and the establishment of permanent offices, the Players Association was now demonstrating its institutional stability.

The pension plan represented the first major concession by major-league owners to the Players Association under the leadership of Marvin Miller, who had been hired as its executive director earlier in the year. As a sign of matters to come, Miller's focus in his comments to the media at the time were not on what they had accomplished, but rather what still needed to be done from the players' perspective. Acknowledging that he did not "know of any comparable plan with comparable benefits," Miller added, "But that does not mean there aren't some areas for improvement."[22] Specifically, the players called for an increase of the minimum salary from $7,000 per year to $12,000. The proposal met with expected opposition by owners and no formal action was taken other than the formation of a committee consisting of Harry Dalton of the Orioles, George Selkirk of the Senators, Buzzie Bavazi of the Dodgers, and Bing Devine of the Mets to study the proposal.[23]

The songs that the Beatles produced in 1966, such as "Eleanor Rigby," "Taxman," and "Yellow Submarine," were significant in their own right and reflected a maturing and diverging sense of musical exploration. Yet, their music that year did not indicate at the time what the group would produce next. Similarly, the business decisions made at the 1966 Winter Meetings were recognized as being important at the time and reflect, at least in hindsight, a maturing sense of the business of Organized Baseball. Yet, the effects of the decisions made in 1966 could not have been accurately predicted at the time.

Who knew at the time, for instance, that by establishing the four-year college rule, Organized Baseball was increasing standout high-school players' leverage in negotiations? If a team could not sign a high-school player it drafted and he went to college instead, that player would usually not be eligible to be drafted again for at least three more years.

Who knew at the time that by trying to sell more novelties, major-league owners were creating an economic engine that could derive additional revenue and would market baseball at levels never previously attained?

And who knew at the time that by gaining concessions from the owners and institutionalizing the Players Association, Marvin Miller would be leading a change in how the game and business of baseball was played, managed, viewed by the public, and ultimately, in many ways, defined?

With the benefit of hindsight, one can see how these decisions laid the foundation for baseball's future. In terms of who knew at the time, though, the title to one of the Beatles' other songs from 1966 provides the answer … "Tomorrow Never Knows."

NOTES

1. For a review of the Beatles' final concert in historical perspective, see Jordan Runtagh, "Remembering Beatles' Final Concert," *Rolling Stone*, August 29, 2016 (available at rollingstone.com/music/features/remembering-beatles-final-concert-w436179).

2. Clifford Kachline, "Everybody Happy After Majors' Meeting: Pension Lift, New College Rule Hailed," *The Sporting News*, December 17, 1966: 19. The Major League Winter Meetings were held in Pittsburgh while the Minor League Winter Meetings were held in Columbus, Ohio.

3. Bob Hunter, "Only 27 Remain of Dodger 1966 Training Roster," *The Sporting News*, December 17, 1966: 25.

4. Les Biederman, "The O'Malley Denies Maury Had to Leave," *The Sporting News*, December 17, 1966: 25.

5. Quoted in Les Biederman, "Wills Trade Triggered by Quail-Hunting Chatter," *The Sporting News*, December 25, 1966: 25.

6. All WAR scores used herein are from Baseball-reference.com. The statistic was developed in the first decade of the twenty-first century, and scores cited here were determined retrospectively.

7. Bailey was sold by the Dodgers to the Expos on October 21, 1968. See "Transaction Information" at retrosheet.org/boxesetc/B/Pbailb103.htm.

8. Mincher actually replaced fellow Pilot Mike Hegan, who was originally selected as Seattle's representative but could not play due to injury.

9. Dick Young, "Young Ideas," *The Sporting News*, December 10, 1966: 14.

10. Runtagh. *Rolling Stone* ranked *Revolver* as the number-3 greatest album of all time.

11. Clifford Kachline, "Everybody Happy After Majors' Meeting: Pension Lift, New College Rule Hailed," *The Sporting News*, December 17, 1966: 19.

12. "Ree, Litwhiler Pleased With New College Ruling," *The Sporting News*, December 17, 1966: 19.

13. "Everybody Happy After Majors' Meeting."

14. Ibid.

15. "Mexico City Tentative Site of '67 Major-Minor Confabs," *The Sporting News*, December 17, 1966: 19. Even though Mexico City was initially named as the "tentative" site, the 1967 winter meetings were in fact held there.

16. "Everybody Happy After Majors' Meeting."

17. Ibid.

18. "Spitball Proof Lacking, Says Rules Group," *The Sporting News*, December 17, 1966: 24.

19. Dick Kaegel, "Dual Cy Young Prizes Okayed in Writer Vote," *The Sporting News*, December 17, 1966: 21.

20. Major League Baseball Properties, Inc. v. Salvino (2nd Cir. 2008) (available at caselaw.findlaw.com/us-2nd-circuit/1198768.html).

21. For a summary of the pension deal, see Clifford Kachline, "Players Land a Real Bonanza—10-Year Men Pension Doubled," *The Sporting News*, December 17, 1966: 20.

22. Ibid.

23. Ibid.

— 1967 —
EXPANSION, INEVITABLY

By Mark Armour

Background

THE 1967-68 OFFSEASON WAS launched in October when Kansas City Athletics owner Charlie Finley was granted permission to move his team to Oakland, California. When Kansas City officials threatened legal action, the American League hastily announced plans on October 18 to add new teams in 1969 in both Kansas City and Seattle. The National League was caught off guard, having believed that the two sides had an agreement to work together on any future expansion or relocation plans. Instead, the American League planned to place a team just across the Bay from the National League's San Francisco franchise, and also in Seattle, considered a plum baseball city.

After holding an emergency meeting at Chicago's Executive House on November 13, the NL agreed to allow the AL plans to stand without further protest. The league owners put off expansion plans of their own, but change was inevitable. "The question," said New York Mets Chairman Donald Grant, "is no longer whether we'll expand—but when."[1] The league agreed to discuss this further at the coming winter meetings.

The 1967 major-league winter meetings were held in Mexico City from Sunday, November 26, through Saturday, December 2. During his opening remarks, Commissioner William Eckert said he was delighted to be in Mexico, to "further the friendship and good relations between our two countries."[2] He stressed the importance of the minor leagues to the health of baseball, and particularly noted that the minor leagues would play a large role in the coming expansion.[3]

The managers and general managers came to Mexico with proposals for several new rules changes to speed up the game. In addition, the usual frenzy of trading was expected—the interleague trading period was limited to November 20 to December 15.

Rule 5 Draft

On November 28 the 20 teams held their annual Rule 5 draft. The first choice, by the Oakland Athletics, was 22-year-old right-handed pitcher Ed Sprague, who had played for Class-A Modesto in the Cardinals farm system.

The most familiar chosen names were infielder Chuck Hiller, drafted by the Pirates from the Phillies, and outfielder Sandy Valdespino, drafted by the Braves from the Twins. Ultimately, though, the most important choice was catcher Elrod Hendricks, taken by the Orioles from the Angels. In the minor-league phase of the draft, the Senators chose infielder Toby Harrah from the Phillies, a choice that would pay big dividends for many years.

The Spitball

One of the biggest stories in baseball in this period was a rampant use of the spitball. It was believed that dozens of pitchers used the pitch, and in September 1967 Mets right-hander Cal Koonce had publicly admitted to doing so. The spitball had been deemed illegal since 1920, but umpires had little means of enforcement. "The publicity over the spitball has always been bad," said White Sox GM Ed Short. "There was that feeling of cheating about it. We certainly didn't think it did the game any good."[4] The clubs felt they had to either give the umpires more authority or legalize the pitch.

On November 27 the team owners unanimously recommended to the Rules Committee support for a rule to penalize pitchers for putting their hands to their mouth. Later that very day, the committee announced that a first violation would cause the umpire to warn the pitcher, and the second would result in his ejection. "The new rule will help baseball 100 percent," said Mets manager Gil Hodges. "It's a great step forward and I'm all in favor of strict enforcement. Pitchers should not be allowed to go to their mouths. That's where the trouble comes in."[5]

Other Rules Changes

Teams also agreed to a number of measures to speed up the game. Umpires were asked to ensure that mound conferences between the pitcher and catcher be curtailed, that batters run back to the plate after a fouled bunt attempt, and that pinch-hitters be already on the bench when the previous batter completed his time at bat, which would eliminate a pinch-hitter from running in from the bullpen. More interestingly, teams were asked to use golf carts to bring relievers in from the bullpen. The Yankees had long refused to use them, but said they would now comply. A committee of general managers and managers was formed to look into and suggest other rules to speed up the game.[6]

After some debate, the owners outlawed deals involving "players to be named later" during the season. If such a deal was made in the offseason, all players must be identified prior to the start of the subsequent season. Because the National League supported the new rule and the American League did not, Commissioner Eckert cast the deciding vote and sided with the NL.[7] As an illustration of what the new rules would prevent, the Baltimore Orioles were still owed players from the Yankees for lefty Steve Barber (dealt during the 1967 season) and the Phillies for right-hander Dick Hall (traded in December 1966, a full year before).

The major leagues agreed to reduce Opening Day rosters to 25 men. Previously teams could carry three additional players until May 15. Many GMs argued that these three players just sat on the bench when they could be playing in the minor leagues. The minor leagues also supported this new rule.

Baseball passed another new rule that barred a club that released a player after August 31 from re-signing him until May 15 of the following season. This rule was to keep teams from using this tactic to free up a roster spot in the offseason. The Yankees deployed this trick with Whitey Ford after the 1966 season. Usually a veteran player is in on the ruse, but when the Houston Astros released Felix Mantilla in November 1966, they assured the infielder they would have a place for him in the spring; however, he thwarted the plan by signing with the Cubs in February.

Hereafter, any player under contract would be required to pass through irrevocable waivers before he could be released. This rule came about because of a situation involving Kansas City outfielder Ken Harrelson. After a dispute with owner Finley in August 1967, Harrelson was summarily released, making him a free agent in the heat of the pennant race. Three days later the Red Sox signed Harrelson to a $150,000 contract. Had the new rule been in effect, Harrelson would almost certainly have been claimed by another AL team and continued under the terms of his old contract.

The clubs further agreed that any incentive bonuses and college scholarship payments that were part of a player's contract would be transferred with the contract if the player was traded. Previously these obligations remained with the club that negotiated the terms into the original contract.[8]

Two new scoring changes were approved. First, a scorer was given the authority to use his discretion if a batter bunts with runners on base—if the scorer believes the batter is trying for a hit but is thrown out, he should not award a sacrifice. Second, if a runner is trapped off base and reaches the next base without an error, the scorer can award a stolen base.[9]

The American League approved, for spring training only, an early form of what would later become the designated-hitter rule. If a manager "designated" a pinch-hitter before the game, the player would be allowed to pinch-hit twice in the game (but not in the same inning).[10]

Expansion

After much internal debate, the National League "unanimously, if grudgingly" voted to expand by two teams by 1971. "We were hoping they would expand at the same time as us," said AL President Joe Cronin, "and maybe they will yet, but there is nothing we can do about it if they don't."[11] The American League had previously decided to expand to Seattle and Kansas City in 1969.

The National League received formal applications from representatives of Milwaukee, San Diego, Dallas-Fort Worth, Buffalo, Toronto, and Montreal, and an informal one from Denver. San Diego, considered a strong choice, had already lured longtime Los Angeles executive Buzzie Bavasi to sign on as one of its owners. Bill DeWitt, a longtime executive with several clubs, was working with the Buffalo group.

The AL, meanwhile, awarded its Seattle franchise to Pacific Northwest Sports Inc., a group led by Pacific Coast League President Dewey Soriano, his brother Max, and Bill Daley, former board chairman of the Indians. The group said that Sick's Stadium, longtime home of the Seattle Rainiers of the Pacific Coast League, could be temporarily expanded to 30,000 seats and that construction on a new stadium would begin by 1970.[12]

The American League owners also heard presentations from four groups hoping to land the Kansas City franchise, and promised to decide between them in January. One of the leading contenders was Ewing Kauffman, president of Marion Laboratories, who, unlike the other Kansas City groups, wanted to buy the entire team with his own money.

The AL also established some details of the expansion draft, to be held in October 1968. Each of the new clubs would be able to select three players from each existing team (a total of 30 players for both Kansas City and Seattle) at a cost of $175,000 per player. The clubs were also required to pay $100,000 to join the league, bringing their initial expenditures to $5.35 million each. In addition, the new clubs would also be required to begin contributing to the player pension fund immediately, but would not be allowed to share in the TV deal for three years.[13]

Player Dealing

Although no blockbuster trades were made in Mexico City, there was enough activity to keep the newspapers filled for a few days.

Starting things off, the Mets acquired catcher J.C. Martin from the White Sox, completing a deal that began in August when they sent third baseman Ken Boyer to Chicago. The Mets also sent right-handed pitcher Bill Denehy and $100,000 to Washington to complete their October acquisition of manager Gil Hodges.

The Dodgers traded catcher John Roseboro and relief pitchers Ron Perranoski (a southpaw) and right-hander Bob Miller to the Twins for right-handed pitcher Mudcat Grant and shortstop Zoilo Versalles. Just over two years earlier, all five men had played key roles for their clubs in the 1965 World Series, but now all would be wearing the opposing uniform. The Dodgers had fallen from first place to eighth in 1967, and manager Walter Alston thought they needed a shortstop most of all. His new shortstop, Versalles, was bitter at the deal: "I'll tell you one thing—they're going to miss me."[14] Roseboro was more sanguine: "If you have to go, it's nice to be going to a pennant contender."[15]

The Dodgers also sold infielder Gene Michael to the Yankees. New York general manager Lee MacPhail had hoped to land a more established starting infielder and was prepared to trade a frontline starter, but he had to settle for Michael, a 29-year-old utilityman.

The Baltimore Orioles traded shortstop Luis Aparicio and outfielders Russ Snyder and John Matias to the Chicago White Sox for infielder Don Buford and right-handed pitchers Bruce Howard and Roger Nelson. Aparicio, who had become expendable with the emergence of Mark Belanger, was thrilled to be returning to Chicago.

The Red Sox, in search of pitching help to back Jim Lonborg, traded minor-league outfielder Bill Schlesinger to the Cubs for veteran righty Ray Culp. Manager Dick Williams said he would put Culp right behind Jim Lonborg in the rotation.

The Cleveland Indians dealt Chuck Hinton to the Angels for Jose Cardenal, in a swap of veteran outfielders looking for a fresh start.

Players Union

The Major League Players Association held their annual meetings in Mexico City as well, with player representatives of all 20 teams present. Drama ensued when the union was told that the owners' Player Relations Committee would not have time to meet with them. The union had made numerous proposals to the owners several months earlier and negotiations had been, in the view of Executive Director Marvin Miller, needlessly slow. "We were told further discussion would be needed in Mexico City," said Miller. "The only reason the players are here is to conclude the negotiation."[16]

The players responded by holding a press conference to lay out the state of the negotiations. The owners claimed to be surprised at the misunderstanding, and said that they never believed there would be time to meet with the players. Most of them claimed that it was much ado about nothing. Atlanta general manager Paul Richards, on the other hand, was more pointed: "Somebody's lying. And I don't think it's the owners. If this guy continues these kinds of antics we might just have to get in the gutter with him."[17]

At their press conference, the players announced that Miller had been given a new contract, through 1970, signaling that the owners could not avoid dealing with the controversial leader. The owners agreed to meet with the players in a couple of weeks in New York.[18]

Miscellaneous

The National Association (the minor leagues) also held their annual meeting, and crowned Mexico City Tigers owner Alejo Peralta, who led the effort to bring the Mexican League into Organized Baseball, as the "King of Baseball." The group also awarded the Larry MacPhail Trophy, as club of the year, to Rochester of the International League.

At the annual meeting of the Baseball Writers Association of America, the group rejected a proposal from Hal Middlesworth of Detroit to rename the Most Valuable Player Award the Player of the Year Award. It was believed by many that the name of the award created confusion every year.

At the annual meeting of team public-relations directors, a committee was formed to plan for an expanded film bureau. All clubs were asked to put together film packages of great moments in their histories.

Paul Richards, the Braves' general manager and a former catcher, proposed moving the pitchers mound back five feet, to 65 feet 6 inches, to help the batter. This was in response to offensive levels being at their lowest since before World War I.

In the National League meeting, Astros President Bill Giles suggested that each club select a candidate for a "Miss Baseball" beauty contest.

C.C. Johnson Spink, publisher of *The Sporting News*, proposed that baseball begin to keep a Game Winning RBI statistic, with a formula to be determined.

Conclusion

The two most pressing issues facing baseball at the end of the 1967 Winter Meetings were the need to finalize expansion plans in each league, and the need to continue and complete negotiations with the players union on what would be the first-ever Basic Agreement. Both issues seemed likely to conclude soon.

NOTES

1. Jerome Holtzman, "N.L. Owners Unload Weapons, Vote Against a Fight for Seattle," *The Sporting News*, November 25, 1967: 30.
2. Stan Isle, "Eckert Cites Key Role for Minors," *The Sporting News*, December 9, 1967: 33.
3. Ibid.
4. Milton Richman, "Majors Start Speed-Up, Clean-Up Campaign," *The Sporting News*, December 9, 1967: 33.
5. Ibid.
6. Ibid.
7. *The Sporting News Official Baseball Guide—1968*, 203.
8. Dick Kaegel, "'Mystery Player' Trades Outlawed," *The Sporting News*, December 16, 1967: 30.
9. *The Sporting News Official Baseball Guide—1968*, 204.
10. Ibid.
11. Stan Isle, "Foot-Dragging N.L. Agrees to Expand," *The Sporting News*, December 16, 1967: 29.
12. Ibid.
13. *The Sporting News Official Baseball Guide—1968*, 180-81.
14. Bob Hunter, "Can Zoilo Instill Go-Go in Dodgers?" *The Sporting News*, December 16, 1967: 36.
15. Arno Goethel, "Ermer Engineer of Trade, Says Shook-Up Zoilo," *The Sporting News*, December 16, 1967: 36.
16. Charles Green, "'Somebody's Lying,' Charges Richards," *Free Lance-Star* (Fredericksburg, Virginia), December 1, 1967.
17. Ibid.
18. Dick Kaegel, "Player-Owner Friction Mounting Rapidly," *The Sporting News*, December 16, 1967: 31.

— 1968 —
DOWN GOES ECKERT

By Mark Armour

Background

BASEBALL WAS GOING THROUGH A time of transition as the 1968 Winter Meetings approached. Most dramatically, the major leagues were about to add four new teams beginning in 1969, and had recently held two expansion drafts to stock the new clubs. On Monday, October 14, the National League held its draft for the Montreal Expos and San Diego Padres, while the following day the American League had its turn to benefit the Kansas City Royals and Seattle Pilots. When the dust settled, each of the 20 existing teams had lost six players and each of the four new teams had added 30.

Expansion also must lead to some reorganization in the minor leagues — both because some of the new teams would supplant minor-league teams, and also because the franchises would need affiliates of their own. In October the general managers approved a plan for 22 Triple-A teams, 20 Double-A, and 24 Single-A teams in 1969, with plans to get to 24 at each level (one for each major-league team) by 1971.

Also of note, the sport had been getting a lot of heat in the national press for its historic lack of scoring, the lowest in 60 years. Most observers believed that baseball would have to act to change the game to generate more offense. "It would be terrible for us to continue on whistling through the graveyard and ignore what is happening," said Cleveland Indians President Gabe Paul.[1] Several possible rules changes were on the agenda for the meetings.

The major-league meetings were held at the Palace Hotel in San Francisco from Sunday, December 1, through Saturday, December 7.

The biggest news to come out of the meetings happened on Friday the 6th, when Commissioner William Eckert was asked for, and soon proffered, his resignation. He had completed just three years of his seven-year contract. The owners wanted a new commissioner who would provide bold and imaginative leadership, traits that Eckert clearly did not have. The owners claimed they were looking for a complete restructuring of the game, changes that would rid baseball of the squabbling between the leagues that had plagued it for years.

"When each league goes its own way on basic matters of policy, what you're left with is the 'law of the jungle,'" said Tigers President John Fetzer. Sounding the same theme, Bill Bartholomay of the Braves added, "We couldn't even agree on a waiver rule change at these meetings. One league wants one thing and one wants something else, and no one in either league knows what the other is thinking."[2]

Mike Burke of the Yankees, one of the "Young Turks" who was angling for the change, thought baseball needed to deal with the fact that it was losing popularity. "We recognize our problem. It's the attitude of the public at large that baseball is not with it, that it's not as contemporary as football, hockey, and basketball, the contact sports. It's an attitude that exists and we've got to decide what to do about it. We need strong, courageous, intelligent leadership."[3]

A three-person committee was created to recommend a reorganization of the management structure of baseball: Jerry Hoffberger, owner of the Orioles; Dick Meyer, representing August Busch of the Cardinals; and John Holland, representing Phil Wrigley of the Cubs. Hoffberger in particular had led the revolt that resulted in the ouster of Eckert.

Rule 5 Draft

On December 2, the 24 teams (including the four expansion teams) held their annual Rule 5 draft. The first choice, by the Houston Astros, was veteran outfielder Gary Geiger, who had spent the 1968 season in the minor leagues and had been left unprotected by the Cardinals, his parent club. Other well-known names included catcher Russ Nixon (taken by the White Sox from the Red Sox), and left-handed pitcher Bob Belinsky (by the Cardinals, from the Astros).

Because the expansion draft had already taken six players from the 40-man rosters of each of the existing 20 teams, the pickings in the Rule 5 draft should have been that much less enticing. On the other hand, the existing teams had six new holes to fill, thus making the draft just as active as it had been in past years.

The most important selections were lesser-known minor leaguers who went on to long careers in the big leagues: corner infielder Darrell Evans (by the Braves from the Athletics), outfielder Cesar Geronimo (by the Astros from the Yankees), and right-handed pitcher Pedro Borbon (by the Angels from the Cardinals). One player who paid off even quicker was Wayne Garrett, whom the Mets selected from the Braves system and who became a platoon regular for them at third base.

Rule Changes

Beginning in 1969 the pitcher's mound was to be 10 inches above the height of the plate, rather than 15 inches, and the strike zone would be reduced to encompass the top of the knees to the armpits, instead of the knees to the top of the shoulder. "All this stuff is trial and error anyway," said Atlanta general manager Paul Richards. "If it works, let's do it." Dodgers manager Walter Alston was less optimistic: "The good hitters are still going to hit and the rotten hitters are still going to strike out."[4]

The Rules Committee agreed to a new rule that would credit a "Save" to a reliever who entered the game with a lead and held that lead until the end of the game, provided he did not get a "Win." The rule would also allow a pitcher to get a Save without finishing the game if he was removed for a pinch-hitter or pinch-runner—in such a case, the official scorer would be allowed to choose from among multiple eligible candidates.[5]

Another new rule would let scorers charge relievers who enter the game in mid-inning with earned runs allowed even if errors before he entered the game would have ended the inning. In this case the runs could be unearned for the team but earned for the relief pitcher.[6]

The baseball clubs created a "temporary inactive list" for players who sustain a bona-fide illness or injury unrelated to baseball activities. A player put on this list would be removed from the roster for at least 21 days and not paid, but would remain under contract to the club. The rule was prompted by injuries like that suffered by right-hander Jim Lonborg, the 1967 American League Cy Young Award winner, who broke his leg skiing in late December 1967.

The rules surrounding suspended games were changed. If a game was suspended after nine innings with the score tied, it would be continued from that point, rather than replayed in its entirety.

The American League agreed to try some experimental rules in spring training: the use of a permanent pinch-hitter for the pitcher; a permanent pinch-runner who could be used any time; and the automatic awarding of first base on an intentional walk. "These tests," said AL President Joe Cronin, "will be made at the discretion of the president."[7]

The leagues rejected a proposal to decrease the roster size from 25 to 23, something the minor leagues (who were losing 100 players with league expansion) were urging.

Major-league teams (and minor-league teams as well) that lost at least two players to military service would be allowed to recall an optioned player.[8]

Player Dealing

Cleveland Indians general manager Gabe Paul went to San Francisco looking for a big bat. He apparently offered five players for Phillies slugger Richie Allen (who was rumored to be going several places), but the Phillies wanted either ace lefty Sam McDowell or All-Star righty Luis Tiant as part of the package. The Indians were also believed to have made a pitch for Senators slugger Frank Howard. All of this came to naught. Instead he settled for acquiring infielder Zoilo Versalles (just drafted from the Dodgers in the October expansion draft) from the Padres to complete an earlier trade. Versalles had won the AL MVP award in 1965, but his career had gone downhill rapidly in the years since.

Ultimately the winter meetings were relatively slow on the big-name front. The Phillies picked up Deron Johnson, the slugging corner infielder-outfielder coming off a couple of down years, from the Braves. The Red Sox, having lost infielders Joe Foy and Jerry Adair in the expansion draft, traded right-handed pitcher Gary Waslewski to the Cardinals for infielder Dick Schofield. The Yankees, coming off an 83-79 record, their best finish in four years, made three small deals, acquiring left-handed pitcher Mike Kekich from the Dodgers for outfielder Andy Kosco; outfielder Dick Simpson from the Astros for right-handed pitcher Dooley Womack; and infielder Nate Oliver from the Giants for third baseman Charley Smith.

In the biggest deal of the meetings, one that would have large ramifications over the game for the next several years, the Baltimore Orioles traded infielder-outfielder Curt Blefary and minor-leaguer John Mason to the Houston Astros for left-handed pitcher Mike Cuellar, infielder Enzo Hernandez, and minor leaguer Tom Johnson. Houston had deemed Cuellar expendable despite three good seasons, and had wanted to trade him for a hitter. They had tried to get Jesus Alou from the Expos for Cuellar but had been turned down. Baltimore, on the other hand, had a surplus in the outfield—Earl Weaver had taken over as Orioles manager in July and had given Blefary's job to Don Buford. Blefary, the 1965 American League Rookie of the Year, had not been happy about it, and the Orioles decided to cash him in.

Player's Union

In September, Players Association Executive Director Marvin Miller had advised the players not to sign their 1969 contracts until a new pension agreement—replacing the one expiring on March 31—was reached. The clubs' pension contribution had traditionally been tied to a percentage of World Series and All-Star Game television revenue, but was replaced with a specific figure in 1966. Since then baseball had signed a new lucrative TV deal ($16.3 million), which included additional revenue for the two League Championship Series. "The players have a right to know what is in their 1969 benefit plan before signing their contracts," reasoned Miller. "The two go hand in hand. Signing without knowing what the new pension plan will offer is like signing half a contract."[9]

During the winter meetings, the union's Executive Board was once again told that the owners were too busy to see them (as they had been in Mexico City a year earlier). After its own meeting, the board called players around the country looking for commitments to not sign contracts without a pension agreement. Miller held a press conference on December 4 and read off the names of dozens of players, including Mickey Mantle, Roberto Clemente, Bob Gibson, and Willie Mays. "Young players have been told to sign now or play in the minor leagues next year," Miller said. "Others have been told they'll never get the necessary five years unless they sign."[10] The owners claimed this was all just a ploy. "A negotiating tactic," said John Gaherin, the owners' chief negotiator, "but it is not conducive to a healthy climate for a settlement."[11]

Also present in San Francisco were the newly organized American League umpires, who were looking for improved salaries and the reinstatement of Al Salerno and Bill Valentine. The two arbiters claimed that they had been fired in September for attempting to organize a union, though AL President Joe Cronin said he made the decision based only on their ability. The Major League Umpires Association (encompassing both leagues) suggested it would strike if the umpires are not given their jobs back.

Centennial

In a meeting of team public-relations directors chaired by Joe Reichler, PR director for the commissioner's office, the group agreed to a plan to celebrate baseball's centennial in 1969. Highlights included:

- A two-trailer caravan containing Hall of Fame memorabilia would visit every major- and minor-league park in the country during the season.
- A baseball digest containing team histories and current players would be published.
- A one-hour television show featuring members of the Hall of Fame and top entertainers would be broadcast on July 21, the eve of the All-Star Game.
- A new US postage stamp would be issued.
- Campbell's Soup would make baseball-oriented labels on 40 million to 50 million cans of company's product.
- Lee Allen and other writers would compile a list of 25 outstanding feats in history, to be part of a publication released during the year.
- Fans in ballparks would vote on the greatest players by position (10 players, including a left- and right-handed pitcher) for their home clubs. Writers would take these teams and pick all-time teams. The living players would be part of the July 21 gala.

Miscellaneous

On December 3, attorneys for the Washington Senators announced the sale of the club by board chairman James H. Lemon to a group led by Robert E. Short of Minneapolis, the treasurer of the Democratic National Committee. Short met with team executives at the winter meetings to discuss the state of the team.

Johnny Mize appeared at the meetings in support of the Global League, a proposed professional circuit that would not compete with the major leagues. According to league plans, there would be teams in Tokyo, Osaka, and Nagoya, Japan, Louisville, Jersey City, and Mobile in the United States. Former Commissioner Happy Chandler would take a leadership role. The league would be supplied with players who had been released by the major leagues. Mize would manage a team, and Roy Campanella was envisioned as the manager for Jersey City. Other interested people included Enos Slaughter, Allie Reynolds, and Bob Turley.[12]

The Global League would also experiment with different rules changes. Hillman Lyons, a longtime major- and minor-league executive and a Chandler associate, elaborated. "Like allowing pinch-hitters to bat more than once, using pinch-runners more than once. Maybe our pitchers won't hit at all."[13]

At the Baseball Writers Association of America annual meeting, the writers urged that the statistics earned in the new league playoffs not count as part of the regular season stats. Past policy was that statistics from league playoffs (after two teams tied for the pennant) counted in regular season statistics.

The two leagues formally agreed to two divisions, 162-game schedules, and best-of-five League Championship Series.

At the annual meeting of the National Association (the minor leagues), outgoing Pacific Coast League President (and incoming Seattle Pilots President) Dewey Soriano was crowned "King of Baseball."

Conclusion

Heading out of the Winter Meetings, baseball had some major problems to deal with. The owners had to find a commissioner, and early indications were that the two leagues were likely not going to agree easily on that score. There was also, for the first time in history, the threat of a player strike over the unresolved pension negotiations. The leagues had agreed to new rules to combat a crisis in run scoring, and no one really knew whether those new rules were going to be sufficient.

With all that going on, baseball was adding four new teams and playing with four divisions for the first time. It was an extraordinarily historic time in the history of the game.

NOTES

1. Bob Sudyk, "Liven Up Ball to Restore Scoring Thrills, Paul Urges," *The Sporting News*, December 7, 1968: 48.
2. Oscar Kahan, "Baseball Groping for New Direction," *The Sporting News*, December 21, 1968: 25.
3. Ibid.
4. Harry Jupiter, "Rules Altered; Now It's Up to Swingers," *The Sporting News*, December 21, 1968: 24.
5. *The Sporting News Official Baseball Guide 1969*, 203.
6. Ibid.
7. Stan Isle, "Players Protest Rule Permitting Pay Suspension," *The Sporting News*, December 21, 1968: 27.
8. Ibid.
9. *The Sporting News* Official Baseball Guide, 1969.
10. Stan Isle, "Threat of Umpire and Player Strikes Hanging Over Majors," *The Sporting News*, December 21, 1968: 24.
11. Ibid.
12. Harry Jupiter, "Mize Goes to Bat for Global League," *The Sporting News*, December 14, 1968: 35.
13. Ibid.

— 1969 —
REORGANIZATION TALK

By Mark Armour

Background

AS THE 1969 BASEBALL WINTER Meetings approached, the central issues on the minds of most owners were the recommendations of the restructuring committee that had been created the year before. At that meeting, in San Francisco, the owners had fired William Eckert as commissioner, and had formed a group to examine ways to restructure the management of the game in an attempt to reduce the league squabbles that had been plaguing baseball over the past decade.

The 1969 Winter Meetings were held from Sunday, November 30, through Saturday, December 6, in south Florida. The minor-league meetings were held at Fort Lauderdale's Galt Ocean Mile Hotel from Sunday night through Wednesday morning, and on Wednesday afternoon the major-league meetings began 25 miles away at the Americana Hotel in Bal Harbour. Most of the teams' top brass attended both sets of meetings.

Restructuring

The restructuring committee, headed by Baltimore owner Jerry Hoffberger, along with Dick Meyer (St. Louis) and John Holland (Chicago Cubs), formally presented highlights of their report (complete details had been prepared by the University of Pennsylvania's Wharton School of management and were mailed to the group after the meeting) to their colleagues on Saturday, December 6. In essence, the committee recommended giving significantly more power to the commissioner by making the two league presidents effectively his deputies, responsible to the commissioner first and the league owners second. The two league presidents (referred to as "deputy commissioners" in the first version of the report) would be nominated by the commissioner and approved by the owners. The minor leagues would also be placed under the commissioner.[1]

Furthermore, the league offices would both move to New York and operate under the commissioner's office. Traditionally the league offices were set up wherever the league president wanted to live. In 1969, the AL offices were in Boston, in deference to league President Joe Cronin, while the NL offices had long been in Cincinnati, home of Warren Giles. The minor-league (formally organized as the National Association of Professional Baseball Leagues) offices would also move to New York and be under the commissioner.[2]

In addition, the two umpiring staffs would be joined and place under the command of the commissioner, rather than managed by the league presidents. The commissioner would also have control of a number of additional people and spheres. He would appoint the chairman of the Playing Rules Committee, a broadcast coordinator, an administrative officer, and various aides, lawyers, and assistants.[3]

Of paramount importance, all playing or operating rules changes or structural changes would require a two-thirds majority of all owners and a simple majority of each league, making it much more difficult for a small group in one league to block a measure favored by most of the owners. Currently the two leagues voted independently and separately and had their own procedures for how their vote was counted. The National League, for example, required unanimous consent on some issues, like relocation or expansion. In 1968 a single owner—Houston's Roy Hofheinz—had reportedly blocked expansion to Dallas, which the rest of the owners wanted.[4]

To a very large degree, the restructuring plan was delivered a blow two days before it was presented when the National League voted 12-0 to hire Charles "Chub" Feeney to replace the retiring Warren Giles as league president. The National League was particularly wary of any loss of independence and power for the league, and it was known that Commissioner Bowie Kuhn wanted Giles to stick around during this transitional period. The sudden appointment of Feeney, who was a member of the restructuring committee and well aware of what was in the coming report, was a significant defeat for Kuhn and the committee.

Feeney, the nephew of San Francisco Giants owner Horace Stoneham, had been an executive with the Giants for more than 20 years. He had been reluctant to take the league presidency because he feared the offices were being weakened, but he now made it clear that he was doing so with assurance that the league's autonomy would be unchanged. "Warren Giles has done a magnificent job of building up the National League during his 17 years," said Feeney. "I will be well satisfied if I can do two-thirds as good a job in my tenure. The National League is having its high point in the cycle. I hope it will continue."[5]

Feeney was opposed to interleague play (something the American League and Kuhn wanted), and also announced that he planned to move his league's offices from Cincinnati to San Francisco, and not to New York. Many were concerned about the time difference. "In the morning," said one observer, "Don Grant (New York Mets), Joe Brown (Pittsburgh), and Don Davidson (Atlanta) will be asking, 'where the hell is Chub Feeney?'"[6]

In any event, many baseball owners, especially in the National League, were leery of the drastic changes as proposed by the restructuring committee. No action was taken at the Florida meetings, but further get-togethers were scheduled to consider the details of the comprehensive proposals point by point.

Rule 5 Draft

On December 1 the major leagues held their annual Rule 5 draft, and 19 players were selected. The first choice went to the Cleveland Indians, who took left-handed pitcher Larry Staab from the Los Angeles Dodgers. Staab had won 13 games for Triple-A Spokane in 1969, and 12 the prior year for the same club.

There were just a handful of players taken whose names were familiar to any but the most rabid of fans. The Astros selected southpaw Jack DiLauro, who had pitched 23 games for the recent champion Mets. The Braves drafted catcher Hal King, who had played parts of two seasons with the Astros and spent 1969 hitting .322 for the Red Sox' Triple-A club in Louisville.

Over the long term, the most important selection was that of infielder Manny Trillo, taken by the Phillies from the Athletics. The 20-year-old was still a few years away.

Rule Changes

The major leagues approved a "caveat emptor" amendment to the existing rules regarding player trades. There had been two high-profile trades in this past year in which a traded player decided to retire rather than report to his new team. The traditional way such matters had been handled in the past was to call off the entire trade.

- On January 22, 1969, the Montreal Expos traded first baseman Donn Clendenon and outfielder Jesus Alou to the Houston Astros for outfielder Rusty Staub. Everything appeared fine for a few weeks, until February 28 when Clendenon announced his retirement. Most observers thought the trade would be called off at this point. In early March, Clendenon suggested that he might be open to returning but not to Houston, though his public stance would change several times over the next few weeks. For his part, Staub was thrilled to be with the Expos, and Montreal was thrilled to have him. After considerable communication with all parties, Commissioner Bowie Kuhn reworked the deal by having Montreal send a couple of additional players to Houston and allowing

Clendenon (who got a big raise) to remain with the Expos.
- In early April the Red Sox made a six-player trade with the Indians, sending popular first baseman-outfielder Ken Harrelson to Cleveland. Harrelson, who had considerable business interests in Boston, announced that he was retiring. Kuhn froze the deal until he could arrange a meeting with Harrelson and executives from each club. After Harrelson got a new contract with a large raise, he "un-retired" and the trade was finalized.

Under the new rule, which even the commissioner believed was necessary, all trades, once agreed upon, would stand. It was up to the teams themselves to persuade their players to report to work.[7] Had this rule been in place a year earlier, both trades would have been final, and Clendenon and Harrelson would have been free to report or not as they wished.

Player Dealing

The New York Mets, fresh off their World Series championship, were willing to trade some of their young pitching (specifically Gary Gentry, Nolan Ryan, and Jim McAndrew) for a hitter if the right deal came along. GM Johnny Murphy did not expect such a deal, and assumed his team would stand pat. Their only need was at third base, where Ed Charles (who had platooned with Wayne Garrett) had retired. "I've talked to every club and they are interested in our kid pitchers," admitted Murphy. "And I've told them all that [Tom] Seaver and [Jerry] Koosman are the only ones we will not trade."[8]

Early in the week the Mets got their third baseman from the Royals in the person of Joe Foy, a 26-year-old who had had a few solid years with Boston and Kansas City. The price was 22-year-old outfielder Amos Otis and right-handed pitcher Bob Johnson, neither of whom was in New York's plans. The Mets were delighted with Foy, considered one of the better young third basemen in the game. "He's a fine defensive third baseman and he gives us speed," said Mets manager Gil Hodges. "I expect him to give us more offense, plus a good glove at third."[9]

The Atlanta Braves traded veteran outfielder Felipe Alou to the Oakland Athletics for right-handed pitcher Jim Nash. Nash was delighted to be playing at home—he had grown up in nearby Marietta and attended the University of Georgia—while the A's hoped Alou would take over either at first base or left field.

The Yankees dealt enigmatic first baseman Joe Pepitone to Houston in exchange for outfielder-first baseman Curt Blefary, the 1965 American League Rookie of the Year. Pepitone had had many off-field issues during his Yankee years, and manager Ralph Houk likely had enough after Pepitone jumped the club twice in 1969. "Pepitone was as good a first baseman as I ever have seen and a fine ballplayer," said Houk. "Joe had his problems, but he was a good guy."[10]

The next day the Yankees continued the teardown of their 1964 pennant winner by dealing left-handed pitcher Al Downing (and catcher Frank Fernandez) to the A's for first baseman Danny Cater and outfielder Ossie Chavarria. Downing, who had had a couple of difficult seasons, had conducted a long holdout in March. The Yankees were hoping that Cater and Blefary would combine to man first base.

Labor issues

After having been rebuffed at the Winter Meetings each of the past two Decembers, the players chose to hold their 1969 annual meeting at a different time and place than the owners, and chose San Juan, Puerto Rico, on December 13 and 14. Bowie Kuhn, who had not become commissioner until February 4, 1969, spoke at the meetings and told the players he hoped they could coordinate their meetings in future years. In fact, Kuhn believed that he was the players' commissioner too. The players voiced a number of grievances to Kuhn, including the increase of artificial playing surfaces, the newer stadium designs, plans to have the fans vote for the All-Star teams, and the stalled contract negotiations.[11] (The very first CBA, agreed upon two years earlier, was to expire on December 31.)

The most important issue discussed at the players' meetings involved star outfielder Curt Flood, who had been traded from St. Louis to Philadelphia in October

> ### "Proposed Reorganization of Baseball"
>
> The formal report, *Proposed Reorganization of Baseball*, drew from information contained in the $80,000 study conducted by the Management Science Center of the Wharton School, and prepared by Russell Ackoff and William Abendroth.* Ackoff, who started out as a math and philosophy professor at Wayne State University, is considered one of the pioneers in operations research—originally designed to solve executive problems in organizations using the application of interdisciplinary techniques, including math, statistics, probability theory, and philosophy.** Ackoff experienced much success in applying operations research to organizations; however, the results of the work with baseball were, arguably, less impactful. While the reported plan may have had a backbone, the delay in action at the Florida meetings mostly foreshadowed long-term avoidance of change and, in some cases, permanent delay.***
>
> ---
>
> * "Baseball Submits a Plan to Centralize Authority," *New York Times*, December 7, 1969: S1.
> ** "Penn Hires 8-Member Research Team," *Philadelphia Inquirer*, May 7, 1964: 31; "IFORS Operational Research Hall of Fame: Russell Ackoff," *International Transactions in Operational Research*, 2005, v12, 129-134.
> *** "The Hottest Issue of All," *The Sporting News*, March 7, 1970: 4; "Is Kuhn Losing Popularity?" *Baltimore Sun*, December 4, 1970: 27.

but now wanted to file suit against baseball to end its hallowed reserve clause. Miller invited Flood to speak to the players, who asked tough questions about his motivations and plans. After hearing from Flood, the players voted unanimously to support his legal case financially and otherwise.[12]

The major-league umpires' union met with league presidents Warren Giles and Joe Cronin to try to iron out the ongoing dispute over their pension plan. "The umpires also are seeking a wage increase and an equalization—certainly an approximation—of benefits in proportion to years of service," said John Reynolds, attorney for the umps. "This meeting, however, was primarily concerned with pensions."[13] While the National League umpires had formed a union in 1963, the American League did not join them until 1968.

Miscellaneous

The National Association named longtime Appalachian League President Chauncey DeVault as the "King of Baseball." At the same banquet, the National Association presented plaques to outgoing NL President Giles, *Sporting News* publisher C.C. Johnson Spink, and Sy Berger, sports director of Topps Chewing Gum Inc. Berger was honored for the company's years of service to the minor leagues, which included a series of annual awards to the top performers in each minor league.

At the annual meeting of publicity directors, plans were discussed to create an annual televised baseball dinner in the wake of the tremendous success of the gala held in Washington on the Monday prior to the 1969 All-Star Game. "We've been told universally," said Joe Reichler, the public-relations aide to Commissioner Kuhn, "that the Washington affair was the biggest sports dinner ever."

At the same meeting, Reichler announced plans to create computerized All-Star ballots, to be distributed to fans at ballparks, gas stations, supermarkets, banks, etc., beginning in June. The fans had not voted on the All-Star Game since 1956. The PR men also discussed setting up a historical library (containing film, photographs, and printed material) in the commissioner's office, a baseball caravan of material that would tour the country, and a Saturday-afternoon TV show for children.

The commissioner asked each of the teams to consider a plan to put names on the backs of their uniforms. While the practice had become common, it was still not universal. At the most recent World Series, the Orioles had their names on their uniforms but the Mets did not.

In a meeting of the baseball writers, the group agreed to expand both the Rookie of the Year and Cy Young Award ballots so that each voter would select a first, second, and third choice, worth 5, 3, and 1 points, respectively. In the recent American League Cy Young Award balloting, Baltimore's Mike Cuellar and Detroit's Denny McLain had finished in a tie, a first in BBWAA history. Additionally, the writers agreed to make their votes public.

The Seattle Pilots had struggled off the field in their inaugural season, to the point where making payroll was not guaranteed. In the fall the club announced that Bill Daley, their principal owner, had an agreement to sell the team to a group led by Jerry Danz, who owned a chain of theaters. Danz met with the American League owners at the winter meetings, but did not make a convincing case that he had sufficient financial backing to come up with the $10.5 million sales price. At least two owners—Jerry Hoffberger of Baltimore and Robert Short of Washington—wanted to give Daley permission to sell the club to a group in Milwaukee who would move the team there right away. The majority disagreed, and urged Danz to go back to Seattle and get some backers immediately.

Conclusion

As baseball concluded its various winter meetings, it was faced with several crucial open issues. One of its franchises—Seattle—was essentially bankrupt and facing an uncertain future after just one season. The game's organizational structure was being debated at the highest levels, and it was uncertain how much power the owners wanted to grant Commissioner Kuhn.

A new CBA was expiring, and the players were looking for an impartial arbiter to hear grievances. And one of the game's marquee players was suing baseball over its reserve clause, one of the underpinnings of the sport.

Another big year loomed.

NOTES

1 Leonard Koppett, "Kuhn Would Have Czar Power if Planners' Ideas Win Okay," *The Sporting News*, 29.

2 Ibid.

3 Ibid.

4 *The Sporting News Official Baseball Guide 1970*, 301.

5 Dick Young, "Giants Lose Ace Exec ... N.L. Prexy Feeney," *The Sporting News*, December 20, 1969: 27.

6 Ibid.

7 Stan Isle, "Buyer Takes Risk in All Deals," *The Sporting News*, December 20, 1969, 28.

8 Jack Lang, "41 Met Hot Sackers, Who'll Be Next?" *The Sporting News*, December 6, 1969: 42.

9 Jack Lang, "Mets Will Toss Reins on Speedboy Foy," *The Sporting News*, December 20, 1969: 30.

10 Jim Ogle, "Trade Winds Puff Out Yank Muscle," *The Sporting News*, December 20, 1969: 31.

11 Stan Isle, "Kuhn 'Well Pleased,' But Miller Isn't," *The Sporting News*, December 27, 1969, 36.

12 Leonard Koppett, "Flood Warms Up for Reserve Clause Attack," *The Sporting News*, January 17, 1970: 33.

13 Stan Isle, "Giles, Cronin Hear Ump Pension Plea," *The Sporting News*, December 13, 1969: 34.

— 1970 —
KUHN THWARTED

By Mark Armour

Background

UNLIKE THE TURMOIL OF THE PREVIous few winters, baseball in December 1970 was relatively calm. Commissioner Bowie Kuhn was secure in his job for at least the next five years, and the owners and players had agreed to a new CBA in May.

The 1970 baseball Winter Meetings were held in Los Angeles, from Sunday, November 29, through Saturday, December 4. The minor-league meetings were in the Biltmore Hotel, while the majors met at the Hilton.

Organizational Matters

One of the significant proposals at the meetings was an attempt by the American and National Leagues to force the National Association (the minor leagues) to relocate its offices from Columbus, Ohio, to New York City, where it would report directly to the commissioner. Phil Piton, who had served as National Association president since 1964 and was set to retire in another year, was opposed, as were both of the league presidents. "Although the majors and minors are engaged in the same primary activity," said Piton, "they differ importantly in that the minor leagues—still comprised largely of independently owned clubs—have the secondary responsibility of furnishing the principal development ground for the players destined to appear on major league diamonds."[1]

Commissioner Kuhn urged the minor leagues to support the move, which was passed by the major leagues. Piton openly asked how the league owners had so freely voted to move the minor-league offices when they had resisted moving the two league offices to New York, as their own planning committee had recommended.[2] In the end, no agreement was reached to move either the National Association offices or the two league offices. Although restructuring had been trumpeted when Commissioner Eckert had been fired at the 1968 meetings, the ensuing two years had brought no significant changes in the organization of the game.[3]

The owners did agree that, beginning in 1971, some weekday World Series and League Championship Series games could be played at night. "The networks are intrigued," said Kuhn, "in terms of potential ratings, with the possibility of telecasting … in prime time. We're also exploring the possibility of blacking out the home city in the championship series."[4]

Although plans to combine the two leagues' umpire staffs into one group were tabled, the leagues did agree to reduce some of the differences between the two groups. "It has been agreed that there will be effort to achieve uniformity in technique and field position as soon as possible," said Commissioner Kuhn.[5]

Rule 5 Draft

On November 30, the major leagues held their annual Rule 5 draft, and it took just 18 minutes for seven clubs to make eight selections. "Frankly, there's very little on the draft list," admitted Yankees general manager Lee MacPhail.[6]

Of the eight players selected, the best known was Joe Foy, selected by the Senators from the Mets. Foy had enjoyed three good seasons as the third baseman for the Red Sox (1966-68), including as a starter on their pennant-winning 1967 team. Lost in the 1968 expansion draft to the Royals, he was traded at the 1969 Winter Meetings to the Mets for outfielder

Amos Otis and right-handed pitcher Bob Johnson. The acquisition of Foy had been considered a key one for the Mets, but just one year later they took him off their 40-man roster.

The St. Louis Cardinals drafted Cecil Cooper, a 20-year-old Single-A first baseman, from the Red Sox. After he failed to make the Cardinals the next spring, he was returned to the Red Sox organization.

Rule Changes

Several proposals for rule changes were rejected at the Playing Rules Committee meetings. During the 1970 season a few rule changes were tried out in the minor leagues, including the designated hitter (Eastern League), an intentional walk without needing to throw four balls (New York-Penn League), and expanded foul lines (Gulf Coast League). In the latter experiment, the foul lines bent outward 3 degrees once they crossed the bases. All three experiments were deemed unsuccessful and were terminated. However, the committee did approve experimentation with wild-card runners in the minor leagues for the coming season.[7]

Charlie Finley, owner of the Oakland Athletics, submitted proposals for colored bases, colored foul lines, and a 20-second clock used to limit time between pitches. All three suggestions were rejected.[8]

On the positive side, the committee passed a rule to require the use of batting helmets, beginning with the 1971 season. Players who had worn a cap liner (the previous requirement) in 1970 would be allowed to continue to do so. Further, Class-A and Rookie League players would have to wear helmets with an earflap.[9]

A rule regarding players interacting with fans was relaxed. Previously, players could not talk with fans or give autographs once batting practice started, but now they could do so up to 30 minutes before the start of the game. This was part of Kuhn's initiative to bring the fans closer to the game.[10]

Statistical Test

Here are some of Lee Walburn's comments from July 1970, when the Atlanta Braves introduced their new computer system:

"Statistics are one of baseball's strongest traditions. In the past, however, we have been limited in the amount of pertinent data which can be updated during and immediately following the contest."

"We are only scratching the surface, but we hope to show with this local test that major league baseball can formulate a joint computer program which will add accuracy, immediacy, volume and prestige to the current methods of baseball data processing."*

Sample statistics the computer instantly reported:

Batting average

Pitching percentages

Number of times a hitter drove in runs with two outs

Number of times a hitter put the Braves ahead in games

Percentage of times a hitter drove in a run with a runner on second or third base

---

* "Braves' New Computer Provides More Stats," *The Tennessean* (Nashville), July 21, 1970: 23.

Rule 5.09B was amended to prohibit baserunners from advancing if the home-plate umpire interfered with a catcher. In Game One of the most recent World Series, umpire Ken Burkhart had become entangled with Baltimore catcher Elrod Hendricks in a controversial play.[11]

Similarly, the use of the disabled list was expanded. Previously a team could have as many as three players disabled at a time—two for 21 days and one for 60. Now a team could also disable a nonpitcher for 15 days, making it permissible to have a total of four at a time.[12]

Player Dealing

On the first day of the meetings the California Angels made a six-player deal with the White Sox. For the Angels, fresh off an 86-win season and hoping to compete, the key acquisition was center fielder Ken Berry, a fair hitter but a Gold Glove-caliber outfielder whom the Angels would play between batting champion Alex Johnson and the newly acquired Tony Conigliaro. "As far as I'm concerned," said Angels general manager Dick Walsh, "we now have a player of record at every position."[13] The White Sox, winners of just 56 games, were rebuilding, and landed catcher Tom Egan, right-handed pitcher Tom Bradley, and outfielder Jay Johnstone.

The Boston Red Sox traded infielders Mike Andrews and Luis Alvarado to the White Sox for veteran shortstop Luis Aparicio. Andrews had become expendable with the October pick-up of Doug Griffin from the Angels. With the acquisition of Aparicio, the Red Sox planned to move Rico Petrocelli to third base, George Scott back to his natural first base, and Carl Yastrzemski back to left field. "We believe these deals give us a chance at the pennant next season," said general manager Dick O'Connell.[14]

In a six-player deal, the World Series champion Baltimore Orioles acquired right-handed pitcher Pat Dobson from the San Diego Padres. The Orioles boasted three 20-game winners—Mike Cuellar, Dave McNally, and Jim Palmer—in 1970, and planned to use Dobson as their fourth starter. The Orioles brass loved Dobson. "He never got a chance to pitch regularly before," said Baltimore general manager Harry Dalton. "That was his problem."[15]

One of the more significant player transactions involved star relief pitcher Hoyt Wilhelm, who was traded from the Cubs to the Braves for minor-league first baseman Hal Breeden. The right-handed Wilhelm, a future Hall of Famer, had been sold from the Braves to the Cubs on September 21 to help in the division race—the Cubs were two games behind the Pirates in the NL East, while the Braves had long been eliminated in the West. Wilhelm pitched just three games for Chicago before being sold back in December. The situation was suspicious enough that the commissioner investigated. "I've satisfied myself that Wilhelm was traded unconditionally by Atlanta to Chicago with no side agreements," reported Kuhn.[16]

Awards Banquet

On Friday evening, December 3, baseball held a huge banquet at the Beverly Hills Hotel, an event much like the Academy Awards show.[17] The 1,200 attendees paid $50 apiece.[18] The event was filmed for a 90-minute special edition of the *Merv Griffin Show* that aired on December 9. Griffin hosted the event as a replacement for an ailing Bob Hope. Hall of Famers present included Carl Hubbell, Joe Cronin, Joe DiMaggio, Stan Musial, Casey Stengel, and Roy Campanella. Award winners included:

- Johnny Bench, player of the year
- Bob Gibson, pitcher of the year
- Brooks Robinson, defensive player of the year
- Willie Mays, for best typifying the game on and off the field
- Danny Murtaugh, manager of the year
- Harry Dalton, executive of the year
- Roger Freed (Rochester), minor-league player of the year

The World Series trophy was presented to Orioles owner Jerry Hoffberger. Special awards were given to Charley Segar, retiring secretary-treasurer of baseball, and Phil Piton, president of the National Association. Astronaut James Lovell, representing the President's

Council on Health and Physical Fitness, recognized Sadaharu Oh, and Tokyo Giants President Toru Shoriki.[19]

Miscellaneous

Faced with a growing concern about drug use in baseball, the owners created the Association of Professional Baseball Physicians. The group, made up of team doctors, was to share information about the care and upkeep of their players, in particular the use of medicine and the distribution of drugs. "Frankly, we don't condone the use of drugs as stimulants," said Dr. Leonard Wallenstein of the Orioles, who was named as the group's president. "In general practice, our trainers are provided with non-addictives that are relatively harmless."[20]

Robert Short, owner of the Washington Senators, informed the American League that he might have to move the Senators if he could not get some relief with his ballpark lease. AL President Joe Cronin said the league would work with Short and local officials on the problem.[21]

Emmett Ashford, the first African-American to serve as a major-league umpire, announced his retirement at the meetings. He had umpired the recent World Series, and thought that a fine way to go out. "Now there are some black umpires in the programs below the majors," he said, "and I'm proud I was the first." His one regret was that it took him so long to get to the majors (age 51) that he got to umpire for only five years. Commissioner Bowie Kuhn said he had talked with Ashford about a public-relations role with the commissioner's office.[22]

George MacDonald Sr., longtime president of the Gulf Coast League and the Florida State League, was crowned the "King of Baseball" at the annual National Association awards banquet. Also on the dais were several entertainers, including singer Dinah Shore and comedian Phil Silvers.[23]

In the annual meeting of publications directors, the All-Star voting procedure was discussed. Baseball had returned the vote to the fans in 1970 and had used computerized ballots. The group agreed to change the number of players on the ballot at each position from six to eight (per league), and also agreed to further discuss allowing fans to vote on the starting pitchers. Joe Reichler, the major leagues' PR director based in the commissioner's office, reported on the success of the Pitch, Hit, and Throw competition, held for the first time in 1970, and said that it would be held again in 1971. Five clubs reported that they would discontinue "bat day" because the bats were being used to hurt people and property.[24]

In the PR directors meeting, Lee Walburn of the Braves reported on his club's use of a computerized statistics program in 1970. He claimed great efficiency at a lower cost, and said it would be expanded in 1971. All clubs were welcome to use the system.[25]

David Dixon, the executive director of the (under construction) New Orleans Superdome, was on hand to make the case for New Orleans as a big-league city, hosting a large cocktail party for Kuhn and the owners, attended by notables like Ernie Banks and Stan Musial. Dixon was open to an existing team moving there, but he also pitched the idea of sharing a team, envisioning the Baltimore-New Orleans Orioles or the Minnesota-New Orleans Twins. His proposal called for New Orleans to host the spring-training season, and then hold up to 40 regular-season games, especially in the cold-weather bookends of the season. "The New Orleans domed stadium," said Louisiana Governor John J. McKeithen, "is going to be the greatest building in the world."[26]

Conclusion

As the winter meetings closed, the biggest news might have been the failure of Commissioner Kuhn to accumulate more power. The umpires remained under the league presidents, and both the league offices and the minor-league offices would remain outside New York City.

The biggest news out of the meetings was Bob Short's news that he might have to move the Senators. Having just gone through a trying ordeal with the Seattle Pilots in 1970, it looked like the American League had more internal discord ahead.

NOTES

1 Stan Isle, "Piton Sounding Battle Call Against Moving Minors' HQ," *The Sporting News*, December 5, 1970: 32.

2 Ibid.

3 Stan Isle, "Majors Balking at Unifying Proposals," *The Sporting News*, December 19, 1970: 33.

4 Ibid.

5 Ibid.

6 Stan Isle, "Short and Sweet: An 18-minute Draft," *The Sporting News*, December 12, 1970: 47.

7 Stan Isle, "Wild-Card Hitter Experiment Junked," *The Sporting News*, December 12, 1970: 48.

8 Ibid.

9 Ibid.

10 Ben Henkey, "Majors Ease Up on Ban—Fan-Player Chats Okayed," *The Sporting News*, December 19, 1970: 35.

11 Associated Press, "Proposals Rejected," *Hartford Courant*, December 2, 1970: 33.

12 Ibid.

13 Ross Newhan, "Berry Fits Into Angel Pennant Scheme," *The Sporting News*, December 19, 1970: 37. The Angels also received infielder Syd O'Brien and right-handed pitcher Billy Wynne.

14 Larry Claflin, "Big-Dealing Bosox Counting on Griffin," *The Sporting News*, December 19, 1970: 41.

15 Phil Jackman, "Pat Dobson Acquired to Fill No. 4 Spot on Oriole Staff," *The Sporting News*, December 19, 1970: 38. The Orioles sent three right-handed pitchers—Tom Phoebus, Fred Beene, and Al Severinsen—plus promising young shortstop Enzo Hernandez to the Padres. Right-handed pitcher Tom Dukes accompanied Dobson to Baltimore.

16 Jerome Holtzman, "Wilhelm Deals Were on Up-and-Up, Kuhn Says," *The Sporting News*, December 19, 1970: 37.

17 Stan Isle, "Bench, Gibson Share Top Laurels at Plush Party," *The Sporting News*, December 19, 1970: 33.

18 Stan Isle, "Fans May Pick the All-Star Pitchers," *The Sporting News*, December 19, 1970: 34.

19 Ibid.

20 Stan Isle, "Team Medics Examining Drug Usage," *The Sporting News*, December 19, 1970: 32.

21 Isle, "Majors Balking at Unifying Proposals."

22 Stan Isle, "Kuhn May Hire Ex-Umpire Ashford," *The Sporting News*, December 19, 1970: 32.

23 Ben Henkey, "MacDonald Crowned 'King of Baseball,'" *The Sporting News*, December 19, 1970: 33.

24 Stan Isle, "Fans May Pick the All-Star Pitchers."

25 Ibid.

26 Stan Isle, "Big League Team in New Orleans," *The Sporting News*, December 19, 1970: 35.

— 1971 —
THE SWAP MEET

By Mark Armour

Background

THE 1971 BASEBALL WINTER MEETINGS took place in Phoenix, Arizona, from Saturday, November 27, through Friday, December 3. As was the custom, the National Association meetings took up the first few days, while the major-league meetings got going on Wednesday.

Rule 5 Draft

In the annual major-league draft, the big-league clubs claimed 13 players at the $25,000 price tag. Cleveland had the first choice and selected Jim Moyer, a right-handed pitcher, from the Giants system. Two outfielders who had recently held down starting positions in the big leagues were also selected: Steve Hovley (by the Royals from the Athletics) and Brant Alyea (by the Athletics from the Twins).

The most interesting name might have been Bob Gallagher, an infielder the Red Sox selected from the Dodgers. Gallagher was the grandson of Shano Collins, who played for and managed the Red Sox in the 1920s and 1930s.[1]

Rule Changes

The rule governing "players to be named later" was modified to prohibit such a player from appearing in the same league as the team to which he was traded, between the date of the trade and the date of its completion. This provision was added to keep a player from directly competing with a club to whom he had been traded. The rule was also modified to require that a cash amount be specified so that the teams could later agree to use the cash consideration instead of the player.[2]

During the 1971 season several players—notably St. Louis outfielders Lou Brock and José Cardenal and San Diego outfielder Ivan Murrell—began using a so-called "Japanese teacup bat," which had a hollow end. NL President Chub Feeney approved its use pending the eventual opinion of the Rules Committee, which met at the meetings and approved. Committee chairman Johnny Johnson, an administrative aide to the commissioner, claimed that the bat did not provide the hitter an advantage.[3]

Johnson also announced that two rules proposals made by the general managers were rejected. One suggested that a line drive intentionally dropped would result in the batter being out, the ball remaining "in play," and no runners able to be retired. The prevalent rule—providing that the runners could advance at their own risk—remained in place. The second rejected suggestion was that the coaches' boxes be lengthened toward the outfield. Coaches rarely place themselves within the box, which the committee determined was acceptable.[4]

The committee ruled that all Double-A players would be required to wear an earflap helmet beginning in 1972, and all Triple-A players by 1973.[5]

Player Dealing

Every year fans across the country anticipate dramatic player dealing, especially trades involving their favorite team, at the winter meetings. The fans were not disappointed—in no year in history was there as much payoff as there was in 1971. What happened on Monday was plenty enough for a few meetings, with three huge deals involving some of the game's biggest stars, and it kept going throughout the week.

BASEBALL'S BUSINESS: THE WINTER MEETINGS

The Oakland Athletics traded center fielder Rick Monday to the Chicago Cubs for left-handed starting pitcher Ken Holtzman. The Cubs had considered center field their biggest weakness, while Holtzman, a two-time 17-game winner, had run afoul of manager Leo Durocher for throwing too many offspeed pitches.[6]

The Cincinnati Reds made a franchise-altering trade, dealing first baseman Lee May, second baseman Tommy Helms, and utilityman Jimmy Stewart to the Houston Astros for second baseman Joe Morgan, infielder Denis Menke, outfielder Cesar Geronimo, right-handed pitcher Jack Billingham, and minor-league outfielder Ed Armbrister. For the power-strapped Astros, the key man was May, who had hit 39 home runs in 1971—26 more than any Astro had hit.[7] The Reds coveted Morgan's speed, his left-handed bat, and his ability to get on base. The deal also allowed the Reds to move Tony Perez from third base to his natural spot at first base, while slotting Menke at third.[8]

The Cleveland Indians traded left-handed pitcher Sam McDowell, a six-time All-Star, to the San Francisco Giants for right-handed pitcher Gaylord Perry and infielder Frank Duffy. "McDowell gives us the left-handed pitcher we needed so badly," said Giants GM Charlie Fox, "a left-hander who can strike someone out. McDowell is 29 and Perry is 33, so the age factor is in our favor." McDowell guaranteed a pennant for the Giants, who had lost in the most recent NLCS.[9] Perry had a long track record of success, but Indians GM Gabe Paul was particularly excited about getting Duffy, a highly sought-after young shortstop.[10]

The Chicago White Sox dealt left-handed pitcher Tommy John and infielder Steve Huntz to the Los Angeles Dodgers for infielder Dick Allen. Allen, the 1964 NL Rookie of the Year, had had a lot of trouble with management and fans when he played in Philadelphia, but the White Sox were excited about his potent bat. "I know when he goes on the field he gives you 100 percent," said manager Chuck Tanner. "He gives you a good day's work. I judge a player strictly on what he does for me."[11]

The Astros, having acquired May, sent young first baseman John Mayberry and a minor leaguer to the Kansas City Royals for lefty Lance Clemons and right-hander Jim York, two of the better pitching prospects in the game.[12]

The New York Yankees dealt starting pitcher Stan Bahnsen, the 1968 AL Rookie of the Year, to the White Sox for infielder Rich McKinney. Yankees GM Lee MacPhail had made it known he would trade a starting pitcher for an infielder, but many were surprised that he settled for an untried player like McKinney.[13]

The American League champion Baltimore Orioles traded their heart and soul, veteran outfielder Frank Robinson (plus left-hander Pete Richert), to the Los Angeles Dodgers for four young players—right-handed pitcher Doyle Alexander and southpaw Bob O'Brien, catcher Sergio Robles, and infielder Royce Stillman. American League rivals cheered the loss of Robinson to the NL, but the Orioles were thinking of the future. "It's a 1974-75 type deal for us," said Baltimore manager Earl Weaver."[14] Robinson took the deal well, saying, "I'm leaving one classy organization and going to another."[15]

The Cincinnati Reds swapped relief pitchers with the Twins, sending right-hander Wayne Granger to Minnesota for Tom Hall. The Reds now believed they had the best bullpen in the game. "Hall gives us balance in the bullpen since he's left-handed," said general manager Bob Howsam.[16]

The Astros traded three minor leaguers—right-handed pitcher Bill Greif and left-handed pitcher Mark Schaeffer and infielder Derrel Thomas—to the Padres for left-handed pitcher Dave Roberts. Roberts had turned in a 14-17 season for a Padres team that had lost 100 games, and his 2.10 ERA was second in the National League only to Tom Seaver's 2.82.[17]

Miscellaneous

On Tuesday, baseball officials met with a congressional delegation from Washington who were concerned with the recent announcement that the Washington Senators were moving to Arlington, Texas. "We just laid it on the table," said B.F. Fisk (Democrat of California). "Of course, there was some discussion of the antitrust laws, and baseball's exemption, and the reserve clause, because they asked about those things."[18]

Governor John L. McKeithen led a Louisiana delegation that presented a plan to the AL for the Cleveland Indians to play 30 games in the New Orleans Superdome in 1974. "The group made a fine presentation," said AL President Joe Cronin, "and we're appointing a committee to look into the main details before the league makes a determination."[19] Oakland owner Charlie Finley, always looking to keep his own options open, voiced his opposition to the plan.[20]

On Friday baseball held its joint meeting between the major and minor leagues, which wrapped up the week. A nine-member committee was formed to study the relationship between the majors and minors — three men from each major league, and three from the minors. "We have long recognized the minor leagues have serious financial problems," said Commissioner Bowie Kuhn. "They have continuously had to ask for more money and we are interested in a better, more lucrative contract for them."[21]

The group consisted of Jim Campbell (Tigers), Joe Cummiskey (Red Sox), Gabe Paul (Indians), Bob Howsam (Reds), Peter O'Malley (Dodgers), Jim Fanning (Expos), Joe Buzas (Pawtucket, Eastern League), Roy Jackson (Eastern League president), and Wallace McKenna (Carolina League president).[22]

The deadline for interleague trading, formerly 10 days after the conclusion of the Winter Meetings, was changed to be midnight prior to the last scheduled day of the meetings. In making the announcement, Commissioner Kuhn said the purpose was to increase trades during the meetings. Given the large number of deals, the press room filled with laughter. "It certainly wasn't needed this year," allowed the commissioner.[23]

The White Sox lobbied the American League to be moved from the Western Division to the Eastern Division. They had previously tried in October, when the Washington franchise moved to Texas and changed divisions, but the Milwaukee Brewers were the team chosen to make the corresponding move to the Eastern.[24] The AL was also granted permission to play a single game prior to the league-wide Opening Day. Previously this privilege had been granted to the Washington club every year.

The American League made a proposal to prohibit exhibition games more than 28 days before the start of the regular season. The purpose of the proposal was to save money, but the National League voted against the change, and Commissioner Kuhn cast the deciding no vote.[25]

There was also a proposal to expand the playoffs to have the second-place teams play each other in a best-of-three series. This proposal was rejected.[26] Kuhn did announce that the middle three games of the World Series (played during the week) would be played at night.[27]

American League President Joe Cronin, whose contract was due to expire in December 1972, received a three-year extension. He was given the additional titles of chairman of the board and chief executive officer.[28]

Phil Piton, the president-treasurer of the National Association (the minor leagues) for nine years, officially

Bird License

The Atlanta Braves were excited about the potential emergence of Ralph Garr, a speedy outfielder. As part of a campaign to recognize his speed, the Braves signed an agreement with Warner Brothers' licensing agent, Licensing Corporation of America. The agreement made Garr the only major-league baseball player who could be called "Road Runner."

According to Jay Emmett of Warner Brothers, "Our contract with the Braves makes Ralph the first licensed nickname to our knowledge anywhere in the world."*

---

*   Richard Dozer, "'Road Runner' Garr Only Speedster with License," *Chicago Tribune*, March 13, 1971: 3.

ended his term and was succeeded by Hank Peters, formerly the Cleveland farm director.[29]

Conclusion

The story of the 1971 winter meetings was the frantic wheeling and dealing. There was little talk of labor negotiations, though concerns about the expiring pension and benefit plan would dominate the game's headlines over the rest of the offseason.

NOTES

1. Stan Isle, "Majors Pay $325,000 to Draft 13," *The Sporting News*, December 18, 1971: 43.
2. Stan Isle, "15 Deals Steal Spotlight at Meetings," *The Sporting News*, December 18, 1971: 43.
3. Stan Isle, "Nippon Bat Okayed by Rules Group," *The Sporting News*, December 18, 1971: 44.
4. Isle, "Nippon Bat Okayed."
5. Ibid.
6. Edgar Munzel, "Cubs See Monday's Bat, Glove Filling a Big Void," *The Sporting News*, December 11, 1971: 46.
7. John Wilson, "Astros See Home-Run Boom With May and Shorter Fences," *The Sporting News*, December 11, 1971: 48.
8. Earl Lawson, "Red Hopes Take Off With Joe the Jet in Tow," *The Sporting News*, December 11, 1971: 49.
9. Pat Frizzell, "'Giants to Win Flag,' Sam Promises," *The Sporting News*, December 11, 1971: 46.
10. Russell Schneider, "Tribe Glad to Have Perry, But Duffy Was Sway Key," *The Sporting News*, December 11, 1971: 51.
11. Jerome Holtzman, "Chisox Crowing Over Allen-Melton Power Duo," *The Sporting News*, December 18, 1971: 51.
12. John Wilson, "Big-Dealing Astros See Contender Role in 1972," *The Sporting News*, December 18, 1971: 52.
13. Jim Ogle, "Yank Fans Are Disgusted Over Bahnsen's Departure," *The Sporting News*, December 18, 1971: 58.
14. Phil Jackman, "Orioles' Rivals Celebrating the Departure of F. Robby," *The Sporting News*, December 18, 1971: 50.
15. Bob Hunter, "Dodgers Thrill Over Flag Insurance at Little Cost," *The Sporting News*, December 18, 1971: 50.
16. "'Tom Hall Gives Us Majors' Finest Bullpen,' Reds Grin," *The Sporting News*, December 18, 1971: 52.
17. Wilson, "Big-Dealing Astros."
18. Isle, "15 Deals Steal Spotlight."
19. Ibid.
20. Ibid.
21. Ibid.
22. Ibid.
23. Ben Henkey, "Majors Shorten Interleague Trading Period," *The Sporting News*, December 18, 1971: 45.
24. Isle, "15 Deals Steal Spotlight."
25. Ibid.
26. Ibid.
27. Henkey, "Majors Shorten Interleague Trading Period."
28. Ibid.
29. Ben Henkey, "Piton Hands the Reins to New Boss Peters," *The Sporting News*, December 18, 1971: 46.

—1972—
CALM BETWEEN STORMS

By Mark Armour

Background

THE 1972 BASEBALL WINTER MEETINGS played host to over 1,300 people at the Sheraton-Waikiki Hotel in Honolulu, Hawaii, from Saturday, November 25, through Friday, December 1. "It looms as the largest in history," said Jack Quinn, general manager of the Pacific Coast League's Hawaii Islanders, "and it marks the first time that all convention activities will be held at the same hotel." Quinn also noted that there were more wives in attendance than usual. "After all, who wants to miss out on a trip to Hawaii?"[1]

At the annual midweek National Association banquet, 1,300 guests feasted on a nine-course Chinese dinner. Several of the speakers pitched Honolulu as a big-league city by 1975. "We in baseball are mindful of the success here in Hawaii," said Commissioner Bowie Kuhn. "We have watched this success with interest, and will continue to do so."[2]

In his annual state of the game speech, Kuhn lamented the past year, which included the first-ever player strike. "There is very little place in baseball for that kind of activity, and every effort is being made to insure that such a catastrophe will not occur again," the commissioner said.[3]

Rule 5 Draft

In the annual major-league draft, big-league clubs claimed a record low of six players, five of them pitchers, for the $25,000 price. The first choice went to the Philadelphia Phillies, who took 21-year-old right-handed pitcher Mike Bruhert, who had won five games in Single A for the New York Mets in 1972. Infielder Bob Gallagher, whom the Red Sox selected from the Dodgers the previous December and had gone 0-for-5 in limited action in 1972, was left unprotected again and went to the Astros.[4]

Rule Changes

The Playing Rules Committee rejected an American League proposal to use a designated pinch-hitter in 1973. The AL had voted 12 to 0 to make the proposal and Commissioner Kuhn backed the plan, intended to combat baseball's decreasing run scoring. However, Kuhn decided not to use his tiebreaking power on such a significant rule change. The committee did allow the AL to use the DH in spring-training games.

But the DH rule was approved for all three Triple-A leagues. In addition, the Double-A Texas League was given permission to use an eight-man batting order (removing the pitcher). "Commissioner Bowie Kuhn has expressed serious concern with the decline in hitting and urged the committee to study the problem and not confine experimentation to a few lower-classification leagues," said John Johnson, rules committee chairman.[5]

(Postscript: In early January the American League requested another joint meeting, this time to request permission to use the DH rule in the AL only. The NL voted no, but this time Kuhn supported the AL. "I hope it works," he said after breaking the stalemate. "I would have preferred that both leagues did it. But if it's successful in one, then I hope the National follows suit."[6])

The Cardinals made a request for adoption of an unspecified tiebreaking procedure that would decide games knotted after 12 innings. This request was tabled.[7]

Player Relations

Having endured a two-week player strike in April, the owners and players since October had been negotiating a new collective-bargaining agreement, designed to replace the one that would expire at the end of December, as well as a new pension agreement to replace the one that would expire on March 31. On November 29, Commissioner Kuhn publicly announced the owners' proposals.[8] (The players were meeting separately in the Bahamas that week.)

- A player with five years of service would become a free agent unless offered a contract of at least $30,000. A player with eight years of service would require $40,000. This was the first time the owners had offered any sort of free agency, as limited as it was.
- Players with 10 years of service, including five with their current club, could not be traded without the player's consent.
- At the end of every year, each club would make three players from its active roster available to be drafted for $35,000. This would give a player a chance to move to a team that would play him more.
- A reduction in the active roster, from 25 to 23, and a corresponding reduction in the list of players under each team's control, from 40 to 38.
- A continuation of the owners' $6 million contribution to the benefit and pension plan (the root of the conflict this past April). Original members of the pension plan (those inactive since 1956) would receive an increase in benefits.
- The minimum salary would be raised from $13,500 to $15,000. Cost-of-living increases would be made to all player allowances, and the size of the World Series pool would be boosted.

"I can't anticipate the reaction of the Players Association," said Kuhn, "but early indications are that they consider it not adequate."[9]

On December 1, in a telephone interview, Miller claimed that Kuhn's press conference went against an agreement Miller had made with chief negotiator John Gaherin not to disclose bargaining details in public. "I consider Kuhn's action misleading, very destructive and mischievous," said Miller.[10]

Kuhn announced that joint talks would continue in New York in a week's time.

Player Dealing

By the end of the Winter Meetings, 21 clubs had made 19 deals involving 68 players. Only the Red Sox, Expos, and Brewers failed to make a deal.[11] Although the trades generally lacked the star power of the previous December, several well-known players did change uniforms.

The New York Yankees went into the offseason hoping to land a hitter. "[Manager] Ralph [Houk] and I honestly believed that we were one good hitter away from being a contending ballclub," said general manager Lee MacPhail.[12] After trying and failing to land Frank Robinson from the Dodgers, the Yankees acquired outfielder Matty Alou from the Athletics for infielder Rich McKinney and left-handed pitcher Rob Gardner. Matty would be joining brother Felipe in pinstripes.

A few days later MacPhail struck again, dealing catcher John Ellis, infielder Jerry Kenney, and outfielders Charlie Spikes and Rusty Torres to the Indians for star third baseman Graig Nettles and catcher Jerry Moses. Spikes was the big loss, a coveted prospect and the jewel of the Yankee system. "I'm not worried about youth," said Houk. "I'm going out to get (the pennant) this season."[13]

The California Angels traded infielder Ken McMullen and ace right-handed pitcher Andy Messersmith to the Los Angeles Dodgers for veteran outfielder Frank Robinson, infielders Billy Grabarkewitz and Bobby Valentine, and right-handed pitchers Bill Singer and Mike Strahler. "I've been close to Robinson a long time," said California general manager Harry Dalton, who had the All-Star in Baltimore. "Any time a man takes you to four World Series, you've got to be close to him. Sure, he's 37 years old and he's not the same player he was five years ago. But he's still a superstar."[14]

The Chicago White Sox traded right-handed pitcher Tom Bradley to San Francisco for outfielder Ken Henderson and right-handed pitcher Steve Stone. White Sox manager Chuck Tanner was ecstatic about getting Henderson, who could play center field and hit. "With Henderson out there, our pitching is going to look even better than it did before," he said.[15]

The Reds traded outfielder Hal McRae and righty pitcher Wayne Simpson for outfielder Richie Scheinblum and right-handed pitcher Roger Nelson. An unusual aspect of this deal was that Scheinblum was coming off an All-Star season in which he finished sixth in the AL in batting, but would now be a reserve outfielder. "Richie isn't walking into a regular job with us," Reds manager Sparky Anderson admitted. "We're simply going to wait and see how Scheinblum fits in."[16]

The Atlanta Braves traded 24-year-old catcher Earl Williams, the 1971 National League Rookie of the Year, and minor-league infielder Taylor Duncan to the Baltimore Orioles for right-handed pitchers Pat Dobson and Roric Harrison, second baseman Davey Johnson, and catcher Johnny Oates. Williams had hit 61 home runs in his two seasons of play, which is why he commanded such a huge outlay. "We weren't jumping over barrels to get rid of him," said Braves general manager Eddie Robinson. "Williams is a fellow who could hit a lot of home runs in his career, and he is a leader type." But Robinson wanted a catcher who was better with pitchers, and he believed Oates fit that bill.

As for the Orioles, the deal reflected significant team needs—a catcher, and power—and their surplus pitching and infield talent. Their best young player, Bobby Grich, would finally have the second-base position all to himself.

The Mets sent veteran outfielder Tommie Agee to the Astros for outfielder Rich Chiles and pitcher Buddy Harris. Agee had been New York's regular center fielder for five years but had balked at sharing playing time with Willie Mays, acquired in May, and had asked to be traded.[17]

Miscellaneous

Both New Orleans and Seattle, with domed stadiums due to open in 1974, sent delegations to Honolulu in support of gaining a major-league team. However, Commissioner Kuhn said there was "no discussion whatsoever of further expansion."[18] Along the same lines, Kuhn said that no progress had been made regarding the prospects for Washington, which had lost its team a year earlier.

Three proposals to increase the pool of playoff teams were offered. All three were withdrawn before voting.[19]

1. Each league's playoffs would include the first- and second-place finisher in each division. The first-place team would play the second-place team in the league's other division, and the winners would face each other in the League Championship Series.
2. The playoffs would consist of the division winners plus the two best remaining teams regardless of division.
3. Leagues would be restructured into three four-team divisions, with the three division winners and best second-place team advancing to the playoffs.

The National League approved a joint proposal, made by Houston, Pittsburgh, and St. Louis, to modify their artificial playing surfaces to include the basepaths, as was already in place in Cincinnati and San Francisco. The NL also recommended that white lines be painted on the surface to delineate the separation between "infield" and "outfield" in all parks. This proposal was discussed but not voted on.[20]

The Triple-A leagues announced a few affiliation changes, the most significant involving the Red Sox. Their Louisville affiliate (International League) was informed late in the season that its expired lease for Fairgrounds Stadium would not be renewed for 1973, so that the park could be reconfigured for University of Louisville football. The Red Sox instead awarded their International League affiliation to the Rhode Island city of Pawtucket, population 70,000, which would become the smallest city in Triple-A baseball, but was part of a metropolitan area of well over a million population and was less than 50 miles from Fenway Park.[21]

The Major League Executive Council approved a budget of $337,500, an increase of $18,000, for the promotion of amateur baseball. About half of that would go directly to boys programs, like the American Legion, and much of the rest to college tournaments. The group also decided to produce a movie with a "Baseball Wants You" theme, to be shown to high schools and colleges.[22]

Conclusion

The biggest story of the 1972 winter meetings was not technically part of the agenda. Kuhn's public announcement of the state of the labor negotiations brought this issue back before a public still reeling from the April strike. And the comments from the players suggested that another strike could be in store for 1973.

NOTES

1. Fred Borsch, "Hawaii Lures Record Turnout," *The Sporting News*, December 2, 1972: 34.
2. Ben Henkey, "Hawaii Makes Pitch for Major Status," *The Sporting News*, December 16, 1972: 42.
3. Ibid.
4. Stan Isle, "A New Low—Majors Draft Only Six Players," *The Sporting News*, December 16, 1972: 45.
5. Stan Isle, "New Designated-Hitter Test Asked in Triple-A," *The Sporting News*, December 16, 1972: 43.
6. Joseph Durso, "American League to Let Pitcher Have a Pinch-Hitter and Stay In," *New York Times*, January 12, 1973: 25.
7. Ibid.
8. Stan Isle, "Kuhn Spells Out the Terms of Owner Offer to Players," *The Sporting News*, December 16, 1972: 41.
9. Ibid.
10. Ralph Ray, "Miller Calls Kuhn's Action 'Disruptive,'" *The Sporting News*, December 16, 1972: 41.
11. Richard Dozer, "Only Three Fail to Make Trades," *Chicago Tribune*, December 3, 1972: E9.
12. Jim Ogle, "Yanks Look for One Good Hitter—and Get Two," *The Sporting News*, December 9, 1972: 42.
13. Ibid.
14. Dick Miller, "Angel Deal Leaves Winkles With Jigsaw Puzzle," *The Sporting News*, December 16, 1972: 47.
15. Edgar Munzel, "Now Chisox Have Thunder, Plus Lightning," *The Sporting News*, December 16, 1972: 48.
16. Earl Lawson, "Scheinblum Likely Red Bench Rider," *The Sporting News*, December 16, 1972: 51.
17. Jack Lang, "Mets Dissolve 'Mobile Unit' in Favor of Question Mark," *The Sporting News*, December 16, 1972: 56.
18. Stan Isle, "Record Swapping Spree at Honolulu," *The Sporting News*, December 16, 1972: 42.
19. Ibid.
20. Ibid.
21. Ben Henkey, "Pawtucket New I.L. City; Division Play Considered," *The Sporting News*, December 16, 1972: 44.
22. "Majors Will Contribute $337,500 to Amateurs," *The Sporting News*, December 16, 1972: 46.

— 1973 —
MANAGERIAL CONFUSION, RON SANTO REACTS, & THE PADRES' DILEMMA

By Donald G. Frank

Introduction and Context

IN 1973, WHEN 24 TEAMS EXISTED IN major-league baseball, the sport conducted its annual Winter Meetings in Houston, Texas, from December 3 to December 7.

Several issues or topics dominated these meetings. A relatively complex managerial situation, featuring Ralph Houk, who had been the manager of the New York Yankees, and Dick Williams, who had been the manager of the Oakland A's, created significant confusion. And surprisingly, Charles O. Finley, the controversial owner of the World Series champion A's, played an important role in the eventual negotiations. Another important issue focused on Ron Santo, the All-Star third baseman of the Chicago Cubs. After playing for the Cubs for 14 seasons, Santo was informed that he was being traded to another team and he refused to go. This was just one of numerous trades and deals that took place at these meetings.

Quite significantly, the possibility of the sale of the San Diego Padres was discussed, which led to controversy before it was ultimately resolved.

The Business Side

As for the managerial brouhaha: Houk had resigned as manager of the Yankees on October 1 with two years remaining on his contract, and then was hired as the manager of the Tigers. Needless to say, the Yankees accused the Tigers of tampering.[1]

After Houk's resignation, the Yankees expressed a degree of interest in Dick Williams, who had resigned as the manager of the A's with one year remaining on his contract. But Finley, the cantankerous owner of the A's, indicated that Williams would not be allowed to go to New York unless the A's received adequate compensation from the Yankees. The Yankees then indicated that Houk would not be allowed to manage the Tigers without receiving adequate compensation from Detroit. Since both Houk and Williams had resigned while under contract, Joe Cronin, the president of the American League, asked representatives of the A's, Tigers, and Yankees to get together at the Winter Meetings to try to come to some agreement.[2]

"As far as I'm concerned, the matter is closed," Finley said after discussing the issues with Cronin, the Yankees, and several attorneys. "Dick Williams will be my manager in 1974 and 1975. If Williams insists on resigning, does not want to manage, should want to go into business with the XYZ Corporation, we would not stand in his way. But, when it comes to managing with another club, we will not permit him to do it unless we get compensation."[3]

Finley named four Yankees minor leaguers and said he'd accept any two as compensation. But the Yankees refused, because the list included outfielder Otto Velez and left-handed pitcher Scott McGregor, whom they viewed as potential stars. The Yankees offered some compensation to Finley for Williams, who was in Florida insisting he was the ex-manager of the A's. But Finley refused the offer, reported to be infielder

Horace Clarke and $50,000. Williams indicated he was disappointed, adding, "Nothing (Finley) does would surprise me." The meetings concluded without resolution of the dispute.[4]

Further negotiations eventually resolved the confusion. Houk did manage the Tigers in 1974, staying with them through 1978, then spent four years directing the Red Sox. Williams never did manage the Yankees, but instead managed the California Angels in 1974, and also led the Expos, Padres, and Mariners in his Hall of Fame career. And Bill Virdon wound up being hired to manage the Yankees in 1974.

C. Arnholt Smith, the owner of the Padres, owed the Internal Revenue Service $22.5 million and was being investigated for alleged illegal campaign contributions. As a result, the National League ordered Smith to sell the Padres. Joseph Danzansky intended to purchase and relocate the Padres to Washington, but after the City of San Diego sued the Padres for $84 million, Danzansky withdrew from the negotiations. Buzzie Bavasi, president of the Padres, recommended selling the team to Marjorie Everett, who intended to keep the team in San Diego, but who also had ties with the Hollywood Park racetrack near Los Angeles. The other National League owners, in discussions at the meetings, opposed the sale of the Padres to someone with potential ties to gambling.[5]

Eventually, the Padres were sold to Ray Kroc, the owner of McDonald's, who asserted that the team would remain in San Diego.

In an interesting sidebar, six managers and general managers at the meetings were randomly selected and asked: "If you could pick one ballplayer right now to add to your roster, who would it be?" They selected César Cedeño, who at the age of 22, had already completed his fourth year in the majors and was viewed as the "player most likely to reach the Willie Mays/Henry Aaron/Mickey Mantle superstar level over the next decade." Cedeño at that point had played in 529 games, was batting .301 and had collected 618 hits, scored 320 runs, driven in 275 runs, hit 64 home runs, and stolen 148 bases. Although Cedeño would win five Gold Gloves and go to four All-Star Games, his career totals fell short of Cooperstown.[6]

The American League's designated hitter rule, used for the first time in 1973, was discussed and it was agreed that this practice would be continued, but only in the American League.

Player eligibility for the World Series was clarified. To be eligible to participate in the World Series, a player would need to be on the team roster on August 31 and must have remained with the team until the end of the season. The American League backed a proposal to extend interleague trading to include the 30 days from May 15 to June 15, in addition to the current period (from five days after the World Series ends to the conclusion of the Winter Meetings), but the National League declined to support it.

Commissioner Bowie Kuhn announced that he would appoint someone from his staff to work with all of the clubs on an energy-conservation program. He also announced the appointment of a committee "to consider changes in the Major League Agreement."[7]

Player Movement

Several rumors circulated in the weeks prior to the meetings, focusing primarily on the Atlanta Braves, New York Mets, and Philadelphia Phillies. The Braves, seeking relief pitching, were said to be willing to trade All-Star outfielder Ralph Garr in order to strengthen their bullpen. In particular, the Braves and Phillies were reportedly considering a deal that would send Garr and right-handed pitchers Ron Reed and Ron Schueler to the Phillies for infielder Larry Bowa, outfielder Bill Robinson, and left-handed relief pitcher Mac Scarce. Another rumor focused on the Mets, who were seeking a center fielder. Yogi Berra, the Mets manager, was reportedly interested in Baltimore's Paul Blair or Houston's Jimmy Wynn.[8]

The Braves did complete a trade with the Phillies, although not quite the blockbuster that had been rumored. Pitcher Schueler (later a major-league general manager) was traded to the Phillies for Barry Lersch, another right-hander, and Craig Robinson, a top prospect at shortstop. The Braves indicated that second baseman Davey Johnson (43 home runs in 1973) would be used as trade bait to obtain additional pitching but, as it turned out, Johnson played for the Braves for two more years.⁹

The Chicago Cubs and Oakland A's completed a trade involving two right-handed relief pitchers, the A's Horacio Piña and Cubs veteran Bob Locker. The trigger for the trade was a promise made by the Cubs to Locker in 1972 to try to trade him to a team on the West Coast to help him with a personal situation. In 1973 Pina had fashioned a 6-3 mark, with eight saves and a 2.76 ERA, while Locker's record was 10-6, with a 2.55 ERA and a team-leading 18 saves.¹⁰

The Detroit Tigers traded left-handed reliever Fred Sherman to the Houston Astros for another bullpen inhabitant, hard-throwing right-hander Jim Ray, plus second baseman Gary Sutherland. Sherman's record in 1973 had been 2-2, with two saves and a 4.23 ERA, while Ray was 6-4 with six saves and a 4.43 ERA. In 54 at-bats in 1973, Sutherland batted .259; he would become the Tigers' regular second baseman for the next two seasons.¹¹

The Houston Astros continued to deal, trading side-arming righty Cecil Upshaw to the Cleveland Indians for right-hander Jerry Johnson. Formerly the feared closer of the Atlanta Braves, Upshaw had joined the Astros in a trade early in the 1973 season. Having compiled a combined record of 2-4 with just one save and a 4.93 ERA, the 31-year-old Upshaw was hoping to return to his former status as an elite closer. The same could be said for Johnson. Sixth in the Cy Young Award voting in 1971, when helped lead the San Francisco Giants to the playoffs, Johnson had been 5-6 for the Indians in 1973 with five saves and a 6.18 ERA.

In a trade involving two standout players, the Astros continued their makeover by sending All-Star center fielder Jimmy Wynn to the Dodgers for right-hander David Culpepper, who pitched in Double A in 1973, and All-Star left-hander Claude Osteen. Wynn, nicknamed the Toy Cannon, had had several great years in Houston, but after he batted .220 in 1973 with 20 home runs and 55 runs batted in, the Astros decided that at 31 he was unlikely to ascend to the next level. Wynn helped the Dodgers get to the World Series in 1974, hitting 32 home runs and driving in 108 runs, but he did decline after that. In 1973, the 34-year-old Osteen was still one of the National League's premier pitchers—only Bob Gibson and Juan Marichal had more National League victories. In 1973, his record was 16-11 with a 3.31 ERA. He was selected to the All-Star team for the third time in his career, and reached double figures in victories for the 10th straight season. But Osteen's best days proved to be behind him; he won just nine games for Houston in 1974 before being traded to St. Louis late in the season, and then pitched for the Chicago White Sox in 1975 before retiring with a 196-195 career record. As for Culpepper, the third player in the deal, he never ascended beyond Triple A and retired in 1976.¹²

Padre Confession

Charges against C. Arnholt Smith were amended to include grand theft from the Padres. Through a series of decisions, Smith allegedly exposed the club to possible debt liability.*

Several federal agencies were pursuing Smith, including the Securities and Exchange Commission, the Internal Revenue Service, the Comptroller of the Currency, and the Department of Justice. After several years of battling the legal ramifications, Smith reportedly told a reporter, "I'm going to write a book about a guy who had a lot of money, then went broke, and went back and tried to start all over again. Trouble is they won't let me out of here to start."**

---

* United Press International, "Tax, Theft Charges Face Ex-Padres Owner Smith," *Kingsport* (Tennessee) *News*, March 24, 1976: 14.
** Norm Clarke, "Changing Times for Fallen Tycoon," *Poughkeepsie Journal*, May 31, 1979: 6.

BASEBALL'S BUSINESS: THE WINTER MEETINGS

Three other blockbuster deals were made. The Dodgers, seeking bullpen help, got one of the best in the game, picking up durable right-hander Mike Marshall from the Montreal Expos in exchange for their longtime center fielder, Gold Glover Willie Davis. Marshall, the Cy Young Award runner-up, had just appeared in 92 games for Montreal, winning 14 and saving 31; he would pitch in a record 106 games and throw 208 relief innings for the Dodgers in 1974, saving 21 games and winning 15 as well as the Cy Young Award. Davis had a good year in Montreal but was traded after just one season, then bounced around to several clubs before he retired.[13]

The St. Louis Cardinals and Boston Red Sox completed a six-player deal that featured five pitchers. The Cardinals traded right-hander Reggie Cleveland, an innings-eater who had won 40 games for them over the past three seasons, righty reliever Diego Segui, and third baseman Terry Hughes to the Red Sox for left-hander John Curtis and righties Mike Garman and Lynn McGlothen. Cleveland, Curtis, and McGlothen all proved to be middle-of-the-rotation starters, Garman and Segui were serviceable arms out of the bullpen (Segui was winding down a long career), and Hughes never had any major-league impact.[14]

The Cubs surprised many by trading their longtime All-Star third baseman Ron Santo to the White Sox for southpaws Ken Frailing and Jim Kremmel, right-hander Steve Stone, and catcher Steve Swisher. Santo, however, refused to be traded and thus became the first player to invoke the new rule that allowed a 10-year man with five consecutive years for his team to veto a trade. Santo, 34, had played for the Cubs for 14 years. His salary in 1973 was $110,000. Santo said that when Cubs GM John Holland called him to discuss a possible trade, "I replied that I elected not to leave Chicago, for personal reasons." Santo eventually agreed to play with the White Sox and the trade stood, but after the 1974 season, he retired as a player and later became a popular radio voice for the Cubs and, a year after his death, was elected to the Hall of Fame. Steve Stone had a middling career except for 1980, when he won 25 games and the Cy Young Award for the Baltimore Orioles, and later, like Santo, became a popular broadcaster. Steve Swisher, considered to be one of the top catching prospects in the game, had a solid career, but neither Frailing nor Kremmel had any major-league impact.[15]

Other trades were made at the meetings and also in the week following. The Cincinnati Reds and Baltimore Orioles traded former top prospects as the Reds sent left-hander Ross Grimsley and minor-league catcher Wally Williams, to the Orioles for outfielder Merv Rettenmund, minor-league catcher Bill Wood, and utility infielder Junior Kennedy. The Pittsburgh Pirates traded right-hander Nelson Briles, who had won 28 games over the previous two seasons, and utilityman Fernando Gonzalez, to the Kansas City Royals for infielder and pinch-hitter deluxe Kurt Bevacqua, utilityman Ed Kirkpatrick, and minor-league first baseman Winston Cole. The Cardinals traded utility player John Wockenfuss to the Detroit Tigers for shortstop Larry Elliott. Elliott would never ascend beyond Double A, but Wockenfuss would go onto a long career, primarily with the Tigers, as a catcher, outfielder, and first baseman.[16]

In other deals that featured notable names, the Yankees traded right-handed pitcher Lindy McDaniel to the Kansas City Royals for outfielder Lou Piniella and righty Ken Wright. An underrated 19-year veteran, McDaniel had yielded his role as closer to Sparky Lyle and was thus deemed expendable. Wright would pitch in only three more major-league games, but Piniella, the 1969 AL Rookie of the Year, spent the next 11 seasons as a key outfielder for the Yankees, helping them win four pennants and two World Series, before becoming a major-league manager, winning the 1990 World Series with the Cincinnati Reds.[17]

The Philadelphia Phillies traded second baseman Denny Doyle to the California Angels for onetime Dodgers prospect Billy Grabarkewitz, whom they expected to replace Doyle, plus outfielder Chris Coletta and right-hander Aurelio Monteagudo. Doyle proved to be the only player in this deal who put up credible numbers in a career that also took him to the Red Sox.[18]

The Cleveland Indians and Texas Rangers exchanged former right-handed pitching prospects. The Indians traded Steve Hargan to the Rangers for Bill Gogolewski. The Dodgers traded lefty Pete Richert to the Cardinals for center fielder Tommy Agee. Richert, a two-time All-Star, had been a key man in the Baltimore Orioles' bullpen during their 1969-1971 championship years, but 1974 would prove to be his final season in the majors. Agee, the 1966 AL Rookie of the Year, had experienced his best years with the New York Mets, anchoring the outfield during their World Series triumph in 1969. He was, however, released by the Dodgers just before Opening Day.

The Montreal Expos traded right-hander Pat Jarvis to the Texas Rangers for outfielder-first baseman Larry Biittner. Jarvis had been a mainstay in the Braves' rotation for several years, five times winning in double figures. His one season in Montreal was disappointing, however, and he was released before Opening Day. Biittner proved to be a serviceable player with a solid bat, especially after he went to the Cubs in 1976. The Cubs and Minnesota Twins traded catchers, with former All-Star and Gold Glover Randy Hundley moving to the American League and George Mitterwald coming to Wrigley. Hundley was at the tail-end of his fine career and would, in fact, play his last few games as a Cub in 1977. Mitterwald fared better, sharing backstopping duties in Chicago for the next four years.[19]

Several players changed teams in straight cash deals. The Texas Rangers purchased Terry Crowley, an outfielder and first baseman, from the Baltimore Orioles. Crowley barely suited up for the Rangers, who traded him to the Cincinnati Reds in the spring, but he eventually returned to Baltimore, his first baseball home, and experienced success as an extraordinary pinch-hitter. The Yankees purchased infielder Jim Mason from the Rangers, and for the next three years he and Gene Michael gave the Yankees excellent defense at shortstop. The Milwaukee Brewers purchased Felipe Alou, an outfielder and first baseman, from the Expos. A .286 lifetime hitter with more than 2,100 hits to his credit, Alou made only three appearances before the Brewers released him; he later won over 1,000 games as the manager of the Expos and Giants. Another member of the Orioles bullpen, Eddie Watt, was sold to Philadelphia. Watt pitched for the Phillies in 1974 and the Cubs in 1975 before becoming a minor-league manager. Supersub César Tovar was purchased by the Texas Rangers from the Phillies, and had two good seasons in Arlington before he began to fade.[20]

Perhaps the most noteworthy straight cash transaction came when the Red Sox purchased All-Star right-hander Juan Marichal from San Francisco. Marichal had won 238 games for the Giants since 1960, but his record in 1973 was only 11-15 with a 3.83 ERA, his second consecutive subpar season, and he had turned 36 after the season. The Red Sox took a chance on him, but he won only five games for them and was released after the season.[21]

In the Rule 5 Draft, a number of players were selected, but only three went on to have decent careers. The Houston Astros drafted infielder Larry Milbourne from the St. Louis Cardinals, and he played nearly 1,000 games for six teams over the next 11 seasons. The Kansas City Royals drafted first baseman Tony Solaita from the Pittsburgh Pirates, and the one-time Yankees prospect, a native of Samoa, had good seasons for the Royals and the Angels. The Detroit Tigers drafted catcher Gene Lamont from the Atlanta Braves. Lamont played only briefly in the majors, but later resurfaced as a major-league coach, and also managed the Chicago White Sox and Pittsburgh Pirates.[22]

Summary

Baseball's 1973 Winter Meetings were active. Managerial confusion involving the Oakland A's, Detroit Tigers, and New York Yankees resulted in significant formal and informal discussions. Ron Santo refused to be traded, although he eventually relented. Officials discussed the possible sale and/or relocation of the San Diego Padres. The skills of César Cedeño were recognized by managers and general managers. Player movement was represented by numerous trades as well as purchases and selections in the Rule 5 Draft.

NOTES

1. Joseph Durso, "A's Refuse to Relax Hold on Williams," *New York Times*, December 6, 1973: 65.
2. Ibid.
3. Ibid.
4. Ibid.
5. Phil Collier, "Only a Prayer Ties Padres to San Diego," *The Sporting News*, December 22, 1973: 29; Collier, "Padres Sweat It Out at Altar of Confusion," *The Sporting News*, December 15, 1973: 45; Joseph Durso, "Padres' Shift to Washington Approved," *New York Times*, December 7, 1973: 51.
6. "Astro Star Accorded Top Rating," *New York Times*, December 12, 1973: 5.
7. Stan Isle, "Avalanche of Trades Tops a Hectic Week at Houston," *The Sporting News*, December 22, 1973: 29; Russell Schneider, "A.L. Will Request One-Year Okay on Designated Runner," *The Sporting News*, December 1, 1973: 32.
8. "Baseball Winter Meetings Open in Houston Monday," *Hartford Courant*, December 2, 1973: 7C.
9. Joseph Durso, "4 Trades Made at Meetings," *New York Times*, December 4, 1973: 57; Stan Isle, "Santo Balks, Halts Cub Bid for Deal," *The Sporting News*, December 22, 1973: 34. (Includes list of transactions.)
10. Ibid.
11. Ibid.
12. Stan Isle, "Santo Balks, Halts Cub Bid for Deal," *The Sporting News*, December 22, 1973: 34. (Includes list of transactions.)
13. Ibid.
14. Ibid.
15. Joseph Durso, "Santo First to Veto Trade by His Club," *New York Times*, December 5, 1973: 57.
16. "Santo Balks, Halts Cub Bid for Deal."
17. Ibid.
18. Ibid.
19. Ibid.
20. Ibid.
21. Ibid.
22. Stan Isle, "Majors Spend $300,000 for a Dozen AAA Players," *The Sporting News*, December 22, 1973: 33.

— 1974 —
DÉTENTE BEORE THE STORM

By Clayton Trutor

Introduction and Context

THE 74TH ANNUAL WINTER MEETINGS were held in New Orleans from Sunday, December 1, to Friday, December 5, 1974. New Orleans hosted the annual meeting on two earlier occasions, in 1916 and 1938, but had not been home to the event in 36 years.

Recent struggles between the Players Association and the owners hung over the 1974 meetings. The work stoppages that affected both the 1972 and 1973 seasons, as well as the impending legal battles over free agency, had led to a change in the way owners in the American and National Leagues regarded one another, not only in terms of labor negotiations with the players union but also on other financial issues that affected both leagues. Writing in the *New York Times*, Leonard Koppett characterized the new spirit of cooperativeness between the American and National Leagues as "détente," mirroring the thaw in US-Soviet relations during the early 1970s.

Owners and officials from the rival leagues worked together in New Orleans to deal with issues affecting them all, most notably with the formation of a joint committee to deal with leaguewide financial concerns, including expansion, franchise relocations, labor relations, and the search for sustainable ownership for teams in ailing markets.[1] Considering the intense focus on league business by baseball leaders at these meetings, it was not surprising that player movement proved to be light, both in terms of volume and in the profile of players traded during the week.

The 1974 Winter Meetings proved to be the final leaguewide gathering before the beginning of the free agency era. Ten days after MLB leaders left Louisiana, arbitrator Peter Seitz ruled on the contract dispute between reigning American League Cy Young Award winner Catfish Hunter and Oakland Athletics owner Charlie Finley. Seitz surprised all interested parties by awarding Hunter outright free agency, not merely bumping up his $100,000 salary from the previous season. Hunter considered a flurry of offers from clubs in both leagues before signing with the New York Yankees on New Year's Eve for a record amount, later reported as five years for $3.35 million and other benefits.[2] Seitz's ruling in the Hunter case proved to be a mortal wound to the reserve clause. A year later, in December 1975, Seitz again served as arbitrator between the owners and the Players Association. This time he heard a grievance filed by the union on behalf of pitchers Andy Messersmith and Dave McNally, and ruled that both players were free to sign with any club, effectively ending the reserve clause.

Player Movement

New Orleans saw 15 trades consummated involving 39 players, a significant drop from the 58 players swapped at the 1973 Winter Meetings and the 68 players dealt in 1972.[3] The focus by baseball's leaders on league business accounted for this in large part, but another reason for the lack of player movement was the unusual vigor of the early offseason trade market. In the six weeks after the Oakland A's victory over the Los Angeles Dodgers in the World Series, a number of deals involving high-profile players made for an interesting beginning to the Hot Stove season. The first major trade involved the St. Louis Cardinals' standout catcher Joe Torre, who was sent to his hometown New York Mets for veteran left-hander Ray Sadecki and young right-handed pitcher Tommy Moore. In late

October, the San Francisco Giants and the Yankees swapped All-Star outfielders, with Bobby Bonds heading east and Bobby Murcer moving west; and in early November, the struggling Atlanta Braves sent aging home-run king Hank Aaron back to the city where he began his illustrious career, dealing him to the Milwaukee Brewers for veteran outfielder Dave May and minor-league pitcher Roger Alexander.[4]

Going into the meetings, trade rumors involving Cleveland's Gaylord Perry, Cincinnati's Tony Perez, and several disgruntled Athletics stars, including Reggie Jackson, Sal Bando, and Vida Blue, circulated in the press.[5] None of these moves came to fruition in New Orleans, yet several trades involving prominent players were concluded that week. The Baltimore Orioles proved particularly successful in their dealings, acquiring in separate transactions Lee May and Ken Singleton, both of whom became major contributors to their championship teams of the late 1970s and early 1980s. The Houston Astros traded the power-hitting first-baseman May, along with outfielder Jay Schlueter, to the Orioles for youthful infielders Rob Andrews and Enos Cabell. The Montreal Expos sent outfielder Singleton and right-handed pitcher Mike Torrez to the Orioles for righty Bill Kirkpatrick, outfielder Rich Coggins, and a three-time All Star, southpaw Dave McNally, who would spend just one season in Montreal before retiring at age 32, never cashing in on the fortune he could have earned in the aftermath of Seitz's decision.[6]

Three other noteworthy deals were completed at the Winter Meetings. The Red Sox sent two-time stolen-base leader Tommy Harper to the California Angels for utility infielder Bob Heise, while the Mets traded their colorful, standout reliever Tug McGraw along with outfielders Don Hahn and Dave Schneck to the Philadelphia Phillies for veteran outfielder Del Unser, heralded rookie catcher John Stearns, and left-handed reliever Mac Scarce.

But the most prominent player involved in a trade at the 1974 Winter Meetings was former AL MVP and reigning home-run champion Dick Allen. In September, Allen, who had been involved in locker-room conflicts throughout the summer, left the White Sox with two weeks remaining in the season. He remained on their roster until teams convened in New Orleans, at which time the White Sox traded the controversial slugger to the Atlanta Braves for $5,000 and a player to be named later.[7] Allen refused to report to the Braves and announced his retirement. Later in the offseason, Allen's original team, the Philadelphia Phillies, persuaded him to return to baseball. He remained Braves property, and in May a convoluted deal was worked out that resulted in Allen rejoining the Phillies.

The Business Side

The most significant event at the meetings was the creation of a joint committee by the American and National Leagues designed to examine the big financial issues that affected the major leagues.

The committee, made up of two members from each league, was to make recommendations to the commissioner on how to deal with the financial issues, including league expansion, franchise relocations, working to ensure the viability of franchises in struggling markets, and finding stable ownership groups for troubled teams. Commissioner Bowie Kuhn, along with AL President Lee MacPhail and NL President Chub Feeney, praised the formation of the committee as a step toward getting the rival leagues to work together permanently to find solutions to leaguewide problems.[8]

Pressing concerns for the new joint committee included the lagging attendance for both teams in the Bay Area, which baseball experts believed was too small to support two teams. Despite the on-field success of the Oakland Athletics, the team struggled to draw even one million fans a year to its ballpark, the football-oriented Oakland Coliseum. The San Francisco Giants, whom longtime owner Horace Stoneham had put up for sale, drew barely 500,000 fans in 1974 and were considered a likely candidate to move to one of the several cities planning to build a domed stadium to lure big-league baseball, among them Seattle, Toronto, and Denver.

The perennially contending Baltimore Orioles also faced significant financial problems, as the team had been drawing lackluster crowds for several years in spite of its on-field success.⁹ Orioles owner Jerry Hoffberger wanted to sell the club or at least move some of its home games to RFK Stadium in Washington in hopes of drawing more fans from the D.C. metropolitan area, which now lacked a team. Other franchises, including the Cleveland Indians and San Diego Padres, struggled mightily at the box office throughout the early 1970s and looked to other cities as a possible solution to their problems.

The formation of the joint committee signaled an end to 20 years of extensive franchise movement and expansion in the major leagues. A consensus had clearly emerged within baseball's leadership that franchise shifts and expansions needed to be considered more carefully than they had been in the 1950s and 1960s. As a result, none of the struggling franchises of the mid-1970s ended up moving. The leagues worked with the cities to find suitable new ownership groups or encouraged the construction of new facilities for the Giants, Orioles, Padres, Indians, and, after Charley Finley's financial troubles, the Athletics. Baseball also slowed down the process of expansion. At the 1974 Winter Meetings, the joint committee told potential expansion cities, including Denver, Seattle, and Toronto, that the sport would need time to carefully consider which cities would provide the most stable homes for two new American League clubs.¹⁰

Temporary labor peace was also achieved at the Winter Meetings. Across the country, the Players Association held its annual meeting in Las Vegas during the same week the owners met in New Orleans. Union representatives from every team except the Athletics (Reggie Jackson was absent) voted for a plan to offer management a no-strike pledge for the 1975 season in return for an agreement to early bargaining on the next labor pact and an agreement to go to binding arbitration if the new deal could not be worked out by December 1, 1975. The owners in New Orleans agreed to the MLBPA's plan, ensuring a strike-free 1975 season.¹¹

Charlie Finley kept the Rules Committee busy at the meetings. Before the 1973 season the American League had adopted the Finley-championed position of the designated hitter. The DH had become popular enough among AL owners that they pushed for its use in All-Star Games and in World Series games played in AL parks. The effort was unsuccessful in New Orleans but a year later, at the 1975 convention in Hollywood, Florida, the Rules Committee approved the proposal for the World Series; its use in All-Star Games played in AL parks would not become a reality until 1989. In New Orleans Finley pushed for the use of orange baseballs, which he declared would be easier to see during night games, and continued championing the idea of a designated runner as an addendum to the designated hitter. The Rules Committee agreed to allow Finley to try out orange baseballs during one spring-training game and to test the designated runner intermittently during the exhibition season. Other rule changes at the 1974 Winter Meetings included a strengthening of the ban on illegal pitches. A pitcher found to be applying a "foreign substance" to the game ball would face immediate ejection. The Rules Committee also agreed to permit the use of cowhide, rather than just horsehide, in the manufacture of baseballs.¹²

Summary

The 1974 Winter Meetings were most noteworthy for the efforts of leaders from both leagues to work together on issues of common concern. The owners kept an eye to the future in their efforts to ensure the stability of the major leagues. Their attempts to stabilize the sport succeeded, as the major leagues witnessed a decade and a half of franchise stability between the 1977 expansions to Seattle and Toronto and the 1993 expansions to Miami and Denver. Owners and players agreed to another season of labor peace. The Rules Committee allowed for more experimentation by Charlie Finley, but held off on more significant changes to the game. Several trades with long-term consequences, including the deals for Ken Singleton, Lee May, and Tug McGraw, took place in New Orleans, yet overall player movement was light after the blitz of early offseason deals.

NOTES

1. Leonard Koppett, "Baseball Meetings End Amid Détente," *New York Times*, December 7, 1974: 35.

2. Murray Chass, "Owners Worry Over Reserve Clause Suit," *New York Times*, January 3, 1975: 44. See also Hunter's obituary in the *New York Times*, September 10, 1999.

3. Joseph Durso, "Harmony Is Keynote of Baseball Owners," *New York Times*, December 8, 1974: 269.

4. Ibid.

5. "Baseball Winter Meetings Set to Open," *Hartford Courant*, December 1, 1974: 9C.

6. Durso.

7. Ibid.

8. Koppett, "Baseball Meetings."

9. Ibid.

10. Durso. The cities that ended up receiving the two expansion teams in 1977, Seattle and Toronto, both kept the pressure on the major leagues until they were awarded their franchises. Seattle agreed to drop its seven-year-old lawsuit on behalf of the departed Pilots in 1976 when the American League voted to place an expansion team in the newly-constructed Kingdome. On the heels of the Labatt Brewing Company's efforts to bring the San Francisco Giants to the newly renovated Exhibition Stadium, Toronto received the other American League expansion franchise. Years later, Denver received a National League franchise for the 1993 season.

11. Leonard Koppett, "A No-Strike Deal Offered by Players," *New York Times*, December 5, 1974: 61.

12. Durso; "Baseball Winter Meetings Set to Open."

— 1975 —
THE THREAT OF FREE AGENCY AND THE RETURN OF THE MASTER SHOWMAN

Gregory H. Wolf

IN AN ATMOSPHERE OF UNCERTAINTY and anxiety, more than 1,400 officials, representatives, and executives of the major and minor leagues held their annual Winter Meetings in Hollywood, Florida, about a half-hour north of Miami, from December 8 to 12, 1975. Prepared to conduct business, entertain trades, and deliberate possible rule changes, many attendees wondered whether there would even be major-league baseball when big-league ballplayers were scheduled to report to their respective spring camps in three months. Arbitrator Peter Seitz's decision on the legality of the reserve clause was expected soon after the meetings were scheduled to conclude. Baseball executives feared that a nullification of the clause, which had limited player movement for almost a century, would cast baseball into perpetual chaos. In addition, the Basic Agreement (the collective-bargaining agreement) between the major-league owners and the Players Association expired at the end of December.

Big-league baseball was coming off one of the most exciting World Series in history. The Boston Red Sox, who had captured their first AL pennant since the "Impossible Dream" team of 1967, faced the overwhelming favorite Cincinnati Reds. The Big Red Machine, winners of 108 games (a new NL record in the "live ball" era) and in its third fall classic in six years, seemed invincible with former MVPs Johnny Bench and Pete Rose as well as 1975 MVP recipient Joe Morgan leading the club. But when Boston's Carlton Fisk blasted a dramatic 12th-inning walk-off home run to win Game Six and tie the Series, Game Seven at Fenway Park was assured. In that deciding contest, which according to some accounts was the most-watched baseball game in history with more than 51.5 million viewers, the Reds emerged victorious, 4-3.

Notwithstanding an exciting World Series, the 1975 season unfolded in what Robert F. Burk, in his groundbreaking biography *Marvin Miller, Baseball Revolutionary* called a "prelude to a reserve-clause showdown."[1] That previous December, Peter Seitz, who had had a 40-year career in arbitrating labor disputes, granted Oakland's Catfish Hunter free agency, the first in baseball history, in light of team owner Charley Finley's violation of the contract terms. Miller, the executive director of the Major League Baseball Players Association, recognized the perfect opportunity to challenge baseball's revered reserve clause and paragraph 10(a) of the Uniform Player's Contract, which gave baseball clubs the right to re-sign an unsigned player "for a period of one year on the same terms." Pitcher Andy Messersmith of the Los Angeles Dodgers agreed to play the entire 1975 season without a contract; veteran hurler Dave McNally of the Montreal Expos, who had decided to retire after the 1975 season, also joined the litigation. The end of the reserve clause would signal the rise of free agency; questions about who could become a free agent, and when, would soon follow. Roger I. Abrams, in his essay "Arbitrator Seitz Sets the Players Free" in SABR's Fall 2009 *Baseball Research Journal*, recounted that the players union filed a grievance on October 1, 1975, and hearings were held on November 21 and 25 and December 1.[2] Seitz's eventual ruling loomed as baseball's 74th annual Winter Meetings got under way in Florida.

Rule 5 Draft: Dwindling Importance

Baseball executives began arriving at the Diplomat Hotel in Hollywood as early as December 4 for a light schedule of meetings on December 5 through 7 before the meetings got underway officially on December 8 with the Rule 5 draft of unprotected players in Triple A. After a high of 27 players were chosen in the 1967 draft at the Winter Meetings in Mexico City, the number of drafted players had dwindled to an all-time low of three at the meetings in New Orleans, in 1974. Business wasn't much better in 1975, as only five players were taken, with a fee of $25,000 each, in a selection process that lasted just 10 minutes. Sportswriter Stan Isle suggested that the winter draft had lost its importance due to a "dearth of talent" in baseball and more "stringent economic policies" since the late 1960s.[3] *New York Times* correspondent Joseph Durso noted that, a generation ago, one out of 22 professional ballplayers was in the majors; that number was one in six in 1975.[4] Harry Dalton, GM of the Angels, offered a grim analysis. "There are no minor leagues to speak of and there aren't enough good players," he said. "Teams just don't have enough money these days to operate farm systems."[5]

Minor-League Draft: Another Record Low

Two days after the Rule 5 draft, the minor-league draft of Double-A and Triple-A players reached an all-time low of seven players. Only three big-league teams made selections. Hank Peters, president of the minor leagues (formally called the National Association of Professional Baseball Leagues) noted that the number of players in Organized Baseball had declined sharply, with 800 fewer players expected to be under contract for the coming 1976 season than there were in 1970. "The lack of participation in the draft," he suggested, "is related to the great reduction of free agent talent.[6]

Labor Disputes: Two Sides of the Basic Agreement and Pension Plan

The first collective-bargaining agreement between the Players Association and the major leagues was signed in February 1968, and others followed in 1970 and 1973. With their perceived loss in the Catfish Hunter free-agency ruling, the owners took a hard stance in negotiating a new Basic Agreement (which included language about minimum salaries, expenses, scheduling rules, and salary arbitration) to replace the one expiring on December 31, 1975. The two sides also had to agree on a new pension and benefit plan, set to expire on March 31, 1976.

While members of the Major League Player Relations Committee met in Hollywood to summarize negotiations already held and plan for the next rounds scheduled over the following weeks, player representatives from all 24 major-league teams met with union director Marvin Miller at the Americana Hotel in nearby Bal Harbour to clarify their positions and labor demands, and develop an effective strategy to achieve their goals. Few people, if anyone, expected a new Basic Agreement to be in place by December 31.

New York Times sportswriter Leonard Koppett reported that there was widespread speculation that owners would delay spring training and lock out players if no agreement was reached by the end of February, when camps were scheduled to open.[7] Such a move would prevent players from striking when the regular season started. "I can't tell what will happen, or what the clubs might do," said Miller. "It is much too early to talk about something like that. Most of our meetings here will be devoted to bringing the players up to date in what has been proposed."[8]

The players and owners both kept the deliberations of the meetings from the press as much as possible, save for sound bites. "We recognize the possibility that the clubs might decide on a lockout," said Miller. "We're proceeding on the basis that sincere bargaining will be carried out."[9] Players and owners alike recognized that Seitz's decision in the Messersmith-McNally reserve-clause case would play a major role in how the two sides ultimately crafted the new CBA and pension contract. "Losing the case," said an anonymous member of the Player Relations Committee, "would be a bigger defeat than winning it would be a victory."[10] No one knew how free agency would affect baseball, though some baseball owners viewed it as economic death. As Burk pointed out in his critically acclaimed biography of Marvin Miller, the players association and major-league owners were charged with the monumental task of determining "the optimal service threshold for free agency" of the new Basic Agreement.[11]

Bill Veeck Buys the White Sox ... Again

"For the man with the mahogany leg, the tireless energy, and friends both well-heeled and needy," wrote Richard Dozer of the *Chicago Tribune* about Bill Veeck, "it was a week of personal triumph."[12] Veeck, who had lost his leg during World War II, accomplished what seemed like a long shot just three months earlier by purchasing the Chicago White Sox—for the second time.

Veeck was no stranger to the major leagues. As SABR member Warren Corbett noted in his biography of the innovative owner, Veeck once said, "I am the only human being ever raised in a ballpark."[13] He got his start as a vendor with the Chicago Cubs, for whom his father, Bill Veeck Sr., served as president until he died in 1933. Veeck Jr. was eventually named treasurer before venturing on his own storied career as an executive who challenged the status quo. He owned the Milwaukee Brewers of the American Association (1941-45), the Cleveland Indians (1946-1949), St. Louis Browns (1951-1953), and Chicago White Sox (1959-1961).

As the 1975 major-league season came to a conclusion, Veeck emerged as the leader of a group of approximately 40 investors interested in acquiring the 80 percent of the White Sox from majority owner John Allyn that Veeck had sold him in 1961. According to the *Tribune*, AL owners met with Veeck on December 3 in Cleveland, shortly before the winter meetings were to begin in Florida, to scrutinize the offer of approximately $8 million. Determining that Veeck's original proposal was underfinanced and too debt-laden, owners gave him a seven-day grace period to obtain additional capital and restructure his financing, setting up a dramatic scene in Hollywood, Florida. Jerome Holtzman reported in *The Sporting News* that Veeck "barely" made the December 10 deadline.[14] Technically Veeck did not fulfill the owners' requirements. Instead of $6 million in cash reserves, Veeck had approximately $3.4 million in bank deposits, with the remainder in subscriptions for preferred stock. Owners voted 8 to 3 with one abstention in favor of the sale. Lacking one vote for the required three-fourths majority to purchase the club, Veeck, whose showmanship and carnival-like promotions had angered conservative owners during his three earlier stints as a big-league owner, seemed doomed.

As reported by *The Sporting News*, Veeck had a stroke of luck. John Fetzer, owner of the Detroit Tigers, concerned that the failure to sell the White Sox to Veeck might result in the franchise's relocation to Seattle, made what Holtzman called a "fiery speech."[15] Despite the validity of the first vote, the AL owners decided to vote again. Apparently moved by Fetzer's cautionary words, they voted 10 to 2 in favor of Veeck's proposal. "It's gonna be a lot of fun," said Veeck soon after learning about the positive vote, and then in a not-so-subtle reminder that the White Sox' last pennant (1959) was on his watch, added. "Yes, even more fun that it was for us the last time."[16] Veeck wasted little time in remaking the White Sox front office. Assuming the title of president, Veeck named Bill DeWitt, one of the investors in the club, as chairman of the board. Veeck trusted his old pal and mentor, the 73-year-old DeWitt, who had sold the Browns to Veeck in 1951 and remained in the club's front office. Veeck also corralled the highly respected Paul Richards, former GM of the Orioles, Colt 45's/Astros, and Braves, as well as one-time White Sox skipper (1951-1954), into the management team, though his exact title was yet unknown. Many speculated that he might replace manager Chuck Tanner (which in fact he did). The *Tribune* reported that Veeck might have given Charley Finley, owner of the Oakland A's, permission to speak with Tanner, and he eventually became the A's skipper for the 1976 season.[17]

The Seattle Giants? The Toronto Giants? The Giants Remain in San Francisco for Now

Major-league baseball's franchise committee had its work cut out in Hollywood. Its members—headed by Donald Grant, chairman of the New York Mets; John McHale, GM of the Montreal Expos; Bud Selig, president of the Milwaukee Brewers; Ewing Kauffman, president of the Kansas City Royals; AL President Lee McPhail, NL President Chub Feeney, and Commissioner Bowie Kuhn—were charged with finding a solution to the continued economic woes of the San Francisco Giants. Majority owner Horace Stoneham, who had moved the Giants from New York to what seemed like guaranteed prosperity in San Francisco in 1958, was on the verge of financial insolvency and was actively trying to sell the club. For the second consecutive season, and third in the last four, the Giants had finished last in the NL in attendance while playing in Candlestick Park, widely derided as the worst ballpark in baseball. "We're still here," quipped the septuagenarian Stoneham. "We're broke. No sale is imminent, but something will have to happen soon. We have bids we are studying. We're in motion."[18]

The National League had infused the Giants with cash during the 1975 season to meet basic expenditures and salary obligations. At the Winter Meetings, the NL voted to continue its financial support of the club through December, and perhaps beyond. "We could carry San Francisco for many years," bragged Dodgers GM Walter O'Malley, whose view seemed to reflect the sentiments of the franchise committee, which was committed to helping Stoneham sell the tradition-laden club, but only under certain circumstances.[19] Labatt's Brewery in Toronto offered $12 million for the club, believed to be at or above the asking price; however, the NL declined the offer when the Canadian concern stipulated that it would relocate the club to Toronto. There were at least three other potential buyers, including a group led by San Jose-based banker Merle Jones, who presented his proposal of a $10 million offer to owners at the Winter Meetings; Bob Lurie, whose group seemed to lack sufficient funds; and an offer from a syndicate based in the state of Washington.

The Giants weren't the only team in the Bay Area experiencing financial duress. Charles O. Finley, majority owner of the Oakland A's, had made it clear that rapidly rising salaries had made operating his club increasingly tenuous. Since relocating the A's from Kansas City to Oakland in 1968, Finley had not enjoyed the financial success or the fan support he had predicted, despite three consecutive World Series championships (1972-1974).

Commissioner Kuhn, keenly aware of the critical financial predicament of these two Bay Area clubs playing in stadiums about 21 miles apart, thought Seattle could be a possible relocation destination for one of them. "In my judgment," said Kuhn, "one must go. And I think that is the view of nearly all of us in baseball."[20] A relocation to Seattle would require either the Giants or A's to initiate expensive litigation to break their lease with the owners of their ballparks.

Seattle was determined to land a big-league club, yet business and governmental leaders felt that the city had been continually betrayed. According to Leonard Koppett of the *New York Times*, Seattle had filled three conditions demanded by major-league baseball in order to be considered for a big-league club.[21] They built a state-of-the-art stadium, the Kingdome; they had a financially sound group ready to purchase a club; and they agreed to drop all litigation against major-league baseball. The last point referred to a $20 million lawsuit Washington state Attorney General Slade Gorton had threatened to file against the AL and the Milwaukee Brewers, charging them with conspiracy in the relocation of the expansion Pilots to Wisconsin after just one season (1969) in the Pacific Northwest. Coincidentally, Bud Selig, a member of the franchise committee, had led Milwaukee's efforts to land the Pilots.

It was a bad week for Seattle in Florida. An ownership group, led by Wes Smith and Danny Kaye, had attended the winter meetings prepared to buy the Chicago White Sox and move them to Seattle, but lost out when Bill Veeck came up with his last-ditch effort to buy them. The franchise committee, as well as the NL, seemed unwilling to let the Giants relocate to Seattle; and Finley apparently lacked the funds to engage in a protracted legal battle to do so. Seattle's best chance of landing a team, according to most reports, was through expansion; however, major-league owners were reluctant to add teams with the player agreement expiring at the end of the month, impending free agency, and other economic factors. "There are no pledges, no commitments beyond good-faith efforts," said Kuhn about expansion.[22] Frustrated by a lack of transparency, Attorney General Gorton announced that he was prepared to proceed with his original lawsuit against the AL, scheduled to be heard as early as January 20, 1976. The *New York Times*'s Leonard Koppett summed up the franchise problems by opining that "business turmoil [is] virtually assured for 1976."[23]

Major League Trades: Veeck Announces His Return

One of the most enduring stories of the 1975 Winter Meetings is Bill Veeck sitting at a desk in the lobby of the Diplomat Hotel. Next to Veeck was White Sox GM Roland Hemond, who famously placed the sign "Open for Business" on the table. Veeck and Hemond, who claimed they slept only four hours a day during the frenzied winter session, went on the trading offensive just hours after Veeck gained control of the club on December 10, making six deals involving 22 players in an attempt to give their club a decidedly youthful composition. The duo was also supported by Paul Richards; Chuck Tanner, who had piloted the club since 1970, left the meetings soon after Veeck was announced as the team's new owner.

The White Sox sent left-handed pitcher Jim Kaat, coming off successive 20-win seasons, and minor-league infielder Mike Buskey to Philadelphia for right-handed pitchers Dick Ruthven and Roy Thomas and utilityman Alan Bannister. The following day they shipped third baseman Bill Melton, a former AL home-run champ and fan favorite, and right-handed pitcher Steve Dunning to the California Angels for outfielder Morris Nettles and first baseman Jim Spencer, setting up a final day of trading that evoked memories of former White Sox GM Frank "Trader" Lane of the 1950s. The club's biggest acquisitions were right-handed reliever Clay Carroll from the Reds in exchange for southpaw reliever Rich Hinton and minor leaguer Jeff Sovern; and All-Star outfielder Ralph Garr (the 1974 National League batting champion) from the Braves for outfielder Ken Henderson, right-hander Dan Osborne, and Ruthven, whom the club had acquired less than 48 hours earlier. The White Sox also acquired infielder Larvell "Sugar Bear" Blanks from Atlanta in that trade, and then shipped him to Cleveland in exchange for infielder Jack Brohamer later that day. Roland Hemond, hoping to keep his job under his new owner, seemed to be in awe of Veeck. "His mere presence has changed me," he said. "I'm basically a conservative person—or at least I thought I was—but being around Bill is a whole different experience. I can't imagine doing these things a month ago."[24]

All told, there were 23 deals involving 64 players at the winter meetings, and all but five teams (Brewers, Cubs, Dodgers, Orioles, and Twins) made at least one trade. The two New York teams were involved in arguably the three biggest trades of the meetings. The Yankees, whose principal owner, George Steinbrenner, was still serving a two-year suspension handed down by Commissioner Kuhn for illegal political campaign contributions, shocked the baseball world by sending All-Star outfielder Bobby Bonds, who had been acquired just a year earlier and had posted a record third season with at least 30 home run and 30 stolen bases,[25] to California in exchange for right-handed pitcher Ed Figueroa and outfielder Mickey Rivers. The trade was widely panned by Yankee supporters and some members of the media; the Associated Press wondered if the Yankees "got their money's worth."[26] Later that day, the Yankees shipped right-hander Doc Medich, winner of 49 games over the three previous seasons, to the Pittsburgh Pirates for second baseman Willie Randolph and pitchers Ken Brett (a lefty) and Doc Ellis (a righty). The Yankees were hoping to revamp a team scheduled to return to Yankee Stadium in 1976 after playing at the Mets' Shea Stadium the previous two seasons while the venerable "House

That Ruth Built" underwent extensive renovation, and they succeeded—Randolph and Rivers strengthened the team up the middle, Figueroa and Ellis won 36 games between them, and the team made the first of three consecutive trips to the World Series. The Mets, who had outdrawn the Yankees every year since 1964, sent fan favorite and dependable right fielder Rusty Staub and southpaw pitcher Bill Laxton to the Tigers for rubber-armed left-hander Mickey Lolich and outfielder Billy Baldwin.

The DH Rule: From Experimental to Optional

Prior to the Winter Meetings, sportswriter Bill Fleishman had predicted a "major battle" over the designated-hitter rule, which had been adopted as experimental three years earlier and had been used by the American League since 1973, and also by 13 of 16 minor leagues in the United States in 1975.[27] The future of the DH rule was entrusted to the 10-member Official Playing Rules committee, which consisted of three members from the AL (Cal Griffith, owner and president of the Minnesota Twins; Rick Ferrell, vice president of the Detroit Tigers; and John Allyn, owner and president of the Chicago White Sox), three from the National League (Chub Feeney, league president; Joe Brown, GM of the Pittsburgh Pirates; and John McHale, president of the Montreal Expos), and well as three from the minor leagues (Bobby Bragan, president of the Texas League; George Sisler Jr., president of the International League; and Vince McNamara, president of the New York-Pennsylvania League). The committee was chaired by nonvoting member John Johnson, deputy to the commissioner. By a vote of 6 to 3, with all three dissenting votes cast by the NL committee members, the status of the designated-hitter rule was changed from experimental to optional. Furthermore, any league (including the NL) could implement the DH by a simple majority vote by its member teams, a change from the previous requirement of a three-quarters majority.[28] Whereas Feeney, Brown, and McHale remained committed to prohibiting the use of the DH even in the minors, their AL counterparts sought to expand the use of the DH to include All-Star games and, importantly, the World Series. However, no action was taken on those points at the Winter Meetings. [At a subsequent meeting of the Rules Committee in 1976, a convoluted compromise was found. The DH was expanded to all games of the World Series, however, it would be used only in alternating years beginning in 1976. The DH was still prohibited in All-Star Games, and was not used in the midsummer game until 1989.]

New Playing Rules: Avoiding Conflicts

The Sporting News correspondent Stan Isle reported that the Official Playing Rules Committee created a panel to study consolidating and standardizing rules of interpretation for major-league umpires.[29] Members of the panel included the AL supervisor of umpires, Dick Butler; his NL counterpart, Fred Feig; and a representative from the minors to be named before the panel was scheduled to meet in January 1976. Reform was prompted by a controversial call in Game Three of the 1975 World Series. In the 10th inning, Cincinnati's Ed Armbrister executed a sacrifice bunt and then collided with Boston's catcher Carlton Fisk in his attempt to field the ball. Armbrister was safe at first on Fisk's throwing error, and ultimately scored the winning run. Home-plate umpire Larry Barnett, who was then in the seventh season of a 31-year career as an AL umpire, did not call interference.[30] Though the call was widely criticized, Barnett's call was correct according to rule 7.06 (a). During the Playing Rules Committee's session at the Winter Meetings, Dick Butler pointed out a glaring discrepancy. The scenario of a collision between catcher and batter was covered in the NL rule interpretation book but not in the AL's book.[31] Butler also noted a few other discrepancies between leagues that needed to be consolidated, such as how long NL and AL umpires must wait before they call games due to inclement weather. Another unusual difference between how leagues interpret rules could have come into play in Game Six of the World Series had Carlton Fisk been mobbed with fans as he ran the bases after his game-winning home run. According to AL rules, a batter must touch all bases; however, NL umpires are permitted to use their judgment if it becomes physically impossible for a player to touch all of the bases.

Signing Collegians: The First Change Since 1967

After meetings between the College Committee, headed by California Angels GM Harry Dalton, and an ad hoc group of the College Coaches Committee, chaired by Rod Dedeaux, head baseball coach at the University of Southern California, Commissioner Bowie Kuhn announced an amended rule permitting college baseball players to sign professional contracts between the end of their junior year and the beginning of their senior year. According to sportswriter Stan Isle, this was the first amendment to the college rule since1967, when college players were prohibited from signing.[32] All 21-year-old collegians, and those who had completed their junior year, would now be eligible to be drafted in the June amateur draft. The rule banning Organized Baseball from signing collegians, including seniors, during the school year remained in effect.

Trading Deadline

Pending approval from the players association, the major leagues passed an amendment to establish a second interleague trading period, running from March 16 until 10 days prior to the opening of the regular season. A similar proposal was passed at the 1974 Winter Meetings, but it was vetoed by the players. The traditional interleague trading period, which began five days after the conclusion of the World Series and extended through the last day of the Winter Meetings, was not affected.

Public Relations Directors: Improving Fan Experience

On Sunday, December 7, public relation and promotion directors met to discuss issues ranging from All-Star Game balloting to televised broadcasts of games. Commissioner Kuhn hailed the All-Star balloting program as a "super-successful promotion" with more than 7.3 million votes cast in 1975.[33] In 1970 fans regained the right to vote for the game's starting lineups for the first time since 1957, but occasionally a bug was found. To eliminate confusion caused by player trades or position changes, the commissioner's office decided to have the ballots printed at a later date in 1976. The public-relations directors for the AL (Bob Fishel) and NL (Blake Cullen) announced plans to publish fan versions of the leagues' Red Book and Green Book, responding to an ever-growing demand for easier accessibility to printed matter about baseball statistics and history. Representatives from the ABC and NBC television networks also gave presentations about their baseball coverage for the coming season.

Minor League Baseball: Attendance and Leagues

At the opening session of the Winter Meetings, outgoing National Association President Hank Peters spoke at length about the state of the minor leagues. He noted that attendance rose by more than 575,000 from the previous year to 11,607,190, its highest mark since 1959, and the fourth consecutive season that attendance had passed the 11 million mark. In 1975 there were 18 leagues, including two in Mexico, with teams in 137 cities. Peters announced the addition of a 19th league, the eight-team Class-A Mexican Pacific League, for 1976. Only two minor-league teams disbanded (Salinas and Visalia of the Class-A California League) and one team moved (Cleveland transferred its affiliate from the Gulf Coast League to the New York-Penn League). Despite the positive news, Peters offered a stark warning: "There's an alarming drop in talent flow coming into baseball, and for the first time, the National Association office found class AAA and AA clubs complaining because major leagues were not providing players."[34]

National Association of Professional Baseball Leagues Banquet: Awards and Recognition

The National Association, established in 1902 as the umbrella organization of the minor leagues, hosted it 74th annual banquet, on December 9 at the Diplomat Hotel.[35] Master of ceremonies Bobby Bragan, president of the Double-A Texas League and newly elected National Association president, greeted 1,200 guests for an evening of festivities, awards, recognition, and fun. Commissioner Kuhn, one of many featured speakers, called the National Association "the heart and soul of professional baseball."[36] The outgoing National Association president, and new Baltimore Orioles GM, Hank Peters, presided over an awards ceremony during which the Tacoma (Washington) Twins, Minnesota's affiliate in the Triple-A Pacific Coast League, were the big winners. Sportswriter Art Voellinger reported that the club received the two most prestigious awards presented by the minor leagues, the National Association Larry MacPhail memorial promotional trophy, and the National Association president's trophy for its "overall operation and contributions to baseball."[37] Praised as a model club, Tacoma drew almost 200,000 fans to its games despite a population of about 156,000.[38] Its GM, Stan Naccarato, received *The Sporting News* Triple-A Executive of the Year Award. In addition, each of the 18 minor leagues presented its executive of the year award. Former big-league pitcher and blues musician Jim "Mudcat" Grant and the Rhodes Brothers provided the entertainment.

Support for Amateur Baseball

The Sporting News reported that the Executive Council of the major leagues appropriated approximately $360,000 to support amateur baseball programs throughout the United States.[39] Included among the 17 recipients were the American Legion, nine boys programs (such as Little League, Babe Ruth baseball, and the American Amateur Baseball Congress), college baseball leagues, and five college summer leagues.

Conclusion

With the Basic Agreement and players pension plan soon to expire, and the prospect of the end of the reserve clause and the rise of free agency, the Winter Meetings concluded with most of the pressing issues facing baseball still unresolved. The sale of the Chicago White Sox to showman Bill Veeck stabilized one club, but franchise situations in San Francisco and Seattle remained muddled and guaranteed that baseball executives would need to address those issues at the beginning of the new calendar year. The DH rule lost its "experimental" designation, but no long-term decision was reached, and its use in the 1976 World Series was still unclear.

Less than two weeks after the Winter Meetings concluded, an old order came crashing down when, on December 23, arbitrator Peter Seitz ruled that clubs could reserve a player for only one year, thereby granting free-agency status to Messersmith and McNally. Commissioner Kuhn immediately filed an appeal. Judge Watkins Oliver of the US District Court in Kansas City upheld Seitz's ruling on February 4, 1976, and a month later, the Eighth Circuit Court of Appeals did the same. A new era had now dawned.

SOURCES

In addition to the sources listed in the notes, the author also consulted the following:

Isle, Stan. "Chisox Top Traders; Made Six Deals," *The Sporting News*, December 27, 1975: 34.

Isle, Stan. "Fans Skip Old-Timers in 'Most Memorable' Vote," *The Sporting News*, December 27, 1975: 36.

Voellinger, Art. "Majors Nix Hike in Minor TV Take," *The Sporting News*, December 27, 1975: 33.

NOTES

1 Robert F. Burk, *Marvin Miller. Baseball Revolutionary* (Urbana, Chicago, and Springfield: University of Illinois Press, 2015), 176.

2 Roger I. Abrams, "Arbitrator Seitz Sets Players Free," *Baseball Research Journal*, Fall 2009. sabr.org/research/arbitrator-seitz-sets-players-free.

3 Stan Isle, "Major Draft Reels In Only 5 Players," *The Sporting News*, December 27, 1975: 38.

4 Joseph Durso, "Only 5 Players Are Drafted as Baseball Meetings Begin," *New York Times*, December 9, 1975: 55.

5 Ibid.

6 Art Voellinger, "'Minors' Draft Reflects Talent Shortage'—Peters," *The Sporting News*, December 27, 1975: 38.

7 Leonard Koppett, "Players to Set Contract Plans," *New York Times*, December 10, 1975: 35.

8 Ibid.

9 Ibid.

10 Ibid.

11 Burk, 183.

12 Richard Dozer, "Week of Triumph for Veeck," *Chicago Tribune*, December 14, 1975: B1.

13 Warren Corbett, "Bill Veeck," SABR BioProject. sabr.org/bioproj/person/7b0b5f10.

14 Jerome Holtzman, "Deluge of Sox Deals Signals Return of Veeck," *The Sporting News*, December 27, 1975: 41.

15 Ibid.

16 Dozer, "Week of Triumph for Veeck."

17 Ibid.

18 Art Spander, "N.L. Will Call Pitches for Giants Until Sale," *The Sporting News*, December 27, 1975: 41.

19 Ibid.

20 Stan Isle, "Majors Still Grappling With Financial Problems," *The Sporting News*, December 27, 1975: 33.

21 Leonard Koppett, "Baseball Meetings End With Problems Unsettled," *New York Times*, December 12, 1975: 50.

22 Isle, "Majors Still Grappling With Financial Problems."

23 Koppett, "Baseball Meetings End With Problems Unsettled."

24 Rick Talley, "Hemond, Peden, in crash course," *Chicago Tribune*, December 14, 1975: B3.

25 Bonds posted two more 30-30 seasons before he retired.

26 Associated Press, "Bobby Bonds Shaken by His Trade to Angels, but Experts Say Yankees Are Improved," *Gettysburg (Pennsylvania) Times*, December 11, 1975: 13.

27 Bill Fleishman, "Majors on Collision Course Over DH Rule," *The Sporting News*, November 22, 1975: 42.

28 Ibid.

29 Stan Isle, "Majors Continue Separate Paths on Use of DH," *The Sporting News*, December 27, 1975: 40.

30 Barnett received death threats for his failure to call interference.

31 Isle, "Major Continue Separate Paths on Use of DH."

32 Stan Isle, "Kuhn Announces Okay of New College Rule," *The Sporting News*, December 27, 1975: 40.

33 Stan Isle, "Majors to Alter All-Star Nominating Setup," *The Sporting News*, December 27, 1975: 35.

34 Art Voellinger, "Mexican Pacific Loop to Hike Minors' 1976 Total," *The Sporting News*, December 27, 1975: 34.

35 The name of the organization was changed to Minor League Baseball in 1999.

36 Art Voellinger, "Tacoma Twins Rendered Dual Honors at Banquet," *The Sporting News*, December 27, 1975: 40.

37 Ibid.

38 According to Lloyd Johnson and Miles Wolff, eds., *The Encyclopedia of Minor League Baseball*, 2nd ed. (Durham, North Carolina: Baseball America, 1997), Tacoma's attendance was 197,583.

39 "Majors Boost Allotment To 17 Amateur Groups," *The Sporting News*, December 27, 1975: 34.

— 1976 —
CHANGING DEMOGRAPHICS AND BROADCAST CHALLENGESS

By Gregory H. Wolf

WHAT A DIFFERENCE A YEAR makes.

When an estimated 1,200 baseball owners, executives, and club representative convened at the Los Angeles Hilton in December 1976 to conduct the 75th annual Winter Meetings, professional baseball had experienced dramatic and history-altering changes in the preceding 12 months. Sportswriter Joseph Durso suggested that the meeting "couldn't have come a worse time."[1] The weeklong event was normally a celebratory occasion and the locus for trades, the discussion of rule changes, and other business-related issues. However, this year the meetings also culminated a tension-filled year which saw the demise of the reserve clause, a lockout, a new Basic Agreement, the establishment of free agency and its corresponding re-entry draft, and an expansion draft. "[B]aseball clans will be fussing and fretting," continued Durso, "and probably wondering about their new values."[2]

A Prelude to the Winter Meetings: Free Agency and a New Basic Agreement

A year earlier, in 1975, baseball's Winter Meetings, in Florida, took place under a cloud of anxious anticipation and uncertainty as arbitrator Peter Seitz's ruling on the legality of the reserve clause was expected any day. About two weeks after the conclusion of the meetings, on December 23, Seitz announced his landmark decision: Clubs could legally reserve players for only one year, after which they would become free agents. Pitchers Andy Messersmith and Dave McNally, both of whom had played the 1975 season without a contract, were declared the first free agents, sending a shiver of doom through the collective spine of club owners. "Make 'em all free agents," said Oakland A's owner Charlie Finley sarcastically.[3] He, like many other owners, predicted that free agency would usher in a new era of high salaries and destroy the sport. Eight days later, on December 31, 1975, baseball's Collective Bargaining Agreement expired. Owners and players now had another concern: Would there be baseball in 1976? A new Basic Agreement between owners and the players union, the Major Leagues Players Association, would necessarily need to define the optimal threshold for free agency. "No one knew what the magical figure was," said Marvin Miller, director of the MLPA.[4]

Commissioner Bowie Kuhn immediately challenged Seitz's ruling. On February 3 Judge John Watkins Oliver of the US District Court in Kansas City upheld Seitz's decision, as did the 8th Circuit Court of Appeals a month later.[5] Unable to reach an agreement with the MLPA regarding free agency, baseball owners ordered a lockout barring players from spring training beginning March 1. Nationally syndicated sportswriter Red Smith called the owners' move "foolish," while Miller denounced it, terming it as "destructive and counterproductive an action as anyone can imagine."[6] According to Robert F. Burke in his exhaustive study, *Marvin Miller, A Baseball Revolutionary*, Kuhn soon thereafter felt pressure from both television networks and owners in big markets (especially George Steinbrenner of the New York Yankees and Walter O'Malley of the Los Angeles Dodgers) to end the lockout, which he did on March 17 with a "unilateral action."[7] The regular season began as scheduled, on April 8, albeit with a shortened training camp, as owners and the MLPA continued to negotiate a new contract.

While the two sides hammered out the details of free agency, Finley took matters into his own hand. Fearful of losing players without compensation, the outspoken owner traded outfielder Reggie Jackson and left-handed pitcher Ken Holtzman to the Baltimore Orioles for right-hander Mike Torrez and outfielder Don Baylor days before the '76 season started. Hours before the June 15 trading deadline, Finley sold three more lame-duck free-agents-to-be, outfielder Joe Rudi and right-handed relief ace Rollie Fingers, to the Boston Red Sox, and left-hander Vida Blue (the 1971 AL MVP and Cy Young Award winner) to the Yankees for $3.5 million in what was then the biggest deal in baseball history. The next day, before any of the three players could take the field for their respective teams, Kuhn voided the sales in the name of preserving the integrity of the game. [In yet another bizarre twist, both Rudi and Fingers had suited up for Boston, coincidentally against the A's in Oakland, and had participated in pregame warm-ups before news of Kuhn's directive reached the Red Sox.] Baseball appeared on the verge of mass chaos. Kuhn's actions "stunned the baseball world," wrote Joseph Durso in the *New York Times*, while Finley promised to take the matter to court.[8]

Re-entry and Expansion Drafts

On July 12 owners and the Executive Board of the MLPA cleared the last major hurdle for the new CBA. The MLPA accepted the owners' offer of a six-year service requirement for free agency. In August the two sides approved a new Basic Agreement. Described in detail by Burke, the new CBA increased minimum salaries to $19,000 in 1977 and $21,000 by 1979, increased each team's annual pension contribution, and defined free agency.[9] All players playing out their option in 1976 would become free agents. They would be eligible to be chosen by up to 12 clubs, whose draft order was based on their record (from worst to best) alternating by league, in a "free agent re-entry draft." According to the new CBA, all teams losing a player would receive a compensatory draft pick in the following annual amateur draft from the team that signed its player. Teams were permitted to sign a maximum of two free agents.

On November 4, the first re-entry draft took place at the Plaza Hotel in New York City. The Montreal Expos chose the Orioles' Reggie Jackson with the first pick. Of the 24 official free agents, only two players, Willie McCovey and Nate Colbert, were not selected by any teams. Thirteen players were selected by the maximum 12 clubs, including A's stars Sal Bando, Don Baylor, Rollie Fingers, Joe Rudi, and Gene Tenace. "It's horse manure," said Finley of the draft. "It's the worst thing that could ever happen to baseball. I don't blame the players. It's the owners who are stupid."[10] Two days after the draft, right-handed reliever Bill Campbell, who had earned $23,000 for the Minnesota Twins in 1976, became the first free agent to ink a pact when he signed a five-year, $1 million deal with the Red Sox. By the opening of the Winter Meetings, 19 of 22 free agents had signed. Contract negotiating with free agents made it clear, suggested sportswriter Ralph Ray, that "newer managements were far more aggressive than veteran operators."[11] The success of clubs like Steinbrenner's Yankees (who signed Jackson and left-handed pitcher Don Gullett), Ray Kroc's San Diego Padres (Tenace and Fingers), and Ted Turner's Atlanta Braves (outfielder Gary Matthews and, earlier, Messersmith) stood in stark contrast to clubs led by what Ray deemed the "old hands," like the Mets, Pirates, Phillies, Dodgers, and Giants, among others, who were shut out.[12] Only the Cincinnati Reds refused to participate in the draft.

On the day after the re-entry draft, the expansion draft took place. Actor and comedian Danny Kaye, a part-owner of the Seattle Mariners, announced his club's first pick, outfielder Ruppert Jones of the Kansas City Royals. The Toronto Blue Jays selected Baltimore's infielder Bob Bailor with the second overall pick. The two teams drafted 60 players.

Oh Yeah, There Was Baseball in 1976, Too

With all of the negotiations over a new CBA, the 1976 baseball season seemed at times to be an afterthought. Cincinnati's Big Red Machine cruised to its fourth pennant in seven seasons. After crushing the Philadelphia Phillies—in the postseason for the first time since the Whiz Kids' pennant in 1950—in three games in the NLCS, the Reds avenged their 1961 World Series loss to the Yankees by sweeping the Billy Martin-piloted club in four games. The Reds' Joe Morgan claimed his second straight NL MVP Award, while Yankees catcher Thurman Munson, who had led his club to its first fall classic since the end of its dynasty in 1964, took home the MVP hardware in the AL. Left-hander Randy Jones, who led the NL with 22 wins for the lowly San Diego Padres, was named the NL Cy Young Award winner; Baltimore's ace right-hander Jim Palmer, also with 22 victories, won his third AL Cy Young Award in four seasons. Detroit Tigers starter and 19-game winner Mark "the Bird" Fidrych, who captured the nation's attention with his entertaining personality on the mound, was named AL Rookie of the Year. And for the first time in the history of the award, two players shared honors: San Diego's right-handed relief ace Butch Metzger and Reds right-handed starter Pat Zachary were named NL Co-Rookies of the Year.

Winter Meetings: The Agenda

The 75th version of baseball's annual Winter Meetings officially started on Friday, December 3. The first three days were dedicated to the National Association (minor leagues), while the major leagues opened their sessions on Monday, December 7, to address the sport described by the *New York Times* as "filled with intrigue, plots, subplots, feuds, lots of money, and cast of thousands."[13] From making sense out of free agency to discussing possible franchise relocation and league alignment, baseball men (and a few token women) had a full slate of meetings through Thursday, December 9.

Kuhn's State of Baseball Address: A Cautionary Tale

In his state of baseball speech at the opening session on Monday, December 6, Commissioner Kuhn was guardedly optimistic. "[T]here should be some real exhilaration in some areas and cause for concern in others," he said. "I am satisfied we have the talent and ability to solve our problems and keep growing."[14] The chief cause of concern was the cost of free agency, which Kuhn claimed was "higher than expected."[15] Owners and executives were still wrapping their heads around salaries that were unimaginable just a year earlier: For example, Reggie Jackson signed for $3 million over five years; Joe Rudi inked a five-year deal worth in excess of $2 million with the California Angels, and pitcher Wayne Garland signed a 10-year contract worth $2 million with the Cleveland Indians. Many around baseball wondered when there would be the first million-dollar-a-year player. Prior to arriving in Los Angeles, Kuhn warned that rising player salaries might have an unintended effect on the quality of players in the future. "You may see some reduction in the expenses of player development," Kuhn suggested ominously in an interview with the *Washington Post*. "I am afraid it could have an effect on our minor leagues."[16] On the other hand, Kuhn noted that baseball was more popular than ever. The major leagues set a new attendance record with 31,318,331 (an increase of more than 1.5 million from the previous season); the minor leagues drew in excess of 11.3 million.[17] Televised baseball was also booming: Viewership of ABC's *Monday Night Baseball* was up 17 percent from a year earlier, and all four games of the World Series between the Reds and Yankees topped the ratings of the 1975 fall classic between the Reds and Red Sox.[18]

Kuhn-Finley Feud

The long-running feud between Charlie Finley and Bowie Kuhn reached a new nadir in 1976 when the commissioner voided the sale of a trio of A's players (Rudi, Fingers, and Blue) at the trading deadline. Finley went on a widely publicized tirade at the Winter Meetings, taking the national stage in anticipation of opening a $3.5 million lawsuit against Kuhn in federal court in Chicago a week after the meetings. At a press conference at the LA Hilton, Finley lambasted Kuhn. "Without leadership, you have no stability. At this point in time, we have no stability," said Finley.[19] Suggesting that neither Kuhn nor the owners were capable of running the game and policing themselves, Finley dropped a bomb: "I'm in favor of the government stepping in, not just in baseball, but in all sports, before the owners destroy sports."[20] Finley vehemently rejected Kuhn's claim that affluent and less affluent and big-market and small-market teams equally benefited from free agency. "In the end," said Finley in remarks that have been repeated by other owners and executives since then, "the rich clubs will end up controlling baseball. There is no way the A's, Minnesota, and a couple of others clubs can survive the battle."[21]

Rule 5 and Minor-League Draft

For a number of years, the major-league draft (also called the Rule 5 draft) had been losing its importance as the official opening of the Winter Meetings. Only eight players combined were drafted in 1974 and 1975. Seven players were drafted in 1976, headlined by former Reds right-handed hurler Tom Carroll, whom the Montreal Expos selected with the first pick. In the minor-league draft, which took place on December 7, 16 players were selected; seven had been drafted in 1975. Sportswriter Oscar Kahan noted that the increase was due primarily to a new rule stipulating that a club could option a drafted player to a lower classification without giving up the rights to the player; formerly, the team had to retain a player on its roster or offer him back to the original club for half the draft price.[22]

Trades: The Effects of Free Agency

Described as a "traditional hotbed of trading activity," the 1976 Winter Meetings produced only 14 trades involving 38 players (and two players to be named later) among 19 clubs.[23] A year earlier 64 players were involved in transactions. "The chief reason for the quiet market is the uncertainly over players' contracts," opined Peter Bavasi, GM of the expansion Toronto Blue Jays. "In the past you were primarily interested in the ability of the players in your trades. Now you have to consider the status of the players — the legal status, their seniority status, their option status."[24] Another reason cited for the slowdown was the addition of the new interleague trading period, from February 15 to March 15, when clubs have a better understanding about the availability of players during spring training. Among the headline-grabbing trades were the following: The Chicago White Sox sent relievers Rich Gossage (a right-hander and two-time All-Star) and southpaw Terry Forster to the Pittsburgh Pirates in exchange for outfielder Richie Zisk and right-handed pitcher Silvio Martinez; the Boston Red Sox shipped first baseman Cecil Cooper to the Milwaukee Brewers for their first baseman, All-Star George "Boomer" Scott, plus outfielder Bernie Carbo; and the Texas Rangers sent outfielder and former AL MVP Jeff Burroughs to the Atlanta Braves in return for a trio of hurlers (right-handers Carl Morton and Adrian Devine and left-hander Roger Moret), outfielders Ken Henderson and Dave May, and cash.

The "Washington Problem"

"We in professional baseball," stated Commissioner Kuhn unequivocally, "think having baseball in Washington is highly important to our interests and to the interests of the people in the Washington community."[25] It was unclear whether Kuhn's "community" referred to baseball fans in the nation's capital or to politicians. In any case, Kuhn and the baseball owners had been acutely feeling the pressure of the US House Select Committee on Professional Sports, which had repeatedly threatened to strip baseball of its antitrust status if an adequate solution to the future of baseball in D.C. was not reached.[26]

The "Washington problem" had its roots in 1971 when the Washington Senators relocated to Arlington, Texas, a suburb of Dallas-Fort Worth. As Leonard Koppett pointed out, Kuhn had made assurances since then that "baseball would make every effort to return to the nation's capital" even though the city had lost two teams in 11 years. (The original incarnation of the Senators had moved to Minnesota for the 1961 season.)[27] The situation seemed to be resolved in 1973 when Washington-based grocery-chain magnate Joseph Danzansky announced his plan to purchase the San Diego Padres for $13 million and promised to move the club to the capital; however, the deal fell through;

Ray Kroc acquired the Padres in 1974 and kept them in Southern California.

At the conclusion of the Winter Meetings, Kuhn announced what he described as a "coordinated resolution that reflected a positive attitude" with regard to baseball in Washington.[28] The NL decided to drop for one year its unanimous-consent provision regarding baseball in the capital, opting instead for a three-fourths vote. In addition, the NL agreed "in principle" to allow any of its 12 members teams to relocate to D.C., and to approve the application of any AL team to relocate to Washington and become a member of the NL.[29] Of course, the latter would create two 13-team leagues, thus raising the distinct probability of interleague play. And finally, Kuhn announced that the Baltimore Orioles would "try to shift" a "suitable" number of their games to RFK Stadium in Washington by 1978.[30] No one knew what a "suitable" number of games would be; however, many reports suggested it would be 13, representing one game against each of the AL teams. [A plan to play a portion of a team's home games in a different nearby city had clear precedence, as owners fully recognized. In 1956 and 1957, the Brooklyn Dodgers played 15 games in Jersey City; in 1968 and 1969, the Chicago Cubs played 20 games in Milwaukee's County Stadium, including one game against all 11 AL opponents in the latter season.]

Contrary to Kuhn's rosy picture of a united front, Orioles GM Hank Peters was livid. He claimed that his club had voted against the AL resolution supporting what the NL had passed, and did not advocate any plan calling for Orioles games to be played in D.C. "I felt that a vote for [the resolution] would have been an indication that the Orioles are all gung-ho for this plan, and that simply isn't the case," said Peters, who also claimed that he was blindsided by the NL's resolution and had no idea that the topic would be discussed.[31] In an effort to reassure the Orioles brass, AL President Lee MacPhail stated, "Our primary concern is the Baltimore franchise and the people of Baltimore," and added that a proposal two years earlier calling for the Orioles to shift 22 games to Washington had been dropped for lack of interest.[32] Sportswriter Jim Henneman suggested that the resolutions were just a "case of baseball buying another year's time with the impatient Congress."[33] [Henneman was correct: Baltimore never shifted any of its games to Washington in 1978, or in subsequent seasons.]

The Washington A's?

Kuhn's announcement of the Washington proposals renewed rumors that the Oakland A's might relocate. For several years, baseball had sought to solve the "Bay Area problem" of two financially distressed clubs, the San Francisco Giants and the A's. One component of the problem seemed to be solved in January of 1976 when real-estate magnate Bob Lurie bought the Giants from Horace Stoneham, who had required financial assistance from the NL to operate the club. However, given the poor attendance by both the Giants and the A's, most experts concluded that the Bay Area couldn't support two teams. [In 1976, the Giants finished last in NL attendance for the third consecutive season, averaging 7,739 per game; despite three World Series championships, the A's had drawn in excess of one million fans only twice since relocating from Kansas City to Oakland in 1968.] One anonymous AL owner said the A's move to Washington was probably impossible as long as Finley owned the club.[34] Two other compelling issues also complicated a shift of an AL team to Washington and the NL: two 13-team leagues would ensure interleague play, and the NL's position against the DH.

AL Realignment: A Possibility

Since expansion in 1969 and the subsequent reorganization of both the NL and AL into two six-team divisions, baseball had a tidy, balanced system. That equilibrium was upset with the addition of two more expansion teams, in Seattle and Toronto, set to begin play in the AL in 1977. Led by Phil Seghi, GM of the Indians, and Angels President Red Patterson, the AL began exploring realignment options. According to sportswriter Stan Isle, American League GMs, at a meeting in Palm Springs a month before the Winter Meetings, overwhelmingly approved a plan calling for a three-division format to begin in 1978.[35] Such a split would necessitate a multi-tiered playoff system involving a wild-card team (which the National Football League had implemented in 1970 after the NFL-AFL merger). The extra revenue from playoff games was especially attractive to owners, so much so that the NL also began to look at possibilities of realigning into three four-team divisions. Isle also reported that owners seemed "likely to approve" a realignment plan at the Winter Meetings;[36] however, the plan stalled. One reason for the proposal's failure was the AL's preference that both leagues realign in the same year to ensure uniformity of a prolonged playoff schedule. [Despite interest in realignment, it took another 17 years for it to become reality when the two leagues split into three divisions in 1994, one year after two expansion teams, the Florida Marlins and the Colorado Rockies, joined the NL.]

Postseason Games: An Earlier Start

Since the division format began in 1969, necessitating a league championship series, the baseball postseason had begun on Saturday to ensure maximum television viewership, widely thought to be greatest on the weekend. That timing was not an issue when the regular season ended on a Wednesday, but since 1973 the season had been ending on a Sunday, which meant that baseball was falling off the collective radar of sports fans across the country because of the six-day layoff. It also became a possibility that the World Series could be extended into late October. In order to remedy the problem, the AL proposed to start the best-of-five League Championship Series on Tuesday, with the World Series beginning the following Tuesday,[37] while the NL proposed a plan with Wednesday as the start date of each. Neither was perfect: The Tuesday start would run the risk of no weekend game for the LCS, and the Wednesday plan could potentially mean no Sunday World Series game in the event of a four-game sweep. However, both plans were subject to the approval of television networks. ABC, which had exclusive television rights for the World Series, subsequently adopted the AL's proposal, and the 1977 NLCS began on a Tuesday.

Rule Changes

John Johnson, a deputy to Commissioner Kuhn and chair of the Official Playing Rules Committee, was concerned about the rash of highly publicized early-season bench-clearing brawls, which he claimed resulted from brushback pitches after home runs. "Anybody who goes head-hunting is putting us all in danger," he said in May. "But the problem is in the rule."[38] He kept his promise to address the rule governing "dusters" at the Winter Meetings. The rules committee, which also included Fred Fleig, secretary-treasurer of the NL and supervisor of umpires, and Dick Butler, AL supervisor of umpires, revised rule 8.02(d) regarding intentionally hit batsmen. Unlike the previously rule, which required an umpire to warn each pitcher separately, thus giving one side the opportunity to retaliate, the new rule enabled the umpire to warn both managers and pitchers simultaneously and to eject the retaliating pitcher immediately.[39] The committee also approved three scoring changes, the most substantial of which required official scorers to make "decisions regarding judgment calls within 24 hours after a game."[40]

New Amendments

From a legislative standpoint, the Winter Meetings were lackluster. Five amendments to the Professional Baseball Agreement and Rules were passed. According to sportswriter Stan Isle, these included the requirement of each major-league team to support "through ownership or Player Development Contract" one minor-league team on the A, AA and AAA level.[41] The two expansion teams, Seattle and Toronto, were exempted until their third year of operation. Another amendment permitted a team to retain a player on its active roster until the newly promoted player reports; the old rule stipulated that the demoted player had to be cut immediately if the club was at its limit. Four amendments to the National Association Agreement were passed. Two amendments dealt with budgets and fees; the two others addressed player limits in Class A (an increase from 25 to 30 players; five of whom could be on inactive lists) and Class AA, increasing the active list from 22 to 23 for the last 20 days of the seasons.[42]

The DH: Another Rejection by the NL

Sportswriter Leonard Koppett opined that baseball paid a lot of lip service to "uniformity," but that was not motivation enough to settle the DH question, which had been simmering since the AL instituted the rule in 1973.[43] The DH study committee (comprising Red Patterson, president of the Angels; Bill DeWitt, president of the White Sox; Phil Seghi, GM of the Indians; Joe McDonald, GM of the Mets; Buzzie Bavasi, GM of the Padres; and Al Campanis, GM of the Dodgers) reported its findings.[44] Showing some signs of weakening its stance, the NL voted 8 to 4 against adopting the DH; Houston, Montreal, San Diego, and St. Louis voted in favor.[45] "We obviously don't like the present situation," said Kuhn, "but we will continue to have the designated hitter in the World Series in alternate years."[46] The 1976 World Series was the first time a DH was used in the fall classic, with Cincinnati's Dan Driessen becoming the first NL batter to serve as a DH.

The Minor Leagues

Bobby Bragan, concluding his first full year as president of the National Association, opined that the minor leagues were stable; he desired, however, a long-term plan to ensure the leagues' prosperity. "I don't ever expect to see a return to the 59 minor leagues we had in 1949," said Bragan. "The Triple-A and Double-A clubs now are more or less stabilized. But the Class-A leagues are flexible."[47] For the fifth straight season, attendance surpassed the 11 million mark; but there was also a decline of approximately 300,000 from 1975 to 1976. There were 19 leagues, including three in Mexico. Perhaps the biggest news in the minor leagues was the announcement that Roy Jackson, president of the Pacific Coast League, was voted president of the International League, becoming the first person ever to hold the top executive position in two Triple-A leagues concurrently.[48] Oscar Kahan reported that many baseball insiders expected Jackson to take over the president's position of the other Triple-A league, the American Association, the following year should his first year go as smoothly as expected.[49] The American Association made news, too, when the circuit, the last remaining holdout against the DH, voted to adopt the rule on a limited basis, namely when both managers agreed to use it.[50] In an issue that had been brought up frequently since the 1950s, the National Association submitted a proposal requesting that a study committee be formed to examine what it considered the "increasingly detrimental effect" of major-league television broadcasts on minor-league markets.[51]

Umpires: A Looming Battle with Owners

Represented by attorney John Cifelli, the Major League Umpires Association met with representatives from the AL and NL, including league presidents Lee MacPhail and Chub Feeney, to negotiate a new contract. "It is our aim," said Cifelli, "and it is long past due—to have the first $50,000-a-year umpire working the major leagues next season." Cifelli also promised to seek "a substantial increase in every economic involvement while maintaining all gains achieved previously."[52] Under the current contract, set to expire on December 31, 1976, umpire salaries ranged from $15,500 for rookies to $47,500 for the most experienced. In addition to the 30 percent increase in salaries, Cifelli proposed that baseball adopt a "gag rule" that would prohibit owners, managers, and players from criticizing umpires publicly. Unrelated to the umpires' contract, the major leagues increased their annual contribution to the Umpire Development Program to $288,000 (up from $264,000).[53]

Banquet of the National Association: The Entertainment Steals the Show

The awards banquet of the 75th Winter Meetings offered a first-class entertainment program that overshadowed the honorees. Vin Scully, broadcaster for the Los Angeles Dodgers, served as master of ceremonies for the event, which took place in the grand ballroom of the Hilton. Frank Sinatra sang, actor Cary Grant spoke briefly about his life in Hollywood, and comedian Don Rickles went through his typically edgy routine. But those three were upstaged, according to one report, by Monty Hall, host of the syndicated game show *Let's*

Make a Deal, who "stole the show" with his version of "The History of Baseball According to the Bible."[54] The big winner of the gala was Don "Bucky" Buchheister, GM of the Cedar Rapids Giants (San Francisco's affiliate in the Midwest League). He was honored as the Class A Executive of the Year, co-winner of the National Association Larry MacPhail Promotional Award (sharing it with Jim Paul, owner and GM of the El Paso Diablos in the Double-A Texas League), and Midwest League executive of the year.[55]

Publicity Men: Recognizing what Fans Want

Public-relations directors for all 26 baseball teams met for a three-day seminar, which one participant characterized as "one of the best sessions in years."[56] Jack Schwadel, longtime photo director of the Associated Press; Dick Enberg, radio-television voice of the California Angels; Ross Porter, member of the Dodgers broadcast team; and LA sportswriter Ross Newhan discussed ways to promote baseball more effectively through all aspects of the media. Additional guest speakers included Commissioner Kuhn and other team executives, who touched on everything from the role of the PR man in everything from free agency to player transactions, the need to promote star players, and scheduling of leaguewide promotions like the All-Star Game.

Conclusion: Few Solutions

"I've been sitting on committees all week and still don't know what's going on," said Minnesota Twins owner Clark Griffith at the conclusion of the 75th annual Winter Meetings. "The world thinks of us as one organization, but in reality we're two—the American and National Leagues—and one is trying to dump its problems on us."[57] After days of discussions, the AL and NL were no closer to solving their most pressing "common problems" (in the words of John McHale, president of the Expos).[58] Those problems included two financially troubled teams in the Bay Area and no definitive plan to bring baseball back to the nation's capital. Charlie Finley, never at a loss for words, described the situation in baseball as "chaos."[59] Perhaps the feisty owner was correct. When the meetings were over Commissioner Kuhn "hurriedly" traveled to Washington, D.C., to meet with members of the House Select Committee.[60] Days later, on December 15, Kuhn was due in federal court in Chicago, where Finley would open his $3.5 million lawsuit against baseball.

SOURCES

In addition to the sources listed in the Notes, the author also consulted Baseball-Reference.com and Retrosheet.org.

NOTES

1 Joseph Durso, "See How They Run," *New York Times*, December 5, 1976: 211.

2 Ibid.

3 Robert F. Burke, *Marvin Miller. A Baseball Revolutionary* (Urbana, Chicago, and Springfield, Illinois: University of Illinois, 2015), 183.

4 Burke, 184.

5 "Appeals Court Upholds Ruling on Free Agents," *Sarasota Herald-Tribune*, March 10, 1976: D1.

6 Red Smith, "Baseball Lockout Childish," *San Bernardino (California) County Sun*, February 26, 1976: D1.

7 Burke, 187.

8 Joseph Durso, "Kuhn Voids Player Sales; Finley Threatens to Sue," *New York Times*, June 19, 1976: 49.

9 Burke, 190.

10 Associated Press, "Finley Watches an Empire Crumble," *Rochester Democrat and Chronicle*, November 5, 1976: 1D.

11 Ralph Ray, "Ex-Agents to Tighten Races—Kapstein," *The Sporting News*, December 18, 1976: 39.

12 Ibid.

13 Durso, "See How They Run."

14 Stan Isle, "Free-Agent Signings Costly, Kuhn Warns Execs," *The Sporting News*, December 25, 1976: 25.

15 Ibid.

16 Kuhn quote in *Washington Post* from C.C. Johnson Spink, "We believe …" *The Sporting News*, December 25, 1976: 14.

17 Isle, "Free-Agent Signings Costly, Kuhn Warns Execs."

18 Ibid.

19 Dick Miller, "Kuhn Sidesteps Finley Offer to Fight," *The Sporting News*, December 25, 1976: 34.

20 Ibid.

21 Ibid.

22 Oscar Kahan, "New Rule Boosts Minors' Draft Picks to 16," *The Sporting News*, December 25, 1976: 36.

23 Stan Isle, "Free-Agent Derby Slows Down Trades," *The Sporting News*, December 25, 1976: 38.

24 Joseph Durso, "Baseball Meetings End, Problems Don't," *New York Times*, December 12, 1976: S1.

25 Stan Isle, "Majors Promise Baseball to Capital in '78," *The Sporting News*, December 25, 1976: 33.

26 Ibid.

27 Leonard Koppett, "Baseball Giving Oriole-Games-in-Washington Plan Another Time at Bat," *New York Times*, December 10, 1976: 51.

28 Isle, "Majors Promise Baseball to Capital in '78."

29 Ibid.

30 Koppett, "Baseball Giving Oriole-Games-in-Washington Plan Another Time at Bat."

31 Jim Henneman, "Orioles Shouted 'Nay' on Shift Resolution," *The Sporting News*, December 25, 1976: 33.

32 Ibid.

33 Ibid.

34 Durso, "Baseball Meetings End, Problems Don't."

35 Stan Isle, "A.L. Seen Ready to Okay 3-Divison Format," *The Sporting News*, December 11, 1976: 37.

36 Ibid.

37 Leonard Koppett, "Tight Postseason Slate Is Proposed," *New York Times*, December 11, 1976: 37.

38 Joseph Durso, "Aftermath of Beanball Controversy," *Wilmington (North Carolina) Star*, May 10, 1976: 1-B.

39 Stan Isle, "Umps Given Muscle to Curb Dusters," *The Sporting News*, December 25, 1976: 34.

40 Ibid.

41 Stan Isle, "Nine Amendments Pass Voter Muster," *The Sporting News*, December 25, 1976: 38.

42 Ibid.

43 Koppett, "Tight Postseason Slate Is Proposed."

44 Isle, "Majors Promise Baseball to Capital in '78."

45 Koppett, "Tight Postseason Slate Is Proposed."

46 Stan Isle, "Majors Promise Baseball to Capital in '78."

47 Oscar Kahan, "Bragan Calls for Long-Term Program for Minors," *The Sporting News*, December 25, 1976: 39.

48 Oscar Kahan, "PCL Boss Jackson Takes on Int Prexy's Post," *The Sporting News*, December 25, 1976: 39.

49 Ibid.

50 "Association Will Use Limited DH," *The Sporting News*, December 25, 1976: 38.

51 "Group Sought to Study Major TV Into Minors," *The Sporting News*, December 11, 1976: 37.

52 Stan Isle, "Umpires Seeking to Shatter $50,000 Barrier," *The Sporting News*, December 18, 1976: 39.

53 Stan Isle, "Majors Promise Baseball to Capital in '78."

54 "Buchheister Carts Away Lots of Hardware at Banquet," *The Sporting News*, December 25, 1976: 36.

55 Ibid.

56 Stan Isle, "Publicity Men Swap Ideas in Three-Day Seminar," *The Sporting News*, December 25, 36.

57 Joseph Durso, "Baseball Meetings End, Problems Don't."

58 Ibid.

59 Ibid.

60 Stan Isle, "Majors Promise Baseball to Capital in '78."

1977
SO MUCH PROMISE, BUT WAIT TILL NEXT YEAR

By Steve Cardullo

THE 1977 MAJOR-LEAGUE BASEBALL season witnessed two new teams—the Seattle Mariners and Toronto Blue Jays—join the American League. George Foster hit 52 home runs for Cincinnati. The Twins' Rod Carew flirted with hitting .400 and Yankees outfielder Reggie Jackson's bat returned the World Series championship to New York City. The 1977 Winter meetings in Honolulu also held some drama and entertainment. Business discussions included talk of the more affluent teams gaining strength under the current free-agent rules, reinstatement by Commissioner Bowie Kuhn of a suspended owner, possible approval of the relocation or sale of one of the two teams in the San Francisco Bay area, and the rejection of the sale of an East Coast team. The Mexican League's longtime association with the majors ended. Owners also held their annual discussion about baseball returning the Washington area. Awards were presented, and a few free agents looking for a new team wandered the halls, along with others seeking any kind of employment with baseball.

The 76th Winter Meetings were held at the Sheraton-Waikiki Hotel from December 4 through 8. Commissioner Kuhn, in his opening address to an audience of 500, lamented the Collective Bargaining Agreement with the players union. Free agency was still new, and Kuhn cited statistics showing that the more affluent clubs were signing most of the free agents.[1] The concern was that eventually the better ballplayers would gravitate to the bigger and more affluent markets, while the smaller-market teams would become far less competitive. Kuhn was also concerned that salaries would challenge revenues.

Kuhn did praise the re-entry draft, saying most players remained in the league "where they had their greatest experience and I think that is a perfectly healthy situation."[2] Players' salaries, however, had risen 60 percent in two years. "That … is a very large gain in a short period of time and there is no way I or anybody else can stand here and say it is not a source of some concern," the commissioner said.[3] He said that the players' salaries plus pension benefits in 1977 represented 26.3 percent of liabilities. This was an 8.1 percent increase since 1950. Looking at the brighter side, he said baseball at all levels—major league, minors, and amateur—had made enormous gains, citing major-league attendance of 38,709,781, a 24 percent increase over the previous year. The Dodgers led all 26 teams, putting 2,955,000 fans through their turnstiles. Minor-league attendance increased 13 percent, to 1.6 million. The 1977 World Series had the highest viewership in the history of televised baseball in four of the six games. Viewership of the League Championship Series increased by 14 percent over the previous year. Citing the Harris Poll, Kuhn declared that baseball had regained its prominence as America's favorite sport. In closing, he cautioned that "[t]here are problems, and we must face up to those problems."[4] When the owners left Honolulu many of these issues remained unresolved, and team ownership was one of them.

A group led by Haywood Sullivan and Edward "Buddy" LeRoux were attempting to purchase the Boston Red Sox. Sullivan, a former catcher with the Sox and A's, was a front-office executive who began working in the Boston front office in 1965, while LeRoux was a former trainer with the team. American

League owners, however, questioned the viability of the group's financial backing.

American League owners did approve the financial reorganization of the Cleveland Indians,[5] led by Cleveland Browns owner and Indians investor Art Modell. The primary stakeholder, millionaire F.J. O'Neill, had to sell his shares in the New York Yankees before he could take on his duties with Cleveland.

The San Francisco/Oakland area market was burdened by low attendance, and many thought that two franchises could not survive there. However, the matter was not discussed at the meetings; any substantive talks would require the presence of Oakland Athletics owner Charlie Finley, and he was not present in the conference room at the time. Finley had recently been in negotiations with several parties who expressed some interest in purchasing the A's, most notably Colorado oil baron Marvin Davis, who would seek to move the club to Denver. Finley actually did sell the club to Davis days after leaving Oahu,[6] but the transaction was nullified by the commissioner as not being in the best interests of baseball. Kuhn did mention that in retrospect it was a mistake to place two teams in the same small market.[7]

The sale

The issue of moving a franchise to Washington was another agenda item. Kuhn had met with several members of Congress in November to discuss specifics.[8] Washington had been without a team since the Senators moved to the Dallas-Fort Worth area after the 1971 season. Back at home after the meetings, Kuhn said that among the difficulties to be ironed out were "the availability of a club, obtaining proper financing and the settling of territorial rights with the Orioles."[9]

Discussing the issue of player bonus incentives, Kuhn said there was "considerable feeling for more flexibility" in the rules.[10] Bonus incentives allowed a team to insert bonus clauses in contracts based on such things as attendance, innings pitched, or games played.[11]

The owners amended the rule dealing with World Series player shares. A player traded from one World Series team to another World Series team would receive a full share with each team paying an amount based on the time he had spent with the team. No player would receive more than a full share.[12]

Commissioner Kuhn announced he had lifted the suspension imposed on Atlanta Braves owner Ted Turner for player tampering ahead of its scheduled expiration on March 23, 1978. Turner had requested an early end to the suspension because the club "needed his abilities,"[13] and the commissioner acquiesced.

Expanding the Championship Series from the best of five games to best of seven was discussed, but support was weak, and the issue was tabled. Kuhn asserted that support for additional games was growing, and predicted that the subject would come up again.[14]

Pay television was also on the agenda, with three teams, the Phillies, Yankees, and Braves, having already entered the new market. Citing a study commissioned by major-league baseball, Kuhn expressed a belief that there was a new national market for major-league baseball.[15]

Kuhn announced that John Gaherin, the owners' negotiator with the players union, would be retiring early and a replacement would be needed. No action was taken.

The owners did come to some agreements. Twins owner Calvin Griffith was re-elected AL vice president. (AL President Lee MacPhail's term would not expire for another year.) NL President Charles "Chub" Feeney's tenure was extended for four years, through 1981. Feeney had originally only received a two-year extension at the 1976 winter meetings because of some owner dissatisfaction, spearheaded by the St. Louis Cardinals' August Busch. These unhappy owners felt that Feeney was in over his head when it came to negotiating with the Players Association. They also expressed dissatisfaction with the way he was handling the Giants franchise problems.[16] In an about-face in 1977, however, Busch praised Feeney, stating he was "doing a terrific job."[17]

Led by their president, Antonio Ramirez Muro, a delegation from the Mexican League announced that they would leave the National Association of Professional Baseball Leagues (the minor-league organization) in 1979. Kuhn had acquired Ramirez's promise not to drop out the previous year, but Mexican

> ### Baseball Dips Feet in TV Production Water
>
> *This Week in Baseball* marked the earliest foray into television production for major-league baseball. Reportedly, Ernie Banks attended the convention for the National Association of Television Program Executives and marketed *This Week in Baseball* wherever he could—including the hotel pool. The program represented a partnership between the commissioner's office, the owners, several production companies, a distributor, and an advertising agency, with the commissioner's office owning half the stock.* Joe Podesta, president of the Major League Baseball Promotion Corporation, said, "This year we will lose quite a bit of money on it. But the show is designed to put people in the stands. We feel if we can show on a weekly basis all the excitement of baseball, we can get people out to the ballpark."**
>
> One of the key technology aspects that made the show possible was placing a video cassette recorder in each ballpark.
>
> ---
>
> * Dan Lewis, "Baseball Plans Own Weekly TV Show," *Muncie* (Indiana) *Evening Press*, March 7, 1977: 12.
> ** Howard Smith, "'This Week in Baseball' Now Becomes Available," *Mitchell* (South Dakota) *Daily Republic*, June 23, 1977: 18.

League interests would not go beyond the one-year agreement. The Mexicans felt that their league was as competitive as major-league baseball, while the major leagues rated them as no higher than Triple A. This issue, festering for years, could not be overcome in discussions. Ramirez cited a pride factor. He also asserted that there were "some problems in our country about our laws that conflict with baseball and labor laws in the United States."[18] In talks later in December, Kuhn tried unsuccessfully to persuade the Mexican League to remain in the National Association. The greatest worry for Organized Baseball was the loss in attendance, with the Mexican League accounting for almost one-quarter of total minor-league attendance. Of the total minor-league attendance of 13 million in 1977, the Mexican League accounted for more than 4 million.[19] Other news from south of the border making the rounds at the meetings dealt with a report that National League President Feeney would meet with a group of Cuban baseball officials in Mexico to negotiate a visit of a major-league all-star team to the island.[20]

The Playing Rules Committee issued a directive to all umpires in Organized Baseball that strict enforcement to end phantom double plays would be "the goal in the 1978 season."[21] The committee believed that strict enforcement would eliminate many injuries. The committee also made four language changes to the scoring rules dealing with how earned runs would be charged to pitchers, including a footnote to clarify how earned runs should be charged to relief pitchers.

On the topic of "head-hunting" and brushback pitches, the committee gave umpires more control in situations involving teams that have a combative history against one another. It added language to the rule on intentional pitches at the batter giving the umpires broader interpretation powers and allowing for warning and ejection before a situation got out of hand. The rationale for the change was the owners' concern that in this era of free agency and rising salaries, the loss of injured players was costly.

There were further discussions on the use of aluminum bats and a new Japanese shoe with golf-type spikes, but no action was taken.[22] The teams' public-relations directors patted themselves on the back for their successes in promoting Organized Baseball, but also highlighted the fact that improvement was still needed, especially in coordinating relations between the media and the players, and the players and the fans.[23] Kuhn praised the PR directors, giving them some credit for the increases in attendance in the 1977 season. Competition against other sports for the entertainment dollar was also discussed, and Kuhn suggested that the public-relations directors monitor fan attitudes and then make the changes that best reflect the fans' feelings. Discussions resulted in authorization of "a program to develop statistical uniformity throughout the major leagues."[24] Bob Wirz, the major leagues' director of information, was to spearhead the effort. Joe Reichler, a special assistant to the commissioner, pledged his support as chairman of the Official Baseball Records Committee.

Baseball memorabilia, soon to bring in added millions to each club, was also on the agenda, with the discussion centering on how to distinguish hobbyist collectors from those looking to make a profit.[25]

The Awards Banquet drew a packed house of 1,700. Two future Hall of Famers, Rod Carew and Lou Brock, received awards for winning the batting crown and setting the major-league record for career stolen bases, respectively. Carew hit .388 to win the American League batting title and also received the league's Most Valuable Player Award. Brock's 35 steals in '77 made him the career leader in stolen bases, with 900 at the end of the season, surpassing Ty Cobb's 897. (Brock finished his career with 938 steals.) Outfielder Ken Landreaux, a California Angels farmhand, was recognized as the Minor League Player of the Year. Between El Paso and Salt Lake City, he batted .357 with 27 home runs.

Each year the National Association recognizes a longtime employee who has shown his dedication and service to the game with its "King of Baseball" award. The honor for 1977 was presented to Bill Weiss, statistician for the Pacific Coast, California, Northwest, Pioneer, and Lone Star Leagues. The Sporting News awards for minor league Executives of the Year went to George Sisler Jr. at Columbus of the Triple-A International League, Jim Paul of El Paso in the Double-A Texas League, and Harry Pells of the Quad City club in the Class-A Midwest League. Stan Isle, associate editor of *The Sporting News*, presented each with a Bulova Accuquartz watch. The President's Award went to Fresno (Class-A California League) for its long-term stability as a franchise and association with the San Francisco Giants for 20 years.

Special awards were also presented to Visalia, California, which owned the city's team in the California League, and Franklin County, Ohio, which owned the Columbus Clippers of the International League. Mary Anne Whitacre, executive secretary of the Hawaii Islanders (Pacific Coast League), was honored by the Rawlings Sporting Goods Co. as baseball's Woman of the Year. George Sisler Jr., general manager of the Columbus Clippers, received the Larry MacPhail Promotion Trophy for outstanding marketing.[26]

Topps presented the award for Outstanding Organization of the year to the Montreal Expos. The award honors accomplishments in a major-league club's farm system.

The owners decided to continue to produce the syndicated TV program *This Week in Baseball*, which premiered in 1977. PR directors voted to hold their spring meetings on March 7, 1978, in Florida and March 14 in Arizona.

The National Association proposed 12 amendments to its agreement with the major leagues, and six of them were adopted.[27] The most important concerned player limits in rookie leagues, increases in National Association fees, payments of incentive bonuses by the parent clubs, and guarantee deposits by Triple-A clubs. The agreement was extended for five years.

The Double-A Eastern League lost two teams and had to play as a six-team league. The Reds announced that they were leaving Quebec City, and the Expos abandoned Three Rivers. Both were moving to the Southern League, with Cincinnati going into Nashville and Montreal to Memphis. The league appealed the shifts, but Commissioner Kuhn eventually ruled that his office would not intervene. Kuhn did, however, strongly suggest that the expansion Seattle clubs, when they fielded Double-A teams in 1980, consider returning baseball to Three Rivers and Quebec City. He also made it plain to the Southern League and Texas League that raiding teams to stock Southern leagues would violate the spirit of the National Agreement set to begin in 1979.[28]

A plan to consolidate the offices of the International League, American Association, and Pacific Coast League into one location and under one CEO failed when the International League failed to muster a majority for the plan. It was thought that consolidation would pass with little or no opposition, but as it turned out, the PCL also had reservations and would have voted to oppose if it was brought to a vote. The plan was opposed by the majors.[29]

Harold Cooper was elected president of the International League. To replace Toronto and Seattle, which expanded into Triple-A cities, Portland and Vancouver each was awarded a team. Portland, however, was a problematic choice. The city was a longtime member of the PCL until the league moved the team to Spokane after the 1972 season. A club the Class-A Northwest League had been moved to Portland, and Bing Russell, owner of the team, wanted $206,000 to give up his territorial rights. No settlement was reached at the meetings, so the question was sent to arbitration.[30]

The arbitration board was made up of two members each from the PCL and NWL, plus a neutral member appointed by the National Association. The board ruled in favor of Russell, awarding him the full $206,000. Several groups expressed interest in owning the Portland club. The Vancouver franchise was awarded to Harry Ornest, a former minor-league baseball player and owner of teams in the NHL and the Canadian Football League.[31]

The American Association had two franchise issues needing to be resolved. The situation in Oklahoma City was settled by an announcement that a local buyer was in the process of purchasing the team and keeping it in town. Less pressing was the announcement that the New Orleans club would be moving to Springfield, Illinois, though the abandoned territory would remain with the league in case a major-league team was ever placed there. New Orleans club owner A. Ray Smith, along with the American Association, would be entitled to compensation if that happened.[32]

Trades are always a major aspect of the Winter Meetings. The 1977 gathering played host to a whopper. Atlanta, Texas, the New York Mets, and Pittsburgh combined to swap 11 players, the biggest player-trade since the Angels and Dodgers pulled off a seven-player deal at the meetings in 1972. Bert Blyleven, Jon Matlack, John Milner, and Willie Montanez were the gems of the deal. Meanwhile, Commissioner Kuhn announced that he would hold a hearing to discuss the deal between the Athletics and Reds, in which Oakland sent left-hander Vida Blue to Cincinnati for their top prospect, first baseman Dave Revering, plus $1 million in cash. Kuhn eventually declined to approve the trade because of the cash amount involved.[33]

Quite a few other well-known players changed teams. Outfielder Bobby Bonds, right-handed pitcher Richard Dotson, and outfielder Thad Bosley went from the Angels to the White Sox in exchange for catcher Brian Downing and right-handed pitchers Chris Knapp and Dave Frost. St. Louis traded colorful left-handed reliever Al Hrabosky to Kansas City for catcher Buck Martinez and right-hander Mark Littell, then sent Martinez to Milwaukee for right-hander George Frazier. Seattle traded outfielder Dave Collins to Cincinnati southpaw Shane Rawley. The Orioles traded pitchers Rudy May, Randy Miller, and Bryn Smith to the Expos for pitchers Don Stanhouse and Joe Kerrigan and outfielder Gary Roenicke. Only the Dodgers and Padres failed to make a deal, as the meeting produced 22 different transactions involving 53 players, the most since 1975, when 64 players changed uniforms in 23 transactions.[34]

One significant swap did not occur. San Diego had come to the meetings looking to trade outfielder Dave Winfield. Two serious negotiations took place, with the Dodgers and the Yankees, but neither was brought to fruition. The Padres rejected what Los Angeles offered, while the Yankees were unwilling to give up third baseman Graig Nettles for the future Hall of Famer, who had let it be known through his agent that he was willing to transfer to the infield.[35] Yankees manager Billy Martin reasoned that if he was deprived of Nettles' services then he couldn't repeat as World Series champion, and if he didn't win then he would lose his job.[36] Winfield, considered to be the holy grail of the trading period and anticipating a swap, had brought his mother to Hawaii to witness the events.

Baltimore manager Earl Weaver walked out for 24 hours after protesting that the Orioles were trading players without his approval or input. The story was that Weaver was taken to a cocktail party and made "unavailable" during the negotiations. When he was tracked down later by sportswriters, the deals had already been finalized, which set off Weaver's famous temper. He returned to the team the next day.[37]

Nothing brings more intrigue than the annual re-entry draft. Seven teams spent $200,000 on eight minor league players. The Cardinals lost three players. "We're either awfully well off or awfully dumb," commented St. Louis general manager Bing Devine.[38] Devine was referring to the wealth of talent in the Cardinals system and how others coveted their players.

Two noteworthy picks that year were first baseman Willie Upshaw, who went to the Toronto Blue Jays with the first pick; and catcher Ned Yost, selected by the Milwaukee Brewers. Both went on to have lengthy major-league careers, and Yost managed the 2015 World Series champion Kansas City Royals. In the Triple-A and Double-A draft, 16 players were plucked. *The Sporting News* speculated that the minor-league draft was full of players whose clubs had lost confidence in them, and that picking one in the draft was perhaps a small wager that some of them would, indeed, work out.[39]

A few side notes

Ralph Houk, former Yankees manager, nearly came to blows with current manager Billy Martin. According to those present at a managers' party hosted by Reds skipper Sparky Anderson, Martin was harassing Houk until the later informed Martin that he was not "screwing with Tom Thumb now!"[40] Martin got the message and quit.

Future Hall of Fame inductee Tony LaRussa was named the new manager of Knoxville in the Southern League.

Dave Dombrowski, a future general manager and major-league club president, got his first baseball employment, with the Chicago White Sox. Dombrowski in two years would be the head of all minor-league scouts in the White Sox system.[41]

NOTES

1. Stan Isle, "Kuhn 'Concerned' as Rich Get Richer in Free-Agent Market," *The Sporting News*, December 24, 1977: 47.
2. Ibid.
3. Ibid.
4. Ibid.
5. Stan Isle, "Owners Shelve Sticky Issues, Bask in Sun," *The Sporting News*, December 24, 1977: 43.
6. Dave Condon, "Finley Agrees to Sell A's," *Chicago Tribune*, December 15, 1977: Section 4, 1 and 3.
7. "Owners Shelve Sticky Issues."
8. Ibid.
9. "Finley Agrees to Sell A's."
10. Ibid.
11. "Owners Shelve Sticky Issues, Bask in Sun."
12. Ibid.
13. "Finley Agrees to Sell A's."
14. "Owners Shelve Sticky Issues, Bask in Sun."
15. Ibid.
16. "Feeney Re-Elected, Will Move Office," *The Sporting News*, December 25, 1976: 34.
17. "Owners Shelve Sticky Issues, Bask in Sun."
18. Oscar Kahan, "Mexican Loop Planning O.B. Divorce," *The Sporting News*, December 24, 1977: 44.
19. Ibid.
20. Ibid.
21. Stan Isle, "Rules Group Puts Umps on Notice—Halt Grid Tactics, End Phantom DP," *The Sporting News*, December 24, 1977: 44.
22. "Rules Group Puts Umps on Notice."
23. Stan Isle, "Public Relations Directors to Step Up Efforts," *The Sporting News*, December 24, 1977: 44.
24. Ibid.
25. Ibid.
26. Chris Mehring, "Timber Rattlers Are Midwest League Nominee for the Larry MacPhail Award," *timberrattlers.com*, December 12, 2016.
27. Stan Isle, "14 Amendments Adopted—Roster Hikes Rejected," *The Sporting News*, December 24, 1977: 45.
28. Oscar Kahan, "Eastern Loses Fight for Two Clubs," *The Sporting News*, December 24, 1977: 45. The Eastern League did pick up two new clubs in 1980, but they were not in Quebec City or Three Rivers, they were in Lynn, Massachusetts, and Glens Falls, New York. Neither Quebec City nor Three Rivers has returned to the National Association.
29. Oscar Kahan, "Majors Spike Triple-A Merger Plan," *The Sporting News*, December 24, 1977: 46.
30. Oscar Kahan, "Russell Demands $206,000 for Loss of Portland to PCL," *The Sporting News*, December 24, 1977: 46.
31. Larry Stone, "Meet the Nuttiest Baseball Team the Northwest Has Ever Seen," *Seattle Times*, July 26, 2014: old.seattletimes.com.
32. "Majors Spike Triple-A Merger Plan."
33. In March, Kuhn approved a deal in which Blue was sent to the Giants in exchange for seven players plus $300,000. baseball-reference.com/players/b/bluevi01.shtml, accessed June 13, 2016.
34. Stan Isle, "11-Player Deal Caps a Swapping Spree," *The Sporting News*, December 24, 1977: 43.
35. Phil Collier, "Padres Fail in Bid to Deal Winfield for Hill Help," *The Sporting News*, December 24, 1977: 55.
36. Ibid.
37. Jim Henneman, "Orioles Blow Logjam and Weaver Blows Top," *The Sporting News*, December 24, 1977: 55.
38. Stan Isle, "Cards Lose Three in Major Draft," *The Sporting News*, December 24, 1977: 48.
39. Oscar Kahan, "16 Players Bring $136,000 in Minors' Draft," *The Sporting News*, December 24, 1977: 48.
40. Dick Young, "Young Ideas/Houk, Martin Near Blows," *The Sporting News*," December 24, 1977: 17.
41. John Feinstein, *Play Ball: The Life and Troubled Time of Major League Baseball* (New York: Villard Books, 1993), 22.

— 1978 —
FIGURING OUT FREE AGENCY

By Dan Levitt

BY THE FALL OF 1978 MODERN FREE agency was entering its third year, and teams were beginning to come to terms with both its existence and its potential, though ownership still hoped to roll it back dramatically. Front offices were figuring out the mechanics of pursuing free agents, how to fit them into their payroll structure, and how to weigh their impact on the future demands of existing players. Yet most teams still had not fully grasped how to manage and build their rosters in this new era in which players were free to leave after six years or at the end of their existing contracts. As baseball's general managers and their owners struggled to make sense of the new player procurement regime, significant trades, often a staple of the winter meetings, were few and far between. Moreover, with both the collective-bargaining agreement and the national television contract not expiring until after the 1979 season, the 1978 winter meetings were relatively quiet on the player-relations and business fronts as well.

Commissioner Bowie Kuhn echoed the sentiments of his owners and focused his opening remarks at these Orlando-based meetings on the dangers of the existing free-agent system to both the financial health of the industry and its competitive balance. "The unfortunate fact," according to Kuhn, "is that these signings fulfill the forecast by many of us that there would be a tendency for the best teams to get the best players. There is also a clear tendency for some of the star players to seek only contending teams. Five clubs have signed 53 percent of the free agents (those who were in the major leagues the previous year and were drafted by at least two clubs). All seven signees this autumn who were drafted by two or more clubs have gone with repeater clubs."[1]

Regarding the overall increase in payroll, Kuhn complained: "Before the reentry draft the approximate average player compensation was $50,000. Today it is approximately $100,000. Some leveling off is vital." As a solution, Kuhn felt, additional compensation to the team losing a free agent from the signing team was necessary. "Amateur draft choices provided under the collective-bargaining agreement as compensation are simply not adequate," he lectured.

Kuhn, however, understood the difficulty of radically changing the new system. "(MLBPA head Marvin Miller) said that it would be suicidal for the owners to start a confrontation on the compensation issue," he said. "That attitude certainly doesn't give much promise of good-faith bargaining on the compensation issue."

Nevertheless, Kuhn also toasted the health of his industry under his leadership. Baseball in 1978 had set another attendance record, breaking the 40 million mark by drawing 40.6 million fans, an increase of 1.9 million over 1977, itself a record year. "A Lou Harris poll shows sports popularity is unmistakably in baseball's favor," Kuhn said. "Today whenever we can get a reading on 1979 season-ticket sales, the readings indicate record levels. Measurements indicate over 70 percent of Americans are sports fans. That means nearly 160 million in the United States alone will be coming our way."

Miller contested Kuhn's economic assertions. In his own news conference (separate from the winter meetings), he produced seven charts to rebut the commissioner. Most pointedly, Miller stressed that in 1978 baseball revenue totaled $278.7 million and the players' portion of that revenue came to only $76.8 million, or 27.6 percent. "What happened to the other $200 million?" Miller challenged.[2]

Business and Administrative

With both the network TV contract and the collective-bargaining agreement with the players set to expire after the 1979 season, the owners had begun considering options to increase revenues and interest. Accordingly, earlier in the year they had created a committee to explore realignment, with an understanding that the emphasis would be on divisional realignment (not interleague play) as a way to promote additional pennant-race excitement and playoff games. Further driving this initiative was the hiring of Tom Villante by the commissioner's office as the executive director of marketing and broadcasting. The man responsible for the phrase "Baseball Fever—Catch It," would now be in charge of increasing broadcast and other revenue sources.[3] The commissioner believed realignment represented "the most significant subject to hit the major league agenda in years."[4] And he expanded: "The main motivation for the change is this: What are you going to do with September? Your hardest selling job in baseball is September, when many teams fall from contention."[5]

At the winter meetings the realignment committee, led by former general managers Joe L. Brown and Frank Cashen, presented their proposal, which entailed expanding from two divisions to three in each league and adding a wild card, increasing the league playoffs from one round to two. After lengthy discussions, seven clubs remained opposed to the scheme, which required unanimous approval. Five were in the National League, including powerful owner Peter O'Malley of the Dodgers. Kuhn put a brave face on the outcome, which unofficially called for more study, but the plan was clearly shelved for the foreseeable future.[6]

The owners also discussed the fallout and potential subsequent actions from the loss to Melissa Ludtke in court. A female sportswriter for *Sports Illustrated*, Ludtke had been barred from the New York Yankees locker room during the 1977 World Series because of her gender. Ludtke sued baseball for the right to equal access and won her case at the federal district court level in September 1978. Baseball's executive council directed the league presidents to poll their respective clubs to learn what stance each individual franchise would adopt if "left to its own devices in this matter."[7] In the end the clubs chose not to push an appeal or further pursue the matter.

Under the National Association agenda, the major-league owners adopted several amendments put forward by the minor leagues, including an increase in the minimum monthly salary in Triple A and Double A to $600 per month, an increase in the maximum monthly salary in the other classifications to $600 per month, and an increase in minor-league meal money. In other business, the owners passed a resolution that no club could opt out of participating in the Major League Promotional Corporation, the arm responsible for coordinating television production, licensing, publishing, and promotional opportunities.[8] In a couple of additional actions, the National Association agreed to bump up the meal money for minor leaguers, and the Major League Executive Committee voted to increase its appropriation for amateur baseball to $402,500.[9]

In the wake of the brief umpire walkout in August, major-league umpires Harry Wendelstedt and Bill Kinnamon met with the major leagues' executive committee on umpires to make the case for better pay and opportunities for minor-league umpires. Wendelstedt, who ran an umpiring school, explained, "It takes five years to develop an umpire, and we are losing many of our finest because they cannot afford to support themselves and their families on what they earn in the minors."[10] Separately, the owners decided that umpiring should be standardized between the two leagues by 1980: The umpires would use the same chest protectors, wear the same uniforms, and officiate from the same places on the field.[11]

At their confab during the winter meetings, the baseball writers responded to a backlash over the Hall of Fame ballot. Historically, a BBWAA screening committee established which newly eligible players would be added to the ballot. Recently, however, there had been criticism when 209-game winner Milt Pappas and slugger Frank Howard and his 384 home runs were left off—a situation that was exacerbated when screening committee member Charlie Feeney said, "(Our) purpose is to keep the Humpy Dumpties off the ballot, and, when compared to real Hall of Famers, guys like Pappas are Humpty Dumpties."¹² In response, the writers voted to abolish the screening committee and put everyone who had played the requisite 10 years on the ballot. For the forthcoming election, that meant 22 additional players would be included. To keep the ballot manageable, however, the writers also ruled that any player who did not receive at least 10 percent of the vote would be permanently removed.¹³

The baseball writers also debated a proposal to add a "team error" to the scoring rules. Its proponents felt the team-error concept would better address situations in which an error should clearly be charged to the fielding team even though it was difficult to single out one particular defender, such as when several fielders circle a popup and let it drop between them, or when a strong, accurate throw by an outfielder hits a baserunner, leading to extra bases. In the end, the writers voted to table the proposal, effectively killing it.¹⁴

Baseball's rules committee tampered with the rain-shortened game rules to address game-changing scores during the visitors' half-inning. In those games in which the visiting team tied the game or took the lead during the top half of the inning and the game was subsequently halted before the home team took the lead or tied the game, the game would now become a suspended game instead of being ended based on the score at end of the previous inning. Such a rule change, however, required the approval of the players union, which was not forthcoming (they neither objected nor approved), so this rule would not take effect until 1980.¹⁵ Other changes to the rulebook included the introduction of the Game Winning RBI—defined as the RBI that gives a team a lead that it never relinquishes—as an official statistic, and the inclusion of statistics from "game 163," used to break divisional ties, in the regular-season statistics.¹⁶

The National Association named a new president, Johnny Johnson, a longtime baseball executive who started as a secretary to Yankees GM George Weiss in 1947 and worked for a time in the commissioner's office. At their annual banquet on December 5, an overflow crowd of 1,400 paid tribute to outgoing President Bobby Bragan. At the event *The Sporting News* presented its Minor League Executive of the Year awards: Willie Sanchez for Triple A, Larry Schmittou for Double A, and Dave Hersh for Single A.¹⁷

On the ownership front, the National League approved the sale of 50 percent of the Houston Astros from GE Credit to Ford Motor Credit, giving Ford Motor Credit full ownership of the team. The two financial institutions had jointly taken possession of the franchise from owner Judge Roy Hofheinz in 1976 as part of a restructuring to help keep Hofheinz out of bankruptcy.¹⁸

Two other franchises reportedly on the block saw little negotiating movement during the winter meetings. Oilman Marvin Davis had been working to buy the A's and move them to Denver, but several issues, most notably the nine years remaining on the Oakland Coliseum lease, lingered as sticking points. A prospective deal with a local purchaser—furniture magnate Sam Bercovich and his son Ed and backed by Oakland Raiders owner Al Davis (no relation)—sputtered over their demand for lease concessions from the Coliseum and an unwillingness (or inability) to prove their financial wherewithal.¹⁹ In Baltimore, owner Jerry Hoffberger had been looking to sell for several years, reportedly at a price of at least $12 million. In early December he was in negotiations with former US Treasury Secretary William Simon, talks that eventually fell through.²⁰

Player Movement Overview

In 1978 owners and general managers were just beginning to adjust to the impact of free agency on the trading market. At the winter meeting meetings only 13 teams consummated trades involving only 31 players—the fewest in at least the last seven years and including no blockbusters.²¹

Year	No. Transactions	Players Involved
1972	19	68
1973	26	58
1974	15	40
1975	23	64
1976	14	39
1977	22	53

"Your key players," summarized Milwaukee general manager Harry Dalton, "are now under long-term contracts and can't be traded easily. Your younger players are not so well-known to other teams, and they're now more important to you, anyway, because they can't leave yet. And your stars who are available in trades are getting paid so much that you can't move them so freely. For all these reasons, the talent is finally getting locked in. Also more players are entering the auction market, so the clubs are put into a position of reacting. They either look for talent in the free-agent market, or they don't get much. You do it, or you die. The old-fashioned system of simply trading players is being crowded out."[22]

Mets manager Joe Torre added, "You're no longer going to take two players of equal ability and make a trade. Not if one of them has four years left on his contract and the other has only one year."[23] His general manager, Joe McDonald, agreed: "In this day and age of the agent, you don't just talk to the player. You find out his seniority status, veto rights, his 5-and-10 situation, whether he's got a no-trade clause, and his salary. I was talking to one general manager about a possible trade, and it suddenly got so complex that he suddenly just started waving his arms in the air."[24]

Indians President Gabe Paul discussed the new environment: "Once all you had to be concerned with were ability and longevity. Now you have to worry about length of contract, special covenants. We used to have one-page contracts, now they're seven or eight."[25] Overall, Paul summarized, "You used to be able to horse-trade. You'd have a roster of 25 players, and all 25 were available to be traded.... Today? Maybe you could trade half the 25 on your roster. The rest are frozen by legal restrictions, veto rights, no-trade clauses or just high salaries that few teams can handle."[26]

The general managers did not get much relief to their dealmaking woes in the Rule 5 draft, which produced little of note. Several teams coveted right fielder Bobby Brown, with the Mets grabbing him with the first pick. The only other draftees to reach 1,000 major-league plate appearances were outfielders Lynn Jones and Max Venable. Oddly, among the seven players drafted, none were pitchers.

Free Agency

Much of the suspense of the winter meetings centered on the pursuit of free agent Pete Rose, arguably the most celebrated name to hit the market since the introduction of free agency. After returning from a monthlong tour of Japan in late November, Rose began a whirlwind tour of his suitors, saying he "wanted everything finished by the winter meetings."[27] He met with Braves owner Ted Turner in Atlanta, Royals owner Ewing Kauffman in Kansas City, Cardinals owner Gussie Busch in his hospital room—who reportedly offered $500,000 per year plus a beer distributorship—and Pittsburgh owners John and Dan Galbreath in both Columbus, Ohio, and Lexington, Kentucky, where they showcased their thoroughbred horses for Rose.[28]

Rose, though, preferred Philadelphia and on Tuesday during the meetings, Phillies owner Ruly Carpenter made the announcement at an overflowing news conference of 250 reporters. Rose signed for $3,225,000 over four years, the largest contract in professional sports up to that time, just above the $800,000 earned by Denver Nuggets star David Thompson. Carpenter employed a little creativity to meet Rose's asking price by inducing television station WPHL, which carried the team's games, to guarantee $600,000 per year of the defined advertising revenues it shared with the Phillies. In effect, WPHL gambled that the impact of Rose would increase station revenues well beyond the breakpoint where they would have to split advertising revenue with the Phillies.[29]

Rose also had several friends on the Phillies, believed the team was close to a pennant, and that his leadership could provide the final impetus to a championship: "They were my first choice all along. They're a great club and I have a lot of friends on it. I've said all along I preferred an offensive team and a contending team."[30] Later he added, "The Phillies need an everyday player with experience. They need leadership. They're a lot like the Reds and Dodgers but they haven't been able to get over the hump. I think I can contribute the little extra they need. If they follow me they'll win."[31]

In other free-agent signings, the Giants re-signed third baseman Darrell Evans to a reported five-year, $1.435 million contract. The Angels landed Giants pitcher Jim Barr on a three-year contract for $860,000 plus a team option for a fourth year at $150,000. Upon his signing, California discussed turning him into a reliever, though he principally remained a starter in 1979.[32]

Trades

On the trade front, the big story of the winter meetings was the pursuit of Twins star Rod Carew. Owner Calvin Griffith knew he would not be able to re-sign Carew after the 1979 season—even if he could afford him, Carew had no interest in coming back after his owner's racially charged remarks as part of a Lions Club speech in September.[33] Complicating the process for Griffith, as a 10-year veteran, five with the same team, Carew had a right to veto any trade, and practically, no team would trade for him unless they could quickly ink him to a long-term contract. Carew provided Griffith with several teams to which he would agree to a trade, but Griffith cut a deal with the Giants, not a team on his list. The Giants agreed to surrender first baseman Mike Ivie, outfielder Jim Dwyer, and minor-league southpaw Phil Nastu, whereupon San Francisco owner Bob Lurie flew to Minneapolis to try to convince the perennial All-Star and seven-time batting champion to accept the deal (the interleague trading deadline ended on December 8, at the end of the meetings). But Carew still spurned the move. The irony of the transformation in player-owner relations that saw an owner supplicantly flying to meet a player during the winter meetings was not lost on observers.[34]

To conclude the Carew saga, Griffith subsequently negotiated with the Angels, who agreed to a five-year, $4 million contract with Carew, but could not come to an agreement with Griffith on player compensation. The Twins owner reportedly wanted third baseman Carney Lansford and righty Chris Knapp, a price California judged too steep. Turning to his third serious negotiating partner, once again with a team not on Carew's approved list, Griffith worked out a deal with the New York Yankees for first baseman Chris Chambliss, outfielder Juan Beniquez, minor-league shortstop Rex Hudler (the Yankees' 1978 first pick in the June draft), minor-league left-hander Chris Welsh, and $250,000. (Commissioner Kuhn, however, ruled that no money could be included in the Carew trade spectacle.) Again Carew turned down the trade, angering Yankees owner George Steinbrenner, who chastised Carew for not "understand[ing] the privilege of playing for the New York Yankees."[35] Finally, in early February Griffith agreed to a deal with the Angels for center fielder Ken Landreaux, right-hander Paul Hartzell, minor-league lefty Brad Havens, and minor-league third baseman-outfielder Dave Engle.

Despite the various new handicaps presented by free agency, several teams consummated notable trades during the meetings. The Red Sox dealt free-spirited left-hander Bill Lee, who had fallen out with manager Don Zimmer, to the Expos for reserve infielder Stan Papi. The Pirates acquired reliever Enrique Romo, who would become a key piece of their 1979 world championship club, by sending several players, including pitcher Odell Jones and infielder Mario Mendoza, to Seattle, where general manager Lou Gorman was hoping to revamp his last-place squad. In another move, Gorman sent 1978 All-Star shortstop Craig Reynolds to Houston for highly touted young lefty Floyd Bannister. Interestingly, both players were heading back to their respective hometowns.

California's Buzzie Bavasi was another active general manager. In addition to free agent Barr, Bavasi landed starting outfielder Dan Ford from the Twins in exchange for corner infielder Ron Jackson and DH Danny Goodwin. Texas owner Brad Corbett was also busy that fall revamping his team. He had made several deals prior to the winter meetings, and in Orlando he swapped third basemen with the Indians, sending Cleveland Toby Harrah in exchange for Buddy Bell.

Cleveland general manager Gabe Paul wanted Harrah because the team "was going for more speed and power. Harrah gives us some of each and has the versatility to play both third base and shortstop."[36] Paul also strengthened his bullpen by trading shortstop Alfredo Griffin (who would become the 1979 co-Rookie of the Year) and minor-league infielder Phil

Lansford to Toronto for righty Victor Cruz. From Toronto's perspective, Griffin brought additional speed and defense to their lineup.

The Mets reluctantly traded veteran lefty Jerry Koosman, who had threatened to retire, to his home-state Minnesota Twins. While the players the Mets initially received reflected the team's lack of leverage, the later underappreciated addition of southpaw Jesse Orosco in February made the trade look much better in retrospect. In one little-remarked trade, Cleveland acquired the contract of outfielder Joe Charboneau from the Phillies (though he actually played with the Twins' Class-A minor-league affiliate in 1978). Charboneau would become a celebrity in 1980 with his Rookie of the Year season and offbeat personality. (He quickly flamed out after his one memorable year.)

As with all trading marts, many anticipated, partially negotiated deals never came to fruition. The Yankees targeted California's Dave Chalk as a backup infielder and either San Diego's Bob Shirley or St. Louis's Buddy Schultz as a lefty reliever but couldn't land any.[37] At the last minute Bavasi backed out of a deal that would have sent All-Star southpaw Frank Tanana to Cincinnati for outfielder Ken Griffey. He had also hoped to swap Tanana to the Brewers for first baseman Cecil Cooper.[38] The Braves wanted a left-handed first baseman, but were unsuccessful in their pursuit of the Yankees' Jim Spencer, the Cubs' Larry Biittner, and the Reds' Harry Spilman.[39]

In one of the more publicized back-and-forth negotiations, the Cubs and Phillies met roughly a dozen times during the fall, hoping to consummate a trade at the winter meetings. The Cubs wanted catcher Barry Foote and either outfielder Jerry Martin or Bake McBride; in exchange the Phillies would receive outfielders Bobby Murcer and Greg Gross, and catcher Dave Rader. Phillies general manager Paul Owens pushed to expand the swap to include Cubs second baseman Manny Trillo, and while a restructured deal appeared resolved by midnight on Thursday, in the end no trade could be worked out.[40] "It has been the most frustrating week of my life," complained Cubs general manager Bob Kennedy. "I've done more running with less results this week that in any week of my life."[41]

Kennedy and Owens eventually worked out a swap in February, with Kennedy getting Foote, Martin, second baseman Ted Sizemore, and two others in exchange for Gross, Rader, and Trillo.

Orioles general manager Hank Peters, who also came up empty, was willing to discuss any player on his roster except Eddie Murray and Jim Palmer: "Of the 38 players on our roster, I mentioned 36 of them at one time or another during the winter meetings. Some of those 36 I really have no intention of trading, but sometimes you have to throw out a name in order to test another player's availability." Peters expanded on his trading approach in some detail: "There was one particular player we were interested in. I won't tell you which one, but we had been told he was unavailable. So I asked the team he is with: 'Suppose I was to offer you pitcher Mike Flanagan?' When I got no response, that told me the player really wasn't available. If I had gotten a reaction to Flanagan's name, then that would have told me the player wasn't untouchable, and that he could be had for the right offer. I had no intention of trading Flanagan (who won 19 games in 1978), but I would have pursued the trade by trying another approach."[42]

Miscellaneous

Mark "The Bird" Fidrych, the one-time youthful pitching sensation of the Detroit Tigers, came to the winter meetings to be examined by a collection of shoulder specialists. In 1976 the 21-year-old Fidrych captured the nation with his stellar pitching (19-9 with a league-leading 2.34 ERA in 250 innings pitched) and quirky habits. But the right-hander developed arm trouble the next year and again struggled with tendinitis in 1978. To gain some insights into his hurler's injuries, general manager Jim Campbell scheduled an examination with the Association of Professional Baseball Physicians, which was holding a symposium on shoulder injuries at the winter meetings.

Unfortunately for Fidrych and the Tigers, the news was disappointing. "He can't pitch until he has built up the strength in his arm," explained Dr. Harvey O'Phelan, Minnesota's team physician and chairman of the association, adding, "It could take all of next year, and it could take longer." Campbell and Fidrych were surprised and angered that these findings were released to the public, and Fidrych chafed at the idea of surrendering another full season. Fidrych had been aiming to be ready for the 1979 season, but after struggling through a few games in May, he was shut down for the year.[43]

At the managers' cocktail party, Whitey Herzog of the Royals underscored the impermanence of their positions, a particularly timely observation as Sparky Anderson, a two-time World Series winner with the Reds, had recently been discharged. "Guys, here's to us," Herzog toasted, "And remember, if you open the season zero and nine, Sparky Anderson's waiting...."[44]

NOTES

1. Stan Isle, "Elite Clubs Endangering Balance, Kuhn Warns," *The Sporting News*, December 23, 1978: 35.

2. Jerome Holtzman, "More Than 40-Million Caught 'Baseball Fever,'" *Official Baseball Guide for 1979* (St. Louis: The Sporting News), 311.

3. 1979 *Official Baseball Guides*, Ibid., 327.

4. Stan Isle, "Majors Warm Up to 3-Division Plan," *The Sporting News*, December 23, 1978: 34.

5. Joseph Durso, "3-Division Proposal for Major Leagues Facing Obstacles," *New York Times*, December 8, 1978: A25.

6. Isle, "Majors Warm Up to 3-Division Plan"; Holtzman, "More Than 40-Million Caught 'Baseball Fever.'"

7. Executive Council Minutes from December 5 Meeting, April 4 1979, Bowie Kuhn Papers, Baseball Hall of Fame, S1-SS1-B2-F1.

8. Bowie Kuhn Papers, Baseball Hall of Fame, S3-SS2-B2-F3.

9. *The Sporting News*, December 23, 1978: 36.

10. Stan Isle, "Plea to Boost Minor Umps' Pay," *The Sporting News*, December 23, 1978: 35.

11. Isle, "Majors Warm Up to 3-Division Plan."

12. Byron Rosen, "Baseball Would Score With Fewer 'Humpty Dumpties' as Screeners," *Washington Post*, December 1, 1978: D7.

13. Jack Lang, "More Names Urged for Shrine Ballot," *The Sporting News*, December 23, 1978: 35; Jack Lang, "Mays Top Name on Shrine Ballot," *The Sporting News*, December 30, 1978: 36.

14. Stan Isle, "Team Error Plan Shelved," *The Sporting News*, December 23, 1978: 34.

15. Stan Isle, "Sub Fielding Rule Change," *The Sporting News*, December 22, 1979: 43.

16. Stan Isle, "Rule Changed on Certain Rain-Halted Games," *The Sporting News*, December 23, 1978: 34. In 1978 baseball had its first-ever divisional playoff game, between the Yankees and the Red Sox. The ruling officially making "game 163" statistics part of the regular season statistics merely confirmed the previous practice in which the league playoff game(s) counted in the regular-season statistics.

17. Oscar Kahan, "Johnson Succeeds Bragan as Minors' Boss," *The Sporting News*, December 23, 1978: 37; "1,400 Salute Bragan at Banquet," *The Sporting News*, December 23, 1978: 37.

18. Holtzman, "More Than 40-Million Caught 'Baseball Fever.'"

19. Tom Weir, "Not a Buyer in Sight for the A's in Oakland," *The Sporting News*, December 23, 1978: 41.

20. Jim Henneman, "Former Treasury Sec in Line to Buy Orioles," *The Sporting News*, December 23, 1978: 51; Holtzman, "More Than 40-Million Caught 'Baseball Fever.'"

21. Press release, Office of the Commissioner, November 22, 1978, Bowie Kuhn Papers, Baseball Hall of Fame, S3-SS3-B3-F6; Stan Isle, "Trades, but No Blockbusters," *The Sporting News*, December 23, 1978: 38.

22. Joseph Durso, "Red Tape Tying the Hands of Horse-Traders," *The Sporting News*, December 30, 1978: 33.

23. Ibid.

24. Ibid.

25. Mike Littwin, "Winter Meetings' Fireworks Fizzle," *Los Angeles Times*, December 8, 1978: E7.

26. Durso, "Red Tape Tying the Hands of Horse-Traders."

27. Mike Littwin, "Rose Decides He'd Rather Be in Philadelphia," *Los Angeles Times*, December 6, 1978: F8.

28. Ibid; Dave Nightingale, "Phillies Have the Inside Track to Landing Rose," *Chicago Tribune*, December 5, 1978: C1.

29. Holtzman, "More Than 40-Million Caught 'Baseball Fever.'"

30. Joseph Durso, "Rose Signed by Phillies to $3.2 Million Pact," *New York Times*, December 6, 1978: B11.

31. Littwin, "Rose Decides He'd Rather Be in Philadelphia."

32. Holtzman, "More Than 40-Million Caught 'Baseball Fever.'"

33. In what he thought were off-the-record comments, Griffith disparaged nearly everyone, but most incendiary were his racist comments regarding the reasons for moving the franchise to Minnesota.

34. The Rod Carew trade saga comes from multiple sources, including Nick Peters, "Carew May Yet Wind Up in a Giants' Uniform," *The Sporting News*, December 23, 1978: 48; Bob Fowler, "Carew Nixes Deal, But Twins Make Two Other Offers," *The

Sporting News, December 23, 1978: 48; Murray Chass, "Carew Rejects Offer; Twins Get Koosman," *New York Times,* December 9, 1978: 17; "Carew Elects to Veto Trade With the Giants," *Los Angeles Times,* December 9, 1978: C1; "Giant Deal Hinges on Carew Nod," *Washington Post,* December 8, 1978: E1.

35 Holtzman, "More Than 40-Million Caught 'Baseball Fever.'"

36 Bob Sudyk, "Big Deal Huge Clinker in Cleveland," *The Sporting News,* December 30, 1978: 42.

37 Phil Pepe, "Yanks' Rosen Went '0 for 4' at Meetings," *The Sporting News,* December 23, 1978: 50.

38 Dick Miller, "Realist Tanana Lowers His 1979 Forecast to 15 Wins," *The Sporting News,* December 30, 1978: 35.

39 Gary Caruso, "Braves See Whiz Kids Coming On With Rush," *The Sporting News,* December 30, 1978: 48.

40 Joe Goddard, "Cubs Got the Foot From Phils—But No Foote," *The Sporting News,* December 30, 1978: 47; Dave Nightingale, "Phillies Have the Key to Locked Trade Mart," *Chicago Tribune,* December 7, 1978: C1; Dave Nightingale, "'Old Pal' Could Dash Cub Plan For Phillie Deal," *Chicago Tribune,* December 8, 1978: E1; Dave Nightingale, "Cubs' Deal With Phillies Fails to Materialize," *Chicago Tribune,* December 9, 1978: C1.

41 Dave Nightingale, "Baseball Confabs Are Becoming Ho-Hum Affairs," *Chicago Tribune,* December 10, 1978: C2.

42 Jim Henneman, "Orioles Fail to Connect in Flyhawk Search," *The Sporting News,* December 30, 1978: 45.

43 Jim Hawkins, "The Bird Will Be Grounded Until 1980," *The Sporting News,* December 23, 1978: 51; Jim Hawkins, "The Bird Disputes Docs, Says He'll Pitch in 1979," *The Sporting News,* January 6, 1979: 36; *Chicago Tribune,* December 5, 1978: C4; "Fidrych Won't Pitch in 1979," *Chicago Tribune,* December 7, 1978: C3; Doug Wilson, *The Bird: The Life and Legacy of Mark Fidrych* (New York: Thomas Dunne, 2013), 185.

44 Bob Sudyk, "Torborg Finds Rock in Gabe's Yule Message," *The Sporting News,* January 6, 1979: 33.

Facts From the Ludtke v. Kuhn Case (1978)

The following facts are pulled from the judge's decision in the *Ludtke v. Kuhn* case.

The court finds that there is no genuine issue as to any material fact and that plaintiffs are entitled to judgment as a matter of law. The undisputed facts, as set forth by the plaintiffs in their 9(g) Statement, and not seriously controverted by defendants, are as follows:

- On April 2, 1975, defendant Bowie Kuhn wrote the general managers of all major league baseball teams indicating that baseball should maintain a "unified stand" against the admission of women sportswriters to major league clubhouses.

- During the 1977 World Series that policy was applied to plaintiff Melissa Ludtke, a sportswriter for *Sports Illustrated*, a weekly sports magazine published by plaintiff Time Incorporated.

- After the 1977 World Series and after the commencement of this action, baseball reconfirmed its policy of excluding women reporters from the clubhouse.

- Kuhn's 1975 "unified stand" letter followed discussions within the Office of the Commissioner triggered by the decision of the National Hockey League All-Star teams to allow women reporters to conduct interviews in the locker rooms following the January 1975 National Hockey League All-Star Game.

- In the course of those discussions, the Commissioner's office questioned no baseball players concerning their opinions. Public relations directors of the major league teams were questioned and their opinions were varied.

- On July 22, 1976, Robert Wirz, Director of Information of the Office of the Commissioner of Baseball, wrote the Public Relations Directors of all Major League Baseball teams a reminder of baseball's stance in opposition to allowing women reporters access to clubhouses and asking whether any women had requested such access.

- On August 4, 1976, by letter, and shortly thereafter orally, the public relations director of defendant New York Yankees told Mr. Wirz that the Yankee players had concluded by an "overwhelming majority" that women could be allowed access to the clubhouse if they conducted themselves professionally.

- Mr. Wirz then told the Yankee public relations director that action by one team to allow women reporters in the clubhouse would be a "definite threat to breaking down the overall barrier."

- Thereafter, Yankee management reversed the position of the players and said "no more" to women reporters in the Yankee clubhouse.

- At the 1977 Baseball World Series games between the New York Yankees and the Los Angeles Dodgers, Melissa Ludtke, an accredited reporter assigned by Sports Illustrated to cover the Series, was informed by the Commissioner's office that she was not permitted, solely on the basis of her sex, to enter either team's clubhouse after the Series games. The Commissioner's office was aware that the Dodgers had already told Ludtke that she would have access to their clubhouse after the games. The Commissioner's office was also aware that Ludtke had been given access to the manager's office in the Yankees' clubhouse during the American League playoff games.

- The Commissioner's office assigned Larry Shenk, the public relations director for the Philadelphia Phillies, to try to bring players out of the clubhouse to speak with Ludtke in the tunnel where she was made to stand. Shenk subsequently stated at the 1977 annual major league public relations meeting, chaired by the Commissioner's Director of Information, that women reporters should be given postgame access to the clubhouse.

- During the World Series, the Commissioner was also told by Henry Hecht, a baseball writer for the *New York Post*, that he and other "regular writers on the beat" thought that women reporters should be given equal access to teams' clubhouses.

- The Commissioner's office spoke to no players concerning their views either during or after the World Series. After the commencement of this action, in January 1978 and again in March, the Commissioner reconfirmed his policy of excluding women reporters from baseball clubhouses.

- Leland MacPhail, the President of the American League, has stated that he supports the Commissioner's policy regarding women reporters.

- In March 1978, at the Yankees' spring training camp in Fort Lauderdale, Florida, the Yankees' manager gave one or more women journalists access to the Yankees' locker room. Shortly thereafter the Yankees were instructed that they were to comply with the Commissioner's policy, and the Yankees' manager stated that women reporters would be excluded from the clubhouse once the regular season began.

- The Annual Notice issued to all major league baseball teams by the Office of the Commissioner of Baseball has, since at least 1974, stated that access to clubhouses "should" be granted to accredited members of the media.

- The World Series Manual issued by the Commissioner's Office for the World Series provides that the clubhouses will be opened to the press within five minutes of the close of each game except after the final game when they will be opened immediately.

- Although the Notices and Manual on their face grant access to accredited reporters without regard to their sex, the Commissioner's Office takes the position that the Commissioner's letter of April 2, 1975, adds a prohibition based upon sex to those Notices and Manual.

- When confronted with situations in which individual players have refused to make themselves available to accredited reporters in clubhouses after major league baseball games, the Office of the Commissioner has urged the clubs of which those players are members to make such players available.

- A significant portion of the news written about baseball emanates from news gathered by male reporters in the clubhouses of professional baseball teams.

- The current president and a former president of the Baseball Writers Association of America indicated to Commissioner Kuhn and his Director of Information during the 1977 World Series that part of their "function" as professional baseball writers was to interview players in the clubhouse.

- By definition, female reporters who are excluded from baseball clubhouses are not given the same access to the news and newsmakers as their male colleagues and competitors. This denial of equal access places female reporters at a severe competitive disadvantage because they miss stories witnessed or heard by male reporters inside the clubhouse, because they are unable to take advantage of the group questioning inside the clubhouse and because they are unable to talk to some players at all.

- Professional hockey teams began to admit accredited female reporters to their locker rooms at the National Hockey League All Star Game in the winter of 1975.

- Professional basketball teams began to admit accredited female reporters to their locker rooms in the spring of 1975.

- As of today, of the 22 teams in the National Basketball Association, all but two or three admit accredited female reporters, including both New York area teams.

- As of today, approximately 14 of the 18 teams in the National Hockey League, including the New York Rangers, give female reporters access to their locker rooms. The Office of the Commissioner was informed by an official of the National Hockey League in January 1978 that "about half" of the NHL teams allowed women reporters into their locker rooms.

- Accredited female reporters have also been given access to the locker rooms of, for example, the New York Cosmos professional soccer team, the Minnesota Vikings professional football team and the University of San Francisco basketball team.

- Women reporters who have been given access to locker rooms in other sports have found that a substantial portion of their material comes from the locker room and thus that access to the locker room is an important part of their job. They are able to compete fully with the male reporters on their beat because they are given equal access to the news and the newsmakers.

- The New York Yankees' clubhouse is divided into nine separate rooms, i. e., the central locker room area which contains cubicles for each player; the manager's office; the players' lounge; the trainer's room; a doctor's office; a sauna; a washroom which contains several individual sinks; a room containing the toilets; and the shower room which includes adjoining drying areas.

- Male reporters have traditionally been granted access only to the central locker room area and the manager's office.
- The shower and toilet facilities are completely hidden from any view from the locker room. Swinging doors could easily be placed in the doorway which leads into the adjacent washroom.
- The individual player cubicles in the central locker room area are approximately four feet wide and three feet deep and a player can comfortably dress in the cubicle. A curtain could be hung across the cubicle's one open side.
- Plaintiff Time Incorporated, is engaged in the communications business and publishes magazines including *Sports Illustrated*. A significant portion of Time's business involves sports coverage.
- After two years of experience as a junior baseball reporter for *Sports Illustrated*, plaintiff Ludtke was assigned by the magazine to attend and report on the 1977 World Series games.
- Defendant Bowie Kuhn is the Commissioner of Baseball, who claims and has been given authority by the New York Yankees to make decisions about access to the clubhouses in Yankee Stadium, and by the American and National Leagues to make decisions about access to the clubhouses of other major league baseball teams.
- Defendant MacPhail is the President of the American League of Professional Baseball Clubs.
- Defendant New York Yankees Partnership is an Ohio Limited partnership and has an office in Yankee Stadium, Bronx, New York. The Yankees are a member of the American League, and together with the American League are a party to the Major League Agreement, which created the Office of the Commissioner of Baseball.
- The City acquired title to Yankee Stadium and the land surrounding it by exercise of its power of eminent domain upon a factual showing, approved by the Supreme Court of the State of New York, Bronx County, that purchase of Yankee Stadium was required for a "public use."
- The City was authorized to lease the Stadium to the Yankees, rather than to the highest bidder, by a New York State statute which found that:
  - ... Yankee Stadium is important to the cultural, recreational and economic vitality of the state and city; ... and that unless the stadium and its supporting facilities are substantially renovated and modernized it is likely that the New York Yankees, the New York Giants and other stadium users will transfer to a location outside the state and the city. ... Chapter 986 of McKinney's 1971 Session Laws of New York.

- Pursuant to the State authorization, on August 8, 1972, the City and the New York Yankees entered into a 30-year lease which gives the Yankees extensive control over the entire stadium and exclusive control year-round over their clubhouse.

- The entire stadium, including the clubhouses, was renovated at a cost to the City of approximately $50 million in time for use by the Yankees during the 1976 baseball season.

- In both 1976 and 1977 the Yankees' obligation for rent due the City was approximately $1 million, as required under a percentage formula whereby the amount paid to the City increases as attendance increases. Accordingly, the City has a stake in increasing attendance at games at Yankee Stadium, and in its lease recognizes the connection between publicity and increased attendance.

- New York City police are on duty at the sporting events held in Yankee Stadium.

- The Yankees are required under the lease to comply with all present and future federal, state and local laws affecting their operations at Yankee Stadium, and the City retains the right to enforce and assure compliance not only with local but also federal and state laws.

---

[1] *Ludtke v. Kuhn*, 461 F. Supp. 86 (S.D.N.Y. 1978), U.S. District Court for the Southern District of New York - 461 F. Supp. 86 (S.D.N.Y. 1978), September 25, 1978. Retrieved from leagle.com/decision/1978547461FSupp86_1532.xml/LUDTKE%20v.%20KUHN on May 16, 2017.

— 1979 —
FIRST CHANCE AT A NEW POST-FREE-AGENCY CBA

By Dan Levitt

TORONTO HOSTED THE 1979 WINTER meetings at the Sheraton Centre, marking the fourth time the winter meetings were held outside the United States (Montreal in 1930 and 1936 and Mexico City in 1967).[1] The owners' discussions, both formal and informal, focused on the game's economics and the coming labor negotiations with the players—only the second of the free-agent era—with baseball's executives plotting to win back some of what many felt they had surrendered too easily four years earlier. Meeting attendance totaled a record 1,600, of whom roughly 150 were members of the media.[2]

In his opening remarks on the state of the game, Commissioner Bowie Kuhn lauded baseball's growing TV audience and attendance but expressed concern over mounting financial stress from the rapid increase in salaries. "The bottom eight clubs in baseball lost on the average of $2 million a club. More than half our clubs are in a loss position," Kuhn said, adding, "In the last year before the 1975 draft you have average salaries of $46,000. Today, or the last time they were measured, they were $121,000 on the average and I can tell you they're higher than that now. All you have to do is look at the recent signings. So there is a time bomb ticking away in our operations as a result of the reentry draft [free agency] and there is reason for concern."[3]

Kuhn also somewhat bizarrely identified a "southern tier" of teams "from Georgia across to California" that were signing a disproportionate number of free agents, in that seven of the 12 free-agent signings so far that offseason were by teams spanning that geographic region. He further expressed unease that teams he viewed as contenders had signed more than their fair share of the free agents.

Kuhn's other principal concern was over the recent phenomenon of regional cable TV "superstations" broadcasting their team's games throughout the country into other teams' markets. The impact of this new delivery channel on major- and minor-league attendance and local TV ratings, along with how the revenue from the broadcast rights should be apportioned, he felt, needed to be tackled.

On the positive side Kuhn highlighted the huge attendance increases in the 1970s over the 1960s; solid television ratings, including 80 million viewers for Game Seven of the 1979 World Series; robust local television viewership; and strong interest from the important 18-34-year-old demographic. Kuhn also emphasized the improvement in marketing, from better international licensing operations to new corporate sponsorships to promoting *This Week in Baseball* into the country's highest rated syndicated TV program.

Business and Administrative

Three amendments relating to minor-league administrative matters that required major-league approval were passed: the payment to teams losing players in the minor-league phase of the Rule 5 draft were doubled, though technically only for 1980 (the first increase since 1968); Triple-A player rosters were increased to 22 (from 21), again technically only for 1980; and if a player was returned to the minors at a higher salary than when initially recalled, the major-league team was responsible for the difference.[4]

The owners also approved a resolution that teams deciding to change their uniform design or colors must give notice by the May 1 prior to the start of the following season, or else indemnify MLB for the "cost of any licensed merchandise which may have become obsolete," plus potential penalties at the commissioner's discretion.[5]

In preparation for the impending labor negotiations, the owners self-imposed a $500,000 fine for any baseball executive speaking publicly about them. Nevertheless, portions of the owners' negotiating position leaked to the press. Most significantly, the owners were reportedly planning to push for direct player compensation between the team signing a free agent and the team losing the player. The owners' proposed scheme would allow the signing team to protect a still-to-be-determined number of players, with the player's former team then allowed to select any unprotected player from the signing team's roster.[6]

Another labor negotiation idea that drew particular scrutiny was the suggestion that all contractual special provisions in player contracts should be cleared through the owners' player-relations committee. Foreshadowing future miscalculations, several legal observers commented that such a scheme was collusive and violated the collective-bargaining agreement, which read in part, "and clubs shall not act in concert with other clubs."[7]

At the baseball writers meeting, the BBWAA discussed the common practice of sportswriters acting as official scorers and the associated potential conflict of interest. The writers resolved that individual sportswriters could continue to act as official scorers if they so wished and their newspaper didn't object. They also concluded, however, that the leagues should be responsible for providing official scorers and that the assignments should no longer be under the purview of the BBWAA. In another decision, the writers changed the calculation methodology for the Rookie of the Year Award, asking the voters to name three players (instead of one) under a 5-3-1 points system, as in the Cy Young Award balloting.[8]

The Official Baseball Records Committee amended the record for most consecutive RBIs, recognizing the Cubs' Oscar Grimes as the major-league record holder with 17 and Taft Wright as the American League titleholder with 13.[9]

On the ownership front, as the meetings opened the long, drawn-out negotiations to sell the Oakland A's to Marvin Davis and move the franchise to Denver appeared closer to fruition. Several Oakland officials, including the mayor and the commissioner-elect of the Oakland Coliseum, had acknowledged that they were willing to let the A's leave in exchange for a $4 million buyout of the lease. Reportedly, the buyout price would be split among Davis, A's owner Charles Finley, San Francisco owner Bob Lurie, and the other American League owners.[10] By the time of the meetings, however, the deal was again hitting some snags: Finley was apparently trying to extract more money out of Davis in the form of consulting fees after the sale, and the Oakland city council voted unanimously to try to keep the team.[11] Nevertheless, the owners left in place a commitment to purchase insurance against third-party claims in the event the team was sold to Davis and moved to Denver.[12]

To pressure Finley to sell the team—whether to Davis or anyone else—the AL owners discussed imposing a minimum $10,000-per-game payment to visiting teams, though no action was taken on this measure. With Finley's low attendance, such a disbursement would have been in excess of the visiting team's percentage of the gate, adding to his financial burden. One report also mentioned that baseball would institute a $50,000 cap on the amount of money that could be included in any trade, well below the $400,000 level Commissioner Kuhn had imposed a couple of years earlier in response to Finley's selling off his players, to further prevent Finley from trying to cash out. Whether this was ever enforced or implemented remains questionable. When Aurelio Rodriguez was sent from the Tigers to the Padres during the meetings, it was first announced that Detroit would receive a player to be named later; it later turned out to be a straight sale for $200,000. In any case, once Finley finally sold the team to Oakland interests the following year, there was no longer a need for this reduced dollar maximum.[13]

Player Movement

As in 1978, the number and significance of trades at the winter meetings remained subdued as teams continued to work through the impact of free agency and other recently acquired player rights. "You just can't make a quick trade anymore," said always aggressive trader Buzzie Bavasi, the GM of the Angels. In speaking about some of his past successes, he added, "I couldn't have made those deals today. It would have taken too long, and something would have stood in the way. It used to be all you had to worry about was, 'Is he healthy?' Now you ask, 'Who's his agent? How many years on his contract? Does he have a no-trade clause? Will he refuse a trade because he's a 10-year player?'" Bob Kennedy of the Cubs agreed, saying simply: "Your hands are tied."[14]

Notorious trader Bill Veeck went so far as to question the continued viability of the meetings as a trading mart: "This year they tell me 39 major-league players were moved between the end of the season and the start of the meetings, and most of these were better known than the ones traded during the meetings." He went on to suggest other possibilities. "We still have a need for the meetings," Veeck said. "And I wish I knew all the answers. But December seems to me to be just too far from everything. Maybe we should have fall and spring meetings instead of winter and summer. Why not have fall meetings during the World Series and the next ones after two or three weeks of spring training?"[15]

The Minnesota Twins dominated the Rule 5 draft, selecting three players, the first time in recent history that any team had selected that many. Overall, 10 players were taken, with two going on to major-league careers of some note. With the seventh pick the Brewers selected outfielder Mark Brouhard, who would log nearly 1,000 major-league plate appearances over a six-year career. The last of the Twins' selections, right-hander Doug Corbett, would be the best, registering 66 saves during his eight-year career. Surprisingly, the best players to come out of the 1979 Rule 5 draft came through the Triple-A phase, where the White Sox grabbed first baseman Greg Walker out of the Phillies organization, and the Blue Jays selected outfielder Mitch Webster from the Dodgers farm system.

Free-agent activity during the winter meetings was relatively quiet as well, particularly when compared to the Pete Rose signing spectacle the previous year. After landing free-agent right-handers Dave Goltz and Don Stanhouse earlier in the fall, the Dodgers had room for one more player in their quota of three free-agent signings. The team wanted to sign Joe Morgan but already had a veteran at second base in Davey Lopes. After some public discussion over possibly shifting Lopes to the outfield, the Dodgers instead elected to sign veteran outfielder Jay Johnstone as their final free agent.[16] Other free-agent signings included left-hander Fred Norman and outfielder Rowland Office by Montreal.

As teams began to come to terms with free agency, they often focused on moving players who would become free agents after the following season and would likely be difficult to sign. Detroit had recently offered free-agent-to-be outfielder Ron LeFlore what they felt was a significant contract of almost $3 million over six years. Leflore reportedly countered at $4 over five years. Unsure of his ultimate ability to re-sign LeFlore, GM Jim Campbell was willing to listen to proposals for his star outfielder, and when Montreal offered lefty Dan Schatzeder, Campbell accepted.[17]

One trade was carelessly announced early, nearly causing Commissioner Kuhn to void the deal. In late November the Rangers swapped third baseman Eric Soderholm to the Yankees for three minor leaguers. Because minor-league rosters were technically frozen until the winter meetings, the teams were prohibited from announcing the minor-league players involved. When the Rangers unthinkingly disclosed their incoming players, Kuhn considered vacating the deal before approving a restructured deal in which the Rangers received only two minor-league players.[18]

The Expos swapped unhappy second baseman Dave Cash, who had been benched for youngster Rodney Scott, to the Padres for utility infielder Bill Almon and outfield reserve Dan Briggs. The Indians traded outfielder Bobby Bonds to the Cardinals for outfielder Jerry Mumphrey and right-hander John Denny. Bonds had demanded a trade during the season (as was his right under the CBA), mostly as a negotiating ploy to sweeten his contract. When Bonds and GM Gabe Paul couldn't reach agreement, Paul worked out the best deal he could at the winter meetings. Cardinals GM John Claiborne hoped to fill three needs at the meetings (in order): left-handed starter, left-handed reliever, and right-handed-hitting outfielder. By landing Bonds just before the deadline, Claiborne could go back to St. Louis with at least one goal met.[19]

Toronto GM Pat Gillick wanted to improve his squad by using one of his veteran first basemen, either John Mayberry or Chris Chambliss, as trade bait. He found a willing partner in Atlanta, who sent him reliever Joey McLaughlin, outfielder Barry Bonnell, and shortstop Pat Rockett for Chambliss and shortstop Luis Gomez.[20] In other action, Texas, always active on the trade front, swapped right-hander Doyle Alexander, infielder Larvell Blanks, and $50,000 to the Braves for righty Adrian Devine and shortstop Pepe Frias. This deal originally had outfielder Jeff Burroughs also going to the Rangers, mostly as a salary dump by the Braves. When he exercised his no-trade right to veto his inclusion, the frustrated Braves complained, "All we can do is hope Jeff's pride takes over."[21]

In a relatively minor swap that highlighted the Twins' trade calculus, manager Gene Mauch pushed for utility infielder Pete Mackanin, whom the team landed for pitcher Paul Thormodsgard. "I know about Mackanin because he played for me in 1975 at Montreal," Mauch said. "He has some power. I don't know if he will give us the power we need for a right-handed DH, but he might. He hit 28 homers for Spokane (PCL) in 1974. He was considered the best prospect in the Texas organization. That's why we traded to get him in Montreal." Minnesota owner and de-facto GM Calvin Griffith, who acknowledged that he knew little about Mackanin, obliged his manager because "we had no plans for Thormodsgard."[22]

Always active Angels general manager Buzzie Bavasi had a frustrating beginning to the winter meetings as an apparently completed deal fell through. After a couple of days of back-and-forth negotiations with his New York Mets counterpart, Joe McDonald, Bavasi had arranged a trade in which California would acquire right-hander Craig Swan, due to be a free agent after the 1980 season, plus outfielder Elliott Maddox in exchange for shortstop Dickie Thon and first baseman Willie Mays Aikens. When Mets manager Joe Torre, who didn't want to trade either of his players, added his voice to the talks, backup catcher Ron Hodges was substituted for Maddox. To formalize the transaction, the Angels and Mets executives, including New York's president, Lorinda de Roulet, retired to the Mets' hotel suite. The Mets were in the process of being sold, but McDonald believed and had publicly announced the team was ready and willing to participate in the trading mart. Nevertheless, de Roulet vetoed the swap, saying it wouldn't be fair to the new owners to make such a significant deal, though Torre may also have influenced her thinking on dealing Swan. Not surprisingly, Bavasi reportedly "unleashed a tirade at the Mets' boss for keeping the Angels hanging for two days during what is a precious time of year for baseball teams."[23]

Bavasi didn't waste any time getting back to working the hotel and a couple of days later dealt Aikens and third baseman Rance Mulliniks to the Royals—in the market for a first baseman with power—in exchange for right fielder Al Cowens, shortstop Todd Cruz, and a player to be named later. Bavasi also signed shortstop Freddie Patek as a free agent, whose agent was former pitcher Jim Bunning, a future Hall of Famer and US senator.[24]

As always, the general managers arranged several blockbuster trades that fell through in the end. Philadelphia GM Paul Owens thought he had worked out a deal for San Diego outfielder Dave Winfield. As negotiated, the swap would have netted the Phillies Winfield and pitchers Gaylord Perry and Bob Shirley in exchange for pitcher Larry Christenson, outfielders Greg Luzinski and Bake McBride, and relief pitcher Ron Reed. Reportedly, the deal unraveled because San Diego wanted to rework the trade to include center fielder Garry Maddox.[25]

Another one of Owens's trades fell through because of a unique clause in reliever Sparky Lyle's contract. Texas GM Eddie Robinson and Owens believed they reached an agreement in which Texas would receive outfielder Bake McBride, pitcher Larry Christenson, reliever Tug McGraw, and a minor leaguer in exchange for Lyle, the just-acquired Devine, outfielder Johnny Grubb, and possibly the just-acquired Frias. But a sticking point popped up in Lyle's contract from when Texas had acquired him in a multiplayer deal in November 1978. Because at the time Texas owner Brad Corbett hadn't realized that Lyle could veto his inclusion in the deal under the CBA rules and the trade would still stand but without him, he had been forced to sweeten the southpaw's contract by adding a 10-year, $50,000-per-year post-career arrangement in which the pitcher would join the Rangers' TV and radio lineup. Since a player could not play for one team and have a financial obligation from another, his contract, therefore, would need to be restructured before this latest trade could be consummated. Lyle and the Phillies discussed several possibilities, including guaranteeing the last couple of years of his existing contract, but with the deadline approaching no deal could be worked out. McBride also used his contract leverage to help scuttle the trade.[26]

Owens summed up his frustration: "It's like getting married, then getting divorced and remarried. It's like the new husband and wife have to settle the conditions of the first marriage. You have to make good on things that were in the first contract that you had nothing to do with. Last year's meetings were slow because of that, but these were even slower. A lot of the deals went by the boards. A lot of people left early because of that. It's getting so I don't see the point of the winter meetings anymore."[27]

White Sox manager Tony LaRussa was another discouraged trader. While sitting in the Sheraton lobby, LaRussa told one reporter he was looking for a policeman. "Why?" the reporter asked. "There are a bunch of people in this hotel who ought to be arrested for attempted theft. They're trying to steal my left-handed pitchers."[28]

The Red Sox had several significant trade opportunities that general manager Haywood Sullivan eventually declined, including a three-way deal that would have netted lefty Frank Tanana and cost them third baseman Butch Hobson, and a straight-up trade of Hobson for pitcher Bob Shirley.[29]

Houston GM Tal Smith also saw his trade opportunities dwindle as the week progressed. On Monday he said, "We have possible matches with eight teams." The next day he told reporters, "That total has been cut in half." On Thursday Smith remarked, "We have less than a 10 percent chance of making a deal with an American League team." Finally, "after Friday he went home."[30]

NOTES

1   Stan Isle, "Player Deals Most Likely News at Toronto Meetings," *The Sporting News*, December 8, 1979: 47.

2   "News and Quotes From Toronto Meetings," *The Sporting News*, December 22, 1979: 47.

3   "Commissioner Kuhn's Address to Opening Session at Annual Meeting in Toronto," December 3, 1979, Bowie Kuhn Papers, Baseball Hall of Fame, S3-SS3-B3-F1; Stan Isle, "Free-Agent System 'Time Bomb'—Kuhn," *The Sporting News*, December 22, 1979: 44.

4   Minutes of the Joint Major League Meetings, BKK Papers. S1-SS1-B2-F2 (1979); 12-18; Stan Isle, "More Money to Flow to Minors," *The Sporting News*, December 22, 1979: 44.

5   Minutes of the Joint Major League Meetings, BKK Papers. S1-SS1-B2-F2 (1979).

6   Murray Chass, "Baseball Clubs Map an Effort to Change Compensation Rule," *New York Times*, December 7, 1979; Murray Chass, "Club Owners Push Compensation Plan," *The Sporting News*, December 22, 1979: 59.

7   Murray Chass, "Owners Adopt $500,000 Muzzle," *The Sporting News*, December 15, 1979: 49.

8   Jack Lang, "Writers Can Keep Jobs as Scorers," *The Sporting News*, December 22, 1979: 44.

9   "An Official Okay for RBI Mark," *The Sporting News*, December 22, 1979: 43.

10 Tom Weir, "Oakland Coliseum Relaxes Its Grip on A's," *The Sporting News*, December 15, 1979: 54.

11 Tom Weir, "Finley Snags Denver Deal," *The Sporting News*, December 22, 1979: 46.

12 Major League Executive Council & Television Committee Meeting December 5, 1979, Minutes distributed April 11, 1980, Bowie Kuhn Papers, Baseball Hall of Fame, S1-SS1-B2-F2.

13 Mike Littwin, "Dodgers May Move to Sign Johnstone," *Los Angeles Times*, December 3, 1979; Tom Weir, "Finley Snags

Denver Deal," *The Sporting News*, December 22, 1979: 46; Phil Collier, "Second-Choice Rodriguez Bolsters Padres at Third," *The Sporting News*, December 22, 1979: 62; *Official Baseball Guide for 1980* (St. Louis: The Sporting News), 392.

14 Richard Dozer, "Meetings Not What Hot-Stovers Imagine," *Chicago Tribune*, December 7, 1979.

15 Richard Dozer, "Winter Meetings Outdated—Veeck," *The Sporting News*, December 29, 1979: 38.

16 Mike Littwin, "Dodgers May Move to Sign Johnstone," *Los Angeles Times*, December 3, 1979; Gordon Verrell, "Dodgers Sidestep Morgan, Land Jay Johnstone Instead," *The Sporting News*, December 8, 1979: 50; Murray Chass, "Mets' Chief Vetoes Swan Trade," *New York Times*, December 5, 1979.

17 "LeFlore to Expos, Palmer to Nowhere," *Washington Post*, December 8, 1979; Richard Dozer, "Expos Obtain Tigers' LeFlore; Indians Send Bonds to Cards," *Chicago Tribune*, December 8, 1979; Tom Gage, "High Pay Demands Made LeFlore Ex-Tiger," *The Sporting News*, December 22, 1979: 57.

18 The Rangers took left-hander Ricky Burdette and infielder Amos Lewis from the Yankees' minor-league system. "Yankees Get Soderholm After All," *Deseret News* (Salt Lake City), November 15, 1979: 36.

19 Rick Hummel, "Cards, Searching for Bat Balance, Invest in Bonds," *The Sporting News*, December 22, 1979: 61; Burt Graeff, "Bad Advice Hastened Bonds Exit," *The Sporting News*, December 22, 1979: 61; Murray Chass, "Bonds Traded Again but Lyle Deal Fails," *New York Times*, December 9, 1979.

20 Neil MacCarl, "Jays' Swap Bait: Mayberry or Chambliss," *The Sporting News*, December 8, 1979: 54; Neil MacCarl, "MacLaughlin Key in Jays' Swap," *The Sporting News*, December 22, 1979: 54.

21 Randy Galloway, "Burroughs Plays It Cool," *The Sporting News*, January 5, 1980: 46; Ken Picking, "Braves Take to Tepee, Smug Over Swaps," *The Sporting News*, December 29, 1979: 34.

22 Bob Fowler, "Twins So-So as Bargain Hunters," *The Sporting News*, December 22, 1979: 62.

23 Murray Chass, "Mets' Chief Vetoes Swan Trade," *New York Times*, December 5, 1979; "Baseball Deals Fall Through," *Washington Post*, December 5, 1979; Jack Lang, "Little Thanks at Empty Met Table," *The Sporting News*, December 8, 1979: 50; Jack Lang, "Mets Blasted for Trade Foul-Up," *The Sporting News*, December 22, 1979: 56.

24 Dick Miller, "Angels to Chart Golden Oldies, Disco Kids," *The Sporting News*, December 29, 1979: 35; Sid Bordman, "Royals Correct Old Pain by Swapping for Aikens," *The Sporting News*, December 22, 1979, 60.

25 "Baseball Deals Fall Through," *Washington Post*, December 5, 1979.

26 Hal Bodley, "Lyle's Radio-TV Pact Killed Swap to Phils," *The Sporting News*, December 29, 1979: 46; Randy Galloway, "Lyle Is Dangled as Bait Despite Corbett's Line," *The Sporting News*, December 29, 1979: 38; Murray Chass, "Bonds Traded Again but Lyle Deal Fails," *New York Times*, December 9, 1979.

27 Hal Bodley, "Lyle's Radio-TV Pact Killed Swap to Phils," *The Sporting News*, December 29, 1979: 46.

28 Richard Dozer, "White Sox Escape Toronto With Lefty Staff Intact," *The Sporting News*, December 22, 1979: 54.

29 Joe Giuliotti, "Red Sox Whiff in Trade Mart—Fans Irked," *The Sporting News*, December 22, 1979: 60.

30 Harry Shattuck, "Astros Black Out in Search for Power," *The Sporting News*, December 22, 1979: 57.

— 1980 —
FUTURE HALL OF FAMERS IN THE SPOTLIGHT

By Kent Henderson and Paul Hensler

Introduction and Context

WITH THE INAUGURATION OF FREE agency in 1976 and the introduction of a second interleague trading period in 1977, the baseball winter meetings had become agonizing to attend. The traditional exchange of players between teams became more limited now that players could bargain for long-term contracts and no-trade clauses. However, the 1980 gathering in Dallas saw a delightful departure from more recent meetings as an overwhelming amount of talent was moved before the sun set on December 12, the official close of business, with more to follow in the coming weeks. The date and location of these meetings had been announced in Toronto the year before, marking the second time that Dallas was the host city, but the first since 1927! For 1980, the magnates set up headquarters at the Loews Anatole Hotel, whose décor was described by some as "Texas—Egyptian."[1]

The current session took place after an exciting regular season in which George Brett of the Kansas City Royals chased the elusive .400 batting mark—he finished at .390—while the Philadelphia Phillies made their first World Series appearance since 1950 and captured baseball's ultimate prize by defeating the Royals in six games.

As the meetings were about to convene, however, an ominous cloud began to form on baseball's horizon. The team physician for the Philadelphia Phillies' Double-A affiliate in Reading, Pennsylvania, along with two other people, was charged with fraudulently prescribing and obtaining amphetamines in quantities "beyond the scope of the patient-doctor relationship and without first conducting physical examinations."[2] Although use of "greenies" had been known in baseball for years, the issue persisted and served as an unfortunate precursor to the cocaine scandal that by 1985 would shake the sport to its core.

The Business Side

When the business meetings convened, a spokesman for the commissioner's office noted, there would be "nothing of significance" on the agenda.[3] However, several executives, including Yankees owner George Steinbrenner, chose to disagree. Steinbrenner was part of a group who felt the time had come for baseball to realign into a three-division format. This was not the first time the subject had been brought up; at the 1978 meetings in Orlando the subject was discussed, and a 10-member study committee presented a recommendation that Commissioner Bowie Kuhn found feasible. In 1978, Kuhn considered the proposal to be "the most significant subject to hit the major league agenda in years."[4]

Steinbrenner expressed confidence that the American League would realign by the beginning of the 1982 season, but he was concerned that the proposal would not meet the commissioner's approval without the National League making a parallel move. At the meetings in Dallas, only one National League executive, Bill Giles, was in favor of the three-division alignment. "The National League has been against it, but I think a majority might be in favor of it now," Steinbrenner said.[5] Skyrocketing operational costs were seen as one factor that could sway the collective thinking of normally conservative owners, and a geographical realignment would make economic sense in helping to reduce travel and operating expenses.

As if to bolster the argument for the economic benefits of three divisions, a recently released audit conducted by Ernst and Whinney disclosed that eight unnamed big-league teams had each lost an average of $2 million in 1978 and 1979. Kuhn used the disclosure of the gloomy financial news as an opportunity to decry the ever-escalating salaries being garnered by players, and express his fear over a potential decline in competitive balance should wealthier clubs succeed in securing the services of the best talent via the signing of free agents. To no one's surprise, Marvin Miller, head of the Major League Baseball Players Association, termed Kuhn's hand-wringing "absurd" and defended the gains made by the players union by pointing out that "every time a franchise changes hands, there are tremendous capital gains [made by the owners who sell their teams]," therefore, it was only fair that the players share in the wealth.[6]

The National Association, the governing body of minor-league baseball, considered 13 amendments to the Professional Baseball Agreement and Rules. Four amendments to the National Association Agreement were discussed as well. Johnny Johnson, president of the National Association, said the proposals involved increases in the size of Double-A and Triple-A rosters, injury rehabilitation assignments, and expanding the high-school rule to cover prospects from Puerto Rico.[7] All of the amendments would need major-league approval. As well as the roster increases, other proposed amendments would bring about improvements in player-development contracts, including an increase in meal allowances for players in each minor-league classification.[8] The International League proposed an amendment to increase the amount of time before a reserve-list player was subject to the December draft, from three years to four years.[9]

Scheduled highlights of the meetings included an instructional clinic for high-school and college coaches moderated by several noteworthy big leaguers: Tom Grieve, Sparky Anderson, Dick Howser, Charlie Lau, Tom Lasorda, and Pat Corrales. Also on tap was a Texas-style Hoedown as well as the annual dinner for the National Association. On December 9, *The Sporting News* Man of the Year was unveiled by St. Louis Cardinals announcer Jack Buck, with the winner, not surprisingly, being the Royals' George Brett.

As the meetings continued, Chicago White Sox owner Bill Veeck petitioned to sell the White Sox to Ohio real-estate tycoon Edward J. DeBartolo Sr. The sale had been vetoed earlier by Commissioner Kuhn due to DeBartolo's horse-racing holdings, but a second attempt by DeBartolo to purchase the White Sox for $20 million was nixed by an overwhelming vote of 11 to 3 by American League owners. Kuhn also felt DeBartolo wouldn't be a good fit for ownership based upon his previous attempts to buy other teams with the intention of moving them to New Orleans, and the commissioner noted the ill-received "pressure tactics" employed by the aspiring owner on several of the AL moguls to support his cause.[10] There were rumblings that DeBartolo was destined to be an absentee owner, which found little favor among his potential brethren. Yet DeBartolo may have felt some degree of entitlement to ownership: It was reported in the *New York Times* that he loaned the White Sox over $500,000 so that the team could sign free-agent outfielder Ron LeFlore two weeks before the winter meetings began.[11] Departing the ranks of ownership for the final time, Veeck ultimately received permission to sell the club to an ownership group headed by Jerry Reinsdorf and Eddie Einhorn in late January 1981.

In matters less controversial, the National League also announced that President Chub Feeney was given a three-year contract extension through 1983, and John McHale of the Montreal Expos was re-elected as the NL's vice president. Commissioner Kuhn announced a 35 percent increase in the budget for the Umpire Development Program, the annual expenditure being raised from $505,000 to $685,000, and the Official Rules Committee made a revision to the designated hitter rule as a means of addressing a scheme employed by Baltimore manager Earl Weaver during the 1980 season. "To counter the possibility of a pitching change by the opposition before his DH came to bat, Weaver on 21 occasions filled the DH spot on his lineup card with the name of a pitcher who wasn't due to play and then used another player in his place."[12] The amendment now forced the player first listed as the DH to bat at least once before he could be removed.

In a move that stunned many at the Dallas gathering, the San Francisco Giants fired manager Dave Bristol, who had expressed displeasure at the team's trade of left-handed pitcher Bob Knepper and a minor leaguer to the Astros for third baseman Enos Cabell. The dismissal, orchestrated by club owner Bob Lurie, came awkwardly "during a luncheon for major-league managers in which the Giants skipper and members of the organization were conspicuously absent from their table."[13] Lurie was also said to be perturbed with Bristol's alleged unflattering statements about first baseman Mike Ivie, which Lurie believed would hurt the Giants' chances to offer Ivie in a trade. Whether coincidental or not, this proved to be the last major-league piloting job Bristol would hold.

In other managerial affairs in the run-up to the winter meetings, Dick Howser in late November became another victim of owner George Steinbrenner's managerial purges when he was jettisoned after New York was swept in the League Championship Series by Kansas City. The owner said that "it will be his [Howser's] decision" whether to return to the Yankees dugout, but Steinbrenner was obviously making the call himself when Howser was axed. In a bizarre press conference, the Yankee owner mendaciously cited Howser's desire to "pursue a real-estate opportunity in Florida," but few were buying this tale.[14] At the same time that Howser was being embarrassed, another of Steinbrenner's past sparring partners, Billy Martin, found a new job near his hometown of Berkeley, California. Following the transfer of ownership of the Oakland Athletics from Charlie Finley to Walter Haas Jr., in August 1980, team President Roy Eisenhardt announced the signing of Martin to a five-year contract to be the A's manager and player-development director.

Several minor-league officials were recognized in Dallas for their contributions in the season just completed. Jim Burris, general manager of the Triple-A Denver Bears; Frances Crockett, GM of the Double-A Charlotte Orioles; and Greensboro Class-A general manager Tom Romenesko were the latest executives to be honored for the success they and their respective clubs achieved. Burris and his team were no doubt helped by the feats of future major leaguers Randy Bass[15]—his MVP performance in the American Association included a .333 batting average, 37 home runs, and 143 RBIs—and Tim Raines, *The Sporting News* Minor League Player of the Year, who swiped 77 bases and led the circuit with a .354 average.

Player Movements

With free agency now in full flower, bidding for the best talent on the market drew the biggest headlines, and the premier player offering his services was outfielder Dave Winfield, late of the San Diego Padres and now seeking a new home and contract. Drawing notice as well was former Dodgers pitcher Don Sutton, who signed with the Houston Astros on the eve of the meetings in Dallas just as the Yankees, with George Steinbrenner's checkbook at the ready, seemed poised to ink the right-hander. The Montreal Expos were also among the serious bidders for Sutton, but the pitcher opted for the chance to pitch his home starting assignments in the spacious Astrodome. Another free-agent hurler, the Phillies' southpaw reliever Tug McGraw, had some anxious negotiations with the club he had just helped propel to the World Series crown, but on the eve of the winter meetings he signed a four-year contract to remain in Philadelphia.

With Red Sox star outfielder Fred Lynn scheduled to be a free agent after the 1981 season, Boston was entertaining trade offers for him. The intriguing possibility of Lynn landing with the New York Mets, who were actively in the bidding for Winfield, left GM Frank Cashen pondering the likely strain on team finances: "Sure it's exciting to think of those two in the same outfield. But could we pay the ushers?"[16] Not only would the payroll rise sharply, but the Mets faced the prospect of surrendering three valued players—outfielder Mookie Wilson and right-handed pitchers Neil Allen and Tim Leary—to the Red Sox, which they declined to do.

Playing the role of consummate dealmaker was St. Louis general manager Whitey Herzog, who had taken the reins of the Cardinals after the midseason dismissal of manager Ken Boyer. Herzog was at the helm for 73 games before moving to the front office and leaving Red Schoendienst in charge of matters on the field. After signing free-agent catcher Darrell Porter from the Kansas City Royals—the backstop's production had fallen precipitously from his stellar 1979 but had played well when Herzog managed the Royals—the White Rat engineered a series of major trades that gave his club a significant makeover. On December 8, Herzog packaged a pair of catchers, Terry Kennedy and Steve Swisher, infielder Mike Phillips, and a quartet of pitchers—right-handers John Littlefield and John Urrea, and southpaws Al Olmsted and Kim Seaman—and sent them to the San Diego Padres in exchange for right-handed relief ace Rollie Fingers, left-hander Bob Shirley, and former World Series hero Gene Tenace, a catcher-first baseman. Yet another catcher, Bob Geren, was sent to St. Louis two days later to finalize the initial deal.

Herzog then moved into the second phase of his maneuvering on December 9. With his sights set on the Cubs' closer, right-hander Bruce Sutter (the 1979 Cy Young Award winner), Herzog swapped first baseman Leon Durham and former Gold Glove third baseman Ken Reitz to Chicago for Sutter. Infielder Ty Waller was also dispatched to the Cubs two weeks later. Moving Reitz could have been difficult as he had a no-trade provision in his contract, but Herzog successfully navigated around it with a $150,000 buyout. Finally completing his frenetic bargaining on December 12, Herzog traded Ted Simmons—the Silver Slugging catcher was expendable with Porter now aboard—along with the just-acquired Fingers along with journeyman right-handed pitcher Pete Vuckovich to Milwaukee. In return, the Brewers sent outfielders David Green and rifle-armed Sixto Lezcano, plus pitchers Dave LaPoint and Lary Sorensen (a lefty and a righty, respectively) to the Cardinals. As was the case with Reitz, Simmons also was able to collect a substantial sum from the Cardinals and Brewers—$750,000 in total—in order for him to waive his no-trade rights. The same buyout situation applied to former National League Cy Young recipient Randy Jones of the San Diego Padres, who was dealt to the New York Mets on December 15 for right-handed pitcher John Pacella and infielder Jose Moreno. In the end, Harry Dalton, the general manager of the Brewers, did not receive the same degree of notoriety as Herzog did on the trading front, but Dalton is due credit for adding players who turned Milwaukee into a pennant winner in 1982.

While it may have seemed that Herzog was stealing most of the thunder in Dallas, a number of other clubs got in on the trading action. Another high-profile pitcher, right-hander Bert Blyleven, was on the move when he was sent to the Cleveland Indians along with veteran Pirates catcher Manny Sanguillen. In return, Pittsburgh received another catcher, Gary Alexander, and a trio of pitchers: left-hander Bob Owchinko, right-hander Victor Cruz, and minor-league right-hander Rafael Vasquez. Pirates manager Chuck Tanner's habit of removing Blyleven from games earlier than the pitcher preferred had soured him on his tenure in Pittsburgh. A bit of intrigue attended this trade because the Indians appeared to have swooped in to grab Blyleven before the California Angels could complete their own trade for the future Hall of Famer. Angels manager Jim Fregosi even admitted that his team was "definitely making progress with the Pirates" as negotiations continued, but the potential deal broke down when Pirates held firm in their refusal to part with infielder Vance Law.[17]

The Angels had dangled right-handed reliever Mark Clear and former American League MVP Don Baylor as bait for the Pirates, but when they failed to consummate a Blyleven trade, they turned their attention to Boston in seeking help for their problem at shortstop. The day after Blyleven slipped away, California traded Clear, third baseman Carney Lansford, and outfielder Rick Miller to the Red Sox for third baseman Butch Hobson and shortstop Rick Burleson. With Burleson likely to become a free agent after the 1981 season, Boston instead chose to avoid the possible loss of his services by trading him to get something of value in return.

BASEBALL'S BUSINESS: THE WINTER MEETINGS

Trades had an impact for several other notable players when San Francisco outfielder Craig Landis and former Rookie of the Year right-hander John Montefusco were swapped to the Braves for another righty, journeyman hurler Doyle Alexander, while the Rangers and Mariners completed a Herzog-sized deal involving 11 players. Heading to Texas were left-handed pitcher Rick Honeycutt, shortstop Mario Mendoza, catcher Larry Cox, outfielder Leon Roberts, and DH Willie Horton, while a quartet of pitchers — righties Ken Clay, Steve Finch, and Brian Allard, plus southpaw Jerry Don Gleaton — joined infielder Rick Auerbach and slugging outfielder Richie Zisk in moving to Seattle.

In a series of moves involving lesser-known players, Oakland swapped shortstop Mario Guerrero to Seattle for a player to be named, but this in actuality was a cash transaction. Outfielder Dave Edwards went from Minnesota to San Diego for infielder Chuck Baker, the Kansas City Royals inked free-agent slugger Lee May, most recently with the Orioles, and the Astros signed infielder Dave Roberts, another free agent formerly with the Texas Rangers. Detroit sent shortstop Mark Wagner to the Rangers for left-handed pitcher Kevin Saucier, and the Angels signed former Expos righty John D'Acquisto as a free agent. Cliff Johnson, a catcher-first baseman, and minor-league infielder Keith Drumright went from the Cubs to Oakland for minor-league left-handed pitcher Michael King, while Twins also dealt outfielder Willie Norwood to the Mariners for right-handed pitcher Byron McLaughlin. Cincinnati and the Cubs exchanged outfielders, Hector Cruz for Mike Vail; outfielder Dave Stegman went from Detroit to the Padres for left-handed pitcher Dennis Kinney; and Toronto infielder-outfielder Bob Bailor was traded to the Mets for right-handed pitcher Roy Lee Jackson. Second baseman Tony Bernazard of Montreal landed with the White Sox, with the Expos getting southpaw Rich Wortham in return.

Free agent Willie Montanez, a National League veteran, opted to re-sign with Montreal as the winter meetings were concluding, and just days later a former Expo, Rusty Staub, returned for a second stint with the Mets. But the plum of the current crop of free agents was Dave Winfield, the lanky outfielder of the San Diego Padres and a five-tool player who was one of the premier players in the game.

Just as the Mets had been in the hunt for Fred Lynn, so too was George Steinbrenner, and the Yankees mogul with the outsized checkbook had spoken with Red Sox GM Haywood Sullivan regarding a possible trade. At the same time, a drama was unfolding regarding the Yankees' quest for Winfield, who was Steinbrenner's primary target. As the meetings in Dallas were wrapping up, the owner's pursuit of Winfield was intensifying, and the *New York Times* reported in mid-December, "Although the likelihood might be remote that the Yankees could have an outfield of Reggie Jackson, Lynn, and Winfield, George Steinbrenner was pictured yesterday as intrigued by that possibility."[18] It was rumored that the Astros might seek the services of Winfield after their own star outfielder, José Cruz, was injured in a recent winter league game, but Steinbrenner was capable of competing financially — which is to say outspending — with his ownership brethren, and despite their stumble in the recent ALCS, the Yankees still fielded a very competitive team that its owner was more than willing to improve.

At the Dallas meetings, Steinbrenner had implored his fellow owners to increase by one year the length of time that clubs could maintain a hold over players in the farm system. He made the argument that he needed this bureaucratic amendment in order to avoid a depletion of his minor-league rosters, but when he came a cropper in this effort, he vowed to find a solution using his wallet. "What I'll have to do is go back home and sign a big raw-boned kid from Minnesota," Steinbrenner said, obviously alluding to Winfield, a native of St. Paul who was educated at the University of Minnesota.[19] This was exactly his course of action, and on December 15 the Yankees announced that they had signed Winfield to a record-setting, 10-year contract worth $25 million, thereby validating Marvin Miller's claim of ownership riches while at once putting a figurative dagger through the heart of Bowie Kuhn and less-wealthy moguls as the proclivity of seemingly frivolous spending apparently knew no limits.

A special footnote is appropriate to the aftermath of the 1980 winter meetings. As mentioned above, Rick Burleson was traded due to his impending free-agent status. And as Fred Lynn was being offered to various teams, he expressed his intent to sign for only the 1981 season and become a free agent thereafter, obviously wanting to take advantage of peddling his services on the open market. This situation held up his potential trade to several teams at the time of the gathering in Dallas. However, when the Red Sox belatedly mailed Lynn his 1981 contract, doing so after the December 20, 1980, deadline, he and teammate Carlton Fisk, whose contract was similarly tardy, filed for free agency. On the eve of an arbitration hearing regarding his filing, Lynn agreed to a trade to the Angels when owner Gene Autry, never bashful himself about spending, signed him to a four-year, $4.1 million deal as part of Lynn's agreement to the trade.[20] For his part, Fisk allowed his grievance to proceed, was granted free agency on February 12, 1981, and subsequently signed with the Chicago White Sox five weeks later.[21]

Summary

The 1980 winter meetings provided a fertile ground for many teams to strike deals and lay the groundwork for others that would be completed in the coming weeks. In total, 58 players were traded in one of the more active sessions since 1977, but the sheer number of personnel swapped was not the only salient factor.

Cardinals GM Whitey Herzog demonstrated a bold sense of confidence in engineering a series of deals involving high-profile talent that was a first step toward giving the St. Louis roster a radical makeover on the way to forging what would be one of the most dominant teams of the 1980s. Herzog's deals also paved the way for the Milwaukee Brewers to acquire talent they needed to compete in the American League in the early part of the decade.

In the area of free-agent signings, liberal spending by well-heeled owners like George Steinbrenner and Gene Autry continued a trend they exhibited in the post-Messersmith era, the former convincing the season's prime free agent, Dave Winfield, to come to the Bronx, while the latter doling out heavily shortly after the Dallas session to head off Fred Lynn's entry into the open market.

Baseball's hierarchy adhered to the status quo of two divisions in each league in spite of discussion of possibly changing to a three-way split, and the ownership ranks stymied the attempts of Edward J. DeBartolo Sr. to purchase the Chicago White Sox.

When taking into account the total time frame of the weeks prior to the winter meetings, the meetings themselves, and their aftermath, it is interesting to note that Winfield, Don Sutton, Bert Blyleven, Bruce Sutter, Rollie Fingers, Bill Veeck, and Whitey Herzog all figured prominently in news emanating from Dallas. In later years they would be figuratively reunited in the Plaque Gallery at the Baseball Hall of Fame.

BASEBALL'S BUSINESS: THE WINTER MEETINGS

SOURCES

In addition to the sources cited in the Notes, the author also consulted Baseball-Reference.com, baseballlibrary.com, and the book by Burton A. and Benita W. Boxerman, *Ebbets to Veeck to Busch: Eight Owners Who Shaped Baseball* (Jefferson, North Carolina: McFarland and Company, Inc., 2003).

NOTES

1. Steve Wulf, "Big Wheels Make Big Deals in Big D," *Sports Illustrated*, December 22, 1980.
2. "Reading Team Doctor Facing Drug Charges," *The Sporting News*, December 6, 1980: 61.
3. Stan Isle, "A.L. May Push for Realignment," *The Sporting News*, December 13, 1980: 39.
4. Ibid.
5. Ibid.
6. Miller quoted in Clifford Kachline, "Labor Strife, Big Salaries Topped '80 News," *1981 Official Baseball Guide* (St. Louis: The Sporting News), 324-325.
7. Stan Isle. "A.L. May Push for Realignment," *The Sporting News*, December 13, 1980: 39.
8. Ibid.
9. A review of records by Minor League Baseball senior communications director Jeff Lantz failed to turn up any evidence as to whether the amendment was actually adopted. Email from Jeff Lantz to author, August 31, 2016.
10. "AL Rejects DeBartolo White Sox Offer Again," *Spokane Spokesman-Review*, December 11, 1980: 35.
11. Murray Chass, "White Sox Had Help in Signing LeFlore," *New York Times*, November 27, 1980: B7.
12. Clifford Kachline, "Labor Strife, Big Salaries Topped '80 News," *1981 Official Baseball Guide* (St. Louis: The Sporting News), 324.
13. "Cards Get Sutter; Dave Bristol Fired," *Sarasota Herald-Tribune*, December 10, 1980: 1D.
14. Dave Anderson, "George Steinbrenner's Revolving Door Sent a Champion to the Royals," *New York Times*, October 18, 2014.
15. Prior to his breakout season with the Denver Bears, Bass had played in 13 major-league games, with 22 at-bats for the Twins, Royals, and Expos.
16. Cashen quoted in "Mets Offered Deal for Lynn," *New York Times*, December 10, 1980: B12.
17. Murray Chass, "Cards Get Sutter; Blyleven to Indians," *New York Times*, December 10, 1980: B9.
18. Murray Chass, "Yankees Press for Lynn and Winfield," *New York Times*, December 14, 1980: A1.
19. George Steinbrenner quoted in ibid. Despite his well-earned reputation as a big spender, Steinbrenner had a point regarding protection of his minor-league prospects. The Yankees' minor-league system in the late 1970s was very capable of producing quality talent, including the likes of Willie McGee, Willie Upshaw, LaMarr Hoyt, Dave Righetti, and Damaso Garcia, most of whom made their mark with clubs other than the Yankees.
20. On January 23, 1981, Boston swapped Lynn and right-handed pitcher Steve Renko to the Angels for right-handed pitcher Jim Dorsey and left-handed pitcher Frank Tanana, as well as outfielder Joe Rudi. California GM Buzzie Bavasi considered Lynn "the complete player," and when the outfielder dropped his grievance by "agree[ing] to a trade to a team of his choice," the Angels were then poised to pull off the deal with the Red Sox. See Dick Miller, "Lynn Adds a Potent Bat to Angel Arsenal," *The Sporting News*, February 7, 1981: 40.
21. Carl Clark, "White Sox Deal a Winning Hand," *1982 Official Baseball Guide* (St. Louis: The Sporting News), 249.

1981

THE POST-STRIKE INTRIGUE OF KUHN, SMITH, AND TEMPLETON

By Paul Hensler

Introduction and Context

THE DISQUIETING YEAR OF 1981 FEAtured the worst upheaval in baseball history—to that point in time—due to a players strike that erased roughly one-third of the regular-season schedule. Play was halted on June 12, and after weeks of acrimonious negotiations between players, club owners, and their respective representatives, a settlement was reached that allowed for a resumption of the championship season on August 10. The key factor in the dispute was compensation demanded by teams that lost players, especially those of the highest quality, to free agency. Newly implemented was a rule that created a pool of players from which those clubs could draft a compensatory replacement to fill the void left by the departed free agent. This rule was opposed by the Major League Baseball Players Association due to concerns about the negative impact it could have on the bargaining rights of players chosen as compensation.

Teams that had been at the top of their division at the time of the strike were declared "first-half" winners, and when play resumed after a delayed All-Star Game on August 9, those clubs that won their division in the "second-half" of the regular season would face the "first-half" victors in a special divisional playoff series that prefaced the normal League Championship Series. When the smoke cleared in late October, the Yankees engaged the Dodgers in the World Series, won by Los Angeles in six games on the heroics of Ron Cey, Pedro Guerrero, and Steve Yeager, all of whom were named co-MVPs of the series. The Dodgers' victory was the capstone to a season in which Los Angeles rode a wave of "Fernandomania," the catchy epithet used to describe enthusiasm generated by the deeds of the team's sensational rookie pitcher, Fernando Valenzuela.

Against this backdrop of labor rancor and the subsequent redemption of a thrilling postseason, major-league baseball held its annual winter meetings from December 7 through the 11th at the Diplomat Hotel in Hollywood, Florida.

The Business Side

With over five years having passed since the landmark Messersmith decision that facilitated free agency, the financial state of the game was less than promising. Addressing the gathering of owners, Commissioner Bowie Kuhn stated that baseball collectively lost $25 million in 1980, and the accounting data for the just-completed season would reveal, according to Kuhn, a $50 million loss.[1] Only nine of the 26 major-league franchises turned a profit in 1980, and some small-market teams, already at a disadvantage because of lower revenue streams, sought some form of revenue-sharing to be modeled on a system used by the National Football League. The pooling and redistribution of a sports league's monies had already taken root in the NFL, and this move had been initiated—successfully so—to ensure the stability of weaker and small-market clubs. Well-funded major-league baseball teams, however, were less than enthusiastic to provide alms for their poorer brethren. Orioles owner Edward Bennett Williams was leading the effort to remedy the disparity and "appear[ed] to have made some progress, but most of the owners in the larger markets ... aren't overly anxious to slice up the pie."[2]

During a quick trip to the nation's capital on December 9, Kuhn fanned the flames of the revenue debate when he testified before a congressional subcommittee and expressed concern about "the potential overexposure of baseball games on cable television [that] threatens the economic viability of the sport."[3] Kuhn's remarks drew a sharp rebuke from Ted Turner, owner of television superstation WTBS and the Atlanta Braves, whose games were beamed to cable outlets nationwide. It was acknowledged at the winter meetings that the American and National League rules dealing with radio and television licensing, some of which were decades old, needed amending in order to account for the "new technology and terminology that didn't exist when the [leagues'] charters were adopted."[4]

Another proposal under consideration by the owners concerned the realignment of each league into three divisions, a concept that would have led to an additional round of playoff games. However, the proposal failed, primarily because of a noticeable lack of support in the National League. The restructuring of the American League required the approval of 10 of its 14 franchises, and informal voting among the junior circuit's moguls seemed to favor the change. But National League bylaws called for unanimous approval, and Dodgers President Peter O'Malley was the most powerful among a bloc of five owners strongly believed to be opposed to three-division league formats.[5]

While the midsummer players strike was thankfully in the past, the owners were beginning to cast a wary eye on negotiations with the umpires union, whose contract had expired at the conclusion of the 1981 season. Bargaining sessions had commenced, noted Blake Cullen, the National League supervisor of umpires, but the progress was slow in the early going.[6]

At the senior level of the uppermost echelon of major-league baseball's power structure, the Executive Council named Baltimore's Edward Bennett Williams, the Brewers' Bud Selig, and Ballard Smith of the Padres as new members, replacing John Fetzer of Detroit, Ed Fitzgerald of Milwaukee, and Peter Bavasi of Toronto. Selig and Eddie Chiles of the Texas Rangers were also named to the Player Relations Committee to replace Fitzgerald and Minnesota's Calvin Griffith. Owners also approved the use of batting helmets with double earflaps, and voted to restrict the size of major-league rosters after August 31 to 28 players rather than 40.[7]

Minor-league business at the meetings created barely a ripple, but several club officials were recognized for their efforts in 1981. Pat McKernan (Triple-A Albuquerque Dukes), Allie Prescott (Double-A Memphis Chicks), and Dan Overstreet (Class-A Hagerstown Suns) were named by *The Sporting News* as the top executives of their respective levels.[8]

The drama receiving the most attention was a nefarious move that threatened to displace Bowie Kuhn from the commissioner's office. Still stung by what was perceived as his aloofness during the summer strike, Kuhn remained in the crosshairs of a cabal of representatives from nine teams seeking his ouster. Kuhn claimed that Lou Susman, an attorney working for the St. Louis Cardinals, was "secretly campaigning" to undermine him.[9] The group of conspirators consisted of Edward Bennett Williams, Ballard Smith, John McMullen (Houston), Bill Williams (Cincinnati), Eddie Chiles, George Steinbrenner (Yankees), George Argyros (Seattle), Nelson Doubleday (Mets), Fred Wilpon (Mets), and Susman. Reporting for the *New York Times*, Joseph Durso listed Edward Bennett Williams as "the leader of the revolt against Kuhn's role as commissioner."[10] Less than two weeks before the winter meetings, Kuhn's detractors had met in New York and drafted what soon became known as the "Hollywood Letter," a missive calling for Kuhn's resignation.

Several days into the gathering in Florida, the anti-Kuhn forces, letter in hand, convened on the evening of Wednesday, December 9, "and decided to press for a restructuring of the high command during Thursday's league meetings."[11] Meanwhile, a group of pro-Kuhn owners, led by the Dodgers' O'Malley and dubbed "the white hats," learned of the plot and held their own confab a few hours the next morning to discuss ways to rally support for the imperiled commissioner. While Kuhn was the most visible figurehead among all baseball executives, he had no control over how owners and teams spent their money. Nonetheless, Kuhn had become the scapegoat for the financial losses of the previous years and the widening gap between richer and poorer teams.

Kuhn retained his composure even when the existence of the letter was revealed, and, defending himself in the face of the onslaught of criticism, he explained that his hands were tied to a great extent during the recent strike because the owners' Player Relations Committee—not the commissioner's office—was tasked with negotiating with the players union.[12] The meeting of National League owners was notably divisive, but a modicum of peace was restored when a new committee of executives was formed to study possible restructuring of the highest offices of baseball. In a superficial attempt to put the matter to rest, the Hollywood Letter was "symbolically torn up by Susman."[13]

Kuhn's term as commissioner was not set to expire until August of 1983, and the terms of his contract held that no discussion of his status could take place until 15 months before its termination. The preemptive assault on the commissioner by his detractors failed, and although he had survived this battle, Kuhn admitted that the shredding of the letter did nothing to dispel the bile among those who ardently sought his removal. This war on Kuhn, initiated by a select group of owners, would continue beyond the conclusion of the 1981 winter meetings.

Personnel Dealings

A prelude to the traditional player transactions at the winter meetings occurred in late November when one trade was completed and another begun. In a swap of former All-Star outfielders, the Detroit Tigers sent former top draft pick and slugger Steve Kemp to the White Sox for Chet Lemon, and ground was broken on a three-way deal involving the Philadelphia Phillies, Cleveland Indians, and St. Louis Cardinals. The Phillies traded outfielder Lonnie Smith and a player to be named later to the Indians for catcher Bo Diaz, and Cleveland immediately shipped Smith to the Cardinals for two pitchers, Lary Sorensen and Silvio Martinez. This trade was completed at the winter meetings when the Indians picked up pitcher Scott Munninghoff from the Phils.

When the action moved to Florida, Yankees owner George Steinbrenner, never shy about amending his roster or management team, announced that manager Bob Lemon would be allowed to pilot the Bronx Bombers for the 1982 season, after which Gene Michael would take over in the Yankee dugout from 1983 through 1985. Another former Yankees skipper, Ralph Houk, had his contract extended through the 1984 season by the Boston Red Sox.

On the ever-popular trading front, activity was relatively slow, leading one major newspaper to comment that most of the winter meetings consisted of "four days of boredom interspaced with rumors."[14] While many clubs may have been waiting until spring training of 1982 to evaluate their squads before ultimately deciding on how to address problem areas, 36 players were nonetheless swapped in 16 separate transactions. This total was off by a substantial margin from the previous winter meetings, at which 59 players were swapped in 18 trades.

Outfielder Clint Hurdle, the bright Royals star who once graced the cover of *Sports Illustrated* but had been disabled for most of 1981, was sent to the Cincinnati Reds for pitcher Scott Brown, who had spent most of his professional career in the Reds' minor-league system.

Pittsburgh sent veteran shortstop Tim Foli to the California Angels for catching prospect Brian Harper. Seeing only limited playing time with the Bucs and three other teams in the mid-1980s, Harper did not start having his best years until 1988 when he joined the Minnesota Twins. But just as he had done for the Pirates in their championship season of 1979, Foli paid a quick dividend for the Angels by helping to anchor their infield during California's drive to the 1982 AL West pennant.

The Mets traded the middle of their infield, exchanging shortstop Frank Taveras for Montreal pitcher Steve Ratzer and cash. The former ironically had been traded in 1979 from Pittsburgh to the Mets for the aforementioned Foli, while the latter, like Scott Brown, appeared in only a handful of major-league games up to 1981 and would never pitch at that level again. New York also sent second baseman Doug Flynn and hurler Danny Boitano to the Texas Rangers for closer Jim Kern. Flynn had been a key acquisition from the Reds as part of the controversial 1977 trade of Tom Seaver to Cincinnati but was a mediocre hitter at best, and Boitano, who pitched for several years in the Phillies and Brewers organizations, pitched only 30 innings for the Rangers in 1982, his last year in the majors. A three-time American League All-Star reliever in the late 1970s, Kern fell victim to injuries in mid-1980 and had become a rehabilitation project. The tall right-hander never pitched for the Mets, as he was traded, along with Alex Trevino and Greg Harris, for Reds slugger George Foster two months later as spring training commenced.

Seattle's Tom Paciorek, whose .326 average was runner-up to Boston's Carney Lansford for the 1981 American League batting crown, was sent to the White Sox for outfielder Rod Allen, shortstop Todd Cruz, and catcher Jim Essian. Allen had no impact for the Mariners, and Essian saw only limited duty behind the plate, but Cruz became Seattle's primary shortstop in 1982 before moving on to Baltimore. First baseman Paciorek, whose two other brothers also played in the major leagues, hit well for the White Sox (.312 in 1982, .307 in 1983) and continued to do so later for the Mets and Rangers in a career that eventually spanned 18 years.

After spending just one season in San Francisco, outfielder Jerry Martin was shipped to the Kansas City Royals for two pitchers, Rich Gale and Bill Laskey. Gale had been a top prospect in the Royals' system but had alternating good and bad years since his 14-win, 3.09 ERA debut in 1978; Laskey blossomed briefly, winning 13 games in both 1982 and 1983. Martin, meanwhile, found a place in the Royals outfield, batting .266 in 147 games during 1982. However, he was swept up in the drug scandal that was soon to plague major-league baseball. Along with fellow Royals Willie Wilson, Willie Mays Aikens, and, most notoriously, Vida Blue, he would serve time in jail for involvement with cocaine.

The Giants added outfielder-first baseman Doe Boyland from the Pirates in exchange for pitcher Tom Griffin, swapped hurler Doug Capilla for the Cubs' Allen Ripley, and traded outfielder Larry Herndon to the Tigers for pitchers Dan Schatzeder and Mike Chris. San Francisco had set out to add one southpaw to its pitching staff at the meetings, but actually ended up with three (Capilla, Chris, and Schatzeder).

Now operating in Chicago, Dallas Green, the new general manager of the Cubs, worked on retooling the team's lineup, first by sending pitcher Mike Krukow and cash to the Phillies—Green's former employer—for pitchers Dan Larsen, Dickie Noles, and catcher Keith Moreland.

It is important to note that one trade that did not take place was a deal involving a prized prospect in the Philadelphia organization. Long rumored to be included in trades for several weeks, Ryne Sandberg was finally acquired in late January 1982 in a trade that brought the future Hall of Famer—along with shortstop Larry Bowa—to the Cubs for shortstop Ivan DeJesus. Based on accounts in *The Sporting News* at that time, one can draw the conclusion that Green had to have been laying groundwork for a deal involving Sandberg but did not complete trade talks until several weeks after the conclusion of the winter meetings.[15]

Former National League Rookie of the Year Rick Sutcliffe, a 17-game winner for the Dodgers in 1979, appeared to be destined more for a minor-league bullpen than continued success at the major-league level after posting two dismal seasons (five total wins with a collective ERA of 5.10, in 1980 and 1981) following his stellar debut. Still perhaps overwhelmed by "Fernandomania" and basking in the glow of its World Series title, Los Angeles decided to move Sutcliffe and second baseman Jack Perconte to Cleveland for outfielder Jorge Orta—a former American League All-Star—catcher Jack Fimple, and pitcher Larry White.

One of the last vestiges of the Big Red Machine, outfielder Ken Griffey, had been traded to the Yankees along with pitcher Brian Ryder a month before the gathering in Hollywood. At the meetings, the Reds completed the deal by acquiring pitcher Fred Toliver from New York.

In a swap of outfielders, the Astros sent Gary Woods to the Cubs for Jim Tracy, with both players immediately assigned to their new team's Triple-A affiliate. The Cardinals signed a pair of pitchers from the Mexican League, Eric Rasmussen of the Yucatan club, and former American Leaguer Vicente Romo of Coatzacoalcos.

American League West rivals Seattle and Oakland completed a trade in which the Mariners shipped infielder-outfielder Dan Meyer, who had twice enjoyed 20-homer seasons, to the Athletics for Rich Bordi, a 6-foot-7-inch reliever who would end up pitching for four other clubs over the following six years. These teams also completed a trade in which the A's sent pitcher Roy Thomas to the Mariners for outfielder Rusty McNealy and pitcher Tim Hallgren.

Legal Hoops

Danny Ainge had a no-basketball clause in the contract he signed in 1980 with Toronto. Boston Celtics general manager Red Auerbach admitted to knowing about the Blue Jays clause and the contract, and being notified twice about it. Still, Ainge's desire to play basketball over baseball landed in the courts. By the beginning of October 1981, a jury decided in favor of Toronto,[*] even though Ainge signed his contract without counsel because he was still in college (Ainge became the first athlete to take advantage of an NCAA rule allowing a college athlete to be a pro in another sport.)[**] However, the possibility of Ainge's playing basketball remained, as Judge Lee Gagliardi questioned the situation:[***]

> Gagliardi: "The affidavit filed by Ainge shows that he wants to play basketball, doesn't it?"
>
> Blue Jays attorney Douglas Parker: "Yes. It says he doesn't want to play baseball. But the Toronto management's position is that Ainge gets confused about his future."
>
> Gagliardi (reportedly smiling): "He's a college man. And an academic All-America. I think he has a very good idea of what he wants."

Toronto agreed to continue working on an agreement with Boston, but progress was slow. Rumors spread of Toronto President Peter Bavasi being an obstacle to negotiations, and hopes emerged after Bavasi resigned in late November, citing the need for a greater challenge.[****] Pat Gillick, Toronto's vice president of baseball operations, suggested that Bavasi's resignation had no impact on the Ainge situation, referring to Toronto's legal team as the driver of negotiations.[*****]

Ultimately, a deal was reached on November 27, with settlement terms not announced.[******]

---

[*] Mike Douchant, "Hands Off Ainge, Jury Tells Celts," *The Sporting News*, October 17, 1981: 62.

[**] Thomas Boswell, "Danny Ainge: A Singular Figure in a Double Play Ainge: Does He Have the Right Stuff for NBA?," *Washington Post*, December 20, 1981: L1.

[***] "Hands Off Ainge, Jury Tells Celts."

[****] Enquirer Wires, "Bavasi (Needing a Challenge?) Resigns from Blue Jays," *Cincinnati Enquirer*, November 25, 1981: 34.

[*****] Neil Singelais, "Bavasi Quits Blue Jays; Ainge Dispute Continues: Resignation May Facilitate Deal with Celtics," *Boston Globe*, November 25, 1981: 33.

[******] Associated Press, "Boston Signs Ainge," *Albuquerque Journal*, November 28, 1981: 32.

BASEBALL'S BUSINESS: THE WINTER MEETINGS

In the annual major-league Rule 5 draft, held on December 7, 10 players were selected by other organizations for $25,000 apiece. Among these, only two players—pitcher and former Cardinal farmhand Jim Gott, and infielder Domingo Ramos, late of the Blue Jays—would enjoy any future success with his new club. While neither Gott nor Ramos racked up big numbers, they did exhibit staying power by each accruing 11 years of service time with four different big-league teams.

Other instances of post-meeting trades that had been initially discussed in Hollywood, were those involving the Houston Astros' Cesar Cedeño, once one of the best all-around players in the game but now in noticeable decline, for Cincinnati third baseman Ray Knight. Knight was the heir-apparent to Pete Rose following Rose's departure to Philadelphia at the end of the 1978 season, but he became expendable after his batting average dropped nearly 60 points from 1979 to 1981. But perhaps the biggest laying of groundwork for a future trade occurred in a transaction between the Cardinals and Padres.

On December 10, St. Louis dealt outfielder Sixto Lezcano to San Diego for pitcher Steve Mura, and these principals were each accompanied by the ubiquitous player-to-be-named from their respective clubs. Having already surrendered two pitchers—Lary Sorensen and Silvio Martinez—in previous trading, Cardinals manager and GM Whitey Herzog stated that he was in the market for more frontline pitching, so it was fair to assume that at least one more hurler would be forthcoming from the Padres. At the onset of the meetings, however, Herzog alluded to possibly dealing his gifted but troubled shortstop, Garry Templeton. Having fallen out of favor with Cardinals fans and his own teammates, especially after a late August home game in which he made obscene gestures to the crowd at Busch Stadium, Templeton was placed on Herzog's trading block.

After weeks of haggling following the initial Lezcano-Mura trade, Templeton and All-Star shortstop Ozzie Smith were announced—on February 11, 1982—as the players swapped to complete the trade first brokered in Hollywood. Smith would go on to anchor the Cardinal infield for three National League crowns and a World Series title while endearing himself to St. Louis fans for the remainder of a career that landed him in Cooperstown. Templeton, feeling more comfortable closer to his home in Santa Ana, California, helped the Padres to the 1984 National League pennant, but he never fulfilled the promise he displayed during his early years when he hit well over .300 in three of his first four seasons as a Cardinal.

Several free-agent signings at the winter meetings involved some well-known names, including former Boston outfielder Joe Rudi and Texas right-hander Fergie Jenkins, who returned to the cities that initially launched them into prominence, Rudi back to Oakland, Jenkins back to Chicago for another stint with the Cubs. Reliever Bill Campbell, also formerly of Boston and a member of the first big free-agent class of 1977, followed Jenkins to Wrigley Field by signing as a free agent. Others, such as outfielder Cesar Geronimo (Kansas City), infielder Jerry Remy (Boston), and catcher Buck Martinez (Toronto), re-signed with their 1981 clubs, and the Cardinals purchased pitcher Mike Stanton from the Indians.

In closing, a few other transactions warrant attention. On December 6, the Angels purchased catcher Bob Boone from the Phillies, and five days later, the Dodgers signed former Orioles shortstop Mark Belanger as a free agent. Both players had been very active as members of the Major League Baseball Players Association, and a third player with a high profile in the players union, Orioles third baseman Doug DeCinces, found himself traded to California in late January 1982. It may be argued that Boone had become expendable in Philadelphia with Bo Diaz about to become the Phillies' backstop. It may also be claimed that Belanger was at the end of his career, and the Orioles were making room for rookie Cal Ripken Jr.; thus, the Phillies and Orioles had little to lose by letting this trio of veterans go. However, the movement of three players prominent in union circles to new addresses may well have been a case in which their former clubs simply chose to rid themselves of some of the reminders of the strike of 1981.

Summary

The first winter meetings following the devastating midseason strike of 1981 were punctuated by a backlash against Commissioner Bowie Kuhn, instigated by a group of owners intent on forcing Kuhn's resignation. Fueled by dissatisfaction over widespread financial problems besetting the national pastime and the ostensible distance at which the commissioner kept himself during the strike, those seeking Kuhn's ouster were unsuccessful in their attempt, but the dissent that surfaced in Hollywood, Florida, did not bode well for Kuhn as baseball's top executive. Trading activity was generally slower than in previous years, but formulation of a deal eventually involving two premier shortstops of the day, Garry Templeton and Ozzie Smith, was set in motion and finally consummated before the opening of spring-training camps in early 1982.

SOURCES

Gillette, Gary, and Pete Palmer, eds. *The ESPN Baseball Encyclopedia*, Fourth Edition (New York: Sterling Publishing Company, 2007).

Kuhn, Bowie. *Hardball: The Education of a Baseball Commissioner* (New York: Times Books, 1987).

Miller, Marvin. *A Whole Different Ball Game: The Sport and Business of Baseball* (New York: Birch Lane Press, 1991).

Siegel, Barry, ed. *Official 1982 Baseball Register* (St. Louis: The Sporting News, 1982).

The Baseball Encyclopedia, Ninth Edition (New York: Macmillan Publishing Company, 1993).

Wigge, Larry, Carl Clark, Dave Sloan, Craig Carter, and Barry Siegel, eds. *Official 1982 Baseball Guide* (St. Louis: The Sporting News, 1982).

NOTES

1 "Kuhn Says Baseball Lost $25 Million in 1980," *Washington Post*, December 8, 1981: C1; Bowie Kuhn, *Hardball: The Education of a Baseball Commissioner* (New York: Times Books, 1987), 362.

2 Jerome Holtzman, "Owners Discuss Sharing Income," *Chicago Tribune*, December 6, 1981: C5.

3 Bart Barnes, "Kuhn Hits Cable TV," *Washington Post*, December 10, 1981: D1.

4 Dave Nightingale, "Chances Dim for 3-Division Play," *The Sporting News*, December 12, 1981: 45.

5 Referring to a gathering of National League executives in October, O'Malley said, "I could have sworn I saw at least five hands in the air (in opposition to three-division play) at the National League meeting in Arizona." See Dave Nightingale, "Chances Dim for 3-Division Play," *The Sporting News*, December 12, 1981: 39.

6 "Chances Dim for 3-Division Play."

7 Clifford Kachline, "Baseball Takes Lumps, Survives Stormy, Strike-Plagued Season," in Larry Wigge, Carl Clark, Dave Sloan, Craig Carter, Barry Siegel, eds., *Official 1982 Baseball Guide* (St. Louis: The Sporting News, 1982), 25.

8 "Top Minor League Execs Packed Their Parks," *The Sporting News*, December 12, 1981: 40.

9 Kuhn, 366.

10 Joseph Durso, "Attack on Kuhn Shook Baseball Talks," *New York Times*, December 13, 1981: S3.

11 Ibid.

12 As Kuhn informed the *New York Times*, "The commissioner's powers are mostly restraining. I don't make labor policy or labor decisions." See Larry Wigge, Carl Clark, Dave Sloan, Craig Carter, Barry Siegel, eds., *Official 1982 Baseball Guide* (St. Louis: The Sporting News, 1982), 24.

13 Kuhn, 10.

14 Mark Heisler, "At Baseball Meetings, There's a Lot of Talk, Not Much Action," *Los Angeles Times*, December 11, 1981: G3.

15 Hal Bodley, "Phils Disgusted; Deals Collapse," *The Sporting News*, January 2, 1982: 38.

— 1982 —
DISPIRITED AND ARGUMENTATIVE

By Dan Levitt

DESPITE THE PICTURESQUE SETTING of Honolulu, baseball's owners were a largely dispirited lot as they headed into the 1982 winter meetings. They were a year and a half removed from a brutal strike in which they had failed to achieve their main objective of direct player compensation for free agents; many teams were losing money; and a minority of frustrated owners had just blocked the reelection of Commissioner Bowie Kuhn. Moreover, the animosity created by the battle over Kuhn's contract renewal had temporarily poisoned some of the relationships among the owners, vitiating the opportunity to implement several long-studied, proposed organizational changes.

In his final state-of-the-game opening address to the convention, Kuhn listed in bullet-point fashion all the unique and appealing reasons he loved the game. He also offered up his "certain commandments, certain articles of faith which should be viewed as imperatives for baseball." Not surprisingly for Kuhn, his first imperative was "protecting the integrity of our game." This was followed by deference to the permanence of the playing rules; improvement in the relationship between players and owners; high-quality ownership that respected the game and its fans; the need to modernize baseball's administrative operations; and a strong commissioner's office. In recognition of his service and his heartfelt remarks, Kuhn received a standing ovation at its conclusion.[1]

Business and Administrative Items

Many of the more far-ranging administrative proposals and initiatives that various study committees had been working on were only halfheartedly considered at the winter meetings, as the owners debated what they wanted in their next commissioner. Over the previous year a significant minority of owners had been campaigning against renewal of Kuhn's contract, which was scheduled to expire on August 12, 1983. Since the commissioner needed at least a three-quarters majority in each league for reelection, the anti-Kuhn faction had considerable clout. On November 1, 1982, despite considerable lobbying from the pro-Kuhn forces, he was formally not renewed—the AL voted 11 to 3 in favor, but the NL vote of 7 to 5 fell two votes shy.[2] Just over a month later at the winter meetings, considerable bad feeling remained between the pro- and anti-Kuhn ownership factions.

The controversy over Kuhn negated much of the effort by the restructuring committee to "bring baseball's superstructure into the Twentieth Century."[3] Co-chaired by Dodgers owner Peter O'Malley and A's owner Roy Eisenhardt, the committee had presented its preliminary findings to a generally positive reception at the summer meetings. The recommendations included items such as creating an eight-man executive committee; incorporating the league offices, the Player Relations Committee, and the Baseball Promotions Corporation under the auspices of the commissioner's office; and eliminating the division of the umpire staffs by league.[4]

The minimal restructuring that did occur consisted primarily of forming some new ownership committees, including Finance and Budget, Employee Relations, and Audit. The owners also agreed that for certain matters, they would count votes in aggregate rather than each league voting separately. To balance out league membership, each NL member's vote would count $1^{1}/16$ of an AL member's vote.[5]

Despite a strong rebound in attendance after the 1981 strike, club financial viability remained a concern. For internal presentation, the clubs divided the teams into thirds: the eight most profitable, the middle ten, and the eight at the bottom. According to their internal figures for 1980 (the most recent year for which all teams had reported their financial results), the top eight teams had an aggregate operating income of $14.7 million, the middle 10 had aggregate operating loss of $8.9 million, and the bottom eight lost $19.8 million.[6]

To solidify the financial viability of the clubs, the owners agreed to require all franchises to "have a ratio of assets to liabilities of not less than sixty (assets) to forty (liabilities)." Penalties for violating this financial covenant ranged from having a team's share of distributions from the Central Fund held in escrow to be counted as an asset in the calculation all the way to the appointment of a custodian to manage the financial affairs of a franchise. The severity of the penalty would depend on how much the team missed the financial covenant by, the reasons for missing the financial target, the previous history of noncompliance, and how hard the team was working to get back into compliance.[7]

In another initiative to bolster the weaker clubs, the owners had put forward various revenue-sharing arrangements in the months leading up to the meetings, but in the end all they could agree on was to share all League Championship Series revenue once each participating club had received $300,000. The other revenue-sharing proposals were tabled.[8]

Because the national TV rights package would be expiring at the end of the 1983 season, the owners also spent considerable time discussing the forthcoming negotiation. For this latest round of talks, the owners wanted more direct control of the process, and as a result baseball's chief TV and radio broadcast negotiator, Tom Villante, resigned in the fall, effective December 1. Instead of bringing in a new executive to lead the negotiations, at the winter meetings the baseball magnates named two of their own, Phillies President Bill Giles and White Sox co-owner Eddie Einhorn, as lead negotiators for MLB's next TV deal. Before leaving, Villante highlighted the intensifying pressure from ownership to increase national TV revenue without limiting the opportunities to also maximize local TV income.[9]

The owners also consented to some nominal amendments to the National Agreement, including extending it by its traditional five years; prohibiting anyone connected with club ownership from acting as a player agent; clarifying some minor-league rehab assignment guidelines; and approving an increase in the caps on player college tuition assistance.[10] Elsewhere, several NL owners and the Yankees' George Steinbrenner proposed removing the $400,000 cap on the cash consideration that could be included in player transactions, but they failed to garner the necessary support.[11]

Player Movement Overview

Teams remained aggressive in their pursuit of free agents to the detriment of trading activity. Winter meetings trades continued their secular decline since the introduction of free agency, novel contract innovations complicated the art of making trades, and the spring interleague trading period gave teams another window in which to make deals. In particular, several teams shied away from the trading mart because they thought they were in the running for two of the key remaining free agents, left-hander Floyd Bannister and coveted first baseman Steve Garvey, neither of whom ended up signing during the winter meetings. In 1982 only 22 players were traded in eight separate deals, down from 36 in 16 in 1981, 59 in 18 in 1980 (a one-time uptick as the first CBA came to an end), and 30 in 11 in 1979.[12] As a further comparison, in 1977 there were 53 players involved in 22 trades, in 1973 there were 58 in 26, and in 1972 there were 68 in 19.[13]

In the Rule 5 draft the Blue Jays selected right-hander Jim Acker with the fifth pick; Acker would go on to a respectable 10-year career, mostly in the bullpen. Other selections who went on to useful major-league careers included Dann Bilardello, who spent eight years as a backup catcher, and pitcher Odell Jones, who had a nine-year career, mostly working out of the pen.

Free Agency

As usual, George Steinbrenner was active and uncompromising in the free-agent market. Prior to the winter meetings he signed DH Don Baylor, and then during the meetings landed two more: lefty

Bob Shirley (four years, $1.5 million) and outfielder Steve Kemp. Kemp was one of the more coveted free agents, and Steinbrenner outbid the White Sox and Orioles by offering $5.45 million over five years. Both runners-up were unhappy. "We never even got to make an offer," complained Orioles GM Hank Peters, who had talked with Kemp's agent and had scheduled a follow-up. Owner Edward Bennett Williams was more philosophical: "If Steinbrenner's giving the kind of numbers I think he is, well, you just have to stop somewhere. I don't know what he's trying to do. It's like he's stockpiling nuclear weapons with all those outfielders—and if somebody doesn't take some of them off his hands, he's going to die with them."[14]

The White Sox responded just after the meetings ended by landing southpaw Floyd Bannister, coveted by the Yankees, for $4.5 million over five years. A spurned Steinbrenner labeled White Sox co-owners Jerry Reinsdorf and Eddie Einhorn "the Abbott and Costello of baseball" for the lavish contract, particularly the clauses that called for an optional additional three years and a payment to the pitcher if the White Sox did not renew him for his option years. "Those two guys come into the league meetings and they never say the same thing. They keep it lighthearted, make us laugh. But I forgave them because they've given me the only laugh in baseball I've had in years." Regarding Bannister, Steinbrenner continued: "Floyd didn't want to tackle the pressures of New York. As far as I'm concerned, his signing with the White Sox is fine."[15]

Reinsdorf responded: "What's the big deal? That's not going to make him the highest-paid pitcher. George doesn't know what he's talking about. He's probably paying Ron Guidry more than that. Nolan Ryan and Steve Carlton are at a million a year, or over. George is just upset because he didn't sign Bannister. After he gets the facts, he'll calm down and everything will be okay. I don't care if he calls us 'Abbott and Costello' or 'The Katzenjammer Kids.' I think it's silly and he ought to stop. But so long as he doesn't call us Hitler and Mussolini, I don't care."[16]

In another notable free-agent signing during the winter meetings, the Astros landed speedy Pirates center fielder Omar Moreno. When Astros GM Al Rosen released Moreno's compensation as $3.25 million over five years, Pirates GM Pete Peterson claimed his offer was only $125,000 less and called out Moreno's agent, Tom Reich, complaining "that he didn't do a

Trading Trends

Prior to the 1982 winter meetings, Oakland A's President Roy Eisenhardt opined on the likelihood of trades: "There are two variables affecting trading, and they work in opposite directions. First, the complexity of trading has increased geometrically. You can't sit down and talk trade anymore without a lawyer, an accountant and an interpreter. The other variable is the climate, literally, of the winter meetings. In Hawaii, there is a loose, easy-going climate. It's a little different from the tension of sitting around during three rainy days in Dallas. It'll be more relaxed, and that will have an effect. Honestly, the single factor most conducive to trading might be rum—mai tais and piña coladas."*

Previous meetings in Hawaii resulted in plenty of action—68 players involved in 19 trades in 1972, and 53 players involved in 22 trades in 1977.** However, the 1982 meetings resulted in under 10 trades,*** consistent with the meetings from the previous year, which resulted in just 16 deals.****

---

* Associated Press, "Baseball Winter Meetings Open Monday in Hawaii," *Shreveport* (Louisiana) *Times*, December 5, 1982: 7.
** Ibid.
*** Associated Press, "Seaver Heads Back to Mets," *Pensacola* (Florida) *News Journal*, December 11, 1982: 13.
**** "Baseball Winter Meetings Open Monday in Hawaii."

good job handling the negotiations." He added that he was also "disappointed in some people in the Houston organization for some things that happened." Reich responded that the contract was for $3.50 million with the ability to earn annual performance bonuses on top of that.[17] In one more winter meeting move, Milwaukee re-signed left-hander Bob McClure for $1.75 million over three years.

Trades

Oakland and Boston found a match early in the meetings. Oakland wanted a third baseman and Boston had a star in Carney Lansford, set to become a free agent at the end of 1983 and looking for a contract beyond what the Red Sox wanted to pay. Moreover, Boston had youngster Wade Boggs ready to step in at third. For their part, next to a number-one starter, Boston wanted a power hitter to bat behind Jim Rice, and Oakland outfielder Tony Armas was one of the league's top power threats. Additionally, from Oakland's point of view, shedding Armas (along with catcher Jeff Newman) freed up payroll that could be used to try to re-sign Lansford. In a swap that also found Boston parting with outfielder/first baseman Garry Hancock and minor-league pitcher Jerry King, Armas for Lansford was the first big trade of the winter meetings.[18]

With Moreno on board, Astros GM Rosen had sufficient outfield depth to trade Danny Heep to the Mets for pitcher Mike Scott, who several years later turned into one of baseball's most dominant pitchers (he won the NL Cy Young Award in 1986). The Mets also reacquired veteran all-time great Tom Seaver from the Reds, though the deal would not become official until several days after the winter meetings when the two sides agreed to new contract terms.[19]

No one orchestrated these winter meetings like Phillies GM Paul Owens, however. In late November he publicly let it be known that he craved Indians outfielder Von Hayes, a young, left-handed outfield bat, and that he was willing to surrender star second baseman Manny Trillo to get him. Moreover, if he pulled this off, Owens acknowledged, Giants second baseman Joe Morgan would make a nice replacement.[20]

Presented all the negotiating leverage by Owens's public remarks, Indians President Gabe Paul and GM Phil Seghi drove a hard bargain for Hayes. They extracted five players from the Phillies, rebuilding their keystone combination with Trillo and top shortstop prospect Julio Franco, plus landing reliever Jay Baller, outfielder George Vukovich, and catcher Jerry Willard. Of the final three, Baller was the key piece for the Indians, viewed as one of the better pitching prospects in baseball. This represented quite a haul for Cleveland despite Trillo's having only one more year on his contract.[21]

The Yankees and Blue Jays also engaged in a noteworthy swap, one Toronto GM Pat Gillick later called one of his favorite deals. The Yankees desperately sought Toronto's relief ace Dale Murray, and after several rounds of negotiations, Gillick agreed to take outfielder Dave Collins and pitcher Mike Morgan in exchange. Gillick initially negotiated with Bill Bergesch, the latest general manager in the Yankees' ever-changing and chaotic front office. But like any savvy trader, he wanted an additional prospect, particularly one with power. Gillick and his scouts liked 18-year-old first baseman Fred McGriff, still in Rookie ball, but didn't mention him right away for fear the Yankees would ask for more. Instead Gillick mentioned outfielder Dan Pasqua and first baseman Don Mattingly, two prospects he knew the Yankees didn't want to surrender. Finally, Steinbrenner stepped in and called Gillick, telling him that he would have to take McGriff as the third player in the deal or there wouldn't be one. Gillick coyly responded that he needed to check with his scouts and would call back in 15 minutes. When he did so, he got the player he wanted all along.[22]

Near the end of the meetings, Owens swapped righty starter Mike Krukow and two minor leaguers (including southpaw Mark Davis, who would later blossom with the Padres) to the Giants for second baseman Joe Morgan and lefty reliever Al Holland, who became the team's closer. (The Yankees also wanted Al Holland, but the Giants turned down their offer of catcher Butch Wynegar.[23]) The trade could not be announced until after the meetings because as a condition of the trade, Morgan needed to wrap up a new contract with the Phillies. In addition to landing a key reliever, Owens thus neatly backfilled his second-base hole after losing Trillo in the Von Hayes deal.[24] "Before we went to the winter meetings in Hawaii," Giles said, "we wrote down the names of the players we wanted most. Those players were Von Hayes, Joe Morgan, and Al Holland, Now, we have them all."[25] With their three new players, the Phillies would win a surprise pennant in 1983.

Texas GM Joe Klein wanted to add pitching and was willing to surrender one of his three coveted position players: third baseman Buddy Bell, catcher Jim Sundberg, or outfielder Larry Parrish. "We would like to add a quality starter," Klein said. "We've got a good list of pitchers who are in competition for starting jobs and I'd feel confident picking two of them. I'm satisfied with Danny Darwin and Charlie Hough and we think we can pick two out of a list that includes Mike Smithson, Frank Tanana, John Butcher, Steve Comer, Rick Honeycutt, Jon Matlack, and Jim Farr. But rather than pick a fifth starter out of that group, I'd rather get a number-one or number-two starter in a trade, depending on what we can concoct."[26]

And he almost did. Despite having two proven catchers on his squad in veteran Steve Yeager and youngster Mike Scioscia, Dodgers GM Al Campanis wanted a defensive stalwart behind the plate. "In this league, a catcher has to be able to throw well," Campanis said. "A catcher can save you a lot of games. We're not just going for a bat, we're going for a lot of things."[27] Sundberg fit Campanis's requirements perfectly, and Klein concocted a great deal: for Sundberg, Texas would receive right-handed pitchers Burt Hooton and Dave Stewart, plus another righty, Orel Hershiser (then in the high minors) and a minor-league outfielder. Unfortunately for the Rangers, Sundberg had some contractual stumbling blocks: he had a no-trade clause requiring a $250,000 buyout; he had the right under the collective-bargaining agreement to demand a trade after the 1983 season; and he wanted to renegotiate his contract, consolidating payments from the later years into a shorter term. Sundberg, the Rangers, and the Dodgers could not come to a mutually satisfactory solution, and the deal fell through.[28]

Klein was also working on a deal to send third baseman Buddy Bell to the Cardinals. St. Louis reportedly offered outfielder George Hendrick, pitcher Steve Mura, and third baseman Ken Oberkfell, but after several days of negotiating, no swap could be finalized. Frustrated Cardinals manager Whitey Herzog complained, "It's amazing that a team can lose 100 games (Texas actually lost 98) and won't make a deal. I feel sorry for people in baseball who have a million-dollar investment and don't know what to do. You mean all these guys are content to go the same way next year? You go to the World Series and teams say, 'Let's wait for free agency before we make a deal.' You go to the winter meetings and they say, 'Let's wait until the interleague trading period in the spring.' They all think they've got pennant winners. I can't believe they won't get off their butts."[29]

As always, a number of other almost fully-baked deals fizzled. The Reds hoped to land a big right-handed bat at the meetings, preferably San Francisco's Jack Clark, but couldn't work out a trade despite

> ### No Big Deal
>
> While much excitement was taking place with the major leagues, John H. Johnson, president of the minor leagues, indicated that he didn't expect much drama during the minors portion of the meetings. "There isn't much legislation on the minor league side," he said. "It's the slimmest I have seen in a long time. Either things are going very well or we are in serious trouble." He added, "We don't have any restructuring problems that the major leagues have. We have just a few adjustments to make—you might say minor matters in the minor leagues."*
>
> ---
> * Ferd Borsch, "Minors' Business Won't Take Long," *Honolulu Advertiser*, December 1, 1982: 105.

offering hurler Frank Pastore, second baseman Ron Oester, and outfielders Mike Vail and Duane Walker.[30] The Mariners had apparently agreed to send second baseman Julio Cruz to Cleveland for first baseman Mark Hargrove before Cleveland landed Trillo in the Von Hayes blockbuster.[31] Dodgers third baseman Ron Cey, whose contract would expire after the 1983 season, was also mentioned prominently in several rumored trades, but none came to fruition.

NOTES

1. Bowie Kuhn Papers, Baseball Hall of Fame, S3-SS3-B6-F1; Stan Isle, "Kuhn Cites 'Imperatives' for Baseball," *The Sporting News*, December 20, 1982: 2.

2. Clifford Kachline, "Baseball Shocks Doomsayers, Attains New Popularity Heights," Official Baseball Guide for 1983 (St. Louis: The Sporting News), 6.

3. Kachline, 8.

4. Kachline, 9-10.

5. Joint Meeting of the Major Leagues, December 9, 1982, Kuhn Papers Baseball Hall of Fame, S3-SS2-B2-F4; Dave Nightingale, "Owners Soak Up Sun, Spin Their Wheels," *The Sporting News*, December 20, 1982: 2.

6. Bowie Kuhn Papers, Baseball Hall of Fame, S1-SS1-B2-F8.

7. Joint Meeting of the Major Leagues, December 9, 1982, Kuhn Papers Baseball Hall of Fame, S3-SS2-B2-F4.

8. Ibid.; Dave Nightingale, "Owners Soak Up Sun, Spin Their Wheels."

9. Nightingale, "Owners Soak Up Sun, Spin Their Wheels"; Kuhn Papers, Baseball Hall of Fame, S3-SS3-B5-F7.

10. Kuhn Papers, Baseball Hall of Fame, S3-SS3-B5-F7.

11. Joint Meeting of the Major Leagues, December 9, 1982; Kuhn Papers, Baseball Hall of Fame, S3-SS2-B2-F4.

12. Murray Chass, "Moreno Signs With the Astros," *New York Times*, December 11, 1982.

13. "Honolulu Plays Host to Baseball," *Washington Post*, December 5, 1982; "Yawns Replace Trades at Baseball Meetings," *Washington Post*, December 12, 1982; Bill Conlin, "A Ho-Hum Session in Hawaii," *The Sporting News*, December 20, 1982: 50.

14. Jim Henneman, "O's Plans Collapse as Kemp Escapes," *The Sporting News*, December 20, 1982: 52.

15. Jerome Holtzman, "Yankee Boss Pans Sox 'Comedy Act,'" *Chicago Tribune*, December 15, 1982.

16. Ibid.

17. Charley Feeney, "Peterson Seething at Reich, Astros," *The Sporting News*, December 20, 1982: 59; Charley Feeney, "Agent Defends Work for Moreno," *The Sporting News*, January 3, 1983: 32.

18. Kit Stier, "Lansford Plugs A's Biggest Gap," *The Sporting News*, December 20, 1982: 53; Peter Gammons, "A's, Bosox, Tribe Deals Look OK," *The Sporting News*, December 20, 1982: 50.

19. The Mets sent right-hander Charlie Puleo and two minor-league utilitymen—Lloyd McClendon and Jason Felice—to the Reds. Jack Lang, "Mets Tab Seaver For 10 to 15 Wins," *The Sporting News*, December 20, 1982: 59; Earl Lawson, "Puleo Could Win Reds Starting Job," *The Sporting News*, December 27, 1982: 41; Jack Lang, "Exile Ends; Mets Welcome Seaver," *The Sporting News*, December 27, 1982: 40.

20. "A Cracker Jack Replay," *Washington Post*, December 1, 1982.

21. Peter Gammons, "A's, Bosox, Tribe Deals Look OK"; Hal Bodley, "Hayes to Give Phillies Muscle," *The Sporting News*, December 20, 1982: 56.

22. Author interview with Pat Gillick, October 2, 2012.

23. Murray Chass, "Moreno Signs With the Astros," *New York Times*, December 11, 1982.

24. "Morgan, Holland Go to Phillies," *Los Angeles Times*, December 15, 1982; "Phils Fill a Void in Deal for Morgan," *Chicago Tribune*, December 15, 1982.

25. Hal Bodley, "Phillies' Wishes All Come True," *The Sporting News*, December 27, 1982: 40.

26. Jim Reeves, "Rangers May Deal Parrish or Bell," *The Sporting News*, December 13, 1982: 57.

27. Gordon Verrell, "Sundberg Trade for Hooton Off," *The Sporting News*, December 20, 1982: 58.

28. Ross Newhan, "Dodgers to Trade Hooton Plus 3 for Sundberg, Maybe," *Los Angeles Times*, December 10, 1982; Jim Reeves, "Sundberg Swaps May Be Revived," *The Sporting News*, December 27, 1982: 43; Jim Reeves, "Rangers May Deal Parrish or Bell"; Gordon Verrell, "Sundberg Trade for Hooton Off"; Jim Reeves, "Collapse of Deal Jolts the Rangers," *The Sporting News*, December 20, 1982: 54.

29. Rick Hummel, "Herzog Annoyed by Timid Traders," *The Sporting News*, December 20, 1982: 56.

30. Earl Lawson, "Reds Fall Short in Bid for Clark," *The Sporting News*, December 20, 1982: 59.

31. Tracy Ringolsby, "M's Are Seeking a Lefthanded Bat," *The Sporting News*, December 27, 1982: 45.

— 1983 —
THE END OF THE BOWIE KUHN ERA

by Michael Huber

Introduction

THE 1983 BASEBALL WINTER Meetings were held at the Opryland Hotel, in Nashville, Tennessee, from December 5 to 10. Trades and free-agent signings usually headline the agenda of the annual gathering of executives, managers, scouts, agents, lawyers, accountants, and media personnel. Going into the 1983 meetings, though, there were several unresolved issues, including the naming of a new commissioner, the selection of a new American League president, and the completion of a restructuring plan that many executives felt was long overdue.

Executive Personnel Changes

Bowie Kuhn had been the fifth commissioner of major league baseball, having first been elected in 1969, but his contract was not renewed in 1983. His tenure as commissioner had been marked by labor strikes (the most noteworthy being the seven-week stoppage during the 1981 season) and the end of baseball's reserve clause. Despite overseeing a doubling of attendance from 1968 to 1983 and a growth in television revenue, Kuhn was forced out by a majority group of disenchanted owners. Kuhn had also been responsible for getting the World Series into prime time; the first World Series night game was played in 1971. Further, Kuhn had a reputation for being hard on players who abused drugs. These were all themes as Commissioner Kuhn gave a valedictory address to officially open the 82nd annual meetings. He viewed the selection of a new commissioner as "a problem and an opportunity."[1] Kuhn called for the new commissioner to be "strong as a personality who will have the necessary courage in the face of relentless problems and pressures and to do what is necessary for the good of the game."[2] He placed emphasis on the problems of drugs and player drug abuse, where "the self-indulgence of a few mars the reputation of the great majority of players who do not use or abuse drugs and mars the reputation of the game."[3] He pushed for collaboration with the Major League Baseball Players Association. He also celebrated the new $1 billion-plus television contracts and increases in attendance, while keeping ticket prices relatively low.

Bud Selig, owner of the Milwaukee Brewers, chaired the Commissioner Search Committee. In early November, Selig told reporters, "I really don't know what will happen in Nashville. It's possible we'll name the new man there, but I won't assure you it's going to happen."[4]

Several names were indeed floating around as candidates for the top job. They included Hall of Famer Henry Aaron (who was the Atlanta Braves' director of player personnel); Congressman Silvio Conte (Republican from Massachusetts); newspaper magnate Francis Dale; Yale University President A. Bartlett Giamatti; Chrysler's Lee Iacocca; United States District Judge Prentice Marshall (presiding in Northern Illinois); Montreal Expos Vice President John McHale; CBS Sports executive Neal Pilson United States Steel's William Resch; United States Olympic Committee President William Simon; Los Angeles Olympic Organizing Committee President Peter Ueberroth; and NBC Sports executive Arthur Watson. Many felt that Giamatti was the front-runner, but Selig refused to comment before the meetings began. Selig later spoke to the press in Nashville, and reporter Peter Gammons wrote wryly, "When Bud

Selig was telling the media that all the stories of his offering the commissionership to various individuals amounted to nothing more than idle and inaccurate speculation, the song playing over the public-address system was Marvin Gaye's version of 'I Heard It Through the Grapevine.'"[5] The Winter Meetings ended without a selection of a new commissioner. Ueberroth told the press he was one of two finalists, but he was withdrawing his name from consideration because of the upcoming Olympics. Kuhn's contract was due to expire on December 31, so he agreed to serve as a 60-day "transitory bridge"[6] during the continuing search.

Candidate Aaron was quoted as saying, "I'm not saying I'm the one who should get the job—maybe I'm not—but I do think we need a baseball man. A baseball man would be more conscious of what is good for the fans. When I interviewed with the search committee for the job, they told me that baseball has grown so much we need a commissioner who understands finance and marketing. If that's what they want, fine. But I think a baseball man knows more about marketing our game—about bringing players into our game and fans into our stadiums—than someone who doesn't know anything about the game." He added, "I'm perfectly satisfied with my job right here [as head of the Braves' farm system]. My main concern is to make sure we have a championship team."[7]

Naming a new commissioner was the top priority, but many felt that even if a decision could not be reached, the owners would be able to find a replacement for Lee MacPhail, who was stepping down as president of the American League in order to direct the owners' Player Relations Committee. *The Sporting News* listed several candidates in the days leading up to the Winter Meetings, and all were either current or former general managers: Peter Bavasi (Toronto Blue Jays), Frank Cashen (New York Mets), Harry Dalton (Milwaukee Brewers), Danny O'Brien (Seattle Mariners), Hank Peters (Baltimore Orioles), and Al Rosen (Houston Astros).[8]

Instead, Dr. Bobby Brown, the former New York Yankees third baseman and now a cardiologist, accepted a five-year contract as the AL's new president. He disclosed to reporters, "I was interviewed twice for the commissioner's job. My appointment (as American League president) came about as a result of my conversations with the search committee."[9] He added, "I will be sorely disappointed if my job is not fun."

The owners also made changes to the Executive Council. Nelson Doubleday of the New York Mets and Roy Eisenhardt of the Oakland Athletics were voted to the council, replacing Bob Lurie of the San Francisco Giants and Haywood Sullivan of the Boston Red Sox, respectively. The remaining Council members were Dan Galbreath of the Pittsburgh Pirates, Peter O'Malley of the Los Angeles Dodgers, Jerry Reinsdorf of the Chicago White Sox, Bud Selig of the Milwaukee Brewers, Ballard Smith of the San Diego Padres, and Edward Bennett Williams of the Baltimore Orioles.

Player Trades and Signings

With the importance of these executive decisions, trading might not have been prominently on the owners' minds at the meetings. In 1980, 59 players changed uniforms in 18 transactions at the annual meetings. In 1982, only eight trades were conducted, involving 22 players,[10] and many considered those trades to be minor. From the end of the 1983 season to the Winter Meetings in December, only six teams adjusted their rosters via the trade or outright purchase of players.

At the Nashville meeting, 18 teams participated in the reshuffling of players. The meetings resulted in 17 trades or purchases featuring 35 major-league players. According to one writer, the teams in the American League West Division "were wheeling and dealing like riverboat gamblers."[11] At the deadline of 5 P.M. CST on December 9, there were 26 new players on the rosters of the seven AL West teams. Their counterparts in the AL East had 17 new roster faces on their seven teams. The National League (both divisions) had just 19 players change uniforms. Only five players were signed as free agents by only four teams: right-handed pitcher Frank LaCorte by the Angels, outfielder Dave Parker by the Reds, outfielder Lynn Jones and catcher Don Werner by the Royals, and catcher Mike Berry by the Yankees.

Milwaukee's Harry Dalton was the general manager who paid the highest price at the meetings. For catcher Jim Sundberg of the Texas Rangers, he gave up catcher Ned Yost and minor-league left-hander Dan Scarpetta. Dalton agreed to pay Sundberg's buyout clause and deferred salary, costing his franchise approximately $1 million. This brought on predictions of two possible outcomes: either a pennant for the Brewers or a "Million Dollar Misunderstanding."[12] The average salary in 1983 was just over $289,000.[13]

Among the whispers as the meetings began was the naming of Yogi Berra to manage the New York Yankees, as owner George Steinbrenner was, for the third time, unhappy with Billy Martin as his skipper.

Policy and Rule Changes

In addition to executive personnel recommendations and player dealings, the Playing Rules Committee was expected to make a decision on a proposal concerning the designated hitter in the postseason. Prior to these Winter Meetings, the designated hitter was used in all World Series games, but only in even-numbered years (the last time in 1982). The Baltimore Orioles won the 1983 World Series without the benefit of a designated hitter. The Executive Council proposed that the DH be employed in every World Series but only in games hosted by the American League. The new rule was passed by the Playing Rules Committee, but it did not gain the approval of the owners. The proposal needed a majority approval in both leagues, and opposition by National League owners prevented its adoption. So, in 1984, the designated hitter would be used under the existing conditions, but there would be no designated hitters in the 1985 Series unless the proposal was revisited.

Along these lines, the owners established a committee to review the designated-hitter rule during the regular season. Commissioner Kuhn said, "Kill it or keep it; frankly, I don't give a hoot which way it's handled. I strongly urge uniformity and, if I had my way, there would be uniformity by the 1985 season."[14]

Baseball owners instructed the Long-Range Planning Committee to undertake a feasibility study regarding expansion. The committee would develop a flexible plan to increase the number of teams in the major leagues by six. This would mean a balanced pair of two 16-team leagues (in 1983, the American League had 14 teams, seven in each division, and the National league had 12 teams, six in each division). This committee consisted of the two league presidents and six team executives: Buzzie Bavasi of the California Angels, Charles Bronfman of the Montreal Expos, Andy McKenna of the Chicago Cubs, Peter O'Malley of the Los Angeles Dodgers, Jerry Reinsdorf of the Chicago White Sox, and Haywood Sullivan of the Boston Red Sox.

Also up for consideration at the meetings was a proposal put forward by the Executive Council to create an additional waiver date of August 1. The rule at this time stated that any player who cleared waivers by the June 15 intraleague trading deadline could be dealt elsewhere until the end of the season. If the new date was adopted, it would be necessary for a player to clear waivers on August 1 before he could be sent elsewhere during the final two months of the regular season. The measure was rejected.

The general managers proposed that the supplemental 15-day disabled list be expanded. Prior to this proposal, a team could place only one player (who was not a pitcher) on the 15-day disabled list. If approved, teams would be allowed to place two players on the 15-day DL, and one of the two could now be a pitcher. This measure was adopted.

One of the more infamous events in recent baseball history was the "Pine Tar Game" between the Kansas City Royals and the New York Yankees. After George Brett had hit a two-out, two-run home run in the ninth inning of a June 24, 1983, contest at Yankee Stadium, giving the Royals a 5-4 lead, New York manager Billy Martin notified home-plate umpire Tim McClelland that Brett's bat was not in conformity with MLB Rule 1.10(c); there appeared to be too much pine tar on the bat's handle. McClelland conferred with the other umpires and then called Brett out, thus giving the Yankees the 4-3 victory. Brett had "hit the game-losing home run."[15] The Royals filed a protest, and American League President Lee MacPhail upheld the protest, ruling in favor of Kansas City. He restored Brett's home run and ordered that play continue with two outs in the top of the ninth. The Royals held on to beat the Yankees by the 5-4 score.

Because of this notable incident, the Playing Rules Committee issued a formal change in the pine-tar rule at the Winter Meetings. Starting with the 1984 season, "a player will neither be ejected nor declared out if he uses a bat with excessive pine tar on the handle. An umpire may eject only the bat."[16]

In other news, the owners adopted an improved pension plan for club nonplaying employees. They also signed a five-year contract for national radio broadcasts with CBS Radio, with the deal covering the 1985 through 1989 seasons. A complicated television plan that supported game-sharing on satellite for local pay-TV venues was approved.

A proposal to require that minor-league postseason games be subject to approval by the Professional Baseball Executive Council was rejected. However, the owners did vote to approve a motion for ballclubs to utilize a service of the Major League Scouting Bureau, beginning in 1984.

Recognizing Achievement

In addition to the player negotiations, the meetings provided opportunities to recognize achievement. Cal Ripken Jr. was selected as the American League's Most Valuable Player by the Baseball Writers Association of America. He also garnered recognition from *The Sporting News* as the 1983 Major League Player of the Year. Ripken was presented with a replica of "The Sandlot Kid," a statue that stands outside Doubleday Field in Cooperstown, New York, at ceremonies during the meetings. The Orioles shortstop played every inning of every game in 1983, and he commented about the award, "To win these awards you have to have been on a very good team. Winning the World Series was the goal of every player, and that is the big thing. That's what is most important."[17] Ripken's general manager, Hank Peters, was named Major League Executive of the Year. This was Peters's second such award in five years.

Since 1951, the "King of Baseball" title had been awarded during the Winter Meetings banquet to a minor-league veteran, and Oscar Roettger was crowned in Nashville. Roettger had played for the Yankees more than 50 years earlier and had coached in their organization. The 85-year-old from St. Louis retired from the game as representative for Rawlings Sporting Goods. He measured hundreds of players for equipment and uniforms and had been attending the Winter Meetings for 50 years.

The United States Olympic baseball team's preliminary roster was announced, naming 44 players to the squad. The tryouts had been held in October in Louisville, Kentucky, and 76 players, mostly from the college ranks, had participated. Hall of Famer Robin Roberts hosted a luncheon for the announcement. The 44-man roster would still need to be trimmed down to 25 by June 1, 1984.

Larry Shenk received the Robert O. Fishel Award, given for excellence in public relations. Shenk was the Philadelphia Phillies' vice president and public-relations director, and he had been in the Phillies organization for 20 years.

Finally, plans were made for an Old-Timers' championship series, which was set to begin on May 26, 1984. Seven stars, including Hall of Famers Henry Aaron, Ernie Banks, Whitey Ford, Juan Marichal, Willie Mays, and Brooks Robinson, had signed up to participate in the best-of-seven series, to be played in cities across the United States and Canada. Harmon Killebrew (who would be inducted into Cooperstown in 1984) had also agreed to play. Details showed that each old-timer would earn a minimum of $1,500 per game.

Future Annual Meetings

The owners decided to hold the 1984 Summer Meetings in Philadelphia and the 1984 Winter Meetings in Houston.

Nashville became a popular site for the owners' annual winter sessions. After this initial gathering in 1983, Opryland would host the National Association of Professional Baseball Leagues' meetings in 1989, 1998, 2002, 2007. The 2015 meetings were also held in Nashville.

NOTES

1. Stan Isle, "Kuhn Calls for Commitment by Owners," *The Sporting News*, December 19, 1983: 46.
2. Ibid.
3. Ibid.
4. Dave Nightingale, "Trades May Steal Show at Nashville," *The Sporting News*, December 5, 1983: 44.
5. Peter Gammons, "A.L. Beat: Deals Appear Most Beneficial to A's," *The Sporting News*, December 19, 1983: 38.
6. Dave Nightingale, "Who'll Follow Kuhn? The Search Goes On," *The Sporting News*, December 19, 1983: 47.
7. "Aaron Still Wants to Succeed Kuhn," *The Sporting News*, December 5, 1983: 46.
8. "Trades May Steal Show at Nashville."
9. "Who'll Follow Kuhn? The Search Goes On."
10. See the chapter on the 1982 Winter Meetings in this book by Dan Levitt, "1982: Dispirited and Argumentative."
11. Dave Nightingale, "A.L. West Is Active in the Trade Market," *The Sporting News*, December 19, 1983: 48.
12. Ibid.
13. sports.espn.go.com/espn/wire?id=3744821. Sundberg made the All-Star team for the Brewers in 1984 but was traded in January 1985 to the Kansas City Royals, where he won a World Series ring in 1985.
14. "Who'll Follow Kuhn? The Search Goes On."
15. Mike McKenzie, "Umpires' Ruling Beats the Tar Out of Royals," *Kansas City Star*, July 25, 1983.
16. "Who'll Follow Kuhn? The Search Goes On."
17. Jim Henneman, "Player of the Year: One More Prize for Cal Ripken Jr.," *The Sporting News*, December 12, 1983: 2.

1984
SUPERSTATIONARY

By Ross E. Davies

THE 1984 WINTER MEETINGS IN Houston, Texas, took place in the midst of important leadership transitions for both major-league baseball and the Major League Baseball Players Association. Baseball had a new commissioner—Peter Ueberroth, an outsider best known for founding First Travel Corporation and for his role in the highly praised and financially successful 1984 Summer Olympics in Los Angeles. He succeeded Bowie Kuhn, whose contract was not renewed after 14 years. The union did *not* have a new executive director. The players had misfired with their selection of Kenneth Moffett to succeed Marvin Miller,[1] and so Donald Fehr, a baseball insider best known for his long and effective service as counsel to the union, was filling the role on an "acting" basis. (In December 1985, Fehr was elected to fill the position permanently.)[2]

Thus, a casual observer might well have assumed that in late 1984, the owners had their house in order while the players were in disarray. The reality was less dramatic, yet more interesting. First of all, owners and players alike were heavily concerned every December with achieving success in the short term, which meant putting together teams that could win games in the coming season. Second, baseball remained both a business and a game, and big changes tended to come slowly and only after much talking and agonizing and maneuvering. Third, no matter what else might be happening in baseball, traditions would be honored. All three of those points had always been present at the winter meetings, and 1984 would be no different. Fourth and finally, while labor-management negotiations loomed—the current collective-bargaining agreement was due to expire on December 31—they would have to wait a few more days.[3]

The Players – Drafting and Dealing

Opening day of the meetings featured the Rule 5 draft. On Monday, December 3, a total of 13 major-league players who'd been left off their teams' 40-man rosters were drafted by other teams.[4] The Mets, who would at the end of the meetings be the big winners in the Gary Carter trade (more about that later), began the meetings as, apparently, the big losers in the draft, with four of their players selected by other teams.[5] But with the benefit of hindsight, it was actually the Toronto Blue Jays and San Diego Padres who gave up players who would turn out to have long and productive careers:

Rule 5 Draft, 1984

PLAYER	FROM	TO
Brian Giles	New York Mets	Milwaukee Brewers
Doug Gwosdz	San Diego Padres	San Francisco Giants
Bill Landrum	Cincinnati Reds	Chicago White Sox
Manuel Lee	Houston Astros	Toronto Blue Jays
Willie Lozado	Milwaukee Brewers	St. Louis Cardinals
Mike Morgan	Toronto Blue Jays	Seattle Mariners
Ed Olwine	New York Mets	Philadelphia Phillies
Junior Ortiz	New York Mets	Pittsburgh Pirates
Mark Salas	St. Louis Cardinals	Minnesota Twins
Lou Thornton	New York Mets	Toronto Blue Jays
Mike Trujillo	San Francisco Giants	Boston Red Sox
Jim Weaver	Minnesota Twins	Detroit Tigers
Mitch Williams	San Diego Padres	Texas Rangers

The minor-league phase of the draft took place the next day. The Mets did some restocking, making five of the 15 picks:[6]

Class AAA

(teams identified by major-league affiliation)

PLAYER	FROM	TO
Omar Bencomo	Boston Red Sox	Toronto Blue Jays
Kevin Burrell	Boston Red Sox	New York Mets
Matt Cimo	San Francisco Giants	Baltimore Orioles
Geoffrey Doggett	Chicago Cubs	New York Mets
Mark Gillaspie	San Diego Padres	Chicago Cubs
Kenneth Jones	Cincinnati Reds	Seattle Mariners
David Nix	Chicago White Sox	New York Mets
Rafael Pimentel	St. Louis Cardinals	Milwaukee Brewers
Jeff Reynolds	Toronto Blue Jays	Montreal Expos
Mark Williams	Montreal Expos	Chicago White Sox

Class AA

(teams identified by major-league affiliation)

PLAYER	FROM	TO
Douglas Barba	Cincinnati Reds	New York Mets
David Haberle	Cincinnati Reds	Pittsburgh Pirates
Angel Morris	Pittsburgh Pirates	Kansas City Royals
Jose Pruneda	California Angels	Chicago White Sox
Scott Thompson	San Diego Padres	New York Mets

Also on December 4, the Montreal Expos purchased first baseman John Daugherty from the independent Pioneer League's Helena (Montana) Gold Sox (which would in 1985 become a rookie-league affiliate of the Milwaukee Brewers).

Trades

The 1984 meetings were low on trade volume, but some of those trades proved to be immediately important and historically significant. Sixteen trades had been completed in 1983 and there would be 12 in 1985, but in 1984 there were just 10 or 11.

Why the uncertainty about the number? Because by 1984 it was not necessarily easy to define what qualified as business conducted at the winter meetings. Put another way, did the meetings really begin with the first official proceedings on Monday morning and end with the last official business on Friday afternoon? Or could there be action before or after those moments that might also qualify as part of the winter meetings?

One of those important 1984 trades nicely illustrates the puzzle. The deal in question sent future Hall of Fame catcher Gary Carter from the Montreal Expos to the New York Mets for infielder Hubie Brooks, catcher Mike Fitzgerald, outfielder Herm Winningham, and minor-league right-handed pitcher Floyd Youmans.

The winter meetings themselves officially began on Monday, December 3, and ended on Friday, December 7, with no word of the transaction sending Carter to the Mets. That's because the pieces were not all in place until Sunday, December 9, and the trade was not made public until December 10 (the date experts commonly use when talking about the deal).[7] Wrote the *New York Times* on Tuesday, December 11:

"The trade was worked out unexpectedly last Friday at the winter baseball meetings in Houston, but was wrapped in absolute secrecy by both clubs. Carter [who had the seniority and service to veto a trade] reportedly gave his assent to the Expos on Sunday, and then Cashen flew to Florida yesterday with Al Harazin, vice president of the Mets. ... An announcement was planned in both Montreal and New York for today. But when the clubs began to receive inquiries late yesterday, they promptly scheduled a joint announcement for 9:30 last night."[8]

So, an important transaction began to take shape on the last day of the winter meetings, was finalized over the weekend after the winter meetings, and was announced and recorded for posterity on Monday. And yet ever since, it has been treated as a

Winter Meetings deal. Nowadays, Carter-to-Mets frequently appears on lists with titles like "The biggest Winter Meetings trades of all time"[9] and "5 most lopsided trades in Winter Meetings history."[10] Similarly, albeit less importantly, business before the Winter Meetings officially opened was treated the same way. The *Hartford Courant*, for example, reported that, "The first deal of the Winter Meetings was made Sunday [December 2]: The Cubs made a conditional purchase of Jamie Nelson, a 25-year-old minor-league catcher, from Milwaukee."[11]

Another one of the really big trades of the 1984 Winter Meetings— future Hall of Fame outfielder Rickey Henderson (and right-handed pitcher Bert Bradley and cash) going from the Oakland Athletics to the New York Yankees for right-handed pitchers Jay Howell and Jose Rijo, outfielder Stan Javier, and two minor-league hurlers, lefty Tim Birtsas and righty Eric Plunk—illustrates the converse of the same puzzle. The Henderson-to-Yankees deal is commonly treated as having been done on Tuesday, December 5, solidly within the official Winter Meetings week.[12] Yet in a December 8 article, the Associated Press reported that as the Winter Meetings ended on December 7, "the New York Yankees still were negotiating with Oakland A's outfielder Rickey Henderson and his agent, Richie Bry, on a contract that could consummate a seven-player deal between the two clubs."[13] Indeed, one *Sporting News* story excluded the Henderson-to-Yankees deal from the tally of Winter Meetings trades (finding there were only nine) precisely because it "took place after the journalists went home" when "the 1984 meeting droned to a close at 5 p.m. on Pearl Harbor Day" (Friday, December 7).[14]

The lesson of these stories may be that the duration of the Winter Meetings had become much like the strike zone: Both the drawing of the boundaries and the identification of what falls within them are at least partly matters of judgment and perspective.

It was a squishiness that was quite reasonable and understandable. By the 1980s (if not earlier), the business of baseball was not a simple, seasonal business for anyone involved. It was so complex, multifaceted, and year-round—a never-ending process of planning and dealing and marketing and managing, as well as training, practicing, and playing—that few things ever got started and finished quickly. As Jeff Barto recounts in his chapter on the 1985 Winter Meetings in this volume (quoting Angels general manager Mike Port), "There's too many complexities involved with today's contracts. It became impossible to take care of all the details in a limited time."[15] In such a world, the moment when a deal is really done will rarely be obvious and incontrovertible.

Despite all this complexity and lengthiness and uncertainty, things did still happen at the Winter Meetings, even if many did not definitely begin or end there. Teams drafted and traded and bought and sold players, players reached agreement on terms with teams, and so on.

In addition to the Carter and Henderson deals, a few other trades qualified, at least in retrospect, as major transactions.

The Chicago White Sox traded right-handed pitcher LaMarr Hoyt and two minor-league righties, Kevin Kristan and Todd Simmons, to the San Diego Padres for left-hander Tim Lollar and right-hander Bill Long, utility player Luis Salazar, and minor-league infielder Ozzie Guillen. In 1983, Hoyt had won 24 games and the American League Cy Young Award, but his 1984 season was, to put it gently, a great disappointment. The Padres were gambling that Hoyt would rebound, and he did in 1985, but then his career came to a sad and speedy end after a series of drug-possession arrests and related problems in 1986 and 1987. The White Sox ended up enjoying both short-term and long-term benefits from the deal, because Guillen turned out to be a great player. He was American League Rookie of the Year in 1985 and, later in his 13-year career with the White Sox, an All-Star and a Gold Glover.

The Detroit Tigers traded third baseman Howard Johnson to the Mets (where Johnson would play for nine years and earn multiple All-Star berths and Silver Slugger awards) for right-handed pitcher Walt Terrell (who would deliver four years of solid pitching for the Tigers).

And while Don Sutton was nearing the end of a long and distinguished pitching career, he wasn't done yet. The Milwaukee Brewers traded the right-hander to the Oakland Athletics for pitcher Ray Burris and two minor league pitchers, left-hander Eric Barry and right-hander Ed Myers.[16] Sutton went on to deliver three solid years for the A's and the Angels, and eventually entered the Hall of Fame (though as a Dodger). In contrast, Burris, who had pitched well for the A's in 1984, was not as effective in Milwaukee as the Brewers had hoped, and he retired after the 1987 season.[17]

Right-hander Bill Caudill had had an All-Star season in 1984, saving 36 games for Oakland. It would prove to be his only year on the East Bay, as the A's shipped him to Toronto in exchange for speedy outfielder-first baseman Dave Collins, infielder Alfredo Griffin (the 1979 American League Rookie of the Year), and cash.

And the Yankees and Pirates began discussing a deal that finally came to fruition a few days before Christmas. Dale Berra, son of the legendary Yogi, would seem to be a perfect fit for the Yankees, so they made it happen by sending infielder Tim Foli, outfielder Steve Kemp, and cash to Pittsburgh. In exchange, the Yankees received outfielder Jay Buhner, left-hander Alfonso Pulido, and Berra, whose time in New York proved to be considerably shorter and less memorable than his father's.[18]

There were five other trades as well:

Right-handers Porfi Altamirano and Rich Bordi, outfielder Henry Cotto, and catcher Ron Hassey went from the Chicago Cubs to the Yankees for outfielder Brian Dayett and southpaw Ray Fontenot.

Right-hander Brian Fisher, once a highly rated prospect, was sent by the Atlanta Braves to the Yankees for catcher Rick Cerone.

Infielder Vance Law, son of Cy Young Award winner Vern Law, was moved by the Chicago White Sox to the Montreal Expos for right-handed pitcher Bob James.

In a separate deal, the White Sox sent right-hander Bert Roberge to the Expos for infielder Bryan Little.

Catcher Ray Smith moved from the Minnesota Twins to the San Diego Padres in exchange for right-hander Floyd Chiffer.

And then, of course, there were the trades—or at least rumors of trades—that got away, including close calls for deals between the Texas Rangers and Pittsburgh Pirates (involving outfielder Larry Parrish and second baseman Johnny Ray);[19] the San Francisco Giants and the Detroit Tigers (involving Giants southpaw reliever Gary Lavelle);[20] and the Philadelphia Phillies and the St. Louis Cardinals (involving catcher Mike LaValliere and pitcher Jeff Lahti).[21]

Free Agency

As Jeff Barto makes clear in his chapter on the 1985 Winter Meetings, the 1984 meetings were the last (for a while) in which free agency functioned at all before the owners sought to shut it down. Even 1984's temporary last hurrah was pretty quiet. (It must be said, however, that shortly after the 1984 meetings, some additional and fairly important free-agent moves were struck, such as outfielder Fred Lynn's December 11 signing with the Baltimore Orioles[22] and pitcher Rick Sutcliffe's December 14 re-signing with the Chicago Cubs.[23])

Five players changed teams via free agency at the 1984 Winter Meetings, but just one of those moves—Bruce Sutter's—was a big deal. With the Cubs and then the St. Louis Cardinals, Sutter had accumulated six All-Star selections, the 1979 National League Cy Young Award, and, in 1984, a share of the major-league saves record. (He had also led the National League in saves from 1979 to 1982.) The Atlanta Braves signed him to what was at the time a huge contract, worth an estimated $44 million spread over 36 years.[24] But plagued by injuries, Sutter's performance begin to decline almost as soon as he arrived in Atlanta. After three disappointing seasons playing for the Braves and a fourth entirely lost to injury, Sutter retired. His years in Atlanta, however, did not affect his overall standing with Hall of Fame voters, and he was inducted into Cooperstown in 2006.

Of the other four deals, only one was productive: The Baltimore Orioles signed outfielder-infielder

Lee Lacy (formerly of the Pittsburgh Pirates), who played for the Orioles for the last three years of his long (1972-1987) career; these were the only three he played in the American League. Designated hitter Cliff Johnson (formerly of the Toronto Blue Jays) signed with the Texas Rangers, but he was back with the Blue Jays (via trade) by the end of August 1985. His major-league career ended when he was released by Toronto after the 1986 season. Outfielder Al Woods, who had been released by the Blue Jays in September 1984, signed with the Minnesota Twins. Other than a pair of brief call-ups in 1986, he spent the rest of his career in the minors and retired after the 1986 season. Catcher Marv Foley (who had been released by the Texas Rangers at the end of the 1984 season), signed with Detroit Tigers, but he never made it back to the majors, playing in the minor-league systems of the Tigers and White Sox before retiring after the 1986 season.

There were also two free agent re-signings at the Winter Meetings. The headliner in this category was the Cleveland Indians' re-signing of Andre Thornton, their All-Star and Silver Slugger designated hitter. He played three more seasons in Cleveland, and retired in 1987.[25] Left-handed pitcher Steve Trout re-signed with the Chicago Cubs and stayed with the team for 1985, 1986, and part of 1987, after which he was traded to the New York Yankees and then to the Seattle Mariners, where his playing career came to a close with his release in June 1989.

The League — Television, Teams, and Rules

In another stretching of the Winter Meetings beyond the Monday-to-Friday zone of official proceedings, new Commissioner Ueberroth met with members of the news media on November 29, the Thursday before the meetings, to present "a 'virtual outline' of his intended speech on December 3 at the Houston conclave."[26] Ueberroth's main message was indeed the same one he would emphasize just a few days later — indeed, as *The Sporting News* reported, "Everything he said in his first State of the Game address [at the Winter Meetings] needed to be said and was well said. But everything he said had been said several days before during a media briefing in New York."[27]

Ueberroth's remarks on the 29th and the 3rd included early public indications of an outlook on the business of baseball that would soon find the commissioner leading the owners into a divisive and expensive exercise in unlawful collusion against the players: "The No. 1 problem of baseball is the owners' inability to work together, their inability to be partners and solve problems. ..."[28]

Of more immediate and concrete interest to most observers in December 1984, however, were two other recurring themes: television and expansion.

Television

Technology — from railroads and radios early on, then to airplanes and television, and on to satellites and cable — has always contributed to the growth and wealth of major-league baseball. But there have always been growing pains, too. When it comes to change, some owners leap more quickly, manage more wisely, and profit more richly than others. Then some of the others complain about the injustice of it all. And eventually, all of them cash in.

In 1984, that pattern was playing out again with the rise of television superstations. The shortest, simplest version of the story is that Ted Turner, owner of the Atlanta Braves, also owned a local television station, WTBS, that carried Braves games. In addition, the station was a pioneer in the use of satellite technology to transmit its local programming to cable networks in distant places, enabling viewers all over the country to watch those local broadcasts without relying on the traditional big networks — ABC, CBS, and NBC. TV stations like Turner's, with a local base and global reach, were soon known, quite appropriately, as superstations. Owners of major-league baseball franchises in Chicago and New York had developed similar setups.

For the rest of the major-league owners, this spelled trouble, for two reasons. First, the owners of the Atlanta, Chicago, and New York team-superstation combos were now making money by transmitting games into the local TV markets traditionally dominated by the

> ### Baseball Contracts with Deferred Money
>
> In April 1965, the boxer Sugar Ray Robinson earned several victories in court against the IRS.[*] The issues at hand related to taxing of money Robinson received in deferred payment for a 1957 bout against Carmen Basilio. In 1968, Buzzy Bavasi pointed out that he only once paid a player in deferred compensation—Don Drysdale.[**] Contracts with deferred portions became more notable in the time leading up to Bruce Sutter. Dave Parker signed a contract in 1979, requiring the Pirates to make payments of more than $5 million into the next century.[***] However, the Pirates later filed suit against Parker, seeking to void the contract due to Parker's potentially drug-impaired performance. The lawsuit was settled in December 1988.[****]
>
> ---
>
> [*] Associated Press, "Sugar Ray Outpoints IRS in Suit, Most of $352,000 Claim Erased," *Washington Post*, April 15, 1965: F4.
> [**] Ross Newhan, "Pro Contracts: A Taxing Means to Profitable End," *Los Angeles Times*, November 13, 1968: D1.
> [***] Gerald Eskenazi, "Athletes' Salaries: How High Will the Bidding Go?," *New York Times*, August 16, 1981: S1.
> [****] "Pirates and Parker Arrive at Settlement," *New York Times*, December 14, 1988: D28.

other 23 major-league baseball teams based in those markets, and the owners of those 23 teams wanted a slice of that pie. Second, in 1983, the major leagues had signed five-year broadcast-rights contracts with ABC and NBC that would bring in a total of more than $1 billion for the owners.[29] The superstations were (or at least were perceived to be) cutting into the networks' viewership, and that meant that when the time came to negotiate with the networks again, more billions might not be forthcoming.

And there was Ueberroth, saying, with respect to the first and more immediate concern:

"(The television superstations) are telecasting into the territories of other major-league teams and it is blatantly unfair."[30]

With respect to the second concern, during his November 29 "pre-meetings" meeting, he had stated:

"I've spoken with network officials and they have told me not to bother to come calling when the current contract expires unless there is a modification of the saturation problem created by the superstations."[31]

At the Winter Meetings, the owners, like Ueberroth, focused on the first concern, and left the second alone for the time being.[32] By a vote of 25 to 1, they resolved to find what Ueberroth called a "business solution" to the conflicts between the teams that had superstations and the teams that did not. "We said," Ueberroth explained, "Here are the two courses. Pool the money and split it up equally, or else cut back the number of games on the air."[33] In the short term, not much would happen. There would be no quick "business solution." A little bit of superstation money did make its way into the pockets of the other owners, but there was no pool and there were no cutbacks. In the long term, the technology cycle would repeat itself yet again. Today, cable is a revenue mainstay for every major-league team.[34] But in 1984, that future was not clear.

Teams

Concerns about declining attendance at ballgames dovetailed with concerns about the rise of the superstations. Were fans in towns with struggling major- or minor-league teams staying home to watch Atlanta Braves games on Ted Turner's superstation instead of taking themselves out to the ballpark to root for the home team? Commissioner Ueberroth said yes; superstation owner Turner said no. No one found an answer at the Winter Meetings, or at least no formal action was taken by the owners there.[35]

The same held true for issues of team ownership. There was a good deal of talk about franchises old and new. According to Ueberroth, seven existing teams were up for sale—presumably Cincinnati, Cleveland,

Oakland, Pittsburgh, San Francisco, Seattle, and Texas.[36] No sales were made, although:

> "In one of the nice little ironies of Houston, while Ueberroth was telling his audience that seven franchises might be for sale, seven groups of well-financed investors were in the hotel, lobbying diligently to acquire franchises. Incredible."[37]

Those investors were, however, mostly there to talk about expansion teams. Eight cities sent delegations to the Winter Meetings: Buffalo, Denver, Indianapolis, Miami, St. Petersburg, Tampa, Vancouver, and Washington.[38] Ueberroth and other major-league officials met with the aspirants, but his comments on the topic were noncommittal:

> "Expansion is a front-burner item which will be looked at seriously as soon as our labor situation is settled. … I'm not going to put baseball on a deadline. Expansion is an owners' decision. But I'd have no objection to have it happen quickly."[39]

It would, in fact, be seven years before the owners approved any expansion, awarding teams to Denver and Miami in 1991, with the Rockies and Marlins playing their first official games in 1993. In contrast, Marge Schott bought a controlling interest in one of the for-sale franchises, the Cincinnati Reds, just a few days after the 1984 Winter Meetings ended,[40] and several more would be sold later in the 1980s.[41]

Rules

Nothing happened to the rules of the game in 1984. But in a sign that they understood their dealings with television were urgent, the owners did adjust the rules governing themselves. They voted 25 to 1 to make decisions on all issues relating to television by a simple majority vote, rather than the usual super-majority (three-quarters) vote in each league.[42]

The Traditions — Honors and Awards

Following longstanding tradition, the National Association of Professional Baseball Leagues honored the winner of its annual "King of Baseball" award for dedication and service to minor-league baseball. Donald Davidson, a long-serving and much-liked and respected official, first with the Braves organization in Boston, Milwaukee, and Atlanta, and then with the Houston Astros, received the 1984 award.

And, launching a new tradition, the first Scout of the Year Award was also presented at the National Association's luncheon, with Howie Haak of the Pittsburgh Pirates deservedly receiving the award.[43] Starting in 1985, it would become a plural award, with East Coast, Midwest, and West Coast honorees.[44]

Other honors bestowed during the Winter Meetings included two by *The Sporting News* — Player of the Year (second baseman Ryne Sandberg of the Chicago Cubs)[45] and Minor League Player of the Year (first baseman Alan Knicely of the Wichita Aeros of the American Association)[46] — and the Robert O. Fishel Award for Excellence in Public Relations (Red Patterson of the California Angels), which will live forever in the annals of public relations for this line from his acceptance: "Thank you, Mickey Mantle."[47]

And, finally, a last word: In a move that may resonate with modern followers of player-safety issues, Gene Coleman, director of conditioning for the Houston Astros, chaired a symposium for team physicians on the subject of batting helmets and reducing head injuries suffered by players.[48]

NOTES

1. As tends to be the case with messy breakups, opposing camps had opposing views. Some in the union felt that Moffett had been an insufficiently engaged and vigorous advocate for players, while Moffett felt that he had been forced out because of his stance on drug abuse by players. Thomas Boswell, "Moffett Links His Firing With Drugs in Baseball," *Washington Post*, February 22, 1984: D1, D6; Lee Lowenfish, *The Imperfect Diamond* (Lincoln: University of Nebraska Press, 2010), 252-253.

2. Marvin Miller, *A Whole Different Ball Game* (Chicago: Ivan R. Dee, 1991; 2004 edition), Chapter 16.

3. Stan Isle, "MacPhail Predicts Agreement Between Players, Management," *The Sporting News*, December 17, 1984: 43.

4. 1984 Rule 5 Draft, baseball-reference.com/bullpen/1984_Rule_V_Draft.

5. "Mets Lose Quartet in Draft," *Binghamton* (New York) *Press and Sun-Bulletin*, December 3, 1984: C1.

6. "Mets Stock Up in Minor Draft," *The Sporting News*, December 17, 1984: 44.

7. See, for example, 1985 MLB Transactions, baseball-reference.com/leagues/MLB/1985-transactions.shtml.

8. Joseph Durso, "Mets Get Expo's Carter for Brooks and 3 Others," *New York Times*, December 11, 1984: B15.

9. AJ Cassavell, "The Biggest Winter Meetings Trades of All Time," m.mlb.com/news/article/158887650/the-best-winter-meetings-trades-of-all-time/.

10. Bryan Mcwilliam, "5 Most Lopsided Trades in Winter Meetings History," thescore.com/news/906624.

11. Claire Smith, "Yanks, Red Sox Reportedly Talk Pitchers Trade," *Hartford Courant*, December 3, 1984: C3.

12. See, for example, 1985 MLB Transactions, baseball-reference.com/leagues/MLB/1985-transactions.shtml.

13. John Nelson, Associated Press, "Braves Sign Sutter as Meetings Close," *Cincinnati Enquirer*, December 8, 1984: C1; ("A flurry of million-dollar signings and multi-player trades wrapped up baseball's 1984 winter meetings Friday. ….").

14. Dave Nightingale, "GMs Enjoy Quiet Week in Houston," *The Sporting News*, December 17, 1984: 43.

15. Tom Pedulla, "Hot Stove League Sees Trade Talks Put on the Backburner," *Battle Creek* (Michigan) *Enquirer*, December 9, 1985: C1.

16. Myers became part of the deal in March 1985 in the role of "a player to be named later."

17. "Burris an Instant Brewers Starter," *The Sporting News*, December 17, 1984: 48.

18. Peter Gammons, "Yanks-A's Swap Benefits Both," *The Sporting News*, December 17, 1984: 51.

19. "Rangers Deal Collapses," *The Sporting News*, December 17, 1984: 49.

20. "Deals Needs Lavelle's OK," *The Sporting News*, December 17, 1984: 50.

21. "Lahti Is Expected to Join Phillies," *The Sporting News*, December 17, 1984: 46.

22. "Fred Lynn Lands with Orioles," *Rochester Democrat and Chronicle*, December 12, 1984: 1D.

23. Fred Mitchell, "A Happy Ending," *Chicago Tribune*, December 15, 1984: section 2, page 1.

24. Associated Press, "Sutter Becomes a Brave," *New York Times*, December 8, 1984: section 1, page 21.

25. "Thornton Re-Signs With Indians," *The Sporting News*, December 17, 1984: 48.

26. Dave Nightingale, "Ueberroth Sees Problem," *The Sporting News*, December 10, 1984: 48.

27. Bill Conlin, "Ueberroth's Repeat Message Falls Flat," *The Sporting News*, December 17, 1984: 45.

28. Dave Nightingale, "Ueberroth Sees Problem."

29. James Edward Miller, *The Baseball Business* (Chapel Hill: University of North Carolina Press, 1991), 278-279; Lee Lowenfish, *The Imperfect Diamond*, 251-252.

30. Dave Nightingale, "The New Commish," *The Sporting News*, December 17, 1984: 42.

31. Dave Nightingale, "Ueberroth Sees Problem."

32. Dave Nightingale, "The New Commish."

33. Thomas Boswell, "Ueberroth on Offensive in Baseball's TV Wars," *Washington Post*, December 6, 1984: F8.

34. Jack Moore, "The Saga of Superstations and Baseball's Historical Resistance to Technology," *Hardball Times*, June 29, 2016, hardballtimes.com/the-saga-of-superstations-and-baseballs-historical-resistance-to-technology/.

35. Ibid.

36. Peter Gammons, "Ueberroth: The Onus Is on Some Owners," *The Sporting News*, December 10, 1984: 54.

37. Bill Conlin, "Ueberroth's Repeat Message Falls Flat."

38. Dave Nightingale, The New Commish."

39. Thomas Boswell, "Ueberroth on Offensive in Baseball's TV Wars."

40. Warren Corbett, "Marge Schott," SABR Baseball Biography Project, sabr.org/bioproj/person/09e49f1e.

41 The other teams to change hands during that period were the Baltimore Orioles (purchased in 1989 by a group led by Eli Jacobs), the Cleveland Indians (purchased in 1986 by Richard E. Jacobs and David H. Jacobs), the New York Mets (purchased in 1986 by Nelson Doubleday and Fred Wilpon), the Pittsburgh Pirates (purchased in 1986 by a group that included the City of Pittsburgh and several local businesses), the Seattle Mariners (purchased in 1989 by a group led by Jeffrey Smulyan), and the Texas Rangers (purchased in 1989 by a group led by George W. Bush).

42 Thomas Boswell, "Ueberroth on Offensive in Baseball's TV Wars."

43 "Baseball Crowns Davidson King," *The Sporting News*, December 17, 1984: 42; milb.com/milb/history/awards.jsp?#king.

44 "History of the Scout of the Year Program," in Jim Sandoval and Bill Nowlin, eds., *Can He Play? A Look at Baseball Scouts and Their Profession* (Cleveland: SABR, 2001), 165; Gary Gillette and Pete Palmer, *The Emerald Guide to Baseball* (Phoenix: SABR, 2011), 242.

45 Joe Goddard, "Hard Work, Improvement Bring Sandberg Top Award," *The Sporting News*, December 10, 1984: 48.

46 Casey Scott, "Player of the Year," *The Sporting News*, December 3, 1984: 56.

47 Dick Young, "Did Kuhn Bend to O'Malley on DH?," *The Sporting News*, December 31, 1984: 9.

48 Stan Isle, "Astros Seek Safer Batting Helmet," *The Sporting News*, December 17, 1984: 42.

— 1985 —
FREE-AGENT FREEZEOUT: COLLUSION I

By Jeff Barto

KIRK GIBSON OF THE DETROIT Tigers and Carlton Fisk of the Chicago White Sox led baseball's free-agent class going into the 1985 Winter Meetings.[1] Kansas City Royals GM John Schuerholz was so interested in slotting Gibson into the team's cleanup spot that he asked a team representative to host him on a hunting trip to gauge his interest in them. New York Yankees owner George Steinbrenner so coveted Fisk that he discreetly proposed a contract that turned out to be the only offer to any free agent that winter. The Yankees soon rescinded their offer to Fisk after White Sox owner Jerry Reinsdorf slapped King George's hand for going rogue with his star catcher.[2] Soon after, Kansas City also cooled on Gibson. As the Royals rep traipsed through the woods hunting birds with Kirk, he sheepishly apologized: "… [L]ook, I'm sorry for misleading you, but I did what I was told to do." The reversal caught Gibson off guard. "They definitely were courting me and then cold-shouldered me big-time," he said.[3]

The two snubs sharply characterized the central issue of the 1985 baseball Winter Meetings, free-agent dormancy. Every player who filed for free agency that fall either re-signed with his original club or was released. Only after clubs freed players did other teams make any offers. Player agents, and the players' union director, Donald Fehr, smelled conspiracy among the owners and general managers. Not long after the meetings, on February 3, 1986, the Major League Baseball Players Association filed a grievance that would later be dubbed Collusion I.[4] Months before the Winter Meetings, a couple of gatherings had taken place among the owners and general managers. It was at these meetings that Commissioner Peter Ueberroth sowed the seeds that forged the first of three collusion grievances filed by Fehr.

On October 16, 1985, Lee MacPhail fired the first subtle shot of collusion. As he neared retirement as president of the owners' Player Relations Committee, he penned a memo to his colleagues. MacPhail's letter included his thoughts on the escalation of players' salaries. It clearly summarized the first 10 years of player free agency that began after the demise of the reserve clause in 1976:

"We must stop daydreaming that one free agent signing will bring a pennant. Somehow we must get our operations back to the point where a normal year for the average team at least results in a break-even situation, so that clubs are not led to make rash moves in the vain hope that they might bring a pennant and a resulting change in their financial position. This requires resistance to fan and media pressure and is not easy. On the other hand, the future health and stability of our game depend on your response to these problems."[5]

MacPhail went on to summarize the folly of signing players to long-term contracts. His data analysis revealed a decline by hitters and pitchers after they signed such agreements. Furthermore, too often these players were injured and were thus not contributing, but they continued to drain the owners' coffers.[6] Specifically, after noting that general managers shelled out $40 million for injured players in 1985 and that no free agents made any major contributions to the last four World Series winners, writer Peter Gammons commented, "That isn't collusion, it's just a dose of realism."[7]

MacPhail sent his memo to the other owners before they met on October 22, 1985, during the World Series. Gussie Busch, the Cardinals hardline owner, opened his Anheuser Busch headquarters for the meeting. Newly appointed Commissioner Ueberroth opened the meeting by addressing the owners with a tone-setting tongue-lashing:

"If I sat each one of you down in front of a red button and a black button and I said, 'Push the red button and you'd win the World Series but lose $10 million. Push the black button and you would have a $4 million profit and you'd finish in the middle.' You are so damned dumb. Most of you would push the red button. Look in the mirror and go out and spend big if you want, don't go out there whining that someone made you do it.... I know and you know what's wrong. You are smart businessmen. You all agree we have a problem. Go solve it."[8]

Two weeks later, on November 6, the general managers met in Tarpon Springs, Florida. Here Ueberroth reinforced MacPhail's caution against signing hitters for contracts longer than three years or pitchers for two years. "It's not smart to sign long-term contracts. They force clubs to want to make similar signings," he wrote. "Don't be dumb. We have a five-year agreement with labor."[9] Ueberroth's terse missive focused on "fiscal responsibility" while his implicit message suggested "collusion."

These two meetings ignited a series of internal memos among the owners that strengthened their resolve to uphold Ueberroth's suggestions. The owners, GMs, and the commissioner then hatched a "gentlemen's agreement" that played out in San Diego at the Winter Meetings in December.

Besides their unspoken agenda, the moguls approached these meetings with a packed agenda. First, Ueberroth pursued a hard line on drug testing in response to baseball's cocaine trials, which had been held in Pittsburgh in September. The Pirates were looking to sell after several years of declining attendance and revenue. In addition, the San Francisco Giants were threatening to move rather than play another year in cold and windy Candlestick Park. Issues slated for less attention included talks on expansion and use of the designated hitter during the World Series. But of all the issues, the free-agent class of 1985 commanded the least attention of all. Since the labor restructuring in 1976, the Winter Meetings had always served as a hub for trades and a flurry of free-agent signings. Now, after a decade of escalating salaries, the lemming-like owners followed Ueberroth's advice to ignore other teams' free agents. In previewing the Winter Meetings, *The Sporting News* foreshadowed the boycott with the headline "Free-Agent Freeze Out?"[10] Eventually the MLBPA labeled the tactic as collusive. The union claimed that the owners acted in concert against signing any of the 62 players who initially filed for free agency. This inaction violated Article XVIII (H) of the Collective Bargaining Agreement between the players and owners. Crafted in 1976, it stated:

"The utilization or non-utilization of rights under this Article XVIII is an individual matter to be determined solely by each Player and each Club for his or its own benefit. *Players shall not act in concert with other Players and Clubs shall not act in concert with other Clubs.*"[11]

The second sentence in the clause eventually backfired on baseball's landlords. First, the owners insisted on including the "Players" piece to prevent player collusion similar to what occurred in 1966. During that preseason, pitchers Sandy Koufax and Don Drysdale tag-teamed their contract negotiations against the Los Angeles Dodgers. Though they eventually negotiated separately, they still doubled their salaries. To stop future player collusion, the owners required language about "Players" collusion in the 1976 CBA. Comforted by a rare win over the union, the owners agreed to the union's request to include a reciprocal piece forbidding collusion on any "Club's" part. Though the "Players" part of the clause alleviated the owner's fears of player collusion, they only envisioned the "Clubs" piece as a bargaining chip. It never occurred to them that they might conspire among themselves. At one point Ueberroth deceptively described his view on any owner consensus: "They aren't capable of colluding. They couldn't agree on what to have for breakfast."[12] But financial promiscuity bled the magnates yearly when free agency rocked their fiefdom in 1976. By 1985 they retaliated by hatching a plot to boycott long-term contracts and ignore other teams' free agents. As the owners' collusion clause was poised to boomerang on them, the 1985 baseball Winter Meetings set the stage on which to play out the owners' scheme.

On Monday, December 9, the Winter Meetings began literally and appropriately in a San Diego fog. A weather system had created a haze so thick on Sunday that several officials chose to fly to Los Angeles and take a bus to Mission Valley in San Diego.[13] The fog also clouded most trading activity. The meetings traditionally ended with a midnight interleague-trading deadline on Friday. The deadline often generated a burst of last-minute deals. But on August 7 baseball's newest collective-bargaining agreement eliminated the interleague-trading deadline. Now the only nonwaiver-trading cutoff date would be July 31.[14] Toronto GM Pat Gillick responded quickly to the new rule, saying, "With no deadline crisis, decisions can be postponed.[15] Dodgers vice president Al Campanis echoed this view, saying, "There's no rush. A lot of clubs may defer trading until they can see what their situation is in spring training."[16] Perhaps the planners of the convention were clairvoyant to book San Diego's Town and Country Hotel—it lacked a lobby in which to make any deals!

Despite predictions of a trade drought, the 1985 meetings eclipsed the bustle of the previous year's meetings, in Houston, by a small margin. When the mist cleared in Mission Valley, 12 deals had been completed, involving 31 major-league players.[17] (The year before, only 10 transactions changed the caps of 25 players.[18]) Though the impact of not having a trade deadline was negligible, "The trading deadline had to go," said Angels' general manager Mike Port. "There's too many complexities involved with today's contracts. It became impossible to take care of all the details in a limited time."[19]

One major trade of note took place early in the meetings, on December 10. That afternoon Oakland dealt left-handed pitcher Tim Conroy and catcher Mike Heath to St. Louis for its temperamental star hurler, right-hander Joaquin Andujar. Many issues surrounding Andujar led to the trade. Though he won 21 games for the Cardinals in '85, he won only one game after August 23. He also refused to pitch in the All-Star Game when he wasn't guaranteed to start. Later he was linked to cocaine during testimony in the September Pittsburgh drug trials. Finally, his emotional breakdown in Game Seven of the World Series led him to charge and bump umpire Don Denkinger. Denkinger had made an erroneous "safe" call the day before, allowing the Royals to force a Game Seven. Andujar's boorish behavior in the final game led to his ejection and a 10-game suspension to start the 1986 season.[20] The embarrassed Cardinals had seen enough. Andujar told a friend before the Winter Meetings that the Cardinals called to tell him he would never pitch for St. Louis again.[21] Oakland was in need of a number-one pitcher and felt that Andujar was worth the risk of an injury-plagued catcher (Heath) and a struggling young pitcher who would be out of the majors two years later (Conroy).

The Major League Rule 5 draft opened the proceedings on December 10. Major-league teams could draft any player left off any other team's 40-man roster. Until this year, $25,000 secured such players, but at the 1985 meetings the price tag doubled to $50,000.[22] Pittsburgh lost infielders Bobby Bonilla to the White Sox and Bip Roberts to San Diego. California claimed right-handed pitcher Carl Willis from Cincinnati and the Reds also surrendered third baseman Eddie Williams to Cleveland. Former first-round pick Clint Hurdle went from the Mets to St. Louis. Texas tried to bolster its pitching by taking righty Scott Patterson from the Yankees' Columbus team. Toronto landed right-hander José de Jesus from Kansas City and right-handed pitcher Jeff Parrett flew from Milwaukee to Montreal. Finally, Minnesota singed the Mets by taking right-handed pitcher Tom Burns.[23] In all, nine prospects switched organizations in the Rule 5 draft, the fewest selected since it began in 1903.[24]

The next day the minor leagues held their phase of the draft. For $12,000, Triple-A teams could select any unprotected player from any Double-A roster, while any Double-A team could raid any Single-A team's exposed players for $4,000. In all, a dozen Triple-A selections were made while nine Single-A players were picked for Double-A teams.[25] Later that day, at its annual banquet, Minor League Baseball presented its "King of Baseball" for lifetime achievement in minor-league baseball to Stan Wasiak in recognition of having managed for 37 consecutive seasons, mainly in the Dodgers' system. During his tenure he amassed the record for most games managed, as well as the most wins and losses in minor-league history.[26]

When Commissioner Ueberroth gave his "state of the game" address to open the meetings on Monday, he unpacked a number of topics to address with the owners. They included the sale of the Pittsburgh franchise, possible drug testing, expansion, the Giants' plight in San Francisco, and the use of the designated hitter during the World Series. Most of the talks took place in a joint meeting between the National and American League owners on Wednesday. Since the lobby-less Town and Country Hotel acted more like a motel, they met at another, undisclosed location. By late afternoon they returned to brief the media on the results of their discussions.[27] One of the first issues the owners resolved was unanimously approving the sale of the Pirates. A public-private partnership of 13 groups, headed by Ryan Homes CEO Malcolm "Mac" Prine, bought the floundering franchise for $23 million. The agreement tied the team and city together through 2011, but an escape clause would allow the new owners to sell the team after five years if they could show continued operating losses.[28]

The Pirates' struggles extended beyond the financial health of the team. A major scandal, centered in Pittsburgh all summer, threatened the franchise and embarrassed the sport. Since free agency in 1976, the players' discretionary income had ballooned, and cocaine had become their drug of choice in the 1980s. Much of the drug activity seemed to swirl around the Pirates' clubhouse, and by 1985 it caught the attention of major-league baseball. In September Pittsburgh hosted drug trials that identified 21 players who used cocaine. Seven of them testified under immunity, and on September 20, seven nonplayers were convicted and took the fall for all the involved players.[29]

Though the players who testified at the trials were protected from criminal prosecution, Ueberroth sought to impose baseball's own punishment on the abusers. After sitting down with each player soon after the Winter Meetings, he ordered suspensions on February 28, 1986. Seven players were banned for a year and four for 60 days.[30] Ueberroth later removed the suspensions when each agreed to community service and to donate 5 to 10 percent of their salaries to drug programs. Seventeen of the 21 players also agreed to undergo drug testing for the balance of their careers.[31] The scandal hastened Ueberroth to try to make drug testing mandatory in major-league baseball. In the spring he ordered such testing for all professional baseball personnel except for the players, who were protected by the CBA.[32] Leading into the Winter Meetings, the owners included as many as 550 mandatory drug-testing clauses into player contracts. Donald Fehr quickly responded that clubs "can't force players to undergo testing as a condition of employment. It has to be negotiated. We're going to take whatever action is appropriate to knock that out, probably within the next two or three weeks."[33] Fehr filed a grievance after the Winter Meetings charging that the drug testing violated the CBA and was subject to collective bargaining; the grievance was upheld in arbitration. Ueberroth was reduced to urging voluntary support among the players, which Fehr advised them to ignore.

After the union broke the reserve clause in 1976, the owners spent a futile decade scrambling to regain control of their assets. Their collusive action during the Winter Meetings was another attempt to control salaries, but it had to remain an unwritten agreement. However, the owners could show open solidarity by manipulating the 25-man roster. The CBA required teams to carry a maximum of 25 players and a minimum of 24. Discussions on roster reduction started at these Winter Meetings but fully flowered in February before spring training. One by one, clubs tested the waters, suggesting they would go to 24-man rosters if all the others did.[34] Union chief Fehr protested this move as another act of collusion. "It's now apparent to us that they've changed the rule," he said. "What clubs have said is you can have 24 players and not more than 24. It's clear that some clubs would go to 25 if others would, but no one wants to be the first. This costs players jobs and affects competition."[35] Fehr felt the CBA language intended for clubs to act independently rather than collectively to reduce rosters. In May he filed a grievance over this issue, the third complaint stemming from the Winter Meetings (drug testing and collusion being the other two). This time the union had no grounds to protest as arbiter George Nicolau granted a rare victory to the owners.[36] The owners cloaked the roster reduction as a cost-cutting move. They pointed to a report by their Player Relations Committee as the basis for the downsizing. The committee estimated losses of $59 million by all 26 teams. Elimination of one player would save each club about $111,000, or $2.9 million total, a saving of only 5 percent of the losses.[37] In the end, these savings paled in comparison to the open victory the magnates managed to maneuver from the players.

Wednesday's off-site meeting also addressed the future of expansion. Earlier in the fall, a dozen groups prepared proposals for a possible expansion team. All 12 groups met on November 7-8 in New York with baseball's Long-Range-Planning Committee, chaired by Ueberroth.[38] The 14-owner committee reported their findings at the joint meeting with the rest of the owners. Since expansion was scheduled to be only a report and not an action item, the discussions proceeded as "staid and straightforward," as described by Cleveland Indians President Peter Bavasi.[39] Reports on each city lasted only a few minutes, with no comments by Ueberroth, or the owners. After this short report the owners tabled expansion, claiming that four struggling clubs (San Francisco, Seattle, Cleveland, and Pittsburgh) still needed to sort out their finances before further growth could be explored.[40] Washington, the leading city hoping for a team, would have to wait until next year again!

San Francisco's ballpark appeared next on Wednesday's eight-hour agenda. Giants owner Bob Lurie again threatened to leave the poor playing conditions of Candlestick Park. The team lost a club-record 100 games in 1985 and Lurie blamed the blustery ballpark.[41] Though nine years remained on his lease with the city, Lurie scrambled to find an alternative. In March of 1985 he had explored the chance to relocate to the San Jose area, but San Francisco Mayor Diane Feinstein intervened, threatening to charge San Jose with tampering.[42] On October 2 Lurie looked to buy out his lease and share the Oakland Coliseum with the A's for three seasons while he built a new ballpark. That plan fell flat when he forgot to mention his plans to Oakland mayor Lionel Wilson, who spelled out a list of reasons to keep the Giants at "Bay."[43] Lurie then asked Denver and then Vancouver to host the team until he could build a downtown replacement. Both cities wanted a permanent team to replace their current Triple-A clubs, so those plans collapsed. By the end of the meetings, the Giants still called Candlestick Park home for the 1986 season.[44]

The DH debuted in the 1973 American League season, but it did not appear in the World Series until 1976. From then through 1984, it was used in World Series games in even-numbered years. By 1985 the use of the DH in the Series troubled Commissioner Ueberroth, who stated, "I think the American League is penalized under the current rule. … When it comes to the Series, I have a firm belief that a team should be able to play with what got it there."[45] Ueberroth proposed changes for the owners to consider at the Winter Meetings. When pressed on what to do if his suggestions failed, Ueberroth affirmed, "Well, I can change the rule independently—and I would consider strongly doing just that."[46] The owners considered his two-pronged proposal to use the DH every year in the Series in games hosted by the American League team. The plan would end the "alternating-year" approach and introduce an "alternating-park" approach.[47] The owners took no action on the issue at the meetings, but Ueberroth leaked his intentions to change the Series DH rule by stating, "[T]hey decided not to do anything about it. But that's not to say I won't do anything about it. For sure, before the next season starts, I will decide on the use of the designated hitter in the World Series."[48] Ueberroth eventually gained a switch to the "alternating-park" format for the 1986 World Series by working with the Major League Baseball Rules Committee in March of 1986.[49]

Baseball's 1985 Winter Meetings appropriately ended on Friday the 13th. The week provided a few peculiar changes: The Pirates changed ownership, Bob Lurie changed his mind, and cocaine changed the game's landscape. But when the fog cleared in San Diego, no free agents changed teams. The Tigers never budged from their three-year, $4.1 million offer to retain outfielder Kirk Gibson, the poster boy for the 1985 free-agent class. Shortly after his honeymoon in January of 1986, he re-signed with the Tigers, eschewing his five-year $8 million demand.[50] His agent, Doug Baldwin, shed the strongest light on the boycott of his client and fellow players: "I think their action speaks louder than any of the announcement the clubs have made about why they're not pursuing free agents. … The best information I have is that not one of the 62 free agents has received offers from any but their former clubs."[51] Baldwin later added, "It's pretty clear there was a directive from somewhere. If the market doesn't open up, I think the agents and the Players Association will be getting together to make charges of collusion."[52] Baldwin's words proved to be prescient by the time 1986 arrived. Union director Donald Fehr filed the first of three collusion grievances against the owners in February. The 1986 Winter Meetings were shaping up as a sequel to the salary slowdown of 1985.

SOURCES

Sources used in addition to those cited in the notes include primary newspaper sources accessed mainly through Google News archives and *The Sporting News* articles accessed through SABR's research link for the Paper of Record.

NOTES

1 Associated Press, "Gibson Claims Royals, Others 'Tampered' With Him," *Owosso* (Michigan) *Argus-Press*, June 24, 1986: 11.

2 Doug Wilson, *Pudge: The Biography of Carlton Fisk* (New York: Thomas Dunne Books, 2015), 257.

3 "Gibson Claims Royals."

4 Gerald W. Scully, *The Business of Major League Baseball* (Chicago: University of Chicago Press, 1989), 9.

5 Roger I. Abrams, *Legal Bases: Baseball and the Law* (Philadelphia: Temple University Press, 2001), 146-147.

6 John Helyar, "Playing Ball: How Peter Ueberroth Led the Major Leagues in the Collusion Era," *Wall Street Journal*, May 20, 1991: A1.

7 Peter Gammons, "Owners Mount Drive for Drug Testing," *The Sporting News*, December 2, 1985: 57.

8 Jerome Holtzman, *The Commissioners: Baseball's Midlife* Crisis (New York: Total Sports, 1998), 220-221.

9 Howard Burman, *Season of Ghosts: the '86 Mets and the Red Sox* (Jefferson, North Carolina: McFarland, 2012), 11.

10 Murray Chass, "Free-Agent Freeze Out?," *The Sporting News*, December 9, 1985: 2-3.

11 Paul C. Weiler and Gary R. Roberts, *Sports and the Law. Test, Cases, Problems.* 3rd Edition. (Eagan, Minnesota: West Publishing Company, 2004), 265.

12 Rob Neyer, *Rob Neyer's Big Book of Baseball Blunders: A Complete Guide to the Worst Decisions and Stupidest Moments in Baseball History* (New York: Touchstone, 2006), 222.

13 Murray Chass, "Owners Working for Control; Free Agents Put on Hold—For Now," *New York Times*, December 9, 1985: D-8.

14 Murray Chass, "Pitching Is the Prime Need as Officials Prepare to Meet," *Spartanburg* (South Carolina) *Herald Journal*, December 9, 1985: B4.

15 United Press International, "Issues, Rather Than Trades, Figure to Dominate Winter Meetings," *Columbus* (Indiana) *Republic*, December 9, 1985: 17.

16 Ross Newhan, "Winter Baseball Meetings: Without Deadlines, There's No Reason to Deal," *Los Angeles Times*, December 8, 1985: 4.

17 Baseball-Reference, baseball-reference.com/leagues/MLB/1985-transactions.shtml (accessed March 31, 2015).

18 Joseph Durso, "Yanks and Mets Disappointed," *New York Times*, December 14, 1985: 48.

19 Ross Newhan, "Winter Baseball Meetings."

20 Fred Mitchell, "Andujar Sent to A's for Heath," *Fort Lauderdale* (Florida) *Sun Sentinel*, December 11, 1985: C1.

21 Peter Gammons, "Andujar Says Brewery Told Him 'Adios,'" *The Sporting News*, December 23, 1985: 35.

22 Associated Press, "Trades Big Topic at Baseball's Winter Meetings," *Toledo Blade*, December 8, 1985: 3E.

23 Stan Isle, "Major League Draft Is Nearly Becalmed," *The Sporting News*, December 23, 1985: 39.

24 Baseball-Reference, baseball-reference.com/bullpen1985_Rule_V_Draft (accessed May 15, 2015).

25 Ibid.

26 Baseball-Reference, baseball-reference.com/bullpen/Stan_Wasiak (accessed May 17, 2015).

BASEBALL'S BUSINESS: THE WINTER MEETINGS

27 Bob Chick, "Baseball Takes Expansion Off the Hot Burner," *St. Petersburg* (Florida) *Evening Independent*, December 11, 1985: 1C.

28 Craig Stock, "A Murky, Intricate Deal to Save a Team," *Philadelphia Inquirer*, January 14, 1986: A1.

29 Aaron Skirboll, *The Pittsburgh Cocaine Seven: How a Ragtag Group of Fans Took the Fall for Major League Baseball* (Chicago: Chicago Review Press, 2010), 195-196.

30 The four players initially suspended for 60 days were Al Holland (Yankees), Lary Sorensen (Cubs), Lee Lacy (Orioles), and Claudell Washington (Braves). The seven players initially suspended for one year were Dave Parker (Reds), Keith Hernandez (Mets), Joaquin Andujar (A's), Lonnie Smith (Royals), Enos Cabell (Dodgers), Jeff Leonard (Giants), and Dale Berra (Yankees).

31 Associated Press, "Pittsburgh Cocaine Trial Baseball's 2nd Biggest Scandal: One Year Later," *Los Angeles Times*, September 21, 1986: 18.

32 United Press International, "Mandatory Drug Tests for Non-Players in Baseball," *The Courier* (Prescott, Arizona), May 8, 1985: 7B.

33 Associated Press, "Union Vows to Take Action Over Drug-Test Clauses in New Contracts," *Gainesville* (Florida) *Sun*, November 20, 1985: 6D.

34 United Press International, "Baseball Rosters: 24 Instead of 25?—Major League Rosters Beginning to Shrink," *The Tennessean* (Nashville), February 8, 1986: 37.

35 Associated Press, "Union Files Grievance Over 24-Man Rosters," *Deseret News* (Salt Lake City), May 14, 1986: 5B.

36 Associated Press, "24-Man Roster Limit Is Upheld," *Gainesville* (Florida) *Sun*, April 16, 1987: 3C.

37 Associated Press, "Teams Agree to Go With 24-Man Rosters," *Sumter* (South Carolina) *Daily Item*, April 5, 1986: 1B.

38 Dave Nightingale, "Expansion Not a Priority Item at Winter Meetings," *The Sporting News*, December 9, 1985: 48.

39 Gary Pomerantz, "Major League Baseball's Decision on Expansion Moves at Snail's Pace," *Washington Post*, December 13, 1985: 1.

40 Dave Sell, "Baseball Owners: Not Showing Their Cards," *Washington Post*, December 4, 1985.

41 William D. Murray, "Plans Scrapped to Build New Stadium for Giants," *Ottawa Citizen*, November 19, 1985: C15.

42 Bob Oates, "The Battle on the Bay: If the Giants Want to Stay in San Francisco and the City Wants the Team to Stay, Then What's All This Talk About San Jose?," *Los Angeles Times*, December 4, 1985: 4.

43 United Press International, "Baseball's Orphans: San Francisco Giants Have No Place to Play," *Los Angeles Times*, October 13, 1985: 1.

44 Chicago Tribune Wires, "Giants to Stay at Candlestick," *Chicago Tribune*, January 30, 1986: 7.

45 Dave Nightingale, "Expansion Not a Priority."

46 Ibid.

47 Richard G. McKelvey, *All Bat, No Glove: A History of the Designated Hitter* (Jefferson, North Carolina: McFarland, 2004), 86.

48 Ibid.

49 Philadelphia Inquirer Wire Services, "Rules Committee Votes to Allow DH in World Series Games in AL Parks," *St. Louis Post-Dispatch*, March 28, 1986: 14.

50 Associated Press, "Gibson Isn't Bitter About 3-Year Pact," *Montreal Gazette*, January 20, 1986: 4D.

51 Murray Chass, "Free Agents Less Free to Move," *Wilmington* (North Carolina) *Morning Star*, December 2, 1985: 4B. The 62 players who filed for free agency in 1985:

American League:

Baltimore: Rich Dauer, Jim Dwyer, Lenn Sakata

Boston: Bruce Kison, Rick Miller

California: Juan Beniquez, Rod Carew, Bobby Grich, Al Holland, Donnie Moore, Don Sutton

Chicago White Sox: Carlton Fisk, Bart Johnson, Dan Spillner

Cleveland: Benny Ayala, Tony Bernazard, Jamie Easterly, Mike Hargrove, Vern Ruhle

Detroit: Tom Brookens, Doug Flynn, Kirk Gibson, Aurelio Lopez

Kansas City: Dane Iorg, Lynn Jones, Hal McRae, Jamie Quirk

Milwaukee: Danny Darwin

New York Yankees: Marty Bystrom, Joe Niekro, Phil Niekro, Butch Wynegar

Oakland: Bruce Bochte, Tommy John, Steve McCatty, Mike Norris, Rob Picciolo

Texas: Alan Bannister, Bill Stein

Toronto: Jeff Burroughs, Steve Nicosia, Al Oliver

National League:

Chicago Cubs: Richie Hebner

Cincinnati: Tony Perez

Houston: Harry Spilman, Dickie Thon

Los Angeles: Steve Yeager

Montreal: Dave Palmer, U.L. Washington

New York Mets: Larry Bowa, Rusty Staub

Philadelphia: Garry Maddox, Derrel Thomas

St. Louis: Doug Bair, Cesar Cedeno, Ivan DeJesus, Mike Jorgensen, Matt Keough

San Diego: Kurt Bevacqua, Al Bumbry, Miguel Dilone

San Francisco: Vida Blue

Two teams in the American League (Minnesota and Seattle) and two teams in the National League (Atlanta and Pittsburgh) did not have any player file for free agency in 1985.

See Associated Press, "Baseball: 62 Free Agents from 1985," *New York Times*, September 22, 1987: A32.

52 Steve Wulf, "Where Have All the Big Spenders Gone?" *Sports Illustrated*, December 9, 1985: 22-23.

— 1986 —
A RIGGED MARKET — COLLUSION II

By Jeff Barto

THE 1985 WINTER MEETINGS HAD showcased a then-record 62 free agents, but the 1986 free-agent class shattered that mark as 82 players filed for free agency by the deadline.[1] Despite the uptick in the number of free agents, however, for the second year in a row none of them signed with a new club at the winter convention. Curiously, this inaction ignored one of the strongest free-agent crops in history. It included two Detroit Tigers stars, right-hander Jack Morris and catcher Lance Parrish, as well as Montreal's two star outfielders, Andre Dawson and Tim Raines. Morris and Dawson garnered the most press over their declaration not to re-sign with their respective clubs. After 10 seasons pitching for the Tigers, Morris was disappointed in the team's salary offer and wanted out. After 10 seasons pounding his legs on Montreal's concrete outfield, Dawson sought a softer surface on which to nurse his knees. Both men anticipated strong bidding for their services from several clubs, just as Kirk Gibson did the previous year. But as Gibson learned, Morris and Dawson saw no interest beyond their original clubs. Spurning these and other stars led to further speculation by the players of collusion among the owners. Their union had already filed a grievance over owner complicity after last year's snub. A second grievance would soon follow these winter meetings, held in Hollywood, Florida.

The Diplomat Hotel kicked off baseball's 1986 winter meetings by hosting a cocktail party from 7 to 9 P.M. on Sunday December 7. Official business began the next morning with Commissioner Peter Ueberroth giving his third annual "state of the game" address. Ueberroth opened by defending accusations of collusion from last year. The players' February grievance on collusion during the 1985-86 offseason had not yet gone to arbitration, so the commissioner and owners continued to justify their free-agent frugality. To buffer against the union's collusion charges, Ueberroth claimed owners had exercised "fiscal responsibility" last year due to two things. First, the three major television networks planned to offer much lower bids for all 26 teams, thus reducing revenue and affecting offers to free agents. Second, the owners were embarrassed by the $50 million-plus lost to players on the disabled list and "dead money" lost on long-term contracts. Specifically, they were stunned by the amount of losses revealed during negotiations of the 1985 collective bargaining agreement.[2] Ueberroth argued that he never suggested that owners offer shorter-term contracts or avoid other clubs' free agents. He bolstered his defense by saying, "[T]he idea of the commissioner being able to manipulate owners of baseball can only be thought by those who don't know baseball very well. If you can tell me that there is any individual on earth who could control a George Steinbrenner and a Ted Turner and a Marge Schott and a Ewing Kauffman, you've got to show that person to me because he certainly is not standing here."[3] This awkward dodge would reprise itself at the following year's meetings, but for now Ueberroth and the owners held firm to their story. Conversely, 1986 marked the first season in history in which every club drew over 1 million fans.[4] As the owners cried poor in the face of rising revenue, another battle loomed between the owners' claim of financial sanity and the players' charge of market manipulation.

Ueberroth quickly pivoted to other topics in his 43-minute address.[5] The 1987 season would mark the 40th anniversary of Jackie Robinson's major-league debut. Ueberroth announced the owners planned to present the Jackie Robinson Foundation with an endowment, co-chaired by the commissioner and actor-comedian Bill Cosby.[6] Furthermore, Ueberroth suggested portraying Robinson's number 42 on second base in each major-league ballpark, as well as on a uniform patch to be worn by all big-league players.[7] After a brief break, he addressed the dearth of minorities in major-league front-office positions. He advised implementing an affirmative-action program to encourage the hiring of more black executives.[8] "We (must) look at ourselves,' Ueberroth said. 'Not on the field, where we have a very fine record, but off the field, and ask the question, 'Are we providing enough opportunities for minorities, particularly blacks, in baseball?' The answer to that question today is 'no.' I am looking for all of baseball to progress in that arena in 1987."[9] By 1986 only three men of color had managed a major-league team (Frank Robinson, Maury Wills, and Larry Doby), one black had been a general manager (Bill Lucas), and only one minority had served as a personnel director (Hank Aaron).[10]

Ueberroth moved down his checklist of nearly a dozen topics to briefly revisit baseball's drug concerns. Pittsburgh's "Cocaine Trials" from 1985 still haunted major-league baseball, but Ueberroth cited evidence of an improving landscape. In February, after sanctioning the 21 players involved in those trials, Ueberroth felt that peer pressure among the players increased their awareness and effectively helped to clean up the game; baseball was now "drug free," he declared.[11]

While cocaine had been the drug of choice among players in the mid-1980s, alcohol had become the drug of choice among the fans. Increasing violence in the stands, due to rising alcohol consumption, concerned the commissioner and owners. Items like 32-ounce beers, hard liquor, and alcohol sales past the seventh inning often contributed to boorish fan behavior.[12] Ueberroth urged each club to consider tackling these issues and to customize a "responsible alcohol management" policy for their fans.[13]

Near the end of his speech, Ueberroth floated a trial balloon that went flat. He suggested a "review board" to help players going bankrupt from associating with dishonest player-agents. Ueberroth said, "There have been people out there who have been picking the pockets of baseball players, players who have earned millions of dollars who are broke when their playing careers have come to an end."[14] The commissioner's office planned to create a board to assist players in handling their agents and investments. However, the players union was a step ahead of the commissioner, having decided a week earlier to begin screening player agents. Those who failed to pass the union's review would not be allowed to represent the players.[15] The union viewed the commissioner's proposal as grandstanding, since he was aware of all this.

After Ueberroth completed his opening speech, there came an unusual sound: applause. His third annual address was a charm as it drew praise from Bill Rigney, three-time manager who currently consulted for the Oakland A's. "He was very good," Rigney offered. "It may have been the best speech we've ever had by a commissioner."[16] Hyperbole aside, Ueberroth earned the owners' ovation by confining his talk to baseball issues, rather than politics as he had in the past.

Major-league baseball's Rule 5 draft followed Ueberroth's opening statements. Until the previous year, the cost to draft a player left off another team's 40-man roster was $25,000, but that had been doubled, so this year was the second using the $50,000 pricetag. Nine teams selected a total of 10 players, eight of them pitchers. The Seattle Mariners were the only team to make two selections, landing a pair of left-handed pitchers, Tony Ferreira from the New York Mets and Stan Clarke from the Toronto Blue Jays. The Blue Jays also lost left-hander Cliff Young to the Oakland A's. Toronto picked up a right-hand pitcher, Jose Nunez, from Kansas City. Milwaukee lost two players, right-hander Robert L. Gibson to the White Sox, and outfielder Bob Simonson to Montreal. The Brewers took right-handed pitcher Vicente Palacios from Pittsburgh, who also lost outfield speedster Cecil Espy to the Texas Rangers. The Los Angeles Dodgers surrendered left-hander Jeff Edwards to Houston while the Mets secured right-hander Charlie Corbell, who had pitched for the San Francisco Giants' Texas League farm club in Shreveport.[17]

The Triple-A phase of the draft followed the next day with six players changing organizations, five of them pitchers. In this draft phase, "teams may select any eligible player left off the major league 40-man roster or the Triple-A reserve roster of 38 players."[18] Players selected this deep from other rosters are theoretically the 79th best player in a team's system. Most teams use this part of the draft to fill special needs in their farm system for a price of $12,000. The Los Angeles Dodgers were the most active. After losing right-handed pitcher Jeff Nelson to Seattle, they replaced him with right-hander Mike Hartley from St. Louis, and then took shortstop Jeff Schaeffer from the California Angels. Toronto selected Cleveland left-hander Gibson Alba. Texas took Philadelphia right-hander Jose Cecena and the Chicago Cubs took a right-hander, Heathcliff Slocumb, from the New York Mets.[19] The minor leagues capped off their day with a banquet that night honoring Hall of Fame Pitcher Lefty Gomez as the "King of Baseball."[20] Gomez, a popular speaker on the banquet circuit, pitched his quips as quickly as his (old) fastball as he accepted the 36th edition of this lifetime achievement award.

While the minor leagues conducted Tuesday's business, the National and American Leagues held their joint meeting on a different floor. First, they unanimously approved the sale of the Cleveland Indians to the Jacobs brothers, Richard and David, for $35 million. The shopping-mall magnates had been seeking the club since May. Former owner Francis J. "Steve" O'Neill had died in 1983 and his estate had owned the team for more than three years. American League President Bobby Brown was pleased when the sale finally materialized. "At no time did we think the completion of this sale wouldn't happen," Brown said. "This is a great day for the American League. We hope it's a great day for Cleveland."[21] It was also a great day for the National League and the New York Mets. Previously, Nelson Doubleday's publishing company had held ownership of the team, but Doubleday requested a transfer of ownership from his company to himself and Fred Wilpon for $81 million. They became equal partners in the club.[22]

Before the end of the meeting, an interesting economic wrinkle emerged. Initially, Hawaii was poised to host the 1987 Winter Meetings, but Ueberroth cited the high expenses required for that venue and suggested a switch to Louisville or Nashville.[23] This small move bolstered the owners' claims of cost-cutting while also diverting attention from their collusive ways.[24] By the end of the meetings, however, the drought of

Let's Make a Deal — Cleveland-style

Lawsuits had previously halted sales of the Cleveland club. On November 14, 1984, David LeFevre withdrew from his attempt to purchase the team. There is an argument to be made that LeFevre had already purchased the team twice.

In June 1984, he bought controlling interest in the team only to have it negated by a lawsuit filed by minority stockholder Walter Laich, who owned about 22 percent of the team. Then, in August 1984, LeFevre and his group increased their purchase offer, but three limited partners, who owned less than one half of one percent, refused to approve the deal. As the case worked its way through the courts, in November, one of the dissenting partners filed an affidavit of prejudice against the judge. Soon LeFevre's group withdrew its intent to buy, leaving Cleveland without a sale for another two years.

Indians President Gabe Paul had this to say about the failed sales: "The so called civic-minded citizens are civic-minded as long as they can squeeze another nickel out of somebody."*

---

* Paul Hoynes, "LeFevre Withdraws Offer to Purchase Indians," *Mansfield* (Ohio) *News-Journal*, November 15, 1984: 21.

trades and free-agent signings would provide more evidence of an owner conspiracy.

Wednesday's meeting featured a host of smaller items of business. Chub Feeney retired as NL president and treasurer. To honor his 17 years of "long and meritorious service to baseball," he was presented the August A. Busch Jr. award.[25] Busch initiated the award in 1978 to be given to "an individual involved with baseball in a non-playing capacity, and has the stature, on the front office level, (as) the Most Valuable Player award has on the playing field."[26] The National League then tapped A. Bartlett Giamatti, the former Yale University president, to replace Feeney. Little fanfare accompanied Giamatti's new position. He was not available to field questions nor was his promotion revealed to the reporters. Only a bulletin-board announcement alerted those in the newsroom who happened to notice.[27]

A few more items of interest rounded out Wednesday's events. Dodgers manager Tommy Lasorda and Tigers skipper Sparky Anderson each won their league's first Milton Richman Award.[28] Richman, a former prize-winning United Press International sports editor and columnist, had died in June and the new award honored those who served former baseball colleagues in financial need. Another writer, Jack Lang of the *New York Daily News*, won the J.G. Taylor Spink Award, earning him recognition by the Baseball Hall of Fame.[29] A less inspiring sight was slugger George Foster wandering through the Diplomat's lobby all week, campaigning for a job. The Mets cut Foster on August 7 after his racial remarks rankled the front office. The White Sox signed him a week later but released him on September 7. Now Foster used the Winter Meetings to find a new team. "Some people put themselves up on a pride pedestal. They wouldn't do this. They feel like they'd be lowering themselves," said Foster. "But I feel I still can play and want to let people know I'm here … creating that visibility, planting that seed."[30] That seed never took root. At $2 million, Foster had earned the most money in 1986, yet said his new demands would not be an obstacle. However, his deteriorating skills and bitter attitude made him the least attractive free agent in a market that ignored everyone. His failure to sign at the meetings marked the end of Foster's career.

A hotel's lobby offers a good setting in which to spin rumors, talk trades, and create deals. The 1985 Winter Meetings saw little such action, in part because the owners inexplicably had selected a lobby-less motel in San Diego. In Hollywood, Florida, the Diplomat Hotel's football-sized lobby offered a better atmosphere in which to conduct business; it did not help. The 1986 Winter Meetings turned into the slowest in history with a record low of seven trades involving 21 major-league players.[31] By early Wednesday, not a single trade of note had been hatched. The old interleague trade deadline in December used to motivate GMs to trade by the last day of the meetings. The new deadline, installed the previous year, pushed the cutoff to July 31. Responding to the lack of trades at the meetings, Dodgers manager Tommy Lasorda said, "There are a lot of reasons. There are no trading deadlines and you're not sure about free agents. Now you call a team about a player and the other team asks you how much he is making and does he have a no-trade contract. It's tough to make a trade."[32]

The inert trade market finally came to life late Wednesday afternoon with three deals. The Dodgers sought pitching and got it in two trades. First they sent their underachieving first baseman, Greg Brock, to Milwaukee, landing two right-hand pitchers, Tim Crews and Tim Leary. They then swapped left-handers with Seattle, trading Dennis Powell and minor-league infielder-outfielder Mike Watters to the Mariners for their best reliever, Matt Young.

In the prior offseason, the Kansas City Royals sought power to energize their cleanup spot, yet they reneged on their interest in signing free agent Kirk Gibson. This year they pulled the trigger on a slugger via the trade route, landing Seattle's powerful outfielder Danny Tartabull. Seattle was happy to part with their "lackadaisical" rookie, who refused to play winter ball.[33] The Royals were eager to accept him along with right-hander Rick Luecken. In exchange for Tartabull's talents, the Mariners received right-handers Scott Bankhead and Steve Shields along with utility outfielder Mike Kingery.[34]

BASEBALL'S BUSINESS: THE WINTER MEETINGS

With most of the scheduled business having been concluded by Wednesday, most executives left the Diplomat on Thursday morning. Staying behind to complete deals, however, the Yankees swapped hitting for pitching by trading designated hitter Mike Easler and infielder Tom Barrett to Philadelphia for right-handers Charles Hudson and minor-leaguer Jeff Knox. Also doing some last-minute trolling, the White Sox sent right-handers Gene Nelson and Bruce Tanner to Oakland for utility infielder Donnie Hill. The last trade of the meetings was also the biggest, in terms of impact and total number of players. Fresh off their World Series win, the New York Mets refused to stand pat. Since 1978 every World Series winner had failed to even win its division the next season, including the previous year's champions, the Royals who, after backing out of that deal with free agent Kirk Gibson, scored fewer runs than any team in the league except for the White Sox.[35]

The Mets looked to break this trend and finally acquired the player they had been seeking throughout the offseason, San Diego Padres slugger Kevin McReynolds. Rumors swirled all week about the outfielder's final landing spot. The Mets and Padres talked every day during the meetings, including several times on Thursday, and finally the Mets got their man in an eight-player trade. For McReynolds, lefty reliever Gene Walter, and minor-league infielder Adam Ging, the Mets gave a bundle of talent to the Padres: Shawn Abner, the first overall pick of the 1984 draft, outfielder Stan Jefferson, third baseman Kevin Mitchell, and minor-league pitchers left-hander Kevin A. Brown and right-hander Kevin Armstrong. It took until late Thursday night, but the eleventh-hour deal was worth the wait, according to Mets vice president Joe McIlvaine. "From our perspective, we set out at these meetings trying to find a right-handed hitter with power to hit in the middle of our lineup with Gary Carter and Darryl Strawberry—without disturbing our pitching staff," said McIlvaine. "We think we've done that with Kevin McReynolds."[36]

The few trades made at the meetings, though, seemed like a flood when compared to the logjam of free agents. Secretly, the owners agreed that all available players were "hands off" until January 8. That was the date by which clubs had to re-sign their own free agents or lose that chance until May 1. After this deadline, the owners would know which players they could go after, since their 1986 clubs now showed no interest in retaining them.

With less competition for their services, players were frequently the ones making the offers, rather than the clubs.

Throughout the meetings, the fate of two free agents simmered in the hands of their agent, Dick Moss. Ten years earlier, Moss had famously represented two other free agents, Andy Messersmith and Dave McNally, when they successfully challenged baseball's reserve clause, and now he was steering Jack Morris and Andre Dawson through the same free-agent jungle. By the last day of the meetings, Moss had received no interest in either client. Earlier in the week Moss made a telling remark to a group of reporters. "I shouldn't say this, but I will," Moss said. "Just before the end of the season, Andre was told by someone in the front office he ought to sign because if he doesn't sign with the Expos, he's not going to play baseball next year."[37] Dawson had upset the Expos when he told them he was seeking another venue on which to patrol center field. His knees ached on Montreal's artificial turf. He declared free agency so that he might play on real grass for his home games, and his first and only choice was in Chicago and Wrigley Field. The Expos had offered Dawson less than the $1,047,000 he made in 1985, proposing $2 million for two years.[38] "He doesn't want to return to Montreal and has been thinking that way for some time. For now, though, the Cubs are as far as we've got," said Moss.[39] Dawson eventually became the first significant player to sign with a new team from the 1986 free-agent class, but it happened only because Moss and Dawson offered the Cubs a blank check on March 6, 1987. The club got to choose the amount and filled out the check for $500,000, with $150,000 in incentives, less than half of what Dawson was worth in an "unrigged" market. After they made the offer, Moss said, "We had hoped that the club's definition of fairness would have been more realistic.

But our offer was unconditional (blank check) and we will, of course, honor our commitment."[40]

Moss's other client, Tigers right-hander Jack Morris, stunned everyone with an announcement near the end of the meetings. Morris had won the most games in the 1980s and was the top prize of the free-agent crop. He made $975,000 in 1986 and sought a five-year deal nearing $9 million.[41] The Tigers, upholding the owners' unwritten rule against long-term contracts, showed no interest in any deal beyond two years. They offered Morris several options: a two-year deal for $2.5 million, accept salary arbitration by the December 19 deadline, or sign elsewhere.[42] Morris was not interested in a lengthy arbitration process with Detroit, so on December 10 he went on the offensive. At a press conference, Moss announced that Morris had ended discussions with the Tigers. He would now only sign with the Twins, Yankees, Phillies, or Angels. "The clubs have said they do not want to negotiate any further," Moss said. "They want us to bring them an offer and they will say yes or no. OK, we will play their game."[43] In effect, Morris reversed the free-agent process by offering his proposals to the teams. He ranked the teams one through four in his order of preference. He then said would sign with the first club that accepted or negotiated an agreement with him. This move agitated the owners by putting four of them in the spotlight. They faced the dilemma of a taboo signing that would anger the other owners, or reject Morris and cause fury for their fans. Morris tried to redirect the market to his terms with this unprecedented move. The uninvolved owners were pleased the pitcher didn't back their team into his corner. When Morris did not list his team, one owner exclaimed, "We're off the hook!"[44] In the end, all four teams rejected multiple offers from Morris, fueling further allegations of owner collusion. By the December 19 deadline, Morris reluctantly submitted to arbitration with Detroit. Fittingly, on February 13, 1987, Morris set a record by winning the largest contract through arbitration, netting the one-year, $1.85 million contract he sought from the Tigers.[45]

As the arbitration deadline passed, another cutoff date loomed, one that had been put in place the previous year. Free agents who refused salary arbitration could still re-sign with their 1986 team by midnight of January 8, 1987. After this date, clubs could not negotiate with their own free agents until May 1. This window invited owners to go after those free agents who appeared to be unwanted by their former clubs. Last year every free agent re-signed with his original club before the January deadline. This year eight players entered a new battlefield by not re-signing.[46] These eight pioneers included outfielders Tim Raines and Andre Dawson, catchers Lance Parrish, Rich Gedman, and Bob Boone, first baseman Bob Horner, and pitchers Ron Guidry and Doyle Alexander. For the most part, the owners continued their hands-off policy as five players re-signed with their clubs after May 1 (Raines, Boone, Gedman, Guidry, and Alexander). Bob Horner received no offers and eventually signed with the Japan's Yakult Swallows. Dawson and Parrish then became two of only four players who signed with new teams before the 1987 season began. Dawson's blank-check ploy paid off as he won the 1987 National League MVP Award and tripled his salary the following year.[47] Before Parrish signed with Philadelphia in March, evidence suggested that American League President Bobby Brown and owners Bud Selig of Milwaukee and Jerry Reinsdorf of the White Sox urged the Phillies president not to sign the catcher.[48]

The 1986 Winter Meetings echoed those of 1985. The lack of free-agent signings and glacial trading marked the gridlock sought by the owners. Donald Fehr, the director of the Major League Baseball Players Association, had smelled conspiracy after the 1985 meetings and filed a grievance in February 1986. Though that grievance was still pending, it did not deter Fehr from filing a second grievance on February 18, 1987. These two protests became known as Collusion I and Collusion II. Yet despite the grievances, the owners felt confident in their cold-market scheme for a number of reasons. First, since both complaints were months from arbitration, they had time to sharpen their defense. Second, they believed that no "smoking gun" existed to convict them. Finally, their free-agent freeze-out was working. Their rigged market reduced free-agent salaries for 1986-87 by 16 percent, and most of the players failed to sign a multiyear contract.[49]

Fehr noted this decline in pay and the 15 percent increase in owner revenues, and suspected collusion.[50] Since the two grievances were in limbo, the owners saw no reason to end their illicit fix. Their new "economics" would continue at the 1987 Winter Meetings, albeit under a new cloak of deception. More free-agent offers would occur during the next winter, but they would be lowball bids and strangely similar. The owners planned to poison the process using an "information bank," in which they shared details of their offers.[51] Collusion III was starting to boil, and soon so would Fehr and the players union.

NOTES

1 Associated Press, "Annual Winter Meetings Open Sunday in Florida," *Rome* (Georgia) *News-Tribune*, December 7, 1986: 13-B. Note: Other sources cite 79 free agents who declared this status. Regardless, this offseason was the largest free-agent class to date.

2 Randy Youngman, "Ueberroth Praises Owners. He Says Good Business Sense Keeps Costs Low," *Orange County Register* (Santa Ana, California), December 9, 1986: C07.

3 Ibid.

4 Associated Press, "Baseball Smashes Attendance Record," *Newburgh-Beacon Evening News* (Newburgh, New York), October 8, 1986: 2B.

5 Jerome Holtzman, "Ueberroth Hits Spending Waste," *Chicago Tribune*, December 9, 1986: C3.

6 Ibid.

7 Youngman, "Ueberroth Praises Owners."

8 Ross Newhan, "Blacks in Major League Baseball Management: Absence or Malice?—The Action Doesn't Look Affirmative," *Los Angeles Times*, April 9, 1987: 1.

9 "Hank Aaron, Monte Irvin Applaud Minority Push," *Jet Magazine*, Vol. 71, No. 15, December 29, 1986: 46.

10 Ross Newhan, "Blacks in Major League Baseball Management."

11 James Edward Miller, *The Baseball Business: Pursuing Pennants and Profits in Baltimore* (Chapel Hill, North Carolina: University of North Carolina Press, 1991), 317.

12 The author experienced Ueberroth's alcohol plan firsthand as a beer vendor at Pittsburgh's Three Rivers Stadium. In 1987, ARAmark, the Pirates concessionaire, stopped beer sales after five innings, two innings sooner than at most ballparks in the league. It truly truncated vendor commissions for the last 14 years of the stadium's life.

13 Youngman, "Ueberroth Praises Owners."

14 Holtzman.

15 Marty York, "Expo GM Plans to Talk New Game," *The Globe and Mail* (Toronto), December 10, 1986: D3.

16 Holtzman.

17 Baseball-Reference, baseball-reference.com/bullpen/1986_Rule_V_Draft.

18 Baseball America, baseballamerica.com/minors/ask-ba-2/#Kkm9OvMp9wLM57BM.97.

19 Baseball-Reference, baseball-reference.com/leagues/MLB/1986-transactions.shtml.

20 Joe Goddard, "Baseball Winter Meeting Bits," *Chicago Sun-Times*, December 10, 1986: 126.

21 Howard Sinker, "Major Leagues Approve Sale of Indians to Jacobs," *Minneapolis Star and Tribune*, December 10, 1986: 6D.

22 Ibid.

23 Ibid.

24 The 1987 meetings eventually were awarded to the Loew's Anatole Hotel in Dallas, Texas.

25 Ibid.

26 Walter O'Malley Biography, walteromalley.com/biog_ref_page83.php.

27 Murray Chass, "Mariners Reinforce the View They Run a Tight Ship," *New York Times*, December 14, 1986: A7.

28 Tom Verducci, "Herzog Adds Spice to Bland Meetings," *Newsday* (Long Island, New York), December 10, 1986: 157.

29 Larry Whiteside, "Busy Mariners Swap Young and Tartabull: Seattle Sends Lefty Reliever to Dodgers, Outfielder to Royals," *Boston Globe*, December 11, 1986: 90.

30 Craig Barnes, "Morris, Dawson Promise to Open Free-Agent Market," *Sun Sentinel* (Fort Lauderdale, Florida), December 11, 1986: 1C.

31 Associated Press, "Baseball Clubs Made Few Deals. Winter Meeting Slowest Ever," *Eugene* (Oregon) *Register-Guard*, December 13, 1986: 8D.

32 Ibid.

33 Associated Press, "Royals Hope Tartabull Fills Void in Lineup," *Lawrence* (Kansas) *Daily Journal-World*, December 11, 1986: 1B.

34 Baseball-Reference, baseball-reference.com/leagues/MLB/1986-transactions.shtml.

35 Associated Press, "Baseball Clubs Made Few Deals."

36 Associated Press, "Mets Acquire Power Hitter They Wanted in McReynolds," *Washington* (Pennsylvania) *Observer-Reporter*, December 12, 1986: B4.

37 Sinker, "Major Leagues Approve."

38 Ryan Allan, "Morris Moves to Thaw Free Agent Freeze-Out," *Toronto Star*, December 11, 1986: F1.

39 Ibid.

40 "Dawson, Cubs Reach Accord," *Newsday*, March 7, 1987: 31.

41 Ryan Allan, "Morris Moves."

42 Murray Chass, "Morris Ends His Tiger Talks," *New York Times*, December 11, 1986: D29.

43 Larry Whiteside, "Morris: Tigers Are Out; Agent Says Pitcher Will Deal Only With Four Teams," *Boston Globe*, December 11, 1986: 89.

44 Murray Chass, "Mariners Reinforce."

45 Ross Newhan, "A Record Judgment for Morris," *Los Angeles Times*, February 14, 1987: 1.

46 Associated Press, "Free Agents' Fight Prepares for a Different Battleground," *Gainesville* (Florida) *Sun*, January 10, 1987: 8C.

47 Baseball-Reference, baseball-reference.com/players/d/dawsoan01.shtml.

48 Murray Chass, "Arbitrator Finds Baseball Owners in Second Free-Agent Conspiracy," *New York Times*, September 1, 1988: A1.

49 John Helyar, *Lords of the Realm: The Real History of Baseball* (New York: Villard Publishing, 1994), 356.

50 Ibid.

51 Scott Rosner and Kenneth Shropshire, *The Business of Sports* (Sudbury, Massachusetts: Jones & Bartlett Learning, 2004), 212.

— 1987 —
CHANGING TIMES — COLLUSION III

By Bob Whelan

I. INTRODUCTION AND CONTEXT

THE 1987 WINTER MEETINGS WERE held at the Loew's Anatole Hotel in Dallas, Texas, in the middle of the "collusion era."[1] Collusion is a complex tale and, as such, only a brief summary is presented here. Peter Ueberroth became commissioner of baseball in 1984, after concluding his successful management of the 1984 Summer Olympic Games in Los Angeles. Ueberroth was quick to tell owners that they were "stupid," particularly in relation to free-agency issues. Undoubtedly, Ueberroth never ordered collusion on free agency, but his comments in owners meetings gave the clear impression that he supported collusion. After the 1985 season, teams announced an end to long-term contracts (i.e., those of more than two years for pitchers and three years for hitters).

Such stars as Kirk Gibson, then a Detroit Tiger, did not receive better offers from other teams. After the 1985-86 offseason, 29 of 33 free agents returned to their former teams.

The four players who did move were marginal players whose original teams weren't interested in retaining their services. In February 1986, the Major League Baseball Players Association (MLBPA) filed its first grievance.[2]

If anything, the 1986-87 offseason was worse for free agents. Such stars as Bob Boone, Andre Dawson, Bob Horner, Jack Morris, Lance Parrish, and Tim Raines attracted little interest, with none of them receiving a larger offer from another team. Indeed, Dawson took a substantial pay cut when he went from the Expos to the Cubs — a decision based on Dawson's bad knees, and a desire to play on grass at Wrigley Field instead of the artificial turf of Montreal's Olympic Stadium.

In February 1987, the MLBPA filed a second grievance. In September of 1987, ruling on the first (February 1986) collusion grievance, baseball's arbitrator, Thomas Roberts, found the major-league owners to be guilty. Teams now took a new approach to collusion, known as the "information bank." A team making an offer to a free agent was supposed to report it to the Player Relations Committee (PRC). A club thinking of making an offer could find out what others had done by first checking with the PRC.[3] The resulting situation was more open than the previous two years, but far from the sometimes outrageous free-agent competition in ensuing years. The greater fluidity was demonstrated in trades and free-agent signings in the period just before the 1987 winter baseball meetings.[4]

II. PLAYER MOVEMENT

Much of the player movement before and during the 1987 Winter Meetings came from the efforts of AL West teams to compete with the World Series Champion Minnesota Twins.

On November 6, 1987, the Kansas City Royals traded left-handed starting pitcher Danny Jackson and infielder Angel Salazar to the Cincinnati Reds for shortstop Kurt Stilwell and right-handed pitcher Ted Power. Jackson proceeded to have his career season, with 23 wins for the 1988 Reds. Salazar appeared in only 34 games for Cincinnati. Stilwell became the Royals' regular shortstop for several seasons. Power had won 10 games for the 1986 and 1987 Reds, but never reached that total again.

Just before the Winter Meetings, there were two major free-agent departures. The first found the San

Francisco Giants signing Cleveland Indians star Brett Butler. One of the outstanding outfielders of his era, Butler was a leadoff man with a high on-base percentage and a knack for disrupting the opposition—between 1983 and 1993, Butler stole more than 30 bases every season. He would play center field for the 1989 Giants World Series team. On the same day, December 1, 1987, the Giants lost outfielder Chili Davis to the California Angels. Davis would go on to have a long and successful stay in the American League as an outfielder and designated hitter, finishing with 350 career home runs.

As the Winter Meetings opened on December 5, 1987, the *Dallas Times-Herald* headline read: "Baseball executives expect sparse trading again this year." With five major trades concluded in the next few days, the reader can draw conclusions as to whether trading was "sparse."[5] Four of the five trades involved AL West teams, as did two of the three moves noted above.

On December 5, 1987, the California Angels traded Gary Pettis to the Detroit Tigers for right-handed pitcher Dan Petry. At a young age, Petry had won 19 games in 1983 and 18 games for the 1984 World Series Champion Tigers. Unfortunately, he was never that pitcher again. (One wonders about his career with more careful handling used today.) Pettis was the prototypical light-hitting, great-fielding center fielder. A two-time Gold Glove winner with the Angels, he would win two more with the Tigers and one more with the Rangers.

The next two trades, made on December 8, 1987, were characterized as "blockbusters" in the Dallas newspapers. In the first, the Oakland A's sent young pitchers Jose Rijo and Tim Birtsas to the Cincinnati Reds for veteran slugger Dave Parker. The old baseball cliché is that the trade helped both teams. The right-handed Rijo became a solid starter, with 14 wins in 1990, followed by two more wins in the World Series, which earned him the World Series MVP award for the champions. After a promising start as a 10-game winner for the 1985 A's, the southpaw Birtsas worked as a reliever for the Reds. Parker, in the twilight of a distinguished career, hit 22 home runs and drove in 97 runs for the A's 1989 championship squad.

The other "blockbuster" trade involved a trio of right-handed pitchers, as the Red Sox sent pitchers Calvin Schiraldi and Al Nipper to the Cubs for star closer Lee Smith. Smith wound up having two good seasons with the Red Sox, and continued a great career in which he led the league in saves on three more occasions. Schiraldi, a great prospect, never developed into a consistent winner. Nipper had been a double-digit winner in both 1986 and 1987 for the Red Sox, but never won that many again.

In another AL West trade, the Kansas City Royals got lefty Floyd Bannister and utilityman Dave Cochrane from the White Sox for four young pitchers: southpaw Greg Hibbard and righties John Davis, Chuck Mount, and Melido Perez. Bannister had won 16 games, a career high, for the White Sox in 1987. He went on to win 12 for the Royals in 1988, but was injured and ineffective thereafter. Both Hibbard and Perez became rotation starters for the White Sox for several years.

The real "blockbuster" trade occurred at the end of the meetings, and it involved three teams and eight players. The Los Angeles Dodgers sent hard-throwing righty pitcher Bob Welch and southpaw Matt Young to the Oakland A's. Another right-hander, Jack Savage, went from the Dodgers to the New York Mets. The A's sent shortstop Alfredo Griffin and right-handed closer Jay Howell to the Dodgers. The A's gave up pitching prospects Kevin Tapani and Wally Whitehurst (both right-handers) to the Mets, while the Mets sent their closer, southpaw Jesse Orosco, to the Dodgers.

This trade had significant results, as the next two world champions—the 1988 Dodgers and the 1989 A's—improved their new teams with this deal. Welch won 211 games in his career, including 27 wins and a Cy Young Award for the 1990 A's. Young never lived up to his early promise as a Mariners starter. Savage recorded only one save in a brief career. "Fettucine" Alfredo Griffin was a good-fielding shortstop for LA for several years, while Howell was a highly successful closer for the 1988 Dodgers, and for several seasons thereafter. Tapani won 143 games in an effective major-league career, but these were for the Twins and Cubs, not the Mets. Whitehurst, who pitched the University of New Orleans to the College World Series in 1984, won only 20 games in a career limited by injuries. Orosco helped the Dodgers win the 1988 championship, but left for Cleveland as a free agent. He remained a top left-handed reliever for many years and, in fact, appeared in more games—1,252—than any other pitcher in history. There were three other trades concluded at the meetings, but in retrospect they don't seem particularly important.

III. BUSINESS SIDE

One change was made in the rules at the 1987 Winter Meetings by the rules committee.

Previously, the upper limit of the strike zone was the batter's armpits. The 1987 rules change redefined the upper limit of the zone as "the midpoint between the top of the shoulders and the top of the uniform pants." The intention of the smaller strike zone was to increase scoring.

Discussion of expansion was perhaps more significant for the future of the major leagues. In 1987, there were 26 teams, and the majors were under pressure from a 14-member US Senate Task Force on Expansion, chaired by Senator Tim Wirth (D-Colorado). The task force was composed of members who hoped that their states would get expansion teams.

The Senate group threatened the end of baseball's antitrust exemption. Phoenix, Tampa Bay, and Buffalo were considered the prime locations for expansion, with Washington, Indianapolis, Miami, and New Orleans also being mentioned. In an interview, Commissioner Ueberroth looked forward to having 32 teams in the major leagues; he even mentioned Havana as a possible franchise site. Expansion was discussed in both owners and league meetings, and Ueberroth appointed an expansion committee. In the 1990s, MLB expanded to its current 30 teams, adding Denver (Colorado Rockies), Miami (Miami Marlins), Phoenix (Arizona Diamondbacks), and Tampa Bay. In addition, the Montreal Expos franchise relocated to Washington after the 2004 season.

Another issue on the business side was the status of Ueberroth. He had previously built a highly successful travel business, and had managed the 1984 Los Angeles Summer Olympic Games. As commissioner, he had increased the amount of baseball's licensing and sponsorship monies significantly. He settled an umpires strike, and a players strike, but the owners were not happy with the results of either settlement. Ueberroth was also the leader of the 1985-1987 collusion effort. Ueberroth's dictatorial approach, and the fact that he wasn't a "baseball man," didn't sit well with club owners. The commissioner was also ahead of his time in proposing a drug-testing plan at the 1987 Winter Meetings. Knowing that he lacked support from a majority of owners, Ueberroth announced that he would not seek a second term in June 1988.

Minority hiring was another important issue for the 1987 meetings. The context was the infamous appearance of Dodgers executive Al Campanis on the television program *Nightline* in April 1987, in which Campanis said that black people lacked the "necessities" for high-level management positions in baseball. At the meetings, Ueberroth met with a group formed to promote the hiring of blacks and Hispanics in managerial positions in baseball. By the end of his tenure as commissioner, He claimed that 180 of 542 baseball hires had been minorities—36 percent in the front office and 30 percent in field-level positions.

Free agency and the salary situation were the overriding concerns at the 1987 Winter Meetings. The owners were pleased that the average salary dropped from $431,521 in 1986 to $408,000 in 1987. At the same time, teams showed a willingness to pursue free agents, under limited conditions (e.g., shorter-length contracts). This was evidenced by the Brett Butler and Chili Davis signings just before the meetings.

IV. SUMMARY AND CONCLUSIONS

In the wake of the arbitrator's decision that collusion had occurred in 1985, there was more movement in free agency and trades than there had been in the previous two years. The 1987 meetings were lively, with several significant trades, involving quality players. A significant rules change—a smaller strike zone—went into place. The owners took steps toward expansion, and the hiring of more minorities. This was a time of transition for baseball, and the Winter Meetings reflected the changes.

NOTES

1. John Helyar, *Lords of the Realm: The Real History of Baseball* (New York: Villard, 1994), especially 354-387.

2. Andrew Zimbalist. *Baseball and Billions* (New York: Basic Books, 1992), 24-25.

3. Helyar, 384.

4. For more detailed accounts of the collusion era, see Helyar, 354-387; Zimbalist, 24-26; and Andrew Zimbalist, *In the Best Interests of Baseball: The Revolutionary Reign of Bud Selig* (Hoboken, New Jersey: John Wiley & Sons, 2006), 90-95.

5. Phil Rogers, "Baseball Executives Expect Sparse Trading Again This Year," *Dallas Times Herald*, December 5, 1987: D6.

— 1988 —
RANGERS MAKE HUGE SPLASH

By Steve West

Introduction and context

THE 1988 WINTER MEETINGS WERE held at the Marriott Marquis Hotel in Atlanta, Georgia, from Sunday, December 4, until Wednesday, December 7. These meetings came at the tail end of the collusion cases, as teams were beginning to open their wallets and spend money again, and a lot of teams were looking at both free agents and trades to get better quickly. The stars of the meetings were both the free agents and the Texas Rangers. Any one of the deals the Rangers made would have been big news, but they made two huge trades, and added a free agent signing, that would redefine the franchise for years to come.

Heading into the meetings, it was becoming apparent that the collusion between owners of the previous few years was breaking apart. In 1985 the owners had met with Commissioner Peter Ueberroth, who had told them not to sign other teams' free agents, because doing so was a waste of money. They held the line during both 1986 and 1987, but an arbitrator had ruled against them in September of 1987 and again in August of 1988, and would do so again the following year.[1]

So now, at the end of 1988, teams were starting to spend money on free agents again. More free agents had signed between the end of the season and the start of the Winter Meetings than had done so in the past couple of years, but there were still several high-profile players waiting for their turn in Atlanta. In addition, several trades were already in discussion, most notably the possibility of the Dodgers acquiring Eddie Murray from the Orioles, and with face-to-face talks, it was hoped that some of those would be resolved in Atlanta.

Before the meetings had even begun, several free agents had signed new contracts. Notably, the A's had signed one of their own free agents, outfielder Dave Henderson, to a three-year deal, and got right-handed pitcher Mike Moore, a free agent from the Mariners, to sign for three years and almost $4 million. The A's then said they were done signing players, and were thankful they hadn't let Moore get to the Winter Meetings, as he would have cost a lot more once the bidding wars began.[2]

Other free-agent deals were happening quickly as the meetings approached. Dodgers second baseman Steve Sax signed with the Yankees for $4 million the week before the meetings began. Infielder Ron Oester re-signed with the Reds, while much-traveled lefthander Dave LaPoint, who had pitched for both the White Sox and Pirates in 1988, chose to move to the Yankees in the run-up to the meetings. Each of these moves took a job from someone and opened another spot somewhere else. Willie Upshaw, for instance, decided to go play in Japan, which opened up first base for the Indians, another hole for them to fill.

With some big free agents still available — the top of the class being Houston right-handed pitcher Nolan Ryan and Boston left-hander Bruce Hurst — there was talk about the possibilities of trades happening during the meetings. The news centered on Orioles first baseman Eddie Murray, who had expressed discontent with the poor performance of the team, and wanted out. Trade talks with the Dodgers were ongoing and received a lot of attention just before the meetings.

There was, of course, both excitement and skepticism among the front-office personnel. Depending on whom you talked to, the opinion might be that nothing was going to happen in Atlanta, or that a lot might happen. Several GMs talked about the old days, when the Winter Meetings were for wheeling and dealing. Prior to 1985 the interleague trade deadline was at the end of the meetings, putting a lot of pressure on teams to get something done. "In the past, you knew if you couldn't get something done at the meetings, there might not be another opportunity," Roland Hemond, the Orioles GM, said.[3]

That rule had been changed, though, and now the pressure was not there to complete a deal so quickly. Teams could get the lay of the land, and then spend weeks or months during the winter working out deals. And with both trades and free agency down, some expected the meetings to be less important, with little happening. "There aren't as many deals being made. There's too much at stake. Too many complications, too many contract problems. And, you know, there's not as much drinking going on," said former American League President Lee MacPhail.[4]

The flip side was with the ballplayers, and with their own agents. "What you'll be running into now is agents. You'll be tripping over them. You won't be able to get through the lobby without running into one. And if you even say hello to them, they're liable to use it against you in arbitration," said an unnamed agent before the meetings.[5]

But some still thought things were going to happen. Angels owner Gene Autry had told Peter Bavasi in November: "I have a lot of money to spend and not a lot of time (to live), and I want a World Series ring."[6] Autry had then instructed his GM, Mike Port, to sign Ryan and Hurst no matter the cost. With the Rangers and Astros also homing in on Ryan, and several teams interested in Hurst (the Cardinals offered him a three-year, $5.1 million offer the Thursday before the meetings, but withdrew it the next day[7]), there were lots of expectations.

Business and politics

On the business side of baseball, much was happening at the meetings regarding ownership, broadcasting, and hiring. Commissioner Ueberroth gave his annual State of the Game speech on Monday. He stated that baseball had cleaned up the drug problems it had faced in the early 1980s, and talked about the progress that baseball had made in hiring minorities, who now made up 10 percent of front-office personnel (up from 2 percent), but he acknowledged that baseball needed to do more in hiring minority managers, general managers, and other visible positions. "We have room to still be critical and, in some areas, very critical," he said.[8]

In response, Hank Aaron blasted baseball's actions. "There are more minorities interviewing, but I don't see them getting the job. You see Joe Morgan, Bill Robinson, Billy Williams. They're all qualified and deserve more than an interview," he said.[9] Aaron said that most of the increase in minorities had been in places like the ticket office, while Bob Watson, new assistant general manager of the Houston Astros, said that minority hires "are mostly window dressing." Aaron also said that Ueberroth's words were "the same old bull, just dressed up a little bit."[10]

After Ueberroth's speech, the owners met for five hours, considering several different issues. Owners were asked to look again at the sale of the Texas Rangers from Eddie Chiles to Edward Gaylord, a deal they had rejected earlier in the year. Owners were afraid that Gaylord would turn his television company, Gaylord Broadcasting, into another superstation, competing with local stations across the country, which would siphon off both fans and local advertising dollars in their own markets. They decided to table the matter, sending it back to committee for further discussion.

The owners did approve the sale of the Baltimore Orioles. Former owner Edward Bennett Williams had died of cancer in August, and had said that he did not want his family to retain ownership of the team. His widow, Agnes, sold the team to a group led by team President Larry Lucchino and New York financier Eli Jacobs, along with former vice presidential candidate Sargent Shriver and Robert Shriver Jr., for $70 million.[11]

Owners did not formally discuss the possibility of major-league expansion, but several cities were on hand for informal presentations. "Expansion. Very simply, it must come, and it must be planned and planned well," said Commissioner Ueberroth.[12] He expected that baseball would be expanding in the 1990s, and representatives from Washington, Denver, Florida, and Buffalo presented their cases to ownership. On the other hand, Commissioner-elect Bart Giamatti said "we're very, very far away from (picking) cities."[13]

The owners had elected Giamatti, the National League president, as the next commissioner in September, and he was due to take office in April, at the start of the new season. The NL met to consider candidates to replace Giamatti, but decided to continue their search and wait until January to decide. "While the annual meeting was a goal, it was never a deadline," said Walter O'Malley, Los Angeles Dodgers owner and head of the search committee. "The committee is being as deliberative as possible so as to make sure it chooses the right person for the position."[14] The committee finally chose former major leaguer Bill White in February. White became the first African American to head a major professional sports league. After his earlier criticism of baseball's minority hiring practices, Hank Aaron was pleased at the appointment of White. "I don't think they could have found anyone more qualified than Bill White. He knows baseball," Aaron said.[15]

One other consideration for owners was a new national television contract. The six-year deal with ABC and NBC was due to expire after the 1989 season, and there was great interest in getting a new agreement done. Although the contract was not completed during the meetings, Ueberroth said he thought it would be accomplished within a week, and it was — on December 14, MLB signed a four-year deal with CBS, which beat out the other networks in a bidding war. The contract, valued at $1.8 billion, was significantly higher than expected,[16] and CBS would end up losing half a billion dollars on the deal.[17] In January baseball completed an additional four-year, $400 million deal with ESPN.[18]

Another announcement was made during the meetings. "The New York Yankees became the first major-league baseball team to sell all of its television rights to a cable network Friday when they announced a 12-year deal with the Madison Square Garden Network. The MSG Network will show 75 games in each of the 1989 and 1990 seasons. WPIX-TV, which has carried Yankees games for 38 years, will broadcast 75 games each of those two years under an existing contract. Beginning in 1991 and through the 2000 season, MSG has exclusive rights to 150 games a season. The value of the package was not announced, but a source familiar with the deal said it was worth about $500 million."[19]

During the meetings several awards were handed out. *The Sporting News* named Orel Hershiser, the Dodgers' star right-hander, the Major League Player of the Year, holding a news conference to honor the player, who had gone 23-8 and was named MVP of both the NLCS and World Series. Hershiser also was awarded his first Gold Glove, joining players like Pirates outfielder Andy Van Slyke, Padres catcher Benito Santiago, Mariners second baseman Harold Reynolds, and Angels outfielder Devon White as Gold Glove rookies, while Mets first baseman Keith Hernandez won his 11th. *TSN* also named Fred Claire, the VP of player personnel for the Dodgers, as their executive of the year.[20]

Bob Hunter of the *Los Angeles Herald Examiner* and Ray Kelly of the *Philadelphia Bulletin* were selected as co-recipients of the J.G. Taylor Spink award by the Baseball Writers Association of America.[21]

On Sunday the meetings got off to a bang with the completion of the trade of Eddie Murray from the Orioles to the Dodgers. Murray had reportedly wanted out of Baltimore for years because he desired to play on a winning team and didn't feel the Orioles were going to get there anytime soon.[22] The two teams had been talking for weeks about the trade, and the Orioles finally accepted shortstop Juan Bell and right-handed pitchers Brian Holton and Ken Howell in return for Murray. In addition, Murray got a new contract with the Dodgers, signing for $6.5 million over three years, along with 20 annual installments of $135,000, beginning in 1992. Ironically the deal was held up a bit at the end: Officials from both clubs were trapped in an elevator on their way to the press conference announcing the deal.[23]

Everybody seemed happy about the trade. "I thought this was going to happen three years ago. It got to the point where I thought I was never coming here," said Murray.[24] Dodgers manager Tommy Lasorda was more prophetic: "It's exciting to get a player we feel will one day be in the Hall of Fame to be on our ballclub," he said.[25] (Murray was inducted into the Hall in 2003).

The Orioles were looking to the future. "This was a very important trade in the reconstruction of the Orioles. We got three talented young players," said Orioles GM Roland Hemond.[26] The acquisition of Bell meant that shortstop Cal Ripken could move to third base. "Whatever I can do for the team, I'll do," said Ripken. "We've never had a shortstop like this come to camp since I've been here. So there's a better chance of (a move to third) happening now than in the past."[27]

The Reds on Sunday announced that they had signed right-handed pitcher Rick Mahler to a two-year, $1,580,000 contract, adding him to a rotation (southpaws Tom Browning and Danny Jackson, and right-hander Jose Rijo) that the Reds felt had the potential to be dominant in the coming season.[28] And the Phillies called a press conference late in the day to announce the resigning of Mike Schmidt to a one-year contract. At the appointed hour, however, Phillies President Bill Giles said there was nothing to announce, that both sides still had contract language to work out, and they were going to think about it overnight.[29]

At the owners meeting on Monday, Commissioner Ueberroth gave his annual State of the Game speech, but the news was dominated by the Texas Rangers. Early in the day they traded outfielder Bob Brower to the Yankees for infielder Bob Meacham, but that was just helping to set up a much bigger deal. Later in the day the Rangers completed a nine-player swap with the Chicago Cubs, the most players in one deal since the Rangers' 1980 trade with Seattle uprooted 11 players. The Cubs sent left-handers Drew Hall and Jamie Moyer and first baseman-outfielder Rafael Palmeiro to the Rangers for minor-league infielder Luis Benitez, minor-league outfielder Pablo Delgado, infielder Curt Wilkerson, and three left-handed pitchers, Paul Kilgus, Mitch Williams, and Steve Wilson. Although most of the players had at least some major-league experience, as a whole the trade was characterized as Palmeiro for Williams. Palmeiro had finished second for the National League batting title in 1988, and was looked upon as a future star. "We were looking for an offensive player, and we felt like we got our cake and can eat it, too," said Grieve.[30] On the other side of the deal, the Cubs felt they were looking at their future closer. "Everybody in baseball knows Mitch Williams has one of the best arms in baseball," said Cubs GM Jim Frey.[31]

The trade was a good matchup for the Rangers, who needed offensive help. They got 24-year-old All-Star Palmeiro, who had hit .307 with 41 doubles and 8 home runs. For his part, Palmeiro was disappointed. "I never expected this, not this early in my career, especially coming off a good year," he said. "I really thought it wouldn't happen this year. I thought maybe two, three, or four years down the road, but things happen and I just have to go on."[32] Jamie Moyer, who had gone 9-15 with a 3.48 ERA for the Cubs, was equally mystified. "I was very surprised. I hadn't heard any rumors. I hadn't heard anything. I look at it as a good opportunity. I couldn't say what Texas's record is, but they've got a good young team, some power and good pitching," he said.[33]

Monday also contained a lot of chatter around Bruce Hurst. With several teams involved, it was starting to look less like a money issue. Boston GM Lou Gorman said that the Hurst situation would probably take a few days to resolve, because "His family wants to go to San Diego but he'd prefer to return to Boston."[34]

Monday also featured the Rule 5 draft, in which teams could select players from other teams' minor-league rosters. A dozen players were taken, with outfielder Geronimo Berroa and utilityman Rich Amaral being the most notable names. The Toronto Blue Jays lost three players during the draft, suggesting that they had a strong farm system and should be improving over the next few years.

Having acquired a new first baseman in Palmeiro on Monday, the Rangers made another blockbuster trade on Tuesday, sending their incumbent first baseman, Pete O'Brien, utilityman Jerry Browne, and outfielder Oddibe McDowell to the Indians for second baseman Julio Franco, the leading hitter among all second basemen in 1988. In two trades the Rangers had upgraded the right side of their infield and remade the heart of their batting order. For their part, the Indians felt they were giving up quality but getting multiple good parts back. "You can't make a trade and improve yourself without giving something up," said Indians GM Hank Peters.[35]

The Phillies traded All-Star right-hander Kevin Gross to Montreal for two other righties, Floyd Youmans and Jeff Parrett, and an agreement that they would not reclaim left-hander Jeff Tabaka, who had been drafted by the Phillies from the Expos in Monday's Rule 5 draft. Having also traded left-hander Shane Rawley in October, the Phillies had now given up two of their better starters. They had, however, finished last in the NL East with their 65-96 mark (10½ games out of fifth place), and new GM Lee Thomas felt they needed to gamble given their position.[36]

The trade for Youmans was risky, given his drug history. Thomas said he believed Youmans to be clean now, even though he had been suspended for 60 days during the season for drug abuse. Thomas acknowledged the perception of a problem. "We think we're making a gamble here, but we think it will work out," he said.[37] (It didn't. Youmans won just one game in a Phillies uniform, was released in late June, and pitched just a handful of games in the minor leagues after that.)

The minor-league draft was held on Tuesday. Thirteen players were selected, nine of them pitchers. One of the oddities was the first pick, right-hander Ben Rivera, by the Braves, who selected him from their own team. They had left him unprotected due to a clerical error, and wanted to make sure they kept him. The other players selected were the usual group of players who might or might not ever make a major-league lineup, but teams paid $50,000 each for the opportunity to give them a chance.

The major-league managers luncheon was held on Tuesday, giving skippers the opportunity to get together to discuss various issues in the game. After the lunch, Pete Rose talked up the Reds, and especially his first baseman, Nick Esasky, who had been the subject of a number of rumors. "I understand he says he lost his confidence here and would rather play elsewhere," Rose said.[38] There continued to be rumors about Esasky throughout the meetings, and sure enough he was traded to the Boston Red Sox a few days after the meetings ended.[39]

The Twins and Yankees had been talking about a trade for Dave Winfield, but the Yankees rejected the Twins' offer and, when they tried to make it something completely different, the Twins took exception. Twins GM Andy MacPhail said the possibility of his team's acquiring Winfield "was as close to being dead as it could be."[40]

Wednesday proved to be the third consecutive day in which the Rangers took the headlines. This time it was the signing of free agent Nolan Ryan to a one-year deal, plus a one-year option, with $2 million guaranteed and various bonuses potentially taking the deal over $3 million.

The Astros had made Ryan an initial offer to return, but when they said they would not budge from that offer they were quickly outbid. The Giants also had some early involvement, but the final decision for Ryan came down to the Rangers and the Angels. Both offers were for similar dollars, and Ryan finally decided to stay in his native Texas. "I am a diehard Texan. It didn't come down to a monetary decision. The overriding fact was what I felt was best for me and my family," Ryan said.[41]

Wednesday at midnight was the deadline for teams to either re-sign their free agents or offer them arbitration, otherwise the teams would not be able to negotiate with the players until May 1. This meant that several players returned to their teams, among them right-handed hurlers Scott Sanderson (Cubs), Greg Harris (Phillies), and Ted Power (Tigers). The biggest name re-signing was Mike Schmidt, who returned to the Phillies on a one-year deal which had a base of $500,000, and incentives that could take it over $2 million. Schmidt, a three-time National League MVP, had had surgery in September for a torn rotator cuff, so the incentives included milestone payments on May 15 and August 15 if he was still on the roster;[42] he reached the first date but not the second, as his Hall of Fame career concluded at the end of May.

Also on Wednesday, having decided that Gregg Jefferies was ready for the major leagues, the Mets traded their starting second baseman, Wally Backman, along with minor-league left-hander Mike Santiago, to the Minnesota Twins for three minor-league right-handed pitchers, Jeff Bumgarner, Steve Gasser, and Toby Nivens.

Although the meetings officially ended on Wednesday, a number of teams stayed in Atlanta for a few extra days, working to complete free-agent signings or continuing with trade discussions. The rumor mill was at full blast. The Braves were reported to be trying to trade All-Star outfielder Dale Murphy, with the Mets and Padres supposedly the prime suitors, but the Braves had a steep asking price. Another buzz had the Mets trying to get outfielder Joe Carter from Cleveland, while the Red Sox were purportedly looking to send third baseman Wade Boggs and infielder Spike Owen to Montreal, getting third baseman Tim Wallach and infielder-outfielder Hubie Brooks in return. A deal between Boston and Montreal was completed on Thursday, but of the players listed, only Owen was actually included, which perhaps tells us how fluid trades can be.[43]

Other teams coming away disappointed were the Indians and Pirates, who both came to the meetings hoping to get a shortstop. The Cubs' Shawon Dunston was the top target, but his price was too high. The Pirates wanted Jeff Blauser or Andres Thomas from the Braves, but Atlanta wanted Barry Bonds in any deal and the Pirates refused to include him. Prior to the meetings, Pirates manager Jim Leyland said the team needed to go to Atlanta with "open ears rather than open mouths,"[44] but it became clear afterward that the opposite had happened. Both Leyland and GM Larry Doughty disparaged their existing shortstops—Rafael Belliard, Felix Fermin, and Al Pedrique—who had combined for just 17 RBIs during the season. Pedrique had been released in November, and both Leyland and Doughty had made it clear they were looking for someone else, which is why the asking price from teams like the Cubs and Braves was so high.

The last available big-name free agent was Bruce Hurst, who had several teams trying to sign him, including the Angels, Padres, and his previous team, the Red Sox. Once Ryan was off the list, Hurst essentially had his pick of teams, and even though the Angels were willing to pay the moon, it came down to the Red Sox and Padres. Although the Red Sox were confident he would return, Hurst finally came to terms with the Padres for a three-year, $5.25 million contract. He cited both the presence of family in San Diego, who were lobbying for him to come, and proximity to his home in Utah as deciding factors.[45]

As the meetings came to an end, two things had become apparent: major-league owners, enriched by television dollars, had returned to their free-spending ways; and some teams had come to Atlanta with a plan in mind. The Texas Rangers' top brass, for instance, had met before the meetings and decided that their internal plan was working and they were ready to take the next step to acquire top talent. "Our goal was to come here and make some changes to make an effort to be a contender," said GM Tom Grieve.[46] They had done that in spades, remaking both their offense (Palmeiro and Franco) and their pitching staff (Ryan and Moyer). Grieve emphasized that this was part of the team's ongoing design to get better. "We were able to keep within the plan. There was pressure not to. There's been times when things have not worked out the last few years and we've been tempted to change for the sake of change, but we haven't. This year, we were ready for the next step," he said.[47]

Other teams were not quite as prepared as the Rangers. As always, too many teams were blowing things up just to look as though they were doing something, or making deals just because they presented themselves, not because they were something the team really needed. There was plenty of pressure to perform, to do something for the local fans to be excited about. Larry Doughty, the new GM of the Pirates, was asked in the first couple of days of the meetings if he was having fun, and replied that "I'd rather have it all done and be watching spring training."[48]

Later in the meetings he was asked again about how things were going, and he responded with something that many GMs might have said: "I'm not even sure if the meetings have any value anymore. You can make rule changes through the mail and you can make trades over the telephone. The only advantage to coming here and negotiating is you do it face to face, and sometimes you can tell by body language or facial expression whether you've struck a nerve or hit a pulse."[49]

BASEBALL'S BUSINESS: THE WINTER MEETINGS

NOTES

1. "Arbitrator Finds Big League Collusion," *Los Angeles Times*, July 18, 1990.
2. Peter Gammons, "And Here We Go Again," *Sports Illustrated*, December 19, 1988: 50.
3. Randy Minkoff, "Major dealing would help heat up winter meetings," *Arlington Heights* (Illinois) *Daily Herald*, December 4, 1988: 3.
4. Bud Shaw, "Baseball Meetings Have Gone Wimpy," *Stars and Stripes*, December 4 1988: 23.
5. "Baseball Meetings to Begin," *New Castle* (Pennsylvania) *News*, December 3, 1988: 14.
6. Gammons, "And Here We Go Again."
7. "Baseball Meetings Have Gone Wimpy."
8. "Minority Job Paces Disappoints Ueberroth," *Stars and Stripes*, December 6, 1988: 25.
9. "War of Words," *Pacific Stars and Stripes*, December 7, 1988: 28.
10. Ibid.
11. "Texas Trading Heavy at Winter Meeting," *Santa Fe New Mexican*, December 7, 1988: B2.
12. "D.C. Lobbies for Baseball Team," *Frederick* (Maryland) *Post*, December 7, 1988: C-2.
13. "Rangers Continue Pace at Winter Meetings," *Titusville* (Pennsylvania) *Herald*, December 8, 1988: 10.
14. "Rangers Latest Team to Make Ryan Offer," *Arlington Heights* (Illinois) *Daily Herald*, December 2, 1988: 3.
15. Michael Martinez, "Bill White a Unanimous Choice to Head National League," *New York Times*, February 4, 1989.
16. Gammons, "And Here We Go Again." Gammons wrote that the new TV contract "is expected to produce revenues of $1.2 billion over the next three years."
17. Phil Jackman, "There's More to CBS's NFL Ouster Than Any 'Gentlemen's Deal,'" *Baltimore Sun*, December 21, 1993.
18. "ESPN Awarded Cable TV Rights for Baseball in $400-Million Deal," *Los Angeles Times*, January 5, 1989.
19. "Grandstand," *Winchester* (Virginia) *Star*, December 10, 1988: 16.
20. "Sporting News Honors Hershiser, Claire," *Santa Fe New Mexican*, December 7, 1988: B1.
21. "Winter Baseball Meeting Notebook," *Tyrone* (Pennsylvania) *Daily Herald*, December 8, 1988: 6.
22. Ross Newhan, "Finally, Deal Is done—Dodgers get Murray," *Los Angeles Times*, December 5, 1988.
23. Richard L. Shook, "LA Finally Seals Murray Deal," *Mount Union* (Pennsylvania) *Daily News*, December 5, 1988: 5.
24. "Murray Traded to LA," *Aiken* (South Carolina) *Standard*, December 5, 1988: 7A.
25. Shook, "LA Finally Seals Murray Deal."
26. Ibid.
27. "Ripken Ready to Make Move," *Winchester* (Virginia) *Star*, December 6, 1988: 11.
28. Shook, "LA Finally Seals Murray Deal."
29. Ibid.
30. Jim Donaghy, "Rangers, Cubs Make a Really BIG Deal," *Elyria* (Ohio) *Chronicle-Telegram*, December 6, 1988: B-6.
31. Ibid.
32. "Rangers Trade For Palmeiro," *Kerrville* (Texas) *Daily Times*, December 6, 1988: 9.
33. Ibid.
34. "Red Sox and Padres Top Contenders for Hurst," *Dixon* (Illinois) *Telegraph*, December 6, 1988: 11.
35. "Tribe Trades Julio," *Elyria* (Ohio) *Chronicle-Telegram*, December 6, 1988: B-6.
36. "Phillies Trade Gross for Pair of Pitchers," *Alton* (Illinois) *Telegraph*, December 7, 1988: B3.
37. Ibid.
38. Tom Saladino, "Rose Offers a New Look, Optimism," *Kokomo* (Indiana) *Tribune*, December 8, 1988: 21.
39. Esasky and left-hander Rob Murphy went to Boston on December 13 in exchange for first baseman-outfielder Todd Benzinger, right-hander Jeff Sellers, and a player to be named, who a month later proved to be minor-league right-hander Luis Vasquez.
40. "Texas Trading Heavy at Winter Meeting," *Santa Fe New Mexican*, December 7, 1988: B2.
41. "Ryan, Schmidt Signed," *Indiana* (Pennsylvania) *Gazette*, December 8, 1988: 21.
42. "Indians Still Searching for Shortstop," *Elyria* (Ohio) *Chronicle-Telegram*, December 8, 1988: D1.
43. Minor-league right-hander Dan Gakeler accompanied Owen to Montreal, with right-hander John Dopson and infielder Luis Rivera going to Boston.
44. "Pirates' Ears Open at Winter Meetings," *Titusville* (Pennsylvania) *Herald*, December 2, 1988: 8.
45. Gammons, "And Here We Go Again."
46. "Texas Leads Way at Winter Session," *Monessen* (Pennsylvania) *Valley Independent*, December 8, 1988: 1B.
47. "Ryan Rejects Bigger $$, Stays in Texas," *Sandusky* (Ohio) *Register*, December 8, 1988: D1.
48. "Doughty looking for shortstop and pitcher," *Indiana* (Pennsylvania) *Gazette*, December 5, 1988: 21.
49. "Cold Winter: No Trades for Pirates," *Monessen* (Pennsylvania) *Valley Independent*, December 8, 1988: 1B.

— 1989 —
MINOR MOVES MAKE MAJOR IMPACTS

By Mark S. Sternman

Dollar Disputes

THE TWIN SPECTERS OF COLLUSION in the recent past, and an expiring deal between the owners and players in the near future (on December 31, 1989), cast the shadow of a seasonal shutdown over the Nashville winter meetings. According to some owners, increasing salaries and revenue differences threatened competitive balance. The eccentric Marge Schott, owner of the Cincinnati Reds, griped, "I think it's dangerous, especially in the smaller areas like Cincinnati. We're hard-pressed. We're going to have to develop more players through our farm system. We just can't go berserk. The solution is to split the money up. More of it should go to the small markets."[1]

Players and their union viewed the owners with suspicion. Yankees player rep Don Mattingly said, "There's a major distrust in the basic agreement we signed in 1985. We basically look at it as having no meaning. Directly after that, collusion came about. There's a lot of problems believing we can trust [that] the things … in the basic agreement are going to be followed through."[2]

Orel Hershiser of the Dodgers agreed, arguing, "The owners have saved hundreds of millions of dollars. They are spending revenues they have saved. They doubled and tripled their profits because of collusion."[3]

Union leader Donald Fehr declared, "I find it odd and troubling that as negotiations begin and on the heels of announcements of 'we've got to have trust, we have to form a new partnership, we're going to persuade players that things are going to be different,' that words like 'economic warfare' are coming [from Commissioner Fay Vincent] and suggestions of setting deadlines, which means lockouts, are coming out."[4]

Asked whether the 1990 season would proceed without interruption, Vincent dodged the question by invoking history, observing, "I think it was (Abe) Lincoln who said, 'The Lord only reveals the future to us one day at a time.'"[5]

Old-school reporter Jerome Holtzman put a pox on both houses but sided with those collecting the money over those who worked for it: "I attended both the owners' winter meetings in Nashville and the meeting of the executive board of the players association in Scottsdale, Ariz., … and my surmise is that both sides are crazy, especially the players."[6]

Columnist Peter Pascarelli dissented, opining, "The point is that baseball is swimming in ever-increasing dollars. All 26 major-league clubs are guaranteed $16 million from network TV next season. … The … market can handle these ludicrous contracts or they wouldn't be offered."[7]

In contrast to their big-league brethren, the minor leagues operated with a much more minimal financial cushion. Five teams in the minors did not have a major-league affiliate, so even though the Atlanta Braves wanted to add a Florida State League club in Daytona Beach, "[N]o expansion will be allowed, according to Sal Artiaga, president of the National Association of Professional Baseball Leagues, the governing body of minor-league baseball. 'Read my lips,' Artiaga … said, borrowing a George Bush tactic, 'there will be no expansion.'"[8]

The affiliation issue notwithstanding, Artiaga expressed optimism about the state of the minors, thanks to record attendance, new ballparks, and improved lighting.[9]

The cheery news at the lower levels did not extend to the major-league owners or their players, as disagreements and dissension would persist throughout the winter before the warring sides reached a deal on March 19, 1990, that was made retroactive to January 1.[10] The great player movements of the 1989 winter meetings would thus prove to be meaningful on the field during the 1990 major-league season.

Player Movements

The Expos had cashed in the biggest chips in the Montreal farm system to acquire Mark Langston in an ultimately futile push to take the 1989 NL East crown, but the first Canadian team in the majors, one of only three teams owned by a billionaire,[11] declined to pursue the flame-throwing southpaw. Any team that wanted to get its fans heated up over the Hot Stove League made noises about going after the prize pitcher, including the Cubs, the team that bested the Expos in taking the 1989 NL East title. "While their interest in … Langston is making headlines, the Cubs expect to make few high-profile moves at the winter meetings … in Nashville," wrote a *Chicago Tribune* correspondent. "Two clubs—believed to be the California Angels and the New York Yankees—reportedly have offered Langston five-year packages … worth between $15 million and $18 million."[12]

Three seasons removed from winning the World Series for the second time, the New York Mets also sought pitching, but in this case bullpen help: The Mets "are likely to create activity in Nashville if they find a team willing to deal for a reliever to complement Randy Myers, the left-hander who saved 24 games," the *New York Times* wrote.[13]

The Angels captured the first headlines after arriving in Nashville by inking Langston to a pact worth $16 million over five years. Knowing more about baseball than capitalism, Boston Red Sox general manager Lou Gorman did not approve, exclaiming, "Good God almighty, I don't know what's happening in this business. We're self-destructing. It's just economic lunacy, that's the best way to describe it."[14]

With Langston fitted for his halo, the focus shifted to trade talks for Cleveland outfielder Joe Carter. Murray Chass of the *New York Times* speculated that Boston, St. Louis, and San Diego had the best chances of capturing Carter: "The Red Sox are willing to trade [Mike] Greenwell for Carter and, if pushed, perhaps [Ellis] Burks. The Cardinals are believed to have offered [Vince] Coleman, their left fielder, and [Willie] McGee, their center fielder. The Padres will give the Indians one of their catchers as the focal point of a multiplayer package."[15]

San Diego dangled catcher Sandy Alomar. The son of the longtime major-league infielder and 1970 All-Star was receiving intense scrutiny although he had played in just eight games over two seasons for the Padres. In receiving the minor-league player of the year award from *Baseball America*, the younger Alomar conceded, "If something happens, that's the way baseball is, it's a weird game."[16]

California sought to acquire Carter in addition to Langston. According to the *Boston Globe*, the Angels were offering center fielder Devon White, right-hander Kirk McCaskill and second baseman Johnny Ray for Carter.[17]

The longer the Winter Meetings lasted, the more possible connections to Carter developed, with the Royals, Blue Jays, and White Sox also reportedly in contention to get him.[18]

Unlike the 28-year-old Carter, Dave Parker's best days were primarily behind him, but that did not deter the Milwaukee Brewers from signing him away from the 1989 World Series champion Oakland A's with a two-year, $3 million contract.

Oakland bemoaned the loss of Parker. "We would like to bring back everybody from our championship team, but the economics haven't made it possible," Athletics general manager Sandy Alderson said. "We also didn't feel we could give him the multiyear contract he was seeking."[19]

Milwaukee manager Tom Trebelhorn praised the Parker pickup, proclaiming, "This gives us a better ballclub than we had yesterday."[20]

At the age of 39, Parker made his last All-Star team in 1990 for the Brewers, but the team went from 81-81 in 1989 to 74-88 in 1990. Meanwhile, thanks to stars like José Canseco and Dave Stewart, Oakland did not miss Parker. Without him, Canseco had an even better year, going from a .269/.333/.542 slash line in 1989 to .274/.371/.543 in 1990 as the A's won the ALCS for the third straight year.

While Milwaukee had its designated hitter, the White Sox needed a first baseman, causing general manager Larry Himes to tout the recently released Keith Hernandez as "a Gold Glove guy. He kind of fits into some things we want to have done defensively with our ballclub."[21]

Instead of Chicago, however, Cleveland signed Hernandez, who hit just .200/.283/.238 with the Tribe in 1990, his final season. In 1990, Chicago brought up 22-year-old rookie Frank Thomas. The future Hall of Famer played 51 games at first base and slugged his way to a .330/.454/.529 line as the surprising White Sox surged into second place.

With Parker gone, Oakland added right-handed pitcher Reggie Harris from Boston in the Rule 5 draft. "We might be able to keep Harris," A's pitching coach Dave Duncan said. "We'll have to see how he does during spring training. All we know now is we've got a good athlete with a good arm. Maybe we can work with him."[22]

With Oakland, Harris went 1-0 with a 3.48 ERA in 1990, the best of his six seasons. The 26th pick overall by the Red Sox in the 1987 draft, Harris would finish his career with a 2-3 record and a 4.91 ERA.

Two other Rule 5 picks proved to be productive players. Plucked from the Padres, Shane Mack hit .299 over a nine-year career and started in right field for the 1991 World Series champion Minnesota Twins. Picked from the Pirates, righty Bill Sampen won 12 games for Montreal in 1990 and 9 in 1991. When he slumped in 1992, the Expos packaged him in a deal with Kansas City for Sean Berry, who made the majority of starts at third base in Montreal for three seasons, including 1994, when the Expos had the best record in the majors.

Minus the more obscure Harris, Boston went after a reliever with a much more impressive pedigree, closer Jeff Reardon, whose agent "expects teams who lose out in the bidding war for National League Cy Young winner Mark Davis to enter into the Reardon hunt."[23]

After criticizing California for paying Langston, Lou Gorman quipped, "I haven't looked at the breakdown of what we've offered"[24] Reardon, thereby making the Boston GM appear clueless rather than hypocritical.

Simultaneously, Boston rejected two fascinating trades with Montreal. "The Expos were willing to send outfielder Tim Raines and lefty Zane Smith to the Red Sox for Mike Greenwell, and also proposed a package of third baseman Tim Wallach and Smith for Wade Boggs," reported the *Boston Globe*.[25]

Leaving Minnesota, the right-handed Reardon took the Boston offer of $6.8 million over three years. A native of Dalton, Massachusetts, Reardon gushed, "I started pitching when I was 6, 7 years old. That's all I ever dreamed was pitching for the Red Sox. I'm so excited to be putting on the uniform. ... I don't even know how to describe it."[26] Reardon said he didn't understand why the Twins didn't offer him a third year: "I am a little surprised after what I did for them. Being 34 years old, I guess that was a factor to them."[27]

Minnesota chose to re-sign slugging first baseman Kent Hrbek over Reardon. Twins general manager Andy MacPhail said, "We're going to miss Jeff, there's no doubt about that. He was instrumental in leading us to a world championship. ... We just didn't feel we could afford to give Jeff that kind of a contract, but with Kent, we had to. He's 29 years old and his prime years are still ahead of him."[28]

MacPhail made the right decision. Reardon had two solid years in Boston before slumping in 1992, when the Sox traded him to Atlanta. Meanwhile, Hrbek played five more seasons for Minnesota and helped the Twins win the 1991 World Series.

Rather than complementing Randy Myers, the Mets moved him to the Reds for pitcher John Franco. Presumably referring more to their star power than to their good looks, New York Vice President Joe McIlvaine called the exchange "the trading of beauty queens,"²⁹ while the "acquisition of Myers … freed the Reds to deal [Norm] Charlton, who relieved [in 1989] after starting the previous summer."³⁰

Sometimes the best trades are the ones that do not happen. The Cubs failed to persuade the Reds to cash in Charlton, a key component along with Myers and Rob Dibble of the Cincinnati Nasty Boys bullpen that keyed the Reds victory in the 1990 World Series.

Likewise, "[T]he Phillies and Yankees and Angels weren't offering the White Sox wonderful players for Bobby Thigpen."³¹ Saving 57 games, Thigpen had a career year in 1990, when he finished fourth in the Cy Young Award voting and fifth in the MVP race.

Chicago Tribune columnist Bob Verdi criticized the White Sox' failure to act more aggressively: "We wonder why the White Sox bothered to attend the winter meetings in Nashville. Were they: (a) There to ask Emmylou Harris if she would sing the National Anthem on Opening Day April 2? (b) There to determine whether Merle Haggard can play third base? (c) There hoping for an Elvis sighting?"³²

If making moves wins games, then San Diego would have had a splendid 1990 season. Since the Indians "couldn't bribe Carter into putting up with the indignity of playing in Cleveland and had to trade him or lose him,"³³ San Diego obtained him for Sandy Alomar, infielder Carlos Baerga, and outfielder Chris James. "It wasn't a tough decision," Carter said. "The situation is right—a contending team, they have a chance to win it all, and it's a great place to play baseball."³⁴

The maestro of the deal, Padres GM Jack McKeon, got his man as part of "a dawn-to-dusk performance December 6 and December 7 at the Opryland Hotel, [where] he juggled about 50 telephone calls, a half-dozen television interviews and went through 18 cigars as he landed Carter and two free agents, outfielder Fred Lynn and lefthanded reliever Craig Lefferts."³⁵

Paybacks …

In August 1989, Judge Thomas Roberts awarded $10.5 million to 139 players for Collusion I, dating back to players who were free agents between 1985 and 1986.* The players union seemed to believe that Barry Rona, the owners' chief labor negotiator, was an instrumental player in collusion, as evidenced a few years later in a lawsuit attempting to prevent Rona from becoming an agent.** Rumors were that the owners shared a similar view as the players union about Rona.*** On the November eve of new labor agreement negotiations in 1989, Rona resigned as chief labor negotiator and was replaced by Charles O'Connor. Commissioner Fay Vincent was asked about Rona's resignation and responded, "That's a subject I'm not going to talk about."****

O'Connor, using a stay-the-course strategy, didn't necessarily earn improved credibility and trust from the players union, either.***** In February 1990, when baseball didn't begin, O'Connor stated that "I concede at this stage it's a lockout."******

    *   Ross Newhan, "Owners Must Pay $10.5 Million," *Hartford Courant*, September 1, 1989: E1.
   **   Murray Chass, "Baseball; Union Sues to Bar Rona as Agent," *New York Times*, December 21, 1993.
  *** Ross Newhan, "A New Man on the Point for Owners Baseball: Charles O'Connor took over at the last minute as lead negotiator for baseball management. Will his outlook affect the outcome of the talks?" *Los Angeles Times*, December 9, 1989: 1.
 **** Manny Topol, "Owners Meet with Union," *Newsday*, November 29, 1989: 125.
***** Michael Hiestand, "Player Meetings; Union Says Baseball Officials' 'Harsh Words' Hurt Negotiations," *USA Today*, December 8, 1989: 04C.
****** Murray Chass, "Negotiators Exchange Outlooks on Talks," *New York Times*, February 16, 1990: A26.

While few liked the trade from the Cleveland perspective, Indians President Hank Peters expressed guarded optimism: "We know Carter will be an impact player in San Diego, but we'd like to think the players we acquired will have some impact, too."[36]

Peters called Alomar "our No. 1 catcher. We've already had three or four offers for him."[37]

In 1990, Carter hit just .232/.290/.391 in his lone season for the Padres, but finished 17th in the MVP balloting. Meanwhile, Alomar won Rookie of the Year in 1990, played 11 seasons for Cleveland, and made six All-Star teams. Less heralded, Baerga played eight seasons for the Indians and made three All-Star teams. Trading Joe Carter put Cleveland on the path to becoming an AL powerhouse during the 1990s.

While the Indians picked up position players, other AL teams tweaked their pitching staffs.

Feeling short-changed by the Red Sox, flamboyant right-hander Dennis "Oil Can" Boyd left Boston for Montreal. "It wasn't like Montreal gave me a billion-dollar deal or anything like that," he said. "Montreal told me they wanted me, and that was the difference."[38]

The Expos had to take the players they could get and find creative ways to compensate them, including incentive pay at a time when the Players Association rejected an industrywide approach that would tie all salaries to statistical rankings.[39] "We're not going to sign the big guys, just because they're going to sign where the weather's warm and the dollars are abundant," said Montreal general manager Dave Dombrowski. "Also, you're dealing with the perception of Canada being a foreign country and all the difficulties associated with that."[40]

Boyd signed for a "guaranteed $400,000, [and] will earn an additional $100,000 for every 30 days ... on the roster ... plus $100,000 for each of five levels of games started or innings pitched, beginning at 24 starts or 140 innings and reaching 32 starts or 220 innings," the *New York Times* reported. "... Whatever Boyd makes ... a tax equalization clause will pay him an extra 5 percent."[41]

Boyd won 10 games for the 1990 Expos, finishing third in the NL with three shutouts.

The big-money Yankees made two trades, which did little for the New Yorkers but provided key parts for both 1990 NL division champions. In Nashville, the Yankees picked up right-handed pitchers Jeff Robinson and Willie Smith from Pittsburgh in exchange for catcher Don Slaught. "We really targeted Slaught," said manager Jim Leyland. "We thought he was the best available."[42]

"I can't believe the Yankees got both those pitchers for Slaught," said Syd Thrift, former general manager of both the Yankees and Pirates. "Robinson's one of the best set-up men if used in that role and Smith has a great arm. He has a chance to be a heckuva closer."[43]

Robinson pitched well for New York in 1990, but an above-average set-up man proved of little use to the worst Yankee team (by winning percentage) since 1913. New York released Smith in 1992 without his ever having appeared for the big-league club.

By contrast, Slaught hit .305 over six seasons in Pittsburgh, which took the NL East crown in each of his first three years with the club, thanks in part due to its effective backstopping duo of the left-handed-hitting Mike LaValliere and the right-handed-swinging Slaught.

In the second deal, the Yankees got right-handed pitcher Tim Leary and minor-league outfielder Van Snider from the Reds for two prospects, right-hander Rodney Imes and first baseman Hal Morris.

The "ace" of the 1990 Yanks, Leary went 9-19, leading the AL in losses and wild pitches. In his three seasons in pinstripes, Leary had an 18-35 record with a 5.12 ERA.

Morris, meanwhile, raked for the Reds for a decade, piling up 1,030 hits and a .305 average. In 1990, he finished third in the voting for Rookie of the Year with a .340/.381/.498 line and started all nine playoff games as Cincinnati won the World Series.

While much of the chitter-chatter at the 1989 winter meetings in Nashville dealt with money, the offseason maneuverings and the subsequent 1990 season proved that the teams with the most dollars do not necessarily triumph on the field.

NOTES

1. Jerome Holtzman, "Owners, Players Begin Posturing," *Chicago Tribune*, December 7, 1989.

2. Murray Chass, "Union Wonders if It Can Trust Owners," *New York Times*, December 7, 1989.

3. Jerome Holtzman, "Collusion 'scar' triggers players' militancy now," *Chicago Tribune*, December 8, 1989.

4. Murray Chass, "Players and Owners Taking Divergent Courses in Talks," *New York Times*, December 8, 1989.

5. Dave Nightingale, "Good News, and Bad, About 1990," *The Sporting News*, December 18, 1989.

6. Jerome Holtzman, "Showered With Millions, Players Still Rip Owners," *Chicago Tribune*, December 10, 1989.

7. Peter Pascarelli, "If Owners Cry Economic Doom, Ignore 'Em," *The Sporting News*, December 18, 1989.

8. Ken Willis, "Expansion Freeze Leaves DB Cold," *Daytona Beach News-Journal*, December 7, 1989.

9. "Artiaga: Minors Going First Class," *The Sporting News*, December 18, 1989.

10. An analysis of this 103-page document lies beyond the scope of this article, but interested readers can find the 1990-1993 Basic Agreement linked at research.sabr.org/business/resources/documents/category/1-agreements-and-settlements# (accessed November 27, 2015).

11. Jerome Holtzman, "Disparity Growing Among Ownership," *Chicago Tribune*, December 5, 1989.

12. Andrew Bagnato, "Cubs Taking a Casual Approach," *Chicago Tribune*, December 1, 1989.

13. Michael Martinez, "Mets Feel Little Trade Urgency," *New York Times*, December 1, 1989.

14. Steve Fainaru, "Angels Dish out $16M: Langston Signed to Five-Year Deal," *Boston Globe*, December 2, 1989.

15. Murray Chass, "In Bizarre Free Agency, Whitey Ford Would Break the Bank," *New York Times*, December 3, 1989.

16. Steve Fainaru, "Lamp Deal Hits a Snag; Expos Hinting That They'll Make a Bid for Free Agent Boyd," *Boston Globe*, December 4, 1989.

17. Steve Fainaru, "Sox Focusing In on Hrbek? Twin May Welcome Change," *Boston Globe*, December 4, 1989.

18. Steve Fainaru, "One Small Trade; Many Big Rumors," *Boston Globe*, December 5, 1989.

19. Ben Walker, Associated Press, "Milwaukee Signs Dave Parker," *Los Angeles Times*, December 4, 1989.

20. Alan Solomon, "Parker Fills 3 Needs for Milwaukee," *Chicago Tribune*, December 4, 1989.

21. Andrew Bagnato and Alan Solomon, "Yount, Lefferts Get 'Substantial' Offers," *Chicago Tribune*, December 4, 1989.

22. Steve Fainaru, "A's Snag Harris From Sox," *Boston Globe*, December 5, 1989.

23. Steve Fainaru and Nick Cafardo, "Expos Appear to Be Serious about Boyd," *Boston Globe*, December 5, 1989. After the winter meetings, Davis signed a four-year contract with the Royals for $13 million.

24. Nick Cafardo, "Red Sox Playing Hardball: Local Ties May Lure Reardon; Hrbek Offer in $10 Million Range," *Boston Globe*, December 6, 1989.

25. Nick Cafardo and Steve Fainaru, "Expos' Bids for Greenwell, Boggs Fail," *Boston Globe*, December 6, 1989.

26. Steve Fainaru, "They're Making Pitch," *Boston Globe*, December 7, 1989.

27. Nick Cafardo, "Reardon Signs On With Red Sox: He Inks Three-Year Deal," *Boston Globe*, December 7, 1989.

28. Nick Cafardo, "Hrbek Takes Twins' 5-Year Plan," *Boston Globe*, December 7, 1989.

29. Dan Castellano, "'Trading of Beauty Queens' Sends Franco to New York," *The Sporting News*, December 18, 1989.

30. Andrew Bagnato, "Cubs; Deal With the Reds Comes Apart," *Chicago Tribune*, December 7, 1989.

31. Andrew Bagnato and Alan Solomon, "Free-Agent 'Show' Helps Put Cubs, Sox on Hold," *Chicago Tribune*, December 10, 1989.

32. Bob Verdi, "Someone Please Wake Up the Sox," *Chicago Tribune*, December 16, 1989.

33. Alan Solomon, "Million-Dollar Question: Why No More Trades?" *Chicago Tribune*, December 8, 1989.

34. Steve Fainaru, "Carter Goes to Padres," *Boston Globe*, December 7, 1989.

35. Barry Bloom, "Trader Jack a Live Wire," *The Sporting News*, December 18, 1989.

36. Moss Klein, "Free Agency Takes Big Bite Out of Dyn-A's-ty," *The Sporting News*, December 18, 1989.

37. Sheldon Ocker, "Indians," *The Sporting News*, December 18, 1989.

38. Steve Fainaru, "Boyd Accepts One-Year Offer From Montreal," *Boston Globe*, December 8, 1989.

39. Murray Chass, "Players Still Seem Cool to Pay-for-Performance," *New York Times*, December 9, 1989. The issue persisted beyond the Nashville winter meetings. In an article that appeared on the last day that the collective-bargaining agreement remained in force, Chass wrote, "[O]wners … will push their pay-for-performance system of salaries for players now eligible for salary arbitration. They would much rather have a statistical scale set salaries than have arbitrators do it or have themselves do it faced with the predictable uncertainty of arbitration." Murray Chass, "Arbitration a Key to Negotiations," *New York Times*, December 31, 1989.

40 Alan Solomon, "Sox Forced to Sell Nostalgia and Hope," *Chicago Tribune*, December 17, 1989. While born in the United States, the author of this article can confirm the accuracy of "the perception of Canada being a foreign country," since for those not born there, Canada is a foreign country.

41 Murray Chass, "As Lockout Threat Looms, Players Lock Up Big Bonuses," *New York Times*, December 17, 1989.

42 John Mehno, "Pirates," *The Sporting News*, December 18, 1989.

43 Bill Madden, "Yankees," *The Sporting News*, December 18, 1989.

— 1990 —
THEY ALMOST DIDN'T HAPPEN

By John Burbridge

Introduction

THE WINTER MEETINGS OF 1990 were held amid a dispute between the major and minor leagues and uncertainty arising from an agreement between the major-league owners and the players union concerning collusion. The minor leagues were mainly asking for additional support for their farm teams from the major-league parent. With respect to the collusion issue, the union had charged that the owners had colluded with each other during the latter part of the 1980s, and such collusion resulted in market issues for free-agent players. An agreement between the owners and the union was announced one month before the scheduled Winter Meetings, but since details of the agreement had not been fully established at the time of the announcement and the subsequent Winter Meetings, a lingering uncertainty remained.

The Dispute

In early May of 1989 David Simon, the president of the Los Angeles Sports Council, announced that the 1990 Winter Meetings would be held in Los Angeles.[1] However, a cloud hovered over these meetings in the form of a dispute between the major and minor leagues concerning the contract between the two parties. The National Association of Professional Baseball Leagues (NAPBL), the minors' umbrella organization, which was in charge of scheduling and organizing the Winter Meetings, was questioning several issues, including the amount of compensation to be paid directly to the minor-league clubs by the major-league parent. Commissioner Fay Vincent also advocated improving salaries and working conditions for minor-league umpires.[2]

Both parties agreed that if an agreement was not reached before November 1, 1990, the combined Winter Meetings would be canceled and the major leagues and minor leagues would meet separately. No agreement was reached, and the 26 major-league clubs pulled out of the Los Angeles meetings.[3] Bill Murray, chief negotiator for the major leagues, said they hoped the dispute would be settled by November 15, but that would be too late to have the combined meetings.[4] Major-league officials also announced that they would attempt to set up alternate meetings for their clubs, while the NAPBL took the position that the meetings would be held in Los Angeles with or without the participation of the major-league clubs.

Quickly reacting to the situation, the commissioner's office rescheduled the major-league portion of the meetings for the Hyatt Rosemont Hotel at O'Hare Airport in Chicago. Reflecting on the situation, Roland Hemond, general manager of the Baltimore Orioles, said there was no substitute for one-on-one trade discussions. "In a face-to-face setting, you have the principals of each club involved," he said. "You might have your club president, your manager, your owner present. That gives you the opportunity to caucus for a few minutes, have a quick discussion and come back and say, 'You've got a deal.' When you do it over the phone, you might have to go back and talk to your people and they have to talk to theirs. There's more time for something to get in the way of a deal."[5]

By November 15 the dispute still was not settled. The contract had an end date of January 12, 1991. As that date neared, it was reported that Major League Baseball was making plans for a reorganized system of minor leagues that could include as many as 170 teams.[6] This never materialized, because an agreement was reached in early December of 1990.

The Collusion Agreement

In September 1990 George Nicolau, an arbitrator, found baseball owners guilty of collusion in their treatment of free agents after the 1987 and '88 seasons. He ruled that baseball club owners must pay players a total of $102.5 million in lost salary for those years. Another arbitrator, Thomas Roberts, had previously awarded $10.5 million for lost salary in 1986, for a total $113 million in damages. The two sides still had to settle or have decided four other issues: (1) damages for lost 1989 and 1990 salaries, (2) interest on all the damages awarded, (3) second-look free agency for 21 former free agents, and (4) damages on individual claims for such matters as lost mobility.[7] On the day the arbitrators announced the award, Charles O'Connor, the owners' chief labor representative, stated that all the details with respect to the collusion agreement could be resolved by the end of 1990.[8]

On November 3, 1990, it was announced that the club owners had agreed to pay $280 million in damages, to end the efforts of the union in its conspiracy cases against the owners.[9] However, no determination had been made as to how many players would share in the settlement, or how money would be distributed. Donald Fehr, director of the players' union, said, "There's been a tentative understanding reached by the lawyers. It's subject to working out a lot of details."[10]

It was also agreed that new-look free agent status would be granted to 16 players who had been free agents after the 1987 season.[11] These free agents and their appropriate teams were:

1. Jack Morris, Detroit
2. Dave Smith, Houston
3. Mike Witt, New York Yankees
4. Dave LaPoint, New York Yankees
5. Dennis Martinez, Montreal
6. Danny Darwin, Houston
7. Larry Andersen, Boston
8. Juan Berenguer, Minnesota
9. Mike LaCoss, San Francisco
10. Charlie Leibrandt, Atlanta
11. Mike Heath, Detroit
12. Jack Clark, San Diego
13. Gary Gaetti, Minnesota
14. Brett Butler, San Francisco
15. Dave Henderson, Oakland
16. Chili Davis, California

However, these 16 players were not to actually become free agents until the two sides ratified the collusion settlement.

While this collusion agreement was not necessarily directly related to the 1990 Winter Meetings, the agreement and the fact that ratification had to occur before the 16 players became free did permeate the atmosphere of the meetings and affected some of the signings and transactions.

First Joint Venture

Against that backdrop, the Major League Winter Meetings kicked off with a state-of-the game address by Commissioner Fay Vincent. The commissioner was at home in Connecticut due to a bout of pneumonia and his address was read at the meeting. Vincent called for the creation of a program to better prepare young players for the pressures of the major leagues. Vincent portrayed this effort, plus the imminent naming of a joint committee to study the economics of baseball, as attempts to improve the relations between the parties. He also commented on the collusion agreement: "Should it be approved, then finally we can put this episode behind us for good and move forward."[12]

Donald Fehr, executive director of the players union, was invited to join the leadership of the joint venture and agreed to present Vincent's proposal to the union. Fehr also offered a note of caution: "The fact is, if the relationship improves, it hinges almost entirely on whether the collusion settlement goes through and whether the free-agent market continues to show signs that it is operating and well. If the relationship does improve, everybody has to be encouraged. It doesn't mean you agree on everything; if it could avoid unnecessary squabbling, that would be a step in the right direction."[13]

Rule 5 Draft

The Rule 5 Draft was a Winter Meetings fixture. Players eligible for the draft were those not on their team's 40-man roster who either signed initial contracts at 19 or older and had spent three or more years in the minor leagues, or signed their initial contract when younger than 19 and had spent four or more years in the minor leagues.[14]

The price to draft a player was $50,000. A drafted player must remain on the drafting team's 25-man roster or be offered back to his original club for $25,000. If a team did not have space on its 40-man roster, it could not participate. The following players were drafted:

Player	Drafting Organization	Prior Organization
Pat Howell	Minnesota Twins	New York Mets
Mike Huff	Cleveland Indians	Los Angeles Dodgers
Greg McCarthy	Montreal Expos	Philadelphia Phillies
Nikco Riesgo	Montreal Expos	Philadelphia Phillies
Frank Seminara	San Diego Padres	New York Yankees
Doug Simons	New York Mets	Minnesota Twins
Ed Taubensee	Oakland Athletics	Cincinnati Reds
Dean Wilkins	Houston Astros	Chicago Cubs

Free Agent Signings

With the meetings occurring just slightly more than a month after the majors and minors chose to hold separate meetings, one might assume that the amount of activity would be less than usual. However, the opposite was true, as the 1990 meetings proved to be memorable in terms of free-agent signings and trades.

On December 3, there was a flurry of free-agent signings. The San Francisco Giants, convinced that their center fielder, Brett Butler, a new-look free agent, would be leaving the club, signed the 1990 National League batting champion, Willie McGee, to a four-year contract worth $13 million and indicated they would not make a serious attempt to re-sign Butler. Not wanting to go into 1991 without a center fielder, Giants president and general manager Al Rosen grabbed McGee.[15]

McGee had actually finished the 1990 season in Oakland, and once he moved across the Bay Bridge, the A's responded by getting Willie Wilson to commit to a two-year contract. Wilson had spent his entire 15-year career with the Kansas City Royals, where he won a batting title (1982) and a stolen-base crown (1979), was named to two All-Star teams, and helped the Royals win the 1985 World Series. Other signings announced on December 3 were third baseman Terry Pendleton signing with the Atlanta Braves for four years at $9.8 million; right-handed pitcher Kevin Gross signing a three-year deal with the Los Angeles Dodgers; and the Detroit Tigers inking right-hander Bill Gullickson. Pitcher Dennis Martinez, another new-look free agent righty, decided not to test free agency but announced that he was staying with the Montreal Expos for a three-year contract believed to be worth $9.5 million.[16]

December 4 saw second baseman Steve Sax sign a four-year deal with the New York Yankees, reportedly worth $12.4 million. Yankees Vice President George Bradley said of the deal, "He is a winning ballplayer and along with Mattingly gives us the start of a solid nucleus to build the club around."[17] The Brewers announced that right-handed reliever Edwin Nunez had signed a two-year contract. The Giants continued being active by signing left-hander Dave Righetti for four years at $10 million, while the Boston Red Sox also signed a southpaw, one-time All-Star Matt Young.

The signings continued on December 5 and 6. On December 5, the Atlanta Braves signed first baseman Sid Bream, the Mets signed outfielder Vince Coleman in an attempt to replace Daryl Strawberry (who had previously signed with the Los Angeles Dodgers), and the Milwaukee Brewers signed first baseman-outfielder Franklin Stubbs. The following day, two outfielders inked new contracts as the Cubs signed

George Bell, the 1987 AL MVP, while the Orioles grabbed eight-time Gold Glove winner Dwight Evans.

The Trade

The 1990 Winter Meetings are mainly remembered today for one of the most significant offseason trades in the history of baseball. The seeds for such a deal were planted during the World Series. Toronto Blue Jays general manager Pat Gillick and Joe McIlvaine, the new general manager of the San Diego Padres, discussed outfielder Joe Carter, who had been acquired by San Diego the year before and had led the Padres in RBIs. Gillick followed up with McIlvaine at the general manager meetings, and their discussion resumed at the Winter Meetings. On December 4 McIlvaine proposed a swap of Joe Carter for Toronto first baseman Fred McGriff. McIlvaine knew that Toronto needed to make room for young first baseman John Olerud, and the Padres needed a first baseman with Jack Clark about to become a new-look free agent. Toronto had also lost outfielder George Bell, who was about to sign with the Chicago Cubs, and needed an outfielder to replace him.

While Gillick was willing to deal McGriff, he had problems with a one-for-one swap given that McGriff was three years younger than Carter. Gillick suggested that Roberto Alomar, the young switch-hitting second baseman for the Padres, be included in the deal. Alomar was already a three-year veteran at the age of 22. McIlvaine was supposedly aware that there were issues between Alomar and his manager, Greg Riddoch. However, McIlvaine was not willing to give up two players for McGriff.

Garry Templeton was the San Diego shortstop and was nearing the end of his career. McIlvaine wanted to replace him and envied Toronto's Tony Fernandez, a smooth fielding, switch-hitting shortstop. McIlvaine was not optimistic that Toronto would trade Fernandez but Gillick supposedly felt his shortstop was somewhat moody and was willing, provided he got Alomar.

On December 5, 24 hours after the initial discussions at the Winter Meetings, McIlvaine mounted a podium in one of the meeting rooms, said, "We thought we'd give you a good old-fashioned baseball trade," and announced that Joe Carter and Roberto Alomar would be going to Toronto for Fred McGriff and Tony Fernandez.[18] No money changed hands.

While the reaction was somewhat mixed as to who got the best of the deal, many realized that Alomar had the highest upside. Jack McKeon, who had been both a manager and general manager for San Diego in 1990, said in 2012 that he would have never considered trading Alomar.[19] Alomar and Carter led Toronto to World Series victories in 1992 and 1993, and Alomar was elected to the Baseball Hall of Fame. McGriff won a home-run title for San Diego in 1991, then was traded to Atlanta, where he helped the Braves win the 1995 World Series. Fernandez, on the other hand, did not last long with San Diego and eventually returned to Toronto.

Other Significant Trades

At the beginning of the meetings, the California Angels traded right-handed pitchers Willie Fraser and Marcus Moore and outfielder Devon White to Toronto for infielder Luis Sojo, outfielder Junior Felix, and a player to be named later, who turned out to be minor-league catcher Ken Rivers.

On December 3, the New York Yankees traded outfielder Oscar Azocar to the San Diego Padres for a player to be named later (outfielder Mike Humphreys).

On December 4, several deals were announced. The Baltimore Orioles traded outfielder Dave Gallagher to the Los Angeles Angels for two minor-league pitchers,

> "Player salaries that have run out of control and collusion damages have forced high-priced tickets and $3.50 hot dogs in big-league ballparks. We will not permit these exorbitant costs to be passed down to the fans in the communities."*
>
> — Sal Artiaga, National Association president
>
> ---
> * Associated Press, "Major, Minor Baseball Leagues Prepared to Sever Ties," *Lancaster* (Ohio) *Eagle-Gazette*, November 19, 1990: 11.

lefty Mike Hook and right-hander Dave Martinez. The Chicago White Sox dealt right-handed pitchers Shawn Hillegas and Eric King to the Cleveland Indians for outfielder Cory Snyder and minor-league infielder Lindsay Foster. The Oakland Athletics traded outfielder Darren Lewis and a player to be named later (minor-league right-hander Pedro Pena) to San Francisco for infielder Ernie Riles.

The following day saw one more deal, as the Giants traded right-handed relief pitcher Steve Bedrosian, the 1987 National League Cy Young Award winner, to the Minnesota Twins for right-handed pitcher Jimmy Ard and a player to be named later (minor-league southpaw Jimmy Williams). This concluded a very active Winter Meetings for the Giants.

Conclusion

Today, the 1990 Winter Meetings are viewed as being quite memorable. What most fans of the game remember is the trade of a future Hall of Famer.[20] There can be no doubt that the trade of Roberto Alomar was a significant factor in the Toronto Blue Jays winning two pennants and two World Series. The business side of the game is also remembered for the major leagues organizing their own meetings in Chicago, independent of the NAPBL. The collusion agreement also cast a cloud over the meetings as it forced teams to evaluate their positions and led to some fascinating free-agent signings. It is also interesting to note that many in the baseball community felt that the collusion agreement would result in greater harmony between the owners and the players union. However, as the history of the 1990s tells us, this wasn't to be the case.

NOTES

1 "Baseball's 1990 Winter Meetings Will Be Held in Los Angeles," *Los Angeles Times*, May 2, 1989.

2 Peter Schmuck, "Major-League Clubs Withdraw From Winter Meetings," *Baltimore Sun*, November 2, 1990.

3 Ibid.

4 articles.philly.com/1990-11-01/sports/25929736_1_major-leagues-minor-leagues-national-league.

5 Peter Schmuck, "Hemond Is Looking to Raise Trade Heat at Winter Meetings," *Baltimore Sun*, November 30, 1990.

6 Claire Smith, "Baseball; Baseball Is Scouting Minor League Homes," *New York Times*, November 20, 1990.

7 Murray Chass, "Players Get $102.5 Million in Collusion Case," *New York Times*, September 18, 1990.

8 Ibid.

9 Ibid.

10 Ibid.

11 Ibid.

12 Claire Smith. "Baseball; Union-Management Plan to Help Young Players," *New York Times*, December 4, 1990.

13 Ibid.

14 baseball-reference.com/bullpen/Rule_V_Draft.

15 Peter Schmuck, "Giants Get McGee as Butler Insurance/Winter Meetings Notes," *Baltimore Sun*, December 4, 1990.

16 Michael Bamberger, "Free-Agent Signings Dot Winter Meetings," *philly.com*, December 4, 1990.

17 Peter Schmuck, "Orioles Make Pitch to Price/Winter Meetings Notes," *Baltimore Sun*, December 5, 1990.

18 Brent S. Gambill, "Anatomy of a Trade: The 1990 Padres-Blue Jays Blockbuster," baseballprospectus.com/article.php?articleid=19068.

19 Ibid.

20 Tyler Kepner, "A Blockbuster That Proved Worthy of the Hall of Fame," *New York Times*, January 5, 2010.

— 1991 —
VINCENT EXPRESSES CONCERN FOR SMALL MARKET CLUBS; MINORS CHOOSE A NEW LEADER

By Tim Rask

MAJOR-LEAGUE BASEBALL WAS coming off a momentous season in 1991. Both the National and American League pennant winners (the Atlanta Braves and Minnesota Twins, respectively) had finished in last place in their division in 1990 before roaring back to life in 1991. The season culminated with a thrilling World Series, during which five of the seven games were decided by one run. Three of the games required extra innings, including a classic Game Seven in which the Twins triumphed, 1-0, behind the brilliant pitching of a hometown hero, right-hander Jack Morris.[1]

In off-the-field news, the National League had announced in June of 1991 that Denver and Miami had been awarded expansion franchises, with the Colorado Rockies and Florida Marlins set to begin play in 1993. When the 1991 winter meetings convened at the Miami Beach Fontainebleau Hilton Hotel that December, it was the first time Miami played host as a major-league city.

The Commissioner's State of the Game

Commissioner Fay Vincent, in his state-of-the-game address on December 9, focused on three areas of concern facing major-league baseball: national television revenue, player salaries, and minority hiring.

Baseball at the time was in the middle of four-year broadcast deals with CBS (for $1.06 billion) and ESPN ($400 million). Both broadcast partners claimed to be losing money on their contracts (as much as $200 million in the case of ESPN) and Vincent warned baseball's owners that they could see a drop in revenue of as much as 50 percent after the 1993 season, when the contracts expired.[2] "If the deal were to be made today, during the worst media advertising recession in recent history," Vincent said, "we would be looking at the unhappy prospect of accepting at least $4 (million) to $5 million less per year than in the present contract."[3]

Vincent expressed concern that without the largess from the national television contracts, smaller markets would face a huge gap in revenue versus big-market franchises. "Because of local revenue disparity our clubs generate considerably different amounts of revenue," he said. "Our most prosperous club will generate $100 million a year while at the other end of the spectrum a club will generate less than $40 million."[4]

Despite the likely future drop in revenue, increases in salaries showed no signs of slowing. Vincent noted that the average major-league player salary was $851,492 in 1991, and was likely to exceed $1 million in 1992.[5] "The present salary situation is out of hand and small-market franchises cannot compete in this environment," he asserted. "Small-market teams must compete on the field and in the player compensation arena with the larger market teams. Small-market clubs simply have no choice but to arrange their payrolls in entirely different scale."[6]

Vincent attacked the arbitration process as the cause of the upward pressure on salaries, saying arbitration "imposes large-market financial judgments on all other clubs, and the trickle-down effect as free-agent signings seep into the salary-arbitration process is like pitching to (Roger) Maris and (Mickey) Mantle back-to-back. If one doesn't get you, the other will."[7]

"The crucial issue for baseball is to find a way to provide fairly for a sharing of revenues between players and owners," Vincent said. "The present salary situation is out of hand, and small-market franchises cannot compete in this environment. The recent rate of escalation of player salaries cannot last. There must be a major change in the system so all of baseball can share properly."[8]

Commissioner Vincent may have projected gloom and doom regarding television deals and player salaries, but he did express some optimism over the future of minority hiring in baseball.

Major-league baseball's annual minority hiring report, compiled by the Washington-based consulting firm Alexander & Associates, showed nonwhite representation in major-league on-field jobs (managers, coaches, trainers, scouts, and instructors) to be 19 percent, unchanged from 1990. (Kansas City's Hal McRae was the only nonwhite manager named in 1991, among 14 openings). Front-office minority hiring fared a little better, according to the report, with 16 percent of front-office positions held by minorities, 1 percent more than at the start of the 1991 season.

Vincent suggested that clubs focus on minority hiring at the minor-league level, to ensure that the system would be well-stocked with candidates who could later move up to positions in the majors.

"I have encouraged all general managers to pay closer attention to minor-league hiring," Vincent said. "If we are successful in adding to the pool of candidates for major-league jobs by increasing the number of minor-league managers and coaches, we will have taken a major step forward. We will increase the pool of candidates and surely more major-league hirings will result."[9]

Other Issues

In league matters, both the American and National leagues faced thorny issues.

The American League had arguably the larger potential headache, with the announcement that Seattle Mariners owner Jeff Smulyan desired to put the franchise up for sale at a $100 million pricetag, thereby opening up the possibility that the Mariners would relocate. The Tampa-St. Petersburg, Florida, area was widely believed to be a potential destination for Seattle's franchise.

Smulyan had 120 days to find a suitable local buyer, so any franchise shift for 1992 was highly unlikely. Furthermore, it was doubtful the American League would be able to alter the schedule to accommodate the Mariners moving from the Pacific Time Zone to the Eastern Time Zone.

Commissioner Vincent had voiced opposition to any franchise movement but noted, "We have to wait and see how things develop in Seattle. This state involves the consideration of whether somebody wants to buy it there. I am sure if the community properly supported baseball for the next three or four years, the problem would go away."[10]

Meanwhile, the National League broached the topic of divisional realignment to coincide with the entry of the Colorado Rockies and Florida Marlins in 1993. The senior circuit proposed moving the Atlanta Braves and Cincinnati Reds from the NL West to the more geographically appropriate NL East, where they would join the new Florida franchise. Moving to the West, along with the Rockies, would be the Chicago Cubs and St. Louis Cardinals, although those two franchises expressed strong reservations about a switch.

At issue was the number of games played on the West Coast by the Cubs and Cardinals. With the two-hour time difference between the Central Time Zone and the Pacific Time Zone, the Cubs and Cardinals stood to lose up to 20 prime-time broadcasts. *The Sporting News* noted that in the 14-team American League, each club played 12 games against its divisional rivals and 13 against each team from the other division. The National League was considering a split of 18 or 20 games against division rivals, leaving six or eight games with opponents from the other division.[11]

No final decision was made regarding realignment, nor was there any information forthcoming regarding a report from the Economic Study Committee. Additionally, no action was reported on the objections that had been raised to the Atlanta Braves and

Cleveland Indians mascots. The mascots, depicting Native Americans, were regarded by many as racist caricatures.[12]

Notable Player Movement

With no immediate resolution forthcoming to the various issues outlined by Commissioner Vincent and the league offices, the action at the winter meetings focused on player movement, whether by free-agent signings or by trades.

Prior to the start of the winter meetings, the New York Mets stole much of the thunder when they signed Pittsburgh outfielder Bobby Bonilla to a $6 million deal. The Mets also signed first baseman Eddie Murray, a future Hall of Famer, before the start of meetings, and knuckleballing right-hander Tom Candiotti also signed, moving from the Blue Jays to the Dodgers, leaving outfielder Danny Tartabull as arguably the biggest free agent remaining.[13]

Still, insiders looked for the meetings to be active with player movement. Baseball scribes predicted that plenty of teams were on the hunt for pitching, and *The Sporting News* noted that 92 free agents were available, though few were of star caliber. *The Sporting News* also noted that an extensive list of "Rent-a-Players" likely would be available by trade—that is, players entering the final year of their current contract in 1992.[14]

"I wouldn't be a bit surprised if a good many star players were traded at the '91 meetings," Cincinnati Reds GM Bob Quinn said. "I know I'll try to do my share to make that come true." Indeed, even prior to the start of the meetings, Quinn had moved outfielder Eric Davis to the Dodgers after having already added left-hander Greg Swindell in a deal with Cleveland.[15]

Undoubtedly, the recent turnaround of the Braves and Twins was thought to encourage some big moves. "All of this last-to-first talk is encouraging, fun for the fans," said Expos GM Dan Duquette. "If you make a couple of big moves you can make a significant change"[16]

On December 9, California Angels GM Whitey Herzog kicked off the wheeling and dealing, but only after launching some vitriol against Bobby Bonilla's agent, Dennis Gilbert. Herzog felt Gilbert had used the Angels merely as leverage to pry more money out of the Mets, and said he would not sign any of Gilbert's clients.

Herzog resorted to some old-fashioned horse-trading by acquiring infielder-outfielder Von Hayes from the Philadelphia Phillies for prospects Kyle Abbott, a southpaw, and outfielder Ruben Amaro Jr.[17]

Just a year after helping to lead Cincinnati to a World Series win as part of the dominating bullpen trio nicknamed "The Nasty Boys," the Reds sent one of them, lefty Randy Myers, to the Padres in exchange for infielder-outfielder Leon "Bip" Roberts and minor-league outfielder, Craig Pueschner.[18]

In a deal that would have much significance in the near future, the Astros sent young outfielder Kenny Lofton and infielder Dave Rohde to the Indians for right-hander Willie Blair and catcher Ed Taubensee.[19] The Indians had finished dead last in the American League East in 1991, but Lofton, installed in center field and at the top of the batting order, helped to revitalize baseball in Cleveland. He finished second (to Milwaukee's Pat Listach) in the Rookie of the Year voting, and would go on to win four Gold Glove Awards while the Indians made the playoffs every year from 1995 through 1999, including two World Series appearances.

It wasn't until the end of the meetings, however, that anything close to a "blockbuster" trade occurred, with two big deals on the final day.

In the first, San Francisco unloaded outfielder Kevin Mitchell, the 1989 National League Most Valuable Player (plus lefty Mike Remlinger), to the Seattle Mariners. The mercurial Mitchell had evidently outstayed his welcome in San Francisco. In exchange, the Giants received three right-handed pitchers: Bill Swift, Mike Jackson, and Dave Burba.[20]

After the trade of a former National League MVP, the meetings concluded with a trade of a two-time American League Cy Young Award winner. Kansas City sent right-hander Bret Saberhagen to the revamping New York Mets, the club that had made so much noise in the free-agent market prior to the winter meetings. Using some age-old baseball logic, Royals GM Herk Robinson reasoned, "We finished sixth in the American League West for two straight years with Bret. Now it's time to see if we can't move up without him." The Royals received three position players form the Mets: infielders Gregg Jeffries and Keith Miller, and outfielder Kevin McReynolds; infielder Bill Pecota joined Saberhagen in going from Kansas City to the Big Apple. *The Sporting News* noted that many baseball minds considered the trade "highway robbery" for the Mets, although columnist Dave Nightingale dubbed the swap "mutually beneficial." Kansas City also bolstered its roster by signing Angels free-agent first baseman Wally Joyner and trading right-hander Storm Davis back to the Orioles, his original team, in exchange for catcher (and future major-league manager) Bob Melvin.[21]

The Minor Leagues

The National Association of Professional Baseball Leagues, commonly referred to as the Minor Leagues, saw a change in leadership at the 1991 winter meetings. Sal Artiaga, who had led the NAPBL since 1988, had announced in the summer of 1991 that he would resign his position. After Artiaga had led the association through the contentious negotiations over the Professional Baseball Agreement (PBA) that was ratified at the 1990 winter meetings, the outgoing president lamented that the job he was hired to do no longer existed.[22]

Four candidates to succeed Artiaga emerged from the executive screening committee. They included one outsider (Washington attorney Stan Brand), two minor-league presidents (Charlie Eshbach of the Eastern League and Joe Gagliardi of the California League), and Mike Moore, the chief administrative officer of the National Association.[23]

In accordance with NAPBL voting procedures, the new president would need 75 percent approval, or 27 of the 36 votes cast. Votes were weighted by minor-league classification, with Triple-A and Double-A leagues having three votes, Class-A leagues having two votes, and short-season and Rookie-league circuits having one vote each.

After the first ballot, Gagliardi was eliminated, having received only the votes from his own league, while Eshbach led by a single vote over Moore, 16-15. On the second ballot, the California and Pacific Coast Leagues switched their support to Moore, who then held a 20-16 lead. Stan Brand was eliminated after round two, leaving Eshbach and Moore as the final two candidates.[24]

After a caucus period, Eshbach withdrew his name from consideration and on December 11, 1991, Mike Moore was elected unanimously as the National Association's 10th president.[25] In announcing his withdrawal, Eshbach called for unity. "I'm not prepared to hold this body up to a long and bitter floor fight, ballot after ballot," he said. "So at this time, I say good luck, Mike Moore."[26] Moore would go on to oversee a reorganization of the governing structure of minor-league baseball. Moore called for a constitutional convention to be held in Dallas six weeks after the winter meetings. Under the new system adopted in February 1992, the National Association president would work with a board of trustees composed of one club owner from each league, along with a newly-created Council of League Presidents.[27]

Conclusions

The selection of a new minor-league president may seem like a momentous occasion, but mainstream press coverage of Mike Moore's election was little more than a footnote to the business transacted by the big leagues.[28] From the perspective of the major leagues, no significant policy decisions were reached at the 1991 meetings, and some writers even expressed dismay that the trade market seemed awfully lackluster.

Miami Herald sportswriter S.L. Price noted that Miami's first hosting since being named a major-league city produced "sorry" winter meetings that "hit the finish line like a fat man out of breath." The scribe concluded, "All in all, it was like watching millionaires pinch pennies. Mostly, baseball's brains played some golf and told some lies and watched each other's wallets very carefully."[29]

That assessment may be a bit unfair, considering that, according to the Associated Press, 14 trades were made during the meetings, with 51 players changing teams. Those 14 trades represented the most since the

1983 edition of the winter meetings. By contemporary comparison, only five trades were completed at the 1989 winter meetings, and teams made six swaps in 1990.

It cannot be denied that the free-agent market was quiet, with a mere eight free-agent signings during the meetings, the fewest since 1986.[30]

What also cannot be denied is that the biggest trade of the 1991 meetings, between the Mets and Royals, didn't yield much return for either club. The Mets finished the 1992 season in fifth place in the NL East, 24 games behind the Pirates. And Herk Robinson did get to see if the Royals could finish sixth in the AL West without Bret Saberhagen—they could and they did. And, just like the Mets, Kansas City finished 24 games off the divisional pace.

While the 1991 World Series is now considered one of the classic championship series, it is doubtful that the '91 winter meetings will be remembered as anything but a largely routine administrative get-together.

NOTES

1. *Baseball America's 1992 Almanac* (Baseball America, 1991), 33-38.
2. Rudy Martzke, "Baseball, Football Take Opposite Tack in Dealing," *USA Today*, December 13, 1991: 3C.
3. Claire Smith, "Baseball: State of Game? Not the Same Everywhere," nytimes.com/1991/12/10/sports/baseball/baseball-state-of-game-not-the-same-everywhere.html.
4. "Salary Structure Draws Vincent's Wrath," *USA Today*, December 10, 1991: 1B.
5. Ibid.
6. Claire Smith.
7. Hal Bodley, "Smaller Markets Feeling the Pinch," *USA Today*, December 10, 1991: 3C.
8. Bill Plaschke, "TV Gravy Will Run Out Soon, Vincent Warns," articles.latimes.com/1991-12-10/sports/sp-296_1_baseball-contracts.
9. Chuck Johnson, "Shut Out? Managers' Score: 14 Openings, 1 Minority," *USA Today*, December 10, 1991: 1C.
10. Hal Bodley.
11. Dave Nightingale, "N.L. Realignment Left on Base," *The Sporting News*, December 23, 1991: 21.
12. Dave Nightingale, "Mariners' Situation Tops Agenda," *The Sporting News*, December 9, 1991: 28.
13. Ken Picking, "Shea-Zam!" *The Sporting News*, December 16, 1991: 30.
14. Dale Nightingale, "Free Trade Zone," *The Sporting News*, December 9, 1991: 28.
15. Nightingale, "Free Trade Zone." Davis was joined on his journey west by right-hander Kip Gross, while a pair of righties, Tim Belcher and John Wetteland, moved from the Dodgers to the Reds. (Two weeks later, Wetteland was flipped to Montreal, along with fellow righty Bill Risley, for outfielder Dave Martinez, infielder-outfielder Willie Greene, and lefty Scott Ruskin.) Cincinnati sent All-Star Jack Armstrong and Scott Scudder, both right-handers, to Cleveland for Swindell and minor-league right-hander Joe Turek.
16. Dan Le Batard, "Baseball's Worst Can Now Dream of First," *Miami Herald*, December 10, 1991: 5D.
17. Murray Chass, "Herzog, Angry Over Bonilla, Acquires Hayes," *New York Times*, December 9, 1991, nytimes.com/1991/12/09/sports/baseball-herzog-angry-over-bonilla-acquires-hayes.html.
18. Chass, "Herzog, Angry Over Bonilla, Acquires Hayes."
19. "Transactions," *The Sporting News*, December 23, 1991: 20.
20. Dave Nightingale, "Hold On, Cowboy!" *The Sporting News*, December 23, 1991: 19-21.
21. Dave Nightingale, "The Heist of Saberhagen," *The Sporting News*, December 23, 1991: 20.
22. *Baseball America's 1992 Almanac* (Baseball America), 1991, 183.
23. *Baseball America's 1993 Almanac* (Baseball America), 1992, 213.
24. *Baseball America's 1993 Almanac*, 213.
25. Lloyd Johnson and Miles Wolff, eds. *The Encyclopedia of Minor League Baseball*, 2nd Edition (Durham: Baseball America, 1997), 607.
26. *Baseball America's 1993 Almanac*, 213.
27. Johnson and Wolff, 640.
28. In *USA Today*, for example, Moore's election is noted in the final sentence in Hal Bodley, "Herzog in His Element With Angels," *USA Today*, December 11, 1991: 12C.
29. S.L. Price, "Dumping of Mitchell Sums Up Sorry Winter Meetings," *Miami Herald*, December 12, 1991: 8D.
30. "Let's Make a Deal: Baseball Winter Meetings Revive Art of the Trade," thecrimson.com/article/1991/12/14/lets-make-a-deal-baseball-winter/.

— 1992 —
THE CIRCUS COMES TO TOWN

By Rodger A. Payne

THE BASEBALL COMMUNITY MET AT the Galt House hotel in downtown Louisville, Kentucky, December 3-9, 1992. Reportedly, 1,800 to 1,900 people registered for the annual meeting, with vendors increasing the size of the meeting to about 2,500. By most accounts, the 1992 Winter Meeting was especially eventful, highlighted by a number of prominent free-agent signings involving past and future Cy Young and MVP Award winners, an ongoing racial controversy about the owner of the Cincinnati Reds, and the tragic sudden death of a team executive during a business meeting. *Time* magazine observed that the "break and circuses" meeting reflected the "greed, rancor, farce and tragedy" of real life.[1]

Business Issues

The Louisville meeting did not involve a great deal of new league business. The biggest business story leading up to and carrying over into the meeting—racist statements attributed to Cincinnati Reds owner Marge Schott—reminded many observers of baseball's racially segregated past. In November, former Reds marketing director Charles Levy, in a deposition in support of fired controller Tom Sabo's suit against the Reds, said Schott referred to former Reds players Eric Davis and Dave Parker as "million dollar niggers."[2] On November 14, Schott issued a statement declaring simply, "I am not a racist." Less than a week later, on the 20th, she released another statement saying her use of the word "nigger" and ownership of a Nazi armband (she called it "memorabilia") were not meant to offend.[3] The story kept gaining traction as the Winter Meeting approached. On November 29, the *New York Times* quoted Schott as saying that "Hitler was good in the beginning, but he went too far." She also claimed that her reference to "niggers" was a joke term, but denied applying it to Davis and Parker. Former Negro League player Hank Aaron, widely beloved as the game's all-time home-run leader at the time, called for Schott to be suspended from baseball.[4]

Because of the Schott controversy, civil-rights leader and former Democratic presidential candidate Reverend Jesse Jackson visited Louisville during the meetings and challenged baseball to regain a leadership role in fair hiring practices and to end its "institutional racism."[5] Jackson met with the small ownership group investigating Schott, but the session ended inconclusively. If baseball did not get its "house in order," Jackson warned, he would call for boycotts of the game and would mount a challenge against its antitrust exemption.[6] While Jackson was calling for structural changes in baseball, he was surrounded at the podium by former players, including Parker and ex-Reds star Frank Robinson, a Baltimore Orioles executive. The following January, Jackson made good on his threat by calling for a boycott of games played by teams that did not have affirmative-action plans in place by Opening Day.[7]

Somewhat unexpectedly, but timed after Jackson's visit, Schott on Wednesday, December 9, issued a tepid apology for her remarks. Reportedly she literally stumbled over the word "apologize":

> "I am not a racist or bigot. I have always believed in equal opportunity for everyone and that individuals should be judged by their merit, not by their skin color, religion or gender. ... I acknowledge that in the past I have, on occasion, made insensitive remarks which I now realize hurt others. On those few occasions, it was my mouth but not my

heart speaking. For any such remarks which were insensitive, I am profoundly sorry and I apologize to anyone I hurt. I can only say that I did not mean them. I love baseball, and if anything I have said caused embarrassment to the game, the Reds, the wonderful fans and city of Cincinnati, I am sorry."[8]

Before ending her statement, like Jackson, Schott pushed some of the blame on baseball itself: "I wish to add that while I am not without blame in this matter, I am also not the cause of the problem. Minority issues have been present in baseball long before I came to the game. They must be resolved. … I pledge to you that I will work with others to accomplish meaningful reform."[9] Throughout the controversy, reporters noted that Schott frequently pointed out that she too was a minority in baseball, a woman in a man's world. However, this fact did not stop baseball from punishing her. On February 3, 1993, Schott was fined $25,000 and banned from day-to-day operations of the Cincinnati Reds during the 1993 season.[10]

The meeting did include some other new business. Owners considered a few fairly small initiatives that served as omens for future changes in baseball. For example, owners reviewed data compiled by market researchers to consider league realignment (which would occur in 1994) and interleague play (which would begin in 1997). Perhaps most importantly for baseball in the 1990s, owners voted 15 to 13 to reopen the Collective Bargaining Agreement with the players union. While some feared this decision was a precursor to a 1993 spring-training lockout of the players, owners also voted to amend their bylaws to require a three-fourths majority vote to authorize such a lockout. Traditionally, owners have more leverage over players in the spring and any lockout would have been intended to force players to accept a salary cap. While owners did not repeat the lockout strategy they had used in 1973, 1976, and 1990, the lack of a settlement about the Basic Agreement did contribute to a midseason 1994 players strike. Players have far more leverage in the middle of the season since owners have every incentive to finish the season and collect revenues from attendance and media contracts. The strike led to the cancellation of the 1994 World Series.

The owners meeting was adjourned early and postponed because of the unexpected death of Carl Barger, the Florida Marlins president and chief operating officer. Barger, a former corporate lawyer, suffered from a ruptured abdominal aortic aneurysm on Wednesday during a joint ownership session in the ballroom of the Galt House East Hotel, and succumbed to the internal bleeding. The *New York Times* reported that he excused himself about 11 A.M. and collapsed just outside the meeting room: "Within seconds, Bobby Brown, the cardiologist who is president of the American League, was at his side administering cardiopulmonary resuscitation, and an ambulance arrived 10 minutes later to take him to the hospital." His doctor at Humana Hospital, however, told the *Times* that Barger never regained consciousness and died before surgery could be performed.[11] Barger had been associated with the Marlins since July 8, 1991, but his new team was yet to play its first game. The team had participated in the expansion draft a few weeks prior to the meeting in Louisville. Before joining the Florida expansion franchise, Barger was widely credited with saving the Pirates franchise in Pittsburgh. The owners adjourned their meeting after Barger's collapse and rescheduled it for January.

Player Movement: Free-Agent Frenzy

Teams reportedly obligated $250 million in free-agent spending at the 1992 meetings. In one of the most prominent moves, the reigning National League Cy Young Award winner, right-hander Greg Maddux, departed the Chicago Cubs for the league champion Atlanta Braves for five years and $28 million.[12] Contemporary news reports suggested that Maddux turned down a New York Yankees offer worth at least $6 million more. Braves general manager John Schuerholz later said that the Maddux signing "was the biggest acquisition I was ever involved with at the meetings."[13]

While the Maddux transaction helped the Braves build a baseball dynasty, it was not the largest free-agent signing at the 1992 Winter Meetings.[14] Peter

Magowan's new ownership group in San Francisco completed a nearly $44 million deal with former Pittsburgh Pirates outfielder and reigning National League MVP Barry Bonds, who had also won the award in 1990. Reportedly, the six-year deal for $43.75 million would be guaranteed even if the proposed sale of the Giants fell through, though departing owner Bob Lurie was quite worried about this aspect of the transaction. Indeed, a hotel-room news conference abruptly ended when a major-league baseball official reportedly whispered Lurie's concerns into the ear of Dennis Gilbert, Bonds' agent. As recounted by then–*San Francisco Examiner* beat reporter Larry Stone, "All of a sudden, the whole group got up and hastily left the ballroom through the kitchen door—Gilbert and his staff of snappily dressed associates; Willie Mays; Bobby Bonds; and a flustered looking Barry—all of whom were seated on the podium, waiting for the triumphant announcement."[15] The highly anticipated news conference occurred three days later.

The Chicago Cubs also said goodbye that winter to outfielder Andre Dawson, a 38-year-old former MVP (1987) with 399 career home runs. The 2010 Baseball Hall of Fame inductee signed with the Boston Red Sox for two years at $9.3 million.

Free-agent designated hitter and former infielder Paul Molitor left Milwaukee after 15 seasons and was an immediate success with his new team. After signing a $13 million, three-year contract with the Toronto Blue Jays, Molitor enjoyed two All-Star seasons with the team before slipping somewhat in the final year of his contract.

A number of teams re-signed their own free-agent stars to lucrative deals. For example, the Minnesota Twins re-signed 31-year-old free-agent center fielder Kirby Puckett to a five-year deal worth $30 million. Reportedly this cost the Twins $2.5 million more than a deal struck months before that was vetoed by Twins owner Carl Pohlad. At the time of the signing, Puckett was briefly the third highest paid player in baseball.

Similarly, 12-time All-Star shortstop Ozzie Smith, age 37, returned to his team, the St. Louis Cardinals for $3 million per year, renewable for each remaining year of his career so long as he remained healthy and achieved 400 plate appearances in the prior year. Smith also signed a six-year personal-services contract worth $1.2 million upon his retirement from baseball. The Detroit Tigers re-signed their five-time All-Star second baseman Lou Whitaker to a three-year contract worth $10 million. They also re-signed their free agent pitcher, righty Bill Gullickson, to a two-year contract for $4.6 million. And All-Star outfielder Joe Carter re-signed with the Toronto Blue Jays for three years and $19.5 million.

By comparison, numerous other signings at the 1992 Winter Meetings involved players who were never major stars of the game. Some impressive sums of cash nonetheless changed hands in these deals. For instance, left-handed pitcher Greg Swindell signed a four-year contract worth $17 million to play for the Houston Astros. On December 8, the Blue Jays signed former Oakland A's right-handed pitcher Dave Stewart, a four-time 20-game winner, to a two-year contract worth $8.5 million. Former St. Louis Cardinals right-handed relief ace Todd Worrell signed with the Los Angeles Dodgers (three years, $9.5 million). In a similar transaction, 30-year-old left-handed reliever Randy Myers signed with the Chicago Cubs for three years and $11 million.

Somewhat less noteworthy, the expansion Florida Marlins signed their first free agents on December 8—infielder Dave Magadan and 44-year-old knuckleball pitcher Charlie Hough. Magadan played only a few months as the Marlins primary third baseman before being traded in late June of 1993 to the Seattle Mariners for right-handed pitcher Jeff Darwin and outfielder Henry Cotto. The right-handed Hough served as the Opening Day starter for the new franchise in both 1993 and 1994, finishing a combined 14-25 in his final two years as a player. After failing to land Greg Maddux and other big-name free agents, the New York Yankees acquired shortstop Spike Owen for a three-year, $7 million contract.

Trades

The 1992 Winter Meetings did not feature a significant number of important trades, but teams were able to agree on a few deals. The first trade of the meetings featured Minnesota trading left-handed pitcher David West, who posted a 6.99 ERA in a limited role during the 1992 season, to the Philadelphia Phillies in exchange for right-handed pitcher Mike Hartley, who had pitched 53 games in relief during the season with an ERA of 3.44. While Hartley performed slightly worse in 1993, West played a significant role in the bullpen of the 1993 National League champion Phillies, finishing with a 2.92 ERA in just over 86 relief innings.

The California Angels traded starting pitcher Jim Abbott, who had finished third in the 1991 Cy Young Award race, to the New York Yankees for a package of players, including first baseman J.T. Snow. The left-handed Abbott's ERA increased significantly in New York as he became a slightly below average starter, though he did pitch a no-hitter in September. Pitcher Charlie Leibrandt, a 15-game winner in each of the prior two seasons, was traded from Atlanta to Texas for his final big-league season. The southpaw finished with a 4.55 ERA in 150 innings and a 9-10 won-loss record.

At 1 A.M. after the busy Wednesday, San Diego Padres general manager Joe McIlvaine announced the final deal of the day, a trade sending right-handed pitcher Jose Melendez to Boston for promising young slugger Phil Plantier. Writer-analyst Bill James predicted that Plantier was the player most likely to slug more home runs in the decade of the 1990s than any other player.[16]

Conclusion

The 1992 meetings are mostly remembered for the large personalities who dominated the headlines — outspoken owner Marge Schott, Jesse Jackson, and Barry Bonds and his entourage. Columnist Hal Bodley later called the 1992 meetings a circus, though this was largely because of the great number of signings involving star players. Indeed, after the 1992 meetings, major-league owners voted 28 to 0 to forbid GMs from attending future Winter Meetings. Executive Council chair Bud Selig pushed for this largely because of frustration with the free-agent marketplace. Baseball management felt that agents and players were using the meetings to create bidding wars for players. Baseball would not reconvene in the same manner until it gathered in Nashville in December 1998.

While most publicity and news coverage about the Winter Meetings focuses on the activities and interactions of a relatively small group of major-league owners and general managers, it is important to keep in mind that the meetings are also a trade show and a job market. Indeed, among those in attendance in 1992 was Dominic Latkovski, a graduate of local Bellarmine University, who had been working since 1990 as the Billy Bird mascot for the Triple-A Louisville Redbirds for a modest $35 per game. In hopes of emulating the famous (San Diego) Chicken and taking the act to audiences nationwide, Dominic and his brother Brennan created a video of their past performances, designed marketing materials, and manned a booth at the meetings hoping to at least break even on their investment by securing four $1,500 bookings for the 1993 season. The Latkovski brothers ended up performing 48 shows in their first year of independent operation and launched a successful business that as of 2017 continued to entertain thousands of people every summer at minor-league ballparks.[17]

BASEBALL'S BUSINESS: THE WINTER MEETINGS

SOURCES

In addition to the sources cited in the Notes, the author also consulted:

Associated Press. "Baseball Meetings Open Today; Clemens, Brown Are Top Names in Marketplace," December 11, 1998. amarillo.com/stories/1998/12/11/spo_166-7052.shtml#.VqvUuvkrL2Q.

Chass, Murray. "Puckett Stays Put With Twins; Swindell Goes Home to Houston," *New York Times*, December 5, 1992. nytimes.com/1992/12/05/sports/baseball-puckett-stays-put-with-twins-swindell-goes-home-to-houston.html.

Chass, Murray. "Jays Re-Sign Carter and Swipe Molitor," *New York Times*, December 8, 1992. nytimes.com/1992/12/08/sports/baseball-jays-re-sign-carter-and-swipe-molitor.html.

Hill, Benjamin. "Latkovski's passion fuels traveling act," MLB.com, May 3, 2013. milb.com/news/article.jsp?ymd=20130503&content_id=46451862&fext=.jsp&vkey=news_milb.

Newhan, Ross. "Baseball Winter Meetings: Marlins' Boss Collapses, Dies," *Los Angeles Times*, December 10, 1992. articles.latimes.com/1992-12-10/sports/sp-2461_1_baseball-winter-meetings.

Schmuck, Peter. "Free-Agent Thaw Floods Baseball Winter Meetings," *Baltimore Sun*, December 11, 1992. articles.baltimoresun.com/1992-12-11/sports/1992346114_1_schott-reopen-executive-council.

Walker, Ben (Associated Press). "Tragedy Marks End of Winter Meetings," *Deseret News* (Salt Lake City), December 10, 1992. deseretnews.com/article/263618/TRAGEDY-MARKS-END-OF-WINTER-MEETINGS.html.

NOTES

1. "The Baseball Barons' Bread and Circuses" *Time*, December 21, 1992. content.time.com/time/magazine/article/0,9171,977306,00.html.

2. John Erardi, "'Bookkeeper' Started It All," *Cincinnati Enquirer*, October 25, 1998. reds.enquirer.com/1998/10/102598sabo.html.

3. Schott's Statement: 'I Am Not a Racist,'" *New York Times*, December 10, 1992, nytimes.com/1992/12/10/sports/baseball-schott-s-statement-i-am-not-a-racist.html; Ira Berkow, "Marge Schott: Baseball's Big Red Headache," *New York Times*, November 29, 1992, nytimes.com/1992/11/29/sports/baseball-marge-schott-baseball-s-big-red-headache.html?pagewanted=all.

4. Berkow. The quotations attributed to Schott are also from this article.

5. Jerome Holtzman, "Jackson Makes Pitch for Minority Hiring," *Chicago Tribune*, December 8, 1992. articles.chicagotribune.com/1992-12-08/sports/9204210874_1_minority-hiring-black-journalists-rev-jesse-jackson.

6. Maryann Hudson, "Jesse Jackson, Looking Beyond Schott, Reprimands Baseball," *Los Angeles Times*, December 8, 1992. articles.latimes.com/1992-12-08/sports/sp-1797_1_jesse-jackson.

7. Danny Robbins, "Jesse Jackson Outlines Boycott: Schott Case Provides Him a Platform to Call for Improvement in Minority Hiring," *Los Angeles Times*, January 13, 1993. articles.latimes.com/1993-01-13/sports/sp-1250_1_jesse-jackson.

8. "Schott's Statement."

9. Ibid.

10. Glen Macnow, "Reds Owner Is Suspended 1 Year, Fined/The Penalty: $25,000. Marge Schott Will Still Pay the Bills. But She Won't Be Able to Run the Team," *Philadelphia Inquirer*, February 4, 1993. articles.philly.com/1993-02-04/sports/25955938_1_cincinnati-reds-owner-marge-schott-inappropriate-language.

11. Robert McG. Thomas, "Carl Barger, 62, Team President With Pirates and Florida Marlins," *New York Times*, December 10, 1992. nytimes.com/1992/12/10/us/carl-barger-62-team-president-with-pirates-and-florida-marlins.html.

12. All signings and trades referenced here are documented at "1993 Major League Baseball Transactions," www.baseball-reference.com/leagues/MLB/1993-transactions.shtml. The player links reveal the terms of contracts.

13. Hal Bodley, "Winter Meetings are no honeymoon," *MLB News*, December 5, 2008. mlb.mlb.com/news/article.jsp?ymd=20081205&content_id=3703507&vkey=perspectives&fext=.jsp&c_id=mlb.

14. For a summary of how these free agents performed through their contracts see, Rodger A. Payne, "Evaluating Free Agent Signings at the 1992 Baseball Winter Meetings," *Rodger A. Payne's Blog*, May 16, 2016. rpayne.blogspot.com/2016/05/evaluating-free-agent-signings-at-1992.html.

15. Larry Stone, "Memories of Winter Meetings Past," *Seattle Times*, December 7, 2009. seattletimes.nwsource.com/html/thehotstoneleague/2010445446_memories_of_winter_meetings_pa.html?syndication=rss.

16. Chad Finn, "Top 50 Red Sox Prospects of Past 50 Years: 30-21," Boston.com, April 2014. archive.boston.com/sports/touching_all_the_bases/2014/04/30-21.html. While Plantier hit 34 home runs for the 1993 Padres, he managed only 53 more over the remainder of his career, including 18 for the 1994 Padres. He never again achieved even 400 plate appearances and was out of major-league baseball by age 29.

17. Press Release, "The ZOOperstars to Perform at Bandits Game Friday," Quad-Cities Online, July 21, 2009. qconline.com/archives/qco/print_display.php?id=449772.

— 1993 —
A COOLING HOT STOVE AND BOILING TEMPERS

By Abigail Miskowiec

AS TENSIONS BETWEEN OWNERS, general managers, and players mounted, the winter meetings of 1993 featured battles over the commissioner's chair, the free-agent process, revenue sharing, and the salary cap. These points of contention collided over four months of meetings that began in early November, when the general managers met in Naples, Florida. The National Association of Professional Baseball Leagues, or minor leagues, followed with a much more subdued meeting in December in Atlanta, while the owners used the months of January and February to settle the revenue-sharing issue before the start of the season.

The multiple meetings did little to save the 1994 season, as the players union and the owners could not come to an agreement regarding the proposed salary cap. Further meetings and clashes came to a head when the union went on strike in August 1994.

New Faces, New Positions in Front Offices

Most seasons of major-league baseball end with front-office shuffles as teams at the bottom of the pile seek to clean house to move up the ladder, and 1993 was no different. Between June 1993 and January 1994, eight teams replaced either a general manager or a manager, and the Baltimore Orioles came under new ownership.

The front-office shakeups started in the midst of the 1993 season when the San Diego Padres' general manager, Joe McIlvaine, resigned and moved to the New York Mets (where he had once been scouting director and assistant general manager) to replace Al Harazin as GM. Randy Smith stepped in to fill McIlvaine's shoes in San Diego, and he would stay there for two years.

In August 1993, a group represented by prominent Baltimore attorney Peter Angelos bought the Orioles at auction for a then-record $173 million. In the midst of their second season at Oriole Park at Camden Yards, the team sat five games off the division lead at the time of the sale. Angelos made no major changes to the organization right off the bat, but he did state that "the primary concern is putting the best ballclub on the field," a goal he would work toward throughout the 1993 offseason.[1] However, after the 1993 season, Larry Lucchino stepped down as president of the club, an office that remained vacant until John Angelos, Peter's son, took the position for one season in 1999.

The remaining front-office moves took place over the course of the offseason and included four general-manager changes and two managerial changes. General manager Dan Duquette jumped from the Montreal Expos to the Boston Red Sox, with Kevin Malone replacing Duquette in Montreal.[2] In Detroit, Joe Klein replaced Jerry Walker as general manager, and Hall of Famer Whitey Herzog retired as general manager of the California Angels with Bill Bavasi reputedly in line for the position.[3]

The Houston Astros, despite a successful season at 85-77, fired manager Art Howe and replaced him with Terry Collins, who had been a bullpen coach for the Pittsburgh Pirates. Similarly, the Chicago Cubs cashiered Jim Lefebvre and brought in Tom Trebelhorn, even though Lefebvre had managed the team to an 84-78 record in 1993.

One final change, or rather, reinstatement, took place early in the 1993 offseason. Cincinnati Reds owner Marge Schott returned to the team after serving eight months of her yearlong ban, imposed for racist comments regarding former Reds players.

GENERAL MANAGERS MEETINGS

After the spending spree of 1992,[4] owners forbade general managers to attend the NAPBL meetings in Atlanta. While the GMs traditionally meet after the season for business, the 1993 meetings in Naples gained more import as a result of the ban. Trade talks and organizational changes dominated the news from the meetings, which took place over the first four days of November.

Trades and Signings

Despite the fact that players who had not cleared waivers would not be on the trading block until November 11, the general managers wheeled and dealed as usual. Without the big-ticket names of 1992 (for example, Barry Bonds and Greg Maddux), the 1993 hot stove contained significantly less spark, but a few teams managed to swing notable trades and signings. Most teams focused on a budding star, right-handed hurler Andy Benes, but the San Diego Padres refused to let the All-Star go.

"We may never see another free-agent crop like the one we saw last winter," said Atlanta Braves general manager John Schuerholz.[5]

The Detroit Tigers and San Francisco Giants kicked off the signings by retaining free agents Eric Davis and Erik Johnson, respectively. The Tigers continued their spending by signing six-time All-Star shortstop Alan Trammell to a one-year contract.[6]

The general managers also worked out a few trades while in Naples, most likely on the links, as is tradition. The Philadelphia Phillies picked up right-handed closer Heath Slocumb from the Cleveland Indians in exchange for outfielder Ruben Amaro. Slocumb saved more than 30 games in 1995 and 1996 but experienced a dropoff in numbers from then on, while Amaro returned to the Phillies in 1996.

The Seattle Mariners and Schott's Reds worked out a four-player deal during the meetings as well. The Mariners sent second baseman Bret Boone and right-handed starter Erik Hanson to the Reds in exchange for right-handed reliever Bobby Ayala and catcher Dan Wilson. Boone, Hanson, and Wilson each made at least one All-Star Game appearance, and Wilson was widely regarded as one of the finest defensive catchers of his era, leading the league in runners caught stealing in 1995 and 1997.

Reasons for Limited Trade Activity

Other than the high price of free agents in 1992, a few factors contributed to the tame market in the 1993 offseason. A new television contract with ABC and NBC cut payouts to clubs by more than $7 million each.[7] Also, the rising price of player contracts[8] threatened to push team payrolls to historic new heights.[9]

As a result, many successful teams sold off or released aging stars and relied on their farm talent to bring success in 1994. The players who debuted in the strike-shortened 1994 season and the 1995 season featured 39 future All-Stars, including Alex Rodriguez, Derek Jeter, Mariano Rivera, and Jason Giambi.[10] Those players also collected a total of 20 Gold Glove Awards, 27 Silver Slugger Awards, and four MVP Awards.

Four future Hall of Famers were among those released at the end of the 1993 season as teams dumped their standard-bearers in favor of young blood: Robin Yount, Eddie Murray, Rickey Henderson, and Goose Gossage. Yount retired rather than play outside Milwaukee, while Gossage threw his final 47 innings in Seattle before the strike. Murray split the next four seasons between four teams, and Henderson played for 10 more years, leading the league in stolen bases when he returned to Oakland in 1998 at the age of 39.

Several other notable players saw the free-agent market in the winter of 1993, including Jack Morris, Bo Jackson, Kirk Gibson, Tim Raines, Harold Baines, Dave Henderson, Tony Peña, Will Clark, Andrés Galarraga, and Rafael Palmeiro. Morris, Jackson, Gibson, and Henderson would all be retired by the end of 1995.

Cleveland Indians' Nightmare Year Continues

Shortly after the general managers adjourned their meetings in Naples, Cleveland Indians GM John

Hart received a heartbreaking phone call. A recently released relief pitcher, southpaw Cliff Young, had been thrown from his vehicle and was pronounced dead at the scene. The 29-year-old appeared in 21 games for the Indians in 1993.

Young was the third Indians pitcher to die in 1993. Relievers Tim Crews and Steve Olin joined starter Bob Ojeda for gator hunting on March 22, the team's only day off during spring training. The boat ran into an unlit dock, and Crews and Olin were killed. Ojeda sustained severe head injuries but remained conscious, reportedly holding Crews as he died. Ojeda sought psychiatric help and returned to the majors on August 7, 1993. He retired the following year with a career record of 115-98 and a 3.65 ERA.[11]

Reflecting on the tragedies, Hart said, "You just shake your head and you wonder, why is this happening?"[12]

The Least Talked About, Most Significant Move of the Offseason

Perhaps the biggest trade of the offseason occurred on November 19, outside of any of the scheduled winter meetings. The Los Angeles Dodgers, who had finished 1993 with an 81-81 record, stepped up to the trading block in an effort to replace second baseman Jody Reed, who decided to test the free-agent market after the season.

The Dodgers were below the league average in almost every offensive category and scored the third fewest runs in the National League. On the other hand, the Dodgers pitching staff, led by right-hander Orel Hershiser, put up above-average numbers in most categories. As a result, Los Angeles used its best bargaining chip, a young relief pitcher named Pedro Martinez.

Montreal Expos general manager Dan Duquette saw the window of opportunity to bolster the team's four-man rotation and make space for utility infielder Mike Lansing in the everyday lineup. In one of his final moves as GM, Duquette sent the team's leadoff hitter and stolen-base specialist, infielder Delino DeShields, to the Dodgers in return for the right-handed Martinez.

Martinez went on to become one of the greatest pitchers of all time, winning three Cy Young Awards, a World Series championship, and a plaque in Cooperstown. DeShields, meanwhile, bounced from the Dodgers to the St. Louis Cardinals, the Baltimore Orioles, and finally, the Chicago Cubs over the course of his 13-year career. DeShields moved on to a successful career as a manager in the Cincinnati Reds organization.

One other deal was made that proved to have some significance. The Astros traded their star outfielder, Eric Anthony, to the Seattle Mariners for outfielder Mike Felder and a young lefty, Mike Hampton. Anthony would bounce around to several teams over the next few years, while Felder played just one more season before retiring. Hampton, on the other hand, became a consistent winner in the majors, including a Cy Young Award runner-up year in 1999, when he won 22 games.

World Series Woes Haunt "Wild Thing"

With a nickname like "Wild Thing," blown saves and late-inning theatrics would be expected from Philadelphia Phillies closer Mitch Williams, but when those collapses come on baseball's biggest stage in front of one of the most hostile fan bases in sports, the failure can be overwhelming and potentially dangerous.

After a record-setting regular season, the left-handed Williams struggled in the 1993 postseason. In Game Four of the World Series against the Toronto Blue Jays, Williams took the loss after allowing the Blue Jays to come back from a 14-9 deficit. When Williams returned to the mound in Game Six, Joe Carter teed off on him for the second World Series walk-off home run in history.

Williams reportedly received death threats throughout the 1993 offseason, which he spent at his ranch in central Texas to escape the fans' fury. Philadelphia general manager Lee Thomas chose to deal Williams to the Houston Astros (for right-handers Doug Jones and Jeff Juden), stating, "I think he'll do well in Houston, but I also think he would have had a difficult time coming back to Philadelphia."[13]

Williams did not do well in Houston. He earned only six saves. In the final three years of his career after the 1993 World Series, Williams appeared in just 52 games, fewer than in any single season with Philadelphia.

MINOR LEAGUE MEETINGS

The annual winter meetings of the National Association of Professional Baseball Leagues, commonly known as the minor leagues, convened December 10-15 in Atlanta. The 1993 meetings were quieter than usual due to the absence of most major-league executives, but scouts and farm directors gathered to conduct business and to oversee the Rule 5 Draft.

Feelings regarding the absence of executives were mixed. Atlanta GM John Schuerholz made an appearance, as did Pittsburgh's Cam Bonifay. Interim Commissioner and Milwaukee Brewers owner Bud Selig argued, "We have enormous problems, but the circus atmosphere took the focus away from what we have to do." Philadelphia general manager Lee Thomas, however, retorted, "It's a week of free publicity and we're throwing it away."[14]

Baltimore Makes a Blockbuster Deal; Seattle Shuts Down Yankees

The Baltimore Orioles went into the 1993 season looking to make good on Angelos's promise to put the best ballplayers on the field. To that end, they targeted one man: first baseman Rafael Palmeiro of the Rangers.

Palmeiro rejected Texas's offer of $26.5 million for five years, and when the Rangers signed former San Francisco Giants first baseman Will Clark, Palmeiro found himself in search of a new team. The Orioles and Palmeiro came to terms on a $30 million deal on December 12, and Palmeiro brought a much-needed bat to the Oriole lineup. In the 1993 season, the slugger had hammered 37 home runs and driven in 105 runs.

Baltimore's division rival, the New York Yankees, missed their intended target when lefty Randy Johnson agreed to a four-year, $20.25 million deal to remain with the Seattle Mariners. Johnson would have been eligible for free agency after the 1994 season. The Yankees were reluctant to pursue such a big-name signing since owner George Steinbrenner allegedly wanted to keep the team's 1994 payroll under $45 million.[15]

Minor Headlines Made Via the Draft

The 1993 Rule 5 Draft, held on December 13, featured few players of note. The New York Mets selected catcher Kelly Stinnett from the Cleveland Indians. Stinnett spent parts of 14 seasons in the majors, working with some of the greatest hurlers of his time, including Cy Young Award winners Dwight Gooden, Bret Saberhagen, Randy Johnson, Zack Greinke, Brandon Webb, Tom Glavine, and Pedro Martinez.

The Florida Marlins picked up Antonio Alfonseca from the Montreal Expos. The right-handed Alfonseca, known for his polydactyly (six fingers on each hand and six toes on each foot), pitched six scoreless innings of relief in three games in the Marlins' 1997 World Series victory. He led the majors in saves in 2000 and was a key piece of the 2002 trade with the Cubs that brought Rookie of the Year phenom Dontrelle Willis to Miami.

More Teams on the Horizon

The successful, smooth expansion of major-league baseball with the addition of the Colorado Rockies and the Florida Marlins in 1993 set the stage for a second round of expansion. While the minor-league meetings commenced in Atlanta, the owners sat down with Jerry Colangelo, owner of the Phoenix Suns in the National Basketball Association, to discuss the possibility of a major-league team in Phoenix.[16] St. Petersburg, Florida, remained in the running thanks to a taxpayer-financed ballpark built in 1990.

The possibility of two more teams in the majors pushed the realignment issue to the fore. Adding Colorado and Florida meant the American and National Leagues each had two seven-team divisions. The surfeit of teams made it increasingly difficult for teams to reach the playoffs; in 1993, the San Francisco Giants won 103 games and finished with the second-best record in the majors but missed out on the playoffs after losing the division by one game.

However, this point of contention remained unsettled until the owners met in early 1994.

OWNERS' MEETINGS

When the owners finally sat down after the new year, they found several pressing issues on their plate. First, the office of commissioner remained vacant after Fay Vincent's resignation following the 1992 season. Second, the looming revenue-sharing agreement and collective-bargaining negotiations threatened the tenuous peace between the owners and the players. Finally, the owners worked on a solution regarding division realignment and league-wide parity.

To solve these issues, the owners met off and on through the offseason, beginning on a blustery January 6 morning in Chicago. The owners would then fly to the warmer climes of Fort Lauderdale to continue the conversation in late January.

Revenue-Sharing Divides Clubs Along Monetary Lines

Club owners butted heads regarding how to share revenue from television broadcasts and playoff games. At the end of the 1993 season, the clubs openly clashed, with large-market teams shutting down meetings and refusing to put increased money into the small-market clubs. To settle the issue, 21 of the 28 clubs would have to be in favor of the revenue-sharing plan. Ten large-market teams (both New York clubs, Baltimore, Boston, Los Angeles, Toronto, Colorado, Florida, St. Louis, and Texas) joined forces to block the plan at meetings in August 1993; the remaining midsize- and small-market teams hoped the Chicago meetings would sway at least three of the 10 clubs.

Interim Commissioner Bud Selig had a significant stake in the agreement. He and his family retained ownership of the small-market Milwaukee Brewers even while Selig oversaw the sport. The Brewers had already dropped mainstays Robin Yount, Paul Molitor, and Jim Gantner, and general manager Sal Bando reportedly needed to cut $5 million off the team's $25 million payroll before the 1994 season. Many Milwaukee fans saw the offseason meetings as a last-ditch effort to keep the club in Wisconsin.[17] Other small-market teams in danger included Cincinnati, Minnesota, Montreal, Pittsburgh, San Diego, and Seattle.

Richard Ravitch, the league's chief negotiator, insisted that the owners come to a decision regarding revenue before entering into discussions with the players union regarding a new collective-bargaining agreement.[18] So important was the revenue deal that many assumed Ravitch would resign if the owners could not resolve the issue in Chicago.[19]

The Chicago meetings featured numerous caucuses (divided by market size), and at least two different plans. The large-market plan received only 11 votes while Ravitch's plan garnered 20. Florida and Texas flipped from their original stance, but the deal still fell a vote short when the meetings adjourned. Essentially, the deal could provide as much as $10 million in subsidies to small-market clubs.

Los Angeles Dodgers President Peter O'Malley summed up the conflict by saying, "I was pleasantly surprised with the movement and the amount of money put on the table by the big-market clubs for the small-market clubs today, but this is not just a debate about money. There are a lot of philosophical issues."[20]

Compromise in Fort Lauderdale

The owners flew south to continue discussions in Fort Lauderdale, Florida, on January 18, 1994. Before the owners even sat down to work out a compromise, rumors indicated that St. Louis and Boston might be the teams to tip the balance in favor of a new revenue-sharing deal.

Two days into the meetings, the owners voted unanimously to approve a revenue-sharing plan proposed by Ravitch. The plan, which would come into effect in 1995, would see the top-earning third subsidizing the bottom third. However, the deal hinged upon the players approving a salary cap, which at the time seemed doubtful.

Players Association executive director Donald Fehr reiterated the union's stance on the salary cap: "[They] want the union to cooperate in adversely affecting the market. That's what a salary cap is."[21]

Due to the uncertainty of the agreement and the salary-cap negotiations, the owners chose to postpone the decision regarding a long-term commissioner. The search committee had reportedly settled on Northwestern University president Arnold Weber, while George Steinbrenner tried to use his significant clout to push US Olympic Committee executive director Harvey Schiller into the position.[22] The owners' inaction left Bud Selig in the position as interim commissioner.

The animosity between the owners and the players hung over the offseason from that point on. Several publications predicted a work stoppage before the 1994 season, and Richard Ravitch geared up for several rounds of clashes with Donald Fehr. In the absence of a commissioner, Ravitch became chief negotiator for ownership.

Realignment Creates More Opportunity in Baseball

In 1993, teams in the majors had a 14.3 percent chance of making the playoffs, with two divisions in each league sending a team to the postseason, but owners saw an opportunity for increased television revenue through realignment and a wild card.

Realignment long hung over the sport, and many teams made moves in the 1993 offseason with new divisions in mind. In the Fort Lauderdale meetings, the owners made this realignment a reality by implementing a Central Division in each league and adding a wild-card slot to the playoffs.[23] This change doubled each team's chance of appearing in the postseason.

The new rounds in the playoffs also served to ease the tension between the owners and the players. Players would receive 80 percent of the ticket sales for the first three games of the Division Series.[24]

CONTINUED COLLECTIVE-BARGAINING DISPUTES

For the remainder of the 1993 offseason and into spring training, Ravitch campaigned tirelessly on behalf of the salary cap. The owners pledged not to lock out players, but the players could strike at any point before or during the 1994 season if a collective-bargaining agreement was not reached. Donald Fehr strongly resisted the idea of a salary cap, arguing that the sharing of revenue would put teams on an even playing field and negate the need for a cap.

Ravitch met with the owners once more during their annual meetings in Scottsdale, Arizona, in late February. He developed a plan to open negotiations with Fehr, and Fehr and Ravitch reconvened after a 13-month hiatus when they met on March 7 at a Tampa, Florida, hotel. Players reported to spring training as usual while their union head came to the negotiating table.

While in Florida, Ravitch met directly with players to further his cause. He presented a rather watered-down version of the owners' plan in hopes that the lack of details would open a dialogue leading to compromise. Fehr, for his part, saw the owners' absence and lack of transparency as a confirmation of their disinterest in the players' demands.

"The players care an awful lot about baseball and working with the owners," Fehr said, "and if the owners shared that view, they would be here. We had 70-odd players here. Not a single owner will come."[25]

The continued meetings did not interfere with the start of the 1994 season, which began on Easter Sunday. A sense of foreboding hung over the games, however, with memories of the 1985 strike and 1990 lockout still fresh in many minds.

In mid-April, the owners finally released detailed economic information about each club, a set of documents the players had requested in spring training. With the new information in hand, the union agreed to meet on July 11, the day before the All-Star Game, in addition to a June 3 meeting of team representatives. Meanwhile, the owners met formally and informally throughout the season to adjust their proposal to the union.

On June 7-9, the owners convened at the Westin Hotel in Cincinnati to work on a final proposal regarding the salary cap and to select a new American League president. At these meetings, owners pushed to amend the Major League Agreement; prior to the 1994 season, a strike could be settled by a simple majority, but the resolution at the Cincinnati meetings changed the rule to a three-fourths approval.

The Players Association criticized the move heavily. Donald Fehr said, "That is not a step in the right direction. It's a direction of people preparing for war."[26]

When the owners' 27-page proposal finally made its way to the players, the union scoffed. The owners hoped to reduce free-agency eligibility to four years and to eliminate arbitration entirely. A more contentious point was revenue-sharing between players and owners. Prior to the 1994 season, the players' share of the revenue from major-league baseball had risen from 42 percent to 58 percent in five years. The owners' proposal would bring that share back down to 50 percent, costing the players $80 million to $90 million.[27]

CONGRESSIONAL ACTION

On top of the ongoing battle between management and the players union in the majors, Senator Howard Metzenbaum (D-Ohio) introduced a bill that, if passed, could change the course of the labor dispute entirely. Metzenbaum sought to repeal baseball's antitrust exemption. Major-league baseball, at the time, was the only sport to have an antitrust exemption, and the passage of this bill would give players a legal avenue to pursue their grievances without a complete work stoppage.

Unfortunately for the union (and for fans who wanted an end to the bickering), the Senate Judiciary Committee shot down Metzenbaum's bill by a vote of 10 to 7. Metzenbaum, discouraged by the loss, accused the owners of buying votes with the promise of expansion franchises, an accusation that was roundly denied by Bud Selig.[28]

A STANDSTILL LEADS TO A STRIKE

Without a meeting of the minds taking place over the All-Star break, Bud Selig pushed the issue even further. He claimed that 19 teams (out of the majors' 28) were operating in the red so far in 1994, a claim that would later be rebutted by Donald Fehr.

Shortly after Selig's statement, the players made their counter-offer. Not surprisingly, they rejected outright the proposal of a salary cap and, instead, requested that eligibility for salary arbitration be reduced from three years of service to two and that the minimum salary be raised from $109,000 to at least $175,000. Within a week, Richard Ravitch rejected the players' proposal.

This final rejection led the Players Association to set August 12 as the strike date. On July 28, the 31 players on the executive board voted to effectively end the season, bypassing the playoffs, on that date.[29] Mike Greenwell of the Boston Red Sox did not mince words, saying, "Let's be honest: We don't plan to give in and they don't. This game is in trouble."[30]

A few owners stood in opposition to the hard line that Richard Ravitch walked. Chicago White Sox owner Jerry Reinsdorf saw the salary cap as a boon to balance his losses under the new revenue-sharing plan, and first-year Baltimore Orioles owner Peter Angelos publicly disavowed Ravitch's stance that the players were to blame for the impending strike.

Baseball fans across the country were understandably dismayed by the threatened strike. Fan groups urged counter-protests. Even President Bill Clinton offered his diplomatic skills to put the conflict to rest.

But as the calendar turned to August, another point of contention rose between the owners and the players. The owners missed the August 1 deadline for their annual payment to the players' pension fund. The payment, based on revenue from the All-Star Game, would have totaled $7.59 million. Ravitch justified the withheld funds by saying, "I think when you're in the midst of collective bargaining and there's no agreement, it's absolutely normal not to make a payment of this nature."[31]

In the waning days before the strike took effect, the owners and union came together to lay ground rules. Players would be paid until the day before the strike, and if they happened to be on the road at midnight on August 11, the players would have to pay their fare home.[32] Players would collectively lose approximately $5 million, but the union's strike fund of at least $175 million would cover those losses. For their part, the owners kept a $260 million line of credit in the event of a strike.[33]

BASEBALL'S BUSINESS: THE WINTER MEETINGS

The day after players walked off the field, Ravitch and Fehr requested a mediator from the Federal Mediation and Conciliation Service in hopes that the intervention would save at least the playoffs, if not the season. Meanwhile, teams like the Montreal Expos and New York Yankees, started to drop nonessential personnel from their payroll.

On September 1, the day that major-league rosters can expand to 40 players, the Pittsburgh Pirates, Texas Rangers, and Chicago Cubs each decided to recall players from their minor-league system. With the strike in effect, those players no longer received the salary that they had been receiving with the lower-level club. For example, Pirates pitcher Randy Tomlin lost out on $5,328 per day after being recalled.[34] This added fuel to the labor-negotiation fire.

On September 14, interim Commissioner Selig declared an end to the 1994 season. A last-ditch effort by the union failed to sway the owners. For the first time since 1904, the World Series was canceled. Selig announced the cancellation with the support of 26 of the 28 owners.[35] (The two dissenting voices belonged to Orioles owner Peter Angelos and Cincinnati Reds owner Marge Schott.)

The financial cost of the strike proved detrimental to both players and owners. Players lost $150 million in salary over the course of the strike, and the cancellation cost the owners an estimated $600 million. The battle continued throughout the 1994 offseason and into the 1995 season, making it the longest strike in major-league baseball history.

NOTES

1. Murray Chass. "Going, Going, Sold: Orioles Auctioned for $173 Million," *New York Times*, August 3, 1993: B9.

2. After the strike-shortened 1994 season, Montreal, led by Malone, sold off most of its talent, leading to a decade of irrelevance and an eventual move to Washington.

3. Herzog spent 38 years involved in MLB in some way, beginning his playing career with the Washington Senators in 1956. He gained fame as a manager, and his philosophy of small ball and hard-nosed defense brought his St. Louis Cardinals a World Series championship in 1982. The Cardinals retired Herzog's number shortly after he was inducted into the Baseball Hall of Fame in 2010.

4. In the three-day span of the 1992 meetings, teams spent $225 million on 35 free agents, according to *USA Today*. See "Winter Meetings Split," *USA Today*, November 1, 1993: 7C.

5. Mark Maske, "Most GMs Prepare to Cut Payrolls; It's New Ballgame During Offseason," *Washington Post*, November 7, 1993: D08.

6. Trammell spent 19 seasons playing for the Detroit Tigers, winning four Gold Glove Awards and three Silver Slugger Awards. He returned to the Tigers as the manager from 2003 to 2005, amassing a 185-298 record.

7. The resultant network, The Baseball Network, paved the way for such sport-owned networks today as the NFL Network and MLB TV. But the network lasted only until 1995, when baseball aligned with Fox Sports, a broadcast partnership that as of 2017 was contracted to last until 2021.

8. Bonds' 1992 contract broke the record for most guaranteed money at $43.75 million, but it wouldn't even fall in the top 100 contracts of all time. Giancarlo Stanton's 2015 deal guaranteed him $325 million over 13 years, the richest contract signed as of July 2016.

9. For example, in 1983, the New York Mets led the league in team payroll at $11.6 million. By 1993, the Toronto Blue Jays took top honors with a team payroll of $51.9 million. Ten years later, in 2003, the New York Yankees paid out $149.7 million, and in 2013, the Yankees paid out $228.8 million.

10. Many of these rookies were implicated in the scandals of the Steroid Era. All-Stars Matt Lawton, Mike Cameron, and Alex Rodriguez each served a ban for violating baseball's drug policy. Jason Giambi, Andy Pettitte, Gregg Zaun, and Paul Byrd were all named in the Mitchell Report but did not serve any bans imposed by major-league baseball.

11. Laura Lippman, "Relief at Last," *Baltimore Sun*, October 19, 1995.

12. "Tragedy Strikes Again for Indians Baseball," *Los Angeles Times*, November 6, 1993: 2.

13. Ross Newhan, "A Wild Day in Baseball Transactions," *Los Angeles Times*, December 3, 1993: 1.

14. Ross Newhan, "Some Baseball Officials Frown at Owners' Curve on Meetings," *Los Angeles Times*, December 9, 1993: 5.

15. The future Hall of Famer, known as "The Big Unit," donned pinstripes for two years, earning a career-high $16 million.

16. Murray Chass, "Baseball Is Considering New Round of Expansion," *New York Times*, December 7, 1993: B15.

17. Tom Haudricourt, "Brewers' Future in Owners' Hands; Important meeting Thursday," *Milwaukee Sentinel*, January 4, 1994: 4B.

18. Murray Chass, "Snow Blows, Fog Arrives, Revenue Meetings Swirl," *New York Times*, January 7, 1994.

19 Haudricourt.

20 Ross Newhan, "One Vote Shy of Accord," *Los Angeles Times*, January 7, 1994: 14.

21 Mark Maske, "Baseball to Share Revenue; Conditional Plan Adopted by Owners," *Washington Post*, January 19, 1994: B1.

22 Mark Maske, "First in Owners' Lineup—a Commissioner; Meetings Lead Off With Search for Boss," *Washington Post*, January 17. 1994: C4.

23 Claire Smith, "Central Divisions Added to Baseball's Lineup," *New York Times*, January 20, 1994.

24 The 1994 season ended in a strike so the divisional alignment experiment would not take place until the 1995 postseason. No further changes to the playoff structure would take place until 2013, when a second wild card was added.

25 Murray Chass, "Owners Promise to Open the Books," *New York Times*, March 8, 1994: B16.

26 Jerome Holtzman, "Union Cries Foul After Owners Pass Strike Amendment," *Chicago Tribune*, June 9, 1994: 3.

27 Larry Whiteside, "Players' Union Not Ready to Play Ball With Owners," *Boston Globe*, June 15, 1994: 52.

28 Richard Justice, "Exemption Survives Senate," *Washington Post*, June 24, 1994: C4A.

29 July 28, 1994, featured another historic baseball moment: Kenny Rogers of the Texas Rangers tossed the 12th perfect game in baseball history (13 if one counts Don Larsen's gem in the 1956 World Series).

30 Bob Berghaus, "Battle Lines Are Drawn as Strike Date Is Set for Aug. 12," *Milwaukee Journal*, July 29, 1994: 1C.

31 "Pension Dispute Latest Snag in Strike Talks," *Chicago Tribune*, August 3, 1994: 2.

32 In solidarity with the players, Donald Fehr refused to be paid his seven-figure salary once the strike began. Richard Ravitch, on the other hand, continued to be paid his $750,000 annual salary.

33 Ross Newhan, "Players Vow Readiness for a Long Strike," *Los Angeles Times*, August 10, 1994.

34 "Recall of Players Sparks More Conflict," *St. Louis Post-Dispatch*, September 2, 1994: 4C.

35 Murray Chass, "Owners Terminate Season, Without the World Series." *New York Times*, September 15, 1994.

1994
YEAR-ROUND LABOR NEGOTIATIONS RESOLVE STRIKE

By Abigail Miskowiec

WITH INTERIM COMMISSIONER BUD Selig calling an end to the 1994 season on September 14 because of the players strike, the baseball offseason commenced earlier than usual. The major feature of the annual winter meetings was, of course, the resolution of the strike, but the issues of offseason transactions and replacement players hung over the sport's head. In addition to the multiple meetings between Donald Fehr, the executive director of the Major League Baseball Players Association, and the owners' negotiator, Richard Ravitch, the general managers convened in Scottsdale, Arizona, while the annual minor-league meetings commenced in Dallas, Texas.

Silence Between Representatives, Congress Gets Involved

As soon as Selig issued his resolution, which also canceled the 1994 World Series, Fehr indicated that, if asked by owners, he would be willing to observe a monthlong waiting period before entering into a legal battle with the owners.[1] Instead, he took to the road and convened a series of regional meetings with players in Atlanta, Tampa, New York, Chicago, Los Angeles, and Dallas. Also on his itinerary was a date with Congress as antitrust hearings continued throughout the winter of 1994.

Fehr's meetings with players served little more than informational purposes. As the fallout of the strike settled, the players received much of the news from media outlets, and Fehr used this one-on-one time to clarify the union's position and to ensure a united front.

As Brett Butler, the Los Angeles Dodgers player representative, put it, "Until they're ready to negotiate, all we can do is inform our players, keep having these meetings and keep them up to snuff on what's going on."[2]

Managerial Moves

Despite the whirl of adversity and uncertainty surrounding the winter months, teams still took steps to better their clubs for the coming 1995 season. Many organizations chose to work from the top down, firing five general managers and seven managers in total.

Baltimore Orioles owner Peter Angelos continued to clean house, firing manager Johnny Oates a week after the season prematurely ended. Oates, sporting a 291-270 record at that point in his career, quickly signed on as manager of the Texas Rangers. Phil Regan stepped in to replace Oates.

Tom Trebelhorn saw the end of his tenuous time with the Chicago Cubs, with Jim Riggleman moving from San Diego to take over the North Side club. Bruce Bochy, former third-base coach of the Padres, oversaw San Diego as the youngest manager in the league in 1995.

Although the Texas Rangers sat in first place at the time of the strike, manager Kevin Kennedy found himself on the job market. Luckily, he found an open position in Boston when Butch Hobson was let go after three mediocre seasons.

The Kansas City Royals similarly experienced managerial changes. Manager Hal McRae made way for Bob Boone.[3] Boone couldn't turn the Royals around and found himself out of work by 1997.

The general-manager front was equally active. The Texas Rangers completed their overhaul, firing Tom Grieve and signing Doug Melvin, who would lead the club to three playoff appearances, the first three in franchise history. The Chicago Cubs likewise made front-office changes when Larry Himes stepped aside for Ed Lynch in October.[4]

St. Louis replaced Dal Maxvill with Walt Jocketty, former assistant general manager of the Colorado Rockies. Just a season removed from back-to-back World Series championships, the Toronto Blue Jays let future Hall of Famer Pat Gillick go and hired Gord Ash.[5] Finally, the Minnesota Twins watched Andy MacPhail accept a position as the CEO of the Chicago Cubs and filled the general-manager role with Terry Ryan.

Free Agent Fracas on the Horizon

Without a new collective-bargaining agreement in place, free-agency filings would start on October 15, and the signing period would begin on October 30. Many players, if they were still on strike, would not sign new contracts, meaning the owners would be forced to reckon with more than 800 free agents from the 40-man rosters.

To avoid this calamity, the owners pushed for a 45-day freeze.[6] Rather than force the clubs to face hundreds of free agents, the freeze would stall only 170 free-agency-eligible players, with whom the owners would not be able to negotiate during the period.[7] This would allow the owners to focus their energies on working out a new free-agency calendar.

Union representatives held off on making a judgment on the freeze. Ultimately, they found that the owners were perfectly willing to come to a conclusion for them. "As for the free agents, Fehr said a letter the union received from O'Connor on Thursday led him to believe the owners plan to unilaterally impose their freeze proposal—which would keep players from filing for free agency and signing contracts before November 30," according to the *Washington Post*.[8]

Adding to the confusion, players at that time needed six years of major-league service to become eligible for free agency. Many of those players who entered the 1994 season with five years of service fell short of the six-year mark because of the strike and subsequent cancellation of the final 52 days of the season. On the first day of the free-agent signing period, Jim Abbott, Jack McDowell, Erik Hanson, and Kenny Rogers tested the waters despite falling short of the required service time. Management's Player Relations Committee rejected the filing immediately, setting up yet another battle in the contentious 1994 offseason.[9]

Among the players most affected by the 1994 strike was Chris Gwynn, brother of Tony Gwynn. Gwynn finished the 1994 season with the Los Angeles Dodgers a mere one day short of the six-year service term. Gwynn attempted to file for free agency on October 17, 1994, but the Player Relations Committee immediately rejected the suit.

The National Pastime in the Nation's Capital

Amid the free-agency chaos and the ongoing strike, the players' and owners' representatives descended upon the nation's capital on October 18 to reconvene overtures that had stalled since September 9. Former Secretary of Labor Bill Usery Jr. joined the discussions at the behest of President Bill Clinton. Usery brought more than four decades of labor-relations experience to the table.

After a day of separate meetings with the union representatives and the owners, Usery brought the two sides together for a formal session. Richard Ravitch appeared with a contingent of 11 owners while Donald Fehr brought six players to the table. While reportedly the sides discussed nothing of grave significance, Ravitch's comments after the meeting inspired optimism. First, he stated that the owners still had not set a date for a potential free-agency freeze, and second, he said, "We have no contemplation of taking any legal steps whatsoever at this point. We reserve our right to do what we're legally entitled to, but we have no current expectation and there was no discussion with the negotiating committee about our proceeding with any legal steps whatsoever."[10]

After the first joint meeting, though, Usery took a backstage role in mediation and would not call the two sides together until November 10 at Doral Arrowwood Resort in Rye Brook, New York. Unlike the October meetings, Commissioner Bud Selig attended the first day of the four-day session but left thereafter due to the death of a close friend.

Richard Ravitch, on the other hand, found his importance to the ongoing negotiations to be waning after John Harrington, Boston Red Sox CEO, stepped into the position of owners' committee chairman. Ravitch's three-year, $2.25 million contract was set to expire at the end of 1994, and the lingering strike threatened his position within baseball. He was in attendance at the meetings in New York, but had little interaction with the press and referred to himself as "an adviser."[11]

The New York meetings adjourned a day early, on November 12, so that the owners could come up with a new proposal for ending the strike. By this point, it had become clear that the union refused to accept any proposal containing a salary cap, so Usery pushed the owners to replace the cap with a luxury tax. But developing the new proposal would take time and compromise.

Alternative League Sees Opportunity

The swirling mass of confusion hanging over baseball opened opportunities for developing leagues. For the first time in 80 years, since the days of the short-lived Federal League, a rival league threatened to steal striking players from the majors. The budding United Baseball League convened a meeting of interested parties on November 1, 1994, in New York City.

This new league focused on rectifying the mistakes of major-league baseball's 1994 season. The owners, led by Congressmen Bob Mrazek and John Bryant, agent Richard Moss, and economist Andrew Zimbalist, proposed a league built on player-owner cooperation. Owners would share 35 percent of pretax revenues with the players on top of a collective 10 percent player share in all teams.

The league eyed international fan bases by placing teams in both Canada and Mexico, with a plan to expand to various Asian countries.[12] The league's 154-game season was set to commence in 1996, but the high hopes fell apart when the league folded.[13]

General Managers' Meeting Quiet

With the free-agent service-time decision still up in the air, the general managers' meeting in Scottsdale, Arizona, on November 16 lacked its usual fervor. Not knowing what kind of economic system they would be operating under or what their respective budgets would be, the GMs had to hold off signing free agents for the time being. For example, the Chicago Cubs stalled on re-signing star first baseman Mark Grace, who filed for free agency prior to the meetings, in case outfielders Sammy Sosa and Glenallen Hill, who fell short of the then-required six years of service time, became eligible due to a restructuring of the system.[14]

Other teams seemed to be operating under similar restrictions. "We're kind of treading water till this new system is in place," said Boston Red Sox general manager Dan Duquette. "Most general managers are waiting to see what the new arrangement will mean."[15]

Even new GMs recognized the bizarre nature of the 1994 meetings. "Coming in as a new general manager," Doug Melvin of the Texas Rangers added, "you want to be aggressive, but now you have to be a little cautious. Without knowing the system, it's a lot tougher than normal."[16]

Melvin shopped around quite a bit for a new home for outfielder Jose Canseco but couldn't find a taker over the three-day span of the meetings. The Houston Astros, likewise, looked to sell off big-ticket stars, including second baseman Craig Biggio and right-handed hurler Doug Drabek.

The sole move of the 1994 general managers' meetings occurred on the last day in Arizona. The Cleveland Indians sent three right-handers—Paul Byrd, Jerry Dipoto, and Dave Mlicki—plus minor-league infielder Jesus Azuaje to the New York Mets in exchange for slugging outfielder Jeromy Burnitz and right-hander Joe Roa. Byrd and Burnitz would make the All-Star Game in 1999, representing the Philadelphia Phillies and Milwaukee Brewers, respectively.

Chaotic Winter Doesn't Affect Trades and Signings

The Texas Rangers completed the first major move of the 1994 offseason just weeks after the close of the general managers' meeting. The Boston Red Sox took the bait and nabbed Jose Canseco in exchange for outfielder Otis Nixon and infielder Luis Ortiz.

The Houston Astros followed with a 12-player deal with the San Diego Padres on December 28. Among the names involved in the trade were third baseman Ken Caminiti and outfielder Steve Finley. Caminiti slugged his way to the MVP Award in 1996 with the Padres while Steve Finley helped the 2001 Arizona Diamondbacks to the World Series championship.[17]

The Los Angeles Dodgers made a splash in the international waters by signing right-hander Hideo Nomo, the first Japanese major-league player to make the jump to the American majors. Nomo took home the Rookie of the Year Award in 1995 with a 13-6 record and a 2.54 ERA.

At an Impasse, Owners Impose Salary Cap

Throughout the last weeks of November, the owners and player representatives gathered again to attempt to settle the strike. Usery once again proposed that the owners postpone the declaration of an impasse and the implementation of a salary cap. In fact, Usery delayed the inevitable until December 23.

The 10-week-old negotiations fell apart when the owners rejected a last-minute proposal from the players. Even Usery admitted defeat: "There was no sense going further tonight and I recessed the negotiations. A deadline was set by owners and it was evident that we weren't going to reach an agreement by that time."[18]

In the week leading up to the final meeting, the owners passed a resolution to allow the executive council to declare an impasse if a deal did not fall into place by December 22. Peter Angelos of the Baltimore Orioles was among the few dissenting voices at the preliminary meeting in Chicago. He called the move "mass financial suicide," a declaration that seemed to hold water when, at the same meeting, the owners learned that the 28 major-league teams owed a collective $600 million.[19]

Both the union and the owners filed charges with the National Labor Relations Board. Union representative Donald Fehr stated, "As the investigation proceeds, we are confident that the board will come to see that the clubs entered into negotiations with no intention of reaching an agreement other than upon the clubs' preconceived terms."[20] The owners, on the other hand, argued that the players refused to negotiate wages on a collective basis, a direct violation of the labor act.

Replacements Cause Further Controversy

As the calendar flipped to 1995, the prospect of spring training filled with unfamiliar faces loomed over the league.[21] The buzz revolved around replacement players who would cross the picket line and suit up in the spring. To preserve solidarity and prevent this from happening, the Major League Baseball Players Association announced that it would impose sanctions on agents who represent any replacement players.

The owners, for their part, drafted and ratified a set of rules governing replacement players. The new guidelines stated that nonprofessional replacement players would be paid $115,000 for the season, and each team could pay up to three former major leaguers with at least three years of experience $275,000. The contracts of current big leaguers who chose to play in the replacement games would be honored as written.[22]

The Players Association strongly suggested that all players listed on teams' 40-man rosters, not just those in the majors at the time of the strike, should abstain from spring training. With the season just a few months away and a settlement possible at any time, striking players struggled to stay in game shape. San Diego Padres outfielder and future Hall of Famer Tony Gwynn commented, "I get 10 or 15 minutes into my workout and sometimes I say, 'The hell with this. They're not going to settle.' It's hard to push yourself when you don't know what's going to happen."[23]

When spring training finally commenced, a motley crew of players took the field. Ken Oberkfell, who made his major-league debut in 1977 and had not played in two years, suited up for the Philadelphia Phillies. The Phillies also featured former major leaguers Jeff Stone (who found work in a steel mill after his baseball career), Todd Cruz, and Marty Bystrom, all in their 30s.

Also among the replacements were a cable-television technician/Pentecostal deacon, a Coca-Cola plant supervisor, and brothers with the monikers "Motorboat" and "Speedboat" Jones.[24]

One of the shining stars of spring training was Pedro Borbon, who stepped in for the Cincinnati Reds. The 48-year-old right-handed pitcher, a member of the Big Red Machine, retired after the 1980 season but continued to pitch in winter ball and in the Dominican Republic. In his spare time, Borbon raised birds in Texas. Borbon, winner of two World Series with the Reds in the 1970s, was the most prominent name on the roster but was released after injuring himself when he slipped while attempting to field a ball.

Joe Girardi, Colorado Rockies player representative, slammed the replacements, saying, "After two or three days of watching UPS drivers trying to play baseball, then what are they going to do? The product is bound to be horrible. It's a slap in the face to the fans to say: 'You will pay for any brand of baseball we put out there.'"[25]

Baltimore Orioles owner Peter Angelos, quickly becoming known as a renegade among the owners, refused to field a team of strikebreakers or play against any team made up of replacements. As a result, all 32 Orioles spring-training games were canceled, and the Orioles instead opted to stage exhibitions between their minor-league affiliates. In the event the strike lingered into the 1995 season, Angelos seemed prepared to forfeit regular-season games.[26]

We, The Owners ...

The following is the owners' announcement that the remainder of the 1994 season would be canceled, and their publicly-stated perception regarding the reasons for the cancellation.

"Whereas the 28 Major League Baseball Clubs ("the Clubs") and the Major League Baseball Players Association ("the MLBPA") have been engaged in collective bargaining over an extended period; and
Whereas, the MLBPA has consistently been unwilling to respond in any meaningful way to the Clubs' need to contain costs and has consistently refused to bargain with the Clubs concerning a division of industry revenues with the players or any other method of establishing aggregate player compensation; and
Whereas, the MLBPA's 33-day strike has caused the cancellation of all games since August 12, 1994, and has made it impossible for the players to resume play at a championship level without a substantial training period.
Now, therefore, be it resolved that:
In order to protect the integrity of the Championship Season, the Division Series, the League Championship Series and the World Series, the 28 clubs have concluded with enormous regret that the remainder of the 1994 season, the Division Series, the League Championship and the World Series must be cancelled and the Clubs will explore all avenues to achieve a meaningful, structural reform of Baseball's player compensation system in an effort to ensure that the 1995 and future Championship Seasons can occur as scheduled and uninterrupted."*

---

* "It's Official. It's Over." *New York Times*, September 15, 1994: B14.

Short-Lived Cap Falls Through

On February 4, a little more than a week before players were to report to spring training, the owners budged. The salary cap implemented by the owners in late December crumpled under threats from the National Labor Relations Board. Had the owners not withdrawn the cap, the NLRB could have filed an injunction against the owners and taken the labor dispute to federal court.

The crux of the issue was the legality of the owners' impasse declaration. The NLRB found that the 25-to-3 vote in Chicago allowing the executive board to declare an impasse on behalf of the owners was unofficial and not a legal basis for the declaration.

The Commissioner Gets Involved

Throughout the offseason meetings, interim Commissioner Bud Selig took a back seat. In late February, though, the overseer and Milwaukee Brewers owner got directly involved in the talks. Selig sat down with Fehr in a series of meetings that spanned the months of February and March. However, the extensive meetings found no common ground, and only the intervention by a federal court would put this conflict to rest.

In a bit of synchronicity, on March 22, the day that owners voted 26 to 2 to use replacement players in the regular season, the NLRB took the side of the Players Association and asked US District Court Judge (and future Supreme Court Justice) Sonia Sotomayor to issue an injunction to restore free-agent bidding and salary arbitration.

Sotomayor granted the injunction on March 31, effectively reinstating the pre-1994 collective-bargaining agreement. In light of the decision, the players extended an offer to end the strike. The offer included a luxury tax in lieu of the salary cap.

"We hope that offer will be accepted and accepted promptly," said Fehr. "If both sides want it to be, this can be an opportunity to bargain this out. It seems to me we need to seize that opportunity."[27]

The owners accepted the agreement on April 2, 1995, and set an April 26 date for Opening Day. The season began without a new collective-bargaining agreement, and in fact a new agreement would not be agreed upon until November 1996. To this day, Major League Baseball remains the only major professional sports league without a salary cap. But the 1995 season began, belatedly, and the experience of the costly strike may have prompted later rounds of collective bargaining to be concluded less acrimoniously. There has not been another work stoppage since the 1994-95 strike.

NOTES

1. Ross Newhan, "Baseball Season, Series Cancelled," *Los Angeles Times*, September 15, 1994: 1.

2. "Players Solidly Behind Strike," *Chicago Tribune*, September 21, 1994: 4.

3. McRae and Boone share more than just their history with the Kansas City Royals; both had the pleasure of managing a son in the major leagues.

4. The 1994 Chicago Cubs season failed on many fronts, illustrated by the sudden retirement of star Ryne Sandberg in mid-June. Sandberg would return to the Cubs for the 1996 and 1997 seasons.

5. Ash would draft All-Stars Roy Halladay, Michael Young, Vernon Wells, and Orlando Hudson.

6. Larry Whiteside, "Baseball Owners Seek a 45-day Freeze," *Boston Globe*, October 5, 1994: 73.

7. According to a January 6 article in the *Washington Post*, only 234 of the 1,069 major-league players were under contract for 1995 and beyond. If all restricted free agents became unrestricted free agents, 835 players would be on the market.

8. Mark Maske, "Ex-Labor Secretary Usery to Mediate Baseball Meetings," *Washington Post*, October 15, 1994.

9. Murray Chass, "Four Players Fire the First Salvo of the Free-Agent Wars," *New York Times*, October 16, 1994.

10. Murray Chass, "A Hint of Hope by Baseball Owners," *New York Times*, October 20, 1994.

11. Murray Chass, "Owners' New Voice Is Peddling Same Line," *New York Times*, November 12, 1994.

12. Murray Chass, "New League Plans Partnership for Clubs and Players," *New York Times*, November 1, 1994.

13. The league folded in April 1996 when Liberty Sports, the television station with whom the UBL had a deal, merged with

BASEBALL'S BUSINESS: THE WINTER MEETINGS

Fox. See "United League Strikes Out," *Gainesville Sun*, April 12, 1996: 2C.

14 Jerome Holtzman, "Between Rounds of Golf, GMs Plan for the Future," *Chicago Tribune*, November 15, 1994.

15 Murray Chass, "Traders Can't Shuffle Their Decks," *New York Times*, November 17, 1994.

16 Ibid.

17 The full deal found the Astros sending shortstop Andujar Cedeño, infielder-outfielder Roberto Petagine, right-hander Brian Williams and a player to be named (who became left-hander Sean Fesh), plus Caminiti and Finley to the Padres, while San Diego shipped outfielder Derek Bell, right-handed pitcher Doug Brocail, infielder Ricky Gutierrez, left-hander Pedro Martinez (not the Hall of Famer), outfielder Phil Plantier, and Australian-born infielder Craig Shipley.

18 Murray Chass, "Baseball Owners Implement a Cap on Players' Pay," *New York Times*. December 23, 1994. [If you can find the chart, perhaps on library microfilm, that could be interesting, but otherwise we can live without it.]

19 Mark Maske, "Even Owners Split on Baseball's Direction," *Washington Post*, December 25, 1994.

20 Murray Chass, "Players and Owners File Complaints With Labor Board," *New York Times*, December 28, 1994.

21 Several big-name players started their career as replacements. As a result, their likenesses and names were banned by the Players Association from licensed merchandise. Additionally, World Series winners Shane Spencer (New York Yankees), Damian Miller (Arizona Diamondbacks), Brendan Donnelly (Anaheim Angels), and Kevin Millar (Boston Red Sox) were banned from commemorative championship merchandise.

22 Mark Maske, "Replacement Rules Approved," *Washington Post*, January 14, 1995.

23 Chuck Johnson, "Players Work to Stay Fit, Focused During Negotiations," *USA Today*, February 3, 1995.

24 Tom Verducci, "The Sham Spring," *Sports Illustrated*, February 23, 2015.

25 Ross Newhan, "Strike Throws Curve Into Start of Spring Training Baseball," *Los Angeles Times*, February 16, 1995.

26 Mark Maske, "Orioles' Opponents Pull Out of Games," *Washington Post*, March 1, 1995: F01.

27 Mark Maske, "Baseball Players Offer to End Strike," *Washington Post*, April 1, 1995: A01.

— 1995 —
INTERLEAGUE PLAY: INNOVATION OR ABOMINATION?

By Paul D. Brown

THE BASEBALL WINTER MEETINGS are usually a time when teams reflect on the past season and plan for the next season. However, 1995 was in the middle of a five-year stretch when major-league baseball did not attend the winter meetings. Instead, the majors held general managers' meetings in November in Scottsdale, Arizona, and owners meetings in November and January. Additionally, the general managers were invited to attend the January 1996 owners meeting held in Los Angeles. This was the first time the GMs and owners met at the same site since the majors stopped attending the annual Winter Meetings.[1] The minor leagues conducted their meeting in December, also in Los Angeles.

The 1995 major-league season was unique in that it consisted of only 144 games because of the players strike, which had begun on August 12, 1994, and lasted until April 2, 1995, when the strike was suspended. The work stoppage resulted in the cancellation of the final months of the 1994 season and the World Series. The 1995 season began on April 25, and it was the first season of expanded playoffs which added a first-round Division Series in each league. In 1994, both the American and National Leagues divided into three divisions instead of two and would have added a wild-card team to the playoffs had the postseason not been canceled due to the strike. In 1995, the Braves, Reds, and Dodgers were divisional champions in the NL and were joined by the Rockies as the wild card, while the AL saw the Red Sox, Indians, and Mariners win their divisions while the Yankees joined them as the wild card.

The Atlanta Braves won the 1995 World Series, defeating the Cleveland Indians in six games. To reach the Series, the Braves swept the Cincinnati Reds in the National League Championship Series. The Braves were in the midst of a 14-year playoff run that began in 1991 and ended in 2006.[2] However, 1995 was their only World Series championship. Cleveland, meanwhile, defeated the Seattle Mariners in six games in the American League Championship Series. For the Indians, this was the first of five consecutive seasons in which they qualified for the playoffs.

Barry Larkin of the Reds was the National League Most Valuable Player and Mo Vaughn of the Red Sox was the American League MVP. Greg Maddux of the Braves and Randy Johnson of the Mariners were the Cy Young Award winners. Don Baylor of the Rockies and Lou Piniella of the Mariners were named Managers of the Year. The Rookies of the Year were Hideo Nomo of the Dodgers and Marty Cordova of the Twins.

The meeting season, beginning with the gathering of general managers in November and ending with the owners' meeting in January, can be considered the apex of the "Hot Stove League." It is during this time that top free agents are signed, trades are made, and rosters begin to be finalized for the coming season. Between November 1, 1995, and January 31, 1996, 272 players signed contracts, either to return to their current team or with a new club. In that same period, 142 players were granted free agency. (It should be noted that 210 players had already been granted free agency in October.) Of the 272 free agents signed during the meeting season, 39 were recent (1993 and 1994), current, or future All-Stars. Seven were future Hall of Famers: Wade Boggs re-signed with the Yankees; Paul Molitor signed with the Twins; Eddie Murray re-signed with the Indians; Craig Biggio re-signed with the Astros; Roberto Alomar was signed by the Orioles; Rickey Henderson signed with the Padres; and Andre Dawson re-signed with the Marlins.

The meeting season can also witness several trades and 1995 was no different. From November 1, 1995, through January 31, 1996, there were 29 deals involving 24 teams and 89 players. Of the 89 players involved, 11 were recent, current or future All-Stars. The most significant name was that of Hall of Fame outfielder Tim Raines, who was traded from the White Sox to the Yankees for a player who never made the major leagues, right-handed pitcher and third baseman Blaise Kozeniewski. At age 37, Raines was no longer the game-changing player he had been, but he continued to be a part-time player for six more seasons (he did not play in 2000). Raines's last game was in 2002 with the Marlins.

Although the major leagues did not attend the December winter meetings in Los Angeles, the Rule 5 draft was held on December 4, and 17 players were drafted by 15 teams, with both the Tigers and Rangers selecting two players each.[3] Of the 17 players drafted, eight made the majors at some point in their careers. Only two of those players, however, appeared in more than 200 games, and one other pitched only one inning in his major-league career.[4]

During the GM meetings, held in November, *The Sporting News* presented the Major League Baseball Executive of the Year Award for the second year in a row to John Hart, general manager of the Cleveland Indians.[5]

During the Minor League meetings, held in December, *Baseball America* announced its awards for the previous season. The awards and winners were:

Major League Organization of Year — New York Mets.

Major League Rookie of Year — Hideo Nomo, Los Angeles Dodgers.

Minor League Player of Year — Andruw Jones, Macon Braves.

Minor League Organization of Year — Norfolk, International League (Mets).

Minor League Manager of Year — Marc Bombard, Indianapolis (Reds).

Bob Freitas Award:
    Albuquerque, Pacific Coast, AAA.
    Midland, Texas, AA.
    Kane County, Midwest, A.[6]

Baseball America also named Todd Helton of the University of Tennessee as the 1995 College Player of the Year.[7] Helton was the eighth overall pick in the amateur draft, selected by the Rockies. He played in the majors for 17 years and was an All-Star five times.

In addition to the *Baseball America* awards, the minor leagues also give out their own annual honors in Los Angeles:

John H. Johnson President's Award	Columbus Clippers (International).
Larry MacPhail Trophy	Kane County (Midwest).
Warren Giles Award	John Hopkins, Carolina League.
Rawlings Woman Executive of the Year	Mary Cain, Portland (Northwest).
King of Baseball	Gene DaCosse, Los Angeles.

While the free-agent signings, trades, Rule 5 draft, and awards occur every year at the Winter Meetings, the 1995 meeting season proved to be unique and historic because, at the January owners' meeting in Los Angeles, the executive committee recommended a fundamental change to major-league baseball and its scheduling. The committee approved a proposal for interleague play to begin with the 1997 season.

"The plan initially calls for a National League club to play three or four games against each American League club in its corresponding division, bunching them around the Memorial Day and Labor Day holidays," *The Sporting News* reported. "Division matchups would rotate year by year, so that once every three years, for instance, the Rockies would play the Mariners."[8]

As owner of the Brewers, Bud Selig had also supported the concept back in the 1970s.[9]

Standing in the way of full implementation, however, was one little thing—the lack of a basic agreement between the owners and players. This was the problem that caused the cancellation of the end of the 1994 regular season and the postseason, and also shortened the 1995 season. However, Donald Fehr, executive director of the players union, was not opposed to the idea. The designated-hitter rule was also seen as a possible obstacle to interleague play, although it had not been a problem in the World Series.[10]

Thus the 1995 series of Winter Meetings, culminating with the gathering of the owners in January, would ultimately have a profound effect on baseball. Indeed, one could argue that it ushered in the biggest change in the game since the American League adopted the designated-hitter rule. No more would a champion in either league be decided solely by games played within that league. No more would the World Series be quite as singular as it had been among American sports—previous participants had not faced each other during the regular season; that now could change. For better or worse, baseball had dramatically changed.

NOTES

1. Murray Chass, "Baseball; Majors' G.M.'s Meet, Greet and Then Retreat," *New York Times*, January 17, 2006. nytimes.com/1996/01/17/sports/baseball-majors-gm-s-meet-greet-and-then-retreat.html, accessed November 12, 2015.

2. It might have been 15 straight years, but the postseason was canceled in 1994 due to the strike.

3. baseball-reference.com/bullpen/1995_Rule_V_Draft, accessed January 11, 2016.

4. baseball-reference.com/players/, accessed January 20, 2016. The two players with over 200 games were Kim Batiste and Kimera Bartee. The pitcher was John Ratliff, who pitched one perfect inning for the A's in 2000.

5. Barry M. Bloom, "Shapiro Tabbed as TSN's Top Exec," mlb.com, November 6, 2015, m.mlb.com/news/article/2293450, accessed September 30, 2015.

6. baseballamerica.com/news/baseball-america-awards/, accessed November 5, 2015.

7. Ibid.

8. Steve Marantz, "The Americanational League," *The Sporting News*, January 29, 1996: 38.

9. Ibid.

10. Steve Marantz, "The Americanational League," *The Sporting News*, January 29, 1996: 39.

— 1996 —
THE YEAR THAT BROUGHT LABOR PEACE

By Chip Greene

IN 1996, FOR THE FIRST TIME IN THREE years, major-league baseball played a full 162-game season.

Few pennant chases in the game's history had ever matched the drama brought by the final pitch of the last complete campaign, when the Toronto Blue Jays' Joe Carter crushed a dramatic three-run home run against the Philadelphia Phillies' Mitch Williams in the bottom of the ninth inning of the 1993 World Series, to deliver Toronto's second consecutive world championship.

But even as Carter's heroics were still reverberating throughout the sport, storm clouds of rancor and mistrust were forming which would lead to one of the most ignominious events in baseball history—the only cancellation of a World Series in the game's annals.[1]

Volumes have been written about the 1994 baseball strike and its aftermath; the reader will find nothing new here. What's significant for the purposes of this essay, however, is to recall that the cancellation of the strike in the spring of 1995 and the subsequent shortened regular season failed to bring about labor peace. After all, the owners hadn't gotten what they wanted, namely a salary cap, and they'd been denied in their efforts to field replacement players. Therefore, while the owners' resentment still simmered, the 1995 season was played without a new collective-bargaining agreement, and the games simply resumed under the old contract, which had expired at the end of 1993.

In 1996, the game finally returned to normal ... to a degree. On the field the New York Yankees won their first pennant in 15 years, but on the business side, nothing had changed, with the season again having been played without a new CBA. And as the offseason commenced, many owners, still agitated, proposed to prolong the labor dispute until the institution of a salary cap. Eventually a majority of the owners realized that it was better to negotiate a new agreement than to continue to play under the old one.[2] Thus, with the conclusion of the playing season, the two sides returned to the bargaining table and tried once again to hammer out something that was agreeable to both sides.

Nothing that took place during that offseason—not a blockbuster trade, a spectacular free agent signing, or even a rookie phenom in the winter leagues—could possibly have been as important to the game's long-term health as a new CBA. Yet at first it appeared negotiations were going to proceed as they had over the previous four years: intransigence that would result in both sides leaving the table. But then, finally, came a glimmer of good news: In the first week of November, Randy Levine, the owners' chief negotiator, and Don Fehr of the players union announced they had finally reached a tentative agreement. Levine took it to the owners ... and they summarily rejected it, citing their dissatisfaction with a few of the provisions.[3] Levine and Fehr steadfastly returned to discussions.

It took several more weeks, but ultimately a deal was done. After four years of acrimony, name-calling, and alienation of the fans, the owners agreed on November 27, in Chicago, to a revised deal, "contingent on resolution of several minor issues,"[4] notably, how to divvy up $2.5 million in postseason bonus money and agreeing upon the qualification dates for 14 players who would gain their rights to free agency. Now, all that remained was for the players to ratify the agreement at their executive-board meeting, to be held in Dorado, Puerto

Rico. It would be up to the Players Executive Council to bring an end to the labor dispute.[5]

On December 5, after several last-minute changes to the agreement, and by a unanimous vote, the Major League Baseball Players Association ratified the agreement.[6] With the lengthy ordeal finally resolved, the principals in the negotiations were each, quite naturally, relieved. "With this unfortunate period behind us," proclaimed an exhausted Fehr, from Puerto Rico, "my fellow players and I can once again focus on the game on the field. We are confident that baseball's best days lie ahead."[7]

Likewise, Levine, expressed gratification with the agreement, noting the efforts of all those involved in the process. "I want to congratulate Don Fehr, the other lawyers and the players on this new contract. It was a lot of hard work by people. Now the owners and players have a chance to work in a real partnership. And that's good for baseball."[8]

Lastly, acting Commissioner Bud Selig offered a thankful but cautionary sentiment as well, noting, "One has to be satisfied that we've made progress. But there is much to be done. The concerns people have about the game are legitimate. When you think back to everything that has happened, this deal reflects a lot of the activity and hopes by both sides. Now it's up to us all to move forward."[9] (Reportedly, Fehr believed that the best way to move forward would be without Selig. At least one newspaper reported that "Fehr called on Selig to resign as quickly as possible to allow for a permanent successor."[10] Little could Fehr have realized that by the time Selig finally left the game in January 2015, Fehr would already be four years into his tenure as executive director of the NHL Players Association, and he would also lead those players into a work stoppage.)

The 1994 strike had been the eighth in 23 seasons. While there was nothing to prohibit future labor actions, the ratification of the new CBA at least precluded any through the year 2000. It also ushered in a radical change on the field, which would take place the following season. Beginning on June 12, 1997, baseball would introduce interleague play on an experimental basis when four National League West Division teams would visit four American League West parks. In the initial version of the CBA, the deal allowed for interleague play only in 1997. However, in the final ratified version, it was stipulated that if the owners agreed to a limit of up to 16 games per team in 1997, the players would then agree to extend interleague play into the 1998 season as well.[11] During interleague games the lineups would be configured according to the rules of the home team, meaning that the designated hitter would be used in American League parks, and pitchers would bat when the National League club was at home. If the owners wanted to expand the schedule beyond 16 games in 1998, though, they would have to allow the designated hitter in all interleague games.

If the introduction of interleague play was going to produce a new look on the field, most of the CBA's other provisions were undoubtedly written in sentences that contained numerous dollar signs. In an effort to address the payroll disparity by increasing revenue-sharing among all teams, the high-revenue teams agreed to forfeit a higher percentage of the profits they generated from local broadcast and ticket money. Also, a 35 percent luxury tax was imposed on the portion of payrolls that exceeded $51 million for the five teams spending the most on players.[12] (In what was seen by his fellow owners as the epitome of hypocrisy, on November 19, before an agreement was reached, Jerry Reinsdorf of the Chicago White Sox, one of the owners most opposed to the players union, signed power-hitting free-agent outfielder Albert Belle to a five-year, $55 million contract, which drew the ire of many of Reinsdorf's fellow owners. That size contract, they railed, was just the type of salary they were trying to eliminate.) In a corresponding gesture by the players, they agreed to reduce their share of money awarded from the first three games of each first-round playoff series from 80 percent to 60 percent, the difference to be deposited into an escrow account. Their minimum salary, however, would increase from $109,000 to $150,000 in 1997.

By the time the CBA was ratified, the free-agent filing period had ended. One provision, though, added 14 free agents to those who had already filed. Those 14, who included such well-known players as left-handed pitcher Jimmy Key, right-hander Alex Fernandez and outfielder Moises Alou, were given credit for service time during the 75 regular-season days that were canceled by the strike, an action that made each one a free agent. And all three went on to sign rich new contracts. Key left the Yankees for a two-year, $7.8 million deal with the Orioles, while Fernandez and Alou signed with Miami. Fernandez got $35 million over five years to leave the White Sox, and Alou agreed to leave Montreal for $25 million over five years.[13] Much to the chagrin of the owners, the players' salaries just kept climbing.

While in the fall of 1996 the CBA ratification in Puerto Rico grabbed the lion's share of the headlines, there was still other baseball business taking place. On Friday, December 6, at Boston's Hynes Convention Center, the National Association of Professional Baseball Leagues, the minor-league association, began their 95th annual winter meetings (which ran through December 10). Initially, in keeping with the prohibition instituted after the 1992 meeting by acting Commissioner Selig, no major-league participation was expected. However, after aggressive lobbying by Boston Red Sox CEO John Harrington (whose team was co-hosting the event), Selig reversed his decision and allowed major-league general managers to attend the winter meetings. "It's an individual club decision," Selig said of his reversal. "It's only if they want to."[14] Only the Orioles, Red Sox, Pirates, and Blue Jays confirmed that they would be in attendance.

With major-league representatives few and far between, minor-league business came to the forefront, with 219 clubs, representing 19 minor leagues, converging on the Hynes Center. Of the 219 clubs, 155, members of 15 leagues, were affiliated with a major-league club. With the Professional Baseball Agreement scheduled to expire after the 1997 season, "movement [was] under way to put all 219 teams under the major league umbrella."[15]

Minor-league business was booming. The labor turmoil of the past three seasons had, understandably, cut into major-league attendance, but in 1996 the minors had drawn 33 million fans, their highest total since 1949, when 448 teams represented 59 cities.

Now, as part of a planned Eastern League expansion, several cities sought franchises and arrived in Boston to eagerly present their case. Eventually the finalists were winnowed to Austin, Texas; Lexington, Kentucky; Springfield, Missouri; Springfield, Massachusetts; and Erie, Pennsylvania, and officials chose the latter two to join the Double-A Eastern League, beginning with the 1999 season.[16]

If, as the press suggested before the event, the lack of major-league participation had made the "Winter Meetings just not what they used to be,"[17] the NAPBL gathering had still undoubtedly been a rousing success.

Since some very important business remained to be completed, one final meeting took place after the 1996 season. On March 9, 1995, in West Palm Beach, Florida, the owners had voted unanimously to make the Arizona Diamondbacks and Tampa Bay Devil Rays the 14th and 15th expansion teams in major-league history. The two teams were slated to begin play in 1998 and now, as the owners met in Scottsdale, Arizona, during the second week of January 1997, it was time to decide which league each team would join.

The process turned out to be more difficult than was probably expected. Coming into the meetings, the anticipated plan was for Arizona to join the National League, with Tampa Bay going to the American. And on Tuesday, January 14, the ruling executive council voted to recommend that plan. However, as a preliminary to the council's official vote, in a straw poll taken the next evening, the American League owners surprisingly voted 8 to 6 to reject the proposal, threatening to block the league assignments. That decision set off a lengthy round of debates.[18]

The following day, the owners met jointly for nine hours. As the proceedings got underway, the reason for the AL's negative vote soon became clear. If Tampa Bay joined the American League, it was noted, the Devil Rays would be the only team in the Southeast. That raised concerns among some AL teams that they would have to play additional games outside their own time zone, a prospect that would "cause early and late TV starts that would decrease ratings and revenue."[19]

As the talks progressed, AL owners repeatedly broke away and huddled. With interleague play scheduled to begin in 1997, some teams suggested that the proposed interleague schedule might be modified for 1998. Currently, that schedule called for each NL East team to play three games against each AL East team; each league's Central Division teams to do the same; and for NL and AL West teams to play a two-game home-and-home series. Once the expansion teams joined, it was further suggested, the NL East teams might play either the AL Central or West; the NL Central could play either the AL East or West; and the NL West might play the AL East or Central.[20]

It was also suggested that more interleague games might be designated in each time zone, resulting in annual games between, for example, the New York Mets and Yankees, the Chicago Cubs and White Sox, the San Francisco Bay-area teams, and other natural rivalries. This called for scheduling creativity, which had never before been an option.

In short order, the AL owners who had vetoed the earlier proposal came around to endorse the plan. Early on Thursday the Yankees, Blue Jays, and Anaheim Angels—among the eight clubs that had voted originally no—changed their votes; later that afternoon, the Chicago White Sox, Seattle Mariners, and Oakland A's also voiced their approval.[21] The impetus for those teams to change their votes had been an agreement among the owners to establish a committee, to be chaired by Red Sox CEO John Harrington, that would examine realignment and the schedule format for 1998. Potentially, a recommendation could be made for some teams to switch leagues, too, although the league constitutions prohibited any club from being forced to switch leagues against its will. The committee agreed to report back to the group by June 30, with the owners casting a vote by September 30.[22]

In the end, with 11 votes in each league needed to approve the league assignments for the two new teams, the National League voted 14 to 0 to put Tampa Bay in the American League and Arizona in the National League. The AL vote was 12 to 2, as Kansas City and Texas remained in opposition. In 1998, major-league baseball would, for the first time, have 30 teams.

While the fate of the expansion teams had absorbed much of the owners' time that week in January, the meetings had also produced one other notable discussion. In September 1992, the owners had forced the resignation of Commissioner Fay Vincent. Since then, the sport had been without a permanent commissioner, with Milwaukee Brewers' owner Bud Selig serving as the acting commissioner. So as the meetings began on Tuesday night, January 15, the search for a replacement commissioner had been one of the main items on the agenda. Selig reportedly wasn't interested. Perhaps the other owners could change his mind.

Commissioner, Commissioner Not

After the bitter battle for a labor agreement, there were mixed feelings regarding whether Bud Selig should remain commissioner, with many off-the-record statements and opinions about who should be able to offer an opinion. The following quotes represent some of the more public statements on the topic.*

"I think a change should take place and will take place within the next six months. The change should be a graceful one. In some respects, he was an effective commissioner in that he could communicate with the clubs in an effective manner. He's taken so much [stuff] over the past few years, he deserves a graceful exit. [But] there's an inherent conflict in having an owner be the commissioner, and I think we need to get someone from outside baseball who hasn't been tarnished by what went on."

—Unnamed baseball executive

"As long as Bud Selig, with his reputation, remains in any central baseball administrative role, that will be a great impediment to baseball's recovery. We need a full-time CEO who actually spends full time running the business, that has experience running a large business and can command the respect of the fans and the corporate advertising community. A new commissioner is absolutely necessary for the recovery process to continue."

—Don Fehr, executive director, MLBPA

"The notion that there will be any cooperation between this office and that office while Bud is commissioner is fantasy."

—Unnamed Players Association source

"I have said that all along, and I haven't changed my mind."

—Bud Selig, in response to the idea that he wouldn't take the commissioner job

"I think he is going to wind up as commissioner, whether he wants it or not."

—Unnamed management official

"That's counterproductive for Don to say that. Now some people will want to keep [Selig] just to [anger] Don."

—Unnamed owner

---

* Mark Maske, "On the Heels of Labor Harmony, Some Commissioner's Shoes to Fill," *Washington Post*, January 11, 1997: F7. See also Maske, "Baseball's Executive Decision," *Washington Post*, January 15, 1997: C2.

NOTES

1. There was no postseason series in 1904, but this was not a cancellation. The first of what we now know as the World Series was played in 1903 between the Boston Americans and Pittsburgh Pirates, by agreement between the two pennant-winners. The Americans won the American League pennant again in 1904, but the New York Giants, who won in the National League, refused to play them in a postseason series.
2. Larry Whiteside, "Players' Ratification Brings Baseball Peace," *Boston Globe*, December 6, 1996: E7.
3. Ronald Blum, Associated Press, *The Capital* (Annapolis, Maryland), December 6, 1996.
4. Whiteside.
5. Ibid.
6. Associated Press, *The Capital* (Annapolis, Maryland), December 6, 1996.
7. Whiteside.
8. Ibid.
9. Ibid.
10. Blum.
11. Whiteside.
12. Ibid.
13. Blum.
14. Associated Press, *Lawrence* (Kansas) *Journal World*, December 3, 1996.
15. Whiteside.
16. Ibid.
17. Associated Press, *Daily Herald Suburban* (Chicago), December 1, 1996.
18. Associated Press, *Burlington* (Iowa) *Hawkeye,* January 17, 1997.
19. Ibid.
20. Ibid.
21. Associated Press, *Joplin* (Missouri) *Globe,* January 17, 1997.
22. Ibid.

— 1997 —
MINOR-LEAGUE CHANGES, MAJOR-LEAGUE IMPACT

By Jessica Frank

ON THE AFTERNOON OF SATURDAY, December 14, 1996, a 700-foot, 70,000-ton bulk cargo ship, fully loaded with grain, lost engine power and glided ominously toward a shopping mall along New Orleans' Mississippi River. Acting quickly, the cool-headed pilot dropped his anchors in an attempt to slow the massive vessel and blasted the emergency horn. As people on shore scrambled frantically, he managed to veer around two docked cruise ships and a floating casino before smacking into a busy section of the mall. Shops and restaurants were demolished by the crushing impact. The Riverside Hilton evacuated 180 of its 460 rooms, reporting major harm to 20. Rescue workers combed the 200-foot swath of mangled steel beams and rubble, prepared for tragedy. But while as many as 140 people needed treatment, most of the injuries were surprisingly minor and there were no deaths. Financial casualties were another story, with damage to the ship listed at over $1.8 million, and reconstruction of the Riverwalk estimated at over $15 million.

OPENING SESSION FIREBRAND

One year later, Will Lingo of *Baseball America* sat in Grand Salon A at the repaired Riverside Hilton and couldn't resist making a comparison. The Opening General Session of the 96th annual Baseball Winter Meetings was underway and, like the ship's pilot, National Association Vice President Stan Brand was sounding his own alarm, trying to alert minor-league executives to impending financial disaster.[1]

Baseball's longstanding antitrust exemption was under attack, he reminded them, and the possibility of repeal was perilously close.

With little going on at this year's meetings, Brand, a Washington-based lawyer who had made the antitrust exemption his primary focus, had an unusually large audience. In an ardent, fiery address, he laid out the danger, and called on the National Association members for a full-throated defense.[2] A brief clause inserted in the December 1996 Collective Bargaining Agreement (CBA) had sparked this most recent threat. In an unanticipated stipulation, owners and the union had committed to petition Congress for a partial repeal that would permit major-league players to file antitrust lawsuits but leave the exemption otherwise intact.[3]

Congress had jumped on the invitation.

In an article evaluating the eventual legislation, Gary R. Roberts explained that since the mid-1950s, various congressmen and senators had regularly proposed bills to undo the Supreme Court's precedent-setting 1922 *Federal Baseball* decision.[4] Normally, such bills failed quickly. But this time, with the pre-approved support of the players union and major-league owners, Congress saw a chance at easy bipartisan success.[5] As soon as the new CBA was in effect, Senator Orrin G. Hatch (R-Utah) and co-sponsoring Senators Patrick J. Leahy (D-Vermont), Strom Thurmond (R-South Carolina), and Daniel Patrick Moynihan (D-New York) worked swiftly to formulate S.53, the Curt Flood Act of 1997. By October 29, 1997 the bill had advanced out of committee and was headed toward a floor vote.[6]

But the minor leagues, who had not been involved in drafting the CBA, were fiercely opposed.[7] The major and minor leagues were a complex, intertwined network, and the minors depended on subsidies from their major-league affiliates. The NAPBL had no tolerance for any change that might weaken the system.[8]

At the opening session, Brand questioned the motives behind the bill and challenged its objective, discounting the right to sue as "an empty threat." Only a year earlier, the Supreme Court had ruled against NFL players in a similar case, he said, establishing that as long as a collective bargaining agreement was in effect, players would be required to take the "radical and disruptive step" of decertifying as a labor union before filing an antitrust lawsuit.[9]

Meanwhile, he was acutely concerned about a likely assault on the amateur draft and reserve clause - the cornerstone for the multimillion-dollar player-development system.[10] Union leader Donald Fehr and the Players Association had a secret strategy, Brand claimed, "to break the amateur draft and redirect the money allocated to the minor leagues to those players and the agents representing them."[11] He feared the current bill was a "Trojan horse" for just such a maneuver, despite language specifically included to shield the minors.[12]

After meeting with Brand in June, Major League Baseball's Executive Council had pledged to pull its support for the bill unless the minor leagues were satisfactorily protected.[13] It was in their interest to stay on friendly terms. If Brand was successful, either the antitrust exemption would be upheld completely, or its most important elements would be preserved, including issues of franchise relocation, control over the minor leagues, and broadcasting and licensing rights.[14] Unfortunately, Brand recounted, when he asked Senator Hatch to postpone a June 17 hearing in order to give the National Association time to draft additional protections, the request had been "summarily denied."[15] Fighting further in committee would be fruitless, he said, describing the members' attitude as stonewalling and noninclusive.[16]

He told the minor-league officials that by working together they still had a chance to protect their industry.[17] Composed of 175 teams scattered throughout the country, most with well-established ties to their communities, the National Association had the ear of hundreds of congressmen.[18] Brand pressed them to make their case. Small towns across America benefited from minor-league baseball, and the antitrust exemption resulted in "increased baseball product at cheaper prices," he argued, cautioning they would need to "stand fast."[19] "This won't be an easy fight," he said. "Defeating a committee recommendation is not an everyday occurrence. It will require a well-organized, sustained and unrelenting effort, and I will be calling on each and every one of you to participate."[20]

Over the next year, in what was described by Gary Roberts as "a long, rancorous, and difficult process,"[21] Brand and the NAPBL battled to ensure that the burgeoning legislation would not ruin their business. Their wide-reaching influence proved to be a powerful weapon. "[T]here was virtually no chance of any bill affecting baseball's antitrust exclusion ever getting to the House floor without the support of the NAPBL," Roberts wrote.[22]

On October 27, 1998, amended with multiple minor-league protections, the Curt Flood Act of 1998 was signed by President William J. Clinton.

Roberts assessed the effect of the amendments in his conclusion:

"[T]he ensuing protections for baseball, and especially the minor leagues, that were put into the Act ... actually expand the scope and strength of the antitrust immunity in most respects and leave it largely unaffected in the major league player-labor market. Thus, legislation that started out to apply antitrust more broadly to baseball has probably caused exactly the opposite effect."[23]

BOOM OR BUST

National Association president Mike Moore also used his opening session platform to issue a warning. If the minor leagues wanted to avoid an economic collapse when the boom ended, he said, they would need to develop a "vision."[24] It was time to take a serious look at their industry and figure out where they wanted to go.[25] For the past 10 years, the financial worth of many teams had been swelling faster than their operating profits. With fewer and fewer buyers willing to pay inflated prices, franchise values were bound to drop.[26] And while some clubs were thriving, others were barely keeping up.

CURT FLOOD ACT OF 1998

Public Law 105-297 105th Congress

An Act

To require the general application of the antitrust laws to major league baseball, and for other purposes. Be it enacted by the Senate and House of Representatives of the United States of America in Congress assembled,

SECTION 1. SHORT TITLE.

This Act may be cited as the "Curt Flood Act of 1998."

SEC. 2. PURPOSE.

It is the purpose of this legislation to state that major league baseball players are covered under the antitrust laws (i.e., that major league baseball players will have the same rights under the antitrust laws as do other professional athletes, e.g., football and basketball players), along with a provision that makes it clear that the passage of this Act does not change the application of the antitrust laws in any other context or with respect to any other person or entity.

SEC. 3. APPLICATION OF THE ANTITRUST LAWS TO PROFESSIONAL MAJOR LEAGUE BASEBALL.

The Clayton Act (15 U.S.C. § 12 et seq.) is amended by adding at the end the following new section:

"SEC. 27. (a) Subject to subsections (b) through (d), the conduct, acts, practices, or agreements of persons in the business of organized professional major league baseball directly relating to or affecting employment of major league baseball players to play baseball at the major league level are subject to the antitrust laws to the same extent such conduct, acts, practices, or agreements would be subject to the antitrust laws if engaged in by persons in any other professional sports business affecting interstate commerce.

"(b) No court shall rely on the enactment of this section as a basis for changing the application of the antitrust laws to any conduct, acts, practices, or agreements other than those set forth in subsection (a). This section does not create, permit or imply a cause of action by which to challenge under the antitrust laws, or otherwise apply the antitrust laws to, any conduct, acts, practices, or agreements that do not directly relate to or affect employment of major league baseball players to play baseball at the major league level, including but not limited to—

"(1) any conduct, acts, practices, or agreements of persons engaging in, conducting or participating in the business of organized professional baseball relating to or affecting employment to play baseball at the minor league level, any organized professional baseball amateur or first-year player draft, or any reserve clause as applied to minor league players;

"(2) the agreement between organized professional major league baseball teams and the teams of the National Association of Professional Baseball Leagues, commonly known as the 'Professional Baseball Agreement', the relationship between organized professional major league baseball and organized professional minor league baseball, or any other matter relating to organized professional baseball's minor leagues;

"(3) any conduct, acts, practices, or agreements of persons engaging in, conducting or participating in the business of organized professional baseball relating to or affecting franchise expansion, location or relocation, franchise ownership issues, including ownership transfers, the relationship between the Office of the Commissioner and franchise owners, the marketing or sales of the entertainment product of organized professional baseball and the licensing of intellectual property rights owned or held by organized professional baseball teams individually or collectively;

"(4) any conduct, acts, practices, or agreements protected by Public Law 87-331 (15 U.S.C. § 1291 et seq.) (commonly known as the 'Sports Broadcasting Act of 1961');

"(5) the relationship between persons in the business of organized professional baseball and umpires or other individuals who are employed in the business of organized professional baseball by such persons; or

"(6) any conduct, acts, practices, or agreements of persons not in the business of organized professional major league baseball.

"(c) Only a major league baseball player has standing to sue under this section. For the purposes of this section, a major league baseball player is –

"(1) a person who is a party to a major league player's contract, or is playing baseball at the major league level; or

"(2) a person who was a party to a major league player's contract or playing baseball at the major league level at the time of the injury that is the subject of the complaint; or

"(3) a person who has been a party to a major league player's contract or who has played baseball at the major league level, and who claims he has been injured in his efforts to secure a subsequent major league player's contract by an alleged violation of the antitrust laws: Provided however, That for the purposes of this paragraph, the alleged antitrust violation shall not include any conduct, acts, practices, or agreements of persons in the business of organized professional baseball relating to or affecting employment to play baseball at the minor league level, including any organized professional baseball amateur or first-year player draft, or any reserve clause as applied to minor league players; or

"(4) a person who was a party to a major league player's contract or who was playing baseball at the major league level at the conclusion of the last full championship season immediately preceding the expiration of the last collective bargaining agreement between persons in the business of organized professional major league baseball and the exclusive collective bargaining representative of major league baseball players. 112 STAT. 2826 PUBLIC LAW 105-297—OCT. 27, 1998 LEGISLATIVE HISTORY—S. 53: SENATE REPORTS: No. 105-118 (Comm. on the Judiciary). CONGRESSIONAL RECORD, Vol. 144 (1998): July 30, considered and passed Senate. Oct. 7, considered and passed House. WEEKLY COMPILATION OF PRESIDENTIAL DOCUMENTS, Vol. 34 (1998): Oct. 27, Presidential statement. Æ

"(d)(1) As used in this section, 'person' means any entity, including an individual, partnership, corporation, trust or unincorporated association or any combination or association thereof. As used in this section, the National Association of Professional Baseball Leagues, its member leagues and the clubs of those leagues, are not 'in the business of organized professional major league baseball'.

"(2) In cases involving conduct, acts, practices, or agreements that directly relate to or affect both employment of major league baseball players to play baseball at the major league level and also relate to or affect any other aspect of organized professional baseball, including but not limited to employment to play baseball at the minor league level and the other areas set forth in subsection (b), only those components, portions or aspects of such conduct, acts, practices, or agreements that directly relate to or affect employment of major league players to play baseball at the major league level may be challenged under subsection (a) and then only to the extent that they directly relate to or affect employment of major league baseball players to play baseball at the major league level.

"(3) As used in subsection (a), interpretation of the term 'directly' shall not be governed by any interpretation of section 151 et seq. of title 29, United States Code (as amended).

"(4) Nothing in this section shall be construed to affect the application to organized professional baseball of the nonstatutory labor exemption from the antitrust laws.

"(5) The scope of the conduct, acts, practices, or agreements covered by subsection (b) shall not be strictly or narrowly construed.".

Approved October 27, 1998.

1 United States Congress. Senate. Committee on the Judiciary. Curt Flood Act of 1998. October 27, 1998 [S53].

Anxious to come up with solutions before the likely slowdown in three to four years, Moore asked for a committee of league officials and presidents to review the records and capital expenses of all the clubs and identify those that might be in danger of facing financial trouble.

And he implored the clubs to shed their greedy tendencies and develop some answers at the league level. "You are not operators of isolated competitive businesses," he reminded them, "You are partners in a joint venture. Those of you operating highly profitable clubs can't make a dime if the other clubs in your league fold."[27]

Earlier in the day, the National Association's vice president of administration, Pat O'Conner, had also expressed concern at the profit disparity. Overall numbers were strong, he said, with attendance and gross revenues at near-record levels, but 60 to 70 percent of the operating income was being generated by 10 percent of the clubs.[28] The 10-year term of the newly adopted Professional Baseball Agreement, with a commitment guaranteeing every club an affiliation through the length of the agreement, would provide minor-league teams with stability, but further increase their financial burden. Moderately optimistic, he praised the National Association's hallmark characteristics of innovation and efficiency, saying it would be up to each team to make the deal as expensive, or inexpensive, as it wished.[29] To help control the costs, he urged NA members to drop their old gripes and join forces with their major-league partner. "The time has come for all of baseball to bury the hatchets of the past and proactively plan for the future," he said.[30]

MAJOR SHUFFLE

Despite being absent at the Winter Meetings, some significant developments kept the major leagues in the news throughout the 1997-1998 offseason. Two new franchises, the Tampa Bay Devil Rays and the Arizona Diamondbacks, had been created, and the expansion affected the majors in a number of ways.

First, there was the discussion of radical realignment.

At the start of November, the executive council voted unanimously to have the Milwaukee Brewers move from the AL to the NL, making them the first team in the history of major-league baseball to change leagues.[31]

In a November 6 article announcing the Brewers' move, Murray Chass summarized the realignment discussion.[32] Adding a new team to each league would have caused both leagues to have 15 teams, and would have necessitated scattering the interleague games throughout the schedule, instead of grouping them in short bunches, an arrangement favored by owners.

Originally, major-league baseball hoped to place the expansion Devil Rays in the AL East, shifting the Detroit Tigers from the East to the Central and the Kansas City Royals from the Central to the West. But when the Royals refused to change divisions, the Devil Rays were dropped in the AL West instead. Royals Chairman David Glass then proposed a complete overhaul based on geographic location. In his bold restructuring, 15 teams would be bumped from one league to the other; the Royals would migrate to the NL Central, generating a rivalry with the St. Louis Cardinals; and all eight Western teams would wind up in the new NL West.

Both the Players Association and the owners said no; San Francisco Giants owner Peter Magowan even threatened legal action. Acting Commissioner Bud Selig and Boston Red Sox CEO John Harrington, who was chairing the realignment committee, suggested a more moderate reshuffling of seven teams. This, too, was rejected.

Owners eventually approved the most minimal realignment possible, having only one team change leagues. The Royals were given the first chance to switch, but turned it down, leading some to question whether they had really been a stalking horse for the Brewers all along.

In the end the Brewers went from the AL Central to the NL Central, becoming the National League's 16th team and the sixth team in the Central Division; the Tigers moved from the AL East to the AL Central, taking the Brewers' spot; and the Devil Rays vacated their original expansion placement in the AL West, and settled in the AL East.[33]

DESIGNATED DISPUTE

The expansion and resulting realignment kicked up the designated-hitter debate.

An Associated Press article published in November 1997 cited results of a recent poll. Almost 80 percent of fans were in favor of a change, with 45 percent calling for the DH to be eliminated, while 34 percent preferred to have the DH in both leagues.[34]

The same November AP article revealed that baseball owners were using both incentive and strong-arm tactics to have the union agree to get rid of the DH. According to the report, management negotiator Randy Levine had contacted the Players Association on August 29 with a proposal/mild threat. Owners wanted to do away with the DH, he told them, and the collective-bargaining agreement gave them the authority to "unilaterally change playing rules with one year advance notice."[35] To ameliorate the expected negative reaction, Levine said that owners would increase active rosters from 25 to 26. But the union rejected that offer, saying they would counter with a grievance that the DH was "more than a playing rule," and that the additional roster spot would likely be filled by a low-priced rookie. "It just aggravates matters," said union leader Donald Fehr.[36]

The union's annual salary report, issued on December 2, 1997, made a strong case for the DH. And an equally strong one against it. Designated hitters, almost all of whom were veteran players, had earned an average salary of $3,585,788 in 1997, making the DH the highest paid position in the American League, and the second highest overall. Only first basemen were paid more, with an average salary of $3,717,579.[37] Clearly, the DH was good for veterans' bank accounts and stressful for owners' payrolls.

Had major league officials attended the Winter Meetings, the bristling controversy might have made for a juicy war of words. According to Fehr, any attempts to get rid of the DH would be interpreted as a bold sign that owners were prepared to fracture the current labor peace. But by April, the debate was dormant once again.[38]

"There is no specific proposal right now to force the American League to consider elimination of the DH," Selig said when asked about the issue. "[Last summer] we were talking about a rather significant amount of realignment. I guess I would call that the event in history, the force that would say we need to have one set of playing rules. At least for the time being, we don't need to do that."[39]

But while Selig and the owners were willing to back off the elimination idea, they were firm on keeping the National League DH-free. "It became clear in the realignment discussion," Selig explained, "that the National League clubs were unalterably opposed to the designated hitter. They are inflexible. If anybody thinks ultimately the National League will go to the DH, they're living in a fairy land. That's not going to happen."[40]

RULE 5 DRAFT

The 1998 expansion also livened up the offseason transactions. A month before the Winter Meetings, an expansion draft had been held in Phoenix for the Devil Rays and Diamondbacks. The draft itself was unremarkable, with both teams choosing young unknowns over high-salaried veterans.[41] But the instant it concluded, a rash of trades were made, with 31 players exchanged in the course of a single night. Joe Hoppel of *The Sporting News* termed it a "swap mart," pointedly criticizing many of the decisions as shamelessly economic.[42]

Rather than working to fortify their rosters, ballclubs were fixated on slashing their budgets, Hoppel asserted, naming the 1997 World Series champion Florida Marlins as the most blatant offenders.

"Perhaps never in sports history has a team so openly acknowledged that the won-lost ledger ... is really secondary to the credits-debits ledger," he wrote.[43] With a payroll that had surged from $25.2 million to $53.5 million between 1996 and 1997, Marlins owner H. Wayne Huizenga had instructed his GM, Dave Dombrowski, to severely reduce their outlay.[44] Dombrowski complied, dispensing with their best hitter, outfielder Moises Alou, right before a predraft trade freeze, and dealing closer Robb Nen, center fielder Devon White, and first baseman Jeff Conine as soon as the weeklong moratorium ended.[45] One columnist called it a "liquidation."[46] "[W]e have our marching orders," Dombrowski said.[47]

And in a separate pair of dollar-driven moves, Montreal Expos GM Jim Beattie swapped Cy Young Award winner Pedro Martinez for one of Boston's top prospects, right-handed pitcher Carl Pavano, plus outfielder Tony Armas, and traded second baseman Mike Lansing to the Rockies for outfielder Mark Hamlin and two Class-A pitchers.[48] "We do not intend to win next year," Beattie said candidly. "We intend to have a championship club when we move into our new stadium in 2001."[49]

During the Rule 5 draft in New Orleans, the one official area of major-league participation at the 1997 Meetings, trading and shuffling continued. Seventy-two players changed teams during the three phases of the draft, though only one, second baseman Jeff Huson, who moved from the Rockies to the Mariners, had any major-league experience.[50]

Under normal policy, teams may not send Rule 5 signees to the minors in the first year without first placing them on waivers or offering them back to the original club at half the $50,000 purchase price. This limitation was lifted for the Devil Rays and Diamondbacks. They were also allowed a "delayed phase" after round two of the major-league phase, in which they had 24 hours to add up to three more players as their rosters permitted.

The Devil Rays, who had signed five free agents since the November 18 expansion draft (southpaw Wilson Alvarez, third baseman Wade Boggs, right-hander Roberto Hernandez, and infielder-outfielders Dave Martinez and Paul Sorrento), arrived in New Orleans with a full roster of 40, unable to select any additional prospects. "Honestly, at the time of the expansion draft, we planned to leave a spot open on our roster for a Rule 5 selection, but with all the free agents we signed that was no longer possible," Devil Rays GM Chuck LaMar said.[51]

Meanwhile, with a roster of only 35, the Diamondbacks had ample space to try out the special draft rules. They chose right-handed pitchers in each of the first two phases, and a righty and lefty in the delayed phase. "The draft was intriguing to us because of the dispensation system in effect this year," said Diamondbacks GM Joe Garagiola Jr. "We looked at it as a one-time opportunity to acquire talent that would not normally be available to us."[52]

But even though there was a lot of action, talent was scarce. The November expansion draft had already ravaged the rosters, and many teams held onto players they ordinarily would have let go. "There's no question there was less quality than normal," said Phillies scouting director Mike Arbuckle.[53] Of the four Diamondbacks picks, the three right-handers — Martin Sanchez, Ynocencio de la Cruz, and Russell Jacobs — never made it to the majors, while the lefty Stephen Randolph pitched a combined three seasons with Arizona and Houston.

The Florida Marlins, whose left-handed starting pitcher Tony Saunders had been snatched by the Devil Rays as the first expansion-draft pick, lost seven more players during the Rule 5 draft, including southpaw Hector Mercado. Hurling for the Marlins' Double-A Portland Sea Dogs, Mercado was one of the better prospects, with a team-leading record of 11-3, and a 3.96 ERA.

He was selected by the Phillies as the second pick of the draft, then immediately sent to the Mets for right-handed closer Mike Welch in a prearranged exchange. "He was right there, he was our 41st guy," Marlins farm director John Boles lamented. "But you can't protect everyone."[54]

A year and a half later, after missing all of the 1998 season due to injury, Mercado was released by the Mets on August 4, 1999. He signed as a free agent with the Cincinnati Reds that December, and made his major-league debut on April 4, 2000, giving up one earned run in a ninth-inning relief appearance. Over a total of four years between the Reds and the Phillies, he would pitch 124⅔ innings in 112 games, with a 5-4 record and a 4.55 ERA.

The number-one draft choice, right-handed pitcher Javier Martinez, was plucked from the Cubs' farm system by the Athletics, then traded to the Pirates for cash. He had a losing record and a less-than-stunning ERA with two of the Cubs' Class-A teams in 1997, but had caught the attention of some scouts, going 5-2, 2.13

in Puerto Rico over the winter.⁵⁵ Martinez lasted only one season in the majors, posting mediocre stats: 41 innings in 37 games, with an ERA of 4.83. Released by the Pirates in December 1999, he remained in baseball for a while, spending two and a half years in the Reds organization and five months signed to the Orioles, but did not pitch in another major-league game.

LUXURY TAX

Players' salaries had soared to an 18.7 percent increase in 1997, totaling over $1 billion for the first time,⁵⁶ and shortly after the Winter Meetings, the five major-league teams with the biggest payrolls received official notice about the sport's very first luxury tax. Added to the 1996 Collective Bargaining Agreement after the 1994 labor dispute and season-ending strike, the tax was an attempt to place limits on ever-increasing payrolls without the imposed harshness of a salary cap, opposed by players.⁵⁷ It had been the main sticking point during negotiations.⁵⁸

In a formula approved for three years, an annual threshold would be calculated by averaging the fifth- and sixth-highest payrolls, and the top five teams would be taxed on every dollar exceeding the threshold. The tax rate would stand at 35 percent for the first two seasons, then be skimmed to 34 percent for 1999.⁵⁹

All five teams penalized in the first year had made the 1997 playoffs. The New York Yankees and Baltimore Orioles owed the most, over $4 million apiece, on rivaling $68 and $67 million-dollar payrolls. The American League champion Cleveland Indians and Atlanta Braves had also been handed significant bills, slightly above $2 million and $1.3 million respectively. And while the World Series-winning Florida Marlins owed just a fraction of the total $12 million due, the $153,046 charge was a result of a paysheet that had more than doubled from 1996 to 1997.

Payrolls had increased so much that the 1997 threshold, set roughly at $51 million in the CBA, was boosted to $55,606,921 once the final figures were in.⁶⁰ At the time of the assessment, eight other teams were spending over $50 million, and only one team, the Pittsburgh Pirates, was under $20 million.⁶¹

As per the agreement, $10 million of the collected funds went toward paying off the revenue-sharing shortfall, and the remaining $2 million-plus was distributed to the five teams with the lowest net revenue from the prior season.⁶²

LAW AND ORDER

Also percolating during the offseason was the question of who would finally assume the duties of full-time commissioner.

A December 1997 article by Murray Chass of the *New York Times* gave some insight into the search process.⁶³ Chass wrote that Bud Selig, who had been maintaining the role on an interim basis for over five years, was helping to lead the search. Selig and search committee chairman Jerry McMorris, owner of the Colorado Rockies, had been conducting interviews, and an unnamed source said the candidates had been narrowed to three. But the process had been so secretive that there were rumblings as to whether a serious search was occurring at all.

McMorris assured reporters that they were getting close. "We have told the Executive Council we would be in with our recommendations at our next meeting," he said. "That meeting will be before the owners' quarterly meetings the middle of next month. I could be very comfortable with several of the candidates. I haven't tried to rank them."⁶⁴

At least one person was pressuring Selig to take the job himself. Paul Beeston, who only months before had resigned as Blue Jays president to become major-league baseball's chief operating officer, reportedly told Selig he might quit his new position if anyone other than Selig was chosen.

"My whole feeling has been that if I could influence Bud to stay by doing my job properly and making it easier for him, then I've done my job," Beeston offered on the record. "I would love for him to stay. I have a great relationship with him. I work well with him. I have no hesitation in telling him what I think or what I think we should be doing." Good friends with Selig, Beeston said he often prodded him playfully, asking "When are we going to end this charade?"⁶⁵

PACE OF GAME INITIATIVE

Prior to the 1998 season, Frank Robinson, VP of on-field operations for major-league baseball, led a pace of game effort for Acting Commissioner Selig. A list of procedures was developed and agreed to by the Players Association and the Umpires Association.

The "primary new procedures," as reported by Dave Anderson in the *New York Times* of March 29, 1998:

- Between-inning breaks will be limited to 2 minutes 5 seconds from the third out to the first pitch of the next half inning; the first batter will be announced after 1 minute 40 seconds.

- In nationally televised games on Fox and ESPN, the break will be 2 minutes 25 seconds with the first batter announced after 2 minutes.

- Television lights in the broadcast booths must be off before the end of the between-inning break so that umpires can start the inning promptly.

- Umpires should not grant time for batters to step out of the box unless, in the umpire's judgment, it is absolutely necessary. When a batter is granted time, he may not stray more than three feet from the batter's box.

- With no base runners, a pitcher must deliver a pitch within 12 seconds after the batter is in the batter's box ready to hit; the former rule was 20 seconds.

- When a manager or a coach leaves the dugout for a second visit to the mound in one inning, which would require a pitching change, he must indicate the new pitcher.

- When possible, pinch-hitters should be warmed up before entering the on-deck circle. Unless there is a reason not to do so, a pinch-hitter should be in the on-deck circle while the preceding hitter is at bat.

- Bat boys should have a second bat readily available in the event a hitter breaks a bat during an at-bat.

- Between-inning announcements and in-park entertainment must conclude after 1 minute 40 seconds so that the public-address announcer may promptly announce the first batter.

- General managers are responsible for monitoring the between-inning break times and public-address announcements.

The *Times* followed two days later with an editorial that began: "Call us crazy, but we think this could be a truly interesting baseball season. For one thing, the commissioner's office has instructed umpires to enforce new procedures aimed at speeding up play. Pitchers will not be allowed to dawdle, and between-inning breaks will be shortened. As long as the basic rules and rhythms of the game are not sacrificed in the rush, this will be an improvement."

1   Dave Anderson, "Time for Crackdown: Enforce Dead Time," *New York Times*, March 29, 1998: SP8.
2   "Topics of the Times: Play Ball!" *New York Times*, March 31, 1998: A22.

McMorris admitted that some of the owners might also prefer Selig over a new choice, but believed Selig would turn down such a request. "I think there's always a chance of a draft movement," McMorris said. "I don't honestly believe Bud will accept even if the draft was strong enough to give it to him. He's made it clear he's not desirous of doing it. I know what I'm saying defies conventional wisdom and in baseball anything can happen."[66]

Seven months later, on July 9, 1998, Chass filed another report. On his 2,130th day of serving in a provisional capacity, Selig had been elected "quickly and unanimously" as major-league baseball's ninth commissioner.[67] Despite his resistance, the owners had been able to wear him down. "We've been working on him as long as I can remember," disclosed Twins owner Carl Pohlad.[68]

Selig told reporters he had made up his mind rather suddenly one day, while driving his car. "You're going to do this," he had realized. He pointed to his strong working relationship with Beeston as pivotal in his decision, explaining that Beeston's capability of handling the "day-to-day, operational things" would free him to tackle the more "global" issues. Developing an equitable method of revenue-sharing and securing the labor peace were both at the top of his list.[69]

"We need to reduce the acrimony from this equation once and for all. ...We've had eight work stoppages. We have to make sure that the next generation doesn't have to endure any more work stoppages," Selig vowed.[70]

MAKING THE WINTER MEETINGS WHOLE AGAIN

Besides the lively opening session, journalists found little to report on. Without major-league participation, news was scarce. Will Lingo described attendees "roam[ing] the lobbies ... ask[ing] baseball friends ... 'Is anything going on?'"[71] And in this fifth consecutive year of major-league absence, much of the chatter was about having the big leagues rejoin the party.[72]

The December get-together had been disrupted in 1990, when a nasty quarrel over the Professional Baseball Agreement provoked an initial split. Rather than attend the Los Angeles meetings planned by the National Association that year, Major League Baseball organized its own gathering in Chicago, drawing away the press and overshadowing the NA.[73]

Majors and minors reconvened in 1991, but after two years back together, major-league owners decided they'd had enough of players and their aggressive agents dominating the activity and pushing prices sky-high.

Acting Commissioner Bud Selig and the Executive Council deliberated, and announced an official boycott, prohibiting GMs from attending future sessions. And with only minor-league news to cover, most reporters went elsewhere.[74]

But by 1997, the majors realized that restricting signing activity at the Winter Meetings wasn't doing anything to control costs.[75] And relations between the major and minor leagues had improved.

Over the previous seven years, the National Association had added staff, modernized operations, and developed a regular working relationship with the major leagues. VP Stanley Brand's antitrust preservation efforts, and the economic success of many of the minor-league franchises further strengthened their position. The majors now viewed the minors as an asset, and as a result, a rumor that Major League Baseball would place a five-affiliate limit on its teams, eliminating many Class-A clubs and thereby reducing money spent on player development, never materialized.[76] Instead, the PBA was settled easily, and was already approved when the Winter Meetings commenced. All that remained to be done in New Orleans was finalize the financial and operational details. Changes included an adjustment in the ticket tax, resulting in some teams having to pay more, and a shift in the distribution of equipment costs.[77] Minor-league teams would share the expense of bats and balls, and pay for their own uniforms.[78] The most notable agreement was to have the minor leagues be responsible for funding umpire development, a program that cost the major leagues $4.8 million in 1997, but that the NA hoped to knock down to $3.5 million.[79]

The smooth dealings left the majors and minors in an amicable, accommodating spirit. Plus, there were signs that Major League Baseball was already reconsidering its voluntary absence. A year earlier, at the 1996 Winter Meetings in Boston, the Red Sox had organized a coinciding fanfest at the same convention center, scheduled appearances by some of their players and coaches, and invited the participation of other major-league executives.[80] Acting Commissioner Selig issued a casual reversal of the ban, allowing GMs to attend the weekend's meetings "merely if they want to."[81]

And the raucous atmosphere at the November 1997 expansion draft reminded some baseball officials of the fun they were missing. "This is the kind of activity we used to have at the old Winter Meetings that the fans love," said Joe Garagiola.[82] Even Selig was beginning to soften. "I thought we got a lot of positive publicity," he said. "Having a day like that makes you rethink things."[83] National Association President Mike Moore confirmed Selig's renewed affection: "There's a lot of interest in (bringing the meetings together). Bud has indicated to me all along that he would like the meetings to be together again. We just haven't figured out what will work for both sides."[84]

The only remaining obstacle seemed to be one of scheduling. Since the breakup, the major leagues had begun holding owners' meetings in January, with the minors keeping the traditional mid-December time. Both groups had their reasons to stay put.[85]

But around the hotel, people seemed willing to change, with some minor-league officials agreeable to shifting to January and others suggesting November as a possibility. The National Association announced that a committee had been formed to resolve the issue and bring the meetings together once again.[86] And at the annual awards luncheon, Maryland Baseball Chairman Peter Kirk added an extra nudge, saying that he had been "taking the postcards in his hotel room and mailing them to major-league officials with a simple greeting: 'Wish you were here.'"[87]

Acknowledgements

Thanks to: Michael Teevan, VP Communications, Major League Baseball, & Jeff Lantz, Senior Director, Communications, Minor League Baseball, for research assistance; and SABR member Mike Hanks, for so generously digging into his personal *Baseball America* archive.

SOURCES

In addition to the sources cited in the Notes, the author also consulted:

Associated Press. "Barge Hits Riverwalk Mall in New Orleans, Scores Injured," *Augusta* (Georgia) *Chronicle*, December 15, 1996. chronicle.augusta.com/stories/1996/12/15/met_201330.shtml.

Bragg, Rick. "Freighter Hits Riverfront Mall in New Orleans," *New York Times*, December 15, 1996. nytimes.com/1996/12/15/us/freighter-hits-riverfront-mall-in-new-orleans.html.

Bragg, Rick. "A Nightmare Along the Mississippi," *New York Times*, December 16, 1996.

nytimes.com/1996/12/16/us/a-nightmare-along-the-mississippi.html.

NOTES

1. Will Lingo. "Brand Warns of Looming Antitrust Threat," *Baseball America*, January 5-18, 1998: 20.

2. Ibid. See also Stan Brand, Address at the Opening General Session of the Baseball Winter Meetings on Friday, December 12, 1997 in New Orleans, NAPBL News Release, officially released remarks.

3. Gary R. Roberts, "A Brief Appraisal of the Curt Flood Act of 1998 From the Minor League Perspective," *Marquette Sports Law Review*, Volume 9, Issue 2, Spring, Article 13 (1999): 416. scholarship.law.marquette.edu/sportslaw/vol9/iss2/13. See: "ARTICLE XXVIII - Antitrust
The Clubs and the Association will jointly request and cooperate in lobbying Congress to pass a law that will clarify that Major League Baseball Players are covered under the antitrust laws (i.e., that Major League Players will have the same rights under the antitrust laws as do other professional athletes, e.g., football and basketball players), along with a provision that makes it clear that the passage of that bill does not change the application of the antitrust laws in any other context or with respect to any other person or entity. ...." (Basic Agreement between the American League of Professional Baseball clubs and the National League of Professional Clubs and Major League Baseball Players Association, effective January 1, 1997, Art. XXVIII: 107).

4. Gary R. Roberts, 413-414. See *Federal Base Ball Club of Baltimore, Inc. v. National League of Professional Baseball Clubs, Inc.*, 259 U.S. 200 (1922). In a unanimous decision, the Supreme Court upheld the Court of Appeals ruling that the Sherman Antitrust Act did not apply to the business of baseball. In the opinion, Justice Oliver Wendell Holmes Jr. reasoned that exhibitions of baseball were strictly state affairs, and therefore did not constitute interstate commerce. "(T)ransport is a mere incident," he wrote, "not the essential thing."

5. Gary R. Roberts, 416.

6. Gary R. Roberts, 416-417. See also Congress.Gov congress.gov/bill/105th-congress/senate-bill/53.

7. Gary R. Roberts, 417-418.

8. Jerold J. Duquette, *Regulating the National Pastime: Baseball and Antitrust* (New York: Praeger Publishers, 1999), 122.

9. Stan Brand. Brand referenced *Brown v. Pro Football, Inc.* (95-388), U.S. 231 (1996), where the Supreme Court, in an 8-to-1 ruling, held that a "non-statutory" exemption, implied from federal labor laws, protected NFL owners from antitrust liability, even after they imposed unilateral terms when negotiations with the NFL Players Association over development squad salaries reached an impasse. "To permit antitrust liability here threatens to introduce instability and uncertainty into the collective bargaining process," Justice Stephen G. Breyer wrote in the majority opinion, "for antitrust law often forbids or discourages the kinds of joint discussions and behavior that the collective bargaining process invites or requires." Jerold J. Duquette argued that *Brown*, along with *Powell v. National Football League*, 678 F. Supp. 777 (D. Minn. 1988) and *National Basketball Association v. L Williams*, 45 F.3D 684 (2D Cir. 1995), "essentially made baseball's antitrust exemption in labor negotiations irrelevant. By ruling that the nonstatutory labor exemption applies so widely," he wrote, "the courts diminished Major League Baseball's need for its exemption in labor matters, allowing them to offer it up in labor negotiations and thereby co-opt the most potent foe of the exemption, the players." Jerold J. Duquette, 119.

10. Ibid.

11. Ibid.

12. "(b) Nothing in this section shall be construed to affect — (1) the applicability or nonapplicability of the antitrust laws to the amateur draft of professional baseball, the minor league reserve clause, the agreement between professional major league baseball teams and teams of the National Association of Baseball, commonly known as the 'Professional Baseball Agreement,' or any other matter relating to the minor leagues." (Excerpted from "Curt Flood Act of 1997" Section 2. Application of the Antitrust Laws to Professional Major League Baseball.)

13. Stan Brand.

14. Jerold J. Duquette.

15. Stan Brand.

16. Ibid.

17. Ibid.

18. Gary R. Roberts, 418.

19. Stan Brand.

20. Will Lingo.

21. Gary R. Roberts, 419.

22 Gary R. Roberts, 418.

23 Gary R. Roberts, 437.

24 Lacy Lusk, "Minors Make Plans for Slower Times," Minor League Notebook, *Baseball America*, January 5-18, 1998: 21.

25 Mike Moore, Address at the Opening General Session of the Baseball Winter Meetings on Friday, December 12, 1997, in New Orleans, NAPBL News Release, officially released remarks.

26 Will Lingo.

27 Mike Moore.

28 Pat O'Conner, Address at the Opening General Session of the Baseball Winter Meetings on Friday, December 12, 1997, in New Orleans, NAPBL News Release, officially released remarks.

29 Ibid.

30 Ibid.

31 Murray Chass, "Brewers Cleared to Shift to N.L. Central in '98," *New York Times*, November 6, 1997. nytimes.com/1997/11/06/sports/baseball-brewers-cleared-to-shift-to-nl-central-in-98.html.

32 Ibid.

33 Ibid.

34 Associated Press, "DH Ban Hot Topic to Owners," *Augusta (Georgia) Chronicle,* November 30, 1997. chronicle.augusta.com/stories/1997/11/30/oth_218326.shtml.

35 Ibid.

36 Ibid.

37 Murray Chass, "Sultans Who Swat: D.H.'s Are Well Paid," *New York Times*, December 3, 1997. nytimes.com/1997/12/03/sports/baseball-sultans-who-swat-dh-s-are-well-paid.html.

38 Murray Chass, "The D.H. Is 25 Years Old, but Now the Question Is Whether It Will Get to 30," *New York Times*, April 5, 1998. nytimes.com/1998/04/05/sports/baseball-notebook-dh-25-years-old-but-now-question-whether-it-will-get-30.html.

39 Ibid.

40 Ibid.

41 Murray Chass. "Unknowns Are Drafted as the Famous Are Traded," *New York Times*, November 19, 1997. nytimes.com/1997/11/19/sports/baseball-unknowns-are-drafted-as-the-famous-are-traded.html.

42 Joe Hoppel, "Upstaging the Expansion Draft," *The Sporting News*, December 1, 1997: 38.

43 Ibid.

44 Murray Chass. "Everybody Must Go! Marlins Are Liquidating," *New York Times*, November 12, 1997. nytimes.com/1997/11/12/sports/baseball-everybody-must-go-marlins-are-liquidating.html.

45 Alou was sent to the Astros for a trio of right-handed pitchers—Manuel Barrios, Oscar Henriquez and Mark Johnson. Nen went to the Giants for righty Joe Fontenot and two minor-league right-handers, Mick Pageler and Mike Villano. White was shipped to the new Diamondbacks for a minor-league left-hander, Jesus Martinez, while Conine headed to Kansas City for minor-league right-hander Blaine Mull.

46 Murray Chass, "Everybody Must Go."

47 Ibid.

48 Jeff Blair, "Montreal Expos Report," *The Sporting News*, December 1, 1997: 41.

49 Joe Hoppel.

50 Allan Simpson, "Rule 5 Keeps Teams Busy," *Baseball America*, January 5-18, 1998: 22.

51 Ibid.

52 Ibid.

53 Ibid.

54 Ibid.

55 Ibid.

56 Murray Chass, "Players' Salaries Passed $1 Billion Mark," *New York Times*, November 14, 1997. nytimes.com/1997/11/14/sports/baseball-players-salaries-passed-1-billion-mark.html.

57 Nathaniel Grow, "MLB's Evolving Luxury Tax," *Fangraphs.com*, May 1, 2015. fangraphs.com/blogs/mlbs-evolving-luxury-tax/.

58 Associated Press, "Baseball Nails 5 Playoff Teams With Luxury-Tax Assessments," *Deseret News* (Salt Lake City), December 26, 1997. deseretnews.com/article/602807/Baseball-nails-5-playoff-teams-with-luxury-tax-assessments.html.

59 Paul D. Staudohar, "The Baseball Strike of 1994-95," *Monthly Labor Review*, March 1997: 27.

60 Associated Press, "Baseball Nails 5 Playoff Teams With Luxury-Tax Assessments."

61 Murray Chass, "Yankees to Pay $4.4 Million as Lion's Share of Teams' 1997 Luxury Tax," *New York Times*, December 25, 1997. nytimes.com/1997/12/25/sports/baseball-yankees-to-pay-4.4-million-as-lion-s-share-of-teams-1997-luxury-tax.html.

62 Ibid. Also see Associated Press, "Baseball Nails 5 Playoff Teams With Luxury-tax Assessments," *Deseret News*, December 26, 1997.

63 Murray Chass, "All Quiet on Some Fronts: Selig Is Silent on Big Question," *New York Times*, December 14, 1997. nytimes.com/1997/12/14/sports/baseball-notebook-all-quiet-on-some-fronts-selig-is-silent-on-big-question.html.

64 Ibid.

65 Ibid.

66 Ibid.

67 Murray Chass, "Take Away the 'Acting' Label: Selig Is Baseball's Commissioner," *New York Times*, July 10, 1998. nytimes.com/1998/07/10/sports/baseball-take-away-the-acting-label-selig-is-baseball-s-commissioner.html.

68 Ibid.

69 Ibid.

70 Ibid.

71 Will Lingo.

72 Will Lingo.

73 Will Lingo, "Minors, Majors Should Get Meetings Back Together," *Baseball America*, December 22, 1997-January 4, 1998: 12.

74 Ibid.

75 Ibid.

76 Jerold J. Duquette, 122-3.

77 Lacy Lusk, "Winter Meetings Should Be Peaceful," Minor League Notebook, *Baseball America*, December 22, 1997-January 4, 1998: 13.

78 Pat O'Conner.

79 Lacy Lusk, "Minors Make Plans for Slower Times," Minor League Notebook, *Baseball America*, January 5-18, 1998.

80 Will Lingo, "Minors, Majors Should Get Meetings Back Together."

81 Ronald Blum, Associated Press, "Most GMs to Avoid Winter Meetings," *Salina* (Kansas) *Journal,* December 3, 1996: 13.

82 Joe Hoppel.

83 Associated Press, "DH Ban Hot Topic to Owners," *Augusta Chronicle,* November 30, 1997. chronicle.augusta.com/stories/1997/11/30/oth_218326.shtml.

84 Will Lingo, "Minors, Majors Should Get Meetings Back Together."

85 Ibid.

86 Will Lingo, "Brand Warns of Looming Antitrust Threat," *Baseball America*, January 5-18, 1998: 20.

87 Ibid.

1998
TEMPERS FLARE, CONTRACTS EXPLODE

By Jessica Frank

"FREE-AGENT FRENZY."[1]
"Meat Market."[2]
Negotiations dominated by "fast-talking, greedy little men."[3]

Memories of the 1992 Winter Meetings in Louisville, Kentucky, were unvaryingly ugly. Over a tumultuous four days, baseball's annual gathering had dissolved into nightmarish chaos and sent major-league executives running.

Among the worst incidents, the Rev. Jesse Jackson denounced baseball's "institutional racism," threatening to organize boycotts and mount a challenge to the owners' coveted antitrust exemption unless substantial changes were made in minority-hiring practices;[4] Cincinnati Reds owner Marge Schott responded to allegations of racist remarks by delivering a statement that was part apology but more defensive denial;[5] and two hours into a concluding meeting of all 28 club owners, Carl Barger, president of the Florida Marlins, suffered a fatal heart attack.[6] But it was the unmitigated greed that left the filthiest impression. Agents swarmed the lobby on behalf of their clients, brokering 35 signings worth a total of $225 million.[7] The most expensive contract of the unprecedented spree: a six-year, $43.75 million deal for Barry Bonds that shattered the record for guaranteed money, made him baseball's best-paid player, and left other owners in shock.[8]

Acting Commissioner Bud Selig reacted diplomatically. "I'm glad this situation has been settled," he said. "There are 28 teams and they all have to make their own judgments."[9] But by the following October, Selig and the owners had come to a unanimous decision, officially pulling out of the meetings and prohibiting major-league GMs from future attendance.[10]

Over the years, though, there had been some changes. Selig, who had repeatedly stated he had no interest in becoming baseball's full-time commissioner, accepted the position in July of 1998.

And his firm opposition to the winter meetings had faded. In 1996 Selig had been coaxed into informally lifting the ban,[11] and by 1998 the commissioner's office was actively encouraging participation.[12] *USA Today*'s Hal Bodley remarked on the news in November: "Sandy Alderson, executive vice president of baseball operations, is trying to renew interest in the winter meetings, once the top event between the World Series and spring training. He has called every GM, reminding each how important the sessions were."[13]

Promoting the event earlier that fall, NAPBL officials even included Commissioner Selig among the expected 3,000 attendees. "It's a very good possibility…" estimated director Tim Brunswick. "This is probably going to be our biggest meeting since 1992."[14]

The 97th session was scheduled for December 11-15 at the Opryland Hotel in Nashville, a dizzying resort complex that boasted 2,884 rooms, multiple Southern-themed lobbies, and three expansive, glass-enclosed garden atriums complete with waterfalls, tropical plants, and Mississippi-style flatboat tours along a quarter-mile-long manmade river.[15]

Both the venue and the expanded agenda seemed an appropriately large, festive way to welcome back the major leagues. There were business seminars and a trade show with exhibitors from over 250 baseball-related companies,[16] hawking everything from tarpaulins, infield dirt, and batting cages[17] to computer programs[18] and the Famous Chicken, a traveling mascot.[19]

There was also an NA-sponsored job fair. For years, handfuls of plucky, baseball-loving job seekers had shown up at the winter meetings on their own initiative, hoping to wrangle low-level positions and internships. Now their loosely-planned searching had become an organized offshoot of the meetings, and hundreds were paying for the chance. In 1994, the NA had established the "Professional Baseball Employment Opportunities" placement program to connect applicants and employers with more efficiency, and by 1998, the PBEO had a full-time director, a quarterly newsletter, and an ongoing databank. There were 535 positions listed at the job fair—the most ever—and the program had gained enough standing to generate a feature in *Baseball America*.[20]

The *Los Angeles Times* relayed three of the postings: "Announcer on the Spanish radio station of the El Paso Diablos," "Picnic management trainee for the Lansing Lugnuts," and "Mascot for the Carolina Mudcats."[21]

CAUTIOUSLY OPTIMISTIC

Selig, who ultimately decided not to travel to Nashville, spoke from his Milwaukee office a week before the session began. "I used to love the Winter Meetings," he explained. "But it got almost impossible to meet and conduct business. It was a terrible thing. Now, with baseball coming off such a great season, we thought there would be more positives than negatives if we did this."[22]

It was also clear that wealthy teams were going to keep dishing out the cash anyway—with or without the Winter Meetings. As noted by Murray Chass in the *New York Times*, in just one week that fall, five free agents secured individual deals that totaled $330 million. "Clubs proved they did not have to be a captive audience to spend lavishly," Chass wrote.[23]

With trades viewed as the one remaining way for small and middle-market teams to be competitive,[24] the big gathering presented a great chance to jumpstart some old-fashioned baseball business.

Many GMs seemed optimistic. "With free agency, it's a few teams doing things and a lot of teams not doing anything," A's GM Billy Beane said. "Maybe it's good to have the winter meetings back—we'll have to remove the cobwebs."[25]

Mariners' GM Woody Woodward was also looking forward to making some trades, after being priced out of the free agent offers. "(N)ot in our wildest dreams did we expect some of these players to sign for what they signed for," Woodward said. "(W)e just made a decision not to get involved in the craziness of the contracts. I don't think you can spend like that. You'll notice that only a few teams are."

"I think there are still a few bargains out there," he added. "And I think there are still trades there."[26]

Even Phillies GM Ed Wade, who had already reshaped his club with a number of moves in November, said he'd be open to a good proposal.[27]

With the meetings about to begin, anticipation was high.[28] Pitcher Kevin Brown was the only "superstar" still floating around, leading major-league VP Sandy Alderson to comment assuredly that agents wouldn't be able to "play the general managers like an instrument."[29] All the major-league GMs were attending, including the Yankees' Brian Cashman in a last-minute organizational decision,[30] and even though there was no indication that the sharks had left the waters, baseball officials were anxious for another dip.[31]

THROWN FOR A LOOP

The Kevin Brown signing made many wish they had stayed ashore.

The ground for his record-splintering deal had been paved in March. Atlanta Braves owner Ted Turner, who had not attended an owners meeting since 1989, made the trip to St. Petersburg, Florida, on March 18, 1998, with one purpose—to try to stop media rival Rupert Murdoch from purchasing the Los Angeles Dodgers. Turner apparently felt strongly enough about the matter to skip a Time Warner board of directors meeting scheduled on the same day,[32] but refused to make his thoughts public, even when pressed by reporters. "Ted made his speech," said one person in attendance, "He made his points that he's against it. He made his arguments."[33] In the *San Diego Union-Tribune*, Tom Cushman predicted trouble. "(If the sale goes through, major-league owners will) have tossed gasoline on a house already in flames. ... If baseball welcomes him, it deserves him."[34] Turner's plea fell flat. Two days later, the *Los Angeles Times* reported that owners voted almost unanimously to approve the sale from Peter O'Malley, whose family had been baseball's oldest dynasty, to Murdoch for a record-setting $311 million. "The vote puts one of baseball's most storied ballclubs in the hands of one of the world's most unsentimental and pragmatic businessmen," the article stated. "The Australian-born Murdoch has gained a reputation for ruthless competitiveness in assembling a worldwide empire of television, newspaper and publishing properties, which were valued in 1997 at nearly $27 billion. Among those assets are broadcast and cable TV rights to games of 22 of the 30 major league baseball teams."[35]

Under this new, well-funded ownership, the club was ready to spend. Earlier in the offseason, they put up a hefty bid for Randy Johnson—a four-year deal, hovering around $50 million. But after weighing three comparable offers from other teams, Johnson chose the Arizona Diamondbacks. The $52.4 million contract, signed on November 30, kept him close to home and made him the second highest paid player in baseball, with an average salary slightly below Mo Vaughn's $13.33 million-per-year deal, inked a week earlier.[36]

Still in need of a premier starter, the Dodgers turned their attention to Brown, who was looking for six years at $80 million-plus. A day into the Winter Meetings, Jason Reid of the *Los Angeles Times* reported that with four teams still in the running, the Dodgers were getting close.[37] The next morning, they crossed the finish line, handing the 34-year-old free agent a deal that far surpassed his $80 million ask, and zoomed past Johnson's. The seven-year, $105 million contract gave Brown both the largest overall and largest annual salary and was loaded with perks. Brown's agent, Scott Boras, said he and Dodgers GM Kevin Malone had worked overnight hammering out the details, and finalized the agreement after a four-mile morning run.[38]

Sweeteners included:

- A no-trade clause for the duration of the contract.[39]

- 12 chartered round-trip flights a year to shuttle his family between Macon, Georgia, and Burbank, California.[40]

- An unspecified number of additional flights to bring his seven- and three-year-old sons along on road trips.[41]

At the press conference, Malone tempered his excitement with a measure of apology. "I've been on the other side," he said, referring to his years as the Montreal Expos GM. "It's unfair in my mind, just like in society, there's a lower class, a middle class and an upper class."[42] But he also defended the signing, saying, "(i)f we didn't do it, someone else would have...."[43]

"We feel like we logically evaluated the marketplace," he continued, adding, "I understand we will be criticized."[44]

Malone could barely get the words out. As Boras took over at the podium, crowing that the Dodgers had, in fact, gotten a bargain, MLB VP of Operations Sandy Alderson began issuing his own statement from the back of the room.[45] With palpable disgust, he lashed into Malone and the Dodgers, scoffing at Malone's show of contrition. "Those comments were a direct affront and an insult to the commissioner of baseball," he told reporters. "To suggest that in spite of this signing they are concerned about the disparity and the fiscal risks associated with the game is (bull)... I don't blame anyone for responding to the dynamics of the market. But don't kid yourself and insult us with those kind of rationalizations."[46]

He wasn't alone in his indignation. "It's truly a tragic day for baseball," said San Diego Padres owner John Moores.[47] "It's a big paradox," Montreal manager Felipe Alou offered. "A number of players made more money last season than our entire payroll."[48] "People say it's monopoly money," Florida Marlins manager John Boles complained. "That's wrong. When we were kids, we never had that much monopoly money."[49]

The clear economic disparity drove Jack McKeon to a more radical idea. "Why not have all the big guys play each other and the little guys play each other and just meet in the World Series," he suggested.[50] Dodgers higher-ups were unsympathetic. "Parity is not the

American way," manager Davey Johnson stated plainly. "The American way is to dominate everyone else."[51]

Only Cleveland Indians GM John Hart sounded unconcerned. "It doesn't guarantee them anything except a long-term commitment," he said.[52]

A couple of days later, fallout continued. Larry Lucchino, San Diego Padres president, accused Brown's agent of providing misinformation to boost the offers.[53]

As proof, Lucchino listed the proposals that the contending teams said they put forward, all five- and six-year deals ranging from $55 to $81 million.[54] Lucchino was incredulous that the Dodgers would offer Brown tens of millions more than any other team, along with an additional year, unless they had been fed false information. But he stopped short of directly attacking Boras, instead suggesting that baseball employ an independent verifier.[55]

"I'm talking about the objective facts about the negotiations," Lucchino argued, "and whether there are flaws in structure of the process that allows for blindman's bluff. There is a growing concern about the process that allows for this type of misinformation circulating."[56]

Boras, quick to fight back, warned that any system of verification would amount to collusion,[57] and classified Lucchino's complaints as "sour grapes."[58] Three other clubs had been ready to pay Brown an equivalent amount, he said, a claim confirmed by insiders. "I spoke to Larry a couple of times in the negotiations and he wasn't too concerned with the situation," Boras revealed. "He kept saying, 'Is he going to St. Louis, is he going to St. Louis?' Then he got wind about the Dodgers. [59]

BLAST-OFF

The Brown explosion shook up the other major negotiation underway at Opryland. In late November, the Toronto Blue Jays' ace, Roger Clemens, had his agents contact the front office.[60] "Clemens Demands to be Traded" read the December 3 headline.[61] Blue Jays GM Gord Ash sprang into action.

The already-elite pitcher had just become baseball's first five-time Cy Young Award winner, capturing consecutive awards in his two years with the Jays. But Toronto remained a midlevel team and Clemens was restless.[62]

"Roger is driven by the one thing he's not accomplished in this game, a ring," Ash said, citing a verbal commitment to deal Clemens if he was unhappy. "I'd say I'm on a fast track with this," he said. "[W]e need to have this clarified before we move on."[63]

But a couple of weeks later, little progress had been made. While a raft of teams had expressed interest (the Indians, Astros, Rangers, Yankees, Rockies, Braves, Mets, and Padres were all listed as possibilities),[64] the separate terms issued by the Blue Jays and Clemens were becoming prohibitive. Toronto was looking for three or four "major-league ready" players, and Clemens was pushing to renegotiate his contract, a move that would essentially make him a free agent. "A double whammy," grumbled executives.[65]

On the first day of the winter meetings, things seemed to be off to a good start. The phone line to the Blue Jays' suite was buzzing with questions Friday afternoon, and Ash was in good humor. "I'm going to stay right here because I can't find my room," he joked. "There's too many numbers."[66]

By Sunday, talks were at a standstill. Clemens, seemingly spurred by the Brown deal,[67] had set the pricetag on his one-year contract extension at $27.4 million.[68] When added to his guaranteed salary of $8 million in 1999 and $8.1 million in 2000, the total three-year deal would average $14.5 million, notably close to Brown's record $15 million a year. Clemens was now also reportedly requesting perks, such as a private box.[69]

Astros GM Gerry Hunsicker was the first to drop out, holding a news conference to publicly express his repugnance. "Quite frankly, we were absolutely stunned and really outraged by the demands," Hunsicker said. "It was mind-boggling."[70] Hunsicker said he was blindsided by the new figure, and complained that the Blue Jays had ceded control of the trade talks to Clemens's agents, brothers Randy and Alan Hendricks. "I'm just extremely concerned for the health of the industry," Hunsicker continued, broadening his criticism. "… What we're creating here is a small country-club type of situation where a handful of teams can compete for the services of the elite players and everyone else takes what is left over. This is just another prime example of how most of us, including the Houston Astros, really can't compete for the services of the elite players."[71] Randy Hendricks dismissed Hunsicker's anger. "The Astros' front office is jealous of the fact that I've been dealing directly with their owner," he said, "so they took the opportunity to call a news conference to try and trash me because their feelings were hurt, that they weren't part of the loop."[72]

Other teams followed the Astros' lead. The Yankees stepped back quietly, with GM Cashman saying they might still be interested if the price was reduced,[73] and a couple of days later, the Mets also withdrew their offer.[74]

Meanwhile, Toronto manager Tim Johnson was facing some tough questions from the media.[75]

Manager press conferences were a new addition to the Winter Meetings, an expansion of an earlier outreach initiative. Following the 1993 lockout, major-league baseball had begun a program of regularly-scheduled telephone conference calls, dubbed "MLB This Week." Different players were featured on the call-in throughout the season, while managers were typically made available in half-hour intervals over one week in December.[76]

During Johnson's obligatory in-person session, reporters pursued an uncomfortable topic. The rookie manager had led the Blue Jays to their first winning record in five years, but ended the season in disgrace after word got out that he had, on numerous occasions, fabricated stories about Vietnam combat experiences in order to motivate players. After initial denials and equivocations, Johnson had eventually owned up to his outright dishonesty in a series of November interviews.[77]

Writing for the *New York Times*, Jason Diamos described Johnson's attitude during the press conference as "apologetic, defensive, and defiant," with Johnson attributing his destructive pattern of lying to guilt over not facing combat, and disavowing the idea that he was one of the factors spurring Roger Clemens's trade wish.[78] (Buddies since their days in Boston, Clemens had inadvertently uncovered Johnson's lies while arranging for a birthday gift to honor his purported service.[79]) "That has nothing to do with anything," Johnson said of the trade request. "I speak to Roger, and believe me, Roger's very close to me."[80]

By the time the meetings ended, Clemens and the Blue Jays were still chained, and Ash had none of his opening cheer. "Gord Ash trudged out of the Opryland Hotel ... with the look of a thoroughly defeated man," wrote Bob Hille of *The Sporting News*.[81] Dozens of trades had been snarled by the inaction, Hille contended. Complex, three-way package deals contingent on Clemens were dangling uncertainly, and the long list of teams looking for pitching had their hands tied. Ash's colleagues were roundly frustrated. "Clemens gummed the whole thing up," one GM told a *Newsday* reporter, "There were a lot of things people wanted to do but couldn't."[82]

Things got even messier the following week. Insulted by the insinuations of greed leveled at him by Hunsicker and Astros President Tal Smith, Clemens withdrew his trade request.

"I have no interest in playing for two individuals like that who would make a statement like that and don't know me," Clemens shot back, in a news conference held near his home in Houston, calling himself "very upset" and "disappointed."[83]

Incongruously, Clemens' agents maintained that a deal with the Astros was still a possibility, praising Astros owner Drayton McLane for his diligence and courtesy.[84] McLane had quickly apologized to the Hendricks brothers after Hunsicker's news conference, and promptly restarted talks.[85] "The goal has been and still is to secure the services of Roger Clemens," Hunsicker affirmed.[86]

From Toronto, Gord Ash also paid Clemens's words little mind, saying he would pick things up again after Christmas.[87]

Then two days later, in an embarrassing side note, the *New York Times* reported that MLB was fining its own COO, Paul Beeston, for "violating established procedures in the Clemens matter."[88] As the Blue Jays' president, Beeston had allegedly supplied Clemens with a detailed, five-point contract addition specifying his trade options, and not just a verbal promise as originally stated. The written addendum, however, had never been submitted to league officials. Toronto and participating clubs also faced potential fines for their loose handling of the trade talks. "We did not follow the letter of the law," Ash acknowledged.[89]

The surprise announcement didn't come until the start of spring training. "In the most significant deal since the purchase of Babe Ruth 79 years ago, the Yankees traded today for Roger Clemens," Buster Olney declared in the *New York Times*.[90] GM Cashman said a persistent Ash had proposed the swap of left-handed ace David Wells, along with relief pitcher Graeme Lloyd and infielder Homer Bush, for the Rocket. Wells, whose lovably gruff, hard-partying posture had made him a fan favorite, had gone 18-4 in 1998, and thrown a perfect game at Yankee Stadium on May 17. Still, the Yankees jumped at the offer.[91] When Wells ambled into the Yankees workout facility at Legends Field the next morning, he acted amused at being immediately summoned to the manager's office.

"I'm in the principal's office already," he quipped, but lost his smile as soon as Cashman and manager Joe Torre broke the news.[92] Only two months earlier, doing some Christmas charity work in the city and feeling secure in his position, he had commented on the prospect of attaining Clemens. "Roger was remarkable," he said. "He was Cy Young. He's got a lot of character and adds a lot wherever he goes, but we did pretty good last year without him. If it takes a lot of players from this organization to get him, is he worth it? If it's a cash thing, give him the cash."[93] Now he was fighting back tears. "Give me a couple days, it's a little tough right now," he said.[94] Meanwhile, Clemens, who agreed to the deal without any extension,[95] was described as "ecstatic."[96] "I know the tradition," he said by phone. "I love it. I love pitching at Yankee Stadium, the monuments, all the stuff that goes with it."[97]

DOUBLE SWITCH

Just like the majors, the minor leagues were facing issues of disparity, and for the second year in a row, VP Pat O'Conner asked minor-league executives to address the imbalance between top-tier and small-market clubs before it was too late. "Financial ruin for the organization is not an imminent threat," he said, "but for many clubs extinction, financially drying up and blowing away, is becoming more of a possibility."[98]

His concern might have seemed unfounded after a year in which gross revenue was close to $16 million, a rise of over 5 percent. As in past years, however, operation costs had also risen, resulting in losses for 36 percent of clubs. And NA President Mike Moore's "task force," formed the prior year to work on the issue, didn't yet have a working plan. While Moore recognized that each club might need an individual solution, O'Conner warned teams to consider the overall organization. "Unless we are able to turn that tide of our smaller markets struggling, it seems even the National Association is in danger of outgrowing small and middle America, something we just cannot let happen. While we may very well need to recognize that baseball in this day and age is not for every community, we cannot idly stand by and lose our smaller communities," he stated.[99]

In their separate league meetings, the minors mostly knocked around the usual topics of franchise moves and team reaffiliations, divisional restructuring, and All-Star Game planning.[100]

The Southern League's discussion was a little more heated. Tampa Bay Devil Rays owner Vincent Naimoli was looking to move his Double-A Orlando Rays into an upgraded facility and had secured a $10 million offer from a group of developers for a brand-new ballpark in Tallahassee.[101] With approval, Naimoli then hoped to relocate his Single-A team, the Florida State League's St. Petersburg Rays, to Orlando. This would nicely separate two competing interests, as the St. Petersburg Rays' current home, Al Lang Stadium, was within spitting distance of the Devil Rays' Tropicana Field.[102]

There was, however, one point of contention: The Southern League wanted restitution for losing the Orlando market. But the rules mandated compensation only when a higher-classification league claimed the territory of a lower-classification league. In this case, the Southern League argued, though a single-A team was moving in, the ultimate beneficiary would be the major-league Devil Rays.

After a lengthy debate, the two sides still seemed to be at odds. SL President Arnold Fielkow emerged from the league's double session without a resolution, only commenting that they'd had a "healthy, lively discussion" and arranged for a follow-up.[103]

And when the Southern League imposed a $1 million relocation fee some time later, the Devil Rays promptly canceled the Tallahassee development deal.[104]

Instead, Naimoli kept his Double-A team in the greater Orlando area, moving them to Disney's Wide World of Sports Cracker Jack Stadium in Kissimmee, a half-hour drive south. But after four losing seasons and a change in ownership, the O-Rays broke their 10-year lease, packed up their equipment, and traveled north to Alabama, where they became the Montgomery Biscuits.[105] And the St. Petersburg Rays played out the rest of their days at Al Lang Stadium, closing down the franchise after the 2000 season.[106]

RULE 5 DRAFT

With the number-one pick in the Rule 5 draft, the Florida Marlins made some news, taking left-handed Venezuelan pitcher Alberto Blanco from the Astros, then handing him off to the Detroit Tigers in a "prearranged deal for cash considerations."[107] But it was pick number four that grabbed the headline. Phillies minor-leaguer and newly minted Heisman Trophy winner Ricky Williams was snapped up by the Expos, and immediately offered for trade. Interested teams were reportedly "lining up" for the University of Texas football star, a rush that surprised Phillies scouting director Mike Arbuckle.

"If he was a little further along with the bat, I could understand it," Arbuckle reasoned. "But he has a long way to go as a baseball player."[108] Drafted by Philadelphia out of San Diego's Patrick Henry High School in 1995 but lured to the University of Texas on a football scholarship, Williams bounced between the diamond and the gridiron, playing four summers in the Phillies' farm system while racking up college football awards during the school year.[109]

The Texas Longhorns' record-breaking running back did manage to turn a few heads as a part-time outfielder. "Fastest guy I ever laid eyes on," minor-league teammate Jimmy Rollins would later say.[110] But his overall baseball performance was unimpressive.

Ted Berg summarized Williams's stats in a short profile for *USA Today*: "Williams batted .211 with very little power across his minor league career, never advancing beyond Class A ball. He struck out 179 times in 568 at-bats. The future NFL star did steal 46 bases in 63 attempts, but never got on base frequently enough to show off his speed on the basepaths."[111]

One day after the Expos' pick, Williams landed with the Texas Rangers, who bought his rights for $100,000. He sat smiling in a Rangers cap, next to manager Johnny Oates, but in the end, the NFL's pull was too strong. He signed with the New Orleans Saints at the April 1999 draft, and never played a game in the majors.[112]

LITTLE WHITE PILLS

One additional piece of news appeared in the papers a few days before the meetings began: a report from AP feature writer Steve Wilstein that baseball was beginning an investigation into androstenedione.[113]

The 1998 season had been supercharged. Pitchers dazzled early: Cubs rookie Kerry Wood struck out 20 in nine innings, tying the mark set twice by Roger Clemens.[114] And at Yankee Stadium a jittery David Wells pounded out his perfect outing before 49,820 on Beanie Baby Day.[115]

But the real jolt came from the hitters. Home runs were flying out of ballparks at a record pace. Mark McGwire, Sammy Sosa, Ken Griffey Jr., and Greg Vaughn were all putting on an electrifying show, chasing Maris's 61.[116] Fans who had been repelled by the 1994-95 players strike returned in droves, the steady launch of red-stitched missiles a thrilling stimulant that hooked them and kept them watching.[117]

Most everybody tried to ignore the other drug.

Wilstein hadn't thought much of the brown bottle when he jotted down a list of personal items on the top shelf of McGwire's locker. But a few weeks later, while reading through his notes, he stopped at the unfamiliar name and made some calls.[118]

A steroid hormone that converts to testosterone in the body, androstenedione was already classified as an anabolic steroid in Canada and banned from use in the NFL, IOC, and NCAA. Numerous doctors viewed it as a dangerous substance, Wilstein learned.[119] Yet in the United States it could be purchased legally as a nonprescription dietary supplement and baseball did not prohibit its use. His article, "Drug OK in Baseball, Not Olympics," was published on August 21, 1998.[120]

The implications were devastating, and Wilstein was made into the villain. McGwire had confirmed his usage of the pills to the AP, along with an amino acid powder, Creatine. But after the article ran he accused Wilstein of "snooping."[121] Cardinals manager Tony La Russa attempted to get him banned from the clubhouse, and even fellow reporters turned on him.[122]

Publicly, Commissioner Selig tried to smooth things over. "I think what Mark McGwire has accomplished is so remarkable, and he has handled it all so beautifully, we want to do everything we can to enjoy a great moment in baseball history," he stated.[123] Quietly, he made some inquiries. Claiming he had not previously known anything about androstenedione, Selig "visited his local pharmacy in Milwaukee where the pharmacist directed him to the bottles of the substance that were openly for sale on the shelves."[124] And he got in touch with Don Catlin, head of the Olympic drug-testing lab at UCLA, who told him that random testing was the only way to clean up the problem.[125] Within the week, Selig and Don Fehr of the Players Association issued a request for a scientific study into the usage of nutritional supplements,[126] hoping to calm the storm. In the midst of a wildly successful, number-smashing year, the last thing baseball wanted to do was call the integrity of the sport into question, or sully one of its big names.[127]

Most sportswriters brushed aside the controversy and focused on the feel-good home-run derby, rejoicing each time McGwire or Sammy Sosa belted another. Over 43 million viewers tuned in to a prime-time Fox telecast of the Cubs-Cardinals game on September 8, and erupted in euphoria when McGwire hit his record-breaking 62nd.[128] He would finish the season with 70 homers and the clear title, ahead of Sosa, who had 66.[129]

Treading carefully, baseball began looking into the matter. Robert O. Millman, medical adviser to the commissioner's office, recommended patience, downplaying the assumption that andro provided a direct boost.[130] And he excused McGwire, saying, "I don't think he was doing anything that was wrong, or that he knew was wrong, or that other people weren't doing. Mark thought of it as sort of a food supplement. And food supplements that you buy in health-food stores are fair game for anyone to take."[131]

Behind the scenes, things weren't so calm. Rick Helling, then a 27-year-old right-handed pitcher and Texas Rangers player representative, spoke out at the 1998 Players Association meeting, held in Las Vegas a couple of days before the gathering in Nashville.[132] "There is this problem with steroids," he told the executive board bluntly. "It's happening. It's real. And it's so prevalent that guys who aren't doing it are feeling pressure to do it because they're falling behind. It's not a level playing field. We've got to figure out a way to address it."[133]

Many team physicians and trainers were also aware of the growing drug problem. At the 1997 Winter Meetings in New Orleans, Astros doctor Bill Bryan had given his colleagues a "list of various supplements and substances, safe and unsafe, with advice about which ones players should avoid." But after voting in favor of passing the information along to their players, they had been stalled by Dr. Millman.[134] This year, with a session entitled "New Drug Policy for Major League Baseball" on the schedule, they thought baseball might be taking action.[135]

Before setting any new policies, baseball officials wanted to know whether ingesting androstenedione tablets did in fact raise testosterone levels.[136] At the meetings, doctors and trainers listened to a proposal from two Harvard Medical School researchers, Joel Finkelstein and Benjamin Leder, for a simple experimental study involving 60 male volunteers, two different doses of the drug, and a placebo.[137]

But then, instead of any further discussion about andro, Millman and Dr. Joel Solomon, medical adviser to the union, proceeded to deliver a high-school-level lecture that seemed to actually promote the benefits of supplementing testosterone while ignoring the documented risk of testicular cancer, heart, and liver disease.[138] Angels GM Bill Stoneman recalled feeling shocked that baseball had allowed such a presentation, and said other executives were similarly vexed by the "message of leniency."[139] And when Cleveland Indians physician William Wilder spoke to players union counsel Eugene Orza, suggesting they provide players with a comprehensive list of supplements, Orza discouraged his efforts.[140] Wilder was incensed. "There is no reason that some preliminary literature can't be sent out to the players concerning the known and unknown data about the performance-enhancing substances," he wrote in a follow-up memo to his GM. "I would like to get something like that out to all players, but when I asked Orza, he said, 'Wait 'til we have more information.' That will be never! Orza and the Players Association want to do 'further study' … so nothing will be done."[141]

Orza, on the other hand, left the meetings in fine spirits, urging open-mindedness. "(T)his is not a time for anyone to be forming firm judgments in such an uncertain area," he told reporters.[142]

On the question of random drug-testing, however, it seemed that his mind was already made up. "I can't imagine the circumstances under which we would do that," he said.[143]

MEETINGS WRAP-UP

After all the build-up the meetings had been disappointing, with only eight trades and 10 free-agent signings.[144] Instead of the positive publicity owners had hoped for, they got pages of bad press about baseball's untenable financial imbalance. Writing for the *Baltimore Sun*, Peter Schmuck skewered baseball's lack of control over its salaries,[145] and Randy Harvey of the *Los Angeles Times* ridiculed owners for allowing Rupert Murdoch to join their ranks, then cry foul when he acted exactly in keeping with his "multinational, multibillion-dollar media empire."[146] In *The Sporting News*, Michael Knisley found fault with the system and baseball's inability to change it. "The game is so fundamentally unfair because its leaders have never figured out a legal way to stop the high rollers from keeping up with the other high rollers, never mind the middle-to-low rollers," he wrote. "Everybody knows these kinds of contracts are wrong, wrong, wrong—unless everybody can pay them. And nobody knows what to do about the teams that can't. You had the sense last weekend at the winter meetings in Nashville that even Malone hated himself for what he was doing with Brown's salary. And he should."[147]

But even though the majors' return had been marred by the same exorbitant contract demands and free agent trouble that had driven them off in 1992, there was no talk of reviving the ban. *Baseball America's* Will Lingo was already looking ahead: "It's probably not necessary, but let me be the last to say that it was great to have the major leaguers back at the Winter Meetings," he wrote. "It added to every aspect of the meetings, bringing more media interest, more major league executives, more managers and players and more fun. Other than the Brown signing, the major leaguers didn't make a whole lot of news, but having them there gave the event a better baseball feel. It's nice to know that almost every significant front-office official in the game was under the same gargantuan roof. It's in Anaheim next year, Mr. Selig. Make your plans to attend now."[148]

Acknowledgements

Thanks to: Michael Teevan, VP Communications, Major League Baseball, & Jeff Lantz, Senior Director, Communications, Minor League Baseball, for research assistance; and SABR member Mike Hanks, for so generously digging into his personal *Baseball America* archive.

BATTING IT AROUND

On Sunday afternoon, one day after the colossal Kevin Brown signing, owner and player representatives faced off again, this time during a town-meeting-style forum hosted by *Baseball America*. The topic of the journal's first "Round Table," an event they hoped to make annual, was the amateur draft. The two-hour-long discussion, moderated by *BA* staff writer Alan Schwartz, was attended by close to 100 baseball people.[1]

Explaining the motivation for the "Round Table," Schwartz wrote that the draft had become an "utter joke." Instead of going in order, the most talented players kept themselves out of the market, waiting for the wealthy teams to sign them to big contracts with even bigger bonuses. Schwartz hoped that an afternoon of open, honest talk might help to identify the problems and get people thinking about solutions.[2]

But despite the friendly name and premise, the two sides were far apart in their ideas.

The physical setup accentuated the divide. On the left: MLB VP of Operations Sandy Alderson, Diamondbacks owner Jerry Colangelo, and Tigers GM Randy Smith sat squarely behind individual microphones at a long, straight, skirted table. Six feet on the right, tilted to face them: an identical table with agent Scott Boras, union second-in-command Gene Orza, and Phillies center fielder Doug Glanville. In the middle, at a tall podium, stood Schwartz.[3]

He started with what everyone knew. Financial disparity was corrupting the draft. Teams with the largest resources seized all the best prospects, year after year, while small-revenue clubs downgraded their expectations. But for each proposed fix—capping bonuses, eliminating free-agent compensation, trading picks, expanding to a worldwide pool—there was a forcible counter-argument.

Even the suggestion that ballplayers might be better off going to college before beginning their careers met with dispute. High-school players, unproven and relatively inexpensive, were being signed in large numbers, and Boras was critical, pointing out that the success rate to have a six-year major-league career was almost double for college athletes. At college, "you learn how to learn," he said. "You learn how to become a professional."[4] Unconvinced, Alderson touted baseball's scholarship program as an alternative, emphasizing that it was irrevocable, with a 70 percent usage rate.[5] When Boras noted that, unlike a fully-covered university scholarship, baseball's program was only "a 60 percent ride," after taxes, Smith stepped in to say that a standard athletic scholarship offered no guarantee in the case of injury, and added that the pressure for college coaches to win caused them to overuse players, especially pitchers.[6]

While the Round Table exchanges stayed civil, certain statements made it clear that underlying philosophies were at issue, not just the particulars of current arrangements.

"From the union's perspective," Orza offered, "the basic problem and concern about the draft is this failure to focus on the draft as a concept to begin with. The draft basically represents an agreement among the clubs to restrict competition for player services. In no other endeavor would we permit someone to do what these clubs do."[7]

A bit further into the discussion, Alderson had a response. "(W)e're creating a competitive environment that leads to a tremendous amount of player compensation," he said. "And while one could argue that for several players there's an artificial limitation on what they get, if it wasn't for this system of compensation we've created, there wouldn't be any money for anyone."[8]

1   Alan Schwartz, "Round One of Round Table Features Polite Jabs," *Baseball America*, January 18-31, 1999: 7.
2   Ibid.
3   Photo by Randy Piland. "Baseball America Round Table '98," *Baseball America*, January 18-31, 1999: 11.
4   Transcript. "Baseball America Round Table '98," *Baseball America*, January 18-31, 1999: 13.
5   Ibid.
6   Transcript. "Baseball America Round Table '98," *Baseball America*, January 18-31, 1999: 14.
7   Transcript. "Baseball America Round Table '98," *Baseball America*, January 18-31, 1999: 11.
8   Transcript. "Baseball America Round Table '98," *Baseball America*, January 18-31, 1999: 12.

NOTES

1   Murray Chass, "After Deals and Signings, What's Left for Winter Meeting?" *New York Times*, December 6, 1998 nytimes.com/1998/12/06/sports/baseball-notebook-after-deals-and-signings-what-s-left-for-winter-meeting.html.

2   Larry Stone, "Trades the Talk at Winter Meeting," *Seattle Times*, December 11, 1998.

3   John Shea, "GMs Are Back, So Let the Meetings Begin," *SF Gate* (sfgate.com), December 6, 1998 sfgate.com/sports/article/GMs-are-back-so-let-the-meetings-begin-3316656.php.

4   Jerome Holtzman, "Jackson Makes Pitch for Minority Hiring," *Chicago Tribune*, December 8, 1992. articles.chicagotribune.com/1992-12-08/sports/9204210874_1_minority-hiring-black-journalists-rev-jesse-jackson.

5   Murray Chass, "Those Tumultuous Winter Meetings Conclude Under a Cloud," *New York Times*, December 10, 1992. nytimes.com/1992/12/10/sports/baseball-those-tumultuous-winter-meetings-conclude-under-a-cloud.html.

6   Ibid.

7   Larry Stone.

8   Peter Schmuck, "Bonds Signs Deal with Giants-to-be/Lurie Protected in $43 Million Pact," *Baltimore Sun*, December 9, 1992. articles.baltimoresun.com/1992-12-09/sports/1992344212_1_barry-bonds-bob-lurie-case-bonds.

9   Ibid.

10 Murray Chass, "The Hot Stove League Cools Off," *New York Times*, October 31, 1993. nytimes.com/1993/10/31/sports/notebook-the-hot-stove-league-cools-off.html.

11 Ronald Blum (Associated Press), "Most GMs to Avoid Winter Meetings," December 2, 1996;

12 personal correspondence: email from Michael Teevan, VP, communications, for major-league baseball, August 15, 2016.

13 Hal Bodley, *USA Today*, November 6, 1998.

14 Keith Russell, "Opryland Hosting Baseball Talks," *Nashville Business Journal*, September 20, 1998 bizjournals.com/nashville/stories/1998/09/21/story1.html.

15 Associated Press, "Clemens, Brown the Hot Topics at Winter Meetings," *Los Angeles Times*, December 12, 1998. articles.latimes.com/1998/dec/12/news/nb-53345; USAToday.com. "The History of Opryland Hotel," traveltips.usatoday.com/history-opryland-hotel-53488.html.

16 Keith Russell.

17 Associated Press, "Clemens, Brown the Hot Topics at Winter Meetings."

18 Will Lingo, "Minors Must Face Up to Financial Concerns," *Baseball America*, January 4-17, 1999: 20.

19 Keith Russell.

20 Lacy Lusk, "Classified Information," *Baseball America*, January 4-17, 1999: 18-19.

21 Associated Press, "Clemens, Brown the Hot Topics at Winter Meetings."

22 John Shea.

23 Murray Chass, "After Deals and Signings, What's Left for Winter Meeting?"

24 Larry Stone.

25 Ibid.

26 Ibid.

27 Jim Salisbury, "Winter Meetings Return, but Phils Don't Plan to Deal," *Philadelphia Inquirer*, December 11, 1998: D02.

28 Keith Russell.

29 Larry Stone.

30 AP, "Clemens, Brown the Hot Topics at Winter Meetings."

31 Murray Chass, "After Deals and Signings, What's Left for Winter Meeting?"

32 "MLB Owners Meetings: Turner in Town to Vote on Dodgers," *Sports Business Daily*, March 18, 1998. sportsbusinessdaily.com/Daily/Issues/1998/03/18/Leagues-Governing-Bodies/MLB-OWNERS-MEETINGS-TURNER-IN-TOWN-TO-VOTE-ON-DODGERS.aspx.

33 Murray Chass, "Turner Has His Say as Owners Weigh Sale," *New York Times*, March 19, 1998. nytimes.com/1998/03/19/sports/baseball-turner-has-his-say-as-owners-weigh-sale.html.

34 Tom Cushman, *San Diego Union-Tribune*, March 17, 1998.

35 Ross Newhan and Michael A. Hiltzik, "Owners Approve Sale of Dodgers to Murdoch," *Los Angeles Times*, March 20, 1998. articles.latimes.com/1998/mar/20/news/mn-30888.

36 Mike DiGiovanna, "Locals Are One Unit Shy," *Los Angeles Times*, December 1, 1998. articles.latimes.com/1998/dec/01/sports/sp-49509& Associated Press. "Johnson Signs with Diamondbacks, Belle with Orioles," *Augusta Chronicle*, December 1, 1998. chronicle.augusta.com/stories/1998/12/01/oth_246225.shtml#.WUh7kdvkeY4.

37 Jason Reid, "Brown Narrows Field to Four," *Los Angeles Times*, December 12, 1998. articles.latimes.com/1998/dec/12/sports/sp-53248.

38 Jason Diamos, "Brown Becomes the Richest in Baseball," *New York Times*, December 13, 1998. nytimes.com/1998/12/13/sports/baseball-brown-becomes-the-richest-in-baseball.html.

39 Ibid.

40 Ibid.

41 Michael Knisley, "A $105 Million Headache," *The Sporting News*, December 21, 1998: 47.

42 Associated Press, "Brown, LA Set Baseball's New Magic Number," *Log Cabin Democrat* (Conway, Arkansas) December 13, 1998. thecabin.net/stories/121398/spo_1213980027.html#.WUh-ztvkeY4.

43 Jason Diamos, "Brown Becomes the Richest in Baseball."

44 Associated Press, "Brown, LA Set Baseball's New Magic Number."

45 Larry Stone, "Memories of Winter Meetings Past," *The Hot Stone League*, December 7, 2009. blogs.seattletimes.com/hot-stoneleague/2009/12/07/memories_of_winter_meetings_pa/ & Ross Newhan, "Baseball; … Or Is It? Despite Industry Backlash, There's No Buyer's Remorse," *Los Angeles Times*, December 13, 1998: D1.

46 Michael Knisley.

47 Jason Diamos.

48 Associated Press, "Brown's Contract Irks the Have-Nots," *Deseret News* (Salt Lake City), December 14, 1998. deseretnews.com/article/668656/browns-contract-irks-the-have-nots.html.

49 Ibid.

50 Ibid.

51 Ibid.

52 Associated Press, "Brown, LA Set Baseball's New Magic Number."

53 Buster Olney, "Tactics in Brown Deal Called Into Question," *New York Times*, December 16, 1998. nytimes.com/1998/12/16/sports/baseball-tactics-in-brown-deal-called-into-question.html.

54 Ibid.

55 Ibid.

56 Ibid.

57 Buster Olney, "Boras Defends Dealings With Brown," *New York Times*, December 18, 1998. nytimes.com/1998/12/18/sports/baseball-boras-defends-dealings-with-brown.html.

58 Ibid.

59 Jason Reid, "Brown's Agent Takes a Swing at the Critics," *Los Angeles Times*, December 18, 1998. articles.latimes.com/1998/dec/18/sports/sp-55252.

60 CBSNews.com Staff. "Clemens Withdraws Trade Demand," *CBS Sportsline*, December 22, 1998. cbsnews.com/news/clemens-withdraws-trade-demand/.

61 Murray Chass, "Clemens Demands to Be Traded," *New York Times*, December 3, 1998. nytimes.com/1998/12/03/sports/baseball-clemens-demands-to-be-traded.html.

62 Ibid.

63 Ibid.

64 Buster Olney, "Owners to Start Meetings as Clemens Saga Winds On," *New York Times*, December 11, 1998. nytimes.com/1998/12/11/sports/baseball-owners-to-start-meetings-as-clemens-saga-winds-on.html.

65 Ibid.

66 Associated Press, "Clemens, Brown the Hot Topics at Winter Meetings."

67 Bob Hille, "Trade Deficit," *The Sporting News*, December 28, 1998: 54-55.

68 Buster Olney, "Astros Won't Meet Clemens's Pay Demand," *New York Times*, December 14, 1998. nytimes.com/1998/12/14/sports/baseball-astros-won-t-meet-clemens-s-pay-demand.html.

69 Ibid.

70 Ibid.

71 Ibid.

72 Ibid.

73 Ibid.

74 "Mets Drop Bid for Clemens," *New York Times*, December 17, 1998. nytimes.com/1998/12/17/sports/mets-drop-bid-for-clemens.html.

75 Jason Diamos, "Jays' Manager Is Hounded by War Tales," *New York Times*, December 15, 1998. nytimes.com/1998/12/15/sports/baseball-jays-manager-is-hounded-by-war-tales.html.

76 Personal correspondence: email from Michael Teevan, VP, communications for Major-League Baseball, August 15, 2016, and February 16, 2017; selected news releases from Major League Baseball—Office of the Commissioner, November 30, 1995-August 26, 1997.

77 Jason Diamos, "Jays' Manager Is Hounded by War Tales."

78 Ibid.

79 Wright Thompson, "Ex-Toronto Manager Pays for Living a Lie," *Chicago Tribune*, August 4, 2003. articles.chicagotribune.com/2003-08-04/sports/0308040180_1_new-friends-pool-hall-tim-johnson.

80 Jason Diamos.

81 Bob Hille.

82 Ibid.

83 Frank Litsky, "Clemens Withdraws Demand for Trade," *New York Times*, December 23, 1998. nytimes.com/1998/12/23/sports/baseball-clemens-withdraws-demand-for-trade.html.

84 Ibid.

85 Bob Hille.

86 Frank Litsky.

87 Ibid.

88 Murray Chass, "Baseball to Fine Beeston Over Clemens's Contract," *New York Times*, December 25, 1998. nytimes.com/1998/12/25/sports/baseball-baseball-to-fine-beeston-over-clemens-s-contract.html.

89 Ibid.

90 Buster Olney, "Yankees Subtract a Star but Add a Legend," *New York Times*, February 19, 1999. nytimes.com/1999/02/19/sports/baseball-yankees-subtract-a-star-but-add-a-legend.html.

91 Ibid.

92 Peter Botte and Dave Goldiner, "Bye, Boomer and Hi, Rocket—Yankees Give Up Wells for Clemens," *New York Daily News*, February 19, 1999. nydailynews.com/archives/news/bye-boomer-rocket-yankees-give-wells-clemens-article-1.831130..

93 Frank Litsky, "For Wells, a New Holiday Uniform," *New York Times*, December 18, 1998. nytimes.com/1998/12/18/sports/baseball-for-wells-a-new-holiday-uniform.html.

94 Peter Botte and Dave Goldiner.

95 "Yankees Trade Wells for Clemens," *Chicago Tribune*, February 18, 1999. articles.chicagotribune.com/1999-02-18/news/9902190037_1.

96 Buster Olney, "Yankees Subtract a Star but Add a Legend."

97 Ibid.

98 Will Lingo, "Minors Must Face Up to Financial Concerns," *Baseball America*, January 4-17, 1999: 20.

99 Ibid.

100 Lacy Lusk, "PCL, SL Dominate Business in Minors," *Baseball America*, January 4-17, 1999: 22-23.

101 Dave Cunningham, "Rays Might Move to Tallahassee," *Orlando Sentinel*, March 14, 1998. articles.orlandosentinel.com/1998-03-14/sports/9803150508_1_orlando-rays-tampa-bay-devil-devil-rays.

102 Lacy Lusk, "PCL, SL Dominate Business in Minors," *Baseball America*, January 4-17, 1999: 22.

103 Ibid.

104 raysbb.com/rbb/Orlando_Rays.

105 Ibid.

106 raysbb.com/rbb/St._Petersburg_Devil_Rays.

107 Allan Simpson, "1998 Heisman Winner Highlights Rule 5 Draft," *Baseball America*, January 4-17, 1999: 24.

108 Ibid.

109 Ted Berg, "Remembering Ricky Williams' Short-lived Baseball Career," *For the Win*, *USA Today*, July 19, 2013. ftw.usatoday.com/2013/07/remembering-ricky-williams-short-lived-baseball-career; baseball-reference.com/bullpen/Ricky_Williams.

110 Ibid.

111 Ibid.

112 Ibid.

113 Steve Wilstein, "Andro Poses Health, Ethical Issues for Baseball," *Southcoast Today*, December 9, 1998. southcoasttoday.com/article/19981209/news/312099937.

114 Mike Lupica, *Summer of '98: When Homers Flew, Records Fell, and Baseball Reclaimed America* (New York: G.P. Putnam's Sons, 1999), 42-43.

115 Mike Lupica, 47-51.

116 Joe Torre and Tom Verducci, "The Man Who Warned Baseball about Steroids," *Time*, February 23, 2009. (Excerpted from "The Yankee Years" by Joe Torre and Tom Verducci. (Doubleday, 2009) content.time.com/time/arts/article/0,8599,1881350,00.html.

117 Ibid.

118 ESPN The Magazine: Special Report "Who Knew?" Part III, 1998-2001 Cause and Effect: The Writer espn.com/espn/eticket/story?page=steroids&num=8.

119 Steve Wilstein, "Drug OK in Baseball, Not Olympics," *AP News Archive*, August 21, 1998. apnewsarchive.com/1998/Drug-OK-in-Baseball-Not-Olympics/id-87e8d2a7928c8de874fdc3f43b53a33a.

120 Ibid.

121 ESPN The Magazine: Special Report "Who Knew?" Part III, 1998-2001 Cause and Effect: The Writer. espn.com/espn/eticket/story?page=steroids&num=8.

122 Mike Bianchi, "Whistle-Blower Finally Receives His Just Reward," *Orlando Sentinel*, December 27, 2004. articles.orlandosentinel.com/2004-12-27/sports/0412270014_1_steroids-in-baseball-mcgwire-locker.

123 ESPN The Magazine: Special Report "Who Knew?" Part III, 1998-2001 Cause and Effect: The Writer espn.com/espn/eticket/story?page=steroids&num=8.

124 George J. Mitchell "Report to the Commissioner of Baseball of an Independent Investigation into the Illegal Use of Steroids and Other Performance Enhancing Substances by Players in Major League Baseball," DLA Piper US LLP, December 13, 2007: 79.

125 ESPN The Magazine: Special Report "Who Knew?" Part III, 1998-2001 Cause and Effect: The Writer. espn.com/espn/eticket/story?page=steroids&num=8.

126 Mitchell: 79.

127 Steve Wilstein, "Andro Poses Health, Ethical Issues for Baseball."

128 Joe Torre and Tom Verducci, "The Man Who Warned Baseball about Steroids," *Time*, February 23, 2009. content.time.com/time/arts/article/0,8599,1881350,00.html.

129 Griffey finished with 56, Vaughn with 50, and nine other players hit 40 or more homers.

130 Steve Wilstein, "Andro Poses Health, Ethical Issues for Baseball."

131 Ibid.

132 Joe Torre and Tom Verducci, "The Man Who Warned Baseball about Steroids," *Time*, February 23, 2009.

133 Ibid.

134 ESPN The Magazine: Special Report "Who Knew?" Part III, 1998-2001 Cause and Effect: The Doctor espn.com/espn/eticket/story?page=steroids&num=9.

135 Ibid.

136 Steve Wilstein, "Andro Poses Health, Ethical Issues for Baseball."

137 Ibid.; Associated Press, "Researchers Will Study Andro Effects," *Deseret News*, December 13, 1998. deseretnews.com/article/668554/Researchers-will-study-andro-effects.html.
The study, funded by an unrestricted grant from Major League Baseball and the Major League Baseball Players Association, was published in February 2000, and concluded that in daily doses of 300 mg, oral androstenedione did increase testosterone levels in healthy men. Benjamin Z. Leder, Joel S. Finkelstein, et al. "Oral Androstenedione Administration and Serum Testosterone Concentrations in Young Men," *Journal of the American Medical Association*, February 9, 2000 — Vol 283, No.6: 779-782.

138 ESPN The Magazine: Special Report "Who Knew?" Part III, 1998-2001 Cause and Effect: The Doctor espn.com/espn/eticket/story?page=steroids&num=9.; Mitchell: 80.

139 Mitchell: 81.

140 Ibid.

141 ESPN The Magazine: Special Report "Who Knew?" Part III, 1998-2001 Cause and Effect: The Doctor espn.com/espn/eticket/story?page=steroids&num=9.

142 Associated Press. "Researchers Will Study Andro Effects," *Deseret News*, December 13, 1998. deseretnews.com/article/668554/Researchers-will-study-andro-effects.html.

143 Steve Wilstein, "Andro Poses Health, Ethical Issues for Baseball."

144 Bob Hille.

145 Peter Schmuck, "Baseball Burned at Hot Stove Fete. Brown, Clemens Focus Gives Winter Meetings High-Priced Black Eye," *Baltimore Sun*, December 16, 1998. articles.baltimoresun.com/1998-12-16/sports/1998350005_1_barry-larkin-pitcher-roger-clemens-kevin-brown.

146 Randy Harvey, "So You Thought Murdoch Would Limit Spending?" *Los Angeles Times*, December 15, 1998: Part D, The Inside Track, Page 2. articles.latimes.com/1998/dec/15/sports/sp-54332.

147 Michael Knisley.

148 Will Lingo.

— 1999 —
ALL ABOUT JUNIOR

By Steve West

THE WINTER MEETINGS OF 1999 WERE held at the Marriott Hotel in Anaheim, California, just down the road from Disneyland. However, "I'm not coming to Anaheim to go to Disneyland," Reds GM Jim Bowden said, stating that his sole goal for going to the winter meetings was to acquire Ken Griffey Jr.[1] Indeed, Griffey was the top prize being offered at the meetings, where teams were expected neither to spend much money on a weak free-agent class nor make many trades until Griffey's future was resolved.

Griffey was everyone's focal point leading up to the meetings. Right after the 1999 season was over, Seattle management had asked his intentions when his contract expired after the 2000 season. Griffey told them he would probably move to a team closer to his home in Florida. When the Mariners said they would prefer to trade him instead of losing him to free agency, Griffey agreed to be traded to one of four teams: Atlanta, Cincinnati, Houston, or the New York Mets.[2] With that, the Griffey deal became the linchpin of the meetings, with everyone expecting the outcome of that transaction to cause a cascade of other transactions.[3]

Although every team was represented at the meetings, not all general managers were there. "There are more lies told in the lobby of winter meetings than anywhere on the face of the earth at any one time," said Braves GM John Schuerholz, which was perhaps the reason he attended for only a couple of days.[4] White Sox GM Ron Schueler said he would skip the meetings because they were just a showcase for agents to bid up the price of their free agents.[5] He sent the club's vice president of player development, Kenny Williams, instead, leading to speculation that the White Sox were going to make a change in the front office, although that was denied by the team. And Yankees owner George Steinbrenner forbade his top lieutenants to go to Anaheim, saying that it was a waste of time, although GM Brian Cashman did work and make deals via the phone.

With a bumper crop of players scheduled to become free agents after the 2000 season—Griffey, Alex Rodriguez, Manny Ramirez, Mike Mussina, and Andy Pettitte among them—numerous teams were holding fire with their money, hoping to snag one of those superstars in a year's time. Because of that, the free-agent market was slow, which in turn made trading a seller's delight, with teams demanding a high price for their players. "I've never seen anything like it," Giants GM Brian Sabean said.[6]

On the other hand, agent Jeff Moorad had coined the term "accelerated free agency" to describe the case of teams trading their players a year before free agency, and those players signing long-term deals with their new team.[7] With all those star players coming to the last years of their pre-free-agency deals, there was the possibility that the winter meetings could see a lot of activity. "It's obviously preferred to make a trade in advance of free agency and presumably get something to help you in the future rather than let a player walk and get nothing in return," said Astros GM Gerry Hunsicker.[8] Agent Barry Meister took a different tack: "I don't suspect a flurry of activity. There might be later, but probably not right now."[9]

There had already been some blockbuster deals earlier in the offseason. At the start of November, the Rangers had jumped ahead of one of their own players with one year left on his contract, two-time MVP Juan Gonzalez, by trading the outfielder to Detroit in a nine-player deal.[10] There was more activity at the general managers' meetings, held in Dana Point,

California, in mid-November. The Blue Jays traded OF Shawn Green to the Dodgers, who quickly signed him to a six-year, $84 million deal. The Blue Jays also sent right-hander Pat Hentgen, the 1996 Cy Young Award winner, to the Cardinals, while the Phillies acquired pitcher Andy Ashby from the Padres.[11] But all that activity wasn't expected to be repeated at the Winter Meetings.

In the days leading up to the Winter Meetings there was some movement. Early in the week first baseman John Olerud left the Mets, signing a three-year, $20 million deal with his hometown Seattle Mariners. The day before the meetings began, the Astros and Craig Biggio signed a three-year, $28 million contract extension, making him the highest-paid second baseman in baseball. "You are talking about a very special player. He probably means as much as any player in the history of this franchise," Hunsicker said.[12] That same day, the Rockies agreed a two-year, $4.15 million contract with catcher Brent Mayne, and the Red Sox signed outfielder Damon Buford for two years and $2.2 million. Then outfielder-DH Harold Baines, whom Baltimore had traded to the Cleveland Indians for the last couple of months of the pennant race, returned to the Orioles for $2 million on a one-year deal.

The Winter Meetings officially began on Friday, December 10, and they began with calamity for Philadelphia. The Phillies had done all their work early, and were headed to the meetings without plans for anything big. They had traded for starter Andy Ashby earlier in the offseason, and signed free agent right-handers Mike Jackson and Jeff Brantley. "Do we have to make a deal? Not necessarily. Do we want to make a deal? Yes, if it makes sense," said GM Ed Wade.[13] Those plans were disrupted on Friday, when the club announced that its top starter, right-hander Curt Schilling, would undergo shoulder surgery and miss the first couple of months of the 2000 season. The Phillies quickly moved to fill that hole, acquiring right-handed pitcher Chris Brock on Sunday from the San Francisco Giants for catcher Bobby Estalella.

Also on Friday, a couple of big deals were announced. In a switch of left-handed relief pitchers, Baltimore traded Jesse Orosco to the Mets for Chuck McElroy. Orosco was returning to the scene of his greatest triumph, having been on the mound when the Mets won the 1986 World Series. Orosco's time in Baltimore came to an end because the Orioles had hired Mike Hargrove as manager. In 1991 while together in Cleveland, Hargrove hadn't used Orosco enough to kick in some bonus money his contract called for, and Orosco was still sore about that. "I had a nice run in Baltimore. I just don't want anything to be a controversy," he said.[14]

Another of the accelerated free-agency deals occurred on Friday, but this time first baseman Carlos Delgado agreed to a three-year, $36 million deal to stay with the Toronto Blue Jays and forgo his free agency, which was a year away. However, Delgado negotiated a clause that allowed him to demand a trade after the 2000 World Series if he wanted, and if the team did not comply, then he could become a free agent.[15]

In other news, catcher Joe Girardi ended his four-year stay with the Yankees, signing with his original club, the Chicago Cubs, for three years and $5.5 million.[16]

The Griffey talks began heating up on Saturday. In the weeks leading up to the meetings, things had been falling apart between the Mariners and their star outfielder. Griffey had given the Mariners the list of four teams he would be willing to be traded to, but after the Mariners brought him several proposals from teams that were not on that list, Griffey decided that it would be Cincinnati—where he went to high school, and where his father was coaching—or nothing.[17] Even so, Mariners GM Pat Gillick was still trying to move him, and not just to the Reds. "I'm optimistic we'll be able to trade (Griffey) at the meetings," said Gillick. "I wouldn't say it's definite, but I do think it's possible."[18]

Because Cincinnati was his hometown, the Reds figured they were in the catbird seat for Griffey, but on Saturday they gave up, breaking off talks between the two teams as they felt the Mariners' demands were too high. "We have a better chance of bringing Goofy back than Griffey," Bowden said.[19] The Reds had tried hard but were frustrated with the Mariners. "We wouldn't have wasted five hours a day for three months not trying to acquire him. But we didn't move a centimeter, let alone an inch," said Bowden.

The biggest obstacle to a deal was the Reds' refusal to give up young second baseman Pokey Reese. Reese said he was flattered. "To get Ken home to Cincinnati, I'd have made the deal. I'm honored my name was used in the same sentence as his."[20]

Mariners GM Gillick said he understood the Reds' position, but indicated things weren't completely closed between the two teams. "I don't think you can ever shut the door on anything," he said.[21] For his part, Bowden's frustration was clear: "I've made 12 to 15 offers. Pat and I have had dialogue almost every day."[22]

Other teams were, of course, still interested in Griffey. The Braves had been on Griffey's original shortlist, and had discussions with Gillick. The Mariners reportedly asked the Braves for both center fielder Andruw Jones and right-handed pitcher Kevin Millwood in return for Griffey. The Braves declined, with manager Bobby Cox saying "I think the price is a little steep."[23]

In a sign that Gillick was working all the angles, he agreed to a deal with the Mets on Monday that sent right-handed pitchers Armando Benitez and Octavio Dotel and outfielder Roger Cedeño to Seattle for Griffey. This reportedly was the same transaction that the Mets had offered Cleveland for Ramirez, one that the Indians had rejected.[24] This trade with the Mariners was also rejected, but this time by Griffey, who had the right to approve any swap as a 10-and-5 player (10 years in the majors, the last five with the same team). When the Mariners called Griffey's agent, Brian Goldberg, to talk about the trade, he told them no. After the Reds had backed out of trade talks, Goldberg said, "I don't know why Seattle is wasting its time talking to a bunch of teams. If he can't go to Cincinnati, then he's going back to Seattle for the final year of his contract."[25]

In other news on Saturday, the Red Sox traded Buford—who just two days earlier had agreed to a two-year contract—to the Chicago Cubs for infielder Manny Alexander. Then, late Saturday night, infielder (and former catcher) Todd Zeile agreed a three-year, $18 million contract with the Mets. Zeile had spent the afternoon in the Rangers' suite, trying to work out a deal to stay in Texas, and went to dinner with his wife and agent to discuss the contract offer, but late in the evening the Mets pounced and quickly got their man. "The fact is I have always wanted the opportunity to play in New York City," Zeile said.[26] The Mets wanted him to move from third base to first to replace Olerud. "That transition will not be a difficult one for him," said Mets GM Steve Phillips. "He's done it in the past."[27]

Sunday was a day of rest, with plenty of talk but little action. The Diamondbacks re-signed infielder-outfielder Tony Womack for four years and $17 million. They planned to move Womack, who had led the National League in steals the last three seasons, from the outfield to become their full-time shortstop.

The Cubs made a move for the third straight day, pushing ahead with their plan to try to become a team made up of more than just Sammy Sosa. They traded right-handers Terry Adams and Chad Ricketts and a player to be named later to the Los Angeles Dodgers for right-handed pitcher Ismael Valdez and second baseman Eric Young. A few days after the meetings the Cubs sent another right-hander, minor-league pitcher Brian Stephenson, to the Dodgers to complete the deal. The Dodgers openly admitted their reasons for the trade — they were cutting payroll. "This is more than a talent issue, cost efficiency is what we're trying to do," said Dodgers GM Kevin Malone.[28]

On the business side of things not much was happening. The biggest story of the week was about third baseman Adrian Beltre. International players were ineligible to be signed until they were 16 years old, but Beltre claimed he was 15 when he originally signed with the Dodgers, and now his agent, Scott Boras, wanted him declared a free agent. Just before the meetings, MLB's executive vice president for baseball operations, Sandy Alderson, said there would be no ruling until the end of the week. This frustrated Boras, who felt that if Beltre was not set free until after the meetings, many teams would have already acted, reducing the potential market for his client.[29] As it happened, Commissioner Bud Selig did not issue a ruling until a week after the meetings, when he penalized the Dodgers with fines and suspensions, and the closing of their Dominican Republic facility for a year. He also awarded Beltre compensation for signing too young, but did not make him a free agent, saying he had been complicit with the Dodgers in falsifying documents that showed him to be a year older than he was.[30]

On Thursday Jeffrey Loria was introduced as the new owner and CEO of the Montreal Expos. The New York art dealer paid $75 million for 35 percent of the club, and said that the Expos would stay in Montreal for the long term.[31] Locals believed that if Loria had not gotten involved the team would have been sold and moved to the United States.[32] Loria also said the team's payroll would jump from $17 million to the mid-$40s by 2002.[33]

In other ownership news, a bid by Mike Prentice to buy the Kansas City Royals had been rejected at the general managers' meetings in November, and Major League Baseball had said it would never approve him because he did not have the funds necessary to cover any potential losses. MLB was aware that the trend of teams wanting to win at any cost, rather than to make money, was a bad one for the future of the sport. "As big a problem as anything in the industry is that a lot of teams are not interested in operating at a profit. If people aren't in business to make money then there's no limit to what they are willing to spend," said Astros GM Hunsicker before the meetings began.[34] The Royals spent the whole winter trying to find local bidders for the team, with CEO David Glass eventually being approved as owner in April.[35]

A man named Socrates Babacus showed up at the Winter Meetings, bringing his personal circus to Anaheim. Babacus, a businessman from Massachusetts, had made several prior bids for professional sports teams, notably in the NFL, and now said he wanted to offer $120 million for the Minnesota Twins. Babacus might charitably be called a dreamer, floating plans for a $350 million retractable-roof stadium for the Twins, similar to other ideas he had for the Philadelphia Eagles and Tampa Bay Buccaneers. His most notable baseball contribution might have been in telling the media at the meetings that Twins officials had told him the team had been taken off the market by owner Carl Pohlad.[36]

During the meetings, umpires were making news across the country in Philadelphia. The Major League Umpires Association had followed a disastrous plan during the 1999 season. Intending to force MLB to open negotiations on a new contract, almost all umpires submitted resignation letters in July, which to their surprise were accepted. After a flurry of activity, many of the umpires were allowed to rescind their resignations, but MLB held out on 22 of them, leading to lawsuits and arbitration, and eventually the decertification of the union, with a group of umpires forming a separate union. Now, the old union was in court fighting for survival and to retain jobs, but eventually the umpires would lose almost every fight and several would never umpire again.

Weekend talks bore fruit on Monday. The Yankees traded Chad Curtis—hero of Game Three of the 1999 World Series—to the Texas Rangers for minor-league right-handed pitchers Sam Marsonek and Brandon Knight. The Marlins swapped outfielders with Pittsburgh, sending Bruce Aven to the Pirates for Brant Brown.

A much bigger deal took place later in the day, with a rare four-team trade going down. Oakland sent right-handed pitcher Jimmy Haynes to Milwaukee. The Brewers sent cash to Oakland, and third baseman Jeff Cirillo and lefty pitcher Scott Karl to Colorado. Tampa Bay sent right-hander Rolando Arrojo and infielder Aaron Ledesma to Colorado. And the Rockies, centerpiece of all the action, sent right-handed pitcher Justin Miller to Oakland, catcher Henry Blanco and right-handed pitcher Jamey Wright to Milwaukee, and third baseman Vinny Castilla—the last of the original Rockies—to Tampa Bay. Even though it took all these moving parts to get the trade done, it could have been even bigger. "There almost was another team involved if I could have gotten another type of player," said Rockies GM Dan O'Dowd.[37] By the end of the Winter Meetings the Rockies had totally overhauled their roster, acquiring 15 players since the World Series.

From the Brewers' perspective, it was a good day. "One of our primary goals at this meeting was to upgrade our pitching and catching situations," GM Dean Taylor said.[38] They did that in one fell swoop, receiving two pitchers and a catcher in the deal.

That same day the Devil Rays also signed outfielder Greg Vaughn to a four-year, $34 million contract. The addition of Vaughn and Castilla to a lineup that already contained Jose Canseco and Fred McGriff had the media calling them a new Murderers Row.[39]

In other news on Monday, Boston closer Tom Gordon had reconstructive elbow surgery, and the Red Sox said he would miss the entire 2000 season. Between 1998 and 1999, the right-hander recorded a major-league record 54 consecutive saves, but then struggled with arm injuries throughout the rest of the 1999 season.

Monday was also the day for the annual Rule 5 draft. Teams are able to take certain minor leaguers from other systems and add them to their major-league rosters. Of the dozen or so players taken each year, one or two occasionally stand out, and it was no different this year. Right-hander Chad Ogea was the rare case of a player with significant major-league experience being taken in the draft. Ogea had pitched six years in the majors, and had even won two games in the 1997 World Series, but had slumped the last couple of years, and been released by the Phillies after the 1999 season. Despite interest from the Rays, he had signed a minor-league deal with the Detroit Tigers. This made him eligible for the draft, and the Rays decided to bring him in after all, although as it would turn out, he would never pitch in the majors again.

It was not known at the time but that draft contained a much more significant pick. The Twins, drafting first, picked a right-handed pitcher named Jared Camp from the Indians' minor leagues. In a prearranged deal, the Marlins then picked southpaw Johan Santana from the Astros, then sent Santana and $50,000 to the Twins for Camp, meaning the Twins essentially got Santana for nothing, as the money covered the draft fee. Camp never pitched in the majors, while Santana went on to win two Cy Young Awards, in 2004 and 2006.

On Tuesday, the last day of the meetings, very little took place as teams began to get out of town. The most notable event was Pittsburgh signing outfielder Wil Cordero to a three-year, $9 million deal. Cordero, joining his fourth team in four seasons, had missed three months in 1999 with a broken wrist, and had not received many offers since recent criminal incidents (a conviction for assaulting his wife in 1997 and an arrest for assault at the start of 1999). The Pirates, though, felt that his past was behind him, with GM Cam Bonifay saying "Since then he's done everything asked of him. ... We did a lot of research about it and we feel very comfortable with him."[40]

A number of discussions begun in Anaheim came to fruition after the meetings were over. The day after the meetings ended, the Astros traded outfielder Carl Everett to the Red Sox for two minor leaguers, shortstop Adam Everett (no relation) and left-hander Greg Miller. The Red Sox had been hoping to delay the deal until they could sign Everett to a long-term contract, but with several teams waiting in the wings on Everett, they decided to go ahead and make the trade.[41]

On Wednesday the Astros also announced that southpaw Mike Hampton had told them he would not sign a contract extension and would become a free agent after the 2000 season. Although Hampton's agent said that it was about opportunity and not a slam on the Astros, the move threw Houston for a loop. "Mike is signed for one more year," said Gerry Hunsicker. "We have to decide if playing him another year makes more sense than trying to trade him."[42] It took them less than a week to decide as they sent Hampton and outfielder Derek Bell to the Mets on December 23, for Dotel and the just-acquired Cedeño, plus left-handed pitcher Kyle Kessel.

In free-agent moves after the meetings, first baseman-outfielder Jeff Conine decided to stay with the Orioles for two years at $5.75 million, right-hander Orel Hershiser returned to the Dodgers for a year and $2 million, and in one of the bigger deals of the offseason, lefty Chuck Finley ended his 14-year tenure with the Angels by signing a three-year, $27 million contract with the Cleveland Indians.

BASEBALL'S BUSINESS: THE WINTER MEETINGS

Looking back, the 1999 Winter Meetings were all about Ken Griffey Jr. There had been some big trades before the meetings, and there were several lesser deals and free-agent signings during the meetings, but for most it was just a matter of waiting for resolution on Griffey, which would cause a domino effect with other deals. As it was, nothing happened with Griffey, which in many ways made the 1999 meetings a dud. It took until February for the Mariners and Reds to finally get together and complete a trade. The Mariners sent Griffey to Cincinnati, and in return got outfielder Mike Cameron, infielder Antonio Perez, and right-handed pitchers Jake Meyer and Brett Tomko. Away from the white-hot spotlight of the Winter Meetings, it all felt a little anticlimactic. So many teams had held fire, waiting for the following year, which would prove to be much more explosive.

NOTES

1. "Griffey Is Top Prize as Baseball Meetings Begin," *Walla Walla* (Washington) *Union-Bulletin*, December 10, 1999: 17.
2. Jeff Horrigan, "Elder Griffey Understands Why Reds Won't Part With Reese," *Laurel* (Mississippi) *Leader-Call*, December 18, 1999: 6B.
3. "Few Moves Expected at Winter Talks," *The Capital* (Annapolis, Maryland), December 10, 1999: D1.
4. "Quote, Unquote," *Lawrence* (Kansas) *Journal-World,* December 12, 1999: 2C.
5. Tracy Ringolsby, "More Teams Turning to Accelerated Free Agency," *Stars and Stripes*, December 12, 1999: 34.
6. "Few Moves Expected at Winter Talks."
7. Ringolsby, "More Teams Turning."
8. Ibid.
9. "Few Moves Expected at Winter Talks."
10. Catcher Gregg Zaun and right-handed pitcher Danny Patterson went to Detroit with Gonzalez, while the Tigers sent utilityman Frank Catalanotto, right-handed pitcher Francisco Cordero, left-handed pitchers Justin Thompson and Alan Webb, catcher Bill Haselman, and outfielder Gabe Kapler to Texas.
11. Green and infielder Jorge Nuñez were sent to the Dodgers for left-hander Pedro Borbon and outfielder Raul Mondesi, the 1994 NL Rookie of the Year. Hentgen and southpaw Paul Spoljaric were shipped to St. Louis in exchange for catcher Alberto Castillo and a pair of hurlers: righty Matt DeWitt and lefty Lance Painter. Ashby went to the Phillies and Adam Eaton, Carlton Loewer and Steve Montgomery—all right-handed pitchers—became Padres.
12. "Astros Make Biggio Second to None at Position," *The Capital* (Annapolis, Maryland), December 10, 1999: D2. Biggio would be elected to the Hall of Fame in 2015.
13. Randy Miller, "Wade Will Tread Cautiously," *Doylestown* (Pennsylvania) *Intelligencer Record*, December 9, 1999: 34.
14. "Orosco Traded to Mets," *Frederick* (Maryland) *News-Post*, December 11, 1999: B1.
15. Ben Walker, "Schilling Set for Surgery, Delgado Stays With Jays," *Rockford* (Illinois) *Register Star*, December 11, 1999: 6E.
16. Bruce Miles, "Baby Steps To Contending Start With Girardi," *Chicago Daily Herald*, December 16, 1999: B-3.
17. Jeff Horrigan, "Elder Griffey Understands."
18. "Griffey is Top Prize as Baseball Meetings Begin."
19. "Reds, Mariners Break Off Talks," *Lethbridge* (Alberta) *Herald*, December 12, 1999: A12.
20. "No New York State Of Mind for Junior," *Kokomo* (Indiana) *Tribune*, December 15, 1999: B2.
21. "Reds, Mariners Break Off Talks."
22. "Griffey Is Top Prize as Baseball Meetings Begin."
23. "Griffey Jr. Price Tag Tough to Meet," *Lethbridge Herald*, December 13, 1999: B3.
24. "Cubs Keep Busy, Swap for Valdes and Young," *Santa Fe New Mexican*, December 13, 1999: B1.
25. Ben Walker, "Griffey Blocks Trade to Mets in Near-Miss," *Daily Sitka* (Alaska) *Sentinel*, December 14, 1999: 6.
26. "Cubs Add Depth With Trade While Dodgers Cut Payroll," *Lethbridge Herald*, December 13, 1999: B3.
27. "Mets sign Zeile; Cubs Make Trade With Los Angeles," *Hutchinson* (Kansas) *News*, December 13, 1999: B1.
28. Ibid.
29. Ringolsby, "More Teams Turning."
30. Murray Chass, "Dodgers Get to Keep Beltre, But are Penalized," *New York Times*, December 22, 1999.
31. "Expos' Saviour Making Plans for New Team," *Brandon* (Manitoba) *Sun*, December 10, 1999: 11.
32. Ibid.
33. Ringolsby, "More Teams Turning."
34. Ibid.
35. "Sale of Royals to Glass Approved," *Aberdeen* (South Dakota) *Daily News*, April 18, 2000: 2B.
36. Ringolsby, "More Teams Turning."

37 "Junior Says No to Mets," *Syracuse* (New York) *Herald-Journal*, December 14, 1999: D5.

38 Ben Walker, "Castilla Traded in Four-Team Deal," *Estherville* (Iowa) *Daily News*, December 14, 1999: 10.

39 Ben Walker, "Tampa Has Devil of Day With Trades, Signings," *Lethbridge Herald*, December 14, 1999: B1.

40 "Cordero Signs Three-Year Deal With Pirates," *Sandusky* (Ohio) *Register*, December 15, 1999: B1.

41 Jimmy Golen (Associated Press), "Astros Trade Everett for Two Minor Leaguers," *Galveston* (Texas) *Daily News*, December 16, 1999: B3.

42 "Hampton Won't Sign as Houston Trades Bat," *Amarillo* (Texas) *Daily News*, December 16, 1999: 4E.

— 2000 —
SHOW ME THE MONEY

By Steve West

THEY SAY EVERYTHING IS BIGGER IN Texas, and when you combine that with the most anticipated free agent in history and a new owner determined to throw money at his team to try to win it all, you get the 2000 Winter Meetings. Over the course of the weekend, nearly a billion dollars was given to players by teams with seemingly more money than they knew what to do with, and once again prognosticators predicted the doom of the sport.

The stars of the show were expected to be shortstop Alex Rodriguez, outfielder Manny Ramirez, and left-handed pitcher Mike Hampton, and so it was. People had been anticipating Rodriguez's free agency for years, reasoning that a young superstar with the numbers he had put up would break all kinds of records both on and off the field.

A lot of free-agent action had already taken place before the meetings, with the Yankees, most notably, giving right-hander Mike Mussina a six-year, $88.5 million contract, taking him away from a division rival (the Orioles.).

Manny Ramirez had asked the Indians for a 10-year deal worth $200 million. Balking at that, the Indians responded with seven years and $119 million.[1] With the two sides far apart, the Indians had signed Ellis Burks to a three-year, $20 million contract, reasoning that they were likely to lose out on Ramirez and would need a replacement, although they said the door was still open for Manny to return.[2]

Rodriguez, for his part, was looked at by every team in the league. Some, of course, just made cursory glances, knowing they had no hope at landing the four-time All-Star. By the time the Winter Meetings arrived, agent Scott Boras said that a number of teams had expressed serious interest in Rodriguez, and thought they might be able to get it done during the meetings. "We've narrowed it down to eight, and I've been negotiating with a smaller group," he said.[3]

Rumors had spread about Rodriguez's demands. Many expected him to become the first $200 million man, with a contract length of at least 10 and perhaps as high as 15 years for the 25-year-old. The Mets reportedly dropped out of the bidding, claiming that Rodriguez wanted an office in the ballpark, his own PR staff, and a billboard as big as Derek Jeter's in New York.[4] Meanwhile, when Rodriguez mentioned on his blog how far back the fences at Safeco were, the Mariners said they were not going to move them, and Boras had to clarify that they were not asking for the fences to be moved as part of the contract.[5]

As the days ticked down to the meetings, things began to happen. Southpaw Denny Neagle, who had won 15 games between the Reds and Yankees during the season, signed with the Rockies for five years and $51.5 million on the Monday before the meetings. The day before the meetings, the Red Sox signed pitcher Frank Castillo for two years and $4.5 million.

Also on Thursday, future Hall of Fame outfielder Tony Gwynn returned to the Padres on a one-year, $2 million deal, keeping him with the only team he'd known for 19 years. "I wanted an opportunity to play my whole career here," he said. "When you think about all the options that you have, that was foremost in my mind. I'm glad that it worked out."[6]

On Friday, December 8, the Winter Meetings opened at the Wyndham Anatole Hotel, near downtown Dallas, Texas. Anticipation ran high, and fans flocked to see what was going on. Neither of the top two free agents was in town yet, with Rodriguez and Boras in Miami meeting with Mariners officials, while

Ramirez's agent, Jeff Moorad, was in California talking to Red Sox people.

Still, news of the first big deal broke right away, that of pitcher Mike Hampton signing with the Rockies. Not formally announced until Saturday, the news raced through the hotel that Hampton had signed for eight years and $121 million, the biggest contract in baseball history, passing the $116.5 million that Ken Griffey Jr. had signed with the Reds in February.

Hampton rejected similar offers from several teams, including the team he was leaving, the Mets, and said he wanted to go to a place where he could raise his family. "What it boils down to is a family decision," he said. "As a whole, this was the place I could move my family to without taking my kid out of school every three months or so."[7]

The New York media—and Mets brass—slammed Hampton for talking about "quality of life" issues in choosing Denver over New York. "I consider that an insult, with a capital 'I,'" one Mets official said. "But if Mike really believes that, (bleep) him, let him go."[8] Hampton was also attacked for his comments about school districts. Mets GM Steve Phillips said, "It's always the money, especially when it's not about the money."[9] But Hampton's agent, Mark Rodgers, said the offers he had received were all equivalent in terms of money. "The New York media want to rake him over the coals. That's fine, but it's not justified."[10]

Major League Baseball Vice President Sandy Alderson said that once again teams had gone too far in giving in to player demands. "There is a benefit to saying no from time to time," he commented. "It would be nice for baseball to experience that benefit occasionally."[11]

On the baseball side of things, Hampton was moving to Coors Field, the worst pitching ballpark in baseball, where he had never done well. "It's a test I look forward to and something that I think will make me a better pitcher in the long run," he said.[12]

The Rockies knew their park was a problem in attracting pitchers, and had decided to offer so much money to top-level talent that it would blow them away. Signing Hampton and Neagle for more than $175 million was all part of their plan. "We added a horse. A number-one starter at the top of the rotation," said Rockies GM Dan O'Dowd. "He's one of the best competitors in the game at his position."[13]

Also on Friday, a few other smaller deals were announced. Andrés Galarraga signed with the Rangers for a year and $6.25 million. Galarraga had missed 1999 because of cancer, then hit .302/28/100 for the Braves in 2000, and was being looked at by several teams after winning *The Sporting News* Comeback Player of the Year Award. "We looked to add a bat with home-run potential, something we sorely missed last year," said Rangers GM Doug Melvin.[14]

Meanwhile, another first baseman, Mark Grace, accepted a two-year, $6 million contract with the Diamondbacks. The Cubs felt they had young first-base talent coming through their farm system and didn't want to block them, so they decided to let Grace go. Grace was unhappy that the Cubs didn't try to re-sign him after he had spent his whole career there, and promised he would get revenge on his old team on the field. "I know we play them nine times this year and I want to kick their (butt) nine times," he said.[15]

For their part, the Cubs were busy looking for pitching, and signed relievers Jeff Fassero (a lefty) for two years at $5.1 million and right-hander Tom Gordon for two years and $5 million. Gordon had missed the whole 2000 season after surgery, and his deal was pending a physical.[16]

After the big start on Friday, Saturday was quiet, although the Hampton deal was formally presented. Instead, everyone was speculating about Rodriguez and Ramirez, reasoning that if Hampton could get so much money, just how far would people go for those two? Teams were beginning to realize just how big a commitment it would take for one of them. "We're not going to get crazy on the Manny Ramirez chase," said Phillips. "We feel that mortgaging our future for an outfielder is not in the best interest of the club."[17]

Not much was happening on the business side of things, either, as everyone was watching the free-agency fireworks. On Saturday, baseball did release its minority hiring report, which showed that minorities had gone from 20 percent to 22 percent of employees overall since the 1997 survey. On the field, minority employees, such as managers, coaches, and scouts, had gone from 26 percent to 30 percent.[18]

Managers and umpires got together during the weekend for a rare discussion. In recent years the top of the strike zone had gotten lower, to the point where anything above the belt was being called a ball. Umpires said they were now being instructed to call the strike zone by the book, while managers said that some movement was okay, but not that much. "We'd all like it to move up an inch or two above the belt. … But 10, 11, or 12 inches? That's wrong. I don't know if the umpires can do that," said Twins manager Tom Kelly.[19]

The discussion was said to be fruitful, but everyone had reservations until they saw the new zone in practice. "There needs to be patience on all parts. We have to live with it. That's what this meeting was about," said umpire Ed Montague, while Alderson said, "There are two things we are looking for in the strike zone. One is accuracy and two is consistency."[20] Managers and umpires also had discussions about the pace of the game, body armor, and other topics.

Managers were also talking about the possibility of a work stoppage when the current labor contract expired after the 2001 season. Commissioner Bud Selig had recently addressed competitive-balance issues and payroll disparity, which led players to believe owners wanted to implement salary caps. "I'm fearful of what might happen," said Cardinals manager Tony La Russa, with Marlins manager John Boles saying, "I'm just petrified."[21]

The minor leagues had their meetings in association with the major-league teams. The Lowell Spinners (a Boston Red Sox affiliate) were awarded the Larry MacPhail Trophy, annually bestowed upon the minor-league team judged to be the best-run.[22] It was also announced that the Triple-A World Series was being canceled. The best-of-five series had been held in Las Vegas for the past three years between the winners of the International League and Pacific Coast League. Due to poor attendance, minor-league officials decided to cancel the event for 2001 and look into future possible formats and locations.[23]

Sunday saw a lot of activity, including the first trade of the meetings, when Anaheim sent right-hand pitcher Seth Etherton to Cincinnati for shortstop Wilmy Caceres. Overall, trading proved to be very quiet during the meetings, with only five swaps being completed. The biggest deal of the meetings, in both quality and quantity, happened on Monday when the Tigers sent catcher Brad Ausmus, and right-handers Doug Brocail and Nelson Cruz to the Astros for outfielder Roger Cedeño, catcher Mitch Meluskey, and right-hander Chris Holt.

Free-agent deals continued to be announced, however. The Pirates gave two-year deals to left-hander Terry Mulholland and right fielder Derek Bell. Shortstop Alex Gonzalez re-signed with the Blue Jays for four years and $20 million, after the team warned him it would move in a different direction if he didn't sign quickly.[24] And catcher Todd Hundley signed for four years and $23.5 million with the Cubs, pending a medical exam, because of the elbow surgery he had undergone three years earlier. It was a return home of sorts for Hundley, who grew up in Chicago while his father, Randy, played for the Cubs. "I've always wanted to play here and to come home to the organization. To play at the place I was at a lot as a kid, missing school. … It's great to be home," he said.[25]

Late on Sunday, the Mets announced they had signed a four-year, $42 million contract with right-handed pitcher Kevin Appier. "New York is a very exciting city," he said. "You can't get a bigger stage than that. If we do great that's only better. I'm glad to have the opportunity."[26]

Also on Sunday, the Rangers gave contracts to right-handed pitcher Mark Petkovsek (two years and $4.9 million) and third baseman Ken Caminiti, the 1996 National League MVP, for one year and $3.25 million, with two option years and bonuses that could take the full contract over $20 million. But the best was just about to break.

Scott Boras spent four hours with Rangers officials during the afternoon, followed by five more hours late into the night.[27] The news broke in the early hours of Monday morning, and was made official a few hours later: The Rangers had come to an agreement with

FIRST PAST THE POST

In December 1998, the commissioner's office and the Japanese baseball commissioner's office reached an agreement governing how Japanese players would reach the major leagues.[*] The terms included:

- Japanese team notifies the Japanese Commissioner's Office they will allow player to be posted.
- Posting is immediately relayed to the US Commissioner's Office.
- U.S. Commissioner lets all 30 major-league organizations know the player is available.
- Major-league clubs then have four business days to bid.
- After the four-day period, the Japanese team is notified of the highest bidder.
- Japanese team then has four business days to accept or reject the offer.
- If Japanese team rejects the offer, the Japanese player plays another year in the Japanese baseball league.
- If the Japanese team accepts the bid, the winning bidder then must come to terms with and sign the player within 30 days; if they can't get this done on time, again the player returns for the next season to the Japanese league.
- If the Japanese player agrees on terms with the major-league team, the club then pays the Japanese team its money within five days of the player's signing.

The first player successfully signed via the new system was Alejandro Quezada, with a winning bid of $400,001.[**] The second player signed through the new system managed to net a winning bid of $13,125,000 for his Japanese team: Ichiro Suzuki.[***]

---

[*] Marty Kuehnert, "Ichiro Trying to Make the Most of Bad System," *Japan Times*, November 5, 2000.
[**] Sean Keeler, "Reds Winning Bidder," *Cincinnati Post*, February 9, 1999: 2C.
[***] Michael Street, "A Brief History of Japanese-American Baseball Relations, Part 3: The Tazawa Effect," *Sports & Recreation Examiner*, December 4, 2008. See also Larry Stone, "M's Win Bid to Woo Suzuki—Seattle Gets 30 Days to Sign Japanese Star at Cost of $13 Million," *Seattle Times*, November 10, 2000: C1.

Alex Rodriguez on a 10-year, $252 million contract, by far the largest deal in the history of baseball, or any other sport, for that matter.

In 1998 Tom Hicks had spent $250 million to buy the Rangers, and now he was spending $252 million on just one player. "I like to win. I like to build things," he said.[28] Hampton's record contract had lasted just two days, with the Rodriguez deal more than doubling the baseball record. It also exactly doubled the dollar total of the previously listed highest contract in sports, the $126 million that Kevin Garnett had received to play for the NBA's Minnesota Timberwolves in 1997.[29]

Reaction across the league was furious. "In two days, we've doubled a new highest salary," said MLB's Alderson. "I don't like the exponentiality of that. … It's a straight upward trend that doesn't look like it will augur at all. Every club will be affected by this."[30] Faced with criticism by the industry about how big and how distorted the deal was, Hicks said, "I think that's a very complicated issue that can't be solved just by the owners but solved collectively by the whole industry."[31]

Meanwhile Rangers players were excited. "If the money wasn't there, it wouldn't be offered," said first baseman Rafael Palmeiro.[32] Galarraga, signed by the Rangers on Friday, reacted with delight to the Rodriguez deal. "With this team, we've got four or five guys who can hit 40 home runs," he said.[33] In the front office they were bullish on the team's future. "Alex is the player we believe will allow this franchise to fulfill its dream of continuing on its path to becoming a World Series champion," said Hicks.[34] "I know expectations will be high. We're ready to meet that challenge," said GM Melvin.[35]

When they saw the price tag for Rodriguez, the other teams that had been finalists for his services learned just how far away they really were. The Mariners were eliminated because they wouldn't offer more than five years. "When they came with a three-year guarantee and a two-year out, I was in disbelief. I just walked away from it, and knew I wouldn't have a real choice," Rodriguez said.[36] "We couldn't go there," said Mariners GM Pat Gillick. "There would have had to have been a major hometown discount to get us into the ballpark."[37] The Braves lost out when they would not give a no-trade clause. "Where (Alex) plays ball, he wants to make his home. So that was really something that directed us in a different direction," Boras said.[38]

Later in the week Rodriguez addressed the Mets' lack of attention during the bidding process. The Mets had dropped out early, citing various requirements by Rodriguez, such as an office in the ballpark and his own PR staff. Reportedly his original first choice, they were never in the running after they made those allegations. "I was intrigued by the way they dropped out of negotiations. That was quite dramatic. All they had to do was say they're not interested. And I would have been very happy with that and moved on," he said.[39] On the other hand, it was suggested in some quarters that the Mets were making excuses, because they had chickened out when the price got so high.[40]

Comparisons of how much money the contract was worth ranged from the sublime to the ridiculous. One note said that you could pay the entire payrolls of the Yankees, Braves, and White Sox for $244 million. Another said that Rodriguez would average $45,000 per at-bat during the course of the contract. And one even pointed out that you could get more than 84 million McDonalds Happy Meals ($2.99 each).[41]

Even the Yankees chimed in on the Rodriguez contract, with their own star shortstop Derek Jeter a year away from free agency. "We expect to no longer hear any criticism from any quarter of the Yankees since our record is absolutely consistent in that we have not broken any barriers. The lion's share of our spending is on retaining our own players," Yankees President Randy Levine said. He also said it would be "the height of hypocrisy" for the teams that had spent big to "ever complain about anything again."[42]

In other action on Monday, right-hander Darren Dreifort decided to stay with the Dodgers for five years and $55 million. Then, late on Monday night, the second superstar contract was agreed on when — almost overshadowed by the Rodriguez deal — Manny Ramirez decided to sign with the Red Sox for eight years and $160 million, the second largest deal ever.

By that point the meetings were coming to a close, with a number of teams having already packed up and left town the day before they were officially scheduled to end on Tuesday. With the circus folding its tent, the news that Ramirez had spurned a $136 million offer from Cleveland barely caused a ripple in the media, exhausted by the huge numbers being thrown around.

Although both sides had given their best pitches to Ramirez, sending players, coaches, and others to talk to him, he decided that Boston had a better chance to win than Cleveland did. The presence of his good friend Pedro Martinez was also cited as a huge factor for Ramirez going to Boston.[43] Both sides gave the obligatory quotes about how well the process had worked, and how good a player the Red Sox were getting. "Dan was a bulldog on this project from Day 1," said Manny's agent, Jeff Moorad.[44] "This kid has been the most gifted hitter in the business. We're a lot stronger than we were," said Red Sox GM Dan Duquette.[45]

Deals continued to be made in the days after the meetings ended, however, following up on events that had begun in Dallas. Having signed a new shortstop in Rodriguez, the Rangers then traded the incumbent, sending Royce Clayton to the White Sox for two right-handed pitchers, Aaron Myette and Brian Schmack.

A week after the meetings ended, the Houston Astros joined the money parade, extending the contract of first baseman Jeff Bagwell for five years and $85 million, tying another first baseman, Toronto's Carlos Delgado, for the third highest average annual salary.

With that, the 2000 Winter Meetings effectively came to an end. It had been a weekend that had shocked the sport, and the ripples from those few days in Dallas would reverberate for years to come. Commissioner Bud Selig said he hadn't been surprised by the money spent at the Winter Meetings. "The inequity in this system is now so apparent," he said. "The question is, how do we fix it and what do we do?"[46] Wendy Selig-Prieb, president and CEO of the Milwaukee Brewers, followed her father's lead, saying that all the money being spent got their attention. "There needs to be meaningful reform in the economics of baseball," she said.[47]

There were renewed calls for the economic restructuring of the game, with owners pointing to other sports as a model. The NFL and NBA, for instance, had salary caps, revenue-sharing, and other limits on player pay that helped them to succeed, and Braves President Bill Bartholomay called for similar structures in baseball. "They have to recognize what other sports have done, bite the bullet and everybody will do better," he said.[48]

With the labor agreement expiring after the 2001 season, people were already looking at the threat of tough negotiations leading to another strike or lockout. "I pray there isn't another work stoppage, because if there is, baseball is in trouble," said Phillies manager Larry Bowa.[49] Donald Fehr, executive director of the players union, heard the discussion of a work stoppage, but dismissed it. "I'm not going to respond to that stuff," he said. "They'll say what they say. I'm not going to play that game."[50]

In total, teams had committed to almost three-quarters of a billion dollars in contracts throughout the Winter Meetings, putting them over a billion dollars for the offseason. "The well's got to run dry. It seems it does for a little bit, but then it starts back up," said Bowa.[51]

A final word may go to the star of the weekend. "Hopefully when it's over, they won't be calling Mr. Hicks a fool but the wisest man in baseball. Only time will tell. But I'm looking forward to the challenge. For me, it revolves around baseball," said Rodriguez.[52] Time would prove him completely wrong.

BASEBALL'S BUSINESS: THE WINTER MEETINGS

NOTES

1. Tom Withers, "Tribe Offers Arbitration to Three," *Ashtabula* (Ohio) *Star Beacon*, December 8, 2000: B1.
2. Ibid.
3. "Amending Fences Not in Mariners' A-Rod Plan," *Lethbridge* (Alberta) *Herald*, December 5, 2000: B3.
4. Jon Heyman, "A-Rod Upset at Mets," *Stamford* (Connecticut) *Advocate*, December 13, 2000: C6.
5. Ibid.
6. Ronald Blum (Associated Press), "Gwynn Stays With Padres; Cone Leaving the Yankees," *Northwest Florida Daily News* (Fort Walton Beach), December 8, 2000: C5.
7. Ronald Blum, "Hampton Gets $121M to Love Coors Field," *Rockford* (Illinois) *Register Star*, December 10, 2000: 9G.
8. Bob Klapisch, "Criticism of Area by Hampton Has Mets' Brass Angry," *Stamford Advocate*, December 10, 2000: C5.
9. Blum, "Hampton Gets $121M."
10. Ibid.
11. Ibid.
12. Ibid. It didn't work out that way. Hampton only spent two years with the Rockies, compiling a 21-28 record, with a 5.75 ERA and a 1.677 WHIP. He would have two good years in Atlanta before injuries derailed his career.
13. Josh Dubow (Associated Press), "Hampton Hoping to Avoid the Curse of Coors Field," *Fitchburg* (Massachusetts) *Sentinel & Enterprise*, December 10, 2000: C3.
14. "Galarraga Finds Home With Rangers," *Chicago Daily Herald*, December 9, 2000: section 2, page 3.
15. "Cubs Get Help for Bullpen," *Rockford* (Illinois) *Register Star*, December 9, 2000: 3E.
16. "Cubs Bolster Bullpen; Galarraga Signs With Texas," *Lawrence* (Kansas) *Journal-World*, December 9, 2000: 10C.
17. Blum, "Hampton Gets $121M."
18. "Baseball Makes Marginal Increases in Number of Minority Employees," *Chicago Daily Herald*, December 10, 2000: section 2, page 4.
19. "Baseball Notes," *Columbia* (South Carolina) *State*, December 11, 2000: C3.
20. "Mets Load Up on Pitchers Appier, Trachsel," *Columbia State*, December 12, 2000: C5.
21. "Baseball Notes," *Columbia State*, December 11, 2000: C3.
22. "Simply the Best," *Lowell* (Massachusetts) *Sun*, December 8, 2000: 9.
23. "No Triple-A Series," *Syracuse* (New York) *Herald-Journal*, December 13, 2000: D2.
24. "Rodriguez Narrows Field," *Doylestown* (Pennsylvania) *Intelligencer Record*, December 11, 2000: B8.
25. "Ramirez Gives Sox a Building Block," *The Capital* (Annapolis, Maryland), December 14, 2000: D5.
26. Ben Walker (Associated Press), "Appier in New York for Physical, Close to Deal With Mets," *Ukiah* (California) *Daily Journal*, December 11, 2000: 6.
27. "Megadeal," *Northwest Florida Daily News*, December 25, 2000: D5.
28. Thomas Stinson, "$252 Million," *Columbia State*, December 12, 2000: C1.
29. Ibid.
30. Ronald Blum, "Owners Deliver $1B to Players," *Rockford* (Illinois) *Register Star*, December 13, 2000: page number unknown.
31. Stinson.
32. "Rodriguez's Deal Shocks Baseball," *Augusta Chronicle*, December 12, 2000: 3C.
33. "Galarraga Should Fit Nicely in Texas," *Stamford Advocate*, December 12, 2000: C5.
34. Ronald Blum, "Rangers Win Rodriguez Sweepstakes—at Record Price," *Chicago Daily Herald*, December 12, 2000: 2.
35. Ibid.
36. "ARod Addresses the Media," *St. Albans* (Vermont) *Messenger*, December 13, 2000: 9.
37. "M's Couldn't Come Close to Texas-Sized Bid," *Walla Walla* (Washington) *Union-Bulletin*, December 12, 2000: 14.
38. Stinson.
39. Jon Heyman, "A-Rod Upset at Mets," *Stamford Advocate*, December 13, 2000: C6.
40. Bob Klapisch, "Despite Signing Mussina, All Not Well With Yanks," *Stamford Advocate*, December 5, 2000: B8.
41. Stinson.
42. "Jeter May Benefit From A-Rod's Deal," *Syracuse* (New York) *Herald-Journal*, December 13, 2000: D2.
43. "Ramirez Gives Thumbs-Up to New Deal With Red Sox," *Augusta Chronicle*, December 14, 2000: 5C.
44. Ibid.
45. Ibid.
46. "Selig: Changes Coming in Game's Economic Structure," *Augusta Chronicle*, December 14, 2000: 5C.
47. Ibid.
48. "Selig Knows Score and It's Not Good," *The Capital*, December 14, 2000: D5.
49. Blum, "Rangers Win Rodriguez Sweepstakes."
50. Ronald Blum, "Salaries, Naysaying on Rise," *Doylestown* (Pennsylvania) *Intelligencer*, December 13, 2000: B6.
51. "ARod Addresses the Media," *St. Albans Messenger*, December 13, 2000: 9.
52. Stephen Hawkins, "Texas Welcomes A-Rod," *Fitchburg* (Massachusetts) *Sentinel & Enterprise*, December 13, 2000: B3.

— 2001 —
ALL QUIET ON THE CHARLES

By Clayton Trutor

Introduction and Context

THE 2001 WINTER MEETINGS WERE held in Boston at the Marriott Copley Place Hotel from Sunday, December 9, to Friday, December 14. This was the second time the city had played host to the meetings, the first time being just five years earlier, in 1996. Commissioner Alan Selig's announcement, made soon after the World Series, that two teams would be dropped from the major leagues (reportedly the Montreal Expos and Minnesota Twins) hung ominously over the Winter Meetings. Representatives of the owners and the players union agreed to postpone further discussion on the time-frame of contraction at the Boston meetings. Owners discussed a new revenue-sharing plan, but action on the issue was pushed back. Similarly, the Major League Baseball Players Association and the club owners put off more concrete discussions of a new labor pact until later in the offseason. Except for perennial big spenders like the New York Yankees and the New York Mets, player movement, either through trades or free agency, lagged at these meetings when compared to the outpouring of spending at the 2000 Winter Meetings in Dallas.

Player Movement

Caution characterized the trade and free-agent markets at the 2001 Winter Meetings. The vast majority of marquee free agents remained available at the end of the week, including Barry Bonds, Chan Ho Park, Moises Alou, Juan Gonzalez, Jason Schmidt, Johnny Damon, and Tino Martinez.[1] Each of them, however, signed a lucrative deal either with their old club or a new club by the middle of January. Whether the reluctance to sign big-name free agents was a product of the economic downturn, the belief by some owners that a dispersal draft was imminent, or, as the union and some prominent player agents suggested, "collusion" on the part of big-league clubs to keep prices down, the six free-agent signings announced at the 2001 Winter Meetings totaled a mere $60 million in salaries. This total differed considerably from the record-breaking $739 million spent on 25 players, including the jaw-dropping Alex Rodriguez and Mike Hampton deals, at the 2000 meetings in Dallas.[2]

The most lucrative free-agent signing negotiated in Boston was the seven-year, $120 million deal the New York Yankees made with Oakland A's slugger Jason Giambi. Giambi and the Yankees finalized the contract over the weekend after the Winter Meetings and announced the move the following week. The Giambi signing came on the heels of the Yankees' inking former Cleveland set-up man Steve Karsay to a four-year, $22.5 million deal in Boston. Other noteworthy free agent signings included those of veteran reliever Norm Charlton, returning to Seattle for 2002, emerging closer Keith Foulke, signing a two-year contract with the White Sox, and pitcher Jay Powell signing for one year with the Texas Rangers. The St. Louis Cardinals signed Oakland's standout closer Jason Isringhausen to a four-year, $27 million contract. The reigning AL West champion Athletics responded by swapping third baseman Eric Hinske, who would win the 2002 AL Rookie of the Year award, and pitcher Justin Miller to Toronto for closer Billy Koch.[3]

The New York Mets proved to be the busiest team on the trade market in Boston, as GM Steve Phillips moved to rebuild the club for another World Series run after a disappointing 2001 season. On the opening day of the Winter Meetings, the Yankees and Mets announced their first trade in eight years. The teams swapped former perennial All-Stars, with the Mets sending third baseman Robin Ventura to the Yankees for outfielder David Justice. Both players had struggled through injury-shortened 2001 seasons. Justice's tenure with the Mets was predictably short-lived, since he was now more of a designated hitter than a position player—Phillips shipped him to the A's for veteran reliever Mark Guthrie and pitching prospect Tyler Yates on the final day of the Winter Meetings.[4] The Mets also sought to improve their pitching staff by acquiring left-hander Shawn Estes from the Giants for outfielder Tsuyoshi Shinjo and middle infielder Desi Relaford. However, the Mets' blockbuster move at the Winter Meetings was an eight-man deal that brought in future Hall of Famer Roberto Alomar, along with two prospects, left-hander Michael Bacsik and slugging first baseman-outfielder Danny Peoples, from the Cleveland Indians in exchange for outfielders Alex Escobar and Matt Lawton, right-hander Jerrod Riggan, and two players to be named later, who turned out to be infielder Earl Snyder and lefty pitcher Billy Traber.[5]

Other significant trades at the 2001 Winter Meetings included the Yankees' acquisition of first baseman-outfielder John Vander Wal from the San Francisco Giants for pitcher Jay Witasick. The Colorado Rockies, one year removed from their eight-year, $123.8 million signing of pitcher Mike Hampton, found themselves looking to sell off expensive assets in Boston. They traded two-time All-Star third baseman Jeff Cirillo and his $30 million contract to the Seattle Mariners for three pitchers—lefty Brian Fuentes and right-handers Denny Stark, and Jose Paniagua.[6]

The Business Side

Major League Baseball faced three major business concerns coming into the Winter Meetings: 1) the proposed contraction of two major-league teams, which press reports indicated were most likely to be the Montreal Expos and Minnesota Twins; 2) the need for the owners and the players union to agree to a new collective-bargaining contract by August 31, 2002, in order to avoid a repeat of the 1994-1995 strike, which had wiped out the 1994 World Series; and 3) the requirement that Major League Baseball implement the recommendations of the Commissioner's Blue Ribbon Panel, which in 2000 declared that revenue-sharing was necessary to ensure the competitive balance of the sport. The revenue-sharing plan had to be approved by the players as part of the coming labor pact. Baseball's leadership tabled concrete action on all three of these issues in Boston, preferring instead to deal with them at a later date.[7]

On November 6, two days after Game Seven of the World Series, Commissioner Selig announced that the owners had voted 28 to 2 at their quarterly meeting in Chicago to eliminate two teams, one from each league, to improve competitive balance. Press reports pointed to the Minnesota Twins and Montreal Expos (or possibly the Florida Marlins) as the most likely candidates to face elimination. Reaction to the announcement proved swift. The players union filed a grievance, arguing that contraction violated their soon-to-be-expiring contract. Legal challenges to contraction from the states of Florida and Minnesota provided additional roadblocks to eliminating two franchises. Threats of an end to baseball's federal antitrust exemption emanated from the halls of Congress. Senator Paul Wellstone (D-Minnesota) led the charge to end baseball's long-standing exemption and to protect his hometown Twins. Commissioner Selig testified before the House Judiciary Committee in late November, at hearings held to examine the antitrust exemption, and claimed that major-league teams lost nearly $500 million in 2001, with 25 of the sport's 30 teams losing money. Contraction, Selig argued, was the only way baseball could improve competition on the field and avoid further financial hardship for its franchises.[8]

Representatives from all 30 teams, therefore, went to Boston not knowing if contraction would be finalized at the meetings. If contraction became a reality, owners also had to consider the possibility that a dispersal draft of players from the two eliminated teams might be held at the Winter Meetings. Speculation about a wild week in Boston was quickly neutralized after representatives of the owners and the Players Association agreed to postpone contraction until at least 2003. The agreement, which was hashed out in a meeting led by Sandy Alderson, executive vice president of Major League Baseball, and Gene Orza, assistant general counsel for the union, took contraction off the table as the two sides inched toward serious discussions of a new collective-bargaining agreement, a process that dragged out until a last-minute, season-saving accord was reached on August 30, 2002. Talk of contraction pushed back serious discussions on other major areas of difference between the players and the owners, including revenue-sharing and the extent of the luxury tax assessed to wealthy franchises. Preliminary talks on both issues were held in Boston, though a consensus on how to deal with them was not reached.[9]

Summary

The 2001 Winter Meetings in Boston lacked the drama many observers had been anticipating. Few major trades or free-agent signings took place. Tangible discussion of league business, including contraction and the new collective-bargaining agreement, were put off for a later date.

NOTES

1 Jack Curry, "At the Winter Meetings, Wheeling, Dealing Will Be High on the Agenda," *New York Times*, December 9, 2001: SP2; Thomas Stinson, "Baseball: Baseball Notebook," *Atlanta Journal-Constitution*, December 16, 2001: 9D; Tracy Ringolsby, "A Winter of Waiting May Thaw Next Week," *Seattle Post-Intelligencer*, December 8, 2001: C2.

2 "Baseball," *New York Times*, December 16, 2001: SP13; Mike Klis, "Players take Center Stage, Trades Focus of Meetings," *Denver Post*, December 9, 2001: SP3.

3 Buster Olney, "Knoblauch May Play at Second for Royals," *New York Times*, December 12, 2001: S5; Ringolsby; Klis; Stinson.

4 Klis; Olney.

5 Olney; Stinson.

6 Klis.

7 Jack Curry, "Talks on Contraction Focus on Postponement," *New York Times*, December 11, 2001: S5; Ringolsby.

8 Ringolsby; Klis; Curry, "Talks on Contraction."

9 Ringolsby; Klis; Curry, "Talks on Contraction."

— 2002 —
RETURN TO NASHVILLE

By Jerry Swenson

Introduction and Context

THE 2002 WINTER MEETINGS WERE held from December 13 to December 16 at the Opryland Hotel in Nashville, Tennessee. This was the fourth time they were held at this venue. Economic conditions in some markets had made contraction—eliminating two or more teams—a concern during the 2001 Winter Meetings. Contraction was not a consideration during the 2002 meetings as two events occurred in 2002 that deferred any discussion of contraction until later in the decade.

On February 5, 2002, Commissioner Alan Selig had issued the following statement: "While the clubs would have preferred to contract for 2002 and begin addressing the economic issues immediately, events outside of our direct control, including yesterday's court decision in Minnesota, have required us to move the date of contraction to 2003."[1] Later that year, the collective-bargaining agreement (CBA), agreed to in August 2002, eliminated contraction as an immediate concern and prohibited it through the 2006 season.[2] The CBA increased local revenue-sharing and provided a revenue-sharing central fund, reinstated the luxury tax, and provided a $10 million discretionary fund for the commissioner.[3]

A series of developments after the 2001 World Series ultimately led to Major League Baseball taking ownership of the Montreal Expos. Shortly after the World Series ended, Selig had announced that two teams would be dropped before the 2002 season. There was not much interest from many owners in getting out of baseball.[4] The owners of the Montreal Expos and the Tampa Bay Devil Rays wanting to remain in baseball were featured prominently in MLB's assuming ownership of the Expos. Jeff Loria, the owner of the Expos, wanted to operate a baseball team as did John Henry, the owner of the Florida Marlins.[5] Also occurring at this time was sale of the Boston Red Sox by the Yawkey Trust. John Harrington of the Yawkey Trust was tasked with selling the club to the highest bidder. There was interest from Charles Dolan (Cablevision) and syndicates headed by Miles Prentice and Joseph O'Donnell in bidding for the Red Sox.[6] Another group of bidders, including Les Otten, Tom Werner, Larry Lucchino, and George Mitchell, did not have enough money to meet the top bids. This group of bidders needed another partner to provide additional money to win the bidding.[7] Meanwhile, Selig was arranging a three-way franchise swap. Henry would swap the Marlins for the Red Sox, Loria would swap the Expos for the Marlins, and Major League Baseball would buy the Expos.[8] The winning bid for the Red Sox (including the New England Sports Network and Fenway Park) was not the highest bid; both Dolan and a group headed by Prentice presented higher bids.[9] No one had ever paid half as much for a baseball team at the time.[10]

Finances continued to play a role in the business plans and strategies of the previous contraction candidates and would affect player movement during the meetings. Major League Baseball implemented a payroll budget and informed the Expos' general manager, Omar Minaya, that the team payroll must be reduced to $44 million. Given this budget requirement, Minaya was not expected to be able to retain the current group of players, who were expected to earn more than $50 million.[11] General managers on other teams hoped that Minaya would quickly identify the players he would make available.

ON HOLD ... FOR FIVE YEARS ... OR MAYBE MORE

Less than a month before the 2002 Winter Meetings, Pete Rose reportedly attended a hearing with Commissioner Bud Selig, with Rose seeking reinstatement to the game, from which he had been banished in 1989. Major League Baseball initially denied that the 2002 meeting took place, and Bob DuPuy, baseball's chief operating officer, later said, "Pete Rose applied for reinstatement several years ago (September 1997) to commissioner Bud Selig and that application has been pending since that time. Given the pendency of the application for reinstatement, neither the commissioner or anyone in our office will comment on the Pete Rose matter further."* After the Winter Meetings, it became clear that a meeting had taken place, when Jeff Idelson of the National Baseball Hall of Fame said, "It was a meeting to bring us up to speed on a number of issues. They gave us an update on Pete Rose. Anything going on is between baseball and Pete Rose. The Hall of Fame has no role in it."**

In the two instances in which Rose was granted a brief exception from banishment — for the 1999 All-Century Team celebration in Atlanta, and the 2002 World Series celebration of Baseball's Top Ten Moments - Rose was cheered and Selig was booed.*** Also, the commissioner's office had recently suffered several potential blows to its reputation - some fans were angry at plans for contraction, members of Congress called Selig a liar during a hearing on baseball economics, *Sports Illustrated* reported that steroid use was widespread in the game, the All-Star Game ended in a tie, and the players nearly went on strike.****

---

*   Hal McCoy, "Actions May Be Under Way for Rose Reinstatement – Baseball, Hit King Say 'No Comment' on Rumor," *Dayton Daily News*, December 11, 2002: 1A.
**   Michael O'keeffe, "Bookie: Bet on Rose Confession," *New York Daily News*, December 19, 2002: 82.
***   McCoy.
**** Michael O'keeffe, "Inside War of Rose's: Answering the Controversy's Red-Hot Questions," *New York Daily News*, December 16, 2002: 58.

Free-agent signings were also very slow heading into the meetings. Referring to the free-agent market, Orioles Executive Vice President Jim Beattie commented, "It's not a quickly developing market, that's for sure. Even with the December 7 deadline [for offering players salary arbitration], I didn't think there was much urgency. People are still tiptoeing into the water. There is a lot of consideration among teams not to be the one to set the market."[12]

The Red Sox operated with an interim general manager, Mike Port, during the 2002 season but elected to search for a new GM after the season. They initially offered Billy Beane the position but he decided to remain with the Oakland A's. The Red Sox promoted Theo Epstein, assistant to team President Larry Lucchino, to general manager on November 25, 2002.[13]

Although many teams were slow to sign free agents before the meetings, the Philadelphia Phillies and New York Mets were exceptions. The Phillies signed free agents Jim Thome and David Bell hoping to improve the team before its move into a new ballpark in 2004.[14] The Phillies also showed interest in Tom Glavine, but he eventually signed with the New York Mets.[15]

The Los Angeles Dodgers were looking for roster flexibility but were hampered by payroll issues and a concern about exceeding the luxury tax threshold. To help alleviate these concerns, they traded infielders

BUCK RODGERS IN THE TWENTY-FIRST CENTURY?

Following declining attendance and World Series ratings for the 2002 season, Bud Selig announced a task force, named Major League Baseball in the Twenty-First Century, to address marketing issues. Selig included the following as his initial task force members:

- David D'Allesando (John Hancock Financial Services Inc.), chairman.
- Terry McGuirk (Turner Broadcasting System), vice chairman.
- Len Coleman (former NL president).
- Gene Orza (Major League Baseball Players Association).
- Bob Daly (Dodgers chairman).
- Tom Werner (Red Sox chairman).
- Peter Chernin (News Corp. chairman).
- George Bodenheimer (ESPN president).
- Sara Levinson (former head of marketing for the NFL).
- George Will (columnist).
- Al Rosen (former player, Yankees, Astros, and Giants executive).
- Tony Ponturo (Anheuser-Busch Cos. Inc. advertising executive).
- Gerald Zaltman (Harvard professor).
- David Reibstein (Wharton Business School professor).
- Irving Rein (Northwestern professor).

Players – Tom Glavine, David Cone, and Al Leiter – were also included on the task force, something Cone suggested was denied during settlement of the 1994 strike, when the players expressed a desire to provide input on the future of the game. The players were also left out of the commissioner's Blue Ribbon Economic Panel, which produced a report in 2000.

The task force met for the first time in late February of 2003, and Selig introduced the essence of the approach with the statement, "For all its perfection, its beauty, its uniqueness and its incomparable historical relevance, baseball, like all institutions, must continually re-evaluate and reassess itself and make necessary changes, no matter how big or slight to sustain its fan base and attract new ones. This is the purpose of my task force, the commissioner's initiative, Baseball in the Twenty-First Century."

Bob DuPuy, MLB's chief operating officer, suggested that baseball was making progress, saying, "I do think we've turned a corner. We needed to ask ourselves what we were going to do to make the game more relevant to the next generation of fans."

1 Associated Press, "Selig Forms Marketing Task Force," *Bucks County Courier Times* (Levittown, Pennsylvania), November 22, 2002: 5D.
2 Ronald Blum (Associated Press), "Selig Opposes More Playoff Teams," Associated Press Archive, January 17, 2003.
3 Jack Etkin, "Here Comes the Pitch – After the Game Nearly Struck Out Last Season, Major League Baseball Decides to Step Up to the Plate and Connect with Fans Again," *Rocky Mountain News* (Denver), March 23, 2003: 6S.
4 Ibid.
5 Rich Thomaselli, "Baseball Tries Makeover – MLB, Sponsors Shoot for Brand Image That Can Regain Fans' Faith," *Advertising Age*, February 3, 2003: 3.

Eric Karros and Mark Grudzielanek to the Chicago Cubs for Todd Hundley in early December.[16]

Player Movement

There was not a great deal of player movement throughout the meetings; only five significant trades were made and seven major-league free agents agreed to deals.[17] The trade market partially hinged on the Montreal Expos, who did not trade some of their more coveted players, including Bartolo Colon and Javier Vasquez. Many teams and agents said this clogged the marketplace.[18]

The Mets continued to be active in the offseason. They traded their Gold Glove shortstop, Rey Ordonez, to Tampa Bay. Both clubs were pleased with the deal. Lou Piniella, the Tampa Bay manager, said shortstop was the team's most pressing need,[19] and Ordonez would help his young pitching staff. The Mets had soured on Ordonez because of his offensive struggles and inconsistent fielding.[20] This move, along with Mets third baseman Edgar Alfonzo signing with the San Francisco Giants, put the Mets in a position to have a new starting left side of the infield in 2003. Jose Reyes and Sanchez were expected to share the primary duties as shortstop while Ty Wigginton was expected to take over at third base.

Oakland's Billy Beane acquired first baseman Erubiel Durazo from the Arizona Diamondbacks in a multiteam deal. Beane called Durazo "almost … my Holy Grail."[21] The Diamondbacks acquired right-handed pitcher Elmer Dessens from the Cincinnati Reds, and the Reds acquired infielder Felipe Lopez from the Blue Jays. The Blue Jays were to acquire a player to be named later (minor-league pitcher Jason Arnold).

Epstein made one trade, acquiring first baseman-outfielder Jeremy Giambi from the Phillies for pitcher Josh Hancock. After the meetings, he made what turned out to be one of his most important signings. The Minnesota Twins, another one of the teams identified as a 2002 contraction candidate, released David Ortiz during the meetings. The Twins could not find a team willing to trade for Ortiz and did not want to go to salary arbitration with him.[22] He signed with the Red Sox on January 22, 2003.

The remaining trades during the meetings included the St. Louis Cardinals acquiring pitcher Brett Tomko from the San Diego Padres for pitcher Luther Hackman and a minor leaguer, while the Atlanta Braves acquired left-handed pitcher Ray King from the Milwaukee Brewers for infielder Wes Helms and lefty John Foster.

The Rule 5 draft included a few players who had played in the major leagues, including Shane Victorino. The Padres selected the future All-Star. However, his stay in San Diego was short and he ended up establishing himself in 2006 as a starting outfielder for the Phillies.

The Business Side

The business aspects of this meeting were much different than the 2001 meetings. There was no talk of contraction but there were payroll restrictions placed upon the Expos. Although the Expos did not move any of their stars during the winter meetings, they did trade right-handed pitcher Bartolo Colon to the Chicago White Sox along with minor leaguer Jorge Nunez before the 2003 season. The Expos received right-handed pitchers Orlando Hernandez and Jeff Liefer, outfielder Rocky Biddle, and cash.

The general managers discussed a minimum age for batboys and eventually decided that further legal advice was needed but that the minimum age would be either 14 or 16.

Also, Bud Selig's idea to have the league winning the All-Star Game would get home field advantage was not discussed.

Finally, Hal McCoy, who covered Reds baseball for more than 30 years, won the Baseball Writers Association of America's Spink Award.

Summary

The 2002 Winter Meetings were noneventful as player signings were slow going into the meetings and continued to be slow during the meetings. Brian Cashman, the Yankees' general manager, said, "Montreal is stagnating things because they have so many players that might be attractive."[23] Teams were slow to offer arbitration to nonstars. The possibility of more free agents on the market acted to slow player movement.

The Atlanta Braves were active shortly after the meetings as they continued to remake their pitching staff. They acquired right-hander Russ Ortiz from the Giants on December 17, traded righty Kevin Millwood to the Phillies for catcher Johnny Estrada on December 20, and re-signed right-hander Paul Byrd. Meanwhile, pitcher Greg Maddux accepted salary arbitration from the Braves.

The free-agent stars were slow to sign, although some signed shortly after the meetings. The Astros signed Jeff Kent on December 18, the Yankees signed Hideki Matsui on December 19 and re-signed Roger Clemens on December 30. The Dodgers signed Fred McGriff on December 20. On January 20 catcher Ivan Rodriguez signed a one-year deal with the Marlins.

NOTES

1. David Schoenfield, "Contraction Time," assets.espn.go.com/mlb/s/2002/0205/1323230.html.
   The Metropolitan Sports Facilities Commission, owner and operator of the Metrodome, sued the Twins and Major League Baseball for an injunction to require the team to honor the remaining year of its lease. Hennepin County District Court Judge Harry Crump granted the injunction because of the "irreparable harm" which would have resulted if the Twins exited early and the "public interest" in assuring that the team play out the final year of its lease. The Minnesota Court of Appeals affirmed the decision. See http://sabr.org/research/play-ball-minnesota-baseball-litigation-lore

2. Doug Pappas, "Summary of New Collective Bargaining Agreement," roadsidephotos.sabr.org/baseball/02-3CBA.htm.

3. Ibid.

4. Doug Pappas, "Why John Henry and Tom Werner Won the Sox," roadsidephotos.sabr.org/baseball/bb02-1.htm.

5. Ibid.

6. Ibid.

7. Ibid.

8. Ibid.

9. Murray Chass, "Owners Give Approval to Sale of the Boston Red Sox," nytimes.com/2002/01/17/sports/baseball-owners-give-approval-to-sale-of-the-red-sox.html.

10. Ibid.

11. Jason Reid, "Expos Find Many Suitors," articles.latimes.com/2002/dec/14/sports/sp-baseball14.

12. Peter Schmuck, "Winter Meetings Might Be All Talk," articles.baltimoresun.com/2002-12-13/sports/0212130046_1_players-teams-signing.

13. Associated Press, "Epstein's Promotion Completes Front Office Overhaul," a.espncdn.com/mlb/news/2002/1125/1466352.html.

14. ESPN.com News Service, "Phillies Beat Out Indians in Pursuit of Thome," a.espncdn.com/mlb/news/2002/1202/1470010.html.

15. Associated Press, "Mets, Glavine Agree to Contract," reds.enquirer.com/2002/12/06/wwwredznote6.html.

16. Jason Reid, "Karros Is Too Much of a Luxury," articles.latimes.com/print/2002/dec/04/sports/sp-dodgers4.

17. Ronald Blum (Associated Press), "Moves Expected After Winter Meetings," peninsulaclarion.com/stories/121702/bas_1217020008.html#.Vty69seZZoU.

18. Ibid.

19. Ronald Blum, "Baseball Winter Meetings," 2.ljworld.com/news/2002/dec/16/baseball_winter_meetings/.

20. Ibid.

21. Ibid.

22. Garry Brown, "Fortunately for Boston, David Ortiz Was Unwanted by the Minnesota Twins," masslive.com/redsox/index.ssf/2013/11/david_ortiz_unwanted_by_minnes.html.

23. Associated Press, "No Trades Made as Winter Meetings Begin," a.espncdn.com/mlb/news/2002/1213/1476554.html.

— 2003 —
BACK IN THE BAYOU

By Jerry Swenson

Introduction and Context

THE 2003 WINTER MEETINGS WERE held from December 12 to 15 at the Marriott Hotel in New Orleans. This was the fifth time the Winter Meetings were held in The Big Easy, with the most recent having been in 1997. Economic conditions in the United States were improving as lower interest rates, the child-tax credit, and lower rates of income-tax withholding provided improved consumer cash flow and enabled a resumption of pre-recession consumption. However, the US-led coalition in Iraq introduced uncertainty about investments and employment.[1] Labor-market concerns loomed large despite the improved financial picture, which economists labeled a "jobless recovery."[2] Additional concerns that economic growth might slow were expressed by Arthur Cashin of UBS Securities: "The consumer has carried the economy on his back like Atlas carried the world, and we don't know if he's going to shrug it off or he's going to get tired."[3]

There was a parallel concern about the economic direction of the baseball industry. In fact, Houston Astros general manager Gerry Hunsicker commented during the meetings, "I think for years we've been talking about the dangerous economic direction the industry was headed. No one wanted to believe it, but now we're at a point where the losses have gotten so large the clubs have no choice [but to cut payroll]. If you look at the trades this winter, most have been motivated by clubs trying to move dollars. If you have cash, you're in the driver's seat. Cash is definitely king this winter because most clubs don't have it. It's a buyer's market because of that."[4]

The meeting took place without any senior executives of the New York Yankees in attendance. A club official said, "George (Steinbrenner, Yankees owner) doesn't want us to go there because we would give away our secrets."[5]

The major theme of the meeting revolved around player movement. In fact, many teams did not wait for the meetings to begin to work on reshaping their rosters. The new owners and management of the Boston Red Sox, in an effort to rid themselves of a massive contract, placed outfielder Manny Ramirez on irrevocable waivers. No team put in a claim. The Red Sox continued their attempts to move the slugger in a potential Manny Ramirez/Alex Rodriguez trade, but in the end, Ramirez was not traded before the start of the 2004 season.[6] Meanwhile, the Red Sox acquired right-hander Curt Schilling from the Arizona Diamondbacks, giving up southpaw Casey Fossum, right-hander Brandon Lyon, and two minor leaguers, left-hander Jorge de la Rosa and outfielder Michael Goss. Schilling had been a second-round pick of the Red Sox in the January 1986 draft but was traded to the Baltimore Orioles in July of 1988. To bring Schilling back, the Red Sox had to get him to agree to remove the no-trade clause in his contract with Arizona, and eventually Epstein persuaded Schilling to agree to the swap and to a contract extension in which Schilling waived the no-trade clause. Epstein was quite effusive in his praise of Schilling: "Curt wasn't out for every last dollar. Very far from it. He wanted to structure the deal so the Red Sox would be competitive for every year of his contract. He deserves a lot of credit, because that's a rare request coming from a player."[7]

The Houston Astros and Anaheim Angels also acquired pitchers before the meetings. The Astros signed lefty Andy Pettitte, the former New York Yankee, and the Angels remade half their starting rotation by signing right-handers Kelvim Escobar and Bartolo Colon away from the Toronto Blue Jays and Chicago White Sox, respectively. The signing of Pettitte sparked rumors that he might be joined by his New York teammate and good friend Roger Clemens. Clemens, who had announced his retirement in 2003, ultimately changed his mind and, a month after the meetings ended, signed with the Astros. He would win 18 games and his seventh Cy Young Award in 2004, and the team would win 92 games and go to the playoffs as the wild card despite having an injured Pettitte pitch in only 15 games.

Although there were free-agent signings before the meetings and some during the meetings, the free-agent market had changed since the Texas Rangers signed Alex Rodriguez to a $252 million deal in 2000. Small-market clubs maintained their budget discipline by trading star players before the Winter Meetings. Slugging first baseman Richie Sexson of the Milwaukee Brewers and right-hander Javier Vazquez of the Montreal Expos were among stars who were moved primarily because lowering payroll became paramount for their teams. "We were faced with the reality of losing Sexson and probably getting nothing in return except for a few draft choices," Brewers general manager Doug Melvin stated as the reason for the trade. The Brewers were looking to trim their payroll to about $30 million.[8]

Likewise, general manager Omar Minaya positioned his Expos to receive high value from the Yankees in the Vazquez deal. "Minaya said, 'I don't have to trade Javier Vazquez. If you (Cashman) are interested, be aggressive.' And to his credit, (Cashman) was aggressive."[9] The Expos were faced with payroll limitations and were willing to trade Vasquez because he was eligible for salary arbitration.[10]

The World Series champion Florida Marlins traded first baseman Derek Lee in an effort to allocate their payroll to core players. General manager Larry Beinfest acknowledged that the Marlins were also managing payroll in the Lee trade. Beinfest said, "There were two main reasons for the move. One is, obviously, we need to achieve our goal of operating within our payroll. Two, we want to make sure we have the appropriate allocations to retain our core pitching."[11]

Trading established stars because of emerging young players was another approach to managing the major-league payroll. The budget-minded Minnesota Twins traded 2002 All-Star catcher A.J. Pierzynski to the San Francisco Giants. "That's all part of the reasons we decided to make this trade," GM Terry Ryan said. "We're dealing from a position of strength. We've got some talent at catching come up and some financial concerns, as far as making sure the pieces fit."[12] The Twins received three pitchers for Pierzynski: left-hander Francisco Liriano and right-handers Joe Nathan and Boof Bonser.

Player Movement

The small-market Oakland A's were hard hit by free agency as they lost two significant contributors from their 96-win team: right-hander Keith Foulke, who had led the league with 43 saves in his only season in the East Bay; and shortstop Miguel Tejada, the 2002 American League Most Valuable Player. The Red Sox signed Foulke to be their closer, and the Orioles signed Tejada to the richest contract (at the time) in Orioles history.[13] He chose Baltimore over the Detroit Tigers and the Seattle Mariners.

The St. Louis Cardinals traded outfielder J.D. Drew and utilityman Eli Marrero to the Atlanta Braves. The Braves were looking to replace free agents Gary Sheffield and Javy Lopez and felt that this trade with the Cardinals was their best available option. "We have great regard for J.D. Drew and of course the versatility that Eli Marrero brings to Bobby (Braves manager Bobby Cox) and his roster," said general manager John Schuerholz. "(This) really helped us in one fell swoop fill several needs that we have on our club. Having said that, we gave up some fine young players to acquire these guys."[14] Cardinals manager Tony LaRussa mentioned the importance of acquiring pitching in the deal: "We felt that without pitching, we weren't going to have a chance to improve in the standings next year."[15] The cost in pitching was quite steep for the Braves, who surrendered two former first-

FUTURE NAME FOR THE EXPOS ... COQUÍ?

In late November 2002, Major League Baseball announced that the Expos would play semi-regularly in Puerto Rico during the 2003 season.* When the Expos released their schedule, it included 22 games that were shifted to Puerto Rico.

Apparently, though, no one invited the players to the fiesta. Gene Orza, the number-two official of the Major League Baseball Players Association, said, "The games require the approval of the players association. They have not yet given their approval. They should not have put out the schedule." Orza had been negotiating with MLB lawyer Rob Manfred and an agreement had not yet been reached with owners on increased meal money for the trip and on having the team pay for families to join players in Puerto Rico for the games, which originally were to be played at Montreal's Olympic Stadium.**

As it turned out, the Expos played 22 games in Puerto Rico in 2003 and 2004.***

---

*   Gabrielle Paese, "It's Official: The Expos Will Play 20 Games in San Juan in 2003," *Puerto Rico Herald*, November 22, 2002.
** Associated Press, "Expos Schedule Set Without Union OK; Montreal Scheduled to Play Mets, Braves and Reds In Puerto Rico 'Homestand,'" *Waterloo* Ontario) *Region Record*, November 28, 2002: C3.
*** "Promoter Wants to Bring More Major League Games to Puerto Rico," Associated Press Archive, December 16, 2004. For coverage of the games played in Puerto Rico, see Mark Souder, "Major League Baseball in Puerto Rico," in Bill Nowlin and Edwin Fernandez, eds., *Puerto Rico and Baseball: 60 Biographies* (Phoenix: SABR, 2017), 396-418.

---

round draft picks, right-handers Adam Wainwright and Jason Marquis, along with southpaw reliever Ray King. "As tough as it is to trade pitching, our scouting and player-development guys keep finding and developing them and filling the pipeline with them," Schuerholz said. "We're blessed to have that kind of talent. Adam was our No. 1 pitching prospect, and that makes this tough to do. But under the circumstances we had no choice."[16]

The New York Yankees, seeking to replace Pettitte and Clemens in their starting rotation, swapped right-handers with the Los Angeles Dodgers, sending Jeff Weaver west in exchange for six-time All-Star Kevin Brown.

Despite all this activity, the rumored Ramirez-Rodriguez trade did not occur during the meetings. The Red Sox and Rangers continued to work on the proposed deal after departing New Orleans, but ultimately no agreement came from these discussions.

The free-agent landscape showed signs of change from just a few years earlier as big-name stars like Vladimir Guerrero, Ivan Rodriguez, Greg Maddux, and Javy Lopez left the meetings without signed contracts. Each would eventually find employment for 2004, with catcher Lopez signing on with Orioles shortly after the meetings and outfielder Guerrero signing with the Angels in early January. (Guerrero would become the 2004 American League Most Valuable Player.) However, two future Hall of Famers had a longer wait. Rodriguez did not land a deal with the Detroit Tigers until February, while the Chicago Cubs did not sign Maddux until late in spring training, thus giving him the opportunity to continue his pursuit of 300 career victories with the team for which he made his debut in 1986.

The Pittsburgh and Cleveland organizations each lost five players in the major-league portion of the Rule 5 draft. A future Blue Jays slugger, third baseman Jose Bautista, was one of the players lost by the Pirates, as well as two other future major leaguers, first baseman Chris Shelton (to the Tigers) and right-hander Jeff

Bennett (to the Brewers).[17] The Indians' most notable loss was outfielder Willy Taveras to the Astros.

The Business Side

The proposed trade of Alex Rodriguez from the Rangers to the Red Sox generated much interest from the Major League Baseball Players Association. Rodriguez agreed to restructure his original deal, signed at the 2000 Winter Meetings,[18] but the Players Association objected, taking the position that a restructured contract would result in a decreased value of the pact. Rodriguez issued a statement in support of the union's decision:

"In the spirit of cooperation, I advised the Red Sox I am willing to restructure my contract, but only within the guidelines prescribed by union officials," Rodriguez said in a statement to the Associated Press. "I recognize the principle involved, and fully support the need to protect the interests of my fellow players.

"If my transfer to the Red Sox is to occur, it must be done with consideration of the interests of all major-league players, not just one. Any statements by club officials suggesting my position is different than stated is inaccurate and unfortunate."[19]

Mike Moore was re-elected to his fourth four-year term as president of the National Association, the minor-league umbrella group.[20]

Speaking at the opening session of the Winter Meetings, Moore announced that the minor leagues had established a Charity Partners Program with Big Brothers and Big Sisters, the YMCA and the ALS Association.[21]

The Baseball Writers Association of America honored longtime *New York Times* sportswriter Murray Chass with the J.G. Taylor Spink Award.[22]

Summary

Small and mid-market teams managed their payrolls and traded players with an eye toward maintaining their budgets and providing opportunities for prospects. The larger-market clubs, especially the Red Sox, were active before and during the meetings. The Oakland A's would win 91 games in 2004 with their excellent starting pitching and the ability of their front office to find productive offensive players despite continuing to lose players to free agency. Although not based upon the 2004 season, their approach to utilizing ballplayers whose characteristics were not properly valued was later documented in the book and film *Moneyball*.

Manager Lou Piniella expressed concern about the inability of the smaller-market teams to compete with the larger-market teams in pursuing free agents. He specifically addressed the situation for his Tampa Bay Devil Rays when he said, "We're improved, but it's disheartening when you look at the improvements of the other teams in this division. ... Invariably, baseball has to do something about this. I don't know what the answer is. The luxury tax hasn't stopped it. It's the same thing as when they put an extra tax on yachts. If you have the money to buy the yacht, you pay the tax. What's the difference?"[23]

The inability to bring the Ramirez-Rodriguez trade to fruition proved to be fortunate, as Ramirez led a potent Boston offense. His league-leading 43 home runs and .613 slugging percentage, in combination with an improved pitching staff, anchored by Schilling's 21 wins and Foulke's 32 saves, brought the first World Series championship to Fenway Park since Babe Ruth was a pitcher and outfielder for the 1918 Red Sox. Ramirez was named MVP of the World Series. Alex Rodriguez was eventually traded to the Yankees, in a blockbuster deal for infielder-outfielder Alfonso Soriano and infielder Joaquin Arias.

BASEBALL'S BUSINESS: THE WINTER MEETINGS

NOTES

1. United States Economy—2003. *Geographic.org* theodora.com/wfb2003/united_states/united_states_economy.html

2. Ibid.

3. Economy 2003: Anxious And Waiting.. *CBSNews.com*. cbsnews.com/news/economy-2003-anxious-and-waiting/.

4. Elliott Teaford and Ross Newhan, "End of an Era as Dodgers Trade Brown to Yankees," *Los Angeles Times,* December 12, 2003. Accessed January 2, 2012. articles.latimes.com/2003/dec/12/sports/sp-brown12.

5. Jack Curry, "Baseball Analysis; What's Up With the Boss?" *New York Times*, December 13, 2003. Accessed January 2, 2012. nytimes.com/2003/12/13/sports/baseball-analysis-what-s-up-with-the-boss.html?pagewanted=all&src=pm.

6. Gordon Edes and Bob Hohler, "Rodriguez Deal Gaining Momentum," boston.com/sports/baseball/redsox/articles/2003/12/16/rodriguez_deal_gaining_momentum.

7. ESPN.com news services, "Schilling Will Waive No-trade Clause," ESPN.com, November 30, 2003. Accessed January 2, 2012. espn.go.com/mlb/news/story?id=1673350.

8. Associated Press, "Brewers Obtain Counsell, Spivey, Overbay," ESPN.com, December 4, 2003. Accessed January 2, 2012. espn.go.com/mlb/news/story?id=1675283.

9. ESPN.com news services, "Yankees Give Up Three Players in Deal," ESPN.com, December 4, 2003. Accessed January 2, 2012. sports.espn.go.com/mlb/news/story?id=1678044.

10. Ibid.

11. Associated Press, "Teams Exchange First Basemen in Trade," ESPN.com, November 26, 2003. Accessed January 2, 2012. sports.espn.go.com/mlb/news/story?id=1671120.

12. Associated Press, "Giants Give Up Nathan in Deal for Catcher," ESPN.com, November 15, 2003. Accessed January 2, 2012. sports.espn.go.com/mlb/news/story?id=1661751.

13. Gary Washburn, "Tejada Excited About Joining O's," MLB.com, December 14, 2003. Accessed January 2, 2012. mlb.mlb.com/news/article.jsp?ymd=20031214&content_id=618126&vkey=news_mlb&fext=.jsp&c_id=mlb.

14. Mark Bowman, "Braves Trade for Drew, Marrero," MLB.com, December 13, 2003. Accessed January 2, 2012. atlanta.braves.mlb.com/news/article.jsp?ymd=20031213&content_id=617176&vkey=news_atl&fext=.jsp&c_id=atl

15. Associated Press, "Braves Acquire Drew in Deal with Cards," ESPN.com, December 14, 2003. Accessed January 2, 2012. http://espn.go.com/mlb/news/story?id=1685436

16. Washburn, "Tejada Excited About Joining O's."

17. Bautista had an interesting few months. The Orioles selected him in the Rule 5 draft in December, but in early June he was picked up by Tampa Bay in a waiver deal. Before the month was out the Rays sold him to the Royals, who a month later traded him to the Mets for infielder-outfielder Justin Huber. The Mets then flipped Bautista, along with infielder Ty Wigginton and minor-league righty Matt Peterson, to the Pirates. Pittsburgh gave up right-handed pitcher Kris Benson (the number-one pick in the 1996 draft) and infielder Jeff Keppinger. Four years later the Pirates sent him to the Blue Jays, where he would blossomed into one of the game's premier sluggers.

18. Associated Press, "A-Rod Stands by Union's Stance," ESPN.com, December 18, 2003. Accessed January 2, 2012. sports.espn.go.com/mlb/news/story?id=1688755.

19. Ibid.

20. milb.com/articles/?id=1544.

21. milb.com/highlights/?id=1538.

22. "BASEBALL: Chass to Enter Hall of Fame," *New York Times*, December 15, 2003. Accessed January 2, 2012. nytimes.com/2003/12/15/sports/baseball-chass-to-enter-hall-of-fame.html.

23. Bill Madden, "Proof in the Payrolls for Some, Price of Dealing Too High," NYDailyNews.com, December 14, 2003. Accessed January 2, 2012. nydailynews.com/archives/sports/proof-payrolls-price-dealing-high-article-1.519153.

— 2004 —
IT'S ALL A GAMBLE

By Hawkins DuBois

Introduction

For many in the baseball world, the 2004 season marked the end of an era. Perhaps it was the Boston Red Sox finally breaking the "Curse of the Bambino" to end their streak of futility, or the Expos playing their final games in Montreal, or Barry Bonds' career finally beginning to wind down as he won the last of his seven Most Valuable Player Awards. The year 2004 was one that brought about changes, but the offseason would be slow to bring about the same transformations that the regular season had brought.

The 2004 Winter Meetings were held in California, at the Anaheim Marriott, less than a mile from Disneyland. While baseball's general managers, agents, and writers were unlikely to spend much time at the "happiest place on Earth," they were hoping to bring joyous news to fans across the country, as they attempted to lure some of the game's best players to join their teams. A long weekend of baseball rumors and transactions lay ahead for these show runners between December 10 and 13 as they looked to improve their rosters.

After the 2003 Winter Meetings in New Orleans that featured Miguel Tejada's six-year megadeal, the 2004 iteration of the meetings ended up being relatively quiet in terms of major player movements. While the Marriott was constantly abuzz with rumors, many of the major deals that were discussed never actually materialized beyond the preliminary stages during the meetings. There was no huge signing or trade in Anaheim, but clubs still made a variety of moves looking to contend in 2005. The hope that transformation was coming was a common theme throughout discussions at the meetings, but the transactions rarely brought on the same optimism as the rumors.

Player Movement

Pitchers were at the heart of much of the movement during the convention. Offense was beginning its decline from the heights of the steroid era, and much of that had to do with the rising value of pitching, the hot commodity of the Winter Meetings.

Right out of the gate, the first big move on Friday was the Arizona Diamondbacks making a splash by signing starting pitcher Russ Ortiz for $33 million over four years. The Diamondbacks were coming off an abysmal 51-111 record in 2004, but they had plans to immediately end what many suspected would be a rebuilding phase for the club. Despite a multitude of claims to the media about their lack of financial flexibility, the Diamondbacks found a way to pay significant dollars to the right-handed Ortiz, and also to the recently signed third baseman Troy Glaus, who received $45 million over four years. At the press conference announcing the signing of the pair, Ortiz made it immediately clear that the Diamondbacks' attempted turnaround into contention was a large part of why he chose to sign with them. "Winning is important. I wanted to be a part of what they're trying to accomplish," he said. "They convinced me from day one they were headed in that direction."[1] The Diamondbacks had decided that now was the time to reenter the fray of the competitive National League West, and so they went out and paid top dollar for one of the big-name free agent pitchers on the market.

In the words of Joe Sheehan of Baseball Prospectus, "You don't usually get the kind of agreement on a transaction that I heard about the Russ Ortiz signing.

No one I talked to likes it, and a few people were calling it the worst signing of the winter."[2] In the eyes of the media, then, the first signing of the Winter Meetings was perhaps also the worst.

Next came a pair of outfielders relocating to the American League West. The Angels announced that they were bringing aboard 40-year-old Southern Californian Steve Finley via free agency, and the Rangers were finalizing a contract with the enigmatic Richard Hidalgo, who would be joining the team after playing parts of eight seasons with the cross-state Houston Astros.

Finley inked his deal for two years at $7 million per season to be the Angels' new center fielder. This effectively took them out of the running for the biggest free agent on the market, Carlos Beltran. Just as with Ortiz, Finley cited the team's ability to win as a large reason for his decision to sign with the Angels, saying, "It's close to home, it's a great team, it's a great organization with a chance to win. You can't ask for any more than that as a player."[3] At 40 years old, Finley was going to be one of the oldest regular position players in baseball, but he had seen minimal decline in production up to this point. The Angels took his age into consideration and picked up the elderly outfielder anyway.

While the Finley signing was made with the hope that an older player would be able to maintain his production, the Rangers' signing of Hidalgo was made with the hope that a young player would return to the flashes of brilliance he had shown in years past. The Rangers picked up Hidalgo for $4.5 million for one year under the belief that he was going to bounce back from a disappointing 2004. Rangers general manager John Hart said, "Richard is a premium young player. With this addition, we have filled one of our needs with an everyday right fielder who can hit in the middle of the order."[4]

As discussion of the two new West Coast outfielders was buzzing throughout the hotel, word began to spread that 42-year-old left-hander David Wells was leaving San Diego, despite his hometown Padres pushing hard to retain his services. Wells had spent several years with the New York Yankees, but was now moving across the biggest rivalry in baseball to join the Boston Red Sox.

Wells was intensely pursued by both Boston and San Diego, but he also gave the Yankees every opportunity to bring him back. Wells made multiple calls to Yankees general manager Brian Cashman in the days before signing to see if they would be interested in striking a deal, but Cashman declined. The two did, however, remain on good terms, with Cashman saying to Wells on the first day of the Winter Meetings, "When I'm in Boston next year, I'll stay out late with you and let [Red Sox general manager Theo Epstein] deal with disciplining you." Wells responded: "I'm game. Perfect."[5]

Wells ended up inking his contract with Boston for two years and a guaranteed $8 million, but with the ability to escalate the value of the contract to as much as $18 million if he reached all of the incentives. He was signed to take over a spot at the back of the rotation, but with Boston moving further out of the running for Pedro Martinez due to their unwillingness to add another year to their offer, it looked as if Wells was going to have to play a larger role in Boston's rotation.

Most of the previous moves on Day One were significant financial commitments by teams to improve their club with a recognizable former star. The forever penny-pinching Marlins, on the other hand, did not spend big but went bargain-bin diving, and came up with a pair of elderly right-handed relievers in Todd Jones and Antonio Alfonseca. Jones and the polydactyly Alfonseca were picked up to compete for the closer's role with fellow veteran right-hander Guillermo Mota. There were some rumors that the Marlins could still be in on Carl Pavano, but as time passed it became more and more apparent that the Marlins ownership was unwilling to spend the money necessary to bring Pavano back.

With six major-league contracts being agreed to on the first day, the Winter Meetings appeared to have quickly jumped into the full swing of things. The market was changing drastically for the front-line players as teams elected to sign cheaper alternatives in their place. The change created by the number of significant moves on Day One led to the final three days of the meetings being generally uninteresting in comparison.

One of the more quiet, but still intriguing, stories on Day Two was the announcement that 2004 National League Cy Young Award Winner Roger Clemens would accept his arbitration offer from the Houston Astros. Although Clemens and his agent would not reveal whether Clemens had plans to play in 2005, the Astros were appreciative of the sign of commitment to their organization.

The Astros reportedly also met with Scott Boras, the agent for Carlos Beltran and many of the other top free agents on the market. The word around the Marriott was that the Astros had offered Beltran five years and $70 million, well under half of Boras's asking price of 10 years and $200 million. Boras was known for being one of the most powerful men in the baseball world, and the Winter Meetings were the perfect arena for him to show off his talents. The superstar agent occupied three rooms in the Anaheim Marriott, and he constantly handed out his signature binders filled with statistics, looking to entice a team into signing one of his elite free-agent clients.[6] Even with his dedicated efforts during the meetings, none of Boras's big clients would agree to contracts, but Boras was not concerned. "Talent doesn't have a wristwatch," he said. Though nothing was finalized in Anaheim, Boras apparently did his usual excellent work because eventually all of his elite clients received the big contracts they were seeking.

Along with Clemens's potential return to Houston, Saturday also brought more big news related to one of the best pitchers of the generation. John Smoltz had been working as the Atlanta Braves closer for several years after his prolific career as a starting pitcher was interrupted by Tommy John surgery. From 2001 to 2004 Smoltz worked out of the bullpen, but after the 2004 season Smoltz and the Braves decided that it was now time to bring him back to the rotation. This meant that the Braves would need a new closer to replace him, which resulted in Dan Kolb and the Milwaukee Brewers being brought into the equation.

Kolb was considered to be a proven closer, having amassed 60 saves and made an All-Star Game appearance over the previous two years. With a track record of being one of the most effective relievers in the league, he seemed like a perfect fit to take over the closer's role in Atlanta. Kolb did not come cheap, however—the Brewers demanded top prospect Jose Capellan (ranked among the top 30 prospects in the game by *Baseball America*[7]), a right-handed pitcher, along with an additional prospect from the Braves (who proved to be outfielder-turned-pitcher Alec Zumwalt). Atlanta didn't like giving up Capellan, but felt Kolb was worth the price, especially since it gave them the ability to move Smoltz back to the rotation.

Along with the trade of Dan Kolb for Jose Capellan, the Pittsburgh Pirates and Cleveland Indians also agreed to a trade, with left-handed reliever Arthur Rhodes going to the Indians and outfielder Matt Lawton moving to the Pirates. Rhodes, 34, was coming off one of the worst years of his career, and just two weeks earlier had been acquired by Pittsburgh in exchange for the former face of the Pirates franchise, catcher Jason Kendall. Cleveland GM Mark Shapiro still saw something in Rhodes that he liked, though, saying "There were a multitude of things that happened to him to explain why he had a bad year. We're still hopeful he's going to be a strong, solid contributor in our bullpen."[8] Lawton was also coming off a year in which he struggled, but the Pirates needed a new leadoff hitter, having dealt Kendall to the A's. By swapping Rhodes for Lawton, the Pirates were able to save some money for the 2005 season, and they were able to pick up a leadoff hitter, corner outfielder, and potential power bat all in one. It was a trade that was praised on both sides, with each team relinquishing someone they didn't need and acquiring a piece that they saw as more valuable than the other team did.

Among the numerous rumors that didn't come to fruition on Day Two of the meetings was the one that had Tim Hudson on the move from Oakland. The frontrunner at the moment was the Los Angeles Dodgers, offering flamethrowing righty Edwin Jackson and infielder Antonio Perez, but the A's knew they had to take advantage of a huge market for their pitcher. The Dodgers were the consensus favorites to acquire Hudson, but nearly half the league was also rumored to be interested in him, including the Red Sox, Yankees, and Braves, all of whom were having serious talks with the A's that would bring several coveted young players to Oakland. The high traffic on Hudson created a major market for the A's, and while talks would be ongoing throughout the meetings, Hudson would still be with Oakland's green and gold when the meetings came to an end.

The Yankees had been involved with the rumors for Hudson from the beginning, but after a flurry of action on Day Two, it seemed they would be exiting the competition for the Oakland pitcher. After having no team officials attend the Winter Meetings in 2003 in New Orleans, both the Yankees and Brian Cashman were ready to make their presence known in Anaheim. On Saturday, the Yankees signed Carl Pavano, one of the top pitchers of the free-agent class. Just before the Winter Meetings, the Yankees had agreed to sign right-hander Jaret Wright to a three-year, $21 million contract, but earlier on Saturday it appeared as though Wright had failed his physical, leading the Yankees to pounce on Pavano for four years and $39 million.

Pavano, pitching in Florida, was coming off the best season of his career, having given the Marlins his first All-Star Game appearance, and a sixth-place finish in the National League Cy Young Award voting. For signing with the Yankees, he cited the same reason numerous other players at the meetings had used in picking their teams (as spoken through their agents): "Number one, he wants to win."[9]

Nobody thought that the Pavano deal was in the same category as the Russ Ortiz signing, but there were certainly some qualms with the amount of money and years being given to an injury-prone pitcher who was coming off a season that looked like an aberration. Wright passed his physical and joined the New York rotation as well.

Day Three was by far the quietest day of the meetings. The Blue Jays made a pair of moves and the Diamondbacks signed another free agent, although this one was on a much smaller scale.

The first move came very early in the morning, as the Corey Koskie signing with the Blue Jays was finalized after reports of the deal had circulated for several days. Koskie got a contract for three years and $17 million from Toronto to take over as the club's third baseman and help take away some of the sting of the team's loss of one of the American League's best offensive players in Carlos Delgado.

As a Canadian, Koskie was incredibly excited to be signing on with Toronto. "I grew up watching the Blue Jays," he said. "Every Canadian kid's dream is to play for a team you grew up watching. This is a real happy day for me and my family."[10] Not many were in favor of the Koskie signing, but Toronto felt it needed to reinsert more offense into its lineup.

The other move of significance made by the Blue Jays that day was a trade sending the Devil Rays their future manager in catcher Kevin Cash and bringing Toronto right-handed pitcher Chad Gaudin. It was a minor trade for both sides, but each player still had the potential to make a minor impact on the big-league team in the near future. Cash was a glove-first catcher who could compete for the backup spot on the Devil Rays roster, and Gaudin offered starting pitching depth for a team with tons of young arms in the rotation.

The final move of the day was the acquisition of Royce Clayton by the Diamondbacks on a one-year, $1.35 million deal. Clayton was expected to take over for Alex Cintron as the Diamondbacks' shortstop. Manager Bob Melvin praised Clayton for both his defense and his offensive flexibility, and Clayton praised the organization for its people like outfielder Luis Gonzalez and hitting coach Matt Williams. Clayton even went as far as to say, "The knowledge of Matt Williams was vital in me making my decision. Having him on board, I think the organization benefits tremendously from his baseball perspective."[11]

Kicking off the final day of the meetings was the signing of first baseman Wil Cordero by the newly anointed Washington Nationals. Cordero was coming off an injury-plagued season in Florida that saw him produce very little either offensively or defensively, but the Nats believed he could provide some pop off the bench and some leadership in the clubhouse, so they brought him aboard for less than a million dollars.

Among the other signings of the day was the finalization of a deal between the San Francisco Giants and defensive-minded catcher Mike Matheny for three years and $10.5 million. Matheny was signed to replace the previous year's starting catcher, A.J. Pierzynski. Newcomer Pierzynski had problems with much of the pitching staff, and was ill-fitted for the Giants clubhouse. The signing of Matheny allowed the Giants to move on from Pierzynski and get a catcher who was widely considered to be one of the best in the game behind the plate. Giants GM Brian Sabean was very excited about Matheny's defense, raving, "There's no telling how many runs he's going to save because he doesn't make any mistakes behind the plate."[12] The Giants hoped the change from Pierzynski to Matheny would lead to a huge turnaround for their pitching staff and an improvement in the overall record of their club. (Pierzynski, for his part, would land on his feet, signing in January with the White Sox, where he would be their regular behind the plate for the next eight years, including their World Series championship season of 2005.)

With rumors of a Tim Hudson blockbuster continuing to swirl around the Winter Meetings for each of the first three days, no one would have been surprised to finally hear that a deal had been agreed to on the last day of the meetings, but the closest that reporters got to a headline-grabbing trade was one that brought Carlos Lee to the Milwaukee Brewers. The consistently productive left fielder of the Chicago White Sox was swapped in exchange for center fielder Scott Podsednik and reliever Luis Vizcaino.

Both sides gloated about what they had acquired in their half of the trade. The Brewers were coming off a season in which they had finished dead last in the National League Central, and were in dire need of an offensive upgrade. Brewers GM Doug Melvin said, "A profile like Carlos's was our biggest need and we felt we accomplished that—but it didn't come cheaply."[13] The Brewers had to give up their speedy center fielder, Podsednik, just a year after he had finished second in the Rookie of the Year voting, and just weeks after leading the league in stolen bases with 70. Podsednik had struggled some in his sophomore season, though (his average dropped 70 points), and it was possible that a change of scenery could turn things around for him.

White Sox GM Kenny Williams said of Podsednik, "His swing got a little long and little bigger. He kind of went away from his strengths. We're looking for something in between last year and the year before. That's plenty good enough for us."[14] The White Sox were able to save millions of dollars by moving Lee to Milwaukee, which allowed them to reallocate their funds in ways that they saw as more fitting to their new-look club. Having seen the long ball fail them during the 2004 season, the White Sox were now looking to mix up their strategy on offense, as they turned to a player like Podsednik to make themselves into more of a small-ball-oriented team.

On the last day of the Winter Meetings the concluding event is always the Rule 5 Draft. Although the draft hadn't generated a significant regular since Johan Santana's selection in 1999, teams continued to rummage through their rivals' minor-league systems in hopes that they could find a diamond in the rough. The 2004 iteration of the draft led to 12 players being selected in the major-league phase, 51 players in the Triple-A phase, and 12 in the Double-A phase.

As is often the case, the popular choice in the Rule 5 Draft was pitching, especially coming from the left side. To go along with the rest of the draft selections, the consensus number-one player available to be picked up in the draft was left-hander Andy Sisco, who ended up going second overall to the Kansas City Royals. The 6-foot-9 Sisco showed immense promise while pitching in the Chicago Cubs system, ranking as high as their fourth-best prospect entering 2004 according to *Baseball America*, but Sisco failed to follow his offseason conditioning, and his season suffered greatly because of this lack of preparedness.[15] Even armed with the knowledge of his makeup issues, numerous teams were still enamored by his potential, and it was clear he was the best player available in the draft, leading to his early selection by the Royals.

The rest of the major-league draft consisted of 11 players: seven pitchers, three outfielders, and a first baseman. The first overall pick in the draft was right-handed pitcher Angel Garcia, by the Devil Rays. Five of the next seven picks were left-handed pitchers. Outfielder Adam Stern was the 11th pick, going to the Boston Red Sox, which gave them the distinction of having the most Jewish players on a major-league roster since the start of the expansion era (they also employed Kevin Youkilis and Gabe Kapler at that time). The last player of note was outfielder Shane Victorino, who ended up being the most successful player to be drafted. Victorino was being selected in the Rule 5 Draft for the second time in his career, having gone 19th in the 2002 draft to the San Diego Padres, but was more likely to stick this time with the Phillies as he was now generating more power in his swing, leading to double-digit home runs for the first time in his career. Victorino wasn't expected to be anything more than a fifth outfielder and pinch-runner according to *Baseball America*, but would end up being much more than that—a key component on the back-to-back National League championship teams and 2008 World Series winner, he had also won three Gold gloves and been selected for two All-Star teams.

The conclusion of the draft ended the Winter Meetings, but this was not the end of player movement during the 2004 offseason.

Business and Politics

The business-oriented news surrounding the 2004 Winter Meetings was primarily focused on potential landing zones for current and future franchises. The big move coming up was the movement of the Montreal Expos to the United States, where they would become the Washington Nationals. While there was not a great deal of talk about Washington, there was some talk stemming from the idea of moving another franchise, or expanding the league to one of the cities that had failed to acquire the Expos. At the center of much of these talks was the flamboyant mayor of Las Vegas, Oscar Goodman.

Arguably the most memorable moment in recent Winter Meetings history was the arrival of the Las Vegas mayor at the Anaheim Marriott, where the meetings were taking place. Goodman slowly emerged from his dark stretch limousine, adjusted the bright "Welcome to Fabulous Las Vegas" sign on his lapel, and waltzed into the lobby with a beautiful Vegas showgirl on each arm, and one of Las Vegas's iconic Elvis impersonators following his every step. Goodman had arrived to sell his city, and he was willing to talk to anyone and everyone who would listen to him, insisting that "someone will have to show interest in Vegas, and then we'll make them an offer they can't refuse." Goodman's flashy entrance caught the attention of all those who could see him, and led one onlooker to fittingly quip, "That's Vegas"[16] as the mayor passed by, but Goodman was hoping to lure the attention of Major League Baseball just as much as he was looking to capture the gaze of the hotel guests.

The big meeting on Goodman's agenda was a get-together with the Florida Marlins leadership. The Marlins were currently in talks to get a new ballpark in the Miami area, following the revelation that Miami Dolphins owner Wayne Huizenga would no longer be willing to share Pro Player Stadium after the 2010 season. This news prompted Marlins President David Samson to tell reporters, "The owner is free to do what he chooses. … What this does is make it very clear the need for the Marlins to have a new place to play is no longer just about economics. It's about survival."[17] The Marlins needed a new ballpark, and Miami Mayor Manny Diaz and his associates were not making negotiations easy, having been dragging their feet since talks began. With Samson and owner Jeffrey Loria feeling that Diaz was not taking the situation seriously enough, Samson decided to have a chat with Goodman to shake things up.

Goodman and the Marlins officials met privately in a hotel room for 90 minutes, but when the chat came to an end, both sides insisted that relocation was not a specific topic that had come up during their conversation. Goodman called the chat a "cordial" one, and told reporters, "I'm not going to allow Las Vegas to be used as a bargaining chip." While Goodman seemed to take the whole meeting very lightly, Diaz felt insulted by the situation, stating, "I'm disgusted because I think it's a showing of bad faith."[18] The meeting was clearly a political move being employed by the Marlins to get the new facility they so badly wanted, but it was unclear what impact it would actually have on their stadium problem. A spokesperson for Jeffrey Loria told the press, "Jeffrey is committed to Miami. At the same time, it's appropriate for Jeffrey and [Marlins' Vice Chairman] Joel Mael to examine all of their options in light of something that's taking so much, much longer than anybody anticipated."[19] Loria was known for being a shrewd businessman, and nobody doubted that he would take his business elsewhere if Miami did not give him what he wanted.

It was clear that the folks around the Winter Meetings had a real interest in Las Vegas as a potential home for a major-league team. Las Vegas had missed out on a chance to acquire the Expos, and the recently concluded meeting with the Marlins was unlikely to actually draw them away from Miami, but Las Vegas was doing everything it could to make itself look like an attractive market for a major-league baseball team. Las Vegas had housed a Triple-A Pacific Coast League franchise since 1983, and was ready to move up to the big leagues. Moments after Goodman arrived at his hotel in Anaheim, he ran into Chicago Cubs manager Dusty Baker, who was emphatic in telling Goodman, "I would love to manage in Las Vegas."[20] Las Vegas was not getting a franchise at the moment, but the glitz and glamour that Goodman put on display clearly had appeal to many people at the meetings, and Las Vegas looked ripe for the picking if a franchise needed a new location in the near future.

Dusty Baker's support of a team in Las Vegas wasn't the only reason he got his quotes into the news while in Anaheim. He also came to the defense of Barry Bonds, making his thoughts on his former player and the BALCO scandal known to the public. Baker believed that it was unfair to defame Bonds, and put an asterisk next to all of his records, until he was confidently and completely proven guilty of the crime for which he was being accused.

Bonds went up in front of a grand jury and told them that he had not used steroids, and for Baker, that was more than enough proof for him to say that Bonds had not used steroids. Baker charismatically defended Bonds' character, and told everyone that if Bonds said he hadn't done it, then Baker believed him. Baker told reporters, "I feel bad for Barry. I've known him and I feel badly because this guy works. I mean, I haven't seen anybody work as hard as Barry."[21] Despite Baker's defense of his former star player, and as the BALCO scandal grew, Bonds' name was constantly met with resentment as word of his involvement spread.

While most of the baseball media wrote negatively about Bonds, *Baseball America* continued to acknowledge his greatness. Among the minor league-sponsored events of the Winter Meetings was the Baseball America Awards Gala, and for the third time in four years Bonds took home the Player of the Year Award. Other major-league award winners included Khalil Greene (Rookie of the Year), the Minnesota Twins (Organization of the Year), Terry Ryan (Executive of the Year), and Bobby Cox (Manager of the Year), while the minor-leagues winners consisted of Jeff Francis (MiLB Player of the Year), Chris Kemple (MiLB Executive of the Year), Marty Brown (MiLB Manager of the Year), and the Lancaster Jethawks (MiLB Organization of the Year). The Freitas Awards for the best minor-league franchises were given to the Sacramento Rivercats (AAA), the Round Rock Express (AA), the Dayton Dragons (A), and the Burlington Bees (Short Season).[22]

Aside from the Awards Gala and a large baseball-related trade show, the minor leagues traditionally sponsor a job fair at the Winter Meetings. Job seekers are especially notorious for their constantly nervous demeanor as they wander the hotel lobby, looking to get just a few moments of face-to-face interaction with a prospective employer. One attendee noted "one [job-seeker] looping by a half-dozen times during a 15-minute conversation [he] was having. Grab a beer and give it a rest, kid" he said.[23] The job fair provides tons of new jobs every year, and despite the anxiety displayed by job-seekers as they meander throughout the lobby, many of them would leave Anaheim with employment.

While many other folks would walk away from the business and political discussions at the Winter Meetings unhappy, Oscar Goodman seemed to leave with the same joy that the successful job-seekers had attained. Goodman did exactly what someone from Las Vegas would be expected to do, when he stole the spotlight at the Winter Meetings. He demanded attention with his flashy appearance, and he showcased business prowess and suavity in his numerous meetings with people in the baseball industry. As Goodman left town, he had to be feeling good about the moves he had made at the Winter Meetings, but only time would tell if it had the impact he wanted.

Conclusion

The 2004 Winter Meetings were dominated by an overall feeling of stubbornness. The headlining acts were an extravagant Las Vegas mayor, the signings of middling free agents, and a general unwillingness for teams and players to back off their high asking prices.

Scott Boras held the fate of many of the top free agents in his hands, and he refused to back off his massive demands; as a result, Carlos Beltran, Pedro Martinez, and Adrian Beltre remained unsigned when he left Anaheim. Billy Beane held onto Tim Hudson and Mark Mulder, two of the biggest trade chips in the game, because nobody was meeting his rising asking prices. Neither the Florida Marlins nor the mayor of Miami were willing at this point to compromise in putting together a deal for a new stadium for the Marlins. Nobody was willing to budge in their negotiations, and the excitement of the meetings suffered because of it.

Despite the belief that everyone in California is laid back and relaxed, Anaheim was unable to do enough to loosen up the general managers of the 30 major-league clubs. Writers and reporters from across the country left the Marriott disappointed, and many teams came away without the players they coveted most. The 2004 Winter Meetings did not bring about the sprawling change that the 2004 season had brought. Fortunately for both fans and teams, though, the major league clubs would adjust from their relative inactivity and make the necessary moves over what remained of the offseason to prepare for what would prove to be another campaign involving the end of a long championship drought.

NOTES

1 "Diamondbacks Sign Ortiz," *Pittsburgh Post-Gazette*, December 11, 2004.

2 Joe Sheehan. "Prospectus Today: The Meetings, Day One," Baseball Prospectus, baseballprospectus.com/article.php?articleid=3669, accessed May 20, 2015.

3 "Newest Angel in OF: Finley Joins Anaheim," ESPN, sports.espn.go.com/mlb/news/story?id=1943279, accessed May 20, 2015.

4 United Press International, "Hidalgo Signs With Rangers," upi.com/Sports_News/2004/12/11/Hidalgo-signs-with-Rangers/58641102778565/, accessed May 20, 2015.

5 Jack Curry, "Wells Joins Other Side With Deal for 2 Years," *New York Times*, December 12, 2004.

6 Jack Curry, "Ultimate Salesman, Pitching the Biggest Stars in Baseball," *New York Times*, December 13, 2004.

7 Jim Callis and Will Lingo, *Baseball America 2005 Prospect Handbook* (Durham: Baseball America, 2005), 10-13.

8 "Rhodes Will Set Up for Wickman," ESPN, sports.espn.go.com/mlb/news/story?id=1944134, accessed June 1, 2015.

9 "Pavano Chooses a Yankee Future," *Los Angeles Times*, December 12, 2004.

10 "Deal Is Worth $17 Million," ESPN, sports.espn.go.com/mlb/news/story?id=1945093, accessed June 9, 2015.

11 "Arizona Signs Veteran Infielders Clayton, Counsell," *USA Today*, usatoday30.usatoday.com/sports/baseball/nl/diamondbacks/2004-12-15-clayton-counsell_x.htm, accessed June 9, 2015.

12 Jorge L. Ortiz, "Giants Like Mike / Signing of Matheny to Three-Year Deal Improves Defense," SFGate, sfgate.com/sports/article/Giants-like-Mike-Signing-of-Matheny-to-2663963.php, accessed June 9, 2015.

13 "White Sox Trade Carlos Lee to Milwaukee for Podsednik, Vizcaino," ESPN, sports.espn.go.com/espn/wire?section=mlb&id=1945634, accessed June 4, 2015.

14 Ibid.

15 Callis and Lingo, 231.

16 "Oscar's Dash for Home," *Las Vegas Sun*, December 13, 2004.

17 Ryan Wilkins, "The Week in Quotes: November 22-December 13," Baseball Prospectus, baseballprospectus.com/article.php?articleid=3671, accessed June 6, 2015.

18 Sarah Talalay. "Marlins Up Stakes With Talks in Vegas," *Sun-Sentinel* (Fort Lauderdale), December 10, 2004.

19 Ibid.

20 "Oscar's Dash for Home".

21 John Shea. "Baseball Winter Meetings / Dusty Defends Bonds," SFGate, sfgate.com/sports/shea/article/BASEBALL-WINTER-MEETINGS-Dusty-defends-Bonds-2629740.php, accessed June 9, 2015.

22 "Baseball America Awards," *Baseball America*, baseballamerica.com/news/baseball-america-awards/, accessed December 30, 2015.

23 "Las Vegas to Host Baseball Winter Meetings for the First Time From Dec. 8-11," MiLB.com, milb.com/gen/articles/printer_friendly/clubs/t400/y2008/m12/d05/c485556.jsp, accessed December 30, 2015.

24 Jay Jaffe, "The Winter Meetings: The Lobbyists," The Futility Infielder, futilityinfielder.com/wordpress/2004/12/the-winter-meetings-the-lobbyists.shtml, accessed December 30, 2015.

— 2005 —
A LOT OF ACTION IN DALLAS

By Robert K. Whelan

INTRODUCTION AND CONTEXT

AS THE TWENTY-FIRST CENTURY began, the commissioner's office and many team owners were concerned about competitive imbalance. After free agency began in the 1970s, some teams were able to use their financial heft to gain a competitive edge, especially those with lucrative local radio and television contracts; the New York Yankees, for instance, won four of five World Series between 1996 and 2000, and appeared in six of eight World Series between 1996 and 2003.

Steps were taken to address this imbalance. In 1994, a wild-card team was added to the playoff system in each league, thus giving more teams an opportunity for postseason success. After the 2002 collective-bargaining agreement was signed, Major League Baseball imposed a luxury tax. In brief, this meant that teams that exceeded a certain payroll level had to contribute to a fund that was redistributed to financially weaker teams.[1] Along with the amateur draft and several new ballparks, more competition resulted. Between 2000 and 2005, 18 of the 30 major-league teams reached the playoffs.

The 2005 postseason produced some surprises. In the American League Division Series, the Chicago White Sox swept the defending World Series champions, the Boston Red Sox, while in the other division series, the Los Angeles Angels of Anaheim beat the perennially contending Yankees, three games to two. In the National League Division Series, the St. Louis Cardinals swept the San Diego Padres and the Houston Astros defeated the Atlanta Braves, three games to one. In the League Championship Series, the White Sox beat the Angels in five games, while Houston ousted the Cardinals in a hard-fought series, four games to two. In the World Series the White Sox, making their first appearance since 1959, swept the Astros, making their first appearance ever. It was the White Sox' first World Series championship since 1917.

As the offseason began, there was every reason for most teams to think that with the addition of the right player, they too could win in the postseason. Even before the Winter Meetings began, there were several major trades and free-agent signings, which presaged a very busy offseason.

In late November, there were three major trades. In the biggest, the Boston Red Sox sent top prospect Hanley Ramirez and right-handers Anibal Sanchez, Jesus Delgado, and Harvey Garcia to the Florida Marlins for right-handers Josh Beckett and Guillermo Mota and third baseman Mike Lowell. Ramirez was a budding star, and he proved to be one for the Marlins, as he led the National League in runs scored in 2008 and in batting in 2009 (.342). With the Marlins, Ramirez became an All-Star shortstop. Sanchez became a dependable starting pitcher for the Marlins and later for the Detroit Tigers. Beckett and Lowell were central to Boston's World Series victory in 2007. Beckett won 20 games that year, and Lowell had a career year at the plate with a .324 batting average, 21 home runs, and 120 runs batted in. This was the proverbial trade that helped both teams.

There were two other consequential trades before the Winter Meetings. The White Sox traded their starting center fielder, Aaron Rowand, and minor-league left-handers Daniel Haigwood and Gio Gonzalez to the Philadelphia Phillies for first baseman Jim Thome. Rowand, an excellent defender, would have his best years with the Phillies, including a .309/27/89 All-Star year in 2007. Gonzalez became a very good starting pitcher, with Oakland and the Washington Nationals (21 wins in 2012). Thome continued as a top-level slugger for several years with the White Sox, with 42 home runs and 109 RBIs as an immediate return in 2006. The other deal saw the Florida Marlins send second baseman Luis Castillo to the Minnesota Twins for two minor leaguers. Castillo, a three-time All-Star and three-time Gold Glove winner who had twice led the National League in stolen bases, continued to be a highly productive player for several seasons with the Twins and the New York Mets. The two right-handed pitchers the Marlins received (Scott Tyler and Travis Bowyer) never made the 25-man roster.

PLAYER MOVEMENT AT THE 2005 WINTER MEETING

The meeting was held December 5-8 at the Wyndham Anatole Hotel in Dallas, Texas. In those four days, 21 free agents signed contracts and 15 trades were completed, with 42 players changing teams. Another 15 players were selected in the Rule 5 draft.

FREE AGENT SIGNINGS

Many of the 21 free agents re-signed with their original teams. For example, All-Star outfielder Brian Giles and star closer Trevor Hoffman returned to the San Diego Padres, and veteran left-handed starter Jamie Moyer went back to the Seattle Mariners.

Five free-agent signings could be characterized as more important than others. Most notably, right-handed starting pitcher A.J. Burnett went from the Florida Marlins to the Toronto Blue Jays. Burnett pitched in Toronto for three years, with 18 wins in 2008. He went on to pitch for the New York Yankees and Pittsburgh Pirates, ending his career with 164 victories in the majors. Paul Byrd, a right-handed starting pitcher, signed with the Cleveland Indians after having spent the 2005 season with the Angels. Byrd spent several seasons in the Cleveland rotation, winning 15 games in 2007. Kyle Farnsworth, a veteran right-handed relief pitcher, left the Atlanta Braves for the Yankees. With Mariano Rivera established as the closer in the Bronx, Farnsworth assumed a setup role. He continued as a major-league reliever with five more teams until 2014, with a career-high 25 saves for Tampa Bay in 2011. The Los Angeles Dodgers added star shortstop Rafael Furcal, the 2000 National League Rookie of the Year, who left the always-contending Atlanta Braves. Furcal had several solid seasons with the Dodgers, and also had an All-Star season (2012) with the St. Louis Cardinals. Relief specialist Tom Gordon signed with the Philadelphia Phillies, a move that paid immediate dividends for the Phils, as the right-handed Gordon recorded 34 saves in 2006, the second-best total of his 21-year career.

TRADES

The first trade of the Winter Meetings saw the Florida Marlins send catcher Paul Lo Duca to the New York Mets for outfielder Dante Brinkley and right-hander Gaby Hernandez. Lo Duca was the Mets' starting catcher for two seasons, making the All-Star team in 2006 when he batted .318 and helped the Mets reach the National League Championship Series. Neither Brinkley nor Hernandez ever played in the major leagues.

In a trade of relief pitchers, the Baltimore Orioles sent the lefty Steve Kline to the San Francisco Giants for right-hander Latroy Hawkins. Kline pitched two more respectable seasons for the Giants, while Hawkins was in the middle of a 21-year career (1995-2015) that saw him pitch with 11 different clubs, highlighted (perhaps) by appearances in the 2007 World Series with the Colorado Rockies. As late in his career as 2014 (with the Rockies), Hawkins recorded 23 saves.

The Colorado Rockies made two major trades at the meetings. They sent outfielder Larry Bigbie and infielder Aaron Miles to the St. Louis Cardinals for left-handed relief pitcher Ray King. Miles started for three seasons with the Cardinals, hitting .317 in 2008. Bigbie played only 17 more games in the majors, while King pitched only a couple more inconsequential years in the majors. The Rockies also sent right-hander Miguel Carvajal to the Seattle Mariners for Yorvit Torrealba. Torrealba was the starting catcher for two postseason teams, the 2007 Rockies and the 2011 Texas Rangers.

BASEBALL'S BUSINESS: THE WINTER MEETINGS

In a trade that was thought to be major at the time, the Arizona Diamondbacks sent right-handed pitchers Lance Cormier and Oscar Villareal to the Atlanta Braves for catcher Johnny Estrada. Cormier pitched, mainly in relief, for six more years in the major leagues, and Villareal had a 9-1 record as a Braves reliever in 2006. Estrada, considered a future star at one time (he was an All-Star in 2004 when he batted .314), hit .302 with 11 home runs and 71 RBIs for the Diamondbacks in 2006. He followed that with a respectable season at Milwaukee in 2007, but was out of the majors before the end of the 2008 season.

The Boston Red Sox traded catcher Doug Mirabelli to the San Diego Padres for third baseman Mark Loretta. Mirabelli, a veteran backup catcher, was known as a specialist in catching the knuckleball pitcher Tim Wakefield. Loretta was an excellent veteran hitter, who finished with a lifetime batting average of .295. It seemed for a time that Mirabelli would be a starter, after several years as a backup receiver, but later in the offseason, San Diego signed future Hall of Famer Mike Piazza to be the regular catcher. Mirabelli requested a return to Boston, and was traded back to the Red Sox early in the 2006 season for catcher Josh Bard, right-handed reliever Cla Meredith, and $100,000. Mirabelli was a member of the 2007 Red Sox champions, in his last year in the majors. Loretta hit .285 and made the All-Star team in his only season with the Red Sox, then spent two years with the Astros and one with Dodgers before retiring.

The very active Florida Marlins sent outfielder Juan Pierre to the Chicago Cubs for right-handers Sergio Mitre and Ricky Nolasco, plus southpaw Renyel Pinto. Pierre was consistently good throughout his career and 2006 proved to be no exception, as he led the NL with 204 hits (including 13 triples), batted .292, and stole 58 bases. In 2010, while playing for the Chicago White Sox, Pierre led the American League with 68 steals. Mitre was part of Florida's starting rotation for a couple of seasons, making 27 starts in 2007, before moving to the Yankees and then to the Brewers. Ricky Nolasco became a good starting pitcher for the Marlins, winning 81 games for the team. By the end of the 2016 season (which he spent with the Twins and Angels), Nolasco had more than 100 wins as a major-league pitcher. Pinto wound up pitching in almost 250 games in his five-year Marlins career.

The Toronto Blue Jays got first baseman Lyle Overbay and right-hander Ty Taubenheim from the Milwaukee Brewers in exchange for right-handed starter David Bush, southpaw Zach Jackson, and outfielder Gabe Gross. Overbay was the Blue Jays' regular first baseman for the next five seasons, posting solid, if not spectacular, numbers during that time. Bush was a regular in Milwaukee's pitching rotation for five seasons, winning 46 games for the Brewers. Gross, who had been Auburn's starting quarterback, never became more than a platoon outfielder in the majors, while Taubenheim and Jackson combined for just five major-league victories.

The Atlanta Braves sent heralded third-base prospect Andy Marte to the Boston Red Sox for shortstop Edgar Renteria. Despite the high expectations, Marte never made it as a regular at the major-league level. Renteria batted .293 and .332 in his two seasons in Atlanta. Indeed, postseason appearances and successes followed Renteria throughout his career—he had been with Florida when it won the World Series in 1997, with St. Louis when it lost the World Series (to Boston) in 2004, and would be the World Series MVP with San Francisco in 2010.

Perhaps the most puzzling trade of the meetings was the Texas Rangers-Washington Nationals deal. The Rangers sent second baseman Alfonso Soriano to Washington for right-handed pitcher Armando Galarraga and outfielders Terrmel Sledge and Brad Wilkerson. For Jon Daniels, the Rangers general manager, who built the team into a consistent contender in the 2010s, this was one of his first trades, and it may be one he would rather forget. Soriano had originally come to the Rangers in the trade of Alex Rodriguez to the Yankees after the 2003 season. Soriano was headed for expensive free agency, but he hit 46 home runs and was selected for the All-Star team for the Nats in 2006. Soriano hit 412 home runs and had almost 2,100 hits, in a career that concluded in 2014. Showing long-term value, Soriano had more than 30 home runs and 100 RBIs as late as 2013 (divided

CUBAN DISMISSAL CRISIS*

One of the surprises related to the World Baseball Classic was that Cuba accepted an invitation to participate. "We will participate and demonstrate that we know what to do in baseball," declared President Fidel Castro.** However, about two weeks after the invitation was accepted, the US Treasury Department refused permission for the Cubans to come to the United States, citing the long-standing embargo against the communist nation. As a result, Cuba was removed from the tournament.

The tournament organizers, Major League Baseball and the Major League Baseball Players Association, weren't thrilled. Spokesmen Gene Orza (for the union) and Paul Archey (for MLB) stated, "We are very disappointed with the government's decision to deny the participation of a team from Cuba in the World Baseball Classic. We will continue to work within appropriate channels in an attempt to address the government's concerns and will not announce a replacement unless and until that effort fails."***

Dick Pound, vice president of the International Olympic Committee, wasn't thrilled either, declaring that, if the Cuba decision weren't reversed, "it would completely scuttle" any bid by the United States for the Summer or Winter Olympic Games."**** And Puerto Rico also expressed dismay. Israel Roldán, president of the Puerto Rico Olympic Federation, said, "If they tell me they are going to do the event in another country, then we will go, because we are no longer the host, and to us they are simply inviting us. I am discharging my responsibility as president of the host-country federation. What bothers and aggravates me is the insult that they told me (initially that) Cuba will be invited."*****

A second application for permit was made on December 22, 2005, and on January 20, 2006, the Treasury Department granted the permit with the statement, "We were able to reach a licensable agreement that upholds both the legal scope and the spirit of the sanctions. This agreement ensures that no funding will make its way into the hands of the Castro regime."******

---

* The title is taken from Kevin B. Blackstone, "Cuban Dismissal Crisis Is Baseball Disaster," *Dallas Morning News*, January 13, 2006: 1C.
** Associated Press, "Cuban President Confirms Team Will Come Here – Castro: Cuba Will Play in WBC," *San Juan Star*, December 3, 2005: 063.
*** "U.S. Government Won't Let Cuba Compete in Classic," *The Capital* (Annapolis, Maryland), December 15, 2005: C7.
**** Juan C. Rodriguez, "Cuba Denial May Hurt USOC Bids," *South Florida Sun-Sentinel* (Fort Lauderdale), December 16, 2005: 12C.
***** Adam Rubin, "P.R.: Won't Host Classic," *New York Daily News*, December 23, 2005: 102.
****** Ed Holland, "US Gives Cuba a Chance to Become Baseball Champions," *Financial Times* (London), January 21, 2006: 8.

between the Cubs and Yankees). On the other side of the deal, Galarraga won just 26 games in the majors and is best known as the pitcher who lost a perfect game to an umpire's missed call while pitching for Detroit. Sledge was shipped to the Padres a month later in a deal that also included first baseman Adrian Gonzalez and 6-foot-10 righty Chris Young, and made only token appearances in the majors after the trade. Wilkerson, the key from the Rangers perspective, had hit 32 home runs for Montreal in 2004, but he barely topped that in his two seasons as a Ranger, and he closed out his career with Seattle and Toronto in 2008. Finances certainly played a role in the trade. Soriano was pending free agency, and would have a high veteran's salary. In addition, the Rangers had an excellent second baseman, Ian Kinsler, ready to play at the major-league level in 2006. Kinsler would earn the major-league minimum salary as a rookie. Nevertheless, the return for Soriano was disappointing.

RULE 5 DRAFT

Fifteen players were selected in the Rule 5 draft. Two turned out to be significant acquisitions. The Texas Rangers picked right-handed pitcher Alexi Ogando from the Oakland A's. Ogando was a successful pitcher for several seasons before he suffered arm injuries. As a starting pitcher, he won 13 games in 2011 for a Rangers team that went to the World Series, but he was primarily an effective setup reliever. In one of the all-time Rule 5 bargains, the Florida Marlins took Dan Uggla from the Arizona Diamondbacks. Uggla, a three-time All-Star second baseman, hit at least 30 home runs in every season from 2007 to 2011.

BUSINESS SIDE OF THE MEETING

Owners at the meeting took a harsher stance toward the use of steroids. By unanimous vote, they instituted a 50-game suspension for the first positive test for steroids, a 100-game suspension for a second positive test, and a lifetime suspension for a third positive (the previous penalties were lighter). The players union, meeting at the same time in Henderson, Nevada, ratified the owners' decision. This was thought to be a good sign for the coming negotiations on a new contract. (The current contract was to expire after the 2006 season.) The players opened up a previously negotiated issue (the penalties for steroid use) under pressure from the owners, Congress, and the public.[2]

Major League Baseball also made a major announcement at the meeting about the World Baseball Classic. Some 177 players, including such stars as Barry Bonds, Roger Clemens, Eric Gagne, Vladimir Guerrero, and Derek Jeter, agreed to play in the WBC. This 16-team international tournament was to be played during spring training in March 2006. A player could play for a country's team if one of his parents was born in the country. Thus, future Hall of Fame catcher Mike Piazza and longtime major-league reliever Jason Grilli were on the Italian roster.[3]

Discussions continued about the definitive ownership of the Washington Nationals. In February of 2002, Major League Baseball had taken ownership of the Montreal Expos, and eventually moved them to Washington for the 2005 season. This, however, was considered to be a temporary solution, and the other 29 club owners were eager to find someone to take permanent possession of the Nationals. Four ownership groups under consideration. A group headed by Tennessee developer Franklin Haney may never have received serious consideration. Two of the groups had major Washington connections: One was headed by real-estate developer Ted Lerner, the other by Fred Malek, an investor and former White House aide. A fourth group, headed by Jeff Smulyan, a communications executive and former owner of the Seattle Mariners, was well-funded but lacked local ties.[4] Ultimately, in 2006, the Lerner group received the franchise.

MINOR-LEAGUE MEETINGS

The minor-league meetings, held in conjunction with the major-league meetings, presented a mixed picture of the state of minor-league baseball. The Trenton Thunder of the Double-A Eastern League won the outstanding franchise award. The Brevard County Manatees of the Class-A Florida State League won the Larry MacPhail award for best promotions. In some respects, there was a darker tone. Mike Moore, president of the National Association, the minor leagues' umbrella group, told a sportswriter that half of the 176 affiliated teams in minor-league baseball in 2005 would lose money. Only a few years previously, two-thirds of the franchises had been profitable. Sixteen successful teams made 60 percent of the profits. The fiscal crisis in the minor leagues was said to be caused by owners having to bear more of the costs of ballparks, and to soaring franchise prices.[5]

SUMMARY

The 2005 Winter Meetings left owners, players, the media, and fans with optimistic feelings. While labor negotiations loomed in 2006, the players' acceptance of the stiffer drug penalties imposed by ownership was viewed as a good sign. Moreover, all of the player movement reflected competitive balance. With almost every team involved in free agency, trades, and the Rule 5 draft, a bright offseason outlook was possible for most teams, and their fans.

SOURCES

In addition to the sources cited in the Notes, the author also consulted Baseball-Reference.com and:

Baseball Information Solutions, *The Bill James Handbook 2016* (Chicago: ACTA Sports, 2015).

Zimbalist, Andrew. *Baseball and Billions* (New York: Basic Books, 1992).

NOTES

1. Andrew Zimbalist, *In the Best Interests of Baseball* (Hoboken, New Jersey: John Wiley & Sons, 2006), 168-169.

2. Barry Bloom, "Players Approve New Steroid Agreement," mlb.com. December 8, 2005.

3. Tim Brown, "Major League Stars Sign Up for World Baseball Classic," *Los Angeles Times*, December 6, 2005.

4. Tim Kurkjian, "Nationals Need an Owner Now," espn.go.com, November 16, 2005.

5. Eric Fisher, "The State of Minor League Baseball 2005," sportsbusinessdaily.com, December 5, 2005.

— 2006 —
A BARRY ACTIVE MEETING

By Jason C. Long

Introduction and Context

THE 2006 BASEBALL WINTER Meetings were held in Orlando, Florida, at the Walt Disney World Swan and Dolphin Resort. The size of the resort—an 87-acre facility featuring two hotels with over 80 meeting rooms and 300,000 square feet of meeting space—matched the big names on the market heading into the meetings. Several star players were free agents, including controversial outfielder Barry Bonds, who finished the 2006 season 21 home runs shy of Hank Aaron's career record. The dollar amounts and lengths of several contracts announced at the general managers' meetings a few weeks earlier created anticipation that the Winter Meetings would result in more star players signing big contracts; also, the Red Sox were openly seeking to trade an "elite position player"—which was Boston's way of referring to slugging outfielder Manny Ramirez without specifically mentioning his name.

In the end, however, all the big fish remained as stationary as the 57-foot-tall dolphin statues atop the Dolphin Hotel. A number of teams and players agreed on contracts during the meetings, but the big names did not sign until later, and there were few trades. The business at the Winter Meetings similarly involved only the players approving the new collective-bargaining agreement, a formality by the time the vote was taken, and the Baseball Writers' Association of America voting Cal Ripken and Tony Gwynn into the Hall of Fame.

On the Field

Almost as soon as the Cardinals closed out the Tigers in the 2006 World Series, the offseason looked as though it could be filled with significant player movement. The Tigers, whose offense sputtered against the Cardinals, got things started on November 10 when they traded three minor-league pitchers to the Yankees for DH-outfielder Gary Sheffield, whom the Tigers promptly signed to a $28 million extension through the 2010 season. The big deals continued at the general managers' meetings, which began on November 13 in Naples, Florida. During those meetings, several players signed significant contracts. These included five-time All-Star outfielder Alfonso Soriano signing an eight-year, $136 million deal with the Cubs, who also re-signed third baseman Aramis Ramirez to a five-year, $75 million pact; the Astros and DH-outfielder Carlos Lee agreeing to a six-year, $100 million deal; and the Angels signing outfielder Gary Matthews Jr., coming off a career year, to a five-year, $50 million contract. In addition, the Red Sox agreed to pay the Seibu Lions of Japan's Pacific League a $51 million posting fee just for the right to negotiate with Seibu's star pitcher, right-hander Daisuke Matsuzaka. But the biggest names—Barry Bonds and A's starting pitcher and 2002 Cy Young winner Barry Zito—remained on the free agent market.

The "Most Intriguing" Subplot of the Winter Meetings

Bonds' situation was the "most intriguing" subplot heading into the Winter Meetings, which began on Monday, December 4.[1] The Giants had decided against offering him salary arbitration after the 2006 season, making him a free agent and creating tension between

Bonds and the team. As the Winter Meetings began, Bonds, who had hit .270 with 26 home runs and 115 walks during 2006 but was surrounded by steroid rumors and the possibility of a federal indictment, was reportedly flying to Oakland to meet with the crosstown Athletics. But an A's official responded, "Someone made that up."[2] Another rumor had the Tampa Bay Devil Rays interested in Bonds. This was so amusing to the cash-strapped Devil Rays that when general manager Andrew Friedman opened his suite at the Swan and Dolphin to reporters, they found an easel with Friedman's handwritten message: "Welcome media and Barry Bonds."[3]

Instead of flying to Oakland, Bonds flew to the Winter Meetings. This was unusual for any player, but especially for a star like Bonds; the only other player at the meetings, in fact, was backup infielder Nick Green, who had hit just .164 during 2006. When Bonds strolled through the Dolphin Hotel lobby on Tuesday afternoon, surrounded by about 10 agents and bodyguards, reporters asked whether he was close to a deal with the Giants, and whether other teams were interested in him. "No comment" was Bonds' only response, but his agent, Jeff Borris, insisted that "Lots of teams are interested in Barry."[4] Bonds' appearance at the Winter Meetings was panned as a "desperate" negotiating ploy, as he sought an $18 million deal for 2007 with an option for 2008, while the Giants were offering a $10 million contract for only 2007.[5]

Bonds' ploy, desperate or not, did result in discussions with the Giants. At the close of the Winter Meetings on Thursday, December 7, Borris announced that the sides were making "significant progress."[6] It was only after the meetings ended, however, that Bonds and the Giants agreed to a one-year deal for $16 million with incentives that could increase the contract's value to $20 million. The deal was not officially announced at the meetings, but there were reports that the Giants had agreed with Bonds only after failing to sign Alfonso Soriano or Carlos Lee, or trade for Manny Ramirez.

Barry Zito and Free Agent Pitchers

With Soriano and Lee signing nine-figure contracts before the meetings, there was anticipation that left-hander Barry Zito would be the next $100 million man. Zito, who had not missed a start "since Tee Ball,"[7] and led the A's to the 2006 American League Championship Series, was represented by super-agent Scott Boras. Boras was advertising that Zito wanted "a six- or seven-year contract, most likely for as much as $17 million per season."[8] The Mets, the Cubs, and the Rangers all showed interest in Zito, but he departed Orlando without a deal. Zito wound up getting his money later in December, agreeing with the Giants on a seven-year, $126 million contract.

Nevertheless, several pitchers did sign big contracts at the Winter Meetings. Despite failing to land Zito, the Cubs got a left-handed starter when they signed Ted Lilly, who had won at least 10 games in each of the previous four seasons, to a four-year, $40 million contract. The Dodgers signed former Giants starter Jason Schmidt, who had led the National League in ERA in 2003, to a three-year deal worth $47 million, and the Royals stunned the baseball world when they signed right-hander Gil Meche to a five-year, $55 million contract. In six years with the Mariners, Meche had compiled just a 55-44 record with a 4.65 ERA. Otherwise, the Rangers signed Vicente Padilla to a three-year, $32 million contract and the Padres signed four-time Cy Young Award-winning right-hander Greg Maddux to a one-year deal for $10 million, with a player option for 2008. The Cardinals meanwhile announced that they had agreed with Chris Carpenter, their ace and the 2005 Cy Young winner, on a five-year extension for $63.5 million. And though not a deal, Andy Pettitte announced during the Winter Meetings that he would play again in 2007, but only for his current team, the Astros, or his former team, the Yankees; Pettitte subsequently returned to New York.

The Tampering Red Sox?

The Red Sox attracted some negative attention at the Winter Meetings as they were looking to retool their outfield following a third-place finish in the American League East. After the 2004 season, outfielder J.D. Drew had signed a five-year contract with the Dodgers that allowed him to opt out and become a free agent following the 2006 season. Drew batted .283 with 20 home runs during the season and, on the advice of his agent, Scott Boras, who indicated there would be a "strong market" for the former Florida State star, Drew opted out.[9] On December 5 Boras announced at the Winter Meetings that the Red Sox had signed Drew to a five-year contract for $70 million.

But there was a little more to the story. As the opt-out deadline was approaching, Drew was providing every indication that he would "stick to" his "commitment" to the Dodgers.[10] When Drew signed with the Red Sox, rumors began to swirl that the Red Sox had let Boras know that if Drew opted out, he could get a better deal in Boston. Dodgers general manager Ned Colletti was "angry" over the Drew situation and had stopped taking calls from the Red Sox, while many executives at the Winter Meetings urged him to file a tampering charge.[11] Indeed, MLB officials pledged to "vigorously investigate" the Drew situation if the Dodgers so requested. But as the meetings ended, the Dodgers had not "reached a decision yet" whether to file a tampering charge.

The Red Sox engaged in other business at the Winter Meetings, too. They signed shortstop Julio Lugo, who hit .278 with 12 home runs in a 2006 season split between the Devil Rays and the Dodgers, to a four-year, $36 million contract.[12] Lugo represented the latest in Boston's efforts to find a shortstop after trading away two-time batting champion Nomar Garciaparra, allowing Gold Glove winner Orlando Cabrera to leave as a free agent, and then trading away All-Star Edgar Renteria just one year after bringing him in as a free agent.

As for the Dodgers, they signed outfielder Luis Gonzalez to a one-year, $7.35 million deal in the wake of Drew's departure. The Winter Meetings also saw the Dodgers sign catcher Mike Lieberthal to a one-year deal to back up regular catcher Russell Martin, and re-sign closer Takashi Saito.

Trades

Although there were great expectations for player movement heading into the Winter Meetings, they did not seem to involve trades. Trading activity at the meetings was light; the biggest trade in Orlando involved the White Sox sending right-handed starting pitcher Freddy Garcia to the Phillies. Garcia had won 17 games in 2006, but posted a 4.53 ERA. Chicago accepted right-handed minor-league pitcher Gavin Floyd, the fourth overall pick in the 2001 amateur draft, and a player to be named, as they sought to create room in their rotation for their own prospect, right-hander Brandon McCarthy. The trade was first announced in the Winter Meetings "workroom" at 10:30 P.M. on Tuesday, and formally announced after 11:00. At the formal announcement, Chicago general manager Kenny Williams "let slip" that the player to be named was minor-league southpaw Gio Gonzalez, whom the White Sox had traded to Philadelphia a year earlier in the Jim Thome-Aaron Rowand deal. After the "slip," Kenny Williams remarked, "It's 11 o'clock at night, what do you want?"[13] Other trades involved swaps of relievers for starters, with the Braves sending left-handed starting pitcher Horacio Ramirez to Seattle for right-handed reliever Rafael Soriano, and the Mets sending starter Brian Bannister to Kansas City for reliever Ambiorix Burgos in an exchange of right-handers.

There were rumors of other trades at the meetings, though none came to fruition. For example, one report had the White Sox sending starting pitcher Jon Garland to the Astros in exchange for pitchers Taylor Buchholz and Jason Hirsh and outfielder Willy Taveras, but no such deal occurred. Another had the Tigers sending an outfielder—either Craig Monroe or Marcus Thames—to Baltimore, but Tigers general manager Dave Dombrowski dismissed the rumors as coming from the Orioles. Notably, there seemed to be no rumors involving the Red Sox trading that "elite position player," whoever he was.

Other Signings

There were a few other noteworthy signings during the meetings. The A's signed slugging catcher Mike

Piazza to a one-year deal for $8.5 million to serve as their DH. Piazza was coming off a relatively disappointing season with the Padres, and the A's sought to catch him on the rebound. A similar deal a year earlier with DH Frank Thomas had helped the A's reach the ALCS during 2006. Also, the Giants signed infielder Rich Aurilia to a two-year, $8 million contract, and catcher Bengie Molina to a three-year, $16 million deal. Aurilia had been a star shortstop with the Giants in the early 2000s, but had mostly scuffled since leaving San Francisco. The Giants brought him back as a first baseman and utility infielder. Molina, on the other hand, had hit .284 with 19 home runs as a Blue Jay in 2006. The Giants brought him to San Francisco because they questioned whether their backup catcher in 2006, former Michigan Wolverine Mike Matheny, would be able play again after suffering a concussion. In fact, Matheny never did play again.

The Business of Baseball

As with player movement, there were no great accomplishments in the business of baseball at the meetings. Perhaps the most important business was the Players Association approving the new five-year collective-bargaining agreement. The agreement had been announced in October, but was subject to the players' formal vote at the Winter Meetings. The new agreement adopted a few changes to the existing system, notably leaving in place the drug testing program. Revised in November of 2005, it was designed to strengthen the program that the parties had initially adopted in their previous Basic Agreement. Other changes involved eliminating the requirement that teams must sign their own free agents by early December or wait until the following May to sign them, advancing the deadline for teams to sign amateur draft picks to August 15 following the June amateur draft, increasing the minimum player salary, and raising the luxury tax threshold.[14]

In addition, MLB announced the institution of a "Civil Rights Game." Commissioner Bud Selig stated that the game was designed to commemorate the Civil Rights Movement, which he described as "one of the most critical and important eras of our social history," and to celebrate baseball's role in the movement beginning with Jackie Robinson breaking the "color barrier" in 1947.[15] The inaugural game was scheduled for March 31, 2007, at AutoZone Park, home of the Cardinals' Triple-A affiliate in Memphis. MLB chose this location because Memphis is home to the National Civil Rights Museum, built on the site where Dr. Martin Luther King Jr. was assassinated in 1968. The Cardinals, not only Memphis's parent club but also historically considered a team that featured many minority players, would host the game against the Indians, whose significance in this event included signing Larry Doby in 1947 to break the color barrier in the American League, and hiring Frank Robinson in 1975 as the major leagues' first African-American manager. As part of the event, MLB would make donations to the museum, the NAACP Legal Defense Fund, the Negro Leagues Museum, and other charities.

Hall of Fame Vote and Other Awards

The two players elected to the Hall of Fame during the 2006 Winter Meetings—Cal Ripken Jr. and Tony Gwynn—hardly require introduction. Ripken, the longtime Orioles shortstop and third baseman, was perhaps best known for his consecutive-games-played streak, which broke Lou Gehrig's long-standing record and eventually reached 2,632 games before Ripken removed himself from the lineup on September 20, 1998. Considered oversized for a shortstop, Ripken stood 6-feet-4-inches tall and weighed 225 pounds when he broke into the big leagues, but proved to be an outstanding defensive shortstop, hitting for average and power before moving to third base late in his career. The 1982 Rookie of the Year and a two-time American League MVP, Ripken played exclusively with the Orioles for 21 years, had a .276 lifetime batting average with 431 home runs, and redefined the shortstop position.

Padres outfielder Tony Gwynn won the NL batting crown eight times and hit .338 for his career. Gwynn constantly studied his swing and pioneered using video to refine his batting. Not just a great hitter, Gwynn amassed 319 stolen bases and was a five-time Gold Glove winner. His all-around play led him to

15 All-Star selections and inclusion on more than 97 percent of the Hall of Fame ballots for 2006, the seventh highest percentage in history. Like Ripken, Gwynn spent his entire career with one team.

Also, *Baseball America* held its awards gala at the Winter Meetings on Tuesday, December 5. The Dodgers were named the Organization of the Year, but the Tigers won four major awards, including Dave Dombrowski as Executive of the Year, Jim Leyland as Manager of the Year, Justin Verlander as Rookie of the Year, and a 2006 Tigers draftee, University of North Carolina left-hander Andrew Miller, as College Player of the Year.

The Minor-League Meetings and the Rule 5 Draft

The minor league organization, the National Association of Professional Baseball Leagues, held their meeting at the Swan & Dolphin too, and had an overflow crowd on hand for the events. The minors celebrated record attendance in 2006 exceeding 41 million fans, and sought to emphasize that minor-league operators should implement programs that would "make kids fans for a lifetime," as the minors' President Mike Moore explained.[16]

The Rule 5 draft was the last official business of the Winter Meetings, on Thursday, December 7, and it involved two players who went on to have big-league success. With the third pick, the Cubs selected outfielder Josh Hamilton from Tampa Bay. Hamilton had been the first overall pick in the 1999 amateur draft, and the Cubs immediately sold him to the Reds. Later in the draft, the Kansas City Royals selected right-handed starting pitcher Joakim Soria from the Padres. Hamilton played well in Cincinnati and was traded to Texas before the 2008 season; he went on to become a bona-fide superstar and the 2010 American League MVP. In Kansas City, Soria moved to the bullpen and became an All-Star closer.

Summary

The 2006 Winter Meetings followed an active early offseason, and perhaps the pre-meeting deals stole some of the meetings' thunder. Those teams that had already completed trades or signed players to significant contracts were less likely to make further moves at the Winter Meetings; meanwhile, that flurry of early activity may have increased expectations among the remaining significant free agents, lowering the possibility of agreements at the Winter Meetings. As for the signings that did take place, most were either not significant for the coming season, or not unexpected. For instance, there was never serious doubt that Barry Bonds would return to the Giants. But the contract that Bonds reportedly agreed to as the Winter Meetings ended was not finalized until February 2007 because the commissioner's office refused to approve personal-appearance clauses related to Bonds' pursuit of Hank Aaron's home-run record. The lack of big signings or trades led Mariners general manager Bill Bavasi to describe 2006 as "one of the more miserable Winter Meetings" he had ever attended.[17] But for the teams that did sign players, including the Dodgers, the meetings were hectic. After agreeing with four players at the meetings, Dodgers general manager Ned Colletti said that the only thing left for him to do after the meetings was to "get some sleep."[18]

SOURCES

In addition to the sources cited in the Notes, the author also consulted:

"Baseball: Dodgers Land Ace Schmidt for $47M," *Detroit Free Press*, December 7, 2006: Sports 2.

"Bonds, Giants Agree on One-Year Deal; Slugger Gets $16 Million to Stay in San Francisco," *Grand Rapids Press*, December 8, 2006: D8.

"Bonds, Ramirez Talk of Meetings," *Orlando Sentinel*, December 4, 2006: D3.

"Busy Red Sox Add Drew, Lugo; Maddux Near One-Year Deal With Padres," *Grand Rapids Press*, December 6, 2006: E9.

Cafardo, Nick. "Green Light: For $51M, Sox Get Go-Ahead on Matsuzaka," Boston.com, November 15, 2006. Accessed July 8, 2011. articles.boston.com/2006-11-15/sports/29244391_1_japanese-ace-daisuke-matsuzaka-red-sox-seibu-lions.

Cantor, George. *The Tigers of '68: Baseball's Last Real Champions* (Dallas: Taylor Publishing Company, 1997).

Chass, Murray. "On Baseball: Winter Meetings a Big Deal? Sometimes," *New York Times*, December 3, 2006. Accessed March 25, 2011. query.nytimes.com/gst/fullpage.html?res=9805E7DD1F3EF930 A35751C1A9609C8B63&pagewanted=all.

"Contract Language Keeps Bonds Deal in Limbo," *The Boston Channel.com*, February 1, 2007. Accessed February 13, 2012. thebostonchannel.com/r/10898772/detail.html.

Curry, Jack. "Baseball: Job Search for Bonds Ends Where It Started, as Expected," *New York Times*, December 9, 2006. query.nytimes.com/gst/fullpage.html?res=9A01E1D61731F93AA35751C1A9609C 8B63. Accessed March 25, 2011.

-----. "Baseball: In Need of Job, Green Decides to Interview," *New York Times*, December 12, 2006. query.nytimes.com/gst/fullpage.html?res=9C0CE2DA1431F932A25751C1A9609C8B63. Accessed March 25, 2011.

-----. "Money Can't Buy Happiness, but the Cubs Hope It Does," *New York Times*, December 8, 2006. nytimes.com/2006/12/08/sports/baseball/08cubs.html. Accessed March 25, 2011.

Czerwinski, Kevin. "Rule 5 Draft Brings Unexpected Results," MLB.com, December 7, 2006. http://mlb.mlb.com/news/print.jsp?ymd=20061207&content_id=1754489&vkey=hotstove2006&fext=.jsp. Accessed March 24, 2011.

Footer, Alyson. "Astros Look for No. 2 Starter at Meetings," December 1, 2006. MLB.com. mlb.mlb.com/news/article.jsp?ymd=20061129&content_id=1747466&vkey=hotstove2006&fext=.jsp. Accessed March 24, 2011.

Henning, Lynn. "Tigers Grab Lefty in Rule 5 Draft; Thames Trade Dies, but Team Pays Brewers to Move Up to Select Well-Regarded Reliever," *Detroit News*, December 8, 2006: 1D.

-----. "Deal or No Deal? It's Complicated," *Detroit News*, December 14, 2006: 1D.

"Iraqi Gunfire Signals Big Soccer Victory; 2-1 Win Puts Team in Asian Games Semifinals," *Grand Rapids Press*, December 10, 2006: D12.

Kepner, Tyler. "Baseball Fan as a Boy, Maier Now Seeks Front Office Job," *New York Times*, December 5, 2006. nytimes.com/2006/12/05/sports/baseball/05maier.html. Accessed March 25, 2011.

-----. "Yanks Appear Close to Signing Pettitte," *New York Times*, December 6, 2011. nytimes.com/2006/12/07/sports/baseball/07yankees.html?ref=tedlilly. Accessed March 25, 2011.

Merkin, Scott, and Alyson Footer. "White Sox Downplay Garland Report," MLB.com, December 7, 2006. mlb.mlb.com/news/article.jsp?ymd=20061207&content_id=1754067&vkey=hotstove2006&fext=.jsp. Accessed March 24, 2011.

Morosi, Jon Paul. "GM Can Afford to Be Patient; Lineup Almost Set as Winter Meetings Begin Monday," *Detroit Free Press*, December 3, 2006: Sports 3.

-----. "Leading Man? Skipper Jim Leyland Ponders Pudge at the Top of the Order in 2007," *Detroit Free Press*, December 7, 2006: Sports 1.

-----. "Tigers Aren't Looking to Deal Pitchers," *Detroit Free Press*, December 5, 2006: Sports 1.

-----. "Tigers Get Left-Hander Via Rule 5 Draft, Trade," *Detroit Free Press*, December 8, 2006: Sports 7.

-----. "Tigers Not Close to Making Trades," *Detroit Free Press*, December 6, 2006: Sports 1.

Muskat, Carrie. "Hendry Has Angioplasty, Feels Fine," The Official Site of the Chicago Cubs, December 7, 2006. chicago.cubs.mlb.com/news/article.jsp?ymd=20061206&content_id=1753071&vkey=news_chc&fext=.jsp&c_id=chc. Accessed March 24, 2011.

"Pitching Takes Over Baseball Meetings; Ramirez Also Being Offered By Red Sox," *Grand Rapids Press*, December 5, 2006: D8.

Robbins, Josh. "Astros, Yankees Will Vie for Pettite," *Orlando Sentinel*, December 7, 2006: D8.

-----. "Even the Mediocre Make Off With Millions," *Orlando Sentinel*, December 9, 2006: C1.

Schwarz, Alan. "Fearing Inflation at the Same Time as Fueling It," *New York Times*, December 10, 2006. nytimes.com/2006/12/10/sports/baseball/10score.html. Accessed March 25, 2011.

Shea, John. "Notebook: Geren, LaRussa do Lunch/Red Sox Sign Drew, Lugo," SFGate.com, December 6, 2006. sfgate.com/cgi-bin/article.cgi?f=/c/a/2006/12/06/SPGECMQBLT1.DTL. Accessed May 18, 2011.

-----. "A's Hope to Choose Manager This Week," SFGate.com. sfgate.com/cgi-bin/article.cgi?f=/c/a/2006/11/15/SPGF8MCQGB1.DTL. Accessed May 18, 2011.

-----. "Schmidt Almost a Dodger," SFGate.com, December 7, 2006. sfgate.com/cgi-bin/article.cgi?f=/c/a/2006/12/07/SPGM7MR5FG1.DTL. Accessed May 18, 2011.

BASEBALL'S BUSINESS: THE WINTER MEETINGS

Sheehan, Joe. "AL Winter Meetings Preview," December 4, 2006. *SI Vault*. sportsillustrated.cnn.com/vault/article/web/COM1046549/index.htm. Accessed March 24, 2011.

Shpigel, Ben. "At the Winter Meetings: Oh Mickey, You're So Fine," *New York Times*, December 5, 2006. nytimes.com/2006/12/06/sports/baseball/06mickey.html?fta=y. Accessed March 25, 2011.

-----. "Baseball: Mets Kick Some Tires, but Make No Deals," *New York Times*, December 6, 2006. nytimes.com/2006/12/06/sports/baseball/06mets.htmlhttp://www.nytimes.com/2006/12/06/sports/baseball/06mets.html. Accessed March 25, 2011.

Slusser, Susan. "Piazza Coming to A's; Trade Talks Continue," SFGate.com, December 7, 2006. articles.sfgate.com/keyword/mike-piazza/featured/5. Accessed May 18, 2011.

"Three Tigers to Receive Awards," *Detroit Free Press*, December 4, 2006: Sports 3.

Whitley, David. "Bonds Sighting Has Nothing on Spitball Gang," *Orlando Sentinel*, December 7, 2006. articles.orlandosentinel.com/2006-12-07/sports/WHITLEY07_1_bonds-spitball-baseball-winter-meetings. Accessed March 24, 2011.

NOTES

1. Josh Robbins, "Bonds Remains Giant Concern," *Orlando Sentinel*, December 6, 2006: C1.

2. John Shea, "On Day 1, Talk Centers on Bonds, Giants," *SFGate.com*, December 5, 2006. sfgate.com/cgi-bin/article.cgi?f=/c/a/2006/12/05/SPGAGMPH981.DTL. Accessed May 18, 2011.

3. Robbins.

4. John Shea, "Bonds Arrives at Hotel, Source Says a Deal Could Be Close," SFGate.com, December 6, 2006. sfgate.com/cgi-bin/article.cgi?f=/c/a/2006/12/06/SPMQMQGL43.DTL. Accessed May 18, 2011.

5. Jack Curry, "In Unemployment Line, Bonds Looks for a Job," *New York Times*, December 7, 2006. nytimes.com/2006/12/07/sports/baseball/07base.html. Accessed March 25, 2011.

6. "Giants, Bonds Gain Ground on Contract," *Orlando Sentinel*, December 8, 2009: D11.

7. Lee Jenkins, "Zito's Father Played His Role to Perfection," *New York Times*, December 4, 2006. nytimes.com/2006/12/04/sports/baseball/04zito.html?_r=1&ref=sports&oref=slogin. Accessed March 25, 2011.

8. Jack Curry, "Drew Agrees to Contract as the Red Sox Reload," *New York Times*, December 6, 2006. nytimes.com/2006/12/06/sports/baseball/06base.html. Accessed March 25, 2011.

9. Murray Chass, "Talk of Misconduct Is Swirling Around Red Sox," *New York Times*, December 8, 2006. nytimes.com/2006/12/08/sports/baseball/08chass.html. Accessed March 25, 2011.

10. Ibid.

11. Ibid.

12. "Red Sox Agree to 4-year, $36M deal with Lugo," ESPN.com, December 6, 2006. espn.com/mlb/news/story?id=2687827. Accessed October 21, 2016.

13. "Sox Unload Garcia for Prospects; Phillies Add Right-Hander to Strengthen Rotation," *Grand Rapids Press*, December 7, 2006: D10.

14. "MLB, MLBPA Reach Five-Year Labor Accord," MLB.com, October 24, 2006. mlb.mlb.com/pa/releases/releases.jsp?content=102406. Accessed August 21, 2016. The new major-league minimum salary was set at $380,000 for 2007, $390,000 for 2008, and $400,000 for 2009, with 2010 to remain constant and a cost-of-living adjustment to apply in 2011. For the minor leagues, the minimum salary was set at $60,000 for 2007, $62,500 for 2008, and $65,000 for 2009. The new agreement set the luxury tax threshold at $148 million for 2007, $155 million for 2008, $162 million for 2009, $170 million in 2010, and $178 million in 2011. The luxury tax continued at the same levels from the prior agreement, which were 22.5 percent of the overage for clubs exceeding the threshold for the first time, 30 percent for the second time, and 40 percent afterward.

15. Barry M. Bloom, "First Civil Rights Game Set for March 31," MLB.com, December 4, 2006. mlb.mlb.com/news/article.jsp?ymd=20061204&content_id=1750068&vkey=news_mlb&fext=.jsp&c_id=mlb. Accessed May 18, 2011.

16. Lisa Winston, "Winter Meetings Bring Flurry of Milb Activity," MLB.com, December 7, 2006. milb.com/gen/articles/printer_friendly/milb/y2006/m12/d07/c147901.jsp. Accessed August 21, 2016. Notably, MiLB President Mike Moore was not the same Mike Moore who pitched for the Mariners, A's, and Tigers.

17. Corey Brock, "Mariners' Tally: Big Bat, Starting Duo," MLB.com, December 7, 2006. mlb.mlb.com/news/article.jsp?ymd=20061207&content_id=1753927&vkey=news_sea&fext=.jsp&c_id=sea. Accessed March 24, 2011.

18. Murray Chass, "On Baseball: Week in Review: Few Trades but Feverish Spending," *New York Times*, December 10, 2006. query.nytimes.com/gst/fullpage.html?res=9502E0DD1431F933A25751C1A9609C8B63&pagewanted=all.

— 2007 —
THE PROMISE AND CURSE OF TECHNOLOGY

By Paul D. Brown

IN GENERAL, THE BASEBALL WINTER Meetings can be viewed as a watershed event, marking both the end of one season and the beginning of the next. Even before the 2007 Winter Meetings got under way in Nashville, however, the offseason had been launched with a major new initiative.

Major-league general managers held their annual meetings from November 5 through 7 at the Grand Cypress Resort in Orlando, Florida, and in a 25-to-5 vote, approved studying the use of instant replay. Their recommendation to the commissioner was to examine the use of replay only in the case of disputed home run calls — whether the ball was fair or foul, or over the fence or not. They also recommended that a replay review ought to take place in one central location, instead of at each individual ballpark. In addition, the unions for both the players and umpires would have a say in whether and/or how replay would be implemented.[1]

The general managers also discussed ways to increase the tempo of the game by enforcing such existing procedures as the 12-second rule for a pitcher to receive the ball, get the sign, and deliver the pitch. In addition, batters would be limited in the number of times they could ask for a timeout.[2]

The Boston Red Sox swept the Colorado Rockies in the 2007 World Series after having beaten the Cleveland Indians in an exciting seven-game ALCS. Nevertheless, during the GM meetings, *The Sporting News* presented the Major League Baseball Executive of the Year award to Mark Shapiro, general manager of the Cleveland Indians.[3]

During the meetings, the general managers experimented with a new concept introduced by Theo Epstein of the Red Sox and Larry Beinfest of the Marlins. One by one, each GM stood up and announced to the group what their goals and needs were and what kind of trade each might consider. No one was permitted to speak for more than two minutes and so all were aware of the environment in around an hour.[4] However, the Players Association had a different take:

"Any such activity with respect to free agents is clearly improper," Don Fehr, executive director of the Players Association, said. "We expect to look into the situation and are prepared to take the appropriate action to respond to any collusive behavior, and to make sure that the rights of free-agent players under the Basic Agreement are fully protected.[5]

"Over the past few days, press reports coming out of the general managers' meetings relating to the sharing of information between clubs as to their plans regarding players potentially raise serious questions concerning the fairness and integrity of the free-agent market. Such questions are amplified by reports stating that the Commissioner is attempting to influence the market for at least one player."[6]

The Associated Press reported that the player in question was Alex Rodriguez, the former Yankees third baseman who had recently opted out of the last three years of his 10-year, $252 million contract.

Rob Manfred, Major League Baseball's executive vice president of labor relations and human resources, told the AP that he was surprised by the union's comments.[7]

BASEBALL'S BUSINESS: THE WINTER MEETINGS

With this as a backdrop, the 2007 Winter Meetings were held from December 3 to 6 at the Gaylord Opryland Resort and Convention Center in Nashville, Tennessee, the 106th time that baseball executives gathered toward the end of the calendar year to begin preparing for a new season.[8]

There are several events held during the Winter Meetings: Major League Baseball meetings, Minor League Baseball meetings, a baseball trade show, and a baseball job fair. But for most of the media and fans, the focus of the Winter Meetings is on the major leagues: trades, Hot Stove League rumors, and possible free-agent signings. The 2007 Winter Meetings provided one blockbuster deal, as well as seven other trades.[9] In addition, there were two player-for-cash deals and five free-agent signings, while two more free agents signed shortly after the meetings ended.

The primary attention-getter was the eight-player trade between the Florida Marlins and the Detroit Tigers. The Tigers received third baseman Miguel Cabrera and southpaw Dontrelle Willis (the 2003 National League Rookie of the Year) in exchange for outfielder Cameron Maybin, catcher Mike Rabelo, left-handed pitcher Andrew Miller, right-handed pitcher Eulogio de la Cruz and two minor-league right-handers, Dallas Trahern and Burke Badenhop.[10] In hindsight, this can be viewed as one of the more one-sided trades in major-league history, with Detroit receiving a likely Hall of Fame hitter in Cabrera (who would win the Triple Crown in 2012) while giving up no more than two decent players (Miller and Maybin). It may be argued that Florida had to trade Cabrera because of impending salary issues, but the prospects the Marlins received did not have much impact.

On the first day of the meetings, December 3, the Chicago White Sox acquired outfielder Carlos Quentin from Arizona for first-base prospect Chris Carter.[11] That same day, the Tampa Bay Rays traded outfielder Elijah Dukes to the Nationals for left-handed pitcher Glenn Gibson. The Rays were willing to trade the talented Dukes to the Nationals for a pitching prospect because of Dukes' off-the-field issues, which included domestic and anger-management problems.[12] And the Orioles completed the player movement for the day by signing free agent Guillermo Quiroz to be a backup catcher.[13]

There were three trades, in addition to the Cabrera blockbuster, on the second day, December 4. The first was between the Nationals and the Yankees, with Washington sending right-handed pitcher Jonathan Albaladejo to the Yankees for right-handed pitcher Tyler Clippard. The second trade also included right-handed pitchers; Detroit's Jose Capellan to Colorado for Denny Bautista.

The third was a three-player deal between the Cubs and the Braves. The Cubs acquired right-handed pitcher Jose Ascanio for infielder Omar Infante and left-handed pitcher Will Ohman. This was the second time Infante had been dealt in less than a month — on November 12, he had been traded by the Tigers to the Cubs for outfielder Jacque Jones. And completing the day's player carousel, the Royals signed free-agent outfielder Jose Guillen to a three-year contract.[14]

There were two trades and a free-agent signing on December 5. First, the Reds acquired right-handed pitcher Justin James from Toronto for outfielder Buck Coats. Then the Texas Rangers received first baseman Chris Shelton from the Detroit Tigers in exchange for outfielder Freddy Guzman. Finally, the Milwaukee Brewers signed free-agent right-handed pitcher David Riske to a three-year contract.

On December 6, the Dodgers signed free-agent outfielder Andruw Jones, and the Nationals signed free-agent infielder Aaron Boone.

December 6 was also the day that both the major-league and minor-league phase of the Rule 5 draft was held, with the most significant player selected being right-handed pitcher R.A. Dickey, chosen by Seattle with the 12th pick of the day. Dickey had had an interesting journey over the previous several weeks. He had spent the entire 2007 season with Milwaukee's Triple-A farm club in Nashville, but was granted free agency at the end of October by the Brewers despite having won 13 games for the Sounds. One month later he was signed by the Minnesota Twins, who did not place him on their 40-man roster, thus making him eligible for the Rule 5 draft. And his long, strange trip would continue, as he was returned to the Twins on

March 29, 2008, and traded back to the Mariners on the same day!

Of all the players selected in the minor-league draft, only right-hander Adalberto Mendez pitched in the major leagues. He appeared in five games for the Marlins in 2010. It is not a big surprise that only three players made the majors from the minor-league phase of the Rule 5 draft, as it is used primarily to fill holes on minor-league rosters.[15]

Major League Baseball also uses the Winter Meetings to make announcements of some importance. On Monday, December 3, MLB declared that the White Sox and the Mets would play in the second Civil Rights game on March 29, 2008.[16] According to baseball-almanac.com, "The intent of the Civil Rights Game was to 'embrace baseball's history of African-American players,' (Bud Selig) as well as to generate interest for future black players. A demographics survey revealed that the percentage of black players in the major leagues has dwindled in the previous twelve years to just 8.4 percent."[17]

Baseball America held its Seventh Annual Baseball America Awards Gala on December 4, at which time the following awards were announced:[18]

MLB Organization of the Year		Colorado Rockies
MLB Player of the Year	Alex Rodriguez	New York Yankees
MLB Rookie of the Year	Ryan Braun	Milwaukee
MLB Executive of the Year	Jack Zduriencik	Milwaukee
MLB Manager of the Year	Terry Francona	Boston
MiLB Player of the Year	Jay Bruce	Louisville (Cincinnati)
MiLB Executive of the Year	Mike Moore	National Association
MiLB Manager of the Year	Matt Walbeck	Toledo (Detroit)
Team of the Year	San Antonio (Texas)	San Diego
Bob Freitas Award[19]	AAA Albuquerque Isotopes	Pacific Coast League
	AA Frisco Roughriders	Texas League
	A Lake Elsinore Storm	California League
	Short Missoula Osprey	Pioneer League
Roland Hemond Award[20]	Art Stewart	Kansas City

Baseball America also presented Lifetime Achievement Awards to former and current Braves pitchers Greg Maddux, Tom Glavine, and John Smoltz, and to Gary Hughes, special assistant to the Cubs' general manager.[21]

While the major leagues always garner most of the headlines during the Winter Meetings, the minor leagues are not idle and they also gather under one roof. At their 2007 convention, also held at Nashville's Gaylord Opryland Resort and Convention Center, they also gave out a series of awards (in addition to the *Baseball America* minor-league awards listed above):

John H. Johnson President's Award[22]	Midland (Texas)
Larry MacPhail Trophy	West Michigan Whitecaps (Midwest)
Warren Giles Award	John Henry Moss, South Atlantic League
Joe Bauman Round-Tripper Award	Craig Brazzell, Omaha & Chattanooga
Rawlings Woman Executive of the Year	Shari Massengill, Kinston (Carolina)
King of Baseball	Dave Walker, Burlington Baseball Assoc.

The most important item for Minor League Baseball, however, was the retirement of longtime President Mike Moore and the election of Pat O'Conner, Minor League Baseball's chief operating officer and vice president of administration, as the organization's 11th president. Moore had been president for 16 years.[23]

During the Baseball Trade Show, attendees were asked to vote for the best new product, and for 2007, the winner was PitchTrack, which follows a pitched ball and gives its velocity, location and movement.

INDEPENDENT INVESTIGATION?

Reportedly driven by the publication of the book *Game of Shadows* (though some point out the intent was to stave off Congress), the steroids probe and Mitchell Report were fraught with issues from inception to publication.[*] George Mitchell was a director of the Boston Red Sox and held a chairmanship at Disney, which had controlling ownership of ESPN – a broadcaster with deep ties to the ratings of MLB.[**] Commissioner Bud Selig defended the choice of Mitchell, saying, "He's on his own. It is really going to be a thorough investigation, unimpeded by anything or anybody."[***]

Additionally, Mitchell had a previous history of leaning toward management, as opposed to the union. He had served as one of four independent members of the Commissioner's Blue Ribbon Panel on Baseball Economics, with the rest of the panel composed of club representatives. Of that report, union head Don Fehr said, "I hope this turns out not to be the case, but you will discover that prior to nearly all the other negotiating sessions, each time we've seen an economic analysis that has suggested problems and then was used as a framework for [the owners' bargaining]. I hope we can begin a bargaining process where conclusions can be drawn collectively and not in advance."[****] Indeed, seven years later, in 2007, Don Fehr again was discussing the publication of a report involving Mitchell, of which the players union had little notice and in which it had little involvement.[*****] Some observers noted that the Mitchell Report did not call out any owners or members of upper management, and lacked a recommendation for the commissioner's recommendation.[******]

Defending Selig and reinforcing the idea that only certain portions of the Mitchell report and its public interpretation should matter were the likes of Jerry Reinsdorf, who said, "The game has prospered. He's done all sorts of great things. And the only thing that has held us back in the steroid and HGH area is Don Fehr."[*******]

---

[*] Troy E. Renck, "Selig Starts Drug Probe – Former Senator to Lead Steroid Investigation," *Denver Post*, March 31, 2006: D-01. See also "Will Mitchell Report Have Any Impact?" *Weekend All Things Considered* [National Public Radio], December 22, 2007.

[**] Steve Zeitchik, "Curve Balls for Mitchell: Mouse Man on Hot Seat," *Daily Variety*, 291 (4), April 6, 2006: 1.

[***] Jim Salter, "Selig Defends Choice of Mitchell for Probe," Associated Press Archive, April 11, 2006.

[****] Eric Fisher, "Report May Widen Differences Between Owners and Players," *Washington Times*, July 16, 2000: A3.

[*****] "Mitchell Blames Players, Management in Baseball Steroid Investigation," *PBS Newshour*, pbs.org/newshour/bb/sports-july-dec07-mitchell_12-13/ accessed September 18, 2017.

[******] Dave Zirin, "Mitchell Report – The Message Is the Messenger," *San Francisco Gate*, December 19, 2007; Jerry Green, "Selig to Blame for Grievous Stain on Baseball History," *Detroit News*, December 16, 2007.

[*******] Ronald Blum, "Selig Has Approval of Owners – Commentary: Baseball's Commissioner Delivers Profits," *Seattle Times*, December 26, 2007: D9.

Second place went to KoolGator, which is a cooler that can be tied around a person's neck or head in order to keep them cool. Third place went to SweetSpots, which helps players improve the accuracy of their throws.[24]

Shortly after the Winter Meetings, on December 13, Major League Baseball released the Mitchell Report, formally known as the "Report to the Commissioner of Baseball of an Independent Investigation into the Illegal Use of Steroids and Other Performance Enhancing Substances by Players in Major League Baseball."[25] The 409-page report described the use of performance-enhancing drugs in baseball, in particular anabolic steroids and human growth hormone. The report states that with the advent of random drug testing in 2004, players switched from detectable steroids to undetectable human growth hormone.[26] In addition to describing the problem and the environment, the report named 89 players who allegedly used steroids or other drugs, including Barry Bonds, Roger Clemens, and Rafael Palmeiro.[27] The report made several recommendations to baseball which in Mitchell's view would help bring the "steroid era" to a close.[28]

Not everything of import happens at the Winter Meetings, but the groundwork is laid for much of the future. With the advent of the general managers meeting and the increasing use of advanced media, the impact of the Winter Meetings may have waned over the years. However, as in other human endeavors, face-to-face interaction becomes the grease that allows advanced media to work. The Winter Meetings may never again be what they once were, but they will remain very important for the overall business of baseball.

NOTES

1. Barry M. Bloom, "GMs Vote in Favor of Instant Replay," November 6, 2007, m.mlb.com/news/article/2293785/ accessed September 30, 2015.
2. Ibid.
3. Barry M. Bloom, "Shapiro Tabbed as TSN's Top Exec," November 6, 2015, m.mlb.com/news/article/2293450 accessed September 30, 2015.
4. Jim Molony, "New Approach Could Speed Hot Stove," November 7, 2007, m.mlb.com/news/article/2295507 accessed September 30, 2015.
5. Barry M. Bloom, "Union Concerned With Info-Sharing," November 8, 2007, m.mlb.com/news/article/2296642 accessed September 30, 2015.
6. Ibid.
7. Ibid.
8. Lisa Winston, "Spirited Winter Meetings Come to a Close," December 6, 2007, milb.com/news/article.jsp?ymd=20071206&content_id=328213&vkey=news_milb&fext=.jsp accessed October 5, 2015.
9. "Majors: Trade Central: 2007," *Baseball America*,, baseballamerica.com/news/trades07 accessed October 6, 2015.
10. Ibid.
11. Ibid. Quentin played for the White Sox for four years and was released by the Mariners on May 1, 2015. He was a two-time All-Star with the White Sox. Carter was subsequently traded (December 14, 2007), along with five other prospects (outfielders Carlos Gonzales and Aaron Cunningham; left-handed pitchers Brett Anderson, Dana Eveland, and Greg Smith) to the Athletics for right-handed pitchers Dan Haren and Connor Robertson.
12. Matt Eddy and Ben Badler, "Embattled Dukes on the Move," December 3, 2007, *Baseball America*, baseballamerica.com/today/majors/trade-central/2007/265298.html accessed October 6, 2015. Gibson never made it to the majors while Dukes lasted two years with the Nationals before being released.
13. Spencer Fordin, "Try as They May, O's Stuck at Status Quo," Orioles.com, m.orioles.mlb.com/news/article/2319981 accessed October 19, 2015.
14. Dick Kaegel, "Guillen Deal Spanned Winter Meetings," mlb.mlb.com/news/print.jsp?ymd=20071206&content_id=2320278&vkey=hotstove2007&fext=.jsp, accessed October 19, 2015.
15. FanGraphs, fangraphs.com/library/rule-5-draft accessed October 12, 2015.
16. Scott Merkin, "White Sox, Mets Get Civil Rights Game Nod," milb.com/news/article.jsp?ymd=20071203&content_id=327397&vkey=news_milb&fext=.jsp accessed September 15, 2015.
17. Baseball Almanac, "Civil Rights Game," baseball-almanac.com/legendary/Civil_Rights_Game.shtml accessed October 14, 2015.
18. MLB.com, brewers.com, "Jack Zduriencik named Baseball America Executive of the Year," December 4, 2007, milwaukee.brewers.mlb.com/content/printer_friendly/mil/y2007/m12/d04/c2316966.jsp accessed October 14, 2015.

19. Ballpark Business, "Tribe Named Triple-A Freitas Winners," ballparkbiz.wordpress.com/tag/bob-freitas-award/ Award given to "…organization with best overall operations at each level of minor league baseball." Accessed October 14, 2015.

20. Baseball Almanac, "Roland Hemond Award," baseball-almanac.com/awards/roland_hemond_award.shtml "The Roland Hemond award is presented annually to recognize baseball executives who have provided at least fifteen years of outstanding service to professional baseball and served the Arizona Fall League in a key leadership capacity." Accessed October 14, 2015.

21. *Baseball America,* baseballamerica.com/majors/t/lifetime-achievement-award accessed October 14, 2015.

22. Minor League Baseball, "Major Award Winners," milb.com/milb/history/awards.jsp accessed November 5, 2015. President's Award given annually to honor "complete baseball franchise—based on franchise stability, contributions to league stability, contributions to baseball in the community, and promotion of the baseball industry."

23. "Minors Baseball: O'Connor New MILB President," *Sports Network,* December 5, 2007.

24. Minor League Baseball, "PitchTrack wins New Product Showcase," December 12, 2007, milb.com/news/article.jsp?ymd=20071212&content_id=328949&vkey=pr_milb&fext=.jsp accessed October 19, 2015.

25. MLB.com, mlb.mlb.com/mlb/news/mitchell/index.jsp accessed October 19, 2015.

26. George J. Mitchell, *Report to the Commissioner of Baseball of an Independent Investigation into the Illegal Use of Steroids and Other Performance Enhancing Substances by Players in Major League Baseball,* Office of the Commissioner of Baseball, 2007, SR-2.

27. Baseball Almanac, baseball-almanac.com/legendary/Mitchell_Report.shtml, accessed November 9, 2015.

28. Ibid., SR-29-SR-35.

— 2008 —
CLOUDS OVER THE GAME

by John Bauer

WHEN THE MOVERS AND SHAKERS of the baseball world descended on the Bellagio Hotel in Las Vegas for the 2008 Winter Meetings, the sport and the country faced economic uncertainty not witnessed since the Great Depression of the 1930s. The economic downturn that became known as the Financial Crisis or the Great Recession began rumbling through housing markets in 2007, brought the banking sector and the global economy to near-collapse in the fall of 2008, and festered through mass layoffs and other dislocations into 2009 and beyond. Baseball was not immune from its impact. More than 78 million fans had attended major-league games in 2008, the second greatest number in history, but at these meetings, baseball people could only speculate on what the full effect of the Financial Crisis would be for the business of professional baseball. Before the Las Vegas congregation, however, there occurred plenty of baseball business to set the table for the Winter Meetings proper.

The business away from the business meetings

The 2008 baseball season concluded with the Philadelphia Phillies defeating the Tampa Bay Rays in a five-game World Series. Late October weather in Philadelphia affected several games, specifically a 90-minute delay before Game Three and a two-day suspension of the deciding Game Five. These factors may have contributed to the worst television ratings in the history of the fall classic, with the 13.6 million average viewership representing a 14 percent drop from the record low established in the 2006 Cardinals-Tigers match-up.[1] Shortly after winning their second championship, the Phillies announced a major front-office move, with Ruben Amaro Jr. replacing Pat Gillick as general manager. The Phillies' announcement was the second such move of the offseason as the Mariners previously hired Jack Zduriencik from Milwaukee as a permanent replacement for general manager Bill Bavasi, who took the fall in June for what proved to be a disastrous 101-loss season. In a more momentous hiring, the Mariners later named Don Wakamatsu as their manager, making him the first Asian-American to manage in the major leagues.

Along with front-office changes, November was, as always, the awards season for baseball's high achievers. Rookies of the Year were the first major announcement, on November 10, and Tampa Bay third baseman Evan Longoria claimed unanimous AL honors, while Chicago catcher Geovany Soto fell one vote short of doing the same in the NL. The following day, San Francisco's Tim Lincecum capped his first full major-league season with the NL Cy Young Award, beating out Arizona's Brandon Webb and New York's Johan Santana. Two days after the NL announcement, Cleveland's Cliff Lee gained the AL Cy Young, ahead of Toronto's Roy Halladay and Los Angeles' Francisco Rodriguez. For Lee it was a remarkable comeback after a 2007 season that saw him pitch in three levels of the minors in an attempt to return to form. Rodriguez had also turned in a spectacular season, establishing a new major-league saves record with 62 for the Angels. Tampa Bay's surprise pennant resulted in its skipper, Joe Maddon, winning near-unanimous AL Manager of the Year honors. Maddon's predecessor in the Rays dugout, Lou Piniella, claimed the NL award for his work with the Cubs, who won the Central Division crown with a league-best 97 victories, though they were swept by the Dodgers in the Division Series. Sweet Lou won a closer race in beating out Philadelphia's

Charlie Manuel and Florida's Fredi Gonzalez. Boston's Dustin Pedroia followed up his 2007 Rookie of the Year season with AL Most Valuable Player honors, finishing ahead of Minnesota's Justin Morneau and teammate Kevin Youkilis to become the first AL second baseman to win the award since Nellie Fox of the White Sox in 1959. Within weeks, the Red Sox rewarded Pedroia with a six-year, $40.5 million contract extension. In the NL, St. Louis's Albert Pujols beat out a fellow first baseman, Philadelphia's Ryan Howard, to claim senior circuit MVP honors for the second time.

Despite the celebration of the game's best, worsening economic conditions clouded preparations for the offseason. On November 20, club owners and executives received a confidential briefing on the economy from Paul Volcker, the former chairman of the Board of Governors of the Federal Reserve and current adviser to President-elect Barack Obama. Volcker appeared at the invitation of Commissioner Bud Selig, and spoke to officials for 45 minutes. Attendees noted that Volcker's assessment "was not upbeat."[2] The state of the economy had clubs paying close attention to their ticket pricing for the 2009 season. The Boston Red Sox, for instance, froze ticket prices at 2008 levels, marking their first offseason without an increase since 1994.[3] Red Sox chief executive Larry Lucchino commented, "We are hearing from fans and seeing for ourselves that these are uncertain, at best, and perilous, at worst, economic conditions."[4] The Yankees would join the Red Sox in announcing that spring-training tickets would remain the same as last season.

The economic belt-tightening would not necessarily extend into the free-agent market as big paydays were forecast for big talents. Even Lucchino foresaw "crazy competition" for elite free agents.[5] Milwaukee left-hander C.C. Sabathia, Angels first baseman Mark Teixiera, and Dodgers outfielder Manny Ramirez entered the offseason as the most coveted available players. Additionally, San Diego and Colorado were shopping right-hander Jake Peavy (the 2007 National League Cy Young Award winner) and outfielder Matt Holliday (the 2007 National League batting champion), respectively, through the trade market.

Holliday became a key figure in the first major deal of the offseason when he was sent to Oakland on November 10 in exchange for three players, outfielder Carlos Gonzalez, right-hander Huston Street and southpaw Greg Smith. The free-agent market opened November 14 and signings were slow to develop. After almost two weeks, only left-hander Jeremy Affeldt (leaving Cincinnati for San Francisco) and right-hander Ryan Dempster (staying with the Cubs) had inked new deals for the 2009 season. The paucity in signings represented the slowest opening to the free-agent market since the 2002-2003 offseason.[6] Commentators offered varying assessments about whether the slow-developing market reflected wider economic problems infecting baseball. Ben Shpigel wrote, "It is unclear how well baseball is insulated from the country's economic troubles, but it is clear people are concerned."[7] With new stadiums under construction in New York and marquee names still expected to collect a bonanza, William Rhoden observed that "[w]ith much of the nation reeling, with banks failing, workers being laid off and homes being foreclosed, sports owners continue to build castles and pay players by the millions."[8]

The Winter Meetings and the business of baseball

As the Winter Meetings formally opened in Las Vegas on December 8, the free-agent market began stirring in earnest. After a quiet first day in which the most significant deals involved the Tigers trading for catcher Gerald Laird[9] and signing veteran shortstop Adam Everett, the Yankees asserted themselves by grabbing one of the market's top players. The 2007 AL Cy Young Award winner, C.C. Sabathia, agreed to a seven-year, $161 million contract with the Yankees to complete a move that took him from Cleveland to Milwaukee to the Bronx in less than six months. Meanwhile, the Mets sought to address the bullpen woes that factored into late-season collapses in 2007 and 2008. To do so, Mets general manager Omar Minaya signed former Angels closer Francisco Rodriguez to a three-year, $37 million contract during the meetings, and also executed a three-team, 12-player trade resulting in the acquisition of right-handed set-up man J.J. Putz from Seattle.¹⁰ Announcing the latter deal to reporters at the Bellagio, Minaya said, "Best thing I can say about this trade, guys, is it's an old-fashioned baseball trade. Here we are in the year 2008 and talking about millions of dollars, and this is how trades were done. Just a pure baseball trade."¹¹

The Winter Meetings were also notable for a trade that did not happen. It was no secret that the Padres were eager to deal starting pitcher Jake Peavy. After a 99-loss campaign, owner John Moores had little interest in spending another $72 million just to finish in the basement again, and removing the $63 million due to Peavy over the next four seasons provided an obvious target for cost savings. As the meetings commenced, the Cubs appeared to be Padres general manager Kevin Towers' likeliest trading partner. Towers, however, would not make a deal just for the sake of doing so, and he asserted his willingness to take Peavy into the 2009 season if the right deal could not be found.¹² Indeed, there would be no deal. Unsuccessful attempts to acquire Peavy left Cubs general manager Jim Hendry muttering, "I'm not trading seven players for one."¹³ Peavy opened 2009 as a Padre before a midseason move to Chicago—the Cubs' crosstown rivals, the White Sox.

Shortly after the Winter Meetings proper, the Yankees added right-hander A.J. Burnett to their rotation with a five-year, $82.5 million deal. After Boston dropped out of the bidding, Mark Teixiera joined the Yankees in an eight-year, $180 million deal completed days before Christmas. (The other major free agent, Manny Ramirez, re-signed with the Dodgers in March.) Including Sabathia, the Yankees committed over $400 million to three players in an active December. Word of the Financial Crisis apparently had not traveled from Manhattan to the Bronx.

Major League Baseball took advantage of the Winter Meetings to showcase the talent and studio set designs for the new MLB Network. The channel was scheduled to debut January 1 in 50 million cable and satellite homes. Matt Vasgersian was introduced as studio host after years as a minor-league broadcaster and stints with the Brewers and Padres. Trenni Kusnierek and Hazel Mae would leave club beats to join the network as reporters, while former players Harold Reynolds, Dan Plesac, and Al Leiter would provide analysis. The network unveiled designs for Studios 3 and 42 that would serve as the broadcasting hub from its headquarters in Secaucus, New Jersey. Network president Tony Petitti viewed the channel as complementing baseball's Internet presence: "We're both 24/7 operations. ... We can come together operationally, driving baseball fans back [and forth] to both places."¹⁴ MLB Network launched New Year's Day with the "Hot Stove" studio show, followed by the first national rebroadcast of Don Larsen's perfect game in the 1956 World Series.¹⁵

The minor-league baseball job fair and trade show also coincided with the Winter Meetings, and the state of the economy dominated discussions. With cumulative attendance of 43 million in 2008, minor-league baseball seemed to have solid foundations. Minor League Baseball president Pat O'Conner announced three initiatives to help promote the sport for the new season. First, clubs would work toward environmental sustainability through a "Team Green" program. Second, Minor League Baseball planned to partner with the National Youth Baseball Organization to enhance youth participation. Finally, diversity programs would target increasing minority employees and minority-owned businesses working throughout the minor-league game. These initiatives did not disguise the challenging economic environment, as the normal raft of job seekers found fewer openings. In addition to constrained headcount, clubs sought creative solutions to find additional cost savings, including reusing the prior season's uniforms and recycling in-game video entertainment. Because the minor-league season ended before the near-collapse of the economy in mid-September, uncertainty was paramount as the minor leagues had yet to labor under the conditions the new season would bring.

The business of baseball included equipment and rules changes for implementation in 2009. The issue of equipment related primarily to bat manufacture. Maple bats were the choice of a clear majority of players; those bats were also more prone to shattering, at a threefold rate over ash bats.[16] During the second day of the meetings, the Safety and Health Advisory Committee issued nine recommendations that were accepted by the owners and players. Some recommendations related to the slope of the grain, which concerned improved straightness in the wood for increased durability, and increased quality inspections through random audits at major-league ballparks. Bat manufacturers would be required to attend workshops on engineering and wood grading practices, track each bat they made, and subject their factories to audits from inspectors. Administration fees and insurance requirements would also increase for manufacturers.[17]

Additional rules changes were discussed in Las Vegas and confirmed a month later at the owners' quarterly meetings. Acting upon complaints from general managers, baseball's executive vice president of operations, Jimmie Lee Solomon, announced in Las Vegas that he would propose for owners to approve a switch from coin flips to head-to-head regular-season records to decide home field in a tiebreaker game. Tiebreaker games had been required the past two seasons, including the Twins having to play the White Sox in Chicago (and losing) for the 2008 AL Central Division title despite winning the regular-season series. The owners adopted this change on January 15 during their meetings in Paradise Valley, Arizona. After Game Five of the World Series was suspended for multiple days because of rain, Selig stated that playing rules would be amended to stipulate that all postseason contests and the All-Star Game would be played in full.[18] This change was confirmed in Arizona, with tiebreaker games included within the coverage of the rule.

The Winter Meetings provided a cause for celebration for two new Hall of Fame inductees. The Veterans Committee announced the results of its two ballots, one for "pre-1943" players and another for "post-1942" players. In the pre-1943 balloting, former Yankees and Indians second baseman Joe Gordon received 10 out of 12 votes to secure his enshrinement in Cooperstown. In the post-1942 poll, however, no one secured enough votes for admission to the Hall of Fame. Former Cubs third baseman Ron Santo garnered the most votes (39 of 64) but fell short of the required 75 percent threshold. Former Yankee Tony Kubek, whose playing career included the 1957 Rookie of the Year award and four All-Star Game appearances, received the Ford C. Frick award for broadcasting excellence, which granted Kubek a spot in Cooperstown. Amid the accolades for past performance, future Hall of Famer Greg Maddux announced his retirement in Las Vegas. Maddux, whose career achievements included 355 wins and four consecutive NL Cy Young Awards, explained making his announcement in Las Vegas: "Everybody has always treated me great, and the friends I made, I really just came here today to say thank you."[19] In January, Rickey Henderson and Jim Rice learned they would also receive Hall of Fame plaques. Henderson earned induction in his first year of eligibility, appearing on 94.8 percent of ballots; Rice, in his 15th and final time on the ballot, crossed the needed threshold with 76.4 percent of the vote.

Baseball business in the home of the Financial Crisis

The offseason business of the Yankees and Mets related to off-field issues as much as, if not more than, on-field matters. Conceived during better economic times, new ballparks would greet the Yankees and Mets when the season started whether or not the Financial Crisis affected their balance sheets and cash flows, and those of their potential ticket buyers. Shortly after the 2008 season and with new Yankee Stadium rising next to its eponymous predecessor, the Yankees completed a planned "passing of the baton." On November 20, the owners voted unanimously to approve the transfer of control from longtime owner George Steinbrenner to his son, Hal. George would remain chairman of the club, but his sons Hal and Hank would oversee the business and baseball operations, respectively, as co-chairmen. Without a championship since 2000 and with plenty of premium seats to sell, the acquisition of premium free agents like Sabathia and Teixeira signaled an intent to win big in a (hopefully) full, new stadium.

The Mets, on the other hand, were having an offseason to forget. Citi Field was scheduled to open next to

Shea Stadium, whose destruction began shortly after the season ended. The Mets hoped that a new ballpark would help fans forget about their recent failures, but it seemed to be doing quite the opposite. Citigroup had agreed to a 20-year, $400 million naming rights deal for the new stadium, but with the onset of the Financial Crisis, the company was forced to become a recipient of federal bailout funds through the Troubled Asset Relief Program. Nonetheless, Citigroup affirmed in November that it would honor its commitment to the Mets. By early 2009, however, Citigroup had accepted billions in taxpayer funds and announced plans to shed over 50,000 jobs, leading some members of Congress to request that the US Treasury Department force the company to abandon its deal with the Mets.[20] In the end, the political pressure abated and the ballpark opened as Citi Field.

The bad news continued for the Mets, this time on a personal level for their ownership. Fred Wilpon and his family financed high payrolls as the Mets enjoyed a run as NL East contenders during the mid-2000s. With the amenities normally afforded by a new stadium, the Mets' financial clout was expected to increase. Any such expectation seemed to come crashing down, however, on December 12 when the Wilpon-owned Sterling Equities announced it had accounts with Bernard L. Madoff Investment Securities. Days before, federal authorities extracted from Madoff a fraud confession related to the collapse of his $50 billion investment firm-cum-Ponzi scheme. Madoff became symbolic of the Wall Street excesses that created the Financial Crisis; he was also a personal friend of Wilpon. One report pegged Wilpon's potential losses in the region of $300 million.[21] Major League Baseball adopted a brave face, as Chief Operating Officer Bob DuPuy asserted, "The Mets are completely self-sufficient, and we have confidence that none of the other investments will affect the team. ... [W]e expect it to be business as usual."[22]

The saga of selling the Cubs

The Chicago Cubs remained for sale for the second straight offseason. Since its acquisition by investor Sam Zell in April 2007, the Tribune Company had been seeking a buyer for the Cubs, Wrigley Field, and its 25 percent stake in the regional Comcast SportsNet channel. With its own bankruptcy an increasing possibility and credit markets seizing up because of the Financial Crisis, the Tribune Company was being forced to reconsider its original $1 billion valuation for the package. It set a November 27 deadline for the latest and, presumably, final round of bidding, but 10 days before bids were due, the Securities and Exchange Commission filed a civil suit against Dallas Mavericks owner and Internet billionaire Mark Cuban, alleging insider trading in a stock sale that purportedly allowed Cuban to avoid a $750,000 loss.[23] Rumored to be the frontrunner to obtain the Cubs, Cuban responded with charges of prosecutorial misconduct and political vendetta, but the ruckus seemed likely to put off other major-league owners who would need to vote to approve the eventual sale.[24] In fact, when the bidding parties were revealed in early December, Cuban's name was missing. Rather, the bidders were groups led by Tom Ricketts, chief executive of investment bank Incapital and son of the man who founded TD Ameritrade Holding; Mark Utay, managing partner with Clarion Capital Partners, a private equity firm; and Hersh Klaff, a Chicago real-estate executive.

The Cubs' offseason and potential sale became complicated when broader financial problems forced the Tribune Company to file for federal bankruptcy protection on December 8. Dealing with significant debt and declining advertising revenue from its media properties, the Tribune Company sought Chapter 11 protection. In doing so, the Tribune Company attempted to shield the Cubs, Wrigley Field, and its Comcast stake by omitting those properties from its bankruptcy petition. While the company asserted that the sale remained unaffected (and inclusion of the Cubs in the petition may have restarted the sale process entirely), the federal bankruptcy judge would have to approve any deal. The Tribune Company targeted Opening Day to complete the Cubs deal.

On January 22, 2009, Ricketts disclosed that the Tribune Company selected his group, composed primarily of family members, to enter into exclusive sale negotiations.[25] While the Ricketts's $900 million offer for the Cubs, Wrigley Field and the Comcast stake fell short of the Tribune Company's aspirations, it represented an unprecedented figure in baseball history. If completed, this deal would exceed the $700 million sale of the Red Sox, Fenway Park, and 80 percent of the NESN regional television network in 2002.[26] Sources explained the factors that set apart the Ricketts bid, noting "that it featured more cash up front than the other bids, promising roughly 50 percent in equity and the rest of the $900 million financed with debt ... mean[ing] more cash in the bank on closing day."[27] For the bankrupt Tribune Company, the extra cash appeared to be decisive. A significant chunk of that cash came from a stock buyback deal with TD Ameritrade in mid-February, where Ricketts family members received $403 million for 34 million shares.[28] The Ricketts family secured additional financing before reaching a formal sale agreement in July; major-league owners unanimously approved the sale in October 2009.

The continuing shadow of the Steroid Era

One offseason removed from the Mitchell Report, the shadow of the Steroid Era continued to hover over baseball.[29] News coverage related to arguably the greatest hitter and greatest pitcher of the last generation concerned legal disputes about their involvement with performance enhancing drugs (PEDs). Barry Bonds was scheduled for trial in March in federal court in Northern California on a 15-count indictment related to false statements made under oath in connection with his alleged use of steroids and human growth hormone. In November, three counts were dismissed but Bonds still faced 12 counts concerning 2003 grand-jury testimony related to the Bay Area Laboratory Co-Operative (BALCO). Bonds' lawyers pressed to have additional counts dismissed because of the alleged ambiguity of the questions posed to Bonds at that time. Additionally, they filed a motion in January to exclude certain evidence from being used against Bonds. Specifically, they argued that the chain of custody related to certain blood and urine tests had been compromised, and that calendars and handwritten notes by Greg Anderson, Bonds' former trainer, allegedly used to track Bonds' drug use, could not be connected directly to Bonds.

US District Judge Susan Illston unsealed certain evidence on February 4 that revealed Bonds tested positive for steroids in 2000 and 2001.[30] On their face, the tests appeared, in conjunction with Anderson's handwritten notes, to connect Bonds directly to steroid use. Anderson's refusal to cooperate with the government jeopardized their admissibility, however. Illston presided over oral arguments on that issue on February 5, and she signaled her inclination to toss the evidence without a witness to connect Bonds to the written materials, thereby connecting the positive tests to Bonds. Illston stated, "[T]he documentation is not hooked up to this case."[31] Prosecutors believed the combination of the positive tests and Anderson's documents would allow them to persuade a jury that Bonds lied when he told the grand jury in 2003 that he never used steroids. Illston issued a formal ruling February 19 that excluded several pieces of evidence without testimony from Anderson to authenticate the materials.[32] Anderson's lawyer indicated he would not provide such testimony, and with the trial date approaching, prosecutors decided to appeal Illston's February 19 ruling, a move that ultimately postponed the trial for several more years.

Roger Clemens had sued his former trainer, Brian McNamee, for defamation concerning McNamee's statements to former Senator George Mitchell about Clemens' alleged PED use. The case resided in federal court in Houston. On November 3, US District Judge Keith Ellison heard oral arguments on whether the suit should be dismissed because McNamee was immune from Clemens' suit. McNamee's lawyer argued that his client was compelled to disclose to Mitchell that he injected Clemens with PEDs by the terms of an immunity agreement with the Department of Justice and the FBI.[33] Within days of the hearing, Ellison ordered McNamee's lawyers to provide evidence to support his contention that the statements were provided in connection with a federal probe. In December, McNamee's lawyers moved for dismissal of the case. Ellison sided with McNamee by dismissing much of

Clemens' suit on February 12. The judge ruled that McNamee's statements were indeed privileged because of their connection to a federal investigation. Later in 2009, Clemens would not only find himself accused of lying to Congress about his alleged PED use, but he was also on the receiving end of a defamation lawsuit filed by McNamee.

Another former witness before the Mitchell commission created headlines with a book depicting Steroid Era practices. Former Mets clubhouse employee Kirk Radomski, who pleaded guilty in 2007 to illegal distribution of certain PEDs, authored *Bases Loaded*, which was released in January. In his book, Radomski detailed his past selling PEDs to ballplayers and the circumstances that led to his statements to the Mitchell commission. Radomski also professed his belief in the truth of McNamee's statements about Clemens.[34] Mitchell publicly disputed certain passages in *Bases Loaded*, but the book's publicity kept the PED issue in the news for several days during the offseason.

In addition to the Bonds and Clemens matters hanging over the game, baseball's highest-paid and arguably best player became confronted by a past that included PED use. In early February, Alex Rodriguez faced revelations about his own positive PED test, conducted in 2003. Rodriguez's sample had been seized in 2004 in connection with a federal investigation into BALCO. Two days after the result surfaced, Rodriguez acknowledged PED use while playing for the Texas Rangers from 2001 to 2003. The positive result occurred during baseball's confidential sampling program in 2003, which included 104 total positives, thereby surpassing the threshold for instituting mandatory testing in 2004. Because of the confidential nature of the test, Rodriguez would not be subject to discipline for his 2003 positive. Unable to punish Rodriguez, Selig could only resort to shame when he commented, "What Alex did was wrong, and he will have to live with the damage he has done to his name and reputation."[35] Any embarrassment or disgrace would have to be deferred, however, as surgery for an injured hip kept Rodriguez out of the lineup until May.

Conclusion

Continuing revelations about PEDs indicated that baseball could not simply outrun its past. The recent past, however, had seen an economic expansion of the business of baseball. On the one hand, events seemed to demonstrate an uninterrupted cycle of growth: sizable free-agent contracts, erection of new palaces to showcase players' talents, growth in baseball's cable and digital presence, and a record deal for one of baseball's most venerable franchises. On the other hand, the business of baseball would face economic conditions not seen in generations. Whether baseball could continue its business growth under these conditions was the great question facing the game as the offseason gave way to the new season.

NOTES

1. Richard Sandomir, "World Series Sets a Low for Viewership," *New York Times*, October 30, 2008, accessed at: nytimes.com/2008/10/31/sports/baseball/31ratings.html.

2. Michael S. Schmidt and Katie Thomas, "Volcker Gives Baseball an Update on the Economy," *New York Times*, November 20, 2008, accessed at: nytimes.com/2008/11/21/sports/baseball/21mlb.html.

3. Ibid.

4. Richard Sandmir, "Red Sox Will Not Raise Ticket Prices," *New York Times*, November 12, 2008, accessed at: nytimes.com/2008/11/13/sports/baseball/13tickets.html.

5. William C. Rhoden, "Recession Is a Relative Term in Baseball," *New York Times*, November 16, 2008, accessed at: nytimes.com/2008/11/17/sports/baseball/17rhoden.html.

6. Ben Shpigel, "All Is Unusually Quiet on the Free-Agent Front," *New York Times*, November 25, 2008, accessed at: nytimes.com/2008/11/26/sports/baseball/26agent.html.

7. Ibid.

8. Rhoden.

9. Guillermo Moscoso and Carlos Melo, a pair of right-handers, were sent to the Rangers in exchange for Laird.

10. It was a blockbuster deal in terms of numbers, and in future big-league talent. The Mariners sent Putz, right-hander Sean Green, and outfielder Jeremy Reed to the Mets, and infielder Luis Valbuena to the Indians. The Mets, in turn, sent six players out to Seattle: slick-fielding outfielder Endy Chavez, southpaw Jason Vargas, right-handers Maikel Cleto and Aaron Heilman, outfielder Ezequiel Carrera and first baseman-outfielder Mike

Carp. They also shipped right-hander Joe Smith to the Indians, who completed the transaction by moving outfielder Franklin Gutierrez to Seattle.

11 Joe Posnanski, "Take Me Out to ... The Winter Meetings in Vegas, Baby, Vegas," *Sports Illustrated*, December 22, 2008, accessed at: si.com/vault/2008/12/22/105764680/take-me-out-to-the-winter-meetings-in-vegas-baby-vegas#.

12 John Schlegel, "Class Acts and Done Deals on Day 1," mlb.com, December 9, 2008, accessed at: m.mlb.com/news/article/3707488//.

13 Ibid.

14 Barry M. Bloom, "MLB Network Introduces On-Air Lineup," MLB.com, December 8, 2008, accessed at: m.mlb.com/news/article/3706838.

15 Richard Sandomir, "Fans Who Can't Get Enough Are Getting More," *New York Times*, December 31, 2008, accessed at: nytimes.com/2009/01/01/sports/baseball/01sandomir.html.

16 Jack Curry, "New Bats to Undergo Testing for Quality Control," *New York Times*, December 10, 2008, accessed at: nytimes.com/2008/12/10/sports/baseball/10bats.html.

17 Ibid. Also, for more information about the changes related to bat manufacture and inspection, see Curry, "Changes for Maple Bats in 2009," *New York Times*, December 9, 2008, accessed at: bats.blogs.nytimes.com/2008/12/09/changes-for-maple-bats-in-2009/.

18 Jack Curry, "Hal Steinbrenner Is Named the Yankees' Boss," *New York Times*, November 20, 2008, accessed at: nytimes.com/2008/11/21/sports/baseball/21hal.html.

19 John Schlegel, "Class Acts and Done Deals on Day 1," MLB.com, December 9, 2008, accessed at: m.mlb.com/news/article/3707488//.

20 "House Members Seek End to Citigroup-Mets Deal," *New York Times*, January 30, 2009, accessed at: query.nytimes.com/gst/fullpage.html?res=9F00E0DA1130F933A05752C0A96F9C8B63.

21 Dealbook, "New York Mets Owner's Firm Was Madoff Client," *New York Times*, December 12, 2008, accessed at: dealbook.nytimes.com/2008/12/12/new-york-mets-owners-firm-was-madoff-client/.

22 Michael S. Schmidt, "Wilpon's Losses in Fraud Case May Affect Mets," *New York Times*, December 13, 2009, accessed at: nytimes.com/2008/12/14/sports/baseball/14wilpon.html.

23 Michael J. de la Merced and Floyd Norris, "Mark Cuban Is Charged With Insider Trading," *New York Times*, November 17, 2008, accessed at: nytimes.com/2008/11/18/business/18insider.html.

24 Ibid.

25 Ameet Sachdev and Michael Oneal, "Meet the Cubs' $900 Million Man," *Chicago Tribune*, January 23, 2009: 1-1.

26 Sachdev and Oneal: 1-11.

27 Ibid.

28 Dealbook, "TD Ameritrade to Buy Stock From Founding Family," *New York Times*, February 18, 2009, accessed at: dealbook.nytimes.com/2009/02/18/td-ameritrade-to-buy-stock-from-founding-family/.

29 Formally titled "Report to the Commissioner of Baseball of an Independent Investigation Into the Illegal Use of Steroids and Other Performance Enhancing Substances by Players in Major League Baseball," December 13, 2007, accessible at: files.mlb.com/mitchrpt.pdf.

30 Michael S. Schmidt, "Positive Drug Tests in Bonds Case," *New York Times*, February 4, 2009, accessed at: nytimes.com/2009/02/05/sports/baseball/05bonds.html.

31 Michael S. Schmidt and Carol Pogash, "Once Again, Bonds Case Circles Back to Trainer," *New York Times*, February 5, 2009, accessed at: nytimes.com/2009/02/06/sports/baseball/06bonds.html.

32 Katie Thomas, "Prosecutors May Appeal in Bonds's Perjury Case," *New York Times*, February 20, 2009, accessed at: nytimes.com/2009/02/21/sports/baseball/21bonds.html.

33 Michael S. Schmidt, "Evidence Sought in Clemens's Defamation Suit," *New York Times*, November 7, 2008, accessed at: nytimes.com/2008/11/08/sports/baseball/08clemens.html.

34 Michael S. Schmidt, "In Book, Radomski Talks About Selling Drugs and Dealing With Mitchell," *New York Times*, January 19, 2009, accessed at: nytimes.com/2009/01/20/sports/baseball/20radomski.html.

35 "A-Rod Gets Only a Selig Scolding," *Chicago Tribune*, February 13, 2009: 2-8.

— 2009 —
CHANGES HERE, CHANGES THERE, CHANGES EVERYWHERE
A BLOCKBUSTER, AN OOPS, A SUCCESSION, AND MAGIC TRICKS BY OWNERS

By Steve Weingarden

Introduction and Context

THE 2009 WINTER MEETINGS WERE held in Indianapolis—representing a Northern host city for just the fifth time in 43 years; in fact, this was the farthest-north host city associated with a minor-league team since the 1966 meetings were held in Columbus, Ohio. While Indianapolis provided amiable temperatures, player movement was only lukewarm. Gloom from the continuing dreary economy provided a shadow over the meetings, and slowed down overall movement. Mostly, the meetings served as a precursor for moves that occurred much closer to Opening Day.

The meetings had been awarded to Indianapolis in 2006. The Winter Meeting decision makers "were worried about the cold weather, our hotel situation and other accommodations," said Indianapolis Indians Chairman Max Schumacher, who was the force behind bringing the meetings to the city.[1] Schumacher had endured rejection three previous times in his quest to host the meetings. For Schumacher and his International League club, however, the value of hosting the meetings drove toward a "no surrender" approach. In a city where the competition for the sporting dollar included the Indianapolis 500 and the NFL's Colts—a team with a strong recent history (they won the Super Bowl in 2007)—it was essential to make an imaging statement about the importance of baseball. Some 5,000 attendees made their way to the Indiana Convention Center for the meetings, held December 7-10, providing a $3.865 million impact for Indianapolis.[2]

Player Movement

Like the 2008 meetings, the 2009 meetings lacked teeming player movement. Going into the meetings, the major player questions involved the eventual homes of two right-handed pitchers, Roy Halladay and John Lackey, and two position players, outfielders Jason Bay and Matt Holliday.[3] Halladay's situation garnered the most pre-meeting discussion. Despite his expressed affinity for the city of Toronto, Halladay sought to pitch for a team that had a realistic chance at the World Series, and held spring training near his home in Tampa, Florida.[4] Halladay was cool toward talks of a contract extension that would keep him with the Blue Jays beyond the 2010 season, and that partly fueled the need to deal the former Cy Young Award winner.[5] The end result was a complicated blockbuster that involved the Blue Jays, Philadelphia Phillies, Seattle Mariners, and Oakland A's. The Phillies acquired Halladay and sent Toronto two top prospects, right-hander Kyle Drabek and catcher Travis d'Arnaud, along with outfielder Michael Taylor. The Jays flipped Taylor to Oakland, receiving third baseman Brett Wallace in exchange. Phillies GM Ruben Amaro Jr. then swapped left-hander Cliff Lee to the Mariners and received three minor-league prospects: right-handers Phillippe Aumont and J.C. Ramirez, plus outfielder

Tyson Gillies.[6] Lee, the reigning American League Cy Young Award winner, had been acquired by the Phillies at the end of July and had been especially valuable in the postseason, winning four of his five starts, including the team's only two World Series victories against the New York Yankees.[7] However, he had only one year left on his contract.[8] These deals began brewing at the Winter Meetings and were consummated just over a week after they ended.[9]

Rumors of a different blockbuster trade emerged on the first day of the meetings. A 12-inning loss to the Twins in a tie-breaking game 163 kept the Tigers out of the postseason, but word leaked out that Detroit was considering sending their All-Star center fielder and fan favorite, Curtis Granderson, to the Yankees, while right-hander Edwin Jackson, a power-armed starting pitcher, was rumored to be on his way to the Arizona Diamondbacks. In both cases, the Tigers would receive top prospects in return, a broad hint that the team might be thinking about the future rather than the present, a situation mostly unfamiliar to the Tigers during the tenure of general manager Dave Dombrowski. The Tigers had initiated each trade discussion separately nearly a month prior to the Winter Meetings, but the needed framework for the three-team deal evolved at the meetings, and the final deal was made toward their end. Indeed, Granderson went to the Yankees, their sole prize from the exchange. Jackson transferred to the Diamondbacks, along with right-handed starting pitcher Ian Kennedy, who came from the Yankees. Meanwhile, the Tigers received center fielder Austin Jackson and lefty Phil Coke from the Yankees; and right-handed starting pitcher Max Scherzer and left-handed reliever Daniel Schlereth from the Diamondbacks.[10]

The Mariners—with the successful acquisition of Lee still a few days away—signed free-agent Chone Figgins, a speedster, All-Star and 2009 American League base-on-balls leader, to a four-year contract. Hopeful that the slick fielding third baseman with defensive versatility would help boost their pathetic 2009 team on-base percentage, the Mariners cautioned that their reshuffling might not be done.[11]

The end of the meetings turned into stories of the "unwanted." The Atlanta Braves had been seeking a new home for reliever Rafael Soriano, and the Tampa Bay Rays obliged, sending Atlanta reliever Jesse Chavez in an exchange of right-handers completed the day after the Winter Meetings concluded.[12] The reported reason the Braves needed to make this deal was interesting. Earlier they had signed two free-agent relievers—southpaw Billy Wagner and right-hander Takashi Saito—for a little more than $10 million.[13] They made these moves because they expected that Soriano would decline their offer of arbitration.[14] When he did accept, however, the chagrined Atlanta front office sought new accommodations for their former pitcher.[15]

The Boston Red Sox tried to send third baseman Mike Lowell to the Texas Rangers. The MVP of the 2007 World Series would turn 36 before Opening Day, and the Red Sox were looking to get younger. Despite Boston's offer to pay a lot of money toward his salary, the trade fizzled a couple of weeks later when Lowell failed a physical and the Rangers stamped him "return to sender."[16] Near the end of the meetings, Jeff Borris, agent for all-time home-run and RBI leader Barry Bonds, announced that Bonds' career was probably complete. Borris noted, "When 2008 came around, I couldn't get him a job. When 2009 came around, I couldn't get him a job. Now, 2010. ... I'd say it's nearly impossible. It's an unfortunate ending to a storied career."[17]

The stories for many of the available players, including Lackey, Bay, and Holliday would not be told until well after the Winter Meetings.

The Business Side

With the growing importance of quarterly meetings, changes in how baseball business was being transacted had become something of a nonstory. Many business stories hit the press before the arrival of the meetings. Red Sox owner John W. Henry publicly grumbled about the revenue-sharing system and paid for it in the sum of a $500,000 fine by the commissioner's office. Henry argued that baseball was funding several teams that were consistently noncompetitive. He proposed a new revenue-sharing system and pointed out that, "It's amazing because owners, some of the most ardent capitalists in the country—who have all made their fortunes through capitalism, have imposed a tax system on baseball they would never sit still for in any of their industries."[18]

The behavior of two other large-market ownership groups made Henry's plea for sympathy more difficult to entertain. The Ricketts family purchased the Chicago Cubs a few months prior to the Winter Meetings.[19] During the meetings, word broke that Cubs Chairman Tom Ricketts had met with the governor of Florida about a possible spring-training move from Arizona to Naples.[20] The Cubs had trained in Arizona since 1952 (with the exception of 1966),[21] and this potential move, seemingly driven by greed, failed to sit well with Cubs fans.[22] In Los Angeles, the co-owners of the Dodgers, Frank and Jamie McCourt, had begun what proved to be a bitter divorce, with their complaints about money being way out of touch with the "average Joe."[23] As the Winter Meetings approached, it was unclear how the Dodgers could even function. Within weeks of the meetings, however, it was almost "magically" announced that Dennis Mannion, and not Frank McCourt, had led the Dodgers over the last year.[24] The announcement, while likely meant to assuage nervous Dodgers fans, probably created more questions and disbelief.

Escaping the madness of the owners was longtime Major League Baseball Players Association executive director Don Fehr. Fehr had announced plans to step down in June 2009, and that transition became complete when the union's executive board approved Michael Weiner as the new executive director at their annual meeting. Coincidentally, one of Weiner's first official statements was to reject Henry's brainchild for a new revenue-sharing plan, a conceptualized team payroll minimum that Weiner opposed because, he felt, it could have been the beginnings of a salary cap.[25]

On the first day of the Winter Meetings, the Hall of Fame revealed new inductees Whitey Herzog and Doug Harvey.[26] Herzog, a longtime manager, led the Kansas City Royals to three consecutive American League West crowns and guided the St. Louis Cardinals to a 1982 World Series triumph. Harvey umpired for 31 seasons and was part of six All-Star Game crews. Both men gained election via the Veterans Committee for Managers and Umpires. The Veterans Committee for Executives and Pioneers failed to induct any candidates, which caused yet another round of questions about what qualifications were lacking in union pioneer Marvin Miller.[27]

In a more sensible public-relations move, Pat Courtney, MLB's vice president of public relations, on the first day of the meetings was named recipient of the Robert O. Fishel Award for Public Relations Excellence.[28]

At the minor-league level, National Association President Pat O'Conner recognized the difficult economy as a challenge to operators, and encouraged considerations around ticket pricing as well as out-of-the-box thinking.[29] He also highlighted three initiatives. O'Conner noted the continuation of Minor League Baseball's diversity initiative, started the year before. The initiative had five focuses: race and gender diversity of ownership within the industry; executive-level management; staff-level employment; diversification of the fan base; and development of business-to-business opportunities between Minor League Baseball and a diverse network of businesses. O'Conner called on Wendy Lewis, MLB's lead diversity executive, to stand up and be recognized as he spoke about the diversity initiative.

A second initiative focused on a partnership with the Baseball Hall of Fame. Included in this work were special membership opportunities for Minor League Baseball employees and fans, ideas for promotions during the season, and unique gifts that could be shared with sponsors, season-ticket holders, and corporate partners. Representatives from the Baseball Hall of Fame were also on hand, and acknowledged by O'Conner.

Finally, O'Conner noted that Minor League Baseball would take over Dodgertown in Vero Beach, Florida, with eyes on the creation of Vero Beach Sports Village. (Minor League Baseball had hoped to use the name Historic Dodgertown, but the Dodgers blocked an agreement.)[30]

BASEBALL'S BUSINESS: THE WINTER MEETINGS

Summary

Like other Winter Meetings from recent years, the 2009 affair was marked by a modest amount of player movement and business activity. However, while limited in amount, the changes were consequential. The blockbuster trade remained a hallmark of Winter Meetings, with deals involving three or more teams being completed, or at least significantly advanced, at this gathering in Indianapolis. As with many meetings in years past, some troublesome and outspoken owners—seemingly all driven by financial futures—added bends in the complexion and provided fodder for all attendees. Leadership in the players' ranks turned over, a fairly rare occurrence; and past leadership within the player ranks continued to be shunned by bodies associated with recognition of the game. Topics like diversity earned more conversation and planning at the minor-league level. The success of Indianapolis as a host city, upending the traditional unsubstantiated mindset that the meetings could only be held in warmer climates, perhaps paved the way for future meetings in the North—although the next three meetings were to be held in Lake Buena Vista (Florida), Dallas (Texas), and Nashville (Tennessee). In all, 2009 proved to be a rich set of experiences, setting the stage for coming seasons.

NOTES

1. Anthony Schoettle, "Baseball Meetings Let Leaders Tout Indianapolis to Influential Audience," *Indianapolis Business Journal*, December 5, 2009, accessed March 11, 2011 ibj.com/baseball-meetings-let-local-leaders-tout-indianapolis-to-influential-audience/PARAMS/article/14930.
2. Indianapolis Visitor & Convention Bureau, email message to author, February 26, 2010.
3. Ken Davidoff, "Winter Meetings Time for Talk, Trades," *Newsday*, December 6, 2009.
4. Geoff Baker, "An Ace of a Deal—Zduriencik's Groundwork Brings Lee to Mariners; Seattle GM Is Catalyst in Complicated Swap," *Seattle Times*, December 17, 2009: C-1.
5. Shi Davidi, "Halladay's Situation With Jays Unchanged," *Guelph* (Ontario) *Mercury*, November 24, 2009.
6. "Phillies Complete Halladay Deal," ESPN.com news services, December 17, 2009, accessed September 19, 2017.
7. Long-awaited Halladay, Lee deal finally completed," *Waterville* (Maine) *Morning Sentinel*, December 17, 2009.
8. "Phillies Complete Halladay Deal."
9. Geoff Baker, "An Ace of a Deal…" *Seattle Times*, December 17, 2009: C-1.
10. Jason Beck, "Tigers Complete Three-Way Blockbuster," MLB.com, December 9, 2009. Accessed March 11, 2011. mlb.mlb.com/news/article.jsp?ymd=20091208&content_id=7778470&vkey=news_mlb&fext=.jsp&c_id=mlb.
11. Associated Press, "Angels Ship Figgins to Mariners," *Daily Local News* (West Chester, Pennsylvania), December 9, 2009: 23.
12. Roger Mooney, "Rays Open Checkbook for Soriano to Close," *Tampa Tribune*, December 11, 2009: 3.
13. Jerry Crasnick, "Soriano's Decision 'Going Down to Wire,'" espn.com/mlb/news/story?id=4717127, December 6, 2009, accessed September 18, 2017.
14. Ibid.
15. Alden Gonzalez and Rhett Bollinger, "Doc Sweepstakes Intensify," MLB.com, December 10, 2009. Accessed March 11, 2011. mlb.mlb.com/news/article.jsp?ymd=20091209&content_id=7781380&vkey=news_mlb&fext=.jsp&c_id=mlb.
16. Jeff Wilson, "Texas Rangers Say No on Trade for Boston's Mike Lowell," *Fort Worth Star-Telegram*, December 20, 2009: C14.
17. John Shea, "Bonds' Agent Concedes Slugger's Playing Days Are Over," *San Francisco Chronicle*, December 10, 2009, accessed March 11, 2011 articles.sfgate.com/2009-12-10/sports/17182403_1_jeff-borris-bonds-career-federal-grand-jury.
18. Nick Cafardo, "Sox Owner Wants to Overhaul MLB's Revenue Sharing System," *Boston Globe*, December 1, 2009, boston.com/sports/baseball/redsox/extras/extra_bases/2009/12/red_sox_owner_j.html
19. *St. Louis Post-Dispatch*, "New Cubs Owner Scoffs at Curse—No Big Changes Are Planned for a Team That He Believes Can Win It All in 2010" *St. Louis Post-Dispatch*, November 2, 2009: B8.
20. Rodney Johnson, "Mesa Faces Stiff Competition to Keep the Cubs: Decision Expected in January," *Phoenix Examiner*, December 5, 2009.
21. "History of the Cactus League," springtrainingmagazine.com/history4.html, accessed September 19, 2017.
22. Ken Belson, "Promises and Perks to Try to Lure Cubs from Arizona," *New York Times*, January 29, 2010: B13.
23. Bob Keisser, "'McCourtship' Will Be Must-See Reality Show," *Daily Breeze* (Torrance, California), October 24, 2009: 3B.

24 T.J. Simers, "Morning Briefing: At End of the Day, It's Mannion," *Los Angeles Times*, December 8, 2009: C2.

25 Ronald Blum, "Players Want Longer First Round of Postseason," Associated Press Archive, December 3, 2009.

26 "Doug Harvey, Whitey Herzog Elected to Hall of Fame by Veterans Committee," National Baseball Hall of Fame and Museum, December 7, 2009. Accessed March 11, 2011. baseballhall.org/news/voting-news/doug-harvey-whitey-herzog-elected-hall-fame-veterans-committee.

27 Mel Antonen, "Herzog, Harvey Receive Hall Call—Ex-union Head Miller Falls Two Votes Short," *USA Today*, December 8, 2009: 2C.

28 "Courtney Named 2009 Fishel Award Recipient," MLB.com, December 7, 2009. Accessed March 11, 2010. mlb.mlb.com/news/press_releases/press_release.jsp?c_id=mlb&content_id=7769496&fext=.jsp&vkey=pr_mlb&ymd=20091207.

29 "Pat O'Conner's Opening Session Speech," MiLB.com, December 7, 2009. Accessed September 23, 2017. milb.com/milb/news/pat-oconners-opening-session-speech/c-7766542

30 Ed Bierschenk, "It's Out With Old, in With New at Vero Beach Sports Village," *Vero Beach* (Florida) *Press Journal*, December 23, 2010: 1.

— 2010 —
BASEBALL'S MOVERS AND SHAKERS CONVENE IN THE SUNSHINE STATE

By Andy Bokser

AMONG THE MORE NOTEWORTHY events in major-league baseball in 2010 were a) the San Francisco Giants winning their first World Series since 1954 (when the franchise was based in New York) when they defeated the Texas Rangers in five games; b) the in-season retirement of several stars, including future Hall of Famers Randy Johnson, Frank Thomas, Tom Glavine, John Smoltz, and Ken Griffey; and c) the retirement of future Hall of Fame managers Bobby Cox and Joe Torre. The major leagues (and minor leagues) culminated the 2010 baseball season with their winter meetings, held at the Walt Disney World Dolphin Resort in Lake Buena Vista, Florida, from December 6 to 9.

Florida Governor Charlie Crist welcomed the attendees to Orlando during the awards luncheon on the first day of the meetings. Governor Crist applauded the major and minor leagues' economic contributions to the state.

"I thank minor-league baseball and major-league baseball for choosing our state as the location for the annual tradition of the winter meetings," Governor Crist said. "Professional baseball means nearly $1 billion annually to Florida's economy, and this event puts a nice ending to a year that saw the economic outlook brighten."[1]

Crist, who had previously served as general counsel for Minor League Baseball, had worked to strengthen professional baseball's presence in Florida.[2] In 2008, he revived the annual Governor's Baseball Dinner after it had not been held for more than a decade. Held at Tropicana Field in St. Petersburg prior to the beginning of spring training, the dinner honored the major-league clubs that hold spring training and fall instructional leagues in the state, and the minor-league affiliates that play in Florida during the spring and summer.[3]

The Winter Meetings in 2010 were more than the gathering of baseball's leaders. There was also a trade show with companies trying to persuade teams to use their products.[4] One example of a trade-show presenter was Pocket Radar, a company that developed a radar gun the size of an iPhone which, according to the company, drew considerable interest from several major-league teams.[5]

One of the topics of discussion at the meetings involved the findings of Commissioner Bud Selig's special committee on rule changes. Among the topics explored by the committee was the idea of expanding the number of teams in the playoffs from eight teams to 10. Torre said he thought the addition of more playoff teams was a good idea because he felt that the team winning the division "didn't have as much clout as it should."[6] Under the existing rules, the wild-card team, while not having home-field advantage during the playoffs, needed the same number of wins to reach the World Series as did the team that won its division. Adding an additional round (or single game between two wild-card teams) would theoretically make it more difficult for the wild-card team to reach the World Series, thus rewarding the division winner for finishing first after 162 games. Torre's support for a change (he was a member of Selig's committee) was echoed by fellow managers Lou Piniella and Cito Gaston.[7] The options contemplated for the new playoff format would be either a best-of-three series or a one-game playoff, which is what was implemented beginning in 2012.[8] Selig's 14-member committee, which also included managers Tony LaRussa (Cardinals), Jim Leyland (Tigers), and Mike Scioscia (Angels), plus Hall of Famer Frank Robinson and future Hall of Famer John Schuerholz, was also charged with discussing the possible expansion of the instant-replay system. Selig (who was voted into the Baseball Hall of Fame Class of 2017),[9] was not at that time in favor of expanding the replay to plays other than home runs or fair/foul calls. However, approval of any changes endorsed by Selig or his committee would only be the first step, with approval needed by both the major-league owners and the Players Association.[10]

Longtime successful managers Joe Torre, Lou Piniella, Bobby Cox, and Cito Gaston were invited to the Winter Meetings by Selig for a special tribute to their managerial careers. (Cox reportedly left before the ceremony due to a family issue.)[11] Cox and Gaston had previously announced their retirements. While neither Piniella nor Torre formally announced their intentions to leave the bench, both made it clear that they were not looking to resume the managerial reins.[12]

In a highlight of the meetings, it was announced that former Toronto Blue Jays executive Pat Gillick had been elected to the Hall of Fame by the Veterans Committee.[13] Gillick spent 27 years as a general manager and was credited with building the 1992-93 Toronto Blue Jays World Series champions; the Seattle Mariners team that reached the American League Championship Series in 2000 and 2001 (winning an AL-record 116 games in 2001 before being dispatched by the New York Yankees in five games in the ALCS)[14] and the 2008 World Series champion Philadelphia Phillies.[15] Prior to his positions as general manager, Gillick also worked as a minor-league player, scout, and scouting director.[16] He was credited with some very successful trades during his career including recommending the acquisition of second baseman Willie Randolph from the Pirates while he was the Yankees' scouting director. When Gillick left the Yankees to become the Toronto Blue Jays' assistant general manager in 1977, George Steinbrenner reportedly unsuccessfully tried to block the move,[17] hoping to keep Gillick in the Bronx.[18] In December of 1982, Gillick was able to outsmart his old boss when he traded right-handed relief pitcher Dale Murray and a minor leaguer to the Yankees for outfielder Dave Collins, right-handed pitcher Mike Morgan, and a minor leaguer Gillick wanted—Fred McGriff, who became a five-time All-Star and hit 493 homers in the majors.[19]

With 16 members on the committee, 12 votes (75 percent) were required to be elected, and Gillick received 13 of 16 votes. Among those who were passed over were Marvin Miller (one vote short), Dave Concepcion (who along with Miller was the only other candidate who received more than half of the votes), Ted Simmons, Vida Blue, Steve Garvey, Ron Guidry, Tommy John, Billy Martin, Al Oliver, Rusty Staub, and Steinbrenner.[20] Miller, who was instrumental in leading the Major League Baseball Players Association from a small struggling entity to one of the strongest unions in all of organized labor, expressed his frustration and anger at the results of the vote. Miller declared, "A long time ago it became apparent the Hall sought to bury me before my time. … Its failure is exemplified by the fact that I and the union have received far more support, publicity, and appreciation from countless fans, former players, scholars, and writers than if the Hall had not embarked on its futile and fraudulent attempt to rewrite history. It is an amusing anomaly that the Hall of Fame has made me famous by keeping me out."[21]

It was reported that Miller did not congratulate Pat Gillick on his election and falsely accused *Sports Illustrated* writer Tom Verducci of not voting for him.[22] Miller did fare better than Steinbrenner, who received fewer than eight votes.[23] Another Veterans Committee member, Hall of Famer Tony Perez, voted for Miller and expressed regret that he had not been elected.[24] Gene Orza, the Players Association's chief operating officer, theorized that Miller's opposition to drug testing may have resulted in his losing votes. He also declared that reasons to vote against Miller were petty.[25] Commissioner Selig said he supported both Miller and Steinbrenner for the Hall of Fame. Former Commissioner Fay Vincent said it was "embarrassing" that Miller did not get in.[26]

Bill Conlin of the *Philadelphia Daily News* won the J.G. Taylor Spink Award for writers, and Dave Van Horne, longtime broadcaster of the Montreal Expos (from 1969 to 2001) and Florida Marlins (since 2002), was named the recipient of the Hall of Fame's 2011 Ford Frick Award.[27] They were honored at the Hall of Fame induction ceremony on July 24, 2011. Conlin covered the Phillies and was *The Sporting News's* National League columnist from 1966 to 1986.[28] In another announcement, the Baseball Writers Association of America reported that it had voted down proposals to delay the voting for manager of the year until November to take the playoffs into account, and to create a new award for relief pitchers.[29]

Minor League Baseball also gave out awards at the meetings. Since 1951, the minors had annually honored one of their own with the "King of Baseball Award" in commemoration of their "long-time dedication and service."[30] The award for 2010 went to former All-Star first baseman Don Mincher, who played with several major-league teams and had been president of the Southern League since 2000.[31] The John H. Johnson President's Award was presented to the Billings Mustangs, the Cincinnati Reds' affiliate in the Pioneer League, for its stability, its contributions to the league's stability, and its promotion of the baseball industry.[32]

The Winter Meetings did not go well for Colorado Rockies manager Jim Tracy. While waiting for an elevator with two of his coaches, Carney Lansford and Tom Runnells, he collapsed and was taken to a hospital, where he was held overnight.[33]

In addition to receiving good news about their manager, the Rockies announced they had signed infielder Ty Wigginton, an All-Star in 2010 with the Baltimore Orioles, to a two-year, $8 million deal.[34]

The Rockies got a bargain in Wigginton when compared to the monster contract signed by Philadelphia Phillies outfielder Jayson Werth. Right before the Winter Meetings, on December 5, Werth's agent, Scott Boras, completed a deal with the last-place Washington Nationals worth $126 million.[35] Werth asserted that the Phillies did not want him after reportedly offering him a mere four-year contract in the vicinity of $66 million. The signing caused more than a stir during the Winter Meetings.[36] New York Mets general manager Sandy Alderson quipped, "I thought they were trying to reduce the deficit in Washington."[37]

It was announced that Los Angeles Dodgers owner Frank McCourt had lost a critical ruling in his divorce action. Superior Court Judge Scott Gordon[38] held that the property settlement reached by McCourt and his wife, Jamie, was invalid. The ruling meant that under California's community-property laws the court could determine after trial that Jamie was a co-owner. That ruling left the future of the Dodgers in turmoil.[39] The troubles with the Dodgers continued after the end of the Winter Meetings when Major League Baseball expressed concerns about how McCourt was running the team, anxieties that led MLB to take over the day-to-day control of the club in April 2011. McCourt filed for bankruptcy protection in June 2011, and in November McCourt agreed to sell the Dodgers to a group that included Magic Johnson, longtime baseball executive Stan Kasten, and controlling owner Mark Walter;[40] they formally took control on March 27, 2012.[41]

Another court proceeding that seemingly had an impact on a team's actions during the meetings involved the Bernard Madoff case in Manhattan Bankruptcy Court. In this case it was the Wilpon family, owners of the New York Mets as well as substantial investors with Madoff, who were involved.

The Bankruptcy Court appointed trustee Irving H. Picard to oversee the distribution of assets from Madoff to his victims. Among the trustee's powers was the ability to reclaim funds from investors who received "profits," and pay the recovered monies into a fund to partially compensate other victims of Madoff's Ponzi scheme. Picard stated that the Mets made nearly $48 million from investing with Madoff.[42] Potentially, the Wilpons would have had to return millions of dollars. As the Winter Meetings began, it was unclear how the Wilpons would be affected by the Madoff litigation. Jeff Wilpon maintained that the Mets were in good shape financially and the family was not looking to sell the team.[43] However, it was not seen as a coincidence that general manager Sandy Alderson said the club was not planning to spend any significant money at the meeting, and that if the Mets were going to improve in 2011 (their 2010 record was 79-83, placing them fourth in the five-team NL East), the current players would have to do better.[44]

However, the Mets did acquire a couple of players during the meetings, including former Miami Marlins catcher Ronny Paulino, who still needed to serve eight games of a 50-game suspension for using performance-enhancing drugs. Alderson, in defending the signing, said the Mets were operating within the system that was in place.[45]

Shortly after the Winter Meetings concluded, the Mets announced that they would explore selling a noncontrolling 20-25 percent interest in the club. Owner Fred Wilpon called it "the right thing to do from a business perspective."[46] (The Madoff chapter with the Wilpons continued until 2012, when the family agreed to return $162 million to the trustee over a five-year period. That amount could have been reduced by any claims they made against Madoff as victims of the Ponzi scheme. The trustee, Picard, reportedly had been seeking to recover up to $386 million from the Wilpons before their settlement.[47])

Amid all of these off-the-field developments, a couple of trades were made, the most significant one involving the San Diego Padres and the Boston Red Sox. The Padres sent their three-time All-Star, first baseman Adrian Gonzalez, to the Red Sox for right-handed pitcher Casey Kelly, Boston's first-round draft pick in 2008, outfielder Reymond Fuentes, first baseman Anthony Rizzo, and a player to be named later who turned out to be infielder-outfielder Eric Patterson. San Diego general manager Jed Hoyer said the Padres had determined that they would not be able to sign Gonzalez after 2011 and decided to act in 2010 rather than risk hoping for a deal to develop the next summer.[48]

The Red Sox' acquisition of Gonzalez and outfielder Carl Crawford, whom they signed to a seven-year, $142 million free-agent contract, was less than successful. They were both packaged on August 25, 2012, along with right-hander Josh Beckett, infielder Nick Punto, and cash, to the Dodgers for infielder Ivan De Jesus, first baseman James Loney, and right-hander Allen Webster, plus players to be named later. The Dodgers later sent right-hander Rubby De La Rosa and outfielder-first baseman Jerry Sands to the Red Sox to complete the trade.[49]

The Baltimore Orioles went to the meetings determined to improve their ballclub, which had just seen three different managers record 96 losses and finish at the bottom of the AL East. On December 6, they traded a pair of right-handers, Kam Mickolio and David Hernandez, to Arizona for third baseman Mark Reynolds and a player to be named, who became catcher John Hester. Three days later, they sent two more righties, Jim Hoey and Brett Jacobson, to the Minnesota Twins for a pair of infielders, J.J. Hardy and Brendan Harris. In 2011 the Orioles won only three more games, but by 2012 they won 93 games and made the postseason.

There was one other major trade involving name players. Right-hander Shawn Marcum, who had just come off a 13-win season for the Toronto Blue Jays, was sent to Milwaukee in a straight deal for infielder Brett Lawrie, who had been the Brewers' first-round draft pick in 2008.

The most significant free-agent signing saw the Yankees bring back their shortstop and captain, Derek Jeter. While that may have seemed to be a no-brainer, Jeter's age (36), his drop in productivity and declining range at shortstop made for some rather contentious negotiations.[50] Jeter agreed to a three-year contract worth $51 million, with an option on a fourth year.[51] After the announcement of the agreement Jeter commented, "I was pretty angry about it and I let it be known." But he added that he was going to move on. "It's over with, and I won't bring it up again. I'm happy because this is where I want to be."[52]

The Seattle Mariners' former closer, right-hander J.J. Putz, left the Chicago White Sox to sign with the Diamondbacks, where he regained his All-Star form in both 2011 and 2012. Two-time All-Star infielder Melvin Mora also signed with Arizona after a season in Denver. Catcher Miguel Olivo also said goodbye to the Mile-High City and hello to the Emerald City of Seattle. Outfielder Jeff Francoeur left the Texas

Rangers for the Kansas City Royals and proved to be very productive in Kansas City. Cincinnati right-hander Aaron Harang signed with the Padres and won 14 games, his best season since 2007. Meanwhile, infielder Miguel Cairo, left-hander Mike Hampton, and first baseman Paul Konerko re-signed with the Reds, Diamondbacks, and White Sox, respectively.

Other reported transactions during the meeting were:

DECEMBER 6

P Brian Bass (Baltimore Orioles) signed with Philadelphia Phillies.

OF Eric Hinske re-signed with Atlanta Braves.

IF Russ Adams re-signed with New York Mets.

DECEMBER 7

OF Trent Oeltjen re-signed with Los Angeles Dodgers.

DECEMBER 8

C Paul Phillips (Colorado Rockies) filed for free agency, then

signed with Cleveland Indians.

P Boof Bonser (Oakland Athletics) signed with New York Mets.

IF Carlos Peña (Tampa Bay Rays) signed with Chicago Cubs.

OF Jack Cust (Athletics) signed with Seattle.[53]

In addition to the team executives and agents trying to make deals, other attendees included agent Scott Boras, who was trying to drum up interest in his many clients, including outfielder Manny Ramirez, who had a poor 2010 season for the Dodgers and White Sox. He did succeed in getting the Chicago Cubs to sign Tampa Bay Rays first baseman Carlos Peña to a one-year, $10 million contract, even though he had batted just .196 in 2010, albeit with 28 home runs.[54]

Newly hired Mets manager Terry Collins was at the meetings, happy to be back running a major-league team, and he expressed his gratitude to Mets former GM Omar Minaya and the man who hired him, general manager Sandy Alderson. Also seen in Lake Buena Vista was former Twins outfielder Bobby Kielty, who had been in the minor leagues for the past three seasons.[55] Kielty attended the meetings after playing winter ball, hoping to stir up interest in having a team sign him for 2011.[56] It didn't happen, and Kielty never again played in a major-league game.

California Angels manager Mike Scioscia, who was at the meetings as a member of Bud Selig's special committee, was touting baseball's number-one prospect, outfielder Mike Trout. He thought Trout would have a great future. (It is clear that Scioscia's perception about his future star was on the money.)[57]

The 2010 Winter Meetings delivered a new Hall of Famer, a future change in the playoff format, several player transactions, awards to deserving members of the baseball family, and every indication that baseball had completed a good year and was set up for a successful 2011 campaign as well.

VOLUME 2 - 1958-2016

NOTES

1. "Governor Crist Applauds Impact of Sports on Florida's Economy," States News Service, December 6, 2010, Infortrac Newsstand, go.galegroupcom/ps/i.do? Gale Document Number: Gale A243664422.

2. Jane Musgrave, "Crist's Career a Continuous Evolution," *Palm Beach Post*, October 17, 2010: 1A.

3. "Governor Crist Applauds Impact of Sports on Florida's Economy," Targeted News Service, December 6, 2010.

4. "Baseball Winter Meetings," Minor League Baseball news release, milb.com/content/page.jsp?sid=t456&ymd=20101205&content_id=16258124&vkey=news.

5. David Waldstein, "Gizmos Come to Play at Winter Meetings," *New York Times*, December 12, 2010: SP8.

6. Ronald Blum, "Ex-Managers Favor More Teams in Baseball Playoff," *Lakeland* (Florida) *Ledger*, December 8, 2010.

7. Ibid.

8. 2012 MLB Postseason Schedule, MLB.com news release, mlb.com/mlb/schedule/ps.jsp?y=12.

9. Craig Muder, "Expanding Hall," *Memories and Dreams* (Hall of Fame publication), Spring 2017.

10. Rick Hummel, "Selig Will Be at Meetings; Commissioner's Panel Will Discuss Expanding the Playoffs," *St. Louis Post-Dispatch*, December 2, 2010: C.3.

11. Bill Madden, "Joe & Lou Manage Futures," *New York Daily News*, December 8, 2010: 64.

12. Ibid.

13. Tyler Kepner, "Gillick Elected to Hall; Steinbrenner and Miller Fall Short," *New York Times*, December 7, 2010.

14. Steve Gietschier, "Year in Review," *The Sporting News Baseball Guide* 2002 Edition.

15. Bill Madden, "On George, Vets Shout Hall No! Boss Gets Less than 50% as Rival Gillick Walks In," *New York Daily News*, December 7, 2010: 65. (The article incorrectly listed the Phillies' championship year as 2005; it was 2008 when they defeated the Tampa Bay Rays.)

16. Ibid.

17. Ibid.

18. Tyler Kepner.

19. Ibid.

20. Paul Hogan, "Celebration Breaks Out at Winter Meetings," *Philadelphia Daily News*, December 7, 2010: 60.

21. Bill Madden "On George, Vets Shout Hall No!"

22. Ken Davidoff, "Winter Meetings Report Card," *Newsday*, December 12, 2010.

23. Bill Madden, "On George, Vets Shout Hall No!"

24. Tyler Kepner.

25. Richard Sandomir, "Miller Says Hall Is Trying to Rewrite History," *New York Times*, December 7, 2010.

26. Associated Press, "Pat Gillick Elected to Hall of Fame," *Pensacola News Journal*, December 7, 2010: 15.

27. baseballhall.org/discover/awards/ford-c-frick/dave-van-horne.

28. "Rocks' Tracy out of Hospital After Collapse," *Detroit Free Press*, December 8, 201: B4.

29. Phil Rogers, "Red Sox Land a Monster haul," *Chicago Tribune*, December 10, 2010: 2-8.

30. "Major Award Winners," Minor League Baseball news release, milb.com/milb/history/awards.jsp.

31. "Don Mincher Stats," baseball-almanac.com/players/player.php?p=minchdo01.

32. Minor League Baseball news release, milb.com/minlb/history/awards.jsp.

33. Ben Walker, "Rockies Manager Collapses at Winter Meetings," *Shreveport Times*, December 8, 2010.

34. Ibid.

35. Gary Gillette and Pete Palmer, "2010 Transactions," *The Emerald Guide to Baseball 2011*.

36. Matt Gelb and Bob Brookover, "Werth's Departure Not Surprising," *Philadelphia Inquirer*, December 6, 2010: D06.

37. Associated Press, "Werthwhile Signing," *Easton* (Maryland) *Star-Democrat*, December 6, 2010: 11.

38. "Baseball Notebook," Associated Press, *St. Louis Post-Dispatch*, December 8, 2010: C002.

39. Richard Sandomir and Ken Belson, "Roundup: Ruling Could Lead to Sale of Dodgers." *New York Times*, December 8, 2010: B-19.

40. Tony Jackson, "Frank McCourt to sell Dodgers," EspnLosAngeles.com, November 2, 2011.

41. "Dodgers Owners Through the Years," *Los Angeles Times*, March 27, 2012.

42. Ronald Blum, "Owners Explore Partial Sale of Mets," *Anniston* (Alabama) *Star*, January 29, 2011: 16.

43. Peter Lattman and Michael S. Schmidt, "Madoff Case Lingers as Menace to Mets," *New York Times*, December 6, 2010: D-2.

44. Ibid.

45. David Lennon, "Alderson Addresses Paulino's PED Suspension," *Newsday*, December 9, 2010.

46. Ronald Blum, "Owners Explore Partial Sale of Mets."

47. Grant McCool and Jonathan Stempel, "NY Mets Owners Settle Madoff Case, Avoid Trial," reuters.com/article/madoff-mets/

ny-mets-owners-settle-madoff-case-avoid-trial-idINDEE-82I0BG20120319, March 19, 2012.

48 Ben Walker, "Gillick Elected to Hall, Big Deals at Meetings," *Shreveport Times,* December 7, 2010: 17.

49 Carl Crawford, baseball-reference.com/players/c/crawfca02.shtml.

50 Ben Shpigel and Michael S. Schmidt, "End of Discussion: Jeter's a Yankee," *New York Times,* December 4, 2010, accessed online September 9, 2017.

51 Ibid.

52 "Baseball Notebook," *St. Louis Post-Dispatch,* December 8, 2010: C002.

53 Gary Gillette and Pete Palmer,"2010 Transactions," *The Emerald Guide to Baseball 2011.*

54 Ben Walker, "Hot Stove Heats Up Winter Meetings," *Bennington* (Vermont) *Banner,* December 8, 2010.

55 Dan Woike and Bill Plunkett. "Updates From Baseball's Winter Meetings," *Orange County* (California) *Register,* December 8, 2010.

56 La Velle E. Neal III, "Winter Confidential: Inside Baseball's Winter Meetings From Lake Buena Vista," *Minneapolis Star Tribune,* December 7, 2010: C10.

57 Dan Woike and Bill Plunkett.

— 2011 —
BREAKING THE BUDGET IN THE OFFSEASON

By Chad Hagan

THE 2011 WINTER MEETINGS TOOK place in Dallas from December 5 to 8 at the Hilton Anatole Hotel. This was the sixth time the hotel had hosted baseball's Winter Meetings, with previous meetings taking place in 1980, 1987, 1994, 2000, and 2005.

Located in the design district of downtown Dallas, the hotel is in the middle of the city, though separated from the pedestrian-friendly areas by a mile or two as well as an interstate, allowing for a resort-like sequestered feel and mentality. Inside the hotel, the Anatole has a cavernous atrium design which allows for groups of people to socialize and congregate in private spots, lounge bars, and gathering areas in the hotel lobby. Separated by partial partitions, water gardens, and contemporary interior decor, delegates are able to retain relative privacy while still being out in the open air of the main level. If talks were taking place outside of hotel and agent hospitality suites, they were happening here.

The preconvention atmosphere was alive with offseason rumors about heavy-hitting trades, $100 million deals, and lineup changes. And when all was said and done, a number of teams committed to big trades and significant roster changes, while the press was busy gathering snippets of information from agents and managers on team adjustments, as well as reading the analyses of their fellow writers.[1]

Player Movement

Going into the winter meetings, Mark Buehrle, Albert Pujols, Prince Fielder, C.J. Wilson, Carlos Beltran, and Jimmy Rollins were universally considered to be the top free agents. It was rumored that the Miami Marlins[2] were planning to spend heavily, but realistically every leading team was open for business and looking to make deals. The Marlins started off strong, acquiring White Sox left-hander Mark Buehrle with a four-year, $58 million contract on the very first night of the meetings. Buehrle, who threw a perfect game in 2009, received his third consecutive Fielding Bible and Golden Gloves Awards after the 2011 season. The Marlins continued to dominate the narrative with marquee moves, acquiring hard-throwing right-hander Heath Bell from the San Diego Padres and shortstop Jose Reyes from the New York Mets. Bell, who had three straight years of 40 or more saves for the Padres, signed a three-year contract worth $27 million.[3] The Reyes signing was a landmark deal, well over $100 million spread over six years. The megabuck signings of Buehrle, Belle, and Reyes did not, however, pan out for the Marlins. In 2011 they had finished last in the NL East with a record of 72-90. After committing nearly $200 million to those three free agents, they finished last again, with a record of 69-93. Less than a year later, Buehrle and Reyes were swapped to Toronto in a deal that saw 12 players change uniforms, just a month after Bell had been shipped to the Arizona Diamondbacks in a deal that also included the Oakland A's.[4]

After finishing below .500, Oakland's Billy Beane made teamwide roster changes. At the Hilton Anatole, he sent All-Star right-hander Trevor Cahill and journeyman left-hander Craig Breslow to the Arizona Diamondbacks for right-handers Jarrod Parker and Ryan Cook, plus outfielder Collin Cowgill. He was engaged in talks with the New York Yankees about left-hander Gio Gonzalez, but nothing materialized there and, after the Winter Meetings, the All-Star was sent (along with minor-league right-hander Robert Gilliam) to the Washington Nationals for right-handers A.J. Cole and Brad Peacock, left-hander Tommy Milone, and catcher Derek Norris.

The New York Mets traded outfielder Angel Pagan to the San Francisco Giants for right-hander Ramon Ramirez and outfielder Andres Torres. Pagan became a 2012 NL MVP contender, as well as a top performer for the 2012 World Series champion Giants, while Torres was traded back to the San Francisco Giants the following year. The Colorado Rockies, meanwhile, traded their closer, right-hander Huston Street, to the San Diego Padres for cash and a player to be named later, who turned out to be southpaw Nick Schmidt.[5] And in a surprise move, the Chicago White Sox sent their closer, right-hander Sergio Santos, to the Blue Jays for minor-league utility player Nestor Molina.

On the last day of the Winter Meetings, the Los Angeles Angels paid well over $300 million to land first baseman Albert Pujols and C.J. Wilson. The left-handed Wilson, who had successfully transitioned from being the Texas Rangers' closer to their winningest starter, had been linked to the Marlins, Red Sox, Angels, Yankees, and Nationals before signing with the Angels for five years and $77.5 million.[6] Pujols, the Cardinals' three-time National League MVP, had been linked to the Marlins, Rangers, and Cubs, but chose the Angels, who paid him $240 million, in what became a 10-year, $250 million deal.

As with almost all previous meetings, not every prediction came true. Jimmy Rollins stayed with the Phillies, though the press had linked the shortstop to the Giants or Brewers. Prince Fielder was considered a prime free agent and his agent, Scott Boras, had held conversations with the Mariners, Brewers, Cubs, Blue Jays, Nationals, Rangers, and Marlins prior to the meetings, but his $200 million asking price seemed to stall any deals. That would eventually change, though not until January of 2012, when the big first baseman, a three-time All-Star, signed a nine-year contract with Detroit worth a reported $214 million.[7]

A similar story played out in the case of Yoenis Cespedes. A Cuban defector, he was rumored to be talking to the Tigers, Red Sox, Marlins, Yankees, and Nationals, but was unavailable until he established a residency outside Cuba. A month after he was declared a citizen of the Dominican Republic, the outfielder signed a $36 million, four-year contract with Oakland.[8]

On the international front, the Hokkaido Nippon Ham Fighters of Japan's Nippon Professional Baseball, posted right-handed pitcher Yu Darvish. After the customary 30-day negotiation period, the Rangers won out and bought the rights to negotiate with him from the NPB, under a system in which major-league teams bid on securing the exclusive rights to talk to the player. In the case of the 25-year-old Darvish, the release fee reached was a record $51.7 million. The Rangers then negotiated with Darvish's agents, Arn Tellem and Dom Nomura, and signed the 25-year-old for six years and $60 million.[9] Hall of Famer Nolan Ryan, then a Rangers executive, said: "When I look at my career and his career and where I was at 25 years old, there's a substantial difference. I still had a control problem. I was very durable, but I didn't have the feel for the baseball or my delivery as he does with his."[10]

Baseball Business

There is always more to the Winter Meetings than player movement, and 2011 was no exception, as the Hilton Anatole hosted baseball's annual trade show, social events, and business seminars.

The annual Bob Freitas Business Seminar was held on December 5. Later in the day there was an awards luncheon and then came the main event—Opening Night at the Baseball Trade Show, a reception for baseball executives, convention exhibitors, and attendees, which is routinely the most-attended event during the conference. The trade show was held in the hotel's 128,000-square-foot Trinity Complex exhibition space.

The next day featured the Women in Baseball Leadership Seminar, a forum held since 2008 and designed to encourage collaboration among women baseball professionals. And the Professional Baseball Employment Opportunities job fair took place throughout the convention. An annual feature of the Winter Meetings, the job fair is a way for young people interested in starting a career in the business end of baseball to meet team executives (primarily on the minor-league level) looking to fill job openings.

On December 8, the Rule 5 Draft was held from 9 to 11 A.M., followed by a closing session and then the awards banquet, which honored the award winners for The King of Baseball (Cuauhtemoc "Chito" Rodriguez), John H. Johnson President's Award (Tennessee, Southern League), Larry MacPhail Promotional Award (Lake Elsinore, California League), Warren Giles Award (Chuck Murphy, Florida State League), Sheldon "Chief" Bender Award (Bob Gebhard, Arizona Diamondbacks), and the Mike Coolbaugh Award (Mike Jirschele, Omaha Storm Chasers manager).

The Rule 5 Draft, baseball's ultimate crapshoot, produced several players who had varying degrees of success in the majors. The prize proved to be infielder Marwin Gonzalez, a Cubs farmhand who was drafted by the Red Sox, then immediately traded to Houston for Marco Duarte, a right-handed pitcher. Since then, Duarte mostly pitched in Mexico, but Gonzalez became a super-sub for the Houston Astros and an important player in the team's rise from one of the worst teams in the majors to one of the best. The Cubs also lost another infielder, Ryan Flaherty, who became a valuable utilityman for the Orioles. Other players who were drafted and spent some time in the majors included right-hander Rhiner Cruz (drafted by the Astros from the Mets), left-hander Lucas Luetge (Mariners from the Brewers), left-hander Cesar Cabral (drafted by the Royals from the Red Sox and traded to the Yankees), right-hander Lendy Castillo (Cubs from the Phillies), and outfielder Erik Komatsu (Cardinals from the Nationals).

In other activity, the Orioles traded a pair of minor leaguers, utilityman Tyler Henson and southpaw Jarret Martin, to the Los Angeles Dodgers for the much-traveled lefty Dana Eveland.[11] The Kansas City Royals, meanwhile, traded utility player Yamaico Navarro, whom they had picked up from the Red Sox at the trading deadline, to the Pirates for minor-league right-hander Brooks Pounders and infielder Diego Goris.

Despite the high volume of trading activity, the meetings were still heavily overshadowed by the Marlins and the Angels. While the Marlins led the effort with their early investment of over $150 million, the Angels ultimately stole the show. Signing Pujols was easily the major story to come out of Dallas, and the Angels' commitment of over $300 million continues to cast a long shadow over major-league baseball's winter meetings.

BASEBALL'S BUSINESS: THE WINTER MEETINGS

SOURCES

In addition to the sources cited in the Notes, the author also relied on Baseball-Reference.com, milb.com/milb/events/winter_meetings/y2011/events.jsp, a 2012 sponsorship information packet for exhibitors presented by Minor League Baseball, and the following:

Calcaterra, Graig. "Greetings From the Winter Meetings," mlb.nbcsports.com/2011/12/05/greetings-from-the-2011-winter-meetings/, accessed February 4, 2017.

Caramela, Vince. "2011 Winter Meetings Preview," hardballtimes.com/2011-winter-meetings-preview/, accessed February 4, 2017.

Moore, Jack. "A Brief History of Winter Meeting Madness," Vice Sports, December 12, 2014, sports.vice.com/en_us/article/vvakvb/a-brief-history-of-baseball-winter-meeting-madness.

NOTES

1. Craig M. Williams, "Winter Meetings Winners and Losers," mlbdailydish.com/2011/12/10/2626011/2011-winter-meetings-winners-and-losers.

2. The Florida Marlins had officially become the Miami Marlins on November 11.

3. Eddie Ravert, "MLB Free Agents 2012: Jose Reyes Signs With the Miami Marlins," bleacherreport.com/articles/968813-mlb-baseball-jose-reyes-signs-with-the-miami-marlins, accessed July 4, 2017.

4. Matthew Pouliot, "Update: Marlins, Jose Reyes Agree to Six-Year, $106 Million Deal," mlb.nbcsports.com/2011/12/04/report-marlins-go-to-111-million-in-bid-for-jose-reyes/. Other sources (see Ravert, above) stated that Reyes received $111 million. Gregor Chisholm, "Blue Jays' 12-player deal with Marlins Official," m.mlb.com/news/article/40363638//, accessed July 4, 2017.

5. baseball-reference.com/players/s/streehu01.shtml, accessed July 6, 2017.

6. "Angels, C.J. Wilson agree to deal," espn.com/los-angeles/mlb/story/_/id/7330909/los-angeles-angels-add-texas-rangers-cj-wilson-5-year-775m-deal, accessed July 4, 2017.

7. Jason Beck, "Prince, Tigers Reach Nine-Year Deal," m.mlb.com/news/article/26452690//, accessed July 5, 2017.

8. Susan Slusser and Demian Bulwa, "The amazing saga of Yoenis Cespedes," sfchronicle.com/sports/cespedes/, accessed July 5, 2017.

9. Richard Durrett, "Rangers, Yu Darvish Reach Deal," espn.com/dallas/mlb/story/_/id/7476104/texas-rangers-japanese-pitcher-yu-darvish-agree-six-year-60m-deal, accessed July 5, 2017.

10. Jeff Wilson, "Not All About Yu: Ryan Loves Rangers' Pitching Potential," *Fort Worth Star-Telegram*, February 22, 2012, star-telegram.com/sports/article3830475.html.

11. "2011 MLB Trade Rumors: Dodgers Interested in Mets Daniel Murphy," calltothepen.com/2011/12/11/2011-mlb-trade-rumors-dodgers-interested-in-mets-daniel-murphy/.

— 2012 —
LAYING GROUNDWORK

By Darren Munk

Introduction

THE 2012 WINTER MEETINGS RE-turned to the Gaylord Opryland Hotel in Nashville for the sixth time, starting on Sunday, December 2, and concluding on Thursday, December 6. While the 2012 edition of the meetings lacked a headline-worthy trade or signing like the Los Angeles Angels of Anaheim picking up Albert Pujols in 2011, the Nashville meetings still resulted in a number of deals that had a significant impact on the 2013 season and beyond.

Player Movement

Perhaps the biggest surprise of the 2012 meetings was that a number of top-tier free agents remained available at the conclusion of the gathering, including Josh Hamilton and Zack Greinke.

The Los Angeles Dodgers came into the meetings flush with cash (after their $2 billion sale to a group headed by Magic Johnson)[1] and needing to compete with a division rival, the San Francisco Giants, who had just won their second World Series title in three years, yet left Nashville without signing a single free agent. Although seen by some pundits as a leading candidate to land Greinke, the 2009 American League Cy Young Award winner,[2] the Dodgers were considering pulling out of the Greinke bidding and moving on to other pitchers to upgrade their rotation by the conclusion of the meetings.[3] However, on December 11 (five days after the meetings ended), the Dodgers inked Greinke to a six-year, $147 million contract.[4]

A deal for Hamilton failed to materialize at the meetings owing to several factors, most notably that the outfielder planned to allow his team, the Texas Rangers, a chance to match any offer he received.[5] Further complicating matters, the Rangers were vying for Greinke, meaning that the market for Hamilton was somewhat dependent upon Greinke's decision.[6] There were rumors that the Seattle Mariners were a fallback option for Hamilton in the event that he didn't re-sign with Texas,[7] but his eventual destination was very much up in the air at the conclusion of the meetings. Hamilton eventually signed with the Los Angeles Angels of Anaheim, getting a five-year deal worth $125 million on December 14.[8]

Although neither Hamilton nor Greinke was signed during the meetings, a number of important deals were completed in Nashville. Catcher-first baseman Mike Napoli, outfielder Angel Pagan, right-handed reliever Joakim Soria, right-handed starter Dan Haren, outfielder Shane Victorino, infielder Marco Scutaro, and righty Joe Blanton all signed new contracts, while outfielder Ben Revere was traded from the Minnesota Twins to the Philadelphia Phillies.

Napoli's deal with the Boston Red Sox, while agreed upon at the meetings (on December 4), ended up being a particularly drawn-out affair.[9] As in a number of delayed or canceled trades and free-agent signings, the phrase "pending a physical" turned out to be more than a mere formality. After his physical revealed a hip issue (avascular necrosis) that concerned Boston's medical staff, Napoli's reported three-year, $39 million contract became a one-year, $5 million deal with an additional $8 million in incentives (which wasn't finalized until January 23, 2013, nearly two months after the initial agreement).[10] In spite of his hip problems, Napoli would go on to post a career-high 578 plate appearances with a 128 OPS+, proving to be a key member on the 2013 World Series champions.

> ### EVERY REVOLUTION WAS FIRST A THOUGHT IN ONE MAN'S MIND
>
> Only weeks before the 2012 Winter Meetings, Marvin Miller died.[*] While there seemed to be no formal recognition of Miller at the meetings, former players had previously created a website ThanksMarvin.com to advance the argument for his inclusion in the Baseball Hall of Fame.[**] Posts on the website included support by Commissioner Bud Selig, former Commissioner Fay Vincent, and MLB's former labor negotiator, Ray Grebey.[***]
>
> ---
>
> [*] Derrick Goold, "Marvin Miller, Father of Baseball's Union, Dies," *St. Louis Post-Dispatch*, November 28, 2012: B1.
>
> [**] "Marvin Miller – Tough Negotiator Who Rewrote the Contract Rules for Baseball Players and Paved the Way for Today's Millionaire Superstars," *The Times* (London), November 29, 2012: 73. See also "Cooperstown Confidential: Bob Locker Talks Marvin Miller," Fangraphs.com, April 30, 2010. Accessed October 5, 2017. fangraphs.com/tht/cooperstown-confidential-bob-locker-talks-marvin-miller/.
>
> [***] ThanksMarvin.com. Accessed October 5, 2017. thanksmarvin.com/.

The other impact acquisition for the Red Sox was Shane Victorino, who received virtually the same deal as Napoli's initial agreement, a three-year deal worth $37.5 million, and, fortunately for both parties, Victorino's physical passed muster and the deal was quickly made official.[11] Like Napoli, Victorino was a big factor in the third Red Sox championship since 2004, as he posted a 118 OPS+ at the plate and won a Gold Glove for his outfield defense.

Other News

The biggest off-field news of the 2012 meetings involved the minor-league clubs. Minor League Baseball President Pat O'Conner announced a new initiative called Project Brand, a marketing program focused on unifying the promotional efforts of all 160 minor-league teams. As *Baseball America* reported, "The change O'Conner envisions is a program that sells minor-league baseball as an entity and promotes the model of affordable, family-friendly entertainment to major companies."[12]

The Project Brand initiative, developed by O'Conner in conjunction with Minor League Baseball's marketing committee, was created with the goal of attracting national sponsors rather than the local and regional sponsors traditionally associated with the minors. This change in focus was driven by the idea that national sponsors could generate more marketing revenue for minor-league clubs, while allowing sponsors to reach fans in 160 markets across the country. Tom Dickson, owner of the Lansing Lugnuts and Montgomery Biscuits, declared, "We need to think big. We will be leveraging our wonderful demographics and product and put them together. We can monetize those efforts with significant sponsorship sales."[13]

Other news announced at the meetings included the election of two new members of the National Association board of trustees: Ken Schnacke of the Columbus Clippers and Marv Goldklang of the Hudson Valley Renegades, representing the International League and New York-Penn League, respectively.

George McGonagle was named the 2012 "King of Baseball," an honor given to one executive at each year's Winter Meetings. He was awarded the title as recognition for helping to run the Bluefield team in the Appalachian League, for more than 50 years, and also for transitioning to a Blue Jays affiliation in 2011 after having been aligned with the Orioles since 1958.

Summary

Although the 2012 Winter Meetings didn't have a nine-figure contract signing or a blockbuster trade, the player movement that happened there was important to the outcome of the 2013 season and beyond. Of particular importance were the Napoli and Victorino signings by the Red Sox, as both players were key pieces of the 2013 World Series champion squad. Similarly, the reigning 2012 champion Giants retained Pagan, their center fielder and leadoff hitter, who would be a key contributor again in 2014 as San Francisco won its third title in five seasons.

Similarly, while the league business conducted at the meetings lacked the drama of a contraction threat or drastic rules changes, the introduction of the Project Brand initiative sought to create a more effective (and lucrative) marketing relationship between the 160 minor-league clubs, helping to sustain the health of the sport by ensuring that fans all over the country have games to attend and teams to support.

NOTES

1 "Sale of Dodgers Finalized," espn.go.com/mlb/story/_/id/7877983/los-angeles-dodgers-sale-guggenheim-group-finalized, accessed December 2, 2015.

2 Jayson Stark, "Grand Ole Winter Meetings Preview," espn.go.com/mlb/hotstove12/story/_/id/8697372/previewing-baseball-grand-ole-winter-meetings, accessed December 2, 2015.

3 Steve Adams, "Zack Greinke Rumors: Wednesday," mlbtraderumors.com/2012/12/zack-greinke-rumors-wednesday.html, accessed December 1, 2015.

4 Ken Gurnick, "Greinke's Six-Year Deal With Dodgers Finalized," m.mlb.com/news/article/40585162/, accessed December 2, 2015.

5 Tim Dierkes, "Josh Hamilton Rumors: Tuesday," mlbtraderumors.com/2012/12/rangers-josh-hamilton-making-progress.html, accessed December 3, 2015.

6 Steve Adams, "Mariners Making Serious Run at Josh Hamilton," mlbtraderumors.com/2012/12/josh-hamilton-rumors-wednesday.html, accessed December 3, 2015.

7 Ibid.

8 Alden Gonzalez, "Angels Agree to Five-Year Deal With Hamilton," m.mlb.com/news/article/40641062/, accessed December 3, 2015.

9 Peter Abraham, "Adding Mike Napoli Was Goal for Red Sox," bostonglobe.com/sports/2012/12/04/red-sox-get-their-man-mike-napoli/Qw4RaLVG3JOImTKI8BRbFJ/story.html, accessed December 10, 2015.

10 Nick Cafardo, "Red Sox Complete Mike Napoli Deal, Despite Hip Ailment," bostonglobe.com/sports/2013/01/23/mike-napoli-despite-avascular-necrosis-hip-signs-with-red-sox/ObbFyAGEJSPLmUfwZvd8lO/story.html, accessed December 10, 2015.

11 Nick Cafardo, "Shane Victorino Agrees to 3-Year Deal With Red Sox," bostonglobe.com/sports/2012/12/04/red-sox-offer-shane-victorino-three-year-deal/G1pHkmHKfelU2yw9BhG8UJ/story.html, accessed December 12, 2015.

12 Josh Leventhal, "Winter Meetings Wrapup," baseballamerica.com/minors/winter-meetings-wrapup-14487/, accessed January 10, 2016.

13 Ibid.

— 2013 —
IT ALL HAPPENED THE WEEK BEFORE

by Luca Rossi

Introduction

THE 2013 BASEBALL WINTER Meetings were held December 9-12 at the Walt Disney World Swan and Dolphin Resort, in Orlando, Florida. The meetings came only 40 days after the Boston Red Sox' Koji Uehara pitched a perfect ninth inning in Game Six of the World Series, striking out Matt Carpenter of the St. Louis Cardinals for the final out of the Series as the Red Sox beat the Cardinals and won the World Series for the first time since 1918.

Along with the traditional business activities (seminars and workshops) and social events, the meetings included the Baseball Trade Show, the 20th edition of the PBEO Job Fair, and the Women in Baseball Leadership Event, held for the sixth consecutive year, created as a networking opportunity for women employed directly in baseball and to promote more gender balance in the game.[1]

Issues on the agenda and opening remarks

On December 9, MiLB President and CEO Pat O'Conner opened the meetings with some reflections on the state of the game and the business of baseball.[2]

O'Conner, elected for his second term in 2011, declared the year to have been successful in spite of a slight decrease in attendance at both minor- and major-league levels. (In minor-league games attendance was recorded above the 48 million mark, while at the major-league level over 74 million tickets were sold, the sixth highest of all time.[3]) Despite an unfavorable economic climate, attendance decreased by only 1.1 percent as more than 122 million fans attended professional baseball games during the 2013 regular season.

O'Conner focused on the difficult commercial environment, especially for small businesses, which represent the large majority of ballclubs in America. "Unlike any other time in our history," he said, "we must deal with troubling issues on a daily basis" as the clubs deal "with increasing costs, mounting frustration of a national health-care system undergoing a historical change" (with its own consequences on player contracts), safety concerns, and antiterrorism measures that impacted operating costs of ballparks and clubs.[4] As a result, the 2013 meeting agenda was focusing more than ever on business seminars and workshops dealing with the above-mentioned issues.

The agenda also emphasized the great contribution of technology to the game as MLB and MiLB platforms were proving to be very successful at offering fan engagement and at the same time providing a growing source of revenues. It is perhaps worthy of note that for the first time the Winter Meetings had its own app for those attending the events.

Player movements

"Has any edition of the winter meetings ever been overshadowed by the week before the winter meetings?" With this question, ESPN's Jayson Stark opened his meetings preview column.[5]

Between Monday night and Tuesday afternoon, only hours before the meetings actually started, there were signings or agreements involving players Joe Nathan, Jacoby Ellsbury, Jarrod Saltalamacchia, A.J. Pierzynski, Paul Konerko, Justin Morneau, Scott Kazmir, and Ryan Vogelsong, in addition to seven trades involving 25 other players. And that does not include a nontender day that released 43 more free agents.

Among the most significant free agents still unsigned at the time were right-handed pitchers Matt Garza, Ubaldo Jimenez, and Ervin Santana; outfielder Shin-Soo Choo, and infielder-DH Kendrys Morales, all of whom had to wait until after the conclusion of the meetings to find new employers.[6] Trade talks involving the likes of David Price, Jeff Samardzija, and Matt Kemp also failed to materialize at the meetings despite strong rumors in the previous weeks.

Possibly the only "big-name" player to sign during the week of the meetings was former Cy Young Award winner Bartolo Colon, who agreed to a two-year, $20 million contract with the New York Mets. Having won just 74 games, they proved to be one of the most active teams during the week, also signing former Yankees center fielder Curtis Granderson to a four-year contract worth $60 million.

The meetings' most notable transaction at the major-league level was a complicated three-team trade between the Angels, Diamondbacks, and White Sox. The Angels sent slugging first baseman-outfielder Mark Trumbo and minor-league right-hander A.J. Schugel to Arizona. The Angels received southpaws Tyler Skaggs (from Arizona) and Hector Santiago (from the White Sox), while outfielder Adam Eaton moved from Arizona to Chicago and minor-league outfielder Brandon Jacobs headed from the White Sox farm system to the Diamondbacks.

Veteran ace Roy Halladay announced his retirement at the meetings, signing a one-day contract with Toronto so he could retire as a Blue Jay, the club with which he spent 12 of his 16 baseball seasons. Halladay was only the second pitcher in history to record a no-hitter in postseason play when he defeated the Cincinnati Reds, 4-0, on October 6, 2010, as a member of the Philadelphia Phillies. He had also tossed a perfect game earlier in the year (against the Marlins), making him only the fifth pitcher in major-league history to throw two no-hitters in a single season. Halladay is one of only five pitchers to win the Cy Young Award in both the American League (2003 with Toronto) and National League (2010 with Philadelphia).

Hall of Fame announcement

On December 9 baseball history was on display, following the Expansion Era Committee's announcement that managers Bobby Cox, Tony LaRussa, and Joe Torre would be inducted into the National Baseball Hall of Fame in 2014.[7] The committee's decision was announced by Hall of Fame Chair Jane Forbes Clark during the first day of the meetings. Cox, LaRussa, and Torre combined for 7,558 regular-season wins, 17 pennants, and 8 World Series championships.

Other relevant stories

Perhaps the biggest story from the 2013 Winter Meetings in terms of its possible impact on the future of the game, was that Major League Baseball was moving toward banning collisions at home plate. The players union would have to approve the rules change for the 2014 season; if it did not, MLB could unilaterally implement the rule for the 2015 season.[8] As it turned out, MLB and the Major League Baseball Players Association agreed on language, and an experimental rule, 7.13 (Collisions at Home Plate), was in place beginning with spring training in 2014.[9]

Minor League Baseball crowned Portland Sea Dogs (Double-A Eastern League) President Charlie Eshbach the 2013 King of Baseball. This title represents a long-standing tradition in which Minor League Baseball salutes a veteran from the professional baseball world for longtime dedication and service.[10] Eshbach celebrated his 40th season in the game in 2013, working for one of the minor leagues' most celebrated and successful franchises, following 11 years as president of the Eastern League.

PRESS RELEASE REGARDING NEW MLBPA EXECUTIVE DIRECTOR TONY CLARK

On December 3, 2013, after Players Association executive director Michael Weiner died less than two weeks earlier, Tony Clark became the first former major-league player to assume the role. Clark was caught off guard by the circumstances: "I expected to be tied to the hip of Michael for 20 years. He rides off into the sunset, I ride off into the sunset. We ride off into the sunset having affected the game positively."

Here is the formal announcement of Clark's appointment:

LA JOLLA, Calif. – The executive board of the Major League Baseball Players Association voted unanimously to appoint Tony Clark as the union's next executive director, pending a vote by the general membership, it was announced today during the MLBPA's annual executive board meeting. The general membership will vote on the matter as soon as practicable.

Clark, 41, has been serving as the MLBPA's acting executive director since former executive director Michael Weiner's passing on Nov. 22, after a 15-month battle with an inoperable brain tumor.

As executive director, Clark, who joined the MLBPA staff in March 2010 as director of player relations, and was promoted to deputy executive director this past July, will oversee all day-to-day aspects of the MLBPA's operations, including labor relations, business affairs and the Players Trust.

"Although the need to name a new executive director was brought about by the tragic passing of Michael Weiner, a man we all loved and respected, we're very happy to have someone like Tony take the helm of our union," stated Jeremy Guthrie, who, along with Curtis Granderson, serves as MLBPA association representative, the union's most senior player-leadership position. "Tony's experience as one of the most respected players of his generation and his knowledge of the union and its bargaining relationship with the clubs will serve all players well as we navigate the future."

"Tony has some big shoes to fill, but we're more than confident that he has the knowledge, experience and passion to serve as our next executive director," added Granderson. "Tony has been actively involved in the last three rounds of bargaining, and his commitment to the brotherhood of players – past, present, and future – makes him uniquely qualified to serve in this role."

"It is with a very heavy heart that I thank the players for providing me the honor and opportunity to follow my mentor and friend, Michael Weiner, as the MLBPA's next executive director," said Tony. "We all wish this decision was not necessary; however, we also know that Michael would urge all of us involved with the union to forge ahead in our efforts to protect the rights of the players. The passion and courage Michael displayed during his inspiring 15-month battle has truly set a tone that further embodies the commitment players have to the Players Association and to one another."

Clark retired during the 2009 season, after spending 15 seasons with the Detroit Tigers, Arizona Diamondbacks, New York Mets, New York Yankees, Boston Red Sox, and San Diego Padres. Originally drafted by the Tigers in the first round (second overall) of the 1990 First-Year Player Draft, Clark made his big-league debut in September 1995 and finished third in 1996 Rookie of the Year voting. Clark, a first baseman, played in 1,559 games, appeared in the 2001 All-Star Game and finished his career with 1,188 hits, 251 home runs, and 824 RBIs.

Clark became active in union affairs after attending his first executive board meeting in 1999. From there he became a team player representative, before spending his last seven seasons as an association representative. As a player, Clark was actively involved in the union's collective bargaining negotiations in 2002 and 2006, as well as in negotiations over the Joint Drug Agreement.

The MLBPA executive board consists of the 30 player representatives, two association representatives, two alternate association representatives, two pension representatives and two alternate pension representatives (38 players total).

1   MLBPA/MLB News Release, "MLBPA executive board appoints Tony Clark executive director pending vote of the general membership," MLB.com, December 3, 2013. Accessed October 5, 2017. mlb.mlb.com/pa/releases/releases.jsp?content=120313
2   Chris Jenkins, "Taking the Reins: Former Aztec, Padre to Head Major League Baseball's Players Group," *San Diego Union Tribune*, December 4, 2013: A-1.

BASEBALL'S BUSINESS: THE WINTER MEETINGS

NOTES

1. 2013 Baseball Winter Meetings, Agenda and Events, Milb.com, milb.com/milb/events/winter_meetings/y2013/agenda_events.jsp.

2. "O'Conner's Opening Session Speech," Milb.com, milb.com/news/article.jsp?ymd=20131209&content_id=64505444&vkey=pr_milb&fext=.jsp&sid=milb.

3. numbertamer.com/files/2013_Prelim_notes-Revised_1_.pdf ; "The Good, the Bad and the Ugly of MLB Attendance," Forbes.com, forbes.com/sites/maurybrown/2013/10/03/the-good-the-bad-and-the-ugly-of-mlbs-2013-attendance/#7ff48b7d3308.

4. https://www.milb.com/milb/news/oconners-opening-session-speech/c-64505444?tid=185364810

5. Jayson Stark, "Winter Meetings Forecast," ESPN.com, December 7, 2013, espn.com/mlb/wintermeetings2013/story/_/id/10084758/mlb-winter-meetings-preview.

6. Matt Snyder, "Wrapping Up the 2013 MLB Winter Meetings," CBSSports.com, December 12, 2013, cbssports.com/mlb/news/wrapping-up-the-2013-mlb-winter-meetings/.

7. Barry M. Bloom, "La Russa, Torre, Cox Going Into Hall of Fame," MLB.com, December 9, 2013, m.mlb.com/news/article/64493980/.

8. "MLB Set to Ban Home-Plate Collisions, Needs MLBPA Approval," CBS Sports.com,

cbssports.com/mlb/news/mlb-set-to-ban-home-plate-collisions-needs-mlbpa-approval/.

9. Tim Brown, "MLB Moves to Eliminate Home Plate Collisions," Yahoo Sports.com, December 12, 2013, sports.yahoo.com/news/mlb-moves-to-eliminate-home-plate-collisions-041253389.html.

10. "Eshbach named '2013 King of Baseball,'" Milb.com, December 12, 2013, milb.com/news/article.jsp?ymd=20131212&content_id=64642892&fext=.jsp&vkey=pr_milb.

— 2014 —
A NEW DAWN RISING

By Tom Cuggino

THE 2014 MAJOR-LEAGUE SEASON ended with the San Francisco Giants winning their third World Series in five seasons, beating the Kansas City Royals in a dramatic seven-game series on the shoulders of a staggeringly dominant performance by their 25-year-old southpaw, Madison Bumgarner. The Giants had established themselves as the decade's model franchise, the Royals emerged from almost three decades of obscurity, and both succeeded despite the absence of high-priced household free-agent names on their rosters. This extended what had in recent years become a new tone of operational thinking, focusing on more organic organizational development. This would have a profound impact at that year's Winter Meetings, held at the Hilton San Diego Bayfront Hotel during the week of December 7-10. It was the first time in nearly 30 years that the event had been held in "America's Finest City," and the surrounding dynamics would not disappoint.

The week kicked off with the game's annual awards banquet, which followed the first day's workshop on the business of baseball. The Bob Freitas Workshop Series was again a staple of the week, covering a broad array of topics from sales and marketing to media and community relations. The format for this workshop had recently changed from a ballroom setting to a series of smaller rooms with speakers on special topics to encourage more productive communication. Also featured was the PBEO Job Fair, which entered its 21st year and continued to offer opportunities for prospective industry job-seekers to meet directly with team executives. Just as the majority of the leagues' player transactions occur during this week, most of the hiring for its 400-plus internships and full-time positions is cemented at this venue. The Trade Show on opening night, and the Gala on the final night, mark the bookends of the event, offering a spectacular and festive display of exhibits, merchandise, and networking for all involved.

Just before the meetings it was becoming clear that after turning themselves into one of baseball's most competitive teams, the Oakland A's were now in the process of shedding some of their best talent in exchange for very little experience but smaller salaries. The first to go was All-Star third baseman Josh Donaldson, who was dealt to the Toronto Blue Jays for infielder Brett Lawrie, left-hander Sean Nolin, right-hander Kendall Graveman, and utilityman Franklin Barreto; Donaldson would go on to win the AL MVP Award the coming season. The A's traded another 2014 All-Star, first baseman-outfielder Brandon Moss, to the Cleveland Indians for second baseman Joey Wendle. Completing a difficult week for the A's fan base, the team lost right-handed starter Jason Hammel to the Chicago Cubs via free agency. This rendered Oakland one of the biggest losers of the winter, a trough from which they would not quickly recover. It would also partially reduce GM Billy Beane's hard-earned stature as the artful champion of "Moneyball," which had still not brought a World Series to the East Bay during his tenure.[1]

Along with Moss, other 2014 All-Stars who found new homes during the week. Catcher Miguel Montero and right-hander Jeff Samardzija headed to different sides of Chicago as the Cubs and White Sox became two of the biggest winter winners in their aggressive rebuilding quests. Montero was signed as a free agent by the Cubs to a three-year, $40 million deal after a solid eight-year stint with Arizona that included a pair of All-Star Game appearances. Samardzija, a former standout wide receiver at Notre Dame, would return to the Windy City after having spent the second half of 2014 in Oakland following a July trade that brought shortstop Addison Russell to the Cubs. Samardzija now found himself once again the centerpiece of a multiplayer deal as he and a one-time top prospect, right-hander Michael Ynoa, were sent to Chicago's South Side to anchor the White Sox starting rotation; the A's, in turn, received infielder Marcus Semien, catcher Josh Phegley, right-hander Chris Bassitt, and minor-league utilityman Rangel Ravelo.

The White Sox continued their pursuit of mound help with short- and long-reliever acquisitions. They added free-agent right-hander Dave Robertson as their closer for the next four years at $46 million, then traded right-hander Andre Rienzo (a native of Brazil) to the Marlins for left-handed middle reliever Dan Jennings. Robertson, after seven effective seasons with the Yankees as both a set-up man and closer, was made available after New York opted for a higher-profile closer, signing left-hander Andrew Miller away from the Orioles before the meetings. While Robertson had established himself as a respectable closer with 39 saves and a 1.06 WHIP in 2014, Yankees GM Brian Cashman was betting instead on a lethal righty/lefty late-inning combination of budding star Dellin Betances and Miller, who would be converted from the set-up to the closing role in the Bronx in 2015. Betances was coming off a spectacular rookie season (5-0, 1.40 ERA, 13.5 strikeouts per nine innings, 5.63 strikeouts per walk), while Miller, after a rather subpar beginning to his major-league career in Detroit and Miami, had put it all together in 2014 with a 0.80 WHIP and 14.9 strikeouts per nine innings for the Red Sox and Orioles.

Arguably the most active team of the week was the Miami Marlins, who were largely unsuccessful in wooing their not-so-faithful to the new ballpark they had opened in 2012. Marlins GM Michael Hill first executed a multiplayer deal with the Los Angeles Dodgers that primarily brought righty Dan Haren, second baseman Dee Gordon, and platoon infielder Miguel Rojas to South Florida for fellow platoon infielder Enrique Hernandez and southpaw Andrew Heaney.[2] The next day the Marlins acquired a workhorse, prying 26-year-old right-handed pitcher Mat Latos away from Cincinnati for right-handed prospect Anthony DeSclafani and minor-league catcher Chad Wallach. In his first six seasons in the majors with the Padres and Reds, Latos had thrown over 900 innings and won 60 games, but had been somewhat rushed back to the rotation by the Reds in 2014 after arthroscopic knee surgery. The Marlins assumed that a healthy and productive Latos would eventually provide a formidable one-two punch with their budding phenom, right-hander Jose Fernandez. A particularly unfortunate ending to this plan unfolded over the next two seasons, though, as injuries continued to erode Latos's velocity, and Fernandez was killed in a boating accident in September 2016 at the age of 24.

Having already lured Joe Maddon to manage the team, the Chicago Cubs then landed one of the most significant free agents off the market when they signed left-hander Jon Lester to a seven-year, $155 million deal at the end of the week.[3] The arrangement reunited Lester with his former Red Sox GM, Theo Epstein, who was in the thick of his most ambitious effort yet in building the Cubs from the ground up. Until this point, Epstein had not had the luxury of the near-blank checkbook he enjoyed in his prior role with Boston, but new Cubs owner Tom Ricketts had begun to show signs that the team was ready to take the next step in adding some high-end payroll. The move would pay off two years later, with Lester as the staff ace on the squad that finally brought a World Series banner to the North Side of town after a 108-year drought.

The bid from the Red Sox to regain Lester, whom they had swapped to Oakland at the 2014 trade deadline, fell about $20 million short. GM Ben Cherington opted instead to pursue mid-rotation assets Wade Miley, a left-hander and Rick Porcello, a righty. Boston also rolled the free-agent dice to bring back oft-injured right-hander Justin Masterson, their former second-round draft pick who had been traded to the Indians five years before. Miley was acquired in a trade with Arizona that cost right-handers Rubby De La Rosa and Allen Webster and minor-league infielder Raymel Flores. Porcello came from the Tigers in exchange for emerging Cuban star outfielder Yoenis Cespedes (acquired in midseason from Oakland in the Lester deal), right-handed middle reliever Alex Wilson, and minor-league southpaw Gabe Speier. The results were mixed: Masterson was released after just half a season in Fenway, Miley was traded to the Seattle Mariners after one season, but Porcello (after inking a four-year, $82 million contract despite a subpar 2015) won the Cy Young Award for the Red Sox in 2016 after posting a 22-4 record, 3.15 ERA, and a league-leading 5.91 strikeout-to-walk ratio. The Red Sox had also signed third baseman-first baseman Pablo Sandoval for six years ($107 million) and infielder-outfielder Hanley Ramirez for five years ($110 million) prior to the meetings, making them a popular pick to go from worst to first again, just as they had done from 2012 to 2013.

Apart from the Masterson signing, perhaps the single riskiest free-agent move of the week came from the Dodgers' landing right-hander Brandon McCarthy for four years and $48 million. McCarthy finished 2014 strong after being traded from the Diamondbacks to the Yankees (7-5, 2.89 ERA, 6.3 strikeouts per walk in his final 14 starts), but was already 30 years old and hadn't won more than nine games in any prior season. He appeared in just 14 games the next two seasons at Chavez Ravine, and proved to be just one of several shaky moves made by Dodgers general manager Andrew Friedman. In addition to the trading away of Dee Gordon, he swapped a still-productive Matt Kemp to the Padres a week later following nine productive years, then signed 36-year-old Jimmy Rollins to be their everyday shortstop, all of which left the Dodgers as one of the winter's losers. Friedman had been named Executive of the Year in 2008 after making the Tampa Bay Rays an AL pennant winner despite having the second-lowest payroll in all of baseball ($43.8 million), and now, having been successfully wooed by the Dodgers, found himself managing a $235 million budget in an attempt to overtake the Giants.

It's also worth noting two other top free-agent signings of the winter, although they did not take place during the meetings themselves. Outfielder Giancarlo Stanton decided to stay with the Marlins, an easy decision when they offered a record 13 years and $325 million. Just 25 years old, the 6-foot-6, 245-pound Stanton had all the makings of becoming the LeBron James of baseball, yet in his first five full seasons none of his stats had been eye-popping except for how hard he hit the baseball. (His exit velocity was regularly above 100 mph, often at launch angles of around 20 degrees, an enticing combination of bat speed and strength.) He had, however, also come off a nearly catastrophic season-ending injury after being hit in the face with a fastball by the Brewers' Mike Fiers in September, making the magnitude of this contract quite risky. Meanwhile, right-hander Max Scherzer signed with the Washington Nationals for a comparatively diminutive $210 million over seven years. Coming off two consecutive years as the AL leader in wins while with the Tigers, Scherzer had collected 230 strikeouts or more in each of the prior three seasons and had won the Cy Young Award in 2013. In his first season with the Nats, 2015, he struck out 16 Brewers in a 4-0 shutout, and then in his next start tossed a no-hitter, coming within single strike of a perfect game against the Pirates. The following season he became just the fourth pitcher in history to strike out 20 batters in a nine-inning game, punishing his former Tigers team in the process, and eventually winning another Cy Young Award. The Nationals, no doubt, consider their investment in Scherzer to be money well spent.

The game also continued to evolve off the field that winter, starting at the top, where baseball was changing commissioners for the first time in 20 years. Bud Selig had manned the post since late in 1992, and though the labor strife of 1994-95 was a black mark on his record, he also was instrumental in reorganizing the leagues and introducing interleague play, playoff expansion, the implementation of instant replay for umpiring decisions, and the creation of the World Baseball Classic. He had also introduced a revenue-sharing model to the game, a concept that had helped lower-payroll franchises bid for free agents, creating more parity in the majors. He was elected to the Hall of Fame in 2016.

The torch was now being passed to Rob Manfred, a Harvard lawyer who had been MLB's chief operating officer since 2013. He had represented baseball owners

> ## GLASS CEILING OR OUTFIELD WALL?
>
> In addition to the other lawsuits filed against MLB in 2014, Sylvia Lind, an employee since 1995, filed suit on December 11 against the Office of the Commissioner, Commisioner Bud Selig, and Frank Robinson. According to the suit, Lind was the highest-ranking Hispanic female at the time, and she charged the defendants with illegal discrimination that included accusations of:
>
> - A poor working relationship with Robinson, which included his neglect of reading her memos, and a sitdown at the 2012 Winter Meetings to let her know she wasn't communicating enough with him.
> - An all-negative and unsubstantiated performance evaluation of Lind by Robinson.
> - Unwarranted reassignment of job duties, including her removal from working on the Futures Game.
> - Rumored drinking and missing of meetings.
> - Direction to work with a non-MLB employee (i.e., Robinson's daughter).
> - A second performance review, positive when discussed orally, but negative when presented in written form; and leading to Lind responding with notice that Robinson's actions were discriminatory in nature, on the basis of age, gender, and national origin. She wrote, "It's unfortunate that my supervisor views the evaluation process as an opportunity for character assassination. What is contained here is merely a pretextual attempt to dismiss my considerable skills and qualifications and justify his supplanting me with a young white male."
> - Retaliatory disciplinary action.

during the 1994 strike, and negotiated the game's first drug-testing program in 2002. It was clear that one of Manfred's charges would be to provide a firmer stance against the use of performance-enhancing drugs (PEDs) than had his predecessor. Baseball's drug-testing program became among the most stringent in professional sports. Upon failing a test, players are suspended for half the season without pay, and there are over 100 banned substances and stimulants on its radar. Manfred would also oversee changes to the All-Star Game, primarily by ending its role as the determinant of home-field advantage in the World Series, and also leveraging a bidding process among cities to host the game each year. He also helped streamline player recruitment from Cuba, which for more than two generations had endured stringent restrictions due to the enmity between the U.S. and Cuba. Despite a concentration of talent few countries could match, only 95 Cuban players had played in the major leagues since the U.S. imposed sanctions against Cuba in 1961. New relaxed regulations would introduce potential new stars like Yasiel Puig, Jose Abreu, and Yoan Moncada. Also under consideration was the banning of the infield shift, as well as the inclusion of a 20-second pitch clock to speed up games.

From a legal standpoint, baseball was also dealing with a major antitrust issue related to how the sport divides up its broadcast territories. A class-action lawsuit known as *Garber v. Office of the Commissioner of Baseball* accused MLB of violating the Sherman Antitrust Act with its blackout and television policies, effectively giving teams monopolies in their territories.

- Unprofessional slanderous conduct.
- A blatant discriminatory remark.

Almost all the allegations were denied by MLB and the case ultimately was settled out of court. What MLB admitted, however, was that Lind was one of the highest-ranking Hispanic females in a management position, and that MLB had not appointed a Hispanic female to an executive position. Its response acknowledged that there were no fewer than 52 individuals holding the title of vice president or above at MLB Properties and the Office of the Commissioner. Additionally, MLB admitted that it had no knowledge of a Hispanic female in a vice president or above position, either currently, or in the previous 19 years.

In 2015, MLB dissolved the baseball development division, which had been created in 2012, and reassigned Robinson to senior adviser to the commissioner, as well as honorary American League president.

1   Sylvia Lind v. Major League Baseball Office of the Commissioner, Allan H. "Bud" Selig, and Frank Robinson, Case 1:14-cv-09786-PAC in the U.S. District Court for the Southern District of New York, Document 1 (December 11, 2014).

2   Sylvia Lind v. Office of the Commissioner of Baseball an unincorporated association doing business as Major League Baseball, Allan H. "Bud" Selig, and Frank Robinson, Answer to the first amended complaint, Case 1:14-cv-09786-PAC in the U.S. District Court for the Southern District of New York, Document 17 (March 30, 2015); Suevon Lee, "Female MLB Staffer, League Agree to Drop Discrimination Suit," *Law360.com*, April 6, 2016, law360.com/articles/781625/female-mlb-staffer-league-agree-to-drop-discrimination-suit. Accessed October 5, 2017.

3   Sylvia Lind v. Office of the Commissioner of Baseball an unincorporated association doing business as Major League Baseball, Allan H. "Bud" Selig, and Frank Robinson, Answer to the first amended complaint, Case 1:14-cv-09786-PAC in the U.S. District Court for the Southern District of New York, Document 17 (March 30, 2015).

4   Associated Press, "Frank Robinson Gives Up MLB EVP Job, Becomes Adviser," *USA Today*, February 2, 2015; "Frank Robinson Named Executive Vice President, Baseball Development," MLB.com, June 26, 2012, m.mlb.com/news/article/33955754/frank-robinson-named-executive-vice-president-baseball-development/. Accessed October 5, 2017.

The blackout rules are unpopular with fans, but are critical to MLB's operating model. Teams are able to generate sometimes hundreds of millions of dollars in local television revenue by offering regional cable networks exclusive local telecast rights. If the policy were struck down in court, each team would have to renegotiate its local contract, which would cost millions of dollars in broadcast fees. After U.S. Appeals Court Judge Shira A. Scheindlin ruled that baseball's historic antitrust exemption did not apply to the case, it was allowed to proceed to trial.[4] The practical issue at hand for the fans was the lack of ability to watch a game of their choice while outside the market to which they have subscribed. If a fan in Boston, for instance, had subscribed to NESN to watch the Red Sox, and then found himself in Seattle for the weekend wanting to stream his team over the internet, he felt entitled to do so because he had already paid for the privilege. Major League Baseball, however, felt that the customer should have to pay a surcharge for watching the game anywhere outside New England. Perhaps a more pitiful example was that of someone in Iowa who would be part of the "home market" for no fewer than six teams. That person would arguably have been a fool to subscribe to MLB Extra Innings or MLB.TV, which were intended to give customers a multitude of live games, as long as the games did not include a team within their market. The Iowan would have no luck seeing the Cubs, White Sox, Brewers, Royals, Twins, or Cardinals without getting access to local noncable channels from those markets. Perhaps because technology and customer mobility made it very possible that the case would be decided in favor of the consumer, compromise prevailed a year later when the case was settled out of court just moments before the trial was scheduled to commence. While the blackouts would continue, MLB.TV subscribers would gain a 15 percent saving on their package, at least through 2020. Comcast and DirecTV would also offer a 12.5 percent discount on MLB Extra Innings through 2017.

MLB was also battling a team relocation case brought about by the city of San Jose, California, which was contesting the league's antitrust claims in preventing the Oakland A's from moving to the city. The Supreme Court, in rejecting San Jose's appeal of an adverse ruling from the US Court of Appeals, cited previous exemptions granted to the majors, which only a high court or Congress could change.[4] MLB lawyers indicated to the Supreme Court that San Jose was asking to unravel "a question that has been firmly settled for decades." While San Jose is about equidistant from both Oakland and San Francisco, it is deemed by MLB to be Giants territory.

Even on the minor-league front a legal battle was brewing, as a federal suit, *Senne v. Office of the Commissioner of Major League Baseball*, was filed on behalf of 34 plaintiffs in the Northern District of California alleging violation of wage and hour laws. Players signed to minor-league contracts are paid far less than their major-league counterparts; the highest Triple-A salary at the times was $10,750 over the course of about 1,296 hours, or about $8.29 per hour. The case ultimately was closed on July 21, 2016, in favor of Major League Baseball, sustaining minor-league pay at its relatively paltry levels.[6]

When all was said and done, the 2014 Winter Meetings had become a big part of one of the game's most unusual offseasons in recent years. Two small-market teams, the Padres and Marlins, were in the middle of it all, adding high-profile players, while the one that typically operates in a different financial stratosphere, the Yankees, were relatively dormant. Chicago had also suddenly rendered New York and Los Angeles second cities, with both teams jockeying to shake off what had been generally losing cultures for over half a century. In a minor subplot, Yankees third baseman Alex Rodriguez was also readying his return after being suspended for the entire 2014 season for taking a multitude of PEDs and then lying about it. A-Rod was hoping to continue his pursuit of the 3,000-hit milestone, as well as fourth place on the all-time home-run list. Opening Day 2015 couldn't arrive fast enough.

SOURCES

Consulted in addition to those cited in the Notes:

Baseball-Reference.com, Major League Statistics and Information. baseball-reference.com.

Bergin, Mark, July 13, 2017 wtsp.com/sports/mlb/why-a-pitch-clock-is-coming-to-major-league-baseball-in-2018/456184169.

Catania, Jason, December 11, 2014. bleacherreport.com/articles/2295655-biggest-winners-and-losers-of-the-2014-mlb-winter-meetings.

Fucilli, David, February 11, 2016. sbnation.com/mlb/2016/2/11/10966352/mlb-tv-lawsuit-settlement-details-extra-innings-mlb-tv-packages-cheaper.

Glazer, Adam J., March 29, 2017. sfnr.com/news/2017/4/12/minor-leaguers-have-ninth-inning-rally-have-chance-for-minimum-wage.

Grow, Nathaniel, January 20, 2016. fangraphs.com/blogs/mlb-settles-tv-lawsuit-preserves-blackouts/.

Justice, Richard, December 12, 2014. sportsonearth.com/article/103869670/2014-mlb-winter-meetings-grades.

MacPherson, Brian, February 21, 2015. providencejournal.com/article/20150221/SPORTS/150229787.

Norris, Josh, July 22, 2016. baseballamerica.com/news/major-league-baseball-scores-win-minor-league-litigation/#TFxfC8otCfA6GkIo.97.

Sanchez, Jesse, December 17, 2014. m.mlb.com/news/article/104325146/shift-in-united-states-cuban-relations-may-affect-major-league-baseball/.

Somolokov, Alex, February 9, 2015. fanragsports.com/mlb/2014-15-mlb-offseason-one-ages/page/984/.

Stark, Jayson, December 12, 2014. espn.com/mlb/story/_/id/12015896/mlb-winter-meetings-winners-losers.

Thurm, Wendy, February 3, 2015. deadspin.com/mlbs-awful-blackout-rules-are-finally-under-attack-in-c-1683259431.

Wells, Adam, May 19, 2016. bleacherreport.com/articles/2641207-rob-manfred-comments-on-ped-speculation-mlb-testing-and-more.

milb.com/milb/events/winter_meetings/y2014/agenda_events.jsp.

baseballhall.org/hof/selig-bud.

NOTES

1. Beane was nonetheless promoted to executive vice president of baseball operations after the 2015 season.

2. Right-hander Chris Hatcher and utilityman Austin Barnes also moved from Miami to Los Angeles. Gordon, who led the NL in triples (12) and stolen bases (64) in 2014 along with earning an All-Star Game appearance, went on to swipe 58 more and lead the NL in hitting (.333) the following season. Haren spent just half the 2015 campaign in Miami before being moved to the Cubs in a minor midseason trade and retiring after a 13-year career.

3. The acquisition was then supplemented by adding Lester's "designated catcher," David Ross, to a two-year, $5 million contract.

4. Shira A. Scheindlin, September 14, 2002, scholar.google.com/scholar_case?case=13043734529765955884&q=garber+v.+office+of+the+commissioner+of+baseball&hl=en&as_sdt=6,34&as_vis=1.

5. Howard Mintz, October 5, 2015, mercurynews.com/2015/10/05/san-jose-loses-legal-fight-against-mlb-over-oakland-as-plan/.

6. Josh Norris, July 22, 2016, baseballamerica.com/news/major-league-baseball-scores-win-minor-league-litigation/#TFxfC8otCfA6GkIo.97.

— 2015 —
THE MUSIC CITY PLAYS GRACIOUS HOST TO BASEBALL'S WINTER MEETINGS FOR THE SEVENTH TIME

By Wayne G. McDonnell Jr.

THE 114TH ANNUAL BASEBALL WINTER Meetings were held in Nashville at the Gaylord Opryland Resort and Convention Center from December 7 to 10, 2015. The 700,000-square-foot resort had played host to baseball on six previous occasions (1983, 1989, 1998, 2002, 2007, and 2012) and the festive holiday ambiance eloquently blended into the background as the game's executives strategically pursued desirable free agents and blockbuster trades. By the time the baseball circus had left the Music City, several ballclubs had vastly improved their chances for postseason glory. However, games are never won or lost on paper in the middle of the winter.

Before the Meetings, several clubs were very active in the free-agent market. Many writers and analysts were amazed at how quickly the Detroit Tigers' executive vice president of baseball operations and general manager, Al Avila agreed to terms with right-handed pitcher Jordan Zimmermann on a five-year, $110 million contract. The deal for the Washington Nationals' two-time All-Star included a full no-trade clause through the first three years of the contract. The amazement continued when another All-Star righty, Johnny Cueto, reportedly turned down a six-year contract from the Arizona Diamondbacks in the neighborhood of $120 million. Cueto and his agent, Bryce Dixon, seemed confident in the free-agent market and believed there would be additional suitors with more lucrative offers for Cueto's services. It was assumed he was seeking a contract in the vicinity of $140 million to $160 million. While you won't find Cueto's name atop any of the key statistical categories for the 2015 season, his achievements from the 2014 season were still fresh in the minds of many evaluating his talents. Also, splitting time between the American and National leagues after the July 26, 2015, trade from the Cincinnati Reds to the Kansas City Royals may have had an impact on his season as well.

Without question, pitching was a topic of considerable conversation at the conclusion of the 2015 season. It was, for instance, anticipated that southpaw David Price would become a very wealthy man, and this became a fact when the Boston Red Sox signed the 2012 American League Cy Young Award winner to a seven-year, $217 million contract on December 4. This move sent the free-agent market for starting pitchers into overdrive as Boston's new president of baseball operations, Dave Dombrowski, was already rebuilding a pitching rotation that had accumulated the second worst earned-run average (4.31) in the American League in 2015. With an average annual value of $31 million and an opt-out clause at the conclusion of the third season (2018) at the age of 33, Price's contract had redefined the compensation package for elite starting pitchers. However, his reign atop the average annual value leader board was short-lived thanks to right-hander Zack Greinke. The 2015 National League Cy Young Award runner-up (and 2009 American League winner) signed a six-year, $206.5 million contract with the Arizona Diamondbacks, for an estimated average annual value of $34,416,666. (After deferrals, the present-day value of the contract was actually closer to $194.5 million.)

As well-traveled baseball writers, network analysts, and credentialed media from across the world began to settle in for four days of nonstop action and sleepless nights chasing rumors, many were astonished at what had already occurred during the offseason. The dominoes had quickly fallen into place as franchises aggressively signed desirable starting pitchers to nine-figure contracts prior to baseball's pilgrimage to Nashville. Upon arrival, it seemed as if some of the buzz had temporarily subsided as the media was trying to figure out what would be happening next with regard to starting pitchers. And immediately rumors began circulating throughout the resort concerning the Los Angeles Dodgers' perceived interest in the Miami Marlins' right-handed phenomenon José Fernandez, as well as a potential blockbuster trade that would significantly bolster a bullpen already headlined by Kenley Jansen.

Then, seemingly within a moment's notice on the first morning of the Meetings, the Dodgers looked to be on the verge of acquiring the Cincinnati Reds' ace closer, Cuban-born southpaw Aroldis Chapman, via a trade. According to MLB's Statcast 2015 leader board, Chapman's four-seam fastball eclipsed 102 miles per hour on 50 occasions during the regular season. Also, he had faced 278 batters in 2015 and struck out 116. Simultaneously, as most of the media was dealing with this potential bombshell, the Pre-Integration Era Committee of the National Baseball Hall of Fame and Museum was beginning its press conference. Once it was learned that the 16-member committee had failed to elect any of the 10 candidates, the focus around the Delta Ballroom immediately shifted to the potent bullpen the Dodgers could have with both Jansen and Chapman. Of course, it was also noted that the Dodgers would be creating a new problem for themselves, with two closers looking to pitch in meaningful situations at the end of games, to say nothing of both of them being eligible for free agency after the 2016 season.

The excitement surrounding the rumored Chapman trade immediately changed once news leaked that he had been involved in a physical altercation with his girlfriend in October in which eight gunshots were allegedly fired. Ultimately, because of conflicting stories and a lack of cooperation by all of the interested parties, there were no arrests. However, under the game's new domestic-violence policy, it was likely that Chapman would receive some form of punishment from MLB, which was probably why the Dodgers backed off. In fact, many now viewed Chapman as damaged goods and within an instant his trade value began to plummet.

Chapman's former manager with the Cincinnati Reds, Dusty Baker, was at the epicenter of a controversy involving comments he made regarding the veracity of the domestic violence allegations. Baker said he did not "believe reports" involving Chapman and domestic violence. He defended his former relief pitcher and said he wasn't someone who should judge what had occurred between Chapman and his girlfriend. Baker was ebullient in his praise of Chapman as a person, ballplayer, and family man. Baker did acknowledge that he hadn't read the allegations against Chapman. However, he did support the new domestic-violence policy. Hours after the comments, the Washington Nationals tweeted a clarification regarding Baker's previous comments. According to an interview on MLB Network Radio, Baker would never condone domestic violence and expressed a hope that Chapman would be found innocent of the allegations.

Baker's controversy didn't end with Chapman. In a conversation regarding speed in the game, Baker discussed the importance of left-handed pitching and hitting. He said there was a better chance of getting speed from ballplayers of Latin and African-American descent. Baker was of the belief that he wasn't being racist, but speaking from the perspective of this is how it is in the game.

But the Chapman controversy did not let the Pre-Integration Era Committee off the hook, and they were left to answer some difficult questions. The committee featured four Hall of Famers, four major-league executives, and eight historians and veteran members of the media, but no one was elected.[1] Doc Adams was the only candidate to get double-digit votes (10) for 62.5 percent,[2] while both infielder Bill Dahlen and first baseman-outfielder Harry Stovey each received eight votes. The other seven candidates received three or fewer votes.

After the announcement, one got the sense from the reporters attending the press conference that another overhaul of the voting process needed to occur when it came to the three newly formed committees (Pre-Integration, Golden Era, and Expansion). The last time the Pre-Integration Committee had met was in December 2012 at the Winter Meetings in Nashville, when umpire Hank O'Day, former Yankees owner Jacob Ruppert, and third baseman-catcher Deacon White each received the necessary 75 percent for induction. However, this was the second consecutive year that an election-based committee had failed to produce a single candidate worthy of enshrinement. In December 2014, the Golden Era Committee failed to elect anyone, with both Tony Oliva and Dick Allen falling one vote shy of the required 75 percent. Thus, there were strong feelings of disappointment and a few were even outraged by the results of the election.[3]

During the afternoon of Day One at the Winter Meetings, Commissioner Rob Manfred entered the Delta Ballroom with his usual entourage of executives, as well as a face familiar to everyone. Cal Ripken Jr. was now a prominent member of the commissioner's traveling party. In his first year as commissioner, Manfred had made it abundantly clear to everyone that he had a deep commitment to youth engagement and participation in baseball. His exuberance regarding this topic was first witnessed in March 2015 when he announced the appointment of Tony Reagins as senior vice president for youth programs. Reagins, a former longtime executive of the Los Angeles Angels of Anaheim, had been charged with being the point person overseeing and expanding baseball's youth participation. A sense of importance accompanied this appointment once it was determined that Reagins would be reporting directly to Tony Petitti, Major League Baseball's chief operating officer.[4]

In the summer of 2015, Major League Baseball and U.S.A. Baseball proudly announced an innovative partnership on a baseball field in the shadows of Yankee Stadium. The "Play Ball" initiative was created to encourage various levels of youth participation. Access, engagement, participation, and physical activity were the principal tenets of the initiative. In its purest form, "Play Ball" is a proactive attempt at cultivating a grassroots approach to solving a legitimate problem that has been felt in both urban and suburban communities across the country. With the influx of sports, entertainment, and technology options available to children, the groups said, it was imperative that baseball make an aggressive attempt at reclaiming a significant portion of this audience through exciting programs and fun activities aimed at active engagement.[5]

Major and Minor League Baseball have partnered with the United States Conference of Mayors to bring the initiative to life across the country. It was taken to 125 cities in 34 states plus Washington, D.C. and Puerto Rico during August 2015. Simple things such as a game of catch or even running the bases were encouraged in communities. Commissioner Manfred's persistence was indeed converting naysayers into believers, but "Play Ball" still needed more support. Another highly regarded voice pushing the message even further for Major League Baseball was needed and it came in the form of an "Iron Man."

Cal Ripken Jr. had been a champion of youth baseball since his retirement from the Baltimore Orioles in 2001. The Hall of Famer has diligently worked to create an environment where young athletes can excel while learning the benefits of community and commitment. He was the perfect advocate for "Play Ball" and it was announced in Nashville that Ripken would become the senior adviser on youth programs. His appointment only enhanced Commissioner Manfred's vision for youth participation. It was announced that Ripken would oversee all aspects of policy development for the initiative as well as make appearances on behalf of the commissioner.

The primary goal for Manfred and Ripken always will revert back to increasing youth participation and the overall competitiveness of children playing the sport. During the press conference, Ripken stressed early exposure and allowing children to participate in multiple sports. He reiterated how important basketball and soccer were to him in his development as an athlete and baseball player.

As Day One wrapped up, the Seattle Mariners acquired left-hander Wade Miley and right-hander Jonathan Aro from the Boston Red Sox for right-hander Carson Smith and southpaw Roenis Elias. The key players in the deal were Miley and Smith. In his five seasons in the major leagues, Miley had made one All-Star team and won in double figures three times, but also had only one complete game in 134 starts and allowed more hits (850) than innings pitched (832⅓). Smith, meanwhile, had become the Mariners' closer in only his first full season in the majors. In another transaction, the Kansas City Royals re-signed one of their free agents, right-handed pitcher Chris Young, to a two-year, $11.5 million contract with a mutual option for the 2018 season at $8 million, with a $1.5 million buyout.

Day Two of the Winter Meetings could be best described as a calm day punctuated by a flurry of dinnertime activity.

MLB's chief baseball officer, Joe Torre, discussed the importance of a rules change to protect middle infielders. Baserunners have always tried to prevent double plays when sliding into second base and it's the middle infielders who have been exposed to injuries. Torre made it clear that he wanted to work with the Major League Baseball Players Association on developing a rule to address this matter. The 2015 National League Division Series incident between Chase Utley of the Los Angeles Dodgers and Ruben Tejada of the New York Mets ignited cries for reform after Tejada's leg was broken in the encounter with Utley sliding aggressively into second base.

Safety at ballparks for fans as well has always been a matter of great concern. The proliferation of injuries due to foul balls compelled MLB to conduct a study and it recommended that all major-league clubs expand netting in their ballparks. A protective barrier of some kind was the overwhelming recommendation since baseball fans sit extremely close to the action. Foul balls and broken bats find their way into the stands with great regularity and it is important that fans have safe choices as to where they want to sit at a ballpark. The hard part is to balance the unique baseball experiences that accompany the close proximity to the field as well as safety. Education is always a critical part of the process and it was recommended that ballclubs constantly communicate with their fans about remaining alert as well as safe places to sit in a ballpark. The Philadelphia Phillies were the first club to announce their desire to comply with the recommendations at both their spring-training facility as well as Citizens Bank Park. The Boston Red Sox, Los Angeles Dodgers, Chicago Cubs, and Tampa Bay Rays publicly supported the recommendation and intended to comply with expanding netting at their ballparks. Some clubs were already in compliance with the recommendations from the study. Even Minor League Baseball endorsed the recommendations and was encouraging implementation among its ballclubs.

For most of the day, hundreds of media members had been anxiously awaiting news regarding free agent Ben Zobrist's decision and its effect on both the free-agent market and several proposed trades. For a while it had seemed as if the New York Mets and the Washington Nationals were the finalists for the services of the multitalented Zobrist. With a rare sighting of Jeff Wilpon, the chief operating officer of the Mets, there was a strong sense among the media that Zobrist was on his way to wearing the orange and blue. The rumor circulating throughout the resort was that Zobrist was in line for a contract similar to that of outfielder Curtis Granderson in terms of both years (four) and value ($60 million).

Just before dinner, Mets manager Terry Collins met with the media, confirmed the rumor that he was texting with Zobrist, and reiterated his desire to secure the services of the quintessential utility player. (Having become an attractive franchise once again due to their run to the 2015 World Series, all things Mets were now drawing considerable media attention.) Collins was clearly enamored with Zobrist and the versatility that he could bring to the Mets, but Zobrist broke the hearts of Collins and the Flushing faithful by signing with the Cubs. He received a four-year, $56 million contract and the opportunity to reunite with his former Tampa manager, Joe Maddon.

After Collins had departed the Delta Ballroom, Yankees manager Joe Girardi met with the media and spent a noticeable portion of his allotted 20 minutes talking about options at second base. Girardi reiterated that there would be an open competition in spring training between Dustin Ackley and Rob Refsnyder. He wasn't opposed to a platoon scenario, but his ultimate preference was obviously defensive prowess. In 2015, the Yankees had used six second basemen and not one had a positive Ultimate Zone Rating (UZR).[6] This statistic has become popular when evaluating a ballplayer's defense. According to MLB.com, UZR takes into account all aspects of a ballplayer's defensive performance and makes an honest attempt at measuring how many runs he has saved for his team. There are four key aspects of the statistic: errors, range, outfield arm, and double-play ability. Girardi felt that developing middle infielders was quite difficult in an era of defensive shifts on every pitch and advanced analytics.

It became clear that Girardi wasn't at all comfortable with the instability at second base. Every other position around the diamond had security for the Yankees, but second base was still an enigma that weighed heavily on him. Neither Ackley nor Refsnyder was viewed as a prototypical major-league second baseman, even though Ackley had played 291 games and over 2,500 innings at the position for both the Yankees and the Seattle Mariners through the 2015 season. And any time Refsnyder had been mentioned in conversations, a focus on his offensive prowess clearly superseded his obvious deficiencies at second base. He was referred to as a ballplayer who could one day grow into the position, but would always be viewed as an offensive second baseman.

Earlier in the day, Cubs manager Joe Maddon was effusive in his praise for Zobrist as well as his own second baseman, Starlin Castro. He discussed the importance of utility ballplayers to teams and how there should be a special roster spot created for them on the All-Star teams. Maddon stressed how it takes a selfless attitude to be a truly special utility ballplayer. He was complimentary of Castro and the transition he had to make during the season (moving from shortstop to second base). However, Maddon was quick to point out that Castro not only had the arm, but also the footwork and lateral movements to be a highly effective second baseman. It appeared as if Maddon was selling Castro to the media just in case the Cubs parted ways with him. With the emergence of the pre-arbitration-eligible Addison Russell, Castro—who was owed $37 million over four seasons (2016-2019), plus a $16 million club option for 2020 (with a $1 million buyout)—obviously had become expendable.

As many gathered for meals and socializing, the Yankees and Cubs were finalizing a trade that sent Castro to the Yankees for right-handed pitcher Adam Warren and a player to be named later (shortstop Brendan Ryan). Castro's contract added $7 million to the Yankees' payroll in 2016, while Ryan's $1 million player option for 2016, as well as Warren's first year of arbitration eligibility, became the responsibility of the Cubs.

The deal, which set up a double-play combination of Didi Gregorius and Castro, provided the Yankees with a sense of infield security. Meanwhile, the acquisitions of Warren and Ryan were only the first step in what would become a very busy and exciting series of events for the Cubs. The same day they signed veteran free-agent right-handed pitcher John Lackey to a two-year, $32 million contract. It seemed as if the Cubs and the Yankees ultimately won on Day Two of the Winter Meetings, while it was back to the drawing board for the Mets and their quest for a second baseman they could call their own.

The Mets didn't wallow in misery over the loss of Zobrist for too long. On Day Three, they traded left-handed pitcher Jon Niese to the Pittsburgh Pirates for second baseman Neil Walker. It was now all but certain that postseason hero Daniel Murphy would not be returning to the Mets, and they needed to land a quality ballplayer immediately to play second base. Walker had a slightly better Ultimate Zone Rating (UZR) of -0.2 than Murphy's -1.3 at second base in 2015.[7]

The big news on Day Three involved the Atlanta Braves and Arizona Diamondbacks. Already having made a big splash with signing Greinke, the Diamondbacks decided to adopt the "win now" mentality by trading for right-handed pitcher Shelby Miller. With Los Angeles and San Francisco constantly battling for control of both the National League West and pitching supremacy within the division, the Diamondbacks felt they needed another quality starter to complement Greinke and southpaw Patrick Corbin. However, the franchise did give up a significant amount of talent to secure a pitcher with a .478 winning percentage and a career Wins Above Replacement (WAR) of 9.1 (2.3 average per season). The Diamondbacks parted ways with outfielder Ender Inciarte, right-handed pitcher (and 2013 first-round draft pick) Aaron Blair, and the number-one overall pick in the 2015 amateur draft, Vanderbilt shortstop Dansby Swanson. The Diamondbacks did receive their fair share of criticism for this move as many felt that parting ways with Swanson was risky and a short-term gain for a potential long-term loss.

Not to be outdone, the Giants agreed to a five-year, $90 million contract with free-agent pitcher Jeff Samardzija. Durability had been a hallmark of the right-hander's career, a highly attractive quality to many franchises looking to capitalize on this currently rare trait in a starting pitcher. Also, Samardzija had been a full-time starter only since the 2012 season and had thrown only 2,998 pitches (3.91 pitches per plate appearance) over the first four years of his career while he was primarily a reliever with the Cubs (2008-2011).[8] Samardzija's skills, the Giants thought, fit perfectly as a number two in a rotation behind the likes of an ace like lefty Madison Bumgarner.

Day Three saw a couple of other significant trades. The Milwaukee Brewers sent first baseman Adam Lind to the Seattle Mariners for Carlos Herrera, Daniel Missaki, and Freddy Peralta, a trio of minor-league right-handers. The Oakland Athletics traded third baseman Brett Lawrie to the Chicago White Sox for two minor-league pitchers, right-hander J.B. Wendelken and lefty Zack Erwin. The Mets also agreed to terms with free-agent infielder Asdrubal Cabrera on a two-year, $18.5 million contract, with a club option for a third year at $8.5 million with a $2 million buyout. However, this deal wasn't officially announced until the day after everyone had left Nashville.

New Miami Marlins manager Don Mattingly met with the media on Day Three and was peppered with questions regarding his team and its hitting coach. Though Mattingly tried to discuss the process he was using to evaluate the Marlins' roster, the reporters were more interested in his views on Barry Bonds. Mattingly shared with the gathered members of the media how Bonds became the Marlins hitting coach during a 90-minute meeting in New York. Mattingly clearly described the job to Bonds and wanted to make sure that he was engaged and fully aware of what he was getting into as a major-league coach.

Day Four of the Winter Meetings is traditionally known as the Rule 5 Draft day. Also, it is usually a getaway day for most members of the media. In the two rounds of the major-league phase, 11 clubs selected 16 players. Five clubs selected twice (Phillies, Reds, Brewers, Padres, and Angels) with outfielder Tyler Goeddel from the Tampa Bay Rays being selected first overall by the Philadelphia Phillies. In the Triple-A phase, 24 teams selected players in the first round. Over the course of five rounds, only the Los Angeles Dodgers had selected a ballplayer in each round. In the one round of the Double-A phase, the Miami Marlins selected a right-handed pitcher from the St. Louis Cardinals, Juan Caballero.

Minor League Baseball held a wide variety of informative events, seminars, and panels over the course of four days. Its president, Pat O'Conner, was re-elected for his third four-year term. He ran unopposed and had received unanimous support from all of the league presidents. The topic of diversity was an issue of great importance for Minor League Baseball too. Wendy Lewis, senior vice president of diversity and strategic alliances for Major League Baseball, sat on a panel entitled "Moving Diversity Forward." Having been an integral voice in the commissioner's office regarding diversity and inclusion, she was now spreading her message among all of the minor-league franchises.[9]

The Baseball Trade Show always attracts an extraordinary amount of interest from ballclubs, vendors, and members of the media, and 2015 proved to be no different. The annual Professional Baseball Employment Opportunities Job Fair, a major attraction for college students and other aspiring sports business professionals, served (as always) as a golden opportunity to secure one of the several internships or entry-level positions that are offered by minor-league ballclubs.

The Bob Freitas Business Seminar and Workshop series offered Minor League Baseball employees an opportunity to learn more about their business and to develop new skills. Over the course of three days, workshops were offered on wide-ranging subjects, from social media and nonbaseball events driving revenues, to analytics and effective management of online stores. Even the Society for American Baseball Research gave a presentation, led by Vince Gennaro and Marc Appleman, on how Minor League Baseball can use SABR as a resource.[10]

On Day One of the Winter Meetings, Minor League Baseball held its annual awards luncheon. Nine major awards and an Executive of the Year were given to owners, general managers, team presidents, vice presidents, and executive vice presidents from 15 different leagues. The South Bend Cubs of the Midwest League won the John H. Johnson President's Award. This award honors a "complete" baseball franchise that has demonstrated stability as well as significant contributions to its community, league and the baseball industry. Another Midwest League club, the Fort Wayne TinCaps, won the John H. Moss Community Service Award. Lindsey Knupp of the Lehigh Valley Iron Pigs won the Rawlings Women Executive of the Year Award.[11]

The key major-league activity from Day Four involved the Kansas City Royals bringing their former closer home by signing free-agent right-hander Joakim Soria to a three-year, $25 million contract, which also included a mutual option for a fourth year at $10 million with a $1 million buyout in 2019. And the Washington Nationals wrapped up a busy week by sending cash and third baseman Yunel Escobar to the Angels for right-handers Michael Brady and Trevor Gott.

SOURCES

The author attended the 2015 Winter Meetings and wrote this summary from his notes and articles written for *Forbes Sports Money* during the course of the meetings.

Baseball-Reference.com, Major League Statistics and Information. baseball-reference.com/players/s/samarjeo1-pitch.shtml (April 24, 2016).

Fangraphs.com, Major League Statistics and Information. fangraphs.com/leaders.aspx?pos=2b&stats=fld&lg=all&qual=0&type=1&season=2015&month=0&season1=2015&ind=0&team=9&rost=0&age=0&filter=&players=0

(April 24, 2016).

Fangraphs.com, Major League Statistics and Information. fangraphs.com/statss.aspx?playerid=7539&position=2B#fielding (April 24, 2016).

Fangraphs.com, Major League Statistics and Information. fangraphs.com/statss.aspx?playerid=4316&position=2B#fielding (April 24, 2016).

Hagen, Paul. MLB.com, December 9, 2015. Online, m.mlb.com/news/article/159233076/mlb-issues-recommendations-on-netting/

Hill, Benjamin. MiLB.com, December 9, 2015. Online, milb.com/news/article.jsp?ymd=20151209&content_id=159274622&fext=.jsp&vkey=news_milb.

James, Chelsea. *Washington Post*, December 8, 2015. Online, washingtonpost.com/news/nationals-journal/wp/2015/12/08/amid-uproar-dusty-baker-clarifies-aroldis-chapman-domestic-violence-comments/?utm_term=.307b3f64d231.

McDonnell, Wayne G. Jr. *Forbes Sports Money*, December 7, 2015. Online, forbes.com/sites/waynemcdonnell/2015/12/07/johnny-cueto-could-become-the-belle-of-the-ball-in-nashville/#2edea201431e April 2016.

—. *Forbes Sports Money*, December 7, 2015; online April 21, 2016. forbes.com/sites/waynemcdonnell/2015/12/07/the-iron-man-is-called-upon-to-assist-commissioner-manfreds-mlb-youth-initiatives/.

—. *Forbes Sports Money*, December 8, 2015. online April 21, 2016. forbes.com/sites/waynemcdonnell/2015/12/08/zobrists-deal-with-the-cubs-helps-solve-a-riddle-for-the-yankees-at-second-base/2/.

Sports Illustrated. si.com/mlb/2015/12/08/dusty-baker-aroldis-chapman-reds-domestic-violence-comments.

USA Today. usatoday.com/story/sports/mlb/2015/12/09/torre-mlb-hopes-for-new-rule-to-protect-middle-infielders/77023302/.

NOTES

1. The Hall of Famers were Bert Blyleven, Bobby Cox, Pat Gillick, and Phil Niekro; the executives were Chuck Armstrong, Bill DeWitt, Gary Hughes, and Tal Smith.

2. Adams was a true baseball pioneer. He was a pitcher and infielder, reputedly the first person to play shortstop, probably in the 1840s. He was president of the Knickerbocker Base Ball Club, and in that capacity in 1848, he headed the Committee to Revise the Constitution and By-Laws. He eventually left baseball to practice medicine. John Thorn, "Doc Adams," SABR Baseball Biography Project, (sabr.org/bioproj/person/14ec7492), undated, accessed April 22, 2016.

3. As indicated in the note on sources, this summary is based on the personal experience of the author working as a reporter at the 2015 Winter Meetings. Rather than document each conclusion with a separate endnote, all information reflects the author's observations unless otherwise noted.

4. Tony Reagins was appointed to the position in March 2015. Here is the press release: m.mlb.com/news/article/113123038/mlb-appoints-tony-reagins-as-svp-youth-programs

5. playball.org/ and usmayors.org/playball/.

6. Defensive statistics for the 2015 New York Yankees second basemen: fangraphs.com/leaders.aspx?pos=2b&stats=fld&lg=all&qual=0&type=1&season=2015&month=0&season1=2015&ind=0&team=9&rost=0&age=0&filter=&players=0.

7. Neil Walker and Daniel Murphy's defensive statistics for the 2015 season: fangraphs.com/statss.aspx?playerid=7539&position=2B#fielding and fangraphs.com/statss.aspx?playerid=4316&position=2B#fielding.

8. Jeff Samardzija's career statistics: baseball-reference.com/players/s/samarje01-pitch.shtml.

9. milb.com/news/article.jsp?ymd=20151209&content_id=159274622&fext=.jsp&vkey=news_milb.

10. bwm.milb.net/images/15/2015_Freitas_Schedule.pdf.

11. Summary of all of the 2015 award winners: milb.com/milb/events/winter_meetings/y2015/awards.jsp.

— 2016 —
HAS A NEW DIAMOND AGE BEGUN FOR BASEBALL?

by Charles H. Martin

Introduction

THE 2016 BASEBALL WINTER Meetings were held at the Gaylord National Resort and Convention Center in National Harbor, Maryland (December 4-8). The meetings took place 32 days after a thrilling Game Seven of the World Series between the Chicago Cubs and the Cleveland Indians. The game went into extra innings tied 6-6, and then was held up by a 17-minute rain delay. When play was resumed, Ben Zobrist's double and Miguel Montero's single scored two runs in the top of the 10th inning to lead the Cubs to an 8-7 victory, their first World Series Championship since 1908.

Hall of Fame and Other Announcements

The Eras Committee (formed in 1937 as the Veterans Committee) of the Baseball Hall of Fame evaluates managers, executives, umpires, and players passed over by the votes of the Baseball Writers Association of America. Four eras are evaluated separately: Early Baseball, 1871-1949; Golden Days, 1950-1969; Modern Baseball, 1970-1987; and Today's Game, 1988-present. Eligible candidates for the two most recent Eras are nominated and voted on every five years, and must receive 75 percent of the votes of the 16-member committee.

The Committee chose Allen H. "Bud" Selig and John Schuerholz as its 2017 inductees.[1] As Chairman of MLB's Executive Council, Selig acted unofficially as Commissioner from September 9, 1992, to 1998. He officially became Commissioner in 1998, and served in that office until 2015, making his tenure the longest since that of Kenesaw Mountain Landis.

Under Selig, the 1994 postseason and World Series were cancelled because of a 232-day players strike that began on August 12, 1994, and ended on April 2, 1995. Since the signing of the 1995 Collective Bargaining Agreement, however, and its subsequent agreements, there have been no baseball strikes or lockouts. Major-league revenues, estimated at $1.2 billion in 1992, were projected to be $10.5 billion in 2016. Four franchises (Colorado, Miami, Arizona, and Tampa Bay) were added in 1993 and 1998.

The American and National Leagues had each been divided into two divisions for a quarter of a century, but under Selig's direction, a third division was added in 1994 and a Wild Card team was added to the playoffs in 1995, expanding the postseason to three rounds. A second Wild Card team was added in 2012, necessitating a one-game playoff.

Financial measures were implemented to increase competitiveness of smaller markets. Revenue Sharing, the Luxury Tax, and equal shares of increasing national television, internet streaming and internet servicing revenues have allowed 28 of the 30 Clubs to play in the postseason in the past ten years. According to *Forbes*, television revenues now exceed attendance revenues.[2]

Prior to the meetings, it was announced that the Walt Disney Company would acquire a 33 percent interest in MLB Advanced Media's spinoff media company, BAMTech, for $1 billion. Disney also received an option to become the majority owner in the future. BAMTech will work with ESPN in internet live-streaming of sports and other Disney content separately from MLB Advanced Media's own continuing live-streaming operations. BAMTech revenue will not be subject to revenue sharing, because it will not be baseball-related revenue.[3]

Before Theo Epstein's Cubs won in 2016, John Schuerholz was the only General Manager to win a World Series in both leagues—as GM of the AL Kansas City Royals in 1985, and the NL Atlanta Braves in 1995.

Claire Smith became the first female recipient of the J.G. Taylor Spink Award from the Baseball Writers Association of America for meritorious contributions to baseball writing.[4] The late Bill King received the Ford C. Frick Award for excellence in baseball broadcasting.[5]

Annual Awards

The John H. Johnson Award for outstanding franchise was presented to Fort Wayne of the Midwest League. The Rawlings Woman Executive of the Year Award was presented to Brandy Guinaugh of the Dayton Dragons (Midwest League). The Larry MacPhail Award for best promotion efforts was presented to Midland of the Texas League. The John H. Moss Community Service Award was presented to the Round Rock Express of the Pacific Coast League. The Charles K. Murphy Patriot Award for support of servicemen and women and veterans was presented for the first time, and awarded to the Charleston RiverDogs of the South Atlantic League.[6] The Warren Giles Award for League President was presented jointly to Charlie Blaney of the California League and John Hopkins of the Carolina League. The King of Baseball Award for longtime dedication and service was presented to minor-league operator David G. Elmore. The Sheldon "Chief" Bender Award for player development was presented to Dan Lunetta of the Detroit Tigers. The Mike Coolbaugh Award for work ethic, knowledge and mentoring was presented to Donald "Spin" Williams of the Washington Nationals.[7]

Contract Extension

Before the Winter Meetings started, the New York Mets reached a four-year $110 million contract extension with outfielder Yoenis Cespedes. This annual average salary of $27.5 million is the second highest ever for a position player, after Detroit's Miguel Cabrera ($31 million).[8]

Free Agents

During the meetings, outfielder Carlos Beltran signed for his 20th major-league season with a one-year deal with the Houston Astros for $16 million. Previously, the Astros added catcher Brian McCann and outfielder Josh Reddick.[9] The Los Angeles Dodgers re-signed left-handed pitcher Rich Hill to a three-year $48 million contract. The Colorado Rockies agreed to a five-year $70 million deal with shortstop-center fielder Ian Desmond. The San Francisco Giants signed the former Pirates' All-Star closer righty Mark Melancon to a four-year $62 million contract.

Shortly after the meetings, the New York Yankees signed closer Aroldis Chapman to a five-year deal worth $86 million. The Chicago Cubs lost their center fielder, Dexter Fowler, to their rivals, the St. Louis Cardinals, who corralled him for a five-year, reported $82.5 million. The Yankees signed outfielder-first baseman Matt Holliday to a one-year deal for $13 million. The Tampa Bay Rays signed catcher Wilson Ramos to a two-year contract worth $12 million.

Trades

In the biggest trade, the Chicago White Sox sent their ace left-hander, five-time All-Star Chris Sale, to the Boston Red Sox on December 6 for infielder Yoan Moncada (the best minor-league prospect according to *Baseball America*), right-handed pitchers Michael Kopech and Victor Diaz, and outfielder Luis Alexander Basabe.[10] On the same day, the Red Sox acquired right-handed reliever Tyler Thornburgh from the Milwaukee Brewers for infielder Travis Shaw, two minor-leaguers (infielder Mauricio Dubon and right-hander Josh Pennington), and a player to be named later.

The White Sox then traded outfielder Adam Eaton to the Washington Nationals for right-handed pitching prospects Lucas Giolito, Reynaldo Lopez, and Dane Dunning. The Chicago Cubs traded outfielder Jorge Soler to Kansas City Royals for right-hander Wade Davis, who had been the Royals' closer.[11]

The New Collective Bargaining Agreement

The regular meeting activities were preceded by the conclusion of negotiations between Major League Baseball and the Major League Baseball Players Association for a new Collective Bargaining Agreement. The deal was reached only four hours before the existing CBA was set to expire. The new five-year agreement will expire on December 1, 2021, giving MLB 27 years of uninterrupted labor peace without a lockout or strike since 1994.[12]

The MLB Players Association unanimously ratified the new CBA contract on December 14. It was approved by 29 of the 30 club owners. Tampa Bay Rays owner Stuart Sternberg voted against it, and said "[A]n opportunity to address the extraordinary and widening competitive gap…between higher and lower revenue clubs….was missed here."[13]

Major changes in the new contract:

Competitive Balance Tax (CBT or "Luxury Tax")—The Competitive Balance Tax was first introduced in 2003. The CBT payroll thresholds increase to $195 million in 2017, $197 million in 2018, $206 million in 2019, $208 million in 2020, and $210 million in 2021. As a trade-off, the base CBT rates will increase from 17.5 percent to 20 percent for first-time payers, remain at 30 percent for second-time payers, and increase from 40 percent to 50 percent for third-time or more payers; and an additional new surtax will be applied as follows:

In addition to the Base Tax Threshold for each Contract Year, there will be two Surcharge Thresholds. A Club with an Actual Club Payroll that exceeds one or both of the Surcharge Thresholds applicable in that Contract Year will be assessed an additional Competitive Balance Tax on the amount by which its Actual Club Payroll exceeds the Surcharge Threshold(s), as set forth below.

(i) First Surcharge Threshold: The First Surcharge Threshold shall be $215 million in the 2017 Contract Year, $217 million in the 2018 Contract Year, $226 million in the 2019 Contract Year, $228 million in the 2020 Contract Year, and $230 million in the 2021 Contract Year.

(ii) Second Surcharge Threshold: The Second Surcharge Threshold shall be $235 million in the 2017 Contract Year, $237 million in the 2018 Contract Year, $246 million in the 2019 Contract Year, $248 million in the 2020 Contract Year, and $250 million in the 2021 Contract Year.

The following chart summarizes the Competitive Balance Tax rate a First-, Second-, and Third-Time CBT Payor would incur on the portions of its Actual Club Payroll exceeding the Base Tax Threshold, the First Surcharge Threshold, and the Second Surcharge Threshold.

Amount Actual Club Payroll Exceeds Base Tax Threshold ($M)	First-Time CBT Payor	Second-Time CBT Payor	Third-Time CBT Payor
≤$20 (Base Tax Rate)	20%	30%	50%
$20–$40 (Base Tax + 1st Surcharge Rate)	32%	42%	62%
>$40 (Base Tax +2nd Surcharge Rate)	62.5%	75%	95%

Previously, clubs exceeding the threshold, even in consecutive years, never paid a tax on excessive payroll of more than 50 percent. Beginning in 2018, clubs with a payroll $40 million or more above the CBT threshold will have their highest selection in the Rule 4 Draft (the basic amateur draft) moved back 10 places, except that the top six selections will be protected, and those clubs will have their second highest selection moved back 10 places. Changes to the CBT will take full effect in 2018, and will be phased in for 2017.[14]

Some observers have described the overall effect of these changes as a "soft salary cap." Union Executive Director Tony Clark said, "The premise of the CBT altogether was a drag at the top to keep teams from running away from the group." Commissioner Rob Manfred said, "There's two dynamics around the threshold: stopping people from running away but also having them low enough that people can aspire to spend a little more to be a little more competitive. … This agreement aims to further improve the game's healthy foundation and to promote competitive balance for all fans."[15]

Revenue Sharing—The total percentage of industry revenue subject to sharing remains the same, but the formula by which individual club revenue sharing is determined was revised. According to *Forbes*, top-paying clubs will not be subject to the multiplier in the current formula.[16] The number of clubs disqualified from revenue sharing will be reduced from 15 to 13, with Oakland phased out over four years beginning in 2017. Atlanta and Houston were unofficially indicated to become eligible for revenue sharing.

Free Agency Club Compensation—1) a club may not tender a Qualifying Offer to a player who has previously received a Qualifying Offer, 2) the time period during which a player can accept a Qualifying Offer is extended from 7 to 10 days; and 3) a club signing a free agent subject to club compensation will no longer forfeit a first-round draft selection, but will surrender picks based on their position regarding the Luxury Tax threshold, market size and revenue sharing status, number of qualifying-offer free-agents signed, won-lost records, and whether the free-agent signs with another club for $50 million or more; and 4) a club signing a free-agent subject to club compensation will forfeit between $500,000 and $1 million in its international amateur pool limitation (see below), and/or forfeit one or more Rule 4 Draft selections, depending on its Luxury Tax position, and the number of free-agents signed. Competitive Balance Round picks are exempt from forfeiture, unless obtained through an assignment from another club.

The effect of these new rules is predicted to reduce the incentive for a Club to make a qualifying offer to a borderline player, because it would not receive a high draft pick as compensation, if he rejects the offer and is signed by another club.[17] The rules also might encourage smaller market/revenue clubs to be more active in the free-agent market. They might discourage larger market/revenue clubs from free-agent activity, given the multiple picks and international pool money at stake.[18] These rules take effect after the 2017 regular season.

Minimum Salaries and Assignments—The major-league minimum salary increases from $507,500 in 2016 to $555,000 in 2019. The minor-league minimum salary increases to $45,300 in 2019 for a player's first contract, and to $90,400 in 2019 for a player's second contract, for a player in his second year on a 40-man roster or for players with at least one day of major-league service time. The time period for a club to designate a player for assignment to a minor-league team is shortened from 10 to 7 days. Clubs no longer must place a player on optional assignment waivers prior to optioning them to the minor leagues.

Major-league players cannot be traded during the final week of the regular season.

International Players—Foreign professional players (mainly Japanese and Cuban) who are at least 25 years of age, with a minimum of six seasons of service in a recognized foreign league, will not be subject to a "signing bonus pool" limitation. This was intended to give them the same free-agency status as domestic players of comparable age. Signing of amateur players will be subject to a "hard cap" signing bonus pool limitation of $4.75 million to $5.75 million, depending on the club's status as a recipient of a Luxury Tax compensation Rule 4 Draft pick.

These amounts will grow with MLB revenues. Previously, pool limitations were based on the previous year's won-lost record, but it was a "soft cap," in that clubs could pay a monetary penalty for exceeding the limitation. Other rules will apply to acquisition of such players by trade and to a limited two-round draft for clubs with lower revenues and finishes in the standings.

It is likely that the salary cap rules will be of most benefit to clubs with the best international scouting and academies in Latin America. Some also believe that the hard cap is intended to prevent future deals like the reported Boston Red Sox 2015 contract with then 19-year-old Cuban National Series infielder Yoan

> ## NO LONGER ABLE TO AVOID THE FAME
>
> Calls for Baseball Hall of Fame votes to become public existed for many years.* However, it took until 2016 for the Baseball Writers Association of America to take the needed action. In an 80-to-9 vote at the 2016 Winter Meetings, the writers decided to make all votes public seven days after the election announcement. The rule was slated to go into effect in 2018.**
>
> ---
> * Bob Sudyk, "Hall of Fame Voting Needs Redesigning," *Hartford Courant*, January 15, 1982: C1B.
> ** Barry Bloom, "Hall of Fame Ballots Will Be Made Public Starting in 2018," *MLB.com*, December 6, 2016, Accessed October 5, 2017, m.mlb.com/news/article/210445566/anonymous-hall-of-fame-balloting-ends-in-2018/

Moncada. Moncada received a $31.5 million signing bonus, and the Red Sox paid MLB another $31.5 million tax for exceeding their bonus pool limitation.[19] (As reported above, Moncada was traded to the White Sox during the Winter Meetings for pitcher Chris Sale.)

Postseason Play, Scheduling, and Disabled List—1) Home-field advantage in the World Series will now be awarded to the club with the higher regular-season winning percentage, rather than based on the result of the All-Star Game; 2) the regular-season will start earlier and cover 187 days to provide four extra offdays for players; 3) start times of games on getaway days will be moved up (likely to the afternoon hours) to allow players to arrive in their next city at an earlier time; and 4) a 10-day disabled list will replace the current 15-day disabled list.

All-Star Game—1) all players on the active roster of the winning team will share equally in a $640,000 bonus ($20,000 per player); 2) each team will have 32 players, with 20 position players and 12 pitchers; 3) following fan and player voting, instead of manager selections, the Commissioner's Office will select seven National League and five American League players; and 4) the Home Run Derby format will remain the same, with increasing player prize money.

Drug Testing—1) the number of in-season random urine tests will increase from 3,200 to 4,800; 2) the number of offseason random urine tests will increase from 350 to 1,550, making all 40-man roster players subject to at least one random offseason test; 3) the number of in-season random blood tests (for human growth hormone) will increase from 260 to 500, and the number of offseason random blood tests will increase from 140 to 400; 4) the penalties for performance-enhancing substance violations will be an 80-game suspension for a first violation, 162-game/183 days of pay suspension for a second violation, from 80 to 100 games for a third violation, and permanent suspension for a third violation, with the right to apply for reinstatement after two years; 5) the penalties for stimulants violations will be follow-up testing for a first violation, a 50-game suspension for a second violation, a 100-game suspension for a third violation, and up to a permanent suspension for a fourth violation; 6) the penalties for dehydroepiandrosterone (DHEA) violations will be follow-up testing for a first violation, a 25-game suspension for a second violation, an 80-game suspension for third violation, and up to a permanent suspension for a fourth violation; and 7) an arbitration panel will have more discretion to reduce penalties based on mitigating circumstances. Any player who violates the drug testing rules will no longer receive major-league service time credit during his suspension, unless reduced by 20 or more games. This new rule was motivated by the suspensions of Alex Rodriguez and similar players.[20]

Pension and Medical Benefits—Players will continue to receive the maximum allowable pensions under IRS rules. Players become eligible for minimum benefits after 43 days of major-league service. After 10 years of service time, they are eligible for $200,000 per year, beginning at age 62. Players with four or more years of service time can continue their health care coverage at a cost of at least 60 percent of their chosen plan. Players will also receive a guaranteed minimum contribution to their individual retirement accounts based on accrued service time.

Under the new CBA, clubs will increase their total annual contribution for medical and pension benefits to about $200 million per year.

Smokeless Tobacco—Use of tobacco products on the field will be banned in all ballparks where it is prohibited by local law or ordinance. Any player making his major-league debut in 2017 or later will be prohibited from using smokeless tobacco on the field in every ballpark. It is already banned in the minor leagues.

Translators—Every club will retain a bilingual media relations professional, and will provide additional English language learning opportunities for Spanish-speaking players.

Anti-Hazing and Anti-Bullying Code of Conduct—The commissioner's office will implement an Anti-Hazing and Anti-Bullying Code of Conduct as a supplement to the Workplace Code of Conduct. A report of an abusive hazing incident involving Texas Rangers prospects surfaced in the weeks prior to the new CBA agreement.[21]

The new code bans "requiring, coercing or encouraging" other players to participate in "dressing up as women or wearing costumes that may be offensive to individuals based on their race, sex, nationality, age, sexual orientation, gender identity or other characteristic." In addition, making players "consume alcoholic beverages or any other kind of drug, or requiring the ingestion of an undesirable or unwanted substance (food, drink, concoction)" is prohibited.

Social Responsibility Outreach

Major-league activity at the Winter Meetings, under the rubric "social responsibility," included a "Pathways to Careers in Baseball" panel featuring Kim Ng, MLB Senior Vice President for Baseball Operations, Dodgers General Manager Farhan Zaidi, Mariners scout Amanda Hopkins and others; a panel on inclusion focusing on minor-league executives; a panel on environmental sustainability in ballpark operations; a "Supplier Diversity Summit" panel; and a "Women in Baseball" networking reception.

"On big things like diversity and social responsibility, you have to keep beating people over the head at meetings," said Dan Halem, MLB's Chief Legal Officer. "Baseball people are so busy, and they're so focused on other stuff, you have to keep reinforcing it in whatever you do. That's why the winter meetings are a good place for it.... Look, we need more diversity at every level, and the only way to get more diversity at the senior level is to have more diversity below, and at the entry level, and by focusing on developing people."[22]

Under Armour and Fanatics Uniform Deals

Under Armour, Fanatics and MLB announced a 10-year partnership naming Under Armour as the official uniform provider to MLB. It will begin in 2020 and it will be Under Armour's first professional league uniform deal. Under Armour became the official performance footwear partner of MLB in 2011. It has more than 400 individual athlete partnerships across the major and minor leagues. Fanatics will receive consumer product licensing rights.[23]

Areas of Disagreement—The owners and players failed to agree on 1) a proposal to expand the regular-season roster from 25 to 26 players in return for limiting the September rosters to 28 players, including minor-league call-ups; 2) new rules on pace of play, including a proposed 20-second pitch clock that has been used in minor leagues; 3) an international amateur draft, which was opposed by several Latin American players who attended the CBA negotiations, because they believed it would lower salaries for foreign players, who can now receive larger bonuses than American amateurs can receive.[24] The Rule 4 Amateur Draft covers only players from the United States, Canada and Puerto Rico.

No Longer Able to Avoid the Fame

Calls for Baseball Hall of Fame votes to become public existed for many years.[25] However, it took until 2016 for the Baseball Writers Association of America to take the needed action. In an 80-to-9 vote at the 2016 Winter Meetings, the writers decided to make all votes public seven days after the election announcement. The rule was slated to go into effect in 2018.[26]

Has a New Diamond Age Begun for Baseball?

The business of baseball has never been better. Attendance and television revenues are stronger than ever. Legal challenges by minor-league players over wages (*Senne v. Kansas City Royals Baseball Corp.*), and by San Jose over MLB rejection of a proposed Oakland Athletics relocation (*City of San Jose v. Office of the Commissioner of Baseball*) have been repulsed. The unique antitrust exemption of baseball that was granted by the Supreme Court in 1922, and partially legislated by Congress in 1998, continues.

Challenges loom, however, for the health of the business and the game. The demographics of baseball fans are the oldest of the major sports. The game is disappearing from the playing fields of American (and Cuban) youth. As younger audiences defect from cable television subscriptions, sports networks reconsider their multiyear contract commitments to baseball games.

The inevitability of success cannot be assumed, whether for society or the recreational ethos of a nation. The continued success of baseball will depend on navigation by wise leaders through the challenges that often grow in the shadows of bright, shining triumphs.

NOTES

1 Barry B. Bloom, "Selig, Schuerholz elected to Hall of Fame," m.mlb.com/news/2016/12/05/210231272/bud-selig-john-schuerholz-elected-to-hall, accessed December 16, 2016.

2 Maury Brown, "MLB Sees Record Revenues Approaching $10 Billion for 2016," forbes.com/sites/maurybrown/2016/12/05/mlb-sees-record-revenues-approaching-10-billion-for-2016/#7ce96de91845, accessed February 20, 2017.

3 Maury Brown, "Disney Buys $1B Stake in MLB's BAMTech, to Launch ESPN Streaming Service," forbes.com/sites/maurybrown/2016/08/09/disney-co-makes-1-billion-investment-becomes-minority-stakeholder-in-mlbams-bamtech/#4d7dad221597, accessed December 16, 2016; Maury Brown, "MLB Sees Record Revenues Approaching $10 Billion for 2016".

4 Barry M. Bloom, "Smith first woman to win Spink Award," m.mlb.com/news/2016/12/06/210386718/claire-smith-wins-jg-taylor-spink-award, accessed December 16, 2016.

5 Barry M. Bloom, "Late A's voice King Honored With Frick Award,, m.mlb.com/news/2016/12/07/210538326/bill-king-wins-2017-ford-c-frick-award, accessed December 16, 2016.

6 Baseball Winter Meetings 2016 Minor League Baseball Awards, milb.com/milb/events/winter_meetings/y2016/awards.jsp, accessed December 16, 2016.

7 Major Award Winners, milb.com/milb/history/awards.jsp, accessed December 16, 2016.

8 Jeff Todd, "Mets Re-Sign Yoenis Cespedes," mlbtraderumors.com/2016/11/mets-to-re-sign-yoenis-cespedes.html, accessed December 16, 2016.

9 The Astros traded minor-league right-handers Albert Abreu and Jorge Guzman to get McCann; Reddick was signed as a free agent.

10 Alex Speier, "An inside look at how the Red Sox landed Chris Sale," bostonglobe.com/sports/redsox/2016/12/10/how-chris-sale-deal-came-about/y54iJcIAj4vtbDvRb8LLLP/story.html, accessed December 17, 2016.

11 Transactions, mlb.mlb.com/mlb/transactions/?tcid=mm_mlb_news#month=12&year=201, accessed December 16, 2016.

12 Richard Justice, "Peace & Glove: Owners, players reach CBA deal," m.mlb.com/news/article/209969472/mlb-owners-players-agree-to-new-labor-deal/, accessed December 16, 2016.

13 Associated Press, "Report: Rays only franchise to Vote Against Ratifying CBA," espn.com/mlb/story/_/id/18272683/mlb-owners-ratify-labor-deal-29-1-tampa-bay-rays-voting-against, accessed December 16, 2016.

14 Details of MLB, MLBPA labor agreement, m.mlb.com/news/article/210125462/details-of-mlb-mlbpa-labor-agreement/, accessed December 16, 2016.

15 Associated Press, "MLBPA Backed Out of Deal to Increase Rosters to 26 players," espn.com/mlb/story/_/id/18189604/mlb-pa-backed-deal-increase-rosters-26-players, accessed December 16, 2016.

16 Maury Brown, "Breaking Down MLB's New 2017-21 Collective Bargaining Agreement," forbes.com/sites/maurybrown/2016/11/30/breaking-down-mlbs-new-2017-21-collective-bargaining-agreement/2/#d38e11d3d1f2, accessed December 16, 2016.

17 Chelsea Janes, "How Will Baseball's New Labor Agreement Affect the Nationals?" washingtonpost.com/news/nationals-journal/wp/2016/12/01/how-will-baseballs-new-labor-agreement-affect-the-nationals/?utm_term=.0a8ac820c0df, accessed December 16, 2016.

18 Jonathan Mayo, "How CBA affects Draft, free agency, international market," m.mlb.com/news/article/210035584/mlb-cba-affects-draft-international-prospects/, accessed December 16, 2016.

19 Ibid.

20 Maury Brown, "Breaking Down MLB's New 2017-21 Collective Bargaining Agreement."

21 SI Wire, "Report: Rangers Investigating Prospects for Sexually Hazing Underage Teammate," si.com/mlb/2016/11/21/texas-rangers-prospects-sexual-assault-hazing-investigation, accessed December 16, 2016.

22 Dave Sheinin, "With New Diversity Goals, MLB Tries to Change Its Image as an Old [White] Boys Club," washingtonpost.com/news/sports/wp/2016/12/13/with-new-diversity-goals-mlb-tries-to-change-its-image-as-an-old-white-boys-club/?utm_term=.c1d2183a0661, accessed December 16, 2016.

23 Alyson Footer, "Under Armour, Fanatics, MLB strike uniform deal," m.mlb.com/news/article/210264854/under-armour-to-make-official-mlb-uniforms/, accessed December 16, 2016.

24 Ben Badler, "Top Prospects Voice Opposition to International Draft," baseballamerica.com/international/top-prospects-voice-opposition-international-draft/#m0CcfwBsP0ugfAgc.97, accessed December 16, 2016.

25 Bob Sudyk, "Hall of Fame Voting Needs Redesigning," *Hartford Courant*, January 15, 1982: C1B.

26 Barry Bloom, "Hall of Fame Ballots Will Be Made Public Starting in 2018," *MLB.com*, December 6, 2016, Accessed October 5, 2017, m.mlb.com/news/article/210445566/anonymous-hall-of-fame-balloting-ends-in-2018/.

BASEBALL'S BUSINESS: THE WINTER MEETINGS

Negro Baseball magnates meet at the Hotel Theresa, in New York City on June 20, 1946. The owners had all attended the Joe Louis boxing bout the night before. The meeting was to plan the second-half schedule for the 1946 season.

Left to right: Syd Pollock (Indy Clowns), Tom Wilson (Baltimore Elite Giants), Tom Baird (KC Monarchs), W.S. Martin (Memphis Red Sox), J.B. Martin (NAL President and Chicago American Giants), Ernest Wright (Cleveland Buckeyes), Fay Young (Chicago Defender writer), Wilbur Hayes (Buckeyes), and Tom Hayes, Jr. (Birmingham Black Barons). Courtesy of the National Baseball Hall of Fame.

1933-1962
THE BUSINESS MEETINGS OF NEGRO LEAGUE BASEBALL

By Duke Goldman

ALTHOUGH THE FIRST ORGANIZED and sustainable Negro League, the original Negro National League (NNL), founded by Rube Foster in 1920, did not survive the Great Depression, it was the forerunner of several other Negro Leagues. In the 1920s, the Eastern Colored League (ECL) was formed as a counterpart to the NNL. It lasted from 1923 through the early part of 1928, then was succeeded by the American Negro League (ANL) for one year in 1929. The first NNL, largely based in the Midwest, continued its operations into the 1930s, but was replaced in 1932 by another short-lived organized league called the East-West League. Like the ANL, the East-West League survived only one year.

In 1933, several events of marked importance occurred—Franklin Delano Roosevelt started his 12-year presidency, Adolf Hitler became chancellor of Germany—and the second NNL began operations. This incarnation of the NNL was a hybrid of Eastern and Western clubs, including the developing twin powerhouse Pittsburgh franchises the Pittsburgh Crawfords and the Homestead Grays, along with Midwestern mainstay the Chicago American Giants (at that time referred to as Cole's American Giants as Robert Cole took over ownership in 1931), the team that Rube Foster pitched for and owned while he started the original NNL.[1] Though this NNL began operations during the depths of the Great Depression, it managed to survive the 1930s, thrive during the wartime '40's, and then begin to struggle as soon as Jackie Robinson signed a contract with the Brooklyn Dodgers in 1945 to begin playing with the Montreal Royals in 1946. It is important to note here that the second NNL started right after "the most harrowing four months" of the Depression, when the US economy had hit rock-bottom.[2] According to historian David Kennedy, African-Americans during the Depression represented one-fifth of the people on federal relief, approximately twice their population percentage at the time.[3] That the 1933 NNL was able to get off the ground during these difficult times for all Americans (but especially for the black population) is a testament to the determination of the owners who were committed to re-establishing organized black baseball at a level at least comparable to the original Negro National League.

As referred to by the Negro Leagues Baseball Museum, the "Golden Years" of Negro League Baseball that began in 1933 with the re-established NNL and was augmented by a second competing Negro League, the Negro American League (NAL), starting in 1937, began to slowly close as the NNL ended operations after the 1948 season.[4] The NAL, however, survived, with yearly fluctuations in the number of teams it fielded, through the 1950s. Many commentators consider 1960 to be the last year of the NAL's operations, but others point to limited activity among NAL teams through 1962.

This article is not meant as a complete history of the 30 seasons of Negro League competition through 1962; although references to the on-field performance of the NNL and NAL during this period will be made, along with the star players who populated the legendary teams in each league, the primary focus will be an examination of the often contentious business dealings of team owners *within* the NNL and NAL as well as the internecine conflicts between the two leagues for their 12-year coexistence. Although what follows will include yearly reports of winter and, when available, in-season meetings of the NNL, NAL, and joint meetings of the two leagues, it will also group the analysis into four distinct periods:

1. **Birth and Growth**—The New NNL and the beginnings of the East-West (E-W) Game (1933) and the birth of the NAL (1936) and fledgling years of two-league play (1937-1940).
2. **War and Prosperity**—The heyday of black league baseball—the two leagues profit and the Negro World Series (NWS) and E-W Game thrive (1941-1945).
3. **Integration and Storm Clouds—The NNL's Demise**—Jackie Robinson signs with Brooklyn and Negro League owners see drastic business decline, culminating in the end of the NNL (1945-1948).
4. **The Surviving NAL –The End of the Negro Leagues**—League membership expands and contracts from the late 1940s through the early 1960s as the Negro Leagues struggle to survive—through the last E-W Game on August 26, 1962 (1949-1962).

The primary source material for this article is the black press; however, as referenced by several reporters and columnists who were frustrated by Negro League owner practices, the owners could be secretive about their boardroom discussions; this meant that sometimes the press reported that a meeting was upcoming along with the planned agenda but then did not cover the meeting afterward. Over time, though, this began to change, especially as those involved wrote their own columns describing conflicts between owners in self-serving ways.[5] It is those columns, as well as several excellent secondary sources that have delved into Negro League operations and the correspondence and meeting minutes found in Newark Eagles owner Effa Manley's files that form the basis of this chronicle.

Part 1 – Birth and Growth (1933-1940)

Pre-1933

Even though Rube Foster, the founder of the first NNL in 1920, had ceased to be involved in its operations by late in the 1926 season due to his own mental breakdown, the league managed to survive—barely—through 1931.[6] It did not take long, however, for "Eastern and Western cities east of Chicago" to plan a meeting in Cleveland for January 20 and 21 of 1932. The cities to be included in this meeting were New York, Newark, Philadelphia, Baltimore, Washington, Pittsburgh, Cleveland, and Detroit. A "Cuban team representative" was also expected, while Kansas City's Monarchs were there to join the league as an associate member.[7] As an associate member, Kansas City would pay a smaller franchise fee and be included in league scheduling, but would not be counted in league standings and therefore could not play in any postseason games.[8] The resulting league, named the East-West League, operated through mid-1932, when it also foundered despite the best efforts of team owners like Cumberland Posey of the Homestead Grays, J.L. Wilkinson of the Kansas City Monarchs, and Syd Pollock of the Cuban House of David.

In addition to the short-lived E-W League, 1932 saw a previously minor-league Negro Southern League (NSL) achieving short-lived major-league status. Though incarnations of the NSL existed prior to 1932, they were exclusively constituted by Southern teams; in 1932, in addition to the Monroe, Louisiana, Monarchs, Louisville Black Caps, Nashville Elite Giants, and teams in Houston, Birmingham, and Pittsburgh, the last of which was an associate member that quit before the end of the season, the league included former NNL teams like the Chicago American Giants, the Indianapolis ABCs, and the Cleveland Cubs. Unlike the E-W League, the 1932 NSL struggled through a fragmented second half to a conclusion culminating in a "World Series" between NSL champion Monroe and E-W League member Pittsburgh Crawfords.[9] The loose, ragged nature of league competition in black baseball in 1932 raised a very simple question: What league or leagues, if any, would there be in 1933?

1933

The remnants of the aborted E-W League and the non-Southern 1932 NSL teams met in the first months of 1933 to see if the NNL could be revived. For one thing, as pointed out by *Chicago Defender* writer Ben Diamond, those Northern teams that played in the NSL in 1932 learned a lesson—that it was futile to "cram inter-sectional games down the throats of 'up North fandom.'" Those fans, Diamond suggested, felt that the South "comprises minor league territory and you cannot make them see it differently."[10] Instead, by the end of 1932 there had already been two meetings including the Northern NSL teams, other E-W League teams, former NSL team representatives, and only one Southern team (albeit one that was reportedly considering moving North), the Nashville Elite Giants.[11]

And faithful reporter and former player and soon-to-be NNL manager of the Columbus Blue Birds William "Dizzy" Dismukes let it be known in the year-end edition of the *Pittsburgh Courier* that an organizing meeting of the new league, the first meeting of 1933, would be held in Chicago on January 10, 1933.[12] Dismukes had some strong opinions about what ailed the prior Negro Leagues, and what was needed going forward. For one thing, he believed that the new league should pick among its owners a single league president or a three-man commission, as hiring an outsider he deemed to be unaffordable. This viewpoint foreshadowed a repeated battle between changing ownership factions who favored an insider as league head and other factions who favored a theoretically unbiased outsider non-owner as the league's chief executive.

Dismukes had other opinions—that there should be no salary limit on an owner's payroll, that a 5 percent pool from league receipts should be awarded to the new league's 1933 pennant winner since there would not be two strong leagues to play a season-ending World Series, and that player averages should be reported twice a month, among other things.[13] Dismukes would get his say as he was chosen to be the secretary of the new NNL along with the league's statistician—he would be the one to report league averages—although he would eventually step down from this position to manage the short-lived Columbus team.[14]

Meanwhile, William A. "Gus" Greenlee, owner of the Pittsburgh Crawfords, was chosen as the temporary chairman of the new incarnation of the NNL at the organizing meeting in Chicago.[15] Greenlee had funded his operations—two hotels, the Crawford Grille restaurant, and his baseball team—through the illegal numbers lottery.[16] But there was another side to the story—Greenlee was seen by the Pittsburgh black community as a benefactor, not a racketeer. There were countless stories of the help he gave poor black citizens, including operating a soup kitchen during the Great Depression.[17] According to Negro Leagues historian Jim Overmyer, the funding derived from "numbers bankers" who enabled the "launching [of] a league in the teeth of the Depression. As Rufus Jackson's widow told an interviewer in Pittsburgh in the 1960s, "Well, of course they were involved—they were the only ones with any money."[18] Rufus Jackson later was recruited by Greenlee's "very bitter baseball rival" Cum Posey to fund the operations of his Homestead Grays, while other numbers operators like Alex Pompez and Abe Manley later became owners of the New York Cubans and Newark Eagles, respectively.[19] It is fair to conclude that Branch Rickey's later characterization of Negro League baseball as a racket, in order to justify his signing of Jackie Robinson without compensation to his Negro League team, the Kansas City Monarchs, was based in part on the illegality of the numbers operations engaged in by owners like Greenlee and Pompez. Rickey, however, was willing to partner with Greenlee in the development of the United States League (USL) when it suited his purposes, as Rickey's involvement in that league provided a subterfuge for his scouting of black players for Brooklyn. In the end, as Overmyer pointed out, the illegality of numbers games at that time was by state statute—whereas today, state governments make money through the lottery, a modern version of the numbers lottery.[20]

In the February 11, 1933, edition of the *Courier*, columnist W. Rollo Wilson reported that chairman Greenlee had recently met in Philadelphia with Eastern owners including teams from Philadelphia,

New York, Baltimore, Washington, Harrisburg, and Newark to form an Eastern division of the new league who would play primarily within their division with some lesser number of games to be played against the "West division," culminating in a "world's title" match at season's end.[21] Several of these teams, including Philadelphia, Baltimore, New York, Newark, and Washington, were represented by proxy at a February 15 league meeting held in Indianapolis, with one more meeting scheduled prior to the league's commencement for schedule-making.

The Eastern division of the 1933 NNL never materialized; according to author Neil Lanctot, Greenlee "abandoned a tentative plan for a separate eastern league after encountering resistance and a general lack of enthusiasm."[22] Already, tensions between ownership factions were evident, as can be seen by contrasting reportage from "Eastern" (in this case, Pittsburgh) and Western (Chicago) sources. Rollo Wilson's *Courier* column of March 4, 1933, praised Greenlee as having the makings of a good president. Wilson suggested that Greenlee was anointed permanent chair of the NNL due to his hard work as the temporary head, spreading the word in various cities of the new league's advent. Wilson extolled Greenlee for the building of Greenlee Park in 1932 and for the force of his vision and willingness to spend to achieve it.[23]

Meanwhile, in a more oblique piece, Al Monroe of the *Chicago Defender*, in his "Speaking of Sports" column of February 25, 1933, questioned why the East was put in "direct control of the league even though its idea was conceived and its first meeting arranged by and in the West."[24] While conceding that the East had more experienced hands for running the ship of the NNL, Monroe also cast a wary eye backward to the failed E-W League operations of 1932 and saw a "mark of similarity" in the 1933 setup. If, Monroe said, the leadership did what they promised, success would ensue but the West had valuable resources ("players and managers") that must also be employed if this league would echo the success of Chicagoan Rube Foster's first NNL. Monroe therefore felt that the newly constituted NNL should be led but not dominated by Pittsburgh's Gus Greenlee and Homestead's Cum Posey.[25]

But enough of the machinations of power; let's talk business. At the Indianapolis meeting on February 15, all the league officials and some of the member teams were finalized. It was announced that Cleveland would not be able to field a team due to its inability to find a ballpark in which to play its home games. Meanwhile, Detroit's owner John Roesink was picked as a league member with Negro League great Bingo DeMoss to manage the team. Columbus, Ohio, was also given membership, and Cincinnati was voted an associate membership "to take care of the jumps from the East to the West."[26]

The unnamed columnist who wrote the *Defender*'s other February 25, 1933, column on the Indianapolis meeting of February 15 also reported (and editorialized) that "there was plenty talk of trades but little was actually done."[27] Although trades *did* occur at various Negro League meetings during the 1933-to-1962 period, it was more often the case that talk occurred without moves being made. In this case, new NNL president and Crawfords owner Greenlee could have pulled off a bombshell—he reportedly offered none other than Satchel Paige to the Nashville Elite Giants for pitcher Jim Willis but Nashville owner Tom Wilson "balked at the thought of sending this favorite of Nashville fans elsewhere."[28] As it turned out, both Paige and Willis were picked for the inaugural East-West All-Star Game that summer of 1933 although neither pitched in the game. For Paige it was the first of numerous All-Star berths, culminating in his appearance in the penultimate East-West Game on August 20, 1961; for Willis, it was his only time to be picked for the team. Clearly, Paige was in the early stages of establishing his stardom, while Jim Willis had reached his peak. For Greenlee, this was evidence supporting the baseball bromide that "the best trades are often the ones you don't complete."

As we shall see, more team maneuverings in and out of the fledging league were to come, presaging a 30-year history of such offseason—and inseason, at times—franchise additions and deletions. But at this formative NNL meeting, league officials

Dismukes, James Taylor, and Robert Cole, owner of the Chicago American Giants, were chosen as secretary, vice chairman, and treasurer, respectively. Now permanent chairman Greenlee was still angling for an Eastern division; he reportedly met with several Eastern owners for a two-hour conference in the days prior to a final preseason "Negro National Association" meeting in Detroit on Saturday, March 11.[29] According to Rollo Wilson, the uncertainty of Sunday baseball in Pennsylvania meant that schedules would not be finalized until early April but meanwhile, Greenlee was talking with Ed Bolden, John Dykes, Otto Briggs, and other Eastern club owners as well as the Baltimore Black Sox and Ben Taylor's Baltimore Stars and the New York Black Yankees.[30]

The *Chicago Defender*'s March 18, 1933, column reported on the March 11 meeting, omitting any mention of the Eastern teams, instead recounting that club owners from teams in Indianapolis, Chicago, Detroit, Pittsburgh (both Crawfords and Grays), Columbus, and Nashville were present and a tentative final schedule for the league's initial weeks was announced, as well as that of the various Southern spring-training sites and some players and managers on each team. Notably, future Hall of Famers Willie Wells, Turkey Stearnes, and Mule Suttles were announced as having signed with the Chicago American Giants; speedster James "Cool Papa" Bell was retained by Gus Greenlee: and "Gentleman Dave" Malarcher, Bingo DeMoss, and possibly Clint Thomas were reportedly going to manage Chicago, Detroit, and Columbus respectively.[31]

According to Neil Lanctot's seminal history of Negro League Baseball as a business institution, "a bizarre series of franchise shifts occurred soon after the outset of the season in May."[32] What it boiled down to, according to Lanctot and the black press, was that the original Detroit franchise's unpopular white owner, John Roesink, withdrew before the season's commencement, but after one game with weak attendance in Indianapolis, the ABCs of that city moved to Detroit but were largely replaced there by the Chicago American Giants, who, having been forced out of Schorling Park in Chicago, relocated to play at Perry Field, home of the (white) minor-league Indianapolis Indians, after playing a few games at Mills Field in Chicago that were unsuccessful financially. However, the now Indianapolis-based team still wore Chicago American Giants uniforms.[33] And, to add to the confusion, in late May a seventh team, the Baltimore Black Sox, was added to the league.

There was clearly a need for a midseason meeting to sort out who was still viable to play the second half of the season. The meeting was held on June 23 at Greenlee Field in Pittsburgh. As reported in the July 8, 1933, edition of the *Norfolk Journal and Guide*, six of the seven teams were represented at the meeting, the glaring exception being the Homestead Grays. Neither Grays owner Cum Posey nor any other representatives of the team appeared to defend themselves against changes "involving violation of Section 7 and Section 28 of the Constitution."[34] Apparently, the membership (absent the Grays) voted unanimously to expel the Grays because they allegedly "acquired" Binder and Williams from Detroit without Detroit's permission. This was not the only charge raised at this meeting but it was the most important and most divisive. There were other player disputes between Baltimore and Nashville and between Columbus and nonleague team the Kansas City Monarchs. And, as befits a fledgling league still figuring out how to operate, "methods of reporting and collecting fees, advertising changes and cancellation of games preceded the work of the schedule makers."[35]

The Grays were now banned from the league's second half but the argument about who caused the rift between the league and Posey and indeed whether Posey withdrew from the league prior to being suspended was waged in the black press for weeks to come.

More importantly, the black press and Greenlee were involved in a major development for the future of Negro League Baseball—the creation of an annual All-Star game which became the signature event of Negro League Baseball. What is undisputed is that the East-West Game did not originate at a meeting of NNL owners. The story of how the game originated is disputed; bitter rivals Posey and Greenlee each placed themselves in prominent roles in its conception, but it is generally acknowledged that sportswriter

Roy Sparrow of the *Pittsburgh Sun-Telegraph* was the "driving force behind the game" and Bill Nunn of the *Courier* was instrumental in its realization; alternatively, some sources report that black Cleveland sportswriter Dave Hawkins claimed to have inspired Greenlee and Cole by staging a game in League Park, home of the Cleveland Indians, between Eastern power Pittsburgh Crawfords and Western power Chicago American Giants.[36]

On the eve of the 10th East-West Game, Cum Posey, in his regular *Courier* column called "Posey's Points," recounted his version of the story — that he had invited sportswriters Sparrow and Nunn to a meeting at Pittsburgh's Loendi club to discuss an idea of Sparrow's that "two All-Star Colored Teams feature the Annual Milk Fund Day at Yankee Stadium, New York City." According to Posey, in the discussion "we suggested that the Milk Fund idea be forgotten and a game be staged at Yankee Stadium between the star players of the North versus the Star players of the South."[37] Supposedly, when Greenlee heard of this from Sparrow and Nunn, he changed both the venue and the name by enlisting Robert Cole of the Chicago American Giants to establish the game in Chicago's Comiskey Park as an East-West game, with Nunn and Sparrow helping to promote it. According to historian Lanctot, Greenlee then paid for an exorbitant ($2,500) rental of Comiskey Park which was essential in making the event happen.[38]

What is particularly remarkable in Posey's 1942 column is his parenthetical statement that Greenlee "was a very bitter baseball rival of everything and persons connected with the Homestead Grays" as he explained why Greenlee purportedly changed the game's name and venue.[39] Was the Posey of 1942 also remembering nine years later that Greenlee as NNL chairman banned the Grays from participating in the second half of the 1933 NNL around the same time of the conception of the East-West Game? In a July 8, 1933, letter published in the Courier, Posey claimed that rather than being expelled from the NNL, the Grays had withdrawn from the league because President Greenlee restricted league teams to getting 35 percent of gross receipts for league games, with 5 percent going to the league, when Posey had never accepted less than 40 percent.[40]

In a column headlined "Cum Posey's Pointed Paragraphs" appearing in the *Courier* a month after the just-mentioned letter, Posey expanded his charges against the league, now stating, "[W]e came out of the Negro National Association because it was not a fair league and was handled to a great extent under the sinister influence of the booking agent of the East. All we need at the head of an association of colored baseball clubs is a man with courage enough to fight for what is due the owners of colored clubs."[41] Posey was now contending that booking agents Nat Strong and Ed Gottlieb were strong-arming his team and others by insisting on 5 percent of the receipts of any league game between Eastern and Western clubs (Gottlieb) and blocking games from being played at Yankee Stadium (Strong). Posey obliquely alleged that these actions not only benefited Gus Greenlee's Pittsburgh Crawfords but also by extension the Columbus Blue Birds and Baltimore Black Sox, who stopped playing league contests and booked games independently in the second half of 1933.[42]

So what really happened at the league's June 23 business meeting at Greenlee Field? One firsthand account by a participant in that meeting was reported. After Dizzy Dismukes relinquished the NNL secretary's job to manage Columbus, John L. Clark took that position. Admittedly not an objective observer, as he was a Crawfords official as well, Clark nonetheless provided a detailed description of how and why the league expelled Posey while meeting at "Greenlee's Gardens." Clark charged that Posey's "case" was a subterfuge for his intention to a) appropriate players directly rather than legitimately acquire them from other league clubs and b) cancel league contests without notice.[43] It is a minor point, but still worth mentioning, that Clark explains why the meeting was held at Greenlee Field, arguably enemy territory for Posey, rather than a more neutral site. According to Clark, the meeting was originally scheduled for 10 A.M. at Center Avenue YMCA but was changed to 1:30 P.M. at the offices at Greenlee Field because several league members were not able to reach the city for the earlier scheduled time and location. In addition, Clark carefully documented that the meeting was not a "special session to pass decision of an unfaithful member"—rather, it was called primarily to draft a schedule for the season's second half and before charges were telegraphed by Greenlee to Posey on June 21 that Posey had taken players Binder and Williams without permission from or compensation given to Detroit. Clark further states that Posey had been requested to attend, but after five other items of business were taken care of, Posey's actions were deliberated without his presence. It was then contended by Chicago at the meeting that Posey had canceled upcoming scheduled league games with them on June 24-26 at Greenlee Field and that his actions were eroding the goodwill of the public.

In Clark's account, after a unanimous vote to expel the Grays at the June 23, 1933, meeting, Posey did appear but failed to satisfactorily explain his actions and evaded direct questions. Clark editorialized that Posey was against league play largely because he did not control the league. But Clark did present the argument that Posey left for financial reasons, with league-mandated player and salary limits having "a great deal to do with Posey's kidnapping of Binder and Williams."[44]

Whether one chooses to believe Posey's version or that of Clark (or a little of both), any observer, contemporary or in retrospect, should realize that a pattern had been established. Not only would Posey and Greenlee largely remain at loggerheads, but fierce battles, with accusations of league violations and decisions to expel teams and/or for teams to declare that they were abandoning the league schedule, would be common throughout the 30 seasons of Negro League play starting in 1933 and ending in 1962. Although there were certainly such issues (and many others) in the prior incarnation of the NNL, league President Rube Foster was such a powerful and revered figure that his rulings tended to be respected and followed. There are many reminiscences in the black press about the "halcyon days" of the 1920s and the founding fathers of league play, indicating that many scribes found the ongoing ownership battles in the successor leagues to be tiresome, divisive, and destructive not only to league operations and league success, but also to the larger cause of promoting black athletics with an eye toward eventual integration into white major league operations.[45]

In the final analysis, the 1933 NNL season was a limited success. Only three teams—Nashville, Chicago/Indianapolis, and Pittsburgh—completed the entire season. The first East-West All-Star Game was played with the West prevailing, 11-7, but seven of the 14 who played for the East were from the Pittsburgh Crawfords, and seven of the nine West players were from the Chicago American Giants. Attendance for the game has been variously reported as 19,568 and about 12,000, a pretty good turnout for the times and for a league limping along to the end of its inaugural season, but far less than several future East-West Games.[46]

Not only did the Homestead Grays, Columbus Blue Birds, Detroit Stars, and Baltimore Black Sox abandon (or in the case of the Grays, were also suspended from) league play, but top teams like the Kansas City Monarchs, the Philadelphia Stars, the New York Black Yankees, the Newark Browns, and the New York Cubans never joined the league. Additionally, there was a short-time member of the 1933 NNL, mostly in the season's second half, called the Akron Black Tyrites, who were 2-9 in league play.[47] Chicago protested a game played against Baltimore and when the protest was upheld, they won the league's first half by one game.[48] The second half was apparently a muddle—down to only three teams, Chicago was eliminated as a second-half contender as a compromise resulting from confusing and competing claims by Nashville and Pittsburgh regarding games each wanted counted in their favor as forfeits by disbanding teams. According to the September 27 edition of the *New York Amsterdam News*, Nashville and Pittsburgh were to play a five-game series, and the winner of that series would play Chicago for the 1933 league championship. This author has found no mention of any of those preliminary or championship games being played.

There was hope, though, for 1934. Even in Cum Posey's "Pointed Paragraphs" of August 12 in which he lambasted the NNL's white booking agents while he indicated that a stronger league leader than Greenlee was needed, Posey stated, "Colored baseball in 1934 will start on the upturn."[49] And Rollo Wilson, while noting that in his opinion the booking agents were against league baseball, seemed to believe that in 1934 the NNL would succeed where it failed in 1933 with a new alignment, including Eastern teams in New York and Philadelphia. "Next year," Wilson said, "always brings something new and better to some few...."[50] Which "few" would they be?

1934

At the end of 1933, it was hardly clear whether the wind was blowing in the direction of an established NNL that would continue operations in 1934 and beyond, or back toward an array of independent clubs like the Monarchs, Grays, and Philadelphia Stars and loose confederations like the NSL existing in an uncertain black baseball universe. After all, recent history involved aborted one-year leagues—the ANL and the E-W League did not survive beyond 1929 and 1932 respectively. Given the way the 1933 NNL season petered out, with only three of seven clubs finishing the season and no apparent postseason playoffs, what indications were there of a sustained NNL? On the one hand, you had a successful start of an all-star franchise in the inaugural East-West Game; on the other hand, the *Pittsburgh Courier* reported that the Nashville Elite Giants, Chicago American Giants, and Pittsburgh Crawfords had very little communication between them during early winter of 1933-34.[51] According to the *Courier*, it was believed that the NSL would operate in 1934 but it was unclear whether that three-team NNL nucleus could join with other Eastern clubs and/or Western clubs to form a circuit, while it was doubtful that all three regions would form a complete confederation. The "moguls" behind all the clubs were operating in secrecy, but it was at least known that a January 13, 1934, meeting in Pittsburgh was planned. The invitation list constituted 12 teams from the East, West, and South which did not even include the Homestead Grays and representatives of Dayton, Columbus, Indianapolis, and Akron.[52]

The turnout was limited to Cum Posey, who was not formally invited but received an oral notification from Chairman and fierce rival Greenlee, and apparently, Greenlee himself and Prentice Byrd of the Cleveland Red Sox attending.[53] The 1933 league secretary (and Crawfords employee) John Clark called this meeting discouraging, as the lack of turnout indicated a desire by most potential league members to wait and see what developed.[54] Posey, on the other hand, seemed to think that the league had potential if Philadelphia, Baltimore, and Newark, who had their own parks and who had owners with experience in Ed Bolden (Philadelphia), Joe Cambria (Baltimore), and Harry Passon (Bacharach Giants, formerly of Atlantic City but now playing in Philadelphia), could be included in the league. Otherwise, Posey planned for the Grays to continue the independent status they assumed when they were expelled in the second half of the 1933 season.[55]

Most importantly, however, Greenlee declared at the January meeting that there would be a subsequent league meeting on February 10 in Philadelphia. At the February meeting, six clubs attained full membership in a planned 1934 league—the three-team nucleus of 1933, the Cleveland Red Sox, Ed Bolden's Philadelphia Stars, and the Newark Dodgers. Bolden objected to there being another Philadelphia team in the league (Passon's Bacharachs), believing that he could not succeed with intracity league competition, and his wishes were granted. He did not succeed, however, in convincing the other owners that a good-faith financial deposit (also called a franchise fee or forfeit) was unneeded. Meanwhile, neither the Grays nor Cambria's Baltimore Black Sox were admitted to the league, in the latter case because he did not attend this meeting.[56]

Although little of substance was accomplished at the February 10 meeting, two important steps were taken—1) a third league meeting was announced for March in Philadelphia at which a schedule of playing dates was to be decided upon; and 2) 1933 Chairman Greenlee requested that Rollo Wilson operate as chair when the new league members were voted on.[57]

On March 10 and 11, the newly reconstituted league did in fact meet and chose *Courier* writer Wilson to be the commissioner of the NNL, although Greenlee was still voted chairman of the board, with Tom Wilson, owner of the Elite Giants, as vice chairman, John Clark as secretary, and Robert Cole as treasurer. According to sportswriter Randy Dixon, the choice of Wilson to head the league deserved high praise, as Dixon believed that Rollo had stellar credentials: "His long experience as a critic and follower of colored baseball, his keen insight of the game, and his wide acquaintanceship and contacts makes him ideally suited to the position."[58] Author Neil Lanctot indicated that it was commonly viewed that Wilson, who was an experienced operative from prior Negro Leagues and who was seen as impartial, could successfully arbitrate league disputes and counteract perceived bias in Gus Greenlee's 1933 league operation.[59]

Wilson Made 'Judge Landis' Of New Negro Ball League
-- *New York Amsterdam News, March 17, 1934.*

And disputes there were—immediately, Wilson became the judge of conflicts between the Homestead Grays (who were made associate members at the March meeting) and the Pittsburgh Crawfords over outfielder Vic Harris and catcher-infielder Leroy Morney, while pitcher Ted Trent was claimed by Chicago and the New York Black Yankees (who were still being debated as potential associate members). Meanwhile, at the meeting a schedule was adopted, with the season to be split into halves—the first half to be played from May 12 through July 4, and the second half ending September 9, to be followed by a playoff between the winners of each half-season. And the Negro Southern League, represented by Nashville owner Tom Wilson at this meeting, agreed to be a farm system for the NNL as NNL clubs could buy NSL players "on a trial basis" with the player chosen returning to the NSL club if he did not succeed in the higher league.

The final preseason meeting of 1934 was held in Pittsburgh on April 14. Along with routine business (booking issues, forfeit fees, authority for disbursements granted to league Secretary Clark), the few members present witnessed "representative" Nat Strong withdraw the application of the New York Black Yankees for membership and rejected Baltimore's application as they again did not appear at the meeting.[60]

But Cumberland Posey was not satisfied with his team's associate status. He still chafed about not being officially invited to the initial 1934 meeting, and he also was greatly dissatisfied with the league's decision not to offer Harry Passon's Bacharach Giants league membership.[61] League secretary Clark used his *Courier* column to answer Posey's "points" pointedly and at times, sarcastically. Clark simply said that Posey was left off the initial invitation list because of his actions giving rise to his team's expulsion in mid-1933 and that his other claims to players and criticisms of league choices on membership and on other matters did not merit equal consideration with opinions of full league members. Perhaps the league's biggest mistake, Clark sarcastically opined, was not picking Posey to be league commissioner, as "everybody has been 'picking' on the Homesteader ever since."[62]

Was it true, as Clark claimed, that Posey wanted that "his every claim should be honored, his views accepted without modification"?[63] Not according to Posey. In his view, the well-intentioned commissioner Wilson was being undermined by the power-hungry league secretary Clark, who, he believed, had no right to decide matters like disputed playing dates between clubs or even whether an associate member like the Grays had as much right to consideration as did a full member. Meanwhile, his rival Greenlee was being "strong-armed" by Nat Strong, white booking agent and part-owner behind the scenes; African-American James Semler was the public franchise representative of the New York Black Yankees.[64] The result, according to Posey, was a league without monthly financial reports and an independent commissioner who could not stop the Crawfords from operating the league in their own best interests.[65]

Despite all the vitriol, the league finished its first half without losing any members. And, in a midseason meeting held in Philadelphia on June 28 and 29, right before the first half ended, the league expanded, adding the Bacharach Giants and Baltimore Sox as full members for the league's second half. Commissioner Wilson, in his June 30, 1934 *Pittsburgh Courier* column, indicated that the main order of business at this meeting was to settle on a second-half schedule but that "certain warring owners" would need to peacefully settle their disputes.[66] Settlement of the main battle, between Posey and Greenlee, was not going to come easily. During the meeting, Posey's "money man [and numbers man]" Rufus "Sonnyman" Jackson, turned down an opportunity for full membership for the Grays that was ostensibly offered by the other teams. Secretary Clark, in his July 14 *Courier* column stated that Commissioner Wilson put membership discussions ahead of the "regular order of business" to bring about harmony and to "perpetuate organized policies in Negro baseball." In the end, according to Clark, Jackson turned down membership while his co-owner Posey's agenda—which, of course, included removing columnist Clark from his league secretary position—was turned down flat by the league.[67] Nevertheless, both the *Atlanta Daily World* and the *Chicago Defender* gave mostly positive reports of this meeting and the status of the league. The *World* characterized the meetings as "for the most part, amicable with the owners disposed to give and take."[68] Meanwhile, the *Defender* opined that "although the league machinery has not operated smoothly, it is a distinct improvement over performances of 1933."[69] Arguably, Posey's repeat performance was no worse and perhaps less disruptive to league operations than that of 1933; and adding rather than subtracting teams constituted distinct progress.

The second half of the 1934 season had its fair share of successes, failures, and ultimately, disputes. The second East-West Game followed up successfully from the first one in 1933 with over 25,000 fans, up considerably from the attendance at the inaugural event, seeing East defeat West by a 1-0 score.[70] The league also staged a four-team doubleheader at Yankee Stadium on September 9 before over 20,000 fans, with the Chicago American Giants defeating the New York Black Yankees 4-3 in the first contest and Satchel Paige dueling Stuart "Slim" Jones to a 1-1 tie in the second game.[71] The American Giants, first-half pennant winner, played the second-half pennant-winning Philadelphia Stars for the league championship. The seven-game series, which ended with the Stars winning 2-0 in Game Seven to take the Series four games to three, was marred by a series of protests, with Chicago saying that Hall of Famer Jud "Boojum" Wilson should have been ejected from Game Six for striking umpire Bert Gholston, and both teams protesting Game Seven.[72] Nevertheless, columnist Ed Harris of the *Philadelphia Tribune* generally praised the league for its two "spectacles of sufficient proportion" (the Yankee Stadium doubleheader and the East-West Game) while noting that the league's biggest challenge was that it needed to book nonleague games to maintain its profitability, thereby undermining the integrity of the league schedule.[73] And columnist Romeo Dougherty of the *New York Amsterdam News* praised Greenlee for his successes in staging games in New York while suggesting that the best future path for the league would be to add two New York teams and form an Eastern association with Greenlee as president and have a Western association based in Chicago, with the league champions playing each other at the season's end for a national championship. The ambivalent fortunes of the league are captured well by Dougherty's statement near the end of his column that he was "looking forward *with anxiety* (emphasis added) to the meeting of the National Negro Baseball League in January.[74]

Before that January 1935 meeting, however, the league had one final abortive session in 1934. In it, only league treasurer and Chicago owner Robert Cole, Chairman Greenlee, and Posey and Jackson of ineligible-to-vote associate member Homestead appeared. The meeting was supposed to resolve the Game Seven protest as well as have members pay off their league obligations. When 5 o'clock came and went without any other members appearing, Greenlee expressed the opinion that league business could be conducted, including bill payments. Treasurer Cole refused to "sign a single check until all members were present — adding that there were several matters that he wanted to be clear on." Clearly, Cole was dissatisfied about the failure of his league to rule on his team's protest — and eventually, the protests by both teams were thrown out and the Stars were awarded the 1934 league championship.[75]

1935

Although 1934 was a successful year compared with 1933, NNL Commissioner (but not for long) Rollo Wilson admitted that "few, if any clubs made any money" while Chairman Greenlee cautioned that "in spite of the success of 1934, we have not arrived."[76]

One potentially lucrative opportunity beckoned. Although the NNL played two successful doubleheaders at Yankee Stadium in September of 1934, the second one interrupting the league championship series, they did not have any New York area teams represented in the 1934 NNL.[77] According to Neil Lanctot, NNL Chairman Greenlee realized that the Eastern market provided better moneymaking opportunities than did the Midwestern ones, in large part because of the sizable black population in the Washington-New York corridor.[78] In addition, the *Atlanta Daily World*, in reporting on the upcoming initial 1935 meeting of the NNL on January 12, stated simply that Eastern clubs were reluctant to play in the West because "they almost lost their shirts when they made Western trips last year."[79]

But there was a potential roadblock in Nat Strong, the white powerhouse in the world of black and semipro baseball in New York City. Strong ran a booking agency which had a virtual monopoly on the New York baseball booking business, charging 5 to 10 percent of the gate receipts to book games in venues like Yankee Stadium and Ebbets Field while offering minimal ($500-$600) flat guarantees to black teams that played Sunday night games at Brooklyn's Dexter Park.[80] Though it was clear that Strong would oppose it, the NNL nonetheless voted in November 1934 to add the Brooklyn Eagles to the 1935 NNL mix. The Eagles, owned by Abe and Effa Manley, were to play at Ebbets Field, thereby competing directly with games that Strong would book at Dexter Park.[81]

Suddenly and unexpectedly, that potential problem disappeared, and an even greater opportunity to expand into the New York market became viable because Nat Strong died of a heart attack on January 10. When the NNL met in New York shortly after Strong's death, the league voted to admit not only the Eagles but also the New York Cubans, owned by Cuban-American Harlem racketeer Alejandro "Alex" Pompez. The league was now a robust eight-team assemblage; in addition to the Eagles and the Cubans, the Homestead Grays were bumped up from associate to full membership, and Nashville, Pittsburgh, Philadelphia, Chicago, and Newark fielded teams as well.[82]

The January 12 meeting could be characterized as celebratory, even though the proceedings were "chilled a bit through the death of Nat Strong.[83] While the league members voted unanimously to include the Cubans, they also dropped the Baltimore and Cleveland teams from the roster. Pompez then spoke, "declaring himself ready to spend $35,000 to make New York baseball-conscious as far as Negro baseball is concerned," with plans for enlarging and improving Dyckman Oval in Upper Manhattan as the Cubans' home venue. In addition to perfunctory league business such as Secretary Clark's 1934 report and scheduling and player salary discussions, there was a radio broadcast Saturday afternoon and a dinner for over 100 people at Harlem's Small's Paradise on Saturday night, with a concluding session for player transactions Sunday afternoon.[84]

Baseball Men Gather For Annual Assembly

—*Atlanta Daily World, January 23, 1935*

The league got down to business in a three-day confab held in Philadelphia from March 8 to 10. The league's managers chose eight umpires out of 24 applicants for the 1935 season, including the umpires who worked the protested games of the 1934 league championship. They also submitted their player lists, with only a couple of players being claimed by more than one club, meaning that player disputes were at a minimum. As usual, a great deal of time and energy was devoted to scheduling, characterized by Cum Posey in his March 16, 1935, *Courier* column as "a matter of give and take all the way with a desire shown by all the members to aid the new clubs in their home cities."[85]

The bombshell revelation of this meeting, however, occurred on Sunday night when it was revealed that 1934 Commissioner Rollo Wilson was voted down for the 1935 post; instead Ferdinand Q. Morton, the first black person chosen to be a New York City Civil Service commissioner—was chosen to succeed Wilson.[86] The choice was not unanimous, as Greenlee and Philadelphia Stars owner Ed Bolden still supported Wilson—but Robert Cole, still bitter about the controversial resolution of the 1934 league championship protests in favor of the Stars, and frequent Wilson (and Greenlee) critic Cum Posey joined the two New York teams in supporting Morton.[87] All the other 1934 league officials, including Chairman Greenlee, were re-elected.

Also at this meeting, it was finally resolved that the 1935 lineup of teams would not include the Bacharach Giants (who had attended the January 12 meeting) and would therefore have eight teams, as the "surprise of the meeting was the inability of the Bacharach Giants of Philadelphia to post the necessary forfeit."[88] All the other teams posted the necessary $500 forfeit, or franchise fee, a perhaps small but yet significant indicator of a newly established financial stability for the league.[89]

And then it all unraveled. This author has found no mention in the black press or in several secondary sources of any formal league meetings during the 1935 season, although presumably some contact between owners happened as traditionally the schedule for the league's second half would have been arranged during the season. But, according to Ed Bolden, the league was in conflict. Bolden was quoted in the *Amsterdam News* of August 31 as follows: "There is too much politics in the league and we are dissatisfied with the way its business has been conducted.... We intend to have a show-down at the fall meeting and rip things wide open."[90] Unfortunately for Bolden, the league did not hold any fall meeting, even though Cum Posey pleaded for a meeting "so things could be ironed out."[91] Posey and the other owners clamored for the return of their $500 forfeits while various league owners, including Gus Greenlee and new owners Pompez of the Cubans and the Manleys of the Eagles experienced financial problems, in whole or in part due to poor league attendance."[92] The Cubans were successful on the field, winning the league's second-half pennant but losing to first-half winner Pittsburgh in an exciting seven-game championship series.[93] Yet despite the successful postseason series, the future of the second NNL seemed to hang in the balance.

1936

In the early days of 1936, Commissioner Morton called for a league meeting on January 10. Chairman Greenlee, however, was not planning to attend this meeting, and in the end it was not held. Since the nonmeeting followed the disarray and dissension of most of 1935, a fair characterization of the status of the league would be "in limbo" at best. Greenlee did finally call for a meeting that was held in Philadelphia on January 26 and 27. According to Courtney Smith's article covering the *Philadelphia Tribune*'s reportage on the Philadelphia Stars from 1933-1938, *Tribune* writer Ed Harris was one of seven writers who attended but were barred from this meeting. In a January 16, 1936, *Tribune* article, Harris expressed surprise that the NNL moguls did not realize that canceling league meetings as they did on January 10 undermined the league's legitimacy. Now Harris expressed a belief that ownership's blocking of press coverage of league operations left the fans lacking information about the league and was a foolish way to alienate the fan base.[94]

Since media could not therefore provide an unfiltered report of the meeting, the fans got a measure of the current league plans that was part conjecture, part observation of the comings and goings of prominent individuals, and part leaked information along with some apparently announced league determinations. Conjecture—there is rampant displeasure with the current slate of league officers, including the commissioner: "[A] clean sweep in the personnel officers is forecast." Observation—Greenlee left the meeting early, at the end of the first day, and then switched places with Secretary Clark, who missed day one. Commissioner Morton stayed away on Saturday "but gave them a very limited amount of his time on Sunday." Leaked information—unofficial word that Greenlee offered his resignation as chairman to Commissioner Morton while "varied opinions on the financial health of the body leaked out to the pressmen." Apparent announcements—Newark Dodgers owner Charles Tyler sold his team to heretofore Brooklyn Eagles owner Abe Manley, while Manley's Brooklyn Eagles were "thrown back into the lap of the parent body" and New York Black Yankees owner James Semler applied formally for membership but the league deferred a vote until a planned March 7 meeting. Conclusion? "Members of the Negro National League deferred until March 7 many important matters which intrigue the diamond fans of the country."[95]

Echoing Harris, this was no way to engage the willing but often impoverished black fan base. So Candy Jim Taylor, manager of the Nashville (soon to be Washington) Elite Giants, spoke out. In a February 15, 1936, *Defender* column Candy Jim criticized the magnates: "[A]fter waiting all winter to call the meeting there was little done to get the clubs together and to get the fans interested."[96] Taylor felt that many leaders of black baseball from its earlier days were missed—some like former manager C.I. Taylor, his older brother, and Rube Foster, had since passed away, but others like J.L. Wilkinson, owner of the independent Kansas City Monarchs, and St. Louis Stars owners Dick Kent, L.A. Brown, and G.B. Key, he thought should be invited to a general baseball conference. Finally, Candy Jim raised a sore point that would continue to be harped on throughout the history of Negro League operations: he suggested that the NNL pick a non-owner of a club, perhaps a sportswriter, as league president, pay him a salary and expect him to use his connections to publicize the game.[97] But why should the wise ownership of NNL franchises follow such eminently good advice?

Owners Are At Fault For Present Plight Of Baseball, Says Taylor
THEY BLEED GAME OF MONEY
— *Chicago Defender, February 15, 1936*

Instead, the *Defender* reported in its February 29, 1936, edition that Chairman Greenlee would reconsider his resignation and remain NNL president.[98] But they were wrong. At the March 7-8 meeting, Greenlee did indeed resign as president and "Chief" Ed Bolden was chosen to replace him. Commissioner Morton was retained for another year. But Abe Manley was chosen as vice president, with former VP Tom Wilson shifting to treasurer, replacing Robert Cole, who had remained league treasurer in 1935 even though he sold his interest in Chicago in mid-1935. Since new American Giants owner Horace Hall kept them independent in 1936, it clearly made no sense for Cole, no longer even affiliated with a team no longer in the league, to remain as treasurer—after all, officials outside of team employees were rarely involved in league operations! John Clark continued as league secretary.

Other decisions made at the March 7-8 parley included rejecting the Black Yankees' membership application, a determination to play another split-season schedule with a seven-game championship playoff between the winners of each half, and allowing Nashville to shift its operations to Washington and play at Griffith Stadium, the home park of the Washington Senators, while the now renamed and shifted Brooklyn Eagles would play in Newark's Ruppert Stadium as the Pittsburgh Crawfords and the Homestead Grays would play at Forbes Field, home of the National League Pirates.[99]

On June 18, 1936, the NNL held a midseason meeting in New York. The meeting followed private ones held between the now (Nat) Strong-less but still strong and independent Black Yankees, represented by African-American owner James Semler and white owner/booking agent William Leuschner (former partner of Nat Strong), and Commissioner Morton, in which the Yankees were persuaded to drop damage suits against Eagles owner Abe Manley and New York Cubans owner Alex Pompez for using players under contract to the Yankees. In the subsequent league meeting, the Yankees, "stormy petrels of Negro baseball," were finally made a full member of the league.[100] This meant that, for the second half of the 1936 schedule, the league would have seven teams, with the Yankees joining the Nashville/Washington Elite Giants, Pittsburgh Crawfords, Homestead Grays, Philadelphia Stars, Newark Eagles, and New York Cubans in league competition.[101]

While mundane league business was also conducted at the June 18 meeting, including continuing the Worth baseball as the official NNL baseball, coming to terms with league umpires, and acknowledging a Homestead Grays protest of a May 24 game in Newark, the real league action was elsewhere. Though Greenlee was out as league chairman, Cum Posey was still at odds with him and league Secretary Clark. Posey refused to play his home games at Greenlee Field, resulting in no Grays-Crawfords contests during the league's first half. Meanwhile, a ruling that each league team had to play the others five times per half led to a dispute over the winner of the first-half pennant. In the end, the Elite Giants were declared first-half winner over the Philadelphia Stars but a "convoluted controversy" over rescheduling two Stars-Elites games was unsatisfactorily handled by Commissioner Morton.[102]

While the first-half controversy raged on, the Crawfords claimed the league's second-half crown. But the planned league championship series was canceled after the playing of only one game. A suggestion that the series be finished in the spring of 1937 was dismissed; meanwhile, Chairman Bolden expressed the opinion that "it is not mandatory that the two champions complete a World Series if it does not pay financially."[103] Not only does this statement of Bolden's indicate that the league's disordered and disputed affairs affected fan interest, he preceded it in his *Defender* column by an even more disturbing statement: "[I]t is news to me that the Negro World Series has been abandoned."[104] Did Bolden really not know what was going on in the league over which he presided?

1937

At the start of 1937, the NNL was in trouble. *Philadelphia Tribune* writer Ed Harris, a particularly strident league critic, had assessed the league thusly: "The league as a league is a flop. It seems that some of the teams in the group are in it the way some people are married —simply because it sounds nice."[105] And the marriage was fractious—according to Posey, the seven members of the league as 1936 ended were arrayed as follows: three pulling one way and four pulling opposite."[106] In addition, they would soon have Western competition. In early October of 1936, a "Negro Western League" had an organizing meeting in Indianapolis, with attendees choosing Major Robert R. Jackson as league head, Kansas City Monarchs owner J.L. Wilkinson as treasurer, and *Chicago Defender* sports editor Al Monroe as secretary. Eight cities were awarded league membership at this meeting: Kansas City, Chicago, Indianapolis, Memphis, Birmingham, St. Louis, Cincinnati, and Detroit.[107] A second meeting was held in Chicago in early December where the league officials were formally installed, a scheduling committee was formed, and statements were made indicating that players who had gone East to play for 1936 NNL teams would be returned to their rightful Western owners in time to prepare for the coming 1937 inaugural "Negro National League."[108] Was the *Defender* simply mistaken in labeling this new venture as a new "NNL," or were they expecting the 1936 NNL to cease operations—or were they harkening back to the original Western-based NNL of the 1920s by calling this new league the NNL and perhaps planning to refer to whatever Eastern association that continued in 1937 as the Negro National Association?

Despite its sagging fortunes, the NNL (Eastern variety) did hold a meeting on January 4, 1937, in Philadelphia. It was reported in one source that the NNL clubs were considering adding yet another New York club to the league, and were also interested in connecting with the nascent Western league, but neither of those initiatives would occur in 1937.[109]

Instead, the meeting "produced little action for the Negro National League," reported embattled Secretary Clark.[110] Clark was himself taking action by declaring his resignation as league secretary effective at the end of January. Clearly, Posey's criticism of Clark's "double-dealing" (working for the league and the Crawfords simultaneously) had taken its toll, though why a secretary should be more unbiased than the other league officials, many of whom owned or worked for teams, remains puzzling.

Announcements involving the Grays, Crawfords, Cubans, and Black Yankees provided some hope that the most bitter disputes were abating, as the Grays said they would play 1937 games at Greenlee Field and the Black Yanks at Dyckman Oval, the home field of the Cubans. Additional news from the January 4 meeting included the announcement of a minimum ticket price of 35 cents for all league games, and that Commissioner Morton was running unopposed for another term and was simultaneously running for league chairman against *Courier* business manager Ira Lewis.[111]

A quick follow-up meeting in New York in late January decided the league officers for 1937. Commissioner Morton stayed on for a third term; instead of Ira Lewis, Leonard Williams, a reputed Pittsburgh underworld figure, was chosen chairman, with Elites owner and 1936 Treasurer Tom Wilson returning to the vice-chair position he held in 1934 and 1935 and Abe Manley, who had been vice chair in 1936, switching with Wilson and becoming treasurer. An important change from prior years (albeit one that was later rescinded) was the decision to play an undivided season from May 15 through September 15—could this be an attempt to avoid another controversy like the previous year's dispute over the first-half winner? Various player trades were discussed, with some rejected and others still pending. Finally, what the *Pittsburgh Courier* described as a highlight of the meeting was a unanimous vote by the members to be covered by the Major-Minor agreement of Organized (white) Baseball. Baseball integration was not even a rumor at this point, but acquiring legitimacy by operating under the same structure as white baseball was a desperate hope of the struggling league.[112]

The NNL held its annual schedule-making meeting in New York in late March, a three-day affair punctuated by a blockbuster trade: The Crawfords sent legendary slugging catcher Josh Gibson and star third baseman Judy Johnson to their rival Homestead Grays for catcher Pepper Bassett, third baseman Henry Spearman, and $2,500, then sold pitcher Harry Kincannon to the Black Yankees for an undisclosed amount.[113] Superficially, the first deal was an equal exchange of players at two positions, but the cash element augmenting the meager return of talent for two future Hall of Fame players along with the sale of Kincannon demonstrated that Greenlee was in dire need of funds. Meanwhile, with Leonard Williams having declined the chairman/president position, the league returned the Crawfords owner to his former position.[114]

During the 1937 season, two major developments threatened the league's viability. First, New York Cubans owner Alex Pompez had to leave the country to avoid arrest for his prior involvements in New York's numbers rackets. While Pompez cooled his heels in Mexico City, he left Roy Sparrow and Frank Forbes in charge of his franchise.[115] At the same time, Dominican Republic dictator Rafael Trujillo commenced his raids on prominent Negro League players including luminaries Satchel Paige, Cool Papa Bell, and player-manager Martin Dihigo of the New York Cubans. Eventually, 18 Negro League players, many of them from the Crawfords and the Cubans, departed for the Dominican Republic in 1937, and by April, it was announced in the *New York Age* that the New York Cubans would not play ball in 1937, leaving the 1937 NNL as a six-team operation.[116]

The NNL did try to take action to either recover the Dominican jumpers or at least punish them and suspend them from the NNL for their actions, while gaining US government support in sanctioning the Dominican Republic. In its June 19, 1937, issue, the *New York Amsterdam News* reported that the NNL held a meeting in Philadelphia on May 27 for the purpose of condemning the raid of their players and to strategize about enlisting US government support in their efforts to get these players to return.[117] Several NNL officials and Negro American League President R.R. Jackson did indeed meet with a State Department official, leading to a fruitless discussion with an emissary of the Dominican government, and the players did not return to the NNL in 1937.[118]

Meanwhile, the newly organized Negro American League (as it was now referred to by the *Chicago Defender*) met in late February of 1937 with its primary purpose being to prepare the league's schedule. The NAL planned a split season and a playoff between winners of its first and second halves. To show that the NAL was for real, league President Jackson "ordered all clubs to post forfeit money to guarantee good faith and to assure the fans that no combats will be canceled at any time."[119] At the meeting, the NAL announced that Ted "Double-Duty" Radcliffe had been traded to Cincinnati by Indianapolis and hurler Thomas had been sent by Chicago to Detroit for an "infielder yet to be selected."[120] The NAL completed its 1937 season with a five-game series between Chicago and Kansas City to settle a tie in the standings of the league's first half. Kansas City won the playoff, which included a 17-inning tie, in the second game, and the league decided that there was no purpose to having another playoff series, as the Monarchs had won the season's second half.[121]

Despite the suggestion mentioned at an early 1937 NNL meeting of maintaining contact with the NAL, the two leagues had player disputes and therefore did not develop much of a working relationship in 1937.[122] The Monarchs, though, did play a nine-game series against a team of NNL pennant-winning Homestead Grays and second-place (in the season's first half) Newark Eagles players, with the Grays/Eagles taking seven of the nine games.[123] As *Defender* writer Frank "Fay" Young editorialized, "I cannot see where it can be called a World Series."[124] NNL President Greenlee chimed in by saying that the games were merely a promotion staged by the owners of the Newark Eagles and Homestead Grays and therefore not sanctioned by the NNL.[125] Nevertheless, the series signified the beginnings of interleague competition at the end of the first year of a fledgling two-league black institution.

While the "World Series" was being played, the NNL held a final 1937 meeting in New York on September 27. Former NNL Secretary Clark characterized this meeting as of little moment. Clearly, ownership battles were evident. Clark reported charges being made by Posey and others that Greenlee refused to allow the Dominican contingent of NNL players to return to the NNL and also used some of these players himself in unofficial 1937 games.[126] Would Greenlee be allowed to continue to lead the NNL in 1938?

1938

As the year started, the NNL was on very shaky footing. According to historian Lanctot, "[B]y 1938 numerous African-American sportswriters, owners, players and fans had begun to doubt whether professional black baseball could ever fulfill its potential as a profitable enterprise."[127] Not only were the conditions of a continuing depression depressing fan turnout, but the weak financial conditions and limited business acumen of most NNL franchises also contributed toward maintaining a state of constant trouble in the league's attempt to remain viable. Figurehead Commissioner Morton called for the first 1938 NNL meeting to be held in New York in mid-January but, according to the *Pittsburgh Courier*, no one showed up. At least Greenlee could still get ownership to meet, which they did on January 28 and 29. In anticipation of the gathering, Greenlee maintained that the league, its teams and its players needed to operate in a more disciplined fashion, and salaries, which he claimed to be two-thirds of operating costs for the league's first five years, needed to be reduced.[128]

Modern Baseball Needs Another Rube Foster!

— *Pittsburgh Courier*, January 29, 1938

In the business files of Effa Manley, a document summarizing this January meeting was found. Following up on Greenlee's concerns, the six teams expected to form the 1938 NNL — Effa and Abe Manley's Newark Eagles, the New York Black Yankees, the Pittsburgh Crawfords, the Homestead Grays, the Elite Giants (who were in flux as to their location—which would explain the missing city next to their name), and the Philadelphia Stars were listed underneath a statement that "for the past seven years, Negro League Baseball has operated at a loss."[129] The document went on to declare that salaries would have to be cut so that even greater losses would not occur in 1938.[130] But this agreement aside, the league was still seen as fundamentally divided: "[T]he Nashville [Elite Giants] Philadelphia, Pittsburgh Crawfords were aligned against Newark, Black Yanks, and Homestead Grays."[131] Not only the *Defender*, but the other leading black newspaper, the *Pittsburgh Courier*, perceived the ongoing conflict, describing it as "petty quarreling, underhanded moves, factional fights and differences, and failure to meet obligations."[132] The NNL responded by electing a three-member board of Greenlee, Abe Manley and Thomas Wilson to head the league, and picked Cum Posey as secretary-treasurer. It was an attempt to bridge the gap between sides by picking two owners from each faction as league officials. In addition, the league declared efforts to reduce expenses other than salaries such as cutting down from six to three traveling umpires and attempting to eliminate the expense of middlemen by clubs doing their own promotions.[133]

On March 6 and 7, a final preseason NNL meeting was held in Philadelphia. Resolved—the league would consist of seven teams, including a new team in Washington called the Black Senators.[134] Postponed—the appointment of a commissioner to preside over both the NNL and the NAL. The NAL had picked a commissioner, their 1937 Chairman R.R. Jackson, at an earlier NAL meeting held in Chicago on Saturday, February 19 and had sent J.B. Martin of the Memphis club to Philadelphia to nominate Jackson to oversee the operations of both leagues.[135] After a heated debate, however, there was a deadlock in the NNL vote for commissioner between Jackson and Judge Joseph Rainey of Philadelphia. It had already been made clear that NNL Commissioner Morton was not under consideration for the job. There were many player sales and trades at this meeting, most notably involving pitcher Chet Brewer being sent to Washington from Pittsburgh and Judy Johnson also being obtained by Washington from Homestead—many of the transactions that were announced involving Washington as they were populating their roster. The league set a 16-player limit, and postponed a vote on a Buffalo team entering the league along with the choice of an NNL/NAL commissioner.[136] And, most importantly, players on the disbanded (in 1937) 1936 New York Cubans were distributed throughout the league while the rights to players who followed Trujillo's siren song to Santo Domingo in 1937 reverted to their former teams as their suspensions were lifted.[137] The players were supposed to pay fines, but they were never enforced, which led to criticism by fans and sportswriters of the league's lack of backbone.[138]

The Senators did not survive the 1938 season, disbanding in August; as Neil Lanctot described it, "[T]he failure of the Black Senators and yet another incomplete playoff series climaxed a nightmarish season for black professional baseball."[139] As in 1937, no official NNL/NAL World Series was held; the Grays won both halves of the 1937 NNL season although the Cubans and Grays both claimed to have won the season's second-half pennant.[140] The rumor mill was busy with speculation that Gus Greenlee would be held accountable for NNL failures and in particular for his poor handling of the Dominican jumpers and would be asked to resign.

The NAL met prior to the 1938 season in Chicago in mid-December 1937. They elected Major R.R. Jackson to a second term as league president, and chose J.B. Martin vice president, *Defender* sportswriter Frank "Fay" Young secretary, and J.R. Wilkinson of Kansas City treasurer. The NAL admitted the Atlanta Black Crackers and Jacksonville Red Caps as associate members at this meeting.[141] When they reconvened on February 19, Atlanta had been raised to a full member, joining the Memphis Red Sox, Chicago American Giants, Indianapolis ABCs, Birmingham Black Barons, and the Kansas City Monarchs in a six-team circuit.[142] The NAL decided not to include franchises from Detroit, Cincinnati, or St. Louis as their representatives failed to attend this meeting and put up forfeit money. Rather than including "weak clubs" in an eight-team league, the members felt that "six fast clubs" would be better for the fans.[143] As far as postseason play was concerned, a two-game playoff was swept by first-half winner Memphis over second-half champion Atlanta.[144]

A joint NAL/NNL meeting was held on June 22, 1938, but did not solve the commissioner issue as the Eastern clubs, who met separately prior to the joint meeting, were now against electing one. What the leagues did agree on was "a set of rules by which both leagues could operate and respect territorial rights as well as forcing players to respect contracts."[145] Would the two leagues respect this agreement in their actions or in the breach?

1939

First, though, the two leagues would have to decide upon whether they planned to continue as two leagues or instead merge into one league with two divisions, one in the East and one in the West, much like the original concept of the second NNL in 1933. On Sunday, December 11, 1938, at Chicago's Appomattox Club, the NAL held its now "regular December meeting" (for the third straight year!) with the principal topic of discussion being the configuration of 1939 Negro League competition.[146] Faithful reporter Cum Posey's *Courier* column noted that the meeting, called to order by NAL President Jackson at "10:30 sharp (Negro National League owners, please take notice)" included re-electing 1938 NAL officers Jackson as well as Vice president J.B. Martin, Secretary Frank (Fay) Young and Treasurer J.L. Wilkinson, and Posey's own conveyance of an NNL proposal to merge into one league composed of the best cities, with regular league games between teams from each 1938 league. Posey reported that Jackson would decide by January 10 about forming one combined league.[147]

The January 14, 1939, edition of the *Chicago Defender* reported that Jackson's league would remain intact, specifying that a merger would have involved only four teams from each league and the NAL would not "desert the other four members and make them associate members for 1939."[148] The NNL would just have to move ahead and plan its own operations, without being joined by any NAL teams, for the 1939 season—and they would be doing it without Gus Greenlee.

Even before the NNL's February 1939 meeting, the rumblings of Greenlee's departure from the NNL were being felt. In December of 1938, Greenlee sold Greenlee Field. He considered operating elsewhere but financial setbacks, particularly in the boxing arena, leading to alleged unpaid debts and bouncing checks, meant that he ultimately decided to disband his team.[149] It was hardly a surprise, then, that Greenlee resigned as league chairman in February, (although he was really a member of a three-man board heading the NNL in 1938) and though the league passed a resolution naming him "honorary chairman," neither Greenlee nor any Pittsburgh Crawfords representative appeared at the meeting.[150] In a missive summarizing this meeting written by Cum Posey, he listed the following as team owners: Tom Wilson of the Baltimore Elite Giants, the Eds (Bolden and Gottlieb) of the Philadelphia Stars, Abe Manley of the Newark Eagles, Rufus "Sonnyman" Jackson of the Homestead Grays, Alex Pompez of the returning Cuban Stars, James Semler of the New York Black Yankees, and finally Hank Rigney of Toledo. The absence of any mention of Greenlee in this summary, along with subsequent events, suggests that Gus Greenlee was no longer a factor in the NNL's operations.[151]

The members also elected Tom Wilson as president, Ed Gottlieb recording secretary, and Posey corresponding secretary, with Abe Manley as treasurer, and Ed Bolden as vice president. Along with various resolutions and discussions involving time between doubleheaders, forfeits, and fines, the most intriguing development was a decision to "inaugurate 'streamline' baseball, that is, no player shall throw the ball around between innings, the pitcher shall be allowed to throw four warm-up pitches between innings."[152] Even in 1939, owners were looking for ways to speed up the game! But, just like twenty-first-century initiatives to limit batters stepping into and out of the batter's box, indications are that umpires were inconsistent in enforcing this "streamlined" format as is suggested by a memo written by Posey asking that owners "kindly see that it (streamline baseball) is enforced."[153]

The NAL also held a February meeting in which it announced its first-half schedule with teams in Chicago, St. Louis, Kansas City, Louisville, Cleveland, and Memphis. Newly elected NNL President Wilson attended and advised the NAL scheduling committee regarding open dates which would enable interleague play.[154]

By April, the NNL took action to finalize the replacement of the Pittsburgh Crawfords in the 1939 NNL, as Cum Posey traveled to Toledo in mid-April with the great Oscar Charleston to meet with the prospective Toledo owners. As Posey related in a letter to Effa Manley, Toledo wanted assurances that they would have all 1938 Crawfords players on their roster in return for their $250 fee, a demand which was agreed to by President Wilson.[155] Unfortunately, Toledo would only play five league games as their failure to get the NNL to fulfill its agreement on providing the Crawford players along with the readmission of the New York Cubans into the NNL ended their NNL membership. Instead, at its June 20 meeting, the NNL unanimously passed a motion to allow Toledo to join the NAL.[156]

The NNL and NAL clearly had conflicts in 1939. NAL President Jackson and NNL club owner Posey were trading charges that the other league was operating in bad faith by taking players from their respective league's teams. Major Jackson referenced a lack of a commissioner overseeing both leagues as part of the difficulty in resolving player disputes. After the NNL briefly met on June 20, they recessed prior to the convening of a joint NNL/NAL session. The most important outcome of this session was a signed agreement "which protects players under contract and a heavy fine is placed on owners who attempt to steal or entice players under contract with one club to another."[157] Specifically, ownership of both leagues agreed to a $50 fine for any club inducing a player to jump his club or league; a second such offense would be fined $100; and "any owner who accepts a player who is the property of another league shall be suspended indefinitely and banned from organized baseball."[158]

Along with this attempt at interleague cooperation on respecting player contracts, both leagues agreed to an East-West game to be held on August 6 in Chicago and an all-star game in Yankee Stadium on August 27.[159]

On August 27, presumably in New York, another joint league meeting produced a motion to punish Toledo for using Homestead Grays outfielder Jerry Benjamin.[160] Along with other ongoing interleague player conflicts, the discord over Benjamin signified that the commitment to protecting player contracts was a "wobbly agreement [that] would not last past 1939."[161] The following day, the NNL met and agreed to two five-game semifinal playoff series between Homestead and Philadelphia and between Newark and Baltimore, the winners to meet in a final playoff.[162] In the end, the Homestead Grays defeated the Baltimore Elite Giants 2-0 in the final series while the Monarchs defeated the St. Louis Stars 3-2 in the NAL final playoff series.[163]

When you consider Cumberland Posey's belief, expressed in a letter to Abe Manley, that the two of them and Ed (presumably Ed Gottlieb) had saved the league when the three men met in Philadelphia in January 1939 and "faced things in a sensible manner," the 1939 season could be characterized as a modest success, considering a full slate of playoff series in each league, attendance of over 33,000 at the annual East-West Game, and a total of over 60,000 fans in attendance for five doubleheaders in Yankee Stadium.[164] Nevertheless, as the year came to an end, Newark owner Abe Manley sent his wife and co-owner Effa Manley to speak at a year-end NAL meeting on December 9 and 10, 1939 and convey his belief that "we must have a better understanding, and freindleir (sic) relations between our two leagues. If we hope to command the respect of the baseball loving public…"[165]

1940

In his thorough examination of the inner workings of Negro League baseball, historian Neil Lanctot opined that "Effa Manley provided a necessary stimulant to the often torpid and stagnant world of black professional baseball."[166] There is no doubt that Effa Manley ignited sparks between and among competing factions of the Negro League owners as she sided first with one and then another of the varying (by the year, by the issue) interest groups debating how best to run the Negro Leagues. While 1939 saw an effort to streamline night baseball, the NAL winter meeting on December 9, 1939 saw Effa Manley leading a "movement to streamline the administration of the industry through a commissioner to oversee both leagues."[167] Her solution to both interleague disputes and ineffectual league operating systems began with her putting the name of Judge William Hastie, at that time the dean of Howard Law School and previously the first black federal judge to serve in the U.S. (albeit in the Virgin Islands) before the NAL as a potential commissioner of both leagues, assuring the meeting that Hastie was supported by the Cuban Stars, New York Black Yankees, and Newark Eagles. According to the meeting notes of NNL Secretary Cum Posey (hardly an unbiased observer, as we shall soon see, when the NNL voted on a 1940 president with Posey in opposition to Manley's choice), "the A.N.L. (sic.) did not accept Mr. Hastie on the grounds that this was not ajoint (sic.) meeting."[168]

What the league generally referred to as the NAL (although ANL is occasionally found in letters like Posey's and in the black press) did do was vote 5 to 2 in favor of Dr. J.B. Martin, owner of the Chicago American Giants, to succeed Major R.R. Jackson after he had served three one-year terms as NAL president. But the NAL still had a place for Jackson, as Posey noted that at the December 9 meeting the league picked the major as NAL commissioner, an action which seemed to suggest that Jackson should be commissioner of both leagues—as well as underscoring that the NAL "wasn't ready to have a hand-picked candidate jammed down their throat."[169]

Before taking up the commissioner issue at a joint meeting of the two leagues in late February, the NNL held its first meeting of 1940 on February 2 in Philadelphia. In what was described by the *Chicago Defender* as "the stormiest meeting in the history of the Negro National League—and there have been many stormy ones…,"[170] the league owners split down the middle, deadlocking on choosing to either re-elect Tom Wilson as president or pick *New York Amsterdam News* publisher C.B. Powell as president. Not only were the NNL owners all at loggerheads, but they were being excoriated by members of the black press for, among other items, being kept in the dark about their business proceedings. In the February 3, 1940, edition of the *Pittsburgh Courier*, columnist Randy Dixon asked a series of scathing, sarcastic questions and offered his own answers about the NNL and its February 2, 1940 meeting, a sample of which follows:

"What is the Negro National League? The Negro National League is much ado about nothing… Does the league accomplish anything at its meetings? No… What, then, does it do at its meetings? That's easy: The formula has been the same, year in and year out. It sees to it that all newspapers are excluded… How does the league accomplish excluding newspapermen?… by bluntly telling them they are neither wanted nor required, and then releasing canned copy from which the newspapermen are expected to erect a story…"[171]

Dixon was known for being particularly critical of the men who, he often referred to as "mag-nuts."[172] In contrast, sportswriter Art Carter, who seemingly reported "just the facts" in his *Baltimore Afro-American* column of February 10, 1940, about the conflict between Posey and Effa Manley regarding her seeking Wilson's dismissal, was nonetheless accused by Manley of misstating her reasons for her positions and enthusiastically criticizing her even though "you were not there to see what I did, or hear what I said."[173] In Manley's letter, she essentially acknowledged limits on access placed on the black press as she stated that Carter was "at no time … in the outer office or the inner office, at the time the press was admitted to listen in on the proceedings."[174] The press heard and saw enough, however, to know that Manley 1) headed the effort by the three New York area clubs to oust Wilson, 2) argued that Wilson should be dismissed because he allowed a white booking agent, Philadelphia Stars co-owner Ed Gottlieb, a prohibitive 10 percent of revenues fee while booking games at Yankee stadium instead of him arranging for a black entity to get the booking fees, and after being insulted by Manley, Posey "left the meeting in a huff, vowing that he would never return as long as Mrs. Manley was the Newark Eagles representative and charging that she, as a woman, took advantage of her sex in the deliberations."[175] From a twenty-first-century view, we can certainly censure the media, league ownership, and league officials for their obvious sexism, but we can also see that the media was hardly being enabled by secretive owners and operatives to do their job reporting and in some sense publicizing the league.

The February 2 meeting left matters unresolved; accordingly, the NNL scheduled a meeting on February 23 prior to a joint NNL-NAL meeting in Chicago on February 24. In the NNL meeting, the deadlock over the league presidency held; the league therefore decided to go along with the same officers as in 1939, retaining Wilson as president, at the recommendation of New York Cubans owner Alex Pompez.[176] Though a decision was made, the NNL was really only "kicking the can down the road" as bickering between the factions would resume at the next annual election of league officers. By then, a pattern of bickering, deadlocking, and ultimately keeping the same oftentimes ineffectual leadership had been well-established, especially in the NNL.

In the February 24 joint meeting, the leagues resolved several NNL/NAL player disputes but also entertained a motion by Posey to elect Major Jackson as commissioner of both leagues, in opposition to the position of the Manleys, but the NNL indicated it was not ready to vote on this and Posey withdrew his motion.[177]

On June 18 and 19 in New York, a midseason NNL meeting was followed by a rancorous joint night session, as the leagues battled over "that elongated individual, Satchel Paige" and whether he belonged to the Newark Eagles or not.[178] While the Manleys held the NAL responsible for Paige not reporting to them, Satchel was pitching for an independent team called the Satchell *(sic)* Paige All-Stars, who had their games booked by Lee Wilkinson, brother of Monarchs owner J.L. Wilkinson.[179] In retaliation, Abe and Effa Manley played infielder Bus Clarkson and pitcher Ernie Carter, who were owned by the now-NAL member Toledo Crawfords. Despite NNL President Wilson having earlier ruled that Clarkson and Carter belonged to the NAL, and NAL President J.B. Martin denying that the two players could be traded to the Eagles before being waived out of the NAL (as Abe Manley claimed that Toledo owner Hank Crawford had authorized them going to Newark), the Manleys later got their way in keeping Clarkson and Carter, although Paige became NAL property. At the meeting, however, "the fur flew" as Memphis owner B.B. Martin "stated that the Negro American League was 'sick and tired of having players taken by the Negro National League clubs and then threatening to break the agreement between the two leagues if the N.A. League did not allow this.'"[180]

Is it any surprise that a World Series between league pennant winners scheduled for mid-September did not materialize, given the contention between the two leagues? The powerhouse Homestead Grays and the Kansas City Monarchs won league pennants in the NNL and NAL respectively, although second half NAL standings were incomplete while the NNL played a "straight season through to September 9."[181] Cum Posey reported that the NNL had a final meeting in New York City on September 3 in which "there was a decided trend toward the idea of one Negro major league." In the same piece, Posey criticized the NAL for choosing an inexperienced owner, J.B. Martin, to succeed Major Jackson as NAL president, noted "internal strife amongst league owners causing irregularities in booking," stated that NNL President Wilson "did a fine job, considering the handicap of starting the season with three antagonistic members, "and concluded that "the 1940 baseball season was not a success, financial or otherwise."[182] One can only conclude that if, as Randy Dixon suggested, "1940 is SHOWDOWN year for National Negro League," the NNL and the NAL, if Posey is to be believed, failed the test.[183]

Part 2 — War- and Prosperity- 1941-1945

As 1941 began, the institution of Negro League Baseball was at a crossroads. There were now two (somewhat) functional leagues—yet there was little cooperation between leagues, and no postseason play between them. But 1941 was a signal year for Negro League operation, even as America moved ever closer to entering the worldwide conflict between fascism and democracy. Although American democracy operated on dual tracks, the disadvantaged world of black America received a boost from the wartime economy, and more citizens of color with money in their pockets meant more patronage of Negro League baseball. Ironically, the most profitable years for Negro League magnates simultaneously highlighted the rampant injustice of black stars playing a segregated game, while a war to end injustice raged on abroad.

During this period Negro League owners and executives continued to be at loggerheads with each other and often with the black media. Problems with white booking agents, players skipping out on their contracts to pursue lucrative adventures south of the border, and ongoing difficulties establishing effective stewardship of the leagues persisted—but black baseball shined like it never had before—until October 23, 1945, when it all changed with a signed contract and the fortunes of the institution of Negro League baseball changed with it.

1941

The annual winter meeting of the NAL was held on Sunday, December 29, 1940, in Chicago, one week prior to that of the NNL. In describing the conduct of the meeting, the *Chicago Defender* mentioned that "the entire meeting was harmonious," a believable characterization in that previously a good deal of the conflict had been within the NNL and between the two leagues.[184] Principal business actions at this meeting were the re-election of 1940 officers J.B. Martin (president), Horace G. Hall (VP), Fay Young (secretary), and Major Jackson (NAL commissioner), a discussion about making an agreement with the NNL for the coming season including each league swinging through the other's territory, and the dropping of the Cleveland Bears because of poor 1940 attendance.[185]

The NNL followed with its first 1941 meeting, held in Baltimore on Friday and Saturday, January 3-4. *Baltimore Afro-American* columnist Art Carter echoed the *Defender*'s NAL meeting depiction by describing the NNL meeting atmosphere as "harmony prevailing on the majority of the important issues at stake."[186] The harmony, though, was clearly relative—Carter saw it as a "striking contrast to last year's hectic session" while the *Courier* vividly characterized the meeting as having "started out in the same manner as a screaming bomb, but ended up as tranquil as the Pacific Ocean."[187] Since Carter and the *Afro-American* were hosts of a sumptuous dinner Friday night, with Carter welcoming guests and NL President Wilson awarding a trophy to the 1940 pennant-winning Homestead Grays, he perhaps viewed the atmosphere a bit more positively than did his *Courier* counterparts. The *Courier* report, though, barely mentioned any club conflicts, recounting a treasurer's report that "showed the league with a clean slate, financially, as all bills were paid" and the agreement of five NNL clubs on lifting a ban against players who jumped their contracts in 1940. Additionally, the clubs defused prior anger at the practices of Ed Gottlieb in booking games at Yankee Stadium by agreeing on a "two percent kickback from the booking agent's fee" to go into the league's coffers.[188] Nevertheless, conflict, overt and implicit, still existed within the NNL ownership and between NNL and NAL positions, as a minority of NNL owners opposed the lifting of the contract-jumping-player ban, which meant that no decision on the ban would be reached until the next joint NNL/NAL session , even though NAL prexy J.B. Martin "stated emphatically that his group was against lifting the ban on the recalcitrant players."[189] Additionally, the NNL's voting in Posey as a combined secretary-treasurer meant that Abe Manley had been voted out as treasurer, "which pushed Manley out of the so-called inner circle."[190] But the NNL re-elected Tom Wilson as president with no reported opposition while developing a robust interleague schedule of 24 out of 74 planned league games, awaiting the NAL's approval at the upcoming joint meeting of the two leagues.[191]

Philadelphia owner Ed Bolden was also re-elected as NNL VP, but without his presence at the January meeting. Bolden was proposing a new solution to the Negro League commissioner problem—a committee including Pennsylvania Judge Joseph Rainey, Philadelphia Elks official Edward Henry, and Philadelphia attorney Raymond Alexander would survey Negro League baseball, with one of them then becoming commissioner![192] In summation, then, three offered suggestions for Commissioner were: a Philadelphia owner promoting Philadelphia officials to oversee Negro League operations, a New York area owner (Effa Manley) having recently (1940) promoted a New York newspaperman (C.B. Powell) to lead the NNL, and the NAL continuing to promote its (Midwestern) former president to become commissioner of both leagues—do we see a pattern here?

Bolden Threatens To Go On Warpath—
CLUB OWNER SAYS HE SMELLS A SKUNK

—*Chicago Defender, January 18, 1941*

Despite Bolden's expectations of a firestorm, the joint meeting in Chicago on February 23 successfully resolved key issues involving returning players, interleague scheduling, and settling on a date for the annual East-West Game. Ten out of 12 owners from both leagues agreed to an amended plan allowing jumping players to return to their original clubs if they paid a $100 fine by May 1. Cum Posey was then able to declare his previous signing of 1940 jumper Josh Gibson to play for the Grays in 1941. Both leagues agreed to add interleague play to their schedules, and to hold the East-West Game on July 27.[193] Meanwhile, the NNL held its own meeting in Chicago. In it, Newark officially rejoined the league as they resolved a dispute over payments allegedly withheld from the Grays for a 1940 contest they played in Newark. And Frank Forbes was picked to replace Roy Sparrow as "secretary to the promoter" of those lucrative and controversial Yankee Stadium games.[194]

Despite steps toward peaceful dispute resolution, there continued to be acrimony between the leagues, according to Cum Posey. In his "Posey's Points" column of March 29, 1941, the Grays owner observed conflict at the recent joint session, suggesting that he expected at one juncture that the joint agreement between the leagues would not be maintained. While the decision by both leagues to end the ban on jumping players preserved the joint agreement, Posey sounded an alarm over the possibility that NAL member Kansas City would play the Ethiopian Clowns, who he believed demeaned Negro League baseball with their clowning and playing to racist stereotypes. Posey suggested that the NNL would abrogate the joint agreement unless NAL president J.B. Martin stopped Kansas City from playing the Clowns. Naturally, the Monarchs went ahead and played two separate series against the Clowns during 1941, albeit without NAL approval.[195]

But the NAL had its own axe to grind as owner Jim Semler of the New York Black Yankees used Satchel Paige, under contract to play for the Kansas City Monarchs, to pitch his 1941 league opener against the Philadelphia Stars. This occasioned a "hurried meeting" by NAL owners in Chicago on Saturday, May 17, in which they agreed to ask NNL President Wilson to stop Paige from appearing again for the Black Yankees the following Sunday in Cleveland. In response, Wilson promised to suspend any NNL club using Paige or any other NAL player.[196] Placated, NAL owners eventually agreed to make Paige available to NNL teams for exhibition games.[197]

Clearly, another joint meeting, held in late June in New York, was needed to sort out and resolve league differences. As reported by the *Pittsburgh Courier*, this meeting "went a long way toward correcting some of the flaws in organized Negro baseball."[198] The East-West Game, which was ostensibly in doubt over Paige's antics, was confirmed at this meeting, and a related incipient controversy—over Harlem Globetrotters owner and Negro League promoter Abe Saperstein's role in promoting the game, was resolved in favor of retaining Saperstein. This decision accorded with NAL desires, although Cubans owner Pompez expressed his viewpoint that no promoter be employed who ridiculed

Negro baseball by booking the Clowns. Rather than voting in opposition, Effa Manley and Ed Gottlieb did not vote, and Saperstein was retained.[199]

But the trouble did not end there—it rarely did when it came to the magnates of the Negro Leagues as they endlessly hashed out their differences and then oftentimes rehashed them; like many academics, they had titanic, bloody battles over their places in the hierarchy and over what appeared to be rather insignificant amounts of money.

Saperstein Accused of Monopoly by Posey
—*Cleveland Call and Post, August 16, 1941*

In this case, Cum Posey felt the need to continue the battle with Saperstein and the NAL owners even after the June joint meetings had resolved the issue. Posey wrote an open letter on August 8, 1941, to the "Sports Editor" in which he critiqued Saperstein's self-serving and self-aggrandizing practices in earning himself over $2,000 booking NAL games and additional money publicizing the upcoming East-West Game: "There should be no place in Negro or any other kind of baseball for a man like this."[200] Despite all this six clubs of Negro Organized Baseball (all from the West) voted to have Saperstein publicize the East-West game on the radio and in the white dailies. His cut of this game was over $1500.00. What Posey wanted was to eliminate outside white operators from making profits on Negro League operations: "we are irrevocably committed to the total obliteration of all opportunitists *(sic)* out of organized Negro baseball."[201]

Following Posey's broadside attack on Saperstein and the NAL owners, the NNL held its final meeting in New York City on September 13, 1941. In the main, the NNL meeting was about passing five resolutions affecting the NNL/NAL relationship. The resolutions concerned monetary issues regarding East-West games and a possible Negro World Series and proscriptions against playing any Cuban team other than the New York Cubans and playing league or postseason games against the Ethiopian Clowns. As Cum Posey recorded it and reinforced in his "Posey's Points" column, the NNL planned to dissolve the joint agreement with the NAL if it did not accept these resolutions.[202]

The key question was whether the NAL would indeed agree to these NNL positions, as columnist Fay Young opined that "for the time being, the West is just about tired of being dictated to by the East."[203] And recall that the Negro League commissioner debate itself remained unresolved—as Major Jackson had a figurehead position as the NAL-only commissioner: "he has sort of an honorary position—and the East ignores him because they have never voted for any commissioner."[204]

Despite the continuing disputes, the leagues had seen dramatic increases in attendance in several league cities in 1941.[205] And in a letter from Effa Manley to Cum Posey dated October 13, 1941, she declared that the Newark Eagles had "a gross business of $61,000.00. That is a lot of money anywhere. If we did that much, I am sure the Grays and some others did even more. All this to say the baseball is a really large business, and growing all the time. It is really high time we started to handle it like a big business."[206]

In 1941 the business of Negro League baseball did not end up including a Negro World Series, as the NAL champion Monarchs, with help from peripatetic Satchel Paige, won both halves of the 1941 NAL season, while first-half NNL pennant winner Homestead defeated the second-half winner Cubans in a playoff series, three games to one.[207] As 1941 ended and 1942 dawned, the U.S. weathered a surprise attack on Pearl Harbor and entered World War II—but would the NAL agree to make peace with the NNL at home while war was waged abroad?

1942

The NAL and NNL prepared for year-end meetings as an uncertain landscape for America—and baseball—unfolded. No one really knew what lay ahead as America mobilized for war on two fronts. Before there were any indications from President Roosevelt as to whether professional baseball could operate during wartime, the NAL went ahead as planned with its usual year-end meeting, this time on December 27 and 28, 1941, in Chicago. While

Cum Posey was given a special invitation to attend the NAL meeting by NAL prexy J.B. Martin, he declined to attend, as he knew that Tom Wilson would be representing the NNL—and Wilson would be pressing the resolutions passed at the September 1941 NNL meeting to a vote of the NAL clubs, with the joint agreement between the two leagues ostensibly at stake.[208]

The NAL blinked—and adopted the NNL resolution to ban teams from both leagues playing the Ethiopian Clowns, albeit after much discussion including Wilson presenting the NNL view that "the painting of faces by the Clowns players, their antics on the diamond and their style of play was a detriment to Negro League baseball." They also agreed not to play any assemblage of Cuban players other than the Harlem-based NNL Cuban Stars.[209] The NAL admitted Cincinnati to its league while deferring any decision on the St. Louis Stars. The league also considered a plan put forward by William G. Nunn, the managing editor of the *Pittsburgh Courier*, who had previously been an officer of the NNL. Nunn wanted to start an annual memorial game, to be called the Rube Foster-C.I. Taylor memorial game, the proceeds to be used to establish a home for disabled former Negro League players. The NAL deferred action on Nunn's idea, with J.B. Martin indicating that he thought it worthwhile while Commissioner-without-portfolio Major Jackson expressed his opposition.[210]

The NNL initially planned to meet in Baltimore on January 3, 1942, but the meeting was postponed several times until it was finally held on February 14 and 15. In a series of letters written by Effa Manley, she expressed the view that there was a need for an earlier meeting due to uncertainties caused by the war but several owners kept delaying the meeting to stop her from persuading the majority to drop Tom Wilson in favor of Judge Joseph Rainey as 1942 NNL president.[211] Effa Manley expressed the belief that the NNL was poorly run by Wilson, needing an "efficient Chairman" because "we have never played the same number of games, our admission prices are all different, our umpire situation is pitiful, our contracts are not anything."[212]

The mid-February kickoff meeting of the NNL's 1942 season was held in Baltimore. In black America, the backdrop to this meeting was the newly instituted Double Victory campaign run by the *Pittsburgh Courier* based upon a letter the *Courier* received and published in its January 31, 1942, edition. The letter suggested that black America should respond to the war by seeking a "Double Victory"—simultaneously battling, and ultimately vanquishing, fascism abroad and racism at home. Beginning with the February 7, 1942, edition of the *Courier*, a Double Victory logo appeared on the masthead, leading to 970 Double Victory items published in the *Courier* by year-end 1942, as Double Victory clubs, hairdos, pin-up girls of the week, parades, and baseball games all emanated from the *Courier*'s crusade.[213]

Manleys Bolt NNL Meeting in a Huff
— *New York Amsterdam News, February 21, 1942*

Cumberland Posey expected that the meeting would be "a lengthy session with everybody raising a rumpus at times"—and he would not be disappointed.[214] The meeting was noteworthy in that 1) The 1941 slate of NNL officers—President Wilson, VP Bolden, and Secretary-Treasurer Posey—were re-elected with but one dissenting vote, that of the Newark Eagles; 2) after Effa Manley could not even get her nomination of Judge Rainey for NNL president seconded, she and husband Abe departed the meeting, an action headlined by the *New York Amsterdam News* thusly: "Manleys Bolt NNL Meeting In a Huff"[215]; 3) according to Art Carter, upon leaving Effa declared that "we are through. We cannot operate under the present setup and so the league will have to go on without Newark."[216]; 4) the NNL agreed to put 5 percent of the receipts of the upcoming 10th annual East-West Game in its treasury; 5) The NNL formalized an agreement with the NAL to resume playing a Negro World Series, last played in 1927 when the combatants were representing the first incarnation of the NNL and the Eastern Colored League; 6) NAL cooperation was not without misgivings, with J.B. Martin expressing his league's dissatisfaction with being strong-armed by the NNL: "We are willing to cooperate with you in all matters to the fullest ... but we just don't like the way you say things."[217]; 7) the league formally acknowledged the "colored press" and voted to endorse a publicity plan to be presented at the next NNL meeting in response to speeches by sportswriters Joe Bostic of the *New York Amsterdam News* and Art Carter of the *Baltimore Afro-American* complaining of the league failing to acknowledge the role of the black press in supporting organized Negro baseball[218]; 8) a renewed application by Gus Greenlee to bring a new Pittsburgh Crawfords franchise into the NNL was tabled; and 9) St. Louis Stars owner Allen Johnson stated that he would merge his NAL club with the New York Black Yankees, with J.B. Martin suggesting that fireworks would occur at an upcoming NAL meeting regarding the disposition of St. Louis players who were, in his judgment, still NAL property regardless of Johnson's actions to become a part of an NNL franchise.[219]

With all that activity, some of it unresolved, the NNL decided to hold a follow-up meeting in Philadelphia on February 28. At the meeting, the Newark Eagles, who had flirted with the possibility of operating independently with the aid and support of Abe Saperstein, declared that they would rejoin the NNL despite losing out on reforming it administratively.[220] Effa Manley was nowhere near done decrying the inefficiency of league operations while Gus Greenlee suggested that Abe Manley would have been the best candidate to oppose Tom Wilson, but the status quo would nevertheless be continued and Newark would participate.[221]

Greenlee would not be allowed to rejoin the league. Not only did he fail to show up at the February 28 meeting, but the players he intended to reclaim now belonged to other clubs.[222] At this meeting, there were indications that the Foster-Taylor Memorial Home for indigent players would be supported by the league; however, this researcher could find no other future references to this initiative in the black press. Perhaps the developing war and efforts to support the military with benefit games took the attention of Negro League ownership away from the dire straits of former players.

The NAL had a final meeting before the beginning of its season on May 10; other than setting its season's schedule, the league declared that it would not allow its teams to play the Black Yankees as long as new co-owner Allen Johnson took former St. Louis Stars players for the Yanks and away from the NAL.[223] That ban was lifted during the season, but the acrimony surrounding this conflict showed that all was not harmonious between the two circuits.

With President Roosevelt having given the "green light" for professional baseball to be played during wartime, all expectations were of a prosperous one for black baseball: "the league should break all attendance records as every city in which the regular league games are played is booming with war workers anxious to find some form of pleasurable relaxation."[224] In fact, many games involving black teams and players drew large crowds, including an attendance of approximately 45,000 fans for the August East-West Game. Other heavily attended games included exhibitions pitting Satchel Paige against military teams, a Yankee Stadium doubleheader involving the Monarchs and three NNL teams, and regular interleague games at Washington's Griffith Stadium between the now Homestead-Washington Grays and the Monarchs.[225]

Midseason saw June NAL and joint NNL-NAL meetings, where routine scheduling of second-half games and the planning of the East-West Game to be held on August 16 and an Army benefit game two days later were discussed. One significant move made at the joint meeting was the removal of Abe Saperstein from the role of publicity director of the upcoming East-West Game.[226] Perhaps this action was in retaliation for Saperstein's decision to form a rival league, the Negro Major League, with mostly Midwestern teams including Syd Pollock's now-Cincinnati Clowns. The new league disbanded in midseason, and the Clowns then played NAL stalwarts Memphis, Birmingham, and Kansas City in August but Saperstein paid the price for the anger of the established leagues at the various actions of "clowning," his attempted takeover of lucrative bookings, as well as creating a rival league—or did he? Even a contemptuous critic like Posey "acknowledged that Saperstein had done a good job booking teams, and pointed out that most of the league owners 'were glad to be booked by Saperstein.'"[227]

Ultimately, NAL President J.B. Martin felt "elated over the success made by the league" in 1942.[228] There were challenges aplenty as gas and rubber rationing made league transportation an issue, and players such as Monte Irvin and Willie Wells abandoned Negro League teams for the more lucrative and relatively less prejudiced Latin American venues. The NAL pennant winner Kansas City Monarchs won the first Negro World Series in 15 years by 4-0 over the perennial champion Grays, the postseason meeting of the two leagues signifying at least somewhat more cooperation between them.[229] Yet lurking in the wake of increasing fan attention to Negro League operations was the start of efforts to integrate white baseball, efforts fostered by the war shining a beacon of light on American hypocrisy as evidenced by fighting a war for freedom abroad while oppression of its black citizens continued at home.

1943

As it prepared hopefully for the 1943 season, the Negro American League held its annual winter meeting on December 27, 1942, a two-day meeting for the six teams expected to play in 1943—the Chicago American Giants, Kansas City Monarchs, Memphis Red Sox, Birmingham Black Barons, Cincinnati Buckeyes, and Jacksonville Redcaps—in which the knotty problem of tire and gasoline rationing would be preeminent in their discussions.[230] NAL President Martin, as noted above, was quite sanguine about his now six-year-old league, as he claimed that "while interest in Negro baseball has increased at least 50 per cent, a greater interest is expected in 1943."[231] Martin stated confidently that the information from the Office of Defense Transportation (ODT) was propitious for planning their operations for the next year.[232] According to author Paul DeBono, that confidence did not extend to the future success of the Negro Leagues if the color line in Organized Baseball fell.[233] As 1943 unfolded, however, the NAL, and especially the NNL, would contend with shifting stances by the ODT that first severely restricted public-transit options for both leagues and later, after extensive lobbying efforts by the leagues and other sympathetic entities, partially relaxed these restrictions.

Members of the black press remained extremely critical of league operations despite the recent financial successes. Fay Young likened black baseball to a "rudderless boat" which, he believed, dismayed its fan base by 1) its practice of picking club owners as league presidents, 2) its players capriciously moving between uniforms, and 3) its failure to create one league with East and West divisions.[234] If Young was correct about such fan sentiments, the leagues in 1943 were not responsive to these concerns. The first NNL meeting of 1943, held on January 23 in Philadelphia, reaffirmed the status quo as Tom Wilson, Ed Bolden, Cum Posey, and Abe Manley were re-elected as president, vice president, secretary, and treasurer, respectively. The NNL discussed potential player shortages, with one suggested strategy being the use of weekend players working in war production industries. The league picked Effa Manley to direct NNL war relief efforts, intending that each club hold at least one benefit game and jointly, an all-star benefit contest.[235]

Everything seemingly was in order for a prosperous season, albeit one where war priorities would take precedence. The January 23, 1943, edition of the *Pittsburgh Courier* reported prematurely that unlimited gas rations for bus travel had been approved for both the Negro and major leagues.[236] Surprisingly, ODT's director Joseph Eastman ordered a ban on the use of private buses by baseball teams and other entities effective March 15.[237] Both Negro leagues now had a problem on their hands, as the alternative of train transportation with a limited supplemental automobile travel allowance of 360-470 miles per month for athletes was deemed unfeasible by J.B. Martin and the NAL.[238]

Immediate efforts at negotiating a solution included a meeting arranged by Washington Senators owner Clark Griffith between the ODT and Posey and Martin, attempts by the leagues to operate and acquire limited travel rights, and even a petition drive launched by Kansas City Monarchs owners Tom Baird and J.L. Wilkinson that was supported by then-Senator from Missouri Harry S. Truman. With none of those measures succeeding to persuade ODT to revise its draconian travel order, both leagues had to adapt to the circumstances. The NAL especially had a big problem as "the more compact NNL was capable of functioning within these limitations."[239] Each held a meeting in late March which in significant part discussed methods of addressing the travel restrictions. Surprisingly, the NNL chose to postpone the drawing up of their schedule until a subsequent meeting, to be held in Philadelphia on April 10, whereas the more seriously affected NAL nonetheless announced its season's schedule at this meeting, which was held in Chicago, the venue for most of the NAL meetings.[240]

The NNL's March meeting was held in Washington, D.C., which had become the primary home of the Homestead Grays. The league decided on seven NNL teams competing in 1943, with one team to be owned by former Black Yankees co-owner George Mitchell and whose location had yet to be determined. The NNL's scheduling plans involved sticking to the bigger cities, as well as holding games "in easily accessible places to Virginia and nearby Maryland where defense workers are congregated, in response to the planned travel restrictions."[241] Fay Young, in reporting on the NAL meeting, provided the contradictory inputs of an announced schedule and quoted J.B. Martin saying that "the Negro American League will not be able to operate this season."[242] Dan Burley, writing for the *New York Amsterdam News*, weighed in with the pronouncement that "Negro Baseball this summer seems doomed," blaming the "dilly-dallying practices of Negro League owners" who were "sitting back smoking big black cigars" while their major-league counterparts wrung concessions from ODT director Eastman.[243]

What was really going on in early 1943? Despite the dark pronouncements of black baseball's viability, both leagues were scrambling in their own ways to put together an operating plan dealing with the significant travel restrictions imposed upon them by ODT, while they hoped to get some relief that would enable them to operate substantially as they did in 1942. Some suggested options were 1) they could sell their buses and travel by rail; 2) they could simply "carry on" while attempting to get "special considerations" from Eastman; or 3) they could use trains and commercial buses.[244]

The NNL held its follow-up meeting and planned to operate within the travel restrictions, even as it joined the NAL in applying for relief. It focused its meeting instead upon its new franchise location and other operating issues. It was decided that the new team, owned by George Mitchell and Allen Johnson, would play its home games in Harrisburg and be called the Harrisburg-St. Louis Stars, succeeding 1942's New Orleans-St. Louis Stars. Still to be figured out was who would control players from last year's Black Yankees since George Mitchell had previously co-owned the Yankees with James Semler—a battle between the Harrisburg-St. Louis and New York contingents was sure to follow.[245] Meanwhile, the NNL decided on its first-half schedule, while choosing their umpires (and raising their pay) and passing provisions protecting players who did not receive timely contract payments by declaring them free agents and penalizing the teams that failed to pay players in a timely fashion.[246]

Despite the challenging conditions, both leagues carried on. According to Neil Lanctot, the NAL succeeded in gaining an allowance of 2,000 miles per month per team by late June because of its acknowledged difficulties in traveling publicly in the South; the NNL was excluded from this arrangement because it did not have significant Southern travel.[247] And, as they often did, the two leagues accused each other of stealing players and battled over the entry of the Ethiopian Clowns into the 1943 NAL. Cum Posey was notified by J.B. Martin on May 1 that Posey was in violation of the joint league agreement as his team fielded players under contract to the Memphis Red Sox and Kansas City Monarchs. He responded with a letter released to the black press countercharging that the NAL had repeatedly broken the joint agreement by stealing NNL players, by playing the Clowns, and by not giving to the NNL East-West Game receipts it had earned.[248]

What ensued was a "five-hour hectic meeting" on June 1 in Philadelphia.[249] In the minutes of the meeting, President Wilson opened up the discussion by trying to operate as a peacemaker between the two leagues. He said, "Tampering with players was bad, and would result in tearing down what it took years to build up. … It was [therefore] necessary under existing conditions for everybody to do some sacrificing to help keep baseball going and avoid fights between the two leagues."[250] But fight they did, as charges and countercharges flew back and forth between clubs of both leagues. Both NNL President Wilson and NAL President Martin signed an order finding four NNL clubs, the Harrisburg Stars, New York Black Yankees, Washington Homestead Grays, and Philadelphia Stars; and the Cleveland Buckeyes of the NAL—were in violation of the joint agreement and ordering a total of 10 players either returned to their original clubs or exchanged for other players.[251] An uneasy peace or at least a truce followed, as the order was largely obeyed and even misgivings by NNL clubs over the presence of the Clowns in the NAL gradually faded.[252]

As the war's tide began to turn toward the Allied forces, so too did the Negro Leagues prosper. The August 1 East-West Game drew 51,723 fans, the most of any East-West contest.[253] On August 2, right after the East-West contest, the two leagues reconvened in Chicago for a joint meeting, rare this late in the season. There were discussions of how to handle the problem of approaching the Mexican government to get cooperation in bringing Negro League players back from Mexico, and NNL President Wilson, at the behest of NAL President Martin, ruled that a Negro League team could not go to another Negro League city to play a game against a different opponent than that city's team without the local team's approval.[254] There was also interleague conflict, as third baseman Marvin Carter was playing alternately for the Harrisburg-St. Louis Stars of the NNL and the NAL's Memphis Red Sox. The issue was settled by Stars owner Mitchell saying "he would not play Carter any longer" after Mitchell stated that he had "intended on using Carter in two important games that he had booked."[255] It was not in dispute that Carter belonged to the Memphis Red Sox all along.

Negro League baseball had its best year ever from a financial standpoint in 1943.[256] The NAL's Birmingham Black Barons won the league's first half and proceeded to win a five-game playoff against the second-half winner Chicago American Giants before losing a seven-game Negro World Series to the Homestead Grays, a series replete with "irregularities and disputes."[257] Despite all the squabbles and strife between and within the two leagues, the year 1943 ended at a high point for the institution of black baseball. But a December 3 meeting—not including Negro League owners, but between a black delegation largely composed of newspaper figures and a delegation of major-league owners and officials—foreshadowed a challenge to Negro League magnates greater than the intense conflicts they had between owners and leagues—the eventual opening of major-league baseball to black ballplayers.

1944

As usual, the NAL planned its winter meeting for a date prior to that of the NNL. The NAL owners and officers were mostly interested in 1) reaping favorable publicity for the success of the prior season, which would hopefully carry over into 1944, 2) planning for the coming season, including working out some of the problems that marred last year's Negro World Series, and 3) settling some of its conflicts with its rival and sometimes partner NNL.[258] Before the December 19 meeting, however, *Pittsburgh Courier* sportswriter and trailblazer for baseball integration Wendell Smith weighed in about the larger issue that the Negro League baseball magnates needed to contend with—preparing for the inevitable day when organized white baseball would come calling for their best ballplayers.

In his December 18, 1943, column entitled "Smitty's Sports Spurts," Smith both lauded the Negro League owners for having "attained 'big business' classification" by having their best financial year ever in 1943 and warned them that such success necessitated "sound business tactics" and "a long range program designed to bring them even larger profits in the future." What Smith (and others) saw coming was a time when the major leagues would come calling— and he believed that currently, "the Negro owners are in no position to bargain with major league teams for their players. The Negro owners will have to accept what they are offered." In essence, he foresaw the refusal of Branch Rickey to pay any money for signing the first black player based on Rickey's claim that the Negro Leagues were disorganized and therefore whatever contracts existed need not be recognized. In Smith's judgment, "the business methods of the Negro American and National leagues are not up to par and it wouldn't take much arguing on the part of a major league owner to prove that the two Negro leagues are not organized. And, if the Negro leagues aren't organized, then a major league owner is in no way compelled to recognize the contracts and agreements which ordinarily apply to trades and sales of ball players."[259]

Smith therefore suggested that the Negro American League would be wise to begin planning for the future at its midwinter meeting, because the current prosperity would not last. He expressed the belief that NAL President J.B. Martin was a good businessman, who would have help from other capable NAL owners, naming Cleveland's Ernest Wright, Birmingham's Abe Saperstein and Tom Hayes, Dr. B.B Martin of Memphis, and Tom Baird of Kansas City as partners in developing a sustainable business model, in today's parlance.[260]

In this author's estimation, the appearance of Smith's blueprint for Negro baseball's future success and suggestions for preparing a plan for baseball integration was at least partly occasioned by the unprecedented meeting between the black press and major-league baseball on December 3, 1943. Smith believed that the timing of future actions by the major leagues to integrate was as yet uncertain. Nevertheless, it was significant that 44 major-league owners and baseball officials, including Commissioner Kenesaw M. Landis, saw fit to meet with publishers Ira Lewis of the *Pittsburgh Courier* and John Sengstacke of the *Chicago Defender*, along with leading sportswriters including Wendell Smith, and even former athlete and current singer/performer Paul Robeson. The meeting suggested that organized white baseball realized that it could no longer ignore the presence of a black baseball world and the potential future interrelationship with its own baseball operations.[261]

The meeting, held at the Roosevelt Hotel in New York, included passionate speeches by publishers Lewis and Sengstacke plus Paul Robeson decrying the color line and pointing to changing attitudes of the American public on integrated performances in sports and in the entertainment world. Judge Landis repeated his claim that there "has never been, formal or informal, or any understanding, written or unwritten, subterranean or sub-anything, against the hiring of Negroes in the major leagues." Ira Lewis pushed back, insisting that an unwritten understanding among the white baseball establishment to bar black players indeed existed.[262]

What did this meeting signify, if anything? According to Brian Carroll, whose book on baseball integration traced the process through the actions of the black press, "[T]hough the meeting failed to produce tangible results, it marked the first time integration was included on big league baseball's formal agenda, and Landis's invitations were major league baseball's first issued to men of color."[263] Similarly, the *New York Amsterdam News*, in its January 1, 1944, edition, provided a summary of major 1943 developments that included the following assessment of the meeting: "Nothing definite was accomplished, but it did mark a step forward.[264]

But how would the Negro League magnates and league officials deal with the potential future implications of this unprecedented contact between representatives of the black press and the white baseball establishment? On the eve of the December 19 NAL meeting, President J.B. Martin provided the NAL response to talk of future integration, stating that "we are not opposed to any movement which would advance Negro players to the major leagues." He went on to say that "we should not be expected to solve this problem. It is solely a major league issue. We cannot force them to admit Negro players, nor will we assume that responsibility."²⁶⁵ Neil Lanctot characterized Martin's response to the issue as "dodging responsibility." Lanctot went on to describe as "evasive" Martin's reaction to suggestions like that of Rollo Wilson that the two league presidents should seek an affiliation with major-league baseball as a precursor to integration."²⁶⁶ What Martin did address was the issue of contractual rights as he made it known that any NAL players desired by major-league owners would only be "released with our permission"—but he added that he did not expect this to happen in 1944.²⁶⁷

Meanwhile, the NNL was doing even less than the NAL in acknowledging any role in promoting the integration of organized white baseball. The *New York Amsterdam News* reported that NNL President Thomas Wilson informed the newspapers that black players entering the major leagues was "none of its concern" as the NNL could not compromise its access to major-league ballparks by raising the issue. Just like Martin, Wilson announced his league's position in advance of the NNL's winter meeting, which was held in New York on January 5 at the Hotel Theresa.²⁶⁸

What, then, did transpire at the first 1944 winter meetings of the NAL and NNL? The NAL reelected President Martin, Vice President Ernest Wright, owner of the Cleveland Buckeyes, Secretary Robert Simmons, traveling secretary of the Chicago American Giants, and Treasurer Wilkinson, owner of the Kansas City Monarchs.²⁶⁹ The NAL clubs also decided to count all games between league clubs in the league standings and to require each team to play at least 30 games in each half of the coming season to be eligible for the league pennant. They also ruled that any player must be on his team 30 days prior to the season's end to be eligible for any postseason play.²⁷⁰ As to postseason play, the NAL decided unilaterally that the Negro World Series would now be seven games and would be played solely in the home cities of the competing teams.²⁷¹

From its own vantage point, the NNL apparently was planning to reexamine its joint agreement with the NAL at its 11th annual meeting.²⁷² Since NAL President Martin, along with his brother B.B. of the Memphis Red Sox, Syd Pollock of the Cincinnati (a.k.a. Ethiopian) Clowns, and Winfield Welch of the Birmingham Black Barons were all in attendance, it was open season for revisiting old grievances, as a heated discussion between NNL owners and their NAL counterparts ensued regarding the Memphis Red Sox having played the St. Louis Stars in September 1943 when the NNL had suspended the Stars. Eddie Gottlieb brought up the 1942 issue of Syd Pollock's Ethiopian Clowns (at that time based in Cincinnati) playing against NAL clubs in accusing the NAL of again breaking their joint agreement.²⁷³ Would the two leagues ever get along?

George Mitchell, manager of St. Louis, attended the NNL meeting, but was "barred from the closed meeting." Not only Mitchell, but the members of the press were also barred from the meeting as "the assembled magnates took all their squabbles behind closed doors" and had a five-hour meeting, after which they took the newspaper reporters out to dinner and announced that they would send out a release to those same papers.²⁷⁴ Why did the magnates yet again keep their best sources for league publicity out of their meeting? Maybe they were tired of having their dirty laundry aired by the league, but leaving them out in the cold would not stop the negative reportage from coming out. The press speculated that Mitchell would come up with the money to pay off St. Louis's 1943 obligations to the NNL and then join the NAL in 1944, otherwise why would he be "walking the Theresa corridors, his hands locked behind him?"—certainly he was not there to accompany the equally locked out press!²⁷⁵

In more mundane business matters, the NNL re-elected the prior year's league officers, and newly renamed President Wilson formed a committee to contact ODT and attempt to arrange to use their own buses in 1944, a plan that came to fruition sometime before the season opened when ODT offered the same 2,000 miles per month per team travel allowance to the NNL that it gave only to the NAL in 1943.²⁷⁶

When the NAL reconvened in Chicago on March 5 and 6 for its last preseason meeting, media reportage was scarce, as the decisions of NAL owners were mostly routine in nature. The *Chicago Defender* reported that the Ethiopian Clowns were allowed to shift their home base to Indianapolis from Cincinnati because of a conflict in bookings in Cincinnati—owner Syd Pollock had wanted to play games at the home of the Cincinnati Reds, Crosley Field, but decided not to because they were not allowed by the Reds to use the clubhouse. According to Rebecca Alpert, Pollock instead arranged to play home games at American Association Park in Indianapolis even though the Clowns still played a few games in Cincinnati.[277] Otherwise, the NAL finalized its league schedule but did not finalize the naming of a league statistician.[278]

In contrast, the NNL's final preseason meeting in New York on March 2 and 3 contained "much debate and discussion"—with an undercurrent of contention between, yet again, different factions of NNL owners. Although most of the meeting was taken up with scheduling, a significant decision was made regarding the hiring of a statistician, as the league rejected Wendell Smith's offer to be its statistical agent and hired the Al Munro Elias agency instead.[279] By virtue of this choice, the NNL rejected the recommendation of Effa Manley, who had encouraged Smith to present his offer to the NNL owners, and simultaneously angered vocal elements of the black press. Back in December, Smith had offered to compile statistics for both leagues for $5,000 or one league for $3,000.[280] Effa Manley believed that getting the fans superior information would mean a great deal to black baseball, but acknowledged resistance to hiring Smith.[281] Smith had made enemies among NNL league owners, Cum Posey in particular, resulting in the choice of Elias, which had substantial experience but also was offering a lower price of $425 for the season.[282]

In particular, Dan Burley, employing the nom de plume of Don Deleighbur, contended that the hiring of white agency Elias and snubbing of black reporter Smith was another example of "complete anti-Negroism" by the NNL, along with its "favoring of the Jim Crow Policy of the major leagues" by refusing to push for baseball integration. Burley/Deleighbur went on to suggest that the hiring of Elias instead of Smith constituted an "affront to Smith's ability" but also a rejection of the Negro press overall, who had given black baseball "thousands of dollars in free space on sports pages throughout the land."[283] Supporting Burley, Bob Williams, sports editor of the *Cleveland Call and Post*, said that the rejection of Smith was a reflection of the "'selfish interests' in Negro baseball in 1944,'" a failure to acknowledge that "the Negro Press has stuck its neck out for Negro baseball" by choosing not to reciprocate for the valuable space given to it in the black newspapers and instead "pass up the opportunity in order to save a few paltry dollars." For Williams, the decision on Smith, along with inaction on supporting integration of black players into major-league baseball, led to "Negro Sports writers raising a question this year: HAVE THE NEGRO LEAGUES BROKEN FAITH WITH THE NEGRO PRESS?"[284]

In his *Cleveland Call and Post* column dated March 25, Williams did acknowledge that "INTEGRATION WOULD DISINTEGRATE THE NEGRO baseball leagues."[285] In reply to Dan Burley's broadside, Posey picked up on Williams's concession, stating that the desire of the black press to foster integration led to its essentially "offering a whole Negro enterprise to white business men" which" would automatically put organized Negro baseball out of business." In Posey's view, he and the other NNL owners were facing "racial antagonism" from members of the black press in part because they were not enthusiastically participating in the push toward integration of baseball championed especially by Wendell Smith and also by many other black sportswriters. The end of Posey's letter to the press, which appeared side-by-side with Williams's Sport Rambler column of March 25 in the *Cleveland Call and Post*, stated thusly: "There is enough race antagonism rampant without members of our race constantly seeking self angrandisement *(sic)*. In sports through race pressure."[286]

Despite the underlying and ever-present tensions between owners, between leagues, and between the leagues and the black press, the March 11, 1944, *Pittsburgh Courier*'s headline for its column on the final NNL preseason meeting was "National League Set for Season." Trades were discussed, and one was completed: Pitcher Percy "Pete" Forrest was traded by the New

York Black Yankees to Newark for pitcher Freddie Hopgood and outfielder Ed Stone.[287] According to gadfly Dan Burley, the NNL had one final meeting just prior to the start of the NNL season on May 21, a Philadelphia confab in which the clubs voted unanimously to take over all St. Louis Stars players as Stars owner George Mitchell had not paid off his debt to the league. NNL President Wilson reportedly wired NAL President Martin asking him to require NAL clubs to release Stars players so they could report to the NNL clubs claiming them.[288] Of course, the two leagues continued to battle over these players.

As the war in Europe reached its "D-Day," the two leagues operated quite successfully in 1944. Attendance was brisk for the fourth straight year and at year's end, sportswriter Alvin Moses characterized the 1944 Negro League season as a "banner year financially."[289] The NNL held a scheduling meeting on June 19 in Philadelphia, where it was decided not to offer Gus Greenlee an associate membership for his revived Pittsburgh Crawfords. Since the Homestead Grays were now playing mostly in Washington, Greenlee requested to play at Forbes Field in Pittsburgh when the Grays were not there. Greenlee's intent was to "build Sunday baseball" and he felt that he was owed an opportunity to rejoin the league because of "my record of past contributions to Negro baseball."[290] While the *Afro-American* reported simply that Greenlee was denied an associate membership, Cum Posey later stated that Greenlee was offered an associate membership, but not in Pittsburgh. Posey insisted that league precedent supported President Wilson's ruling that a team could not play home games in a city where another team (his Homestead Grays) had their home grounds unless that team consented.[291]

Rebuffed, Greenlee would not go away quietly. He announced the signing of several players from each league during the weekend of the annual East-West Game, and met secretly with the All-Stars of both leagues, encouraging them to strike for a larger profit share. And Greenlee announced his plans to form a rival league in 1945.[292] Clearly, Gus Greenlee would be a force to be reckoned with in 1945—and nobody yet knew that Branch Rickey would be a partner in Greenlee's new league, mostly as a subterfuge for approaching Negro League players to sign with the Brooklyn Dodgers.

At the June 19 meeting, the NNL also decided to refuse to allow Abe Saperstein, now part owner of the NAL's Birmingham Black Barons, to promote its games, which included the upcoming East-West contest. According to Neil Lanctot, the NNL and NAL had drafted a new joint agreement in early 1944 limiting a promoter to 10 percent of the net receipts for a game he promoted; Cum Posey charged that Saperstein had taken more than 40 percent in some instances.[293] Finally, Posey reported that he surveyed all the NNL owners at this meeting and they unanimously agreed that Negro League baseball needed a "commissioner to straighten out matters between the two leagues and rule organized Negro baseball.[294] Posey stated that the NNL was in accord with the Negro press on the need for a commissioner; he was in this instance agreeing with Wendell Smith, who had written to Effa Manley earlier in 1944 that the only way to get the owners to follow rules and regulations was to elect a commissioner. Would the leagues finally listen to Smith, who had "constantly pleaded for a Commissioner"?[295] If all the discord between the black press and black baseball since the December 3, 1943, meeting between the major leagues and the delegation of black publishers was a guide, the answer was a likely "no"—unless ownership and current leadership in both leagues had finally come to their senses.

The NAL also had one more league meeting during the 1944 season. As was often the case, the NAL's June 13 Chicago meeting had little notable news, if the *Chicago Defender*'s brief reportage was to be believed. In addition to setting second-half schedules, the NAL announced the release of catcher Bruce Petway and the purchase of right fielder Jimmie Crutchfield by Cleveland.[296]

Ultimately, the 1944 season ended with the NNL pennant winning Homestead Grays besting the NAL pennant winning Birmingham Black Barons 4 games to 1. The Negro World Series had now been played for three straight years after a 14-year hiatus—and even though Wendell Smith had been rejected as statistician for the leagues, he had been appointed to a three-man commission with noted sportswriters Fay Young of the *Chicago Defender* and Sam Lacy of the *Baltimore Afro-American* to rule on any disputes arising from a now officially-designated championship series.[297] J.B. Martin was so pleased with the lack of controversy over the World Series that he called it "the finest thing that has happened in Negro baseball. … It is the first time we've had a Series in which the fans, leagues, and clubs could look toward it with confidence and pride."[298]

The 1944 season should have given both the NNL and NAL reasons for optimism for a successful and prosperous future. But there had been a Thanksgiving surprise—Commissioner Kenesaw Mountain Landis suddenly died on November 25, 1944. The baseball world was turned on its ear—and change, in an America poised to imminently defeat the forces of evil abroad and confront those same forces at home, was in the offing.

1945

For the first time in the eight years of a two-league structure in black baseball, the NNL and NAL scheduled their annual first winter meetings as preludes to a subsequent joint meeting the following day. Ordinarily, the leagues met jointly in midseason (although in 1944 there was no reported joint meeting of the two leagues at any time of the season), to work out in-season disputes as well as iron out plans for the annual East-West Game and, more recently, plan a postseason World Series. In 1940, there was a joint session on February 24, though this meeting followed earlier NNL and NAL meetings, the NAL back in December and the NNL in early February. Why was there a need for a two-league gathering at the beginning of the winter offseason?

Clues can be found in a December 6, 1944, letter reading like a press release found in Effa Manley's files. This letter, which lists league Presidents Wilson and Martin and NNL Secretary Posey at bottom, announces the calling of a joint meeting in New York on Friday, December 15, in New York at the Theresa Hotel. The letter mentioned the airing of grievances of two or three teams, clearing up the still ongoing battle between the leagues over the "St. Louis situation which caused a rift between the two leagues," discussing the potential blacklisting of players who jumped their teams and "outlaw clubs" they jumped to, as well as issues involving the East-West Game, in which the players' 1944 strike threat had earned them a substantial raise to $200 from $25 that they had gotten previously.[299]

The final paragraph of the December 6 meeting announcement, however, may have been the most critical. It mentioned "rumors of a third league of Negro Baseball" which NNL and NAL franchise holders were determined not to allow.[300] The specter of Gus Greenlee and other independent clubs organizing a rival league still existed, and the NNL and NAL would be prepared.

Related to the concern over Greenlee, however, was the reality of major-league Commissioner Landis's recent death. In describing the agenda for this early joint meeting, the *New York Amsterdam News* suggested that among matters to be discussed was "the effect the death of baseball czar Judge Kenesaw Mountain Landis will have on park owners and what will be the attitude of Landis' successor as high commissioner of baseball."[301] The immediate concern was threats to the NNL and NAL on getting playing dates at major-league ballparks; but lurking in the background, at least implicitly, were the rumblings of movement on ending the color line by signing Negro League players. Would Landis's successor have a different attitude about allowing black players into the major leagues? Negro League owners saw threats to their viability everywhere—but the operations of the major leagues were arguably the biggest threat to their existence both in the short term and in the long run.

The press also found itself cooling its heels outside of the two league meetings on December 15. According to Wendell Smith, after the black sportswriters threatened to "give the moguls some 'very bad press' the media was "welcomed with open arms" at the joint meeting on Saturday, December 16.[302] What the "assembled scribes" missed witnessing at the league meetings was tension and disputes in the hitherto cooperative NAL environment and smooth and untroubled proceedings in the usually raucous NNL atmosphere.[303] The NAL meeting included a split vote on the re-election of J.B. Martin, as owners Thomas Hayes of Birmingham and Syd Pollock of Cincinnati/Indianapolis voted for attorney and former Negro League player James Shackleford to replace Martin.[304] In addition, the brothers Martin, president J.B. and owner B.B. of the Memphis Red Sox, voted to retain Robert Simmons as secretary, but the other four teams prevailed in replacing him with Fay Young, sportswriter for the *Chicago Defender*. According to the *Defender*, the voting process was animated, with objections given to Martin calling for a vote to succeed himself as NAL president, while his brother B.B. "strenuously objected" to an alternative suggestion of Hayes (a friend of B.B. Martin's) as president, and a "lengthy speech" made by J.B. Martin in favor of retaining Simmons as secretary which was ultimately voted down.[305]

In contrast, the NNL again re-elected its entire slate of officers, although the *New York Amsterdam News* relied on "reports that sifted in from the smoke-filled room where the boys talked over secret league maneuvers."[306] Wendell Smith, in his column entitled "Caught on the Fly at the Baseball Meeting," quoted Syd Pollock and his secretary Bunny Downs as saying that "bad publicity is better than no publicity."[307] One can only speculate whether the periodic keeping of the news hounds out of meetings generated controversy and thereby publicity, or whether it ultimately discouraged the media from giving full support to promoting black baseball.

Otherwise, though, the big news from these winter meetings was the forming of two committees. At the Saturday afternoon joint session, the leagues chose Cum Posey and Ed Bolden to represent the NNL and B.B. Martin and Tom Hayes to represent the NAL to form a group deputized to present a list of candidates to be commissioner overseeing the two leagues. They also chose Abe Manley and Alex Pompez as NNL representatives, and Tom Baird of the Kansas City Monarchs and Ernest Wright of the Cleveland Buckeyes as NAL representatives on a committee tasked with detailed planning for the annual East-West Game, with special attention to avoiding a repeat of the labor dispute that marred the 1944 contest. The previous afternoon, both leagues also met jointly and listened to William Nunn, managing editor of the *Courier* (and former NNL secretary) declare that Negro League baseball had grown into a big business, necessitating ownership action in "building your fences" and specifically, choosing a baseball czar to oversee the game and a planning committee for a successful East-West affair.[308] Apparently, ownership responded with alacrity to Nunn, as they had not done to the suggestions of Wendell Smith and others over the years. But nothing was simply executed when it came to the operations of the Negro Leagues.

Finally, trades and trade rumors filled the air. James "Soldier Boy" Semler, owner of the Black Yankees, purchased Ted "Double-Duty" Radcliffe from the Birmingham Black Barons. Kansas City sent catcher Quincy Trouppe to Cleveland for pitcher Theolic "Fireball" Smith. And Memphis hoping to make James "Cool Papa" Bell their manager, offered outfielder Cowan "Bubba" Hyde to the Homestead Grays in return for Bell, but Posey turned that deal down. Cleveland owner Ernie Wright also rejected what he characterized as "a bad deal" that would have sent outfielder Buddy Armour to Kansas City for pitcher Jack Matchett.[309]

Before any more NNL or NAL meetings were held, one more "Black baseball" league meeting was held—one that was not at all welcomed by the existing leagues. On December 27, 1944, in Pittsburgh, the formative meeting of the "United States Negro Baseball League" (usually referred to as the United States League or USL) was held. The league, which included six formerly independent teams, chose Gus Greenlee as its vice president and Wendell Smith as secretary, but left the president slot open for a "nationally known lawyer and athlete "who they wished to convince to accept."[310] That individual turned out to be James Shackleford, the losing candidate at the recent NAL meeting for the NAL presidency.

The new league included the controversial St. Louis Stars, the Philadelphia/Hilldale Daisies (to be moved to Brooklyn in May and renamed the Brooklyn Brown

Dodgers), the Chicago Brown Bombers, the Detroit City Motor Giants, the Atlanta Black Crackers, and Greenlee's Pittsburgh Crawfords.[311] According to Greenlee, once he had been rejected by the NNL for an associate membership in 1944, he was also rejected by the NAL as "the American league owners were afraid of creating trouble by taking me after the National has rejected my bids."[312] Though Greenlee claimed that he was not competing with the two existing Negro Leagues, the *Courier* believed otherwise, suggesting that his entry would be problematic for the NNL and NAL, who would need to "launch a new and vigorous program" to compete with Greenlee's league.[313] Both leagues, therefore, should have had plenty of incentive to straighten out some of their more dysfunctional elements within their own structures and between the NNL and NAL.

When the NNL reconvened in New York late February or early March for their second and last preseason meeting, however, it primarily focused on undermining the fledgling structure of Greenlee's new circuit. As reported by the *New York Amsterdam News*, the "biggest bombshell of mid-winter baseball palavering" was the announcement by Birmingham manager Winfield Welch that Abe Saperstein would not book games nor would he be "connected with the newly-formed (Gus Greenlee & Co.) U.S. League," even though it mentioned that Saperstein was part of the financing of the St. Louis Stars, one of the six teams in the new league.[314] In other activities, NNL owners turned down an application for associate membership from an Indianapolis contingent, saying that the presence of an Indianapolis team in the NAL in essence meant that the NAL had authority over any black baseball to be played in that city. And the newly-reorganized Negro Southern League's President R.R. Jackson declared his league to a be a minor-league circuit, offering to develop players for the NNL and NAL in return for their protection of his operations.[315]

The NAL followed suit, holding its final preseason meeting on March 5 and 6 in Chicago. One notable difference in this year's proceedings was the degree to which each league participated in each other's meetings, as it was NAL team manager Welch of Birmingham who, accompanied by NAL President J.B. Martin, prominently participated in the prior NNL discussion by declaring Saperstein's independence from the new USL, while NNL league owners Pompez, Abe Manley, Ed Gottlieb, and NNL President and Baltimore owner Wilson all attended the NAL conference. It certainly seemed that the threat of a new operation (one that would soon be joined by Branch Rickey) in black baseball was effectively bringing the rival NNL and NAL together in protection of their legitimacy in the eyes of black fans as well as the black press.[316] In fact, at this meeting the NAL "fell in line with the Negro National League's action" in rejecting a franchise bid of the same Indianapolis interests who had applied for an associate membership at the recent NNL confab, even though this could mean that the NAL Clowns would not have access to the American Association park in Indianapolis that it had previously used, as the failed bidders were now expected to join the USL and had "'tied' the ball park up. ..."[317]

Dizzy Dismukes, now the business manager of the Kansas City Monarchs, announced at this meeting that the Monarchs had signed Jackie Robinson to play the infield, noting that he had been a "top-notch baseball player before joining the Army." In reality, Robinson had batted .097 for the 1940 varsity UCLA baseball team, and shared the team lead in errors committed; his prowess as an all-around athlete, starring in football, basketball, and track, had more to do with his reputation as a quality baseball player invoked by Dismukes.[318] Finally, the NAL declared at this meeting that it would adhere to a 25 percent mileage reduction in scheduling the 1945 season in accordance with the request of the ODT.[319]

That mileage reduction also applied to the major leagues and resulted in the cancellation of the 1945 major-league All-Star game, according to Neil Lanctot.[320] So what would be the fate of the East-West contest in 1945? The East-West contest could have been canceled, but it was apparently saved by J.B. Martin claiming that it was "ninety-eight percent a Chicago affair" and would therefore not involve heavy travel.[321] According to correspondence between William Nunn of the *Pittsburgh Courier* and Abe Manley, however, a significant discrepancy existed between Martin's view of the East-West Game committee's authority and that of the committee members. Nunn proposed that the committee decide upon allocation of the game's receipts, perform a thorough study of the game's promotion, consider increasing pricing, stage a banquet on the night prior to the game, and underwrite the sportswriter's expenses[322] Manley responded by agreeing with all of Nunn's proposals, but informing him that the East-West committee was told by J.B. Martin at the NAL meeting that their sole responsibility for the East-West Game was to solve any problems associated with players striking as they did in 1944.[323] More correspondence ensued, with Nunn making clear that he wanted no part in chairing the East-West committee if it was limited to dealing with player compensation,[324] and Posey weighed in by declaring in a May 5, 1945, *Norfolk Journal and Guide* column that "there is too much control over this game in the hands of one man, Dr. J.B. Martin."[325]

While this conflict played out, the major leagues held an April 24 meeting in which they announced that they had elected Albert B. "Happy" Chandler the new commissioner of baseball, and also that the American and National Leagues had agreed to a request by Sam Lacy of the *Baltimore Afro-American* to set up a committee to study "colored baseball" with an intention of exploring how to incorporate it into "the organized game" and eventually, bring black ballplayers to the major leagues.[326] And on May 7, Branch Rickey held a press conference in which he announced his involvement with the USL through the Brooklyn Brown Dodgers, and simultaneously blasted the Negro Leagues for being "leagues in name only and not in practice" due to their need for booking agents and their shaky player contracts.[327] When you add in tryouts at Dodgers training camp for pitchers Terris McDuffie and first baseman Dave "Showboat" Thomas, as well as the infamous Red Sox tryout of Jackie Robinson, outfielder Sam Jethroe, and infielder Marvin Williams, one could easily conclude that there was more going on that affected the status of Negro League baseball than ever before—and on June 12, the leagues would be deciding how to proceed on the choice of a black baseball commissioner.

Negro League historian Neil Lanctot considered the June 12, 1945, joint meeting of the NNL and NAL to be one of critical importance in the history of the Negro Leagues.[328] In addition to the vote on commissioner of the two leagues, the response of the leagues to Sam Lacy's committee and the handling of preparations for the East-West Game would be decided. Effa Manley reported as the lone NNL or NAL club owner to have attended Branch Rickey's May 7 USL press conference, and representatives of the Mexican League were "lurking in Chicago" with their assumed intent being "taking star players from both Leagues to play in Mexico."[329]

If this meeting was a test of the strength of conviction of both Negro Leagues to work together and address their myriad challenges and organize systems to handle internal conflicts and outside threats, the leagues would get a failing grade. Although NNL President Wilson "spoke for three minutes asking for a harmonious meeting," what he got was no agreement on a new commissioner and inaction on most of the other burning issues.[330]

Two candidates ran for commissioner: Bob Church, a black millionaire and Tennessee political figure with no previous baseball experience, and Judge William Hueston, a former federal official and also president of the first Negro National League from 1927 through 1931.[331] Predictably, Church was nominated by Memphis Red Sox officer (and third Martin brother) W.S. Martin while Hueston was proposed by Posey as "the East's candidate for baseball commissioner." As described by Posey in his "Posey's Points" column of June 23, 1945, Effa Manley defected from the Eastern bloc in supporting Church, so that it was "only an aggressive fight by the remaining Negro National League members ... that kept Memphis, Tenn.—the weakest baseball city in organized Negro baseball—from becoming the capital of Negro baseball." Not only was it decided to require a three-fourths majority, but also to have a written ballot—and once the 7-to-5 vote for Church failed to achieve the necessary approval, a motion for a second ballot failed.[332] In describing the ultimate inaction by the leagues, Rollo Wilson, who had been observing league proceedings since the second NNL began, commented as follows: "The National and American League clubmen showed that they want no commissioner. … No second vote was taken which would seem to evidence that nobody except the fans, the newsmen and possibly a minority of the owners want a check-rein on Negro baseball."[333]

Other nonresponses from this crucial joint meeting included: 1) In response to Effa Manley's report on the USL/Branch Rickey press conference, a suggestion, but no subsequent vote, on a proposed committee of two players and two club representatives to question Rickey and the two major-league presidents, Ford Frick and William Harridge, about what they expected from the two Negro Leagues, 2) an instruction to NAL Chairman Martin to let Sam Lacy know that his letter forming the committee to study black baseball that included major-league officials and known black figures and asking for a Negro League representative "had been received and read" as the joint membership took no position on it, 3) a motion "putting the East-West [Game] up to Dr. J.B. Martin" was made by Kansas City owner Tom Baird and seconded by Cleveland owner Wilbur Hayes but no vote was recorded. The only mention of the East-West Game committee was that it had previously allocated $100 compensation for each player chosen; a motion carried to allow each team $300 to split among players who were not chosen for the contest.[334]

Only one other in-season meeting was covered by the black press in 1945. The NNL held a special meeting in early July in New York, one characterized by the *Baltimore Afro-American* as "one of the most progressive in the history of the organization," in which the league imposed a $500 penalty on the New York Black Yankees for causing two forfeits of games in the past month along with $50 fines on manager George Scales and infielder Buddy Barker for refusing to leave the field after being thrown out of the game. In addition, the league decided to impose a five-year suspension on players who either had already jumped to the Mexican League or planned to do so in the future.[335] That the league announced a punitive action against the Black Yankees clearly surprised Sam Lacy, who predicted that "the NNL officials ain't agoing to do nothing to the Black Yankees" because Bill Leuschner, booking agent owner of the Black Yankees and the Bushwicks, had power over them.[336]

Despite the organizational paralysis and contention that continued to beset the two leagues, they continued to be prosperous in 1945. Attendance around the league continued to be solid; particularly noteworthy was the attendance of 101,818 fans to nine weeknight Negro League games at Philadelphia's Shibe Park, when its two major-league tenants, the A's and the Phillies, only drew 773,020 fans combined *for their entire home seasons.*[337] The Cleveland Buckeyes swept the Homestead Grays, four games to none, in the 1945 Negro World Series, played in the immediate aftermath of V-J Day.[338] Cleveland Buckeyes general manager Wilbur Hayes had predicted correctly that his team would win the 1945 NAL pennant back in December 1944 at the NAL's winter meeting; but who could predict the firestorm of excitement, condemnation, and pressure (the last on Negro League owners and officials) that would be unleashed with the October 23, 1945, announcement of the signing of Jackie Robinson by Branch Rickey and the Brooklyn Dodgers?[339]

Part 3 - Integration and Storm Clouds- And the Demise of the NNL- 1945-1948

Robinson Signs

Although Jackie Robinson signed an agreement with the Brooklyn Dodgers organization on August 28, 1945, the actual signing of a contract to play with the Montreal Royals in the International League for the 1946 season occurred and was announced on October 23, 1945.[340] The signing was hailed in most public pronouncements, including the initial response of NAL President J.B. Martin, whose league had employed Robinson in 1945. The October 27, 1945, *New York Times* published a letter that Martin sent to Branch Rickey in which he wrote: "I take great pleasure on congratulating you for your moral courage in making the initial step which will give the Negro ball players a chance to participate in the major leagues."[341]

The early comments by the Kansas City Monarchs owners were mixed. Both J.L. Wilkinson and Tom Baird indicated that they were "happy to see any Negro player make the major league grade."[342] Wilkinson, though, also noted that "we have been out some expense in training players such as Robinson" and that "something should be done to prevent white organized baseball from just stepping in and taking our players."[343] According to the November 3, 1945 *Baltimore Afro-American*, "Baird was reported to have protested the signing of Jackie and threatened an appeal to Baseball Commissioner A.B. (Happy) Chandler."[344] The *Afro-American* went on to say that Baird had wired them to say that he had been "misquoted and misinterpreted. We would not do anything to hamper or impede the advancement of any colored player, nor would we do anything to keep any colored player out of the white major leagues."[345]

Behind the scenes, Effa Manley and J.B. Martin exchanged letters discussing how to handle this monumental turn of events. Manley suggested to Martin that John Johnson, chair of New York Mayor Fiorello LaGuardia's Committee on Unity, which had a baseball subcommittee that had been part of the impetus toward baseball integration, could arrange a meeting with National League President Ford Frick and Branch Rickey to see what could be done about getting compensation for any of their ballplayers signed by the major leagues. Effa Manley realized that "the future of Negro Baseball was in question" as Jackie's signing threatened the livelihood of Negro League owners, yet she also seemed to get that diplomatic efforts must be made to work with white Organized Baseball to set precedents for future such signings.[346] In return, Martin agreed that Frick and not Chandler should be approached and that some compensation should be received for Robinson "to set up a principle for the ones to follow. There will be no price named, for we are not going to jeopardize Robinson's chance."[347]

Martin also realized that he needed to say more publicly about the signing and its ramifications. Accordingly, he put out a statement in early November denying that the NAL objected to Robinson's signing and once again lauding Rickey for the stand he took which would provide opportunity for black players to advance to the majors, while expressing the belief that Rickey "must have a big heart" and "is too big not to compensate the Kansas City Monarchs for Jackie Robinson." At the same time, he acknowledged that Rickey had called the Negro Leagues "a racket" and felt the need to mention various business procedures of the Negro Leagues that indicated that "we have an organization" with "By-Laws and Constitution, contracts and Gentlemen's Agreements which have always been carried out by the two leagues" although "we will admit that we do not have a commissioner."[348] In reporting on Chandler's statement, the *Cleveland Call and Post* editorialized that Martin's statement "indicates the usual slipshod technique of the Negro leagues"—and there is no doubt that Branch Rickey would have agreed with the *Call and Post*.[349]

Further steps were needed, in the eyes of the black press as well as the Negro League owners and operators. In the November 10 *Call and Post*, sports editor Bob Williams had a lot to say about Martin, Monarchs ownership, and the two leagues—and none of it was pretty. He characterized the initial NAL statements on the signing as "confusing, asinine, or at best, irrational" and added that "Dr. J.B. Martin, league prexy, hemmed, hawed and beat around the bush in typical presidential style, while, on a tangent of his own, T.Y. Baird injected the first sour note of the development" by questioning the signing without compensation. Williams acknowledged that both Baird and Martin found "safer ground" but indicated that they were in danger of permanently damaging Negro baseball unless they gave unqualified support to the Robinson deal. And what about the NNL? When Williams wrote his commentary, the NNL apparently had released no public statements—Williams ironically stating that "they have never been quite so silent on matters heretofore which were definitely none of their business."[350]

Cum Posey was indeed busy behind the scenes. He sent a letter to Commissioner Chandler dated November 1, 1945, along lines similar to that of Martin's public statement, but going a bit further. Posey not only enumerated factors that indicated organized business practices on the part of the NNL (and said that he assumed the NAL "operates in the same manner" given their joint agreement) but mentioned that other NNL players had been recently approached by the Dodgers. He made it clear that "we are not protesting the signing of Jackie Robinson or any other player of organized Negro baseball. We are protesting the manner in which he was signed. We feel that the clubs or Organized Negro Baseball … should be approached, and deals made between clubs involved. … That is the only way in which we can be assured that Negro Organized Baseball can continue to operate."[351]

Posey sent a copy of his letter to Chandler to Washington Senators owner Clark Griffith, who responded to Posey by saying that "Organized Baseball has no moral right to take anything away from [your two leagues] without their consent" while calling Rickey's characterization of Negro League baseball as a racket an "assertion you can prove not to be true."[352] Griffith expressed a hope that Commissioner Chandler would protect the rights of the Negro League clubs to their players and suggested to Posey that "you folks should leave no stone unturned to protect the existence of your two established Negro Leagues."[353] It is important to remember that Posey's Grays were tenants of Griffith's Senators and lucrative ones at that—so Griffith had a vested interest in the viability of the Negro Leagues, and a desire to keep mining cheap talent from Joe Cambria's scouting of Latin countries without competition from this new resource. Griffith had not shown any interest in signing Negro Leaguers, nor would the Senators bring their first black player Carlos Paula, to the majors until September 1954, almost nine years after Branch Rickey signed Jackie Robinson.[354] No, Clark Griffith was not going to make it any easier for Branch Rickey to pave the way for the signing of more Negro Leaguers—and, therefore, he was sympathetic to the arguments of Posey and the other Negro League owners.

Clearly, a special meeting was in order—and so the leagues held a joint meeting on November 9 at their usual New York venue, the Hotel Theresa in Harlem. And not just the NNL and the NAL were meeting. The USL was originally scheduled to meet in Chicago on the same day, then shifted to New York to accommodate Branch Rickey. The USL was also going to meet at the Hotel Theresa on the 9th, and ultimately moved their gathering to the YMCA to avoid confusion over "rooms 102-3 at the Hotel Theresa where such meetings were held."[355] USL President Shackleford attempted to get NNL and NAL members to come to his meeting, but got little response to his invitations. According to Dan Burley's account in the *New York Amsterdam News*, "Negro League Baseball's troublesome course seemed heading for a violent explosion" as the three leagues (and also the minor-league NSL) strategized about how to deal with the major leagues and each other. At the joint NNL/NAL meeting, the announced intent was to strategize about how to stop "Organized White Baseball from raiding Organized Negro Baseball."[356]

Negro Baseball Plots All-Out War On Rickey, Others Seeking Players

—*New York Amsterdam News, November 17, 1945*

Apparently, those terms were used advisedly, as Burley noted the sending of a letter to Chandler at this meeting in which the league magnates described black baseball as having been organized for 15 years and having followed white Organized Baseball's rules, and suggesting that Branch Rickey was now violating those rules by not dealing directly with the black owners.[357] While Burley also expressed the belief that all three leagues were attempting to become a part of organized white baseball, the November 17 *Chicago Defender* made no mention of this goal, saying that the NNL and NAL "sought to have white organized baseball owners deal with Negro organized baseball owners in a businesslike manner and to halt the tampering with their players."[358] At the end of 1945, organized Negro baseball was in quite a pickle.

1946

For the second year, the NNL and NAL decided that their first winter meeting would include a joint meeting. This time, the undercurrent of change was now a tidal wave that could sweep both leagues aside if they did not come up with a survival strategy. Accordingly, the two-day meeting, held in Chicago on December 12 and 13, was an attempt to organize and "get their house 'in order.'"[359] In its individual meeting, the NAL re-elected last year's slate of officers, while the NNL deferred its election to a later meeting because of the absence of Cum Posey. Each league considered, but did not act upon, possible new entrants: in the NAL, a team in Detroit, and in the NNL, a team owned by Gus Greenlee possibly in Montreal and the Brooklyn Brown Dodgers. Together, the two leagues agreed to adopt both the constitution of and uniform player contracts of the major leagues as a prelude to applying for recognition as official organizations of black baseball, with the possibility of eventually becoming part of the current system of white Organized Baseball. According to the December 22, 1945, *Pittsburgh Courier*, "When the two-day meeting was over, their disorderly house still had big leaks in the roof and its foundation was still resting precariously on quicksand."[360]

COLORED AND WHITE MAJOR LEAGUE OWNERS HOLD ANNUAL WINTER MEETINGS AT CHICAGO

— *Atlanta Daily World*, December 22, 1945

In its analysis of the same meeting, the *Atlanta Daily World* said that the two leagues "completely ignored the touchy colored baseball question" occasioned by Robinson's signing.[361] The evidence suggests, however, that the two leagues were preparing an approach to Chandler, the league presidents and National Association President William Bramham to gain legal recognition of their rights to black ballplayers. Shortly after the joint meeting, the two Negro leagues sent a resolution to those individuals asking them to promote action at the first 1946 white baseball meetings to agree to negotiate with Negro League clubs before procuring black ballplayers for their respective leagues.[362] NNL President Wilson and NAL head Martin did succeed in gaining an audience with Chandler, American League President Will Harridge, and National League President Ford Frick on January 17, 1946. The result was that Chandler offered hope that, once the Negro Leagues were better organized, they could apply to be a part of a system of Organized Baseball that would put all—white major and minor leagues, black major and minor leagues, and even amateur baseball—under Commissioner Chandler's jurisdiction.[363]

President Martin, however, put out a press release after this conference because he wanted to underscore the desire of the Negro Leagues for being a part of one system of Organized Baseball but make clear that they had no desire to segregate their ballplayers within the Negro Leagues, thereby impeding their advancement into major-league baseball. Chandler had also said that "The Negro Leagues favor keeping their own boys and with their leagues on a sound basis. … [T]hey expect those boys to want to stay in their class."[364] Organized black baseball was trying to walk a tightrope, ensuring their future by gaining legitimacy from white baseball but also appearing to support opportunities of black players to leave the Negro Leagues and play integrated baseball, as long as appropriate compensation was arranged for releasing the players from their Negro League contracts. Martin needed to make clear that he did not support the expressed views of Chandler which made it appear that Chandler "viewed a strong black organization as a substitute for integration" or Martin would be lambasted by the black press for obstructing the advancement of black civil rights in favor of the selfish business interests of the two Negro leagues.[365]

One thing Martin and Wilson did not support was the recommendation by Chandler that the leagues would be better off with presidents who were not also club owners.[366] Wilson had been ill until recently, but he still ran for another term as NNL president at the February 20-21 meeting of NNL owners in New York. This time, Cum Posey and Effa Manley together backed an opposition candidate, Samuel Battle, a parole board commissioner who had been a New York City patrolman as far back as 1911 and was one of the first black appointees to that post.[367] Posey had been critical of the two league presidents looking to reinforce their power through their dealings with Chandler.[368] Unfortunately, Posey was seriously ill, so it was his co-owner Rufus Jackson who nominated Battle; Posey would die in March of 1946. The other four NNL teams still backed Wilson, and even Rufus

Jackson, after the 4-to-2 vote for Wilson, did not want it recorded that he supported Battle. The league also replaced Ed Bolden, voting in Alex Pompez as the new vice president, and chose Curtis Leak as acting secretary given Cum Posey's declining health.[369]

Both Wilson and J.B. Martin, who attended the meeting, discussed their January 17 session with Chandler. Wilson reported that Chandler approved the new contracts modeled after those of the major leagues but said that the old contracts were not acceptable.[370] Chandler offered consideration of a petition for the Negro Leagues to be recognized by organized white baseball as a minor league; Wilson indicated that he considered black baseball to be below major league but above the International League in caliber.[371] Martin added that Chandler's public statements were "contrary to the ones he had made in his meeting with Mr. Wilson and myself."[372] It was reported in the *Courier* that J.B. Martin said that NAL owners would wait for the Joe Louis fight with Billy Conn in June to come back to New York for their next joint meeting—giving an indication of the priorities of the NAL magnates.[373]

During the second day of the meeting, the league voted to limit fees for renting ballparks to 25 percent of receipts, to play 40 games in each half of the 1946 schedule, to petition Organized Baseball for recognition, to approve a working agreement with the NSL, to invite sportswriter Art Carter to their next meeting to "discuss the possibility of a public relations set up," and to postpone deciding on applications for two new franchises in the NNL from Gus Greenlee and USL President John Shackleford. In the minutes, a "long drawn out discussion" of applications by Greenlee for a team in Montreal and possibly Rickey for a Brooklyn team led to a conclusion (without Greenlee and Shackleford present) to ask for a $2,500 franchise fee for either team and judgment that the owners "morally wanted to do something for Gus Greenlee."[374]

The NAL held its next meeting on February 24 and 25 in Chicago. In this meeting, whose primary purpose was to set the 1946 NAL schedule, the league turned down an application from Greenlee and Shackleford for an NAL team in Detroit because they could not provide assurance that Briggs Stadium, home of the Detroit Tigers, was available. There was discussion of granting an associate membership to W.S. Welch for a team in either Detroit or Cincinnati—the league was apparently willing, but Welch could not decide whether to accept it or have an independent club.[375]

Before holding its June joint meeting with the NAL, the NNL had two more special meetings in 1946. The first, on March 12, was held in Baltimore. The NNL decided at this meeting to turn down Gus Greenlee's request to rejoin the NNL with two franchises, one in either Boston or Brooklyn and the other in Montreal, as it saw "no benefit to the league members" by adding any franchises, although it went on record as giving Greenlee first preference in the future "if he obtained a city that would be beneficial to league members."[376] Both the decision and the process through which the NNL made this decision to exclude Greenlee were heavily criticized by William Nunn. In his *Courier* column of March 23, Nunn called the decision a breach of ethics. He charged that the NNL knew it would turn Greenlee down when it deferred its decision on Greenlee's application in February and delayed it to do damage to the USL, which was trying to set up operations for 1946 even though it had "limped through its first season" in 1945.[377] Nunn expressed the belief that Greenlee was an innovative owner who would have contributed a great deal to the Negro Leagues going forward; rejecting him indicated that the all the Negro League owners "won't see the light. Some just can't keep pace with the changing trends. Others continue stubbornly in the same old pattern because they're sore with those who so correctly advocated for a change."[378] As the managing editor of the *Pittsburgh Courier* and a man who had been chairman of the ill-fated East-West Committee, which had "never been permitted to function and the details were handled by the President of the [Negro] American League," Nunn may have had an axe to grind but he also had a respected voice among the press.[379]

Another respected voice of the press, Art Carter, was hired for $1,000 for the season by the NNL at the March 12 special meeting. Carter was asked to do public relations for the league, which included tracking of the club standings and creating good will for the league with the press, something sorely needed.[380] The league did get some positive press immediately for this hiring and for moving "towards other reforms to make the league a more practicable working organization" including a players pool with compensation for third- and second-place clubs, cash prizes to the league's leading pitcher, hitter and "home run clouter," and the forming of a constitution committee to revise the NNL constitution along the lines of the National League constitution, preliminary to applying for recognition from Commissioner Chandler.[381]

The second NNL special meeting was held in Philadelphia on May 6, 1946, right at the start of the NNL season. The primary focus of this meeting was cracking down on players who had been thrown out of a game by an umpire or had struck an umpire as well as players who had abandoned the Negro Leagues for Mexico. The league ruled that players would be fined $100 and suspended 10 days for striking an umpire, and fined escalating amounts of $10, $25, and $50 for first, second, and third ejections from games. The league banned eight players, including future Hall of Famers Ray Dandridge and Raymond Brown, for jumping to Mexico.[382]

The meetings were coming fast and furious this year, so that six weeks after its second special meeting, the NNL met jointly with the NAL on June 19 and then followed with its own meeting on June 20. The NAL had its own league meeting on June 20 as it set its second-half schedule and "were in New York in time to witness the Louis knockout of Billy Conn", the previous night.[383] In the joint meeting, the two leagues not only decided on August 18 as the date for the annual East-West Game in Chicago, but they also agreed on a second East-West Game (sometimes referred to as the Dream Game) to be played in Washington on August 15. There was also discussion of the lack of coverage the two leagues were getting from the *Pittsburgh Courier*. When William Nunn acknowledged the validity of the complaint and promised that the *Courier* would give the NNL more publicity, an order to have Art Carter investigate was dropped.[384] The need to pressure the *Courier* to increase its coverage of Negro League baseball was an ominous sign for the future of the Negro Leagues, as there was an obvious shift toward covering Jackie Robinson, and also John Wright, Roy Partlow, Don Newcombe, and Roy Campanella, all of whom were playing in the minor leagues of organized white baseball in 1946.

The NNL had still one more special meeting in 1946, this one held in Philadelphia on July 15, in order to organize the second East-West Game in Washington (which had been decided on at the joint meeting). The July 27, 1946, edition of the *Norfolk Journal and Guide* listed players from the six NNL teams that were being considered for selection for the game, including Josh Gibson, Buck Leonard, and Sam Bankhead of the Homestead Grays, Monte Irvin, Leon Day, and Larry Doby of the Newark Eagles, Orestes Minoso and Silvio Garcia of the New York Cubans, Bill Byrd of the Baltimore Elite Giants, and Gene Benson of the Philadelphia Stars.[385]

This illustrious group of players, including several future Hall of Famers, was an indication of the continuing vitality of the NNL in 1946. Another indication of the quality of the league was the quality of the seven-game Negro World Series won by the NNL pennant winner Newark Eagles over the NAL pennant winner Kansas City Monarchs. That World Series was later characterized by longtime New Jersey sportswriter Jerry Izenberg as "the greatest World Series ever played between the Negro National and American Leagues."[386] The Series was a back and forth struggle, with Kansas City winning games 1, 3, and 5 to take a 3-2 series lead, and the Eagles winning games 6 and 7., the latter a 3-2 win in front of "more than 13,000 vociferous fanatics" at Newark's Ruppert Stadium.[387] The series featured pitchers Satchel Paige and Hilton Smith for the Monarchs and Leon Day for the Eagles (all future Hall of Famers) as well as 1946 NAL batting leader Buck O'Neil and Hall of Famer Monte Irvin in a starring role. Monte swatted 3 home runs, 2 of them in the crucial Game 6, and drove in the first run and scored the winning run in Game 7.[388] Author Brian Carroll described the 1946 Negro League as having had a "banner season" but also reported his own content analysis that showed that the *Pittsburgh*

Courier and *Chicago Defender*'s coverage of the Negro Leagues "sharply declined in 1946 as Robinson's major league debut approached."[389]

Negro League owners realized that their window of opportunity was closing—and without any concrete encouraging news from Chandler, they arranged a September 26, 1946, meeting between Effa Manley, Alex Pompez, and Curtis Leak and National League attorney Louis Carroll. In the meeting, they asked Carroll about their prospects for recognition by the major leagues. As reported in a document found in Effa Manley's files, Carroll said it was premature to assess, but that the NNL "needed a concrete program and proof that [we] were operating our business along the lines of established business principles." Carroll said that Commissioner Chandler would want to see the new Negro League constitution and Carroll would keep them informed of developments.[390] But 1947 would bring Jackie Robinson to the major leagues—and Wendell Smith, so instrumental in Jackie's signing, opined that although recent seasons had been profitable ones for the Negro Leagues, "the lush days haven't been here long and they won't be here much longer" as he expressed sympathy even for those owners who "aren't wholly in support of this campaign to bring more Negro players into the majors. But we'll forgive them and go along with them because they can't do anything about it anyway."[391]

1947

"As 1947 dawned, most owners, players, fans, and sportswriters had little reason to recognize that an era in black baseball had ended and the future of the once prosperous institution would soon be in doubt."[392] So said Neil Lanctot in his coverage of the period of baseball integration, combined with the changing postwar world that faced the institution of black baseball. Lanctot was pointing out that 1946 was also, for the sixth straight year, one of strong attendance figures for the Negro Leagues, so that when the owners of the NAL and NNL convened for their late 1946/early 1947 league meetings, they were not inclined to fully grasp how perilous their future path would be.[393] Nor would Negro League players, who had yet to appear in the white major leagues, or even black sportswriters, who had long warned the Negro League owners to get their house in order when postwar prosperity and the beginnings of baseball integration converged, be likely to fully realize just how fast the future prospects of the Negro Leagues would decline in 1947.

As was generally the case, the NAL held the first winter meeting on December 26 and 27 in Chicago. In reporting on the meeting, the January 4, 1947, *Chicago Defender* focused on the mundane details of a meeting in which the previous slate of NAL officers was re-elected, the league decided to defer any decision on Abe Saperstein's application to enter the Cincinnati Crescents as a 1947 NAL franchise, W.S. Martin announced that his newly built $250,000 ballpark in Memphis would be ready for the new season, and R.S. Simmons resigned his position as the traveling secretary of the Chicago American Giants. The NAL owners wanted six or eight clubs in the league for 1947 and were also waiting to hear whether teams in Detroit and St. Louis would apply.[394]

The NNL held its first winter meeting on January 5, 1947, in the Hotel Theresa in New York, as it usually did. The major piece of news of this meeting was a change in leadership—the league elected John H. Johnson, a pastor and police chaplain, to succeed Tom Wilson, who was co-president of the Negro League in 1938 and thereafter, had been president for the past eight years, despite numerous attempts, usually involving the Manleys, to unseat him. This time around, the Manleys were again involved in finding an alternative to Wilson—and their efforts to elect someone different were enhanced by Wilson being advised to give up the job by his personal physician for reasons of poor health.[395] Several challengers to Wilson's presidency were discussed. In addition to Johnson, they included Judge William C. Hueston, who had been president of the first NNL from 1927 through 1931 and had been a candidate for Negro Leagues commissioner in 1945; sportswriter and 1946 NNL publicity agent Art Carter; Frank Forbes, formerly business manager of the 1935 New York Cubans among other positions in black baseball and currently a judge on the New York

State Athletic Commission; Samuel Battle, last year's challenger to Wilson's throne; and a Harlem lawyer named John Doles. That Johnson was the "handpicked candidate" of the Manleys influenced his being chosen to successfully run against Wilson.[396]

Johnson's victory was generally welcomed by the press, not only because it meant that the NNL had finally picked a non-owner to head their operations, but also for the actions he promised to work for that would ostensibly strengthen the league. In his "The Sports Beat" column of January 11, 1947, Wendell Smith welcomed the new president, seeing him as a "righteous man … a non-owner … who will not be vulnerable to charges of favoritism and gerrymandering. … [H]is hands are clean and he will make decisions as he sees fit."[397] Johnson addressed the need for the league to "get its house in order," for quite some time a favorite exhortation to the league from various members of the black press, and specifically develop a balanced schedule of league games, and redraw the league's constitution with an eye toward gaining recognition from Organized Baseball.[398] Although Dan Burley saw Johnson as a "conservative choice" with limited prior connections to baseball, Effa Manley believed that Johnson's election "will also give the lie to hints that we don't want Negroes to go to the major leagues because our new commissioner was one of the most forceful fighters on former Mayor LaGuardia's committee [on baseball]. … [W]e want them to go in an organized fashion and not be virtually "kidnaped" *(sic)*."[399]

In his 'Confidentially Yours' column of January 11, 1947, Burley did cynically suggest that the NNL owners hiring Pastor Johnson was "a long step forward in eliminating the practice of cussing out loud at their powwows, especially when splitting up the money is the main agenda at such gatherings." More seriously, Burley asked a crucial question: "Will the hardheaded club owners give Johnson all the authority he demands, and will they abide by his decisions?" Burley was doubtful that the owners would cede control to Johnson, given their failure to follow the rulings of Commissioner Ferdinand Morton, the last independent ruler of black baseball back in the early years of the second NNL.[400]

There was no doubt that Johnson, as pastor of St. Thomas Episcopal Church in Harlem, a chaplain of the New York City Police Department as well as a former member of Mayor LaGuardia's well-respected Committee on Unity (which has since been credited by many researchers as being influential in the process of baseball integration) had the potential to earn respect while introducing needed reforms. The real question was whether Johnson could create sufficient change in league practices to fully replace what the *Pittsburgh Courier* once called "the loose-leaf organizational structure of the two leagues" which enabled Branch Rickey to sign Jackie Robinson and eschew compensation to the NAL's Monarchs because he deemed the two leagues as "in effect … not actually organized."[401] The jury was out, and it was worth noting that the NAL still had J.B. Martin, owner of the Chicago American Giants, as its president, and the two leagues still had not chosen an independent commissioner to oversee their joint operations.

In 1947 the two leagues chose to have their first joint meeting on February 24 and 25, this time in Chicago, NAL territory, at the Appomattox Hotel on the 24th and the Hotel Grand on the 25th.[402] The realities facing the two leagues seemed to be leading them to more and earlier joint sessions in which a mutual decision process was vital. Each league was also holding its own session in Chicago, although these were to be primarily for arranging their first-half schedules.[403]

In the joint sessions, returning NAL President Martin acted as chairman, which was not surprising given that the NNL had a new leader in Johnson. The leagues decided to more closely coordinate their respective schedules, starting their season on the first Sunday in May and ending it on September 15, and playing the same number of games in each circuit.[404] The March 1, 1947, *New York Times*, reporting on this joint meeting, added that the two leagues were planning on adopting the major-league model of playing all World Series games in the two home cities of the competing teams, departing from their typical practice of playing in several league cities. They also mentioned the banning for five years of several players who had jumped to the Mexican League including the Philadelphia Stars' star second baseman Marvin "Tex" Williams and the infamous Ted "Double Duty" Radcliffe.[405] The *Atlanta Daily World*'s reporting of the same meeting was especially focused on Radcliffe, who was "seen in the lobby of the hotel" with his younger brother and fellow Negro Leaguer Alex. "Double Duty" was described as being known by the owners as the "Peck's bad boy" of Negro League baseball, and he "felt the wrath" of the NNL and NAL owners as they banned him from playing any league or nonleague club in league games or in exhibitions.[406]

In the individual league meetings, the NAL admitted two new franchises, the Detroit Senators and the perennially-wanderering St. Louis Stars, while denying Abe Saperstein a franchise for his Cincinnati Crescents. Employing a bit of hyperbole, the *Cleveland Call and Post* described the NAL meeting as "a sensational history making session" with the adding of two teams along with upholding the 1946 ban on ballplayers who jumped to Latin American countries, demonstrating that the NAL "has a planned program for maintaining its high standards among the nation's top-notch baseball leagues." The *Call and Post* also described an "elegant plea" by Saperstein for a Cincinnati franchise that would play at the Cincinnati Reds ballpark, Crosley Field. Despite the "impressive style" of Saperstein's presentation, the NAL decided that St. Louis had more advantages.[407] In contrast, the *Atlanta Daily World* must have been singularly unimpressed with Saperstein's pitch or have missed it entirely, as it reported that Saperstein missed the meeting.[408]

The NNL meeting, naturally presided over by new President Johnson, centered upon the adoption of a new constitution and bylaws using those of the International League as a model.[409] The NNL also declared that the Black Yankees would play at Yankee Stadium when at home, that the Cubans would play at the Polo Grounds, and that the Newark Eagles would play some games at Ebbets Field.[410]

One could conclude that, as the 1947 season commenced, both the NNL and the NAL were in their own way attempting to legitimize their operations, the NNL with more formalized methods of operations and tighter bonds with major-league owners through their park operations, the NAL with an expanded league and the enforcement of discipline on jumping players that may have been modeled after the five-year ban instituted by Chandler against major-league players who had jumped to Mexico. They were also continuing to work together to mimic major-league operations with an eye toward getting formal recognition by Chandler, as Effa Manley believed they would get more money from major-league owners for their black players if they were recognized as part of major-league operations, and without such significant compensation, they would have a very bleak future.[411]

The 1947 Negro League season was played against the backdrop of Jackie Robinson debuting as the first African-American major leaguer of the twentieth century, with Larry Doby soon following as the first American League player of color. Staying in the limelight, even in the eyes of black America, would prove to be quite a challenge. In his "The Sports Beat" column of June 14, 1947, Wendell Smith reported that the Negro Leagues were experiencing "a definite decline in interest and probably at the turnstiles, too." He blamed the "moguls of the Negro American and Negro National League" for not sending their standings to the black press with regularity and generally not keeping the black public informed of their doings, claiming that the owners were "dodging the issue" by saying that Jackie Robinson's advance to the majors had destroyed their former prosperity.[412] But Smith was also dodging the issue as he failed to acknowledge that the *Courier* and other black newspapers were no longer giving comprehensive coverage to the Negro Leagues.[413]

There was at least some recognition by Negro League owners that they needed to curry favor with the black press, as the second joint NNL/NAL meeting of 1947, which was held June 10 and 11 in New York, included a banquet at Small's Paradise, a venerable New York black nightclub, with the black sportswriters as guests of honor. Although J.D. Martin ended up being the keynote speaker, the two leagues attempted to get Branch Rickey to attend and accept an award for breaking the color barrier with the signing of

Jackie Robinson. That Martin's speech spoke of black baseball's full support for integration did not negate the missed opportunity to "score a public relations coup" that Rickey's presence and participation would have engendered.[414]

The joint meeting included the usual determination of the date of the East-West All-Star Game, which would be held on July 27, and the planning of each league's second-half schedule. In addition, the leagues announced that Ray Brown of the Homestead Grays and Creed McGinnis of the Chicago American Giants were being reinstated after previously being banned for not returning from Mexico before a set deadline date. Earlier, NNL President Johnson had temporarily banned Claro Duany, a Cuban who had played in Mexico in 1946, but Cubans owner Pompez protested that ban, saying Duany had been released by the Cubans and had not jumped to Mexico. Banning Duany was an indication that Johnson was meting out appropriate discipline, thereby keeping them in line with major-league rulings by Chandler. But at the joint meeting, Duany was also reinstated. Whatever the merits of each case, rescinding the bans indicated that the leagues needed returning players desperately, as owners like Pompez pressured the leagues to reinstate their players so they could compete successfully for postseason berths and draw fans who came out to see the star players on Negro League rosters.[415]

Two other issues raised at the June 10 and 11 joint meetings showed the spreading cracks in the façade of the Negro League operations. Manager Homer Curry of the Philadelphia Stars appeared as a spokesperson for a player committee to create a pension plan for retired Negro League players. According to the *Norfolk Journal and Guide*, the owners first expressed interest but then determined that the financial outlay of $75,000 to $100,000 made it too expensive for them. Also, the two leagues decided to eliminate free passes for visiting players because it reduced the owners' profit margin.[416]

The season concluded with a bang—and several whimpers. The New York Cubans won their first league pennant, and dispatched the 1945 World Series winner the Cleveland Buckeyes in five games. An exciting series saw the Cubans lose the first game at home in New York and then win four straight games on the road—but those road games were played in Philadelphia and Chicago before the series finale in Cleveland, contrary to the declaration at the February joint meetings that all World Series games would be played in the home cities of the competing teams, as the Negro Leagues reverted to the traveling cities model they had previously used to reach enough fans. The first two games drew decent crowds of 5,500 for a rained-out game at the Polo Grounds and 9,000 for a game at Yankee Stadium, but the rest were sparsely attended.[417]

Financially, the solid gains that the Negro Leagues had made in solvency over the past six years were largely wiped away in one year. According to Lanctot, "the overall attendance decline in black baseball during 1947 was startling" even though the leagues still drew from a core of loyal fans despite competition from the major leagues.[418] While author Carroll, in his exposition focused on the role of the black press in baseball integration, stated that only two teams, the World Series contestants Cleveland Buckeyes and New York Cubans, made money in 1947, evidence suggests that the Cubans actually lost money, with Pompez claiming to have lost $20,000.[419]

Before beginning what would turn out to be the final season of the Negro National League in 1948, the Negro Leagues were beset with two essential truths. The first, as expressed by Joseph Pierce in his 1947 tome *Negro Business and Business Education*, was what he described as a Negro businessman's dilemma—"he disapproves of racial segregation but as a business man has a vested interest in segregation because it creates a convenient market for his goods and services."[420] This dilemma captures the essence of the apparent unwillingness of Negro League owners to prepare for the eventuality of integration as well as their slow and inconsistent response to its early stages—they did not want to give up the captive audience they had as a result of organized white baseball's institutional racism.

The second truth, which was devastating to their future prospects, was expressed by Neil Lanctot as a summary of 1947: "[T]he year also exposed the essential weaknesses of black business when subjected to outside competition."[421] The competition from the major leagues was not going to recede, and even though the rest of the teams (besides the three who brought black players to the major leagues in 1947) would do so with "deliberate speed," the audience for Negro League baseball would, for the most part, never return.

1948

The Negro Leagues did indeed survive 1947 intact. The year had been wildly successful for Jackie Robinson in the major leagues, as he won the Rookie of the Year Award and competed—and starred—in a losing World Series effort, but the other four black players who made their major-league debuts in 1947—Dan Bankhead for the Dodgers, Larry Doby for the Indians, and Willard Brown and Hank Thompson for the St. Louis Browns—had very little success. There was every reason to expect more debuts of black major leaguers in 1948—at least, for the Dodgers and the Indians (the Browns could easily describe their first integration efforts as a fiasco)—but the other major-league organizations were still rather hesitant to move forward and sign black players. Horace Stoneham, for one, had told *The Sporting News* in early 1948 that he had yet to find a black player to "fit in our plans."[422] At the end of the 1947 season, the Negro League owners and officials still had high hopes that they would be incorporated into the system of white Organized Baseball, and that they would become a well-paid conduit for black talent to the major leagues. They could also anticipate that the process of baseball integration would be slow to develop, meaning that the Negro Leagues would not lose their most talented players precipitously, and they would have time to develop more young, outstanding black players to first star on their teams before they were sold to white organizations.

Before the Negro Leagues held their annual year-end winter meetings, the National Association of Professional Baseball Leagues, the organization that governed minor-league baseball, held its three-day convention from December 3 through 5 in Miami. On the eve of the three-day meeting, George Trautman, entering his second year as president of the minor leagues after succeeding William Bramham at the end of 1946, announced that he saw no need for further expansion of the minor leagues, saying that "our main job is not to seek additional leagues but to strengthen all our existing leagues."[423] During the three days, the minor leagues dealt with business items such as guaranteeing a minimum salary for umpires and also discussed a resolution by the Pacific Coast League to become a third major league.[424] What the various newspapers reporting on the National Association convention did not report for some time was the decision by an executive committee of the National Association made during the Miami convention to turn down a written application of the two Negro Leagues to join organized white baseball. A letter written on December 17, 1947, to NNL President Johnson and NAL President Martin said that "the committee was of the opinion that it would be impossible to do anything with these applications at this time."[425] The main obstacle was territorial rights in that Negro League clubs played in major- and minor-league parks in the same territories played in by those major- and minor-league teams.[426]

In examining the actions taken by both Negro Leagues in their initial winter meetings prior to the 1948 season, knowing that the leagues now knew that their hopes of affiliating with organized white baseball had been dashed informs the actions that they took to desperately shore up the foundation of their now sinking ship, though they were not yet ready to publicly acknowledge the devastating news.

As always, the NAL held the first winter meeting, on December 29 in Chicago. Unlike the meetings of previous years, which were usually held at hotels, this one was held at 910 Michigan Avenue, Room 612. The January 3, 1948, *Chicago Defender* reported that, along with re-electing 1947's NAL officers, there was discussion about possible player trades, Chicago city tax increases, and rises in hotel and restaurant prices.[427] Were rising costs, 1947 financial losses, and most recently the National Association's denial of affiliation for the Negro Leagues with Organized Baseball leading league magnates to economize on their meeting space?

What was not speculative was that an uncertain economic future led to a decision to turn down applications for new franchises in New Orleans and Nashville in favor of staying with six clubs, as the owners were "not caring to venture out too far in 1948 as the season looked uncertain for such a move."[428] Economics were also responsible for the NAL passing a $6,000 club salary cap for the 1948 season.

The NAL announced several managerial changes for the new season, including Buck O'Neil replacing Frank Duncan as manager of the Kansas City Monarchs, Lorenzo "Piper" Davis taking over the managerial duties of the Birmingham Black Barons from Tommy Sampson, and Quincy Trouppe, after being sold by the Cleveland Buckeyes to the Chicago American Giants, leaving Cleveland's manager post to Alonzo Boone and taking over the position in Chicago.[429] And President J.B. Martin announced that the team he owned, the Chicago American Giants, was accusing the San Diego Padres of the Pacific Coast League of tampering with the 1947 NAL batting leader—catcher John Ritchey—by signing him to a 1948 contract, while simultaneously owner J.L. Wilkinson repeated his now more than two-year-old accusation regarding Rickey violating the Monarchs' contractual rights to Jackie Robinson. Unfortunately, Martin's charge was investigated and quickly found to be invalid by Commissioner Chandler, because Chicago could not produce a 1947 contract for Ritchey, further underscoring the similar circumstance of Robinson not having a written contract. Martin was clearly embarrassed, claiming that all the other American Giants were signed, and it was simply a "costly oversight" that defeated his claim.[430] Luckily for Martin, the Padres decided to honor the nonexistent contract and pay a "satisfactory sum" to the Giants for Ritchey, but Wendell Smith commented that the dubious claim of tampering underscored that Negro League operations were still "slipshod" long after Robinson was signed without compensation.[431]

The NNL held its first winter meeting on January 19, 1948, in New York at its usual haunt, the Hotel Theresa. The league joined the NAL in creating a $6,000 per team salary limit, as it was responding to its own economic straits along with the problems it shared with the NAL.[432] In particular, Dan Topping, who succeeded Larry MacPhail as owner and front man of the New York Yankees, had recently released attendance figures showing that attendance at Negro National League games at Yankee Stadium had dropped to over 63,000 patrons in 1947 from in excess of 155,000 in 1946—and Dan Burley estimated that such Yankee Stadium contests in 1945 drew over 200,000 fans. Burley's conclusion—"when Robinson went into big league baseball he took the Negro attendance at all-Negro contests with him."[433]

In addition to saving money through team salary limits, the NNL saw the potential of economic gain in selling younger players that they developed to the major and minor leagues, mentioning as an example the $15,000 that Bill Veeck paid the Newark Eagles for Larry Doby.[434] One could argue, however, that the recent failed attempt to gain recognition from the National Association, combined with the disastrous attempt by the NAL to challenge the major leagues on the Ritchey and Robinson signings, cast doubt that the Veeck signing of Doby would be a successful model for future sales of black players to Organized Baseball. In addition, Effa Manley's success in selling Doby to Veeck in 1947 was a marked contrast to her failure to get Rickey to pay her for the Dodgers signing Newark Eagles pitcher Don Newcombe in 1946, and their failed attempt to sign star infielder-outfielder Monte Irvin without compensating the Eagles in 1948—and the Newark Eagles did have all of their players signed to written contracts at least since the early 1940s.[435]

Otherwise, the NNL decided to continue to ban players who had jumped to Mexico (despite the exceptions it made for Brown, McGinnis, and Duany in 1947) as the Homestead Grays failed to persuade the other owners to overturn it. The league re-elected its 1947 officers, which meant that the owners were reasonably satisfied with the efforts made by Johnson in his first term as NNL president. The league also entertained the possibility of expanding to eight teams, but for the time being it passed on the application of the Richmond Giants, as it could not convince the

Asheville, North Carolina, Blues to apply and was not interested in having seven teams.[436]

In his commentary on the January 19 meeting, Dan Burley revealed the previously unreported failure of the two leagues to affiliate with Organized Baseball. Burley published two columns in the January 24, 1948, *New York Amsterdam News*. His "Confidentially Yours" column, which was more of a notes column, expressed his opinions of the important decisions the league had made and added that "the meeting featured little else but re-electing all officials and some discussions they didn't want made public," while his news column was the first published account to report the rejection of the affiliation application, which could well have been one discussion the NNL was trying to keep private for the time being.[437]

It was not until February 23, 1948, that NNL President John Johnson expressed the anguish of his league over its rejection by the National Association. That day, he released a statement outlining the tangled history of two years of failed promises and dashed hopes for the Negro Leagues. Johnson had been a member of the subcommittee on baseball integration that was part of New York Mayor Fiorello LaGuardia's Committee on Unity, when in mid-September 1945, fellow committee member and Yankees owner Larry MacPhail submitted his own written statement regarding "The Negro in Baseball." MacPhail's statement that he would support admitting the Negro Leagues to Organized Baseball "IF and when the Negro leagues put their house in order—establish themselves on a sound and ethical operations basis—and conform to the standards of Organized Baseball" was now cited in Johnson's statement of February 23 as the basis for a two-year process of attempting to conform to MacPhail's—and later Commissioner Chandler's—requirements. Johnson stated that the Negro leagues had taken the active steps of formulating a new constitution and adopting uniform contracts, yet "in spite of improved organization, when these two Negro leagues made formal application for admission to organized baseball.... They were turned down cold. ...Two years after MacPhail's recommendations were made, the Negro leagues still possess no status, no voice, no rights, no relationship at all to the major or minor leagues."[438] Johnson praised Rickey's signing of Robinson as a contribution to solving the "question of the Negro in baseball," in sharp contrast to the inaction of Organized Baseball to the fulfillment of MacPhail's recommendations. The result, according to Johnson, was that the Negro Leagues were currently in a "precarious situation" after the "wellnigh disastrous season" of 1947.[439]

At this point, it hardly mattered who the real villain was—MacPhail for suggesting a false pathway to major-league recognition in September 1945; Chandler for reinforcing that possibility in a meeting with the NNL and NAL presidents on January 17, 1946; National League attorney Louis Carroll for suggesting that there was still some purpose to continuing to apply for recognition when he met with NNL officials on September 26, 1946; or Branch Rickey for setting the precedent for denying that the Negro Leagues were sufficiently organized to deserve compensation when he signed Jackie Robinson on October 23, 1945.[440] The two Negro Leagues now knew that they had no future as a part of the white baseball establishment—they would have to find their own way to survive.

The NAL and the NNL continued to meet and (later on) compete—separately and jointly—throughout 1948. The NAL quietly held its schedule meeting in Chicago back at the Hotel Grand on February 21 and 22. The most important news had already been announced prior to the meeting—that J.L. Wilkinson had sold his half-interest in the Kansas City Monarchs to co-owner Tom Baird due to his failing eyesight.[441]

The NNL had its next meeting at the end of February or the beginning of March. There was inconclusive discussion of adding two more teams, now including a possible Brooklyn franchise along with earlier applicant Richmond, and temporary approval of Jim Semler's proposal to move his New York Black Yankees to Rochester, New York, leaving New York City venues to Alex Pompez's New York Cubans. In addition, the league promised to consider a proposal to create an interlocking schedule with the Negro American League, which would mean that interleague games would be formally included in each other's league schedules and count in their respective league standings.⁴⁴² As was frequently the case when new league proposals were considered, neither proposal ever materialized.⁴⁴³ The NNL reconvened in New York on March 14 and 15 to finalize its first-half schedule.

The two leagues had their annual midseason joint meeting on June 23 and 24 in New York, preceded by an NNL gathering on the morning of the 23rd. They announced their annual East-West all-star contest would be held in Chicago on August 22, followed by the third (and last) Eastern All-Star Dream Game in Yankee Stadium on August 24. Other declared actions prior to the meeting were the lifting of a ban against the Negro American Association because they stopped exploring the possibility of a franchise in Baltimore, which would infringe on the territorial rights of the NNL's Baltimore Elite Giants, and retaining a 10-day suspension against Thomas Butts, shortstop for those same Giants, for striking an umpire. The leagues now rejected the interlocking schedule, the possibility of including interleague contests within each league's standings, because they could not work out the extensive bus travel required to include such contests in a regular slate of games. They also met with a representative of the Caribbean Federation of Leagues, who wanted an accord with the Negro Leagues on banning ineligible players as an adjunct to their being given "special classification by the National Association"—since the Negro Leagues had a "tacit understanding with Organized Baseball to conform with its law and regulations and therefore wanted to be in harmony with them."⁴⁴⁴ It certainly seemed that everyone—the Mexican League, the Caribbean Federation, even the Pacific Coast League—had a better chance of getting what they wanted from Organized Baseball than did the Negro Leagues.⁴⁴⁵

The 1948 season culminated in a five-game triumph by the Homestead Grays, still featuring first baseman Buck Leonard, in his 16th of 18 successive seasons playing for Homestead, over the Birmingham Black Barons, for whom 17-year-old Willie Mays drove in the winning run in their only triumph. Two of the all-time great Negro League teams contesting the Negro League Fall Classic with an all-time-great ballplayer and several other top-notch talents still drew limited attention from the black press. Though newspapers including the *Baltimore Afro-American*, *Pittsburgh Courier*, and *Chicago Defender* did run some stories on the Grays-Black Barons series, they did not run box scores and paid a great deal more attention to the Cleveland Indians, featuring Larry Doby and Satchel Paige, triumphing over the Boston Braves in the 1948 major-league World Series.⁴⁴⁶

The season was not without its highlights, but it was also replete with failures and indignities. Starting with the February 1948 announcement by NNL President Johnson of the denial of major-league affiliation, the Negro Leagues were simultaneously dealing with Jackie Robinson telling a reporter that "Negro baseball needs a housecleaning from bottom to top," followed by an article written by Robinson appearing in the June 1948 issue of *Ebony* magazine entitled "What's Wrong with Negro Baseball?" in which Robinson "outlined the unpleasant lifestyle in black baseball" along with the questionable business dealings of Negro Leagues owners. Newark Eagles owner Effa Manley pushed back very forcefully against Robinson's charges, suggesting that he was "ungrateful" and did not comprehend how much had been sacrificed by the operators of black baseball. But the damage had been done—arguably, Manley only succeeded in widening the distance between those who were working toward integration and the owners of a declining black baseball institution just trying to survive.⁴⁴⁷

Attendance continued to drop significantly in 1948, limited only by how far it had previously fallen in 1947 from its peak years from 1941 through 1946. The 1948 East-West Game held on August 22 still drew more than 42,000 fans, but the Dream Game at Yankee Stadium held two days later drew fewer than 18,000 fans, far fewer than the expected crowd of 40,000 reported in the August 21, 1948, *New York Amsterdam News*.⁴⁴⁸

By September 1948 the shoes were beginning to drop. First, the New York Black Yankees "discontinued league activities in late August."⁴⁴⁹ Next, Homestead Grays owner Rufus Jackson lamented that "something must be done. We are experiencing our worst season in years and I don't know what the solution is."[450] On September 9, five days before the opening game of the Negro World Series, Effa Manley held a press conference at which she announced that the Newark Eagles were for sale. While she negotiated with various buyers, the future of the Grays also appeared in doubt, even as they were winning the Negro World Series.[451] Effa Manley "said that more than $100,000 had gone through her fingers the past three years" while Jackson's books had recorded losses of $35,000 in 1947 and another $10,000 in 1948, for a total of $45,000.[452]

While Rome was burning, NAL President J.B. Martin declared that Negro baseball had not been hurt by the advancement of black players to the major leagues, and that the "million dollar business" of "our baseball" was "here to stay." While he acknowledged vaguely that "Negro baseball has become a paramount issue," he evinced the belief that "since we can now furnish players for the majors, we are now stronger, especially financially." Martin's pronouncements were reported in the November 24, 1948, *Atlanta Daily World* and it is important to note that he did not mention the NNL in his reassurances of the future viability of "our baseball."[453]

The final disposition of the Negro National League was determined in a special two-day joint meeting held in Chicago on November 29 and 30, 1948. The facts were that at the meeting, the New York Black Yankees, the now-Washington Homestead Grays, and the Newark Eagles formally dropped out of the Negro National League, while the other three 1948 NNL clubs, the Philadelphia Stars, the Baltimore Elite Giants, and the New York Cubans, along with the new Houston club, purchased from the Manleys and transplanted from Newark, were added to the NAL to form one 10-team circuit.[454]

A survey of the headlines of some of the leading black newspapers revealed somewhat different perspectives on the ending of a 16-year run by the second Negro National League and the early prospects for a successful 1949. The *Cleveland Call and Post* headline was the most positive: "Negro Baseball Leagues Merge Into Ten-Team Circuit."[455] There was no mention of disbanding teams, rather a merger of forces. The *Chicago Defender* and the *Baltimore Afro-American* were balanced, each including a reference to one or more teams quitting but also indicating a future entity: "2 More Teams Quit Baseball, Keep Single Loop" headlined the *Defender* piece, while "Grays Quit League; New Circuit Formed" was the headline in the *Afro-American*.[456]

The *Pittsburgh Courier* headline only spoke of failure—"National Circuit Folds Up." In evocative and telling language, the *Courier* article describing the demise of the longest-lasting league in Negro League history started as follows:

> Like a ship without a rudder, Negro baseball was drifting wildly in a deep sea of utter confusion this week as owners of teams in the Negro National and American Leagues met here in a joint meeting designed to save the battered hull of what was once a profitable financial vessel."[457]

According to Negro League historian John Holway, the great Rube Foster, having brought together owners of top black clubs of the Midwest on Friday, February 13, 1920, and convinced them of the need to organize into a Negro National League, told them "We are the ship ... all else the sea."[458] Twenty-eight years later, the leading black newspaper in America described a now leaky vessel with one of its two engines no longer working. But the surviving Negro American League would not breathe its last breath until 1962.

Part 4
The Surviving NAL- The End of the Negro Leagues- 1949-1962

The Last Years of the Negro American League

> Some one *(sic)* ... has to make the public realize that Negro baseball must go on. It is horrible to think that just because four Negroes are accepted into the major leagues, Negro baseball is doomed. If that happens, no less than 400 young men will lose their jobs as players in our league. We can't let that happen.[459]

So stated Effa Manley, the "One-Woman Riot" of Negro baseball, in her newly self-defined role as the unofficial ambassador of black baseball, now that she was no longer a Negro League owner.[460] Outspoken to the end, Effa Manley would now operate from the sidelines as the Negro American League operated in an environment of declining interest from the black press and the black fan base as they attempted to put a competitive product on the field and remain financially viable. Manley was not wrong that abandoning black baseball was premature given the preliminary steps that major-league baseball had taken to incorporate black athletes into their system. Only Jackie Robinson, Roy Campanella, the ageless Satchel Paige, and Larry Doby, the four Negroes she referenced, had established themselves in the major leagues by the end of 1948. In its new one-league format with 10 teams competing, it was an exaggeration to claim that 400 players still would make their livelihood from Negro American League baseball in 1949, but about half of that—200 or more—was certainly accurate.[461] The Negro American League owners therefore trudged onward, fulfilling the obligation Effa Manley outlined and continuing to provide a showcase for the skills of many black ballplayers as the development of an operating pipeline to the major leagues for the best of these individuals continued.

This article's final part will provide a brief summary of the basic operations and the slow yet relatively steady decline of the NAL, the final remaining Negro major league. The league continued to exist in some form through the 1962 season—starting with 10 teams in 1949 and ending up with but three in 1962. The NAL continued to have one or two winter meetings every year until the 1962 season, and usually had a midseason meeting to schedule games for the season's second half. These meetings tended to be limited to basic operations such as working out the schedule, planning for the annual East-West Game, and especially trying to maintain the number of teams in the league from season to season. On August 26, 1962, when the last of 30 East-West All-Star Games was played, not in Chicago, but in Kansas City, the Negro Leagues had essentially staged their last contest.[462]

1949

As noted earlier, the first winter meeting of 1949 was on November 29 and 30, 1948, an earlier date than usual, occasioned by the NNL's dissolution. When the NAL reconvened on February 7 and 8, 1949, at 910 Michigan Avenue, Room 612, the same location as its December 29, 1947, meeting, the league was primarily concerned with establishing the framework for its new operations.[463] The recorded minutes of this meeting noted that "by common consent, it was agreed that there be an East and West Division and the standing be carried separately" but did not actually specify the teams that would play in each division.[464] Since the league approved the moving of owner Ernest Wright's Cleveland Buckeyes to Louisville and was also adding the Houston Eagles to replace the Newark Eagles while dropping the Homestead Grays and the New York Black Yankees from the former NNL, the Indianapolis Clowns were now placed in the East so that each division would have five teams.[465] The East Division included the Baltimore Elite Giants, New York Cubans, Philadelphia Stars, Indianapolis Clowns, and the Louisville Buckeyes, while the West Division had the Chicago American Giants, Memphis Red Sox, Kansas City Monarchs, Birmingham Black Barons, and Houston Eagles.[466]

Naturally, the one-league, two-division setup did not eliminate ownership battles. The February meeting discussed but did not resolve an ownership dispute among the three Martin brothers, NAL President J.B., who in addition to owning the Chicago American Giants had a partial ownership stake in the Memphis Red Sox and his brothers W.S. and B.B. Martin. J.B. wanted to relinquish his rights in the Memphis club equally to his brothers, who were arguing over their resulting share percentages of the team.[467]

At the midseason scheduling meeting, held at the same location as the February meeting on June 22 and 23, 1949, the discussed ownership battle was between new Houston owner Doctor Young and New York Cubans owner Alex Pompez over the rights to Negro League star Ray Dandridge. In this instance, the dispute was resolved with Pompez giving Young $750 for Dandridge.[468] Otherwise, the NAL discussed the process of player selection for the 1949 East-West contest, to be held on August 14, 1949 at the usual venue, Chicago's Comiskey Park, while deciding not to continue the Eastern Dream Game, which had been held for the past three years.[469]

At year's end, the Kansas City Monarchs swept a four-game Negro World Series from the Baltimore Elite Giants. The Giants won both halves of the East Division's split season; the Monarchs won the West Division's first half, but the second-half-winning Chicago American Giants forfeited a playoff series, leaving Kansas City as the West's contestant in this last Negro League fall classic.[470] Not only did Chicago and Kansas City not play each other for the West Division pennant in 1949, but the West Division did not publish their standings.[471] It was not an especially good harbinger for 1950 and beyond.

1950–1955

The first half of the 1950s saw the Negro American League start with its full 1949 complement of 10 teams in two divisions, East and West, at the beginning of 1950. By the end of 1950, the East Division had one team, the Cleveland Buckeyes, drop out after playing only two games and two others, the New York Cubans and the Philadelphia Stars, play shortened schedules.[472] The 1951 season saw the league deciding to form four-team East and West divisions, with Cleveland not returning and the New York Cubans also being dropped from the league.[473] It was not surprising that by 1952, the league had further consolidated into one six-team division; by 1953 it was down to four teams. In 1954, the league added two teams, Detroit and Louisville, but by 1955 the NAL was again a four-team outfit, where it would essentially remain through the end of the decade.[474]

Prior to the first scheduled meeting on January 14 and 15, 1950, owner Tom Hayes of the Birmingham Black Barons suggested that the NAL "confine its operations to the Deep South," primarily playing in cities like Atlanta, Memphis, New Orleans, and Birmingham, and thereby "seek refuge and security behind the jim crow curtain of the Deep South."[475] As the January 5, 1950, *Atlanta Daily World* put it, the "owners will grapple with the problem of completely surrendering the Eastern section of the United States to major league baseball or finding a way to lure customers through the turnstiles to see their teams play."[476]

The league ended up postponing this meeting to February 7 and 8, by which time the "Southern strategy" was no longer being considered, other than continuing to play in Memphis, Birmingham, and Houston, as the other Northern teams were still a part of the league. Wendell Smith, in his "Sports Beat" column of February 18, 1950, described the NAL as "on the ropes and ready for the killing," while in contrast, the owners at the meeting were expressing optimism that their "roughest days" were in the past, and, as the headline to the *Pittsburgh Courier*'s February 18 piece suggested, 1950 would be their best season since 1945.[477] By the time of the NAL's midseason schedule meeting, it was clear that the league still had a "serious problem of making the turnstiles click more often," and according to the June 24, 1950, *Norfolk Journal and Guide*, "the league was ready to call it quits but J.B. Martin … persuaded the owners to carry on."[478]

It never really got any better after that. As year by year the number of teams declined, ownership of the remaining teams continually changed hands. For example, in 1951 J.B. Martin, while continuing on as NAL president, announced at the January 3 and 4 winter meeting held in Chicago (where almost all NAL meetings were now held) that he had sold the Chicago American Giants to former Giants manager Winfield Welch for $50,000.[479] Then, at the midseason meeting held on June 14 and 15, the league announced (but ultimately did not succeed in) the selling of the Baltimore Elite Giants to William S. Bridgforth of Nashville from Henryene Green, the widow of Bill Green, who in turn had acquired the team after longtime NNL President Tom Wilson died in 1947.[480] According to Cal Jacox's column in the May 17, 1951, *Norfolk Journal and Guide*, "Today, the Negro American League is concentrated solely on developing future talent for the majors and the minors."[481] And, it would seem, trying to avoid a total failure of the institution.

At the first meeting of 1952, the Eagles, who had shifted operations to New Orleans from Houston in 1951, withdrew from the NAL.[482] With only six teams remaining and down to one division, Birmingham Black Barons owner Tom Hayes, one of those promoting a Southern-based NAL in 1950, said at the league meeting that things were "up in the air" as he expressed doubts about the league's future.[483] Hayes had tried to sell the franchise at the end of 1951, and though he continued to own the team in 1952, he brought in William Bridgforth, who had supposedly bought the now-disbanded Baltimore team to move it to Nashville but would instead be "affiliated" with the Barons.[484]

Tom Hayes, Black Barons' Owner Sees Dim Future For Negro Loop

—*Atlanta Daily World, January 10, 1952*

By 1953, the league was down to four teams—longtime members the Kansas City Monarchs, Birmingham Black Barons, and Memphis Red Sox, and the Indianapolis Clowns, who became NAL members in 1944 for the first time after overcoming the opposition of primarily NNL owners to their extensive clowning and presenting of racial stereotypes. The league postponed its first meeting in December, with several owners unable to attend, but President J.B. Martin, in announcing that the meeting would be held in February, proclaimed, "I do believe that 1953 will be the best year the Negro American League has had in many years."[485] While Martin maintained a show of optimism, the black press covered the NAL less and less. This researcher could not find any reports of a midseason meeting, and although press coverage continued, many of the articles were shorter and less detailed about league operations.

In 1954, hope sprang anew as the NAL, "anticipating a boom in Negro baseball interest this year," admitted Detroit and Louisville as the fifth and sixth league members at its February meeting.[486] Rumors were afoot, however, that the Kansas City Monarchs, a member of the original Negro National League of 1920 and thereafter a steady presence in the successor leagues, would leave the NAL and go independent.[487] Though sources conflict about whether Kansas City stayed in the league, merely considering leaving it was an ominous sign for the future.

Whether or not Louisville and Kansas City participated in the 1954 NAL, the Indianapolis Clowns and the Louisville club (called the Buckeyes back in 1949 but later referenced in the media without a club name) dropped out of the NAL at the 1955 winter meeting.[488] The big announcement of this meeting was the relocation of the annual East-West Game to Kansas City after 22 successive—and generally successful—years at Chicago's Comiskey Park. Monarchs owner Tom Baird had been reportedly seeking the transfer of venue for the past four years, as attendance at the annual classic had dropped from above 50,000 at its peak during World War II to around 10,000 in 1954.[489] In a rare Milwaukee midseason meeting, the league reversed its earlier vote at the behest of NAL President Martin and decided to keep the game in Chicago.[490]

According to Neil Lanctot, by the end of the 1955 season the league was truly in trouble. The Monarchs suffered their worst season now that they were competing with the newly relocated Kansas City Athletics for fans, as owner Tom Baird stated that the Athletics had "cut our … crowd over 2/3."[491] By the beginning of 1956, Baird sold off most of his players to major- and minor-league teams, and the remainder of his team to Ted Rasberry, a man who became heavily involved in the very final years of NAL operations. As Rasberry would primarily operate out of Michigan with rare dates in Kansas City, the cornerstone franchise of the NAL was largely gone.[492] But the league would go on.

1956–1959

Negro baseball, a sport that appears to be wobbling on its last legs, will hold a league meeting in Memphis, Tenn., Feb. 18. The Negro American League confab will be chaired by Dr. J. V. *(sic)*. Martin, president of the four-team loop.

> The NAL was handed a severe jolt recently when it was announced that Tom Baird, owner of the Kansas City Monarchs, had decided not to field a team during the coming season. The departure of the Monarchs leaves only three teams in the loop. Unless a fourth team can be added it appears as if the NAL will have died.[493]

The above constituted the entire column of the February 18, 1956, *Pittsburgh Courier*, reporting that the NAL was just about dead. But it was wrong. With the selling of three teams, the league reconstituted as a four-team loop and limped onward. At the meeting, Detroit Stars owner Ted Rasberry purchased the Kansas City Monarchs while he attempted to sell his Detroit team. The Birmingham Black Barons were sold to Dr. Anderson Ross, road secretary of the Memphis Red Sox in the 1920s.[494] The league now consisted of Detroit, Kansas City (but in name only), Memphis, and Birmingham, which would soon be renamed the Birmingham Giants.[495]

Although by now there was very little reportage in the black press on the operations of the league, the February 23, 1957, *Chicago Defender*, reporting on an upcoming March 15 meeting of the NAL in Memphis at the offices of Dr. B.B. Martin, quoted NAL President J.B. Martin as saying, "I believe it will be a better year than we've had for a long time" as he said that some independent clubs had expressed interest in joining the league.[496] Martin lacked credibility in his assessment, as he had been saying for years that the league was in good shape, and now was indirectly acknowledging that prior years had not been successful. Nevertheless, at a meeting in April, the league announced that teams in Mobile and New Orleans would join Memphis, Birmingham, Kansas City, and Detroit in a six-team circuit.[497] It seemed that the attempt in 1950 to make a league concentrated in the South might become reality—but Mobile and New Orleans did not finish the second half of the season.[498]

In 1958, the NAL held a spring meeting in which Arthur Dove, a potential team owner from Raleigh, was turned down in his attempt to get a franchise as the league had no interest in an odd number of teams and would continue with the same four clubs—Birmingham, Memphis, Detroit, and Kansas City, the last two represented by Ted Rasberry, who operated primarily out of Michigan and would represent both Detroit and Kansas City at meetings.[499] On May 7, 1958, *New York Times* reporter Roscoe McGowen reported that two NAL doubleheaders were planned for June 1, when the Memphis Red Sox would take on the Detroit Clowns and June 29, when the Memphis Red Sox would play the Kansas City Monarchs. McGowen also said that the four NAL teams were planning a 140-game season.[500] Although it is very unlikely that such a long season, at least in league play, was completed by any NAL team, the two doubleheaders at Yankee Stadium were played, with the Detroit Clowns splitting their June doubleheader with Memphis in front of 15,000 spectators, and the Kansas City Monarchs sweeping the Memphis Red Sox with an attendance of 7,500.[501]

So there was still a bit of life in the NAL at the end of 1958. And 1959 brought the possibility of new franchises, with five applications reportedly being considered at the upcoming February 10 NAL meeting in Memphis as possible new league members.[502] Unfortunately, by season's end, of the six teams that opened the campaign, the two new teams in Raleigh, North Carolina, and Newark, New Jersey, "threw in the towel" while only the stalwart Memphis Red Sox, Kansas City Monarchs, Detroit Stars, and Birmingham Black Barons "managed to keep swinging until the last ball was pitched."[503] As 1959 ended, the NAL was still alive—but not for very long.

1960–1962

The Negro American League's remaining four franchises—the Raleigh Tigers, who were apparently revived for the 1960 season, the Detroit-New Orleans Stars, the Kansas City Monarchs, and the Birmingham Black Barons—met again sometime in early April to plan for the 1960 season.[504] Not only had the Newark Indians, who made a brief appearance in the 1959 NAL, dropped out of the league, but the Memphis Red Sox also ceased operations, a "crushing blow" for the league.[505] At this juncture, J.B. Martin was still the titular head of the NAL, but he reportedly had "limited his duties mainly to presiding over league meetings, keeping an eye on team personnel, and sponsoring the East-West All-Star Baseball Game. ..."[506] The real power behind the throne was Ted Rasberry, the NAL vice president, who "has virtually taken over the field operations of the circuit and controls many of the administrative functions."[507] In his May 27, 1960, column in the *Atlanta Daily World*, sportswriter Marion Jackson expressed the view that Rasberry had new ideas of how to make the league profitable. These included limiting travel, finding useful old ballparks to play in, creating new associate memberships, and finding new talent by playing in areas like Atlanta and Philadelphia.[508]

Unfortunately, most of the ideas suggested by Jackson were not new—and by now, with all 16 major-league teams finally integrated, the sources for black talent were being mostly tapped into by Organized Baseball. The league played on, and held its final Chicago East-West Game on August 21, 1960. The West defeated the East by a score of 8-4 in front of approximately 5,000 fans.[509] In the August 23, 1960, *Defender* there was a picture of J.B. Martin shaking hands with longtime Chicago Mayor Richard Daley, but there was no article on the game, just a few lines under the photograph reporting the score and mentioning the deciding four-run rally.[510]

At the beginning of 1961, representatives of the four surviving teams—the Raleigh Tigers, Detroit Stars, Kansas City Monarchs, and Birmingham Black Barons—met in Chicago in late February or early March to go over league plans.[511] The league decided to switch its East-West Game for the first time to a place outside Chicago—to Yankee Stadium, a locale with a rich history of well-attended Negro League doubleheaders and years of league contests.[512]

Cal Jacox's August 12, 1961, column in the *Norfolk Journal and Guide* began as follows: "Though there are many fans who are unaware of its present existence, the Negro American League is still active on the baseball front."[513] Jacox talked about Satchel Paige pitching for the Monarchs that year, but noted that publicity was virtually nonexistent for the league, a seeming contradiction given that Satchel was always a one-man publicity machine![514] No doubt the highlight of the penultimate season of the NAL was Satchel Paige pitching three scoreless innings to start the August 20, 1961, East-West contest, getting the win in a 7-1 triumph for the West.[515] J.B. Martin estimated that more than 20,000 people would show up, much more than in recent years of East-West Games, given a large advance sale.[516] Once again President Martin was unrealistic, just like his yearly expressed expectations of another outstanding NAL season, as attending the contest were a mere 7,245 fans—a pale shadow of the throngs that used to attend this yearly highlight of the Negro League season.[517]

In 1962 the league had only three teams—the Birmingham Black Barons, Kansas City Monarchs, and Raleigh Tigers—though the Philadelphia Stars were an associate member. J.D. Martin stepped down as league president, and reportedly Ted Rasberry became president.[518] There is no record of league meetings, league officials other than Rasberry, or a regular season slate of games, as the teams apparently operated by barnstorming.[519] The league held a 30th—and final—East-West All-Star Game, this time in Kansas City. On August 26, 1962, the West All-Stars defeated the East by a score of 5-2. Jackie Robinson was given two plaques and a key to the city, and local resident Satchel Paige, who had won last year's East-West Game at the age of 55 but did not pitch in this one, was honored as well.[520] Although the NAL never declared that it had disbanded, the Center for Negro League Research has found no evidence to suggest that there was any operating NAL in 1963.[521] The era of black baseball had ended.

Conclusion

The January 27, 1961 Memphis-based *Tri-State Defender* published an article entitled "Dark Shadows." The article described the demolition of Martin Stadium on Crump Boulevard in Memphis.[522] Martin Stadium was built in 1947 with an estimated $250,000 spent by the Martin brothers, owners of the Memphis Red Sox, to create one of the two most significant ballparks built for Negro League play, the other being Greenlee Field, built for the powerhouse NNL Pittsburgh Crawfords back in 1932, the year prior to the start of the second NNL.[523] The stadium had an 8,000 seating capacity but attendance had typically been only a few hundred people at Memphis Red Sox games in their last three years of play until they closed operations at the end of the 1959 season.[524]

"The dream that was Martin stadium was predicted *(sic)* on the belief that there would always be a place in the American scheme of things for organized Negro baseball."[525] A poetic statement, but one that flies in the face of the hopes and aspirations of a subjugated race of people. The *Tri-State Defender* was expressing nostalgia for bygone days of great performances, great performers, and stadiums filled with people, mostly black people, who celebrated the outstanding stars of their race who were denied the privilege of playing in white Organized Baseball.

Negro League Baseball was a contentious, disorganized, immensely important institution, run by owners who made it possible for those great contests to happen. The story of this era is still being studied and must continue to be told.

NOTES

1. Leslie Heaphy, *The Negro Leagues 1869-1960* (Jefferson, North Carolina: McFarland, 2003), 98,103,106.

2. William Leuchtenberg, *Franklin Roosevelt and the New Deal* (New York: Harper and Row, 1963) as quoted in Neil Lanctot, *Negro League Baseball: The Rise and Ruin of a Black Institution* (Philadelphia: University of Pennsylvania Press, 2004),18.

3. David Kennedy, *Freedom From Fear: The American People in Depression and War, 1929-1945* (New York: Oxford University Press, 1999), 1964.

4. *See* https://www.nlbm.com/s/current.htm ; Thomas Aiello, *The Kings of Casino Park: Black Baseball in the Lost Season of 1932* (Tuscaloosa, Alabama: University of Alabama Press, 2011), 3.

5. See Heaphy, *The Negro Leagues*, 133-34.

6. Ibid., 54; Neil Lanctot, *Negro League Baseball*, 9; https://www.nlbm.com/s/team.htm

7. *Pittsburgh Courier*, January 16, 1932; see also Alan J. Pollock, *Barnstorming to Heaven: Syd Pollock and His Great Black Teams* (Tuscaloosa, Alabam,a: University of Alabama Press 2006),77-78. Syd Pollock, later the owner of teams in various cities that were called the Clowns, was at that time proprietor of a team called the Cuban House of David or the Cuban Stars. Pollock's Cuban Stars were entered in the 1932 East-West League; Alejandro "Alex" Pompez launched an earlier team called the Cuban Stars which was a member of the ECL. Adrian Burgos, Jr., *Cuban Star: How One Negro-League Owner Changed The Face of Baseball* (New York: Hill and Wang, 2011), 45-67.

8. Heaphy, *The Negro Leagues*, 42.

9. *Pittsburgh Courier*, December 31, 1932; *Chicago Defender* December 24, 1932; Aiello, *The Kings of Casino Park*, 5.

10. *Chicago Defender*, December 24, 1932.

11. Ibid.

12. *Pittsburgh Courier*, December 31, 1932.

13. *Pittsburgh Courier*, January 7, 1933.

14. *Chicago Defender*, February 25, 1933.

15. *Pittsburgh Courier*, March 4, 1933.

16. Lanctot, *Negro League Baseball*, 10.

17. Rob Ruck, *Sandlot Seasons: Sport in Black Pittsburgh* (Urbana, Illinois: University of Illinois Press, 1987), 149-51.

18. Email, Jim Overmyer to Bill Nowlin, October 2, 2017.

19. *Pittsburgh Courier*, August 15, 1942.

20. Email, Jim Overmyer to Bill Nowlin, October 2, 2017.

21. *Pittsburgh Courier*, February 11, 1933; In Wilson's March 4, 1933 Courier column, he reported that "reports from the West last week" indicated that Greenlee had been elected permanent chairman of the NNL- he was clearly referring to the February 15 meeting in Indianapolis. *Pittsburgh Courier*, March 4, 1933.

22. Lanctot, *Negro League Baseball*, 23-24.

23. *Pittsburgh Courier*, March 4, 1933.

24. "Speaking of Sports," *Chicago Defender*, February 25, 1933.

25. Ibid.

26. *Chicago Defender*, February 5, 1933.

27. Ibid.

28. Ibid.

29. *Pittsburgh Courier*, March 11, 1933. The NNL in 1933 was sometimes referred to as the Negro National Association.

30. Ibid.

31. *Chicago Defender*, March 18, 1933.

32. Lanctot, *Negro League Baseball*, 20.

33. Paul DeBono, *The Chicago American Giants* (Jefferson, North Carolina: McFarland, 2007),133.

34. *Norfolk Journal and Guide*, July 8, 1933. This was the first reference found to a league constitution.

35. Ibid.

36. Lanctot, *Negro League Baseball*, 22; "Posey's Points," *Pittsburgh Courier*, August 15, 1942.

37. "Posey's Points," *Pittsburgh Courier*, August 15, 1942.

38. Lanctot, *Negro League Baseball*, 22.

39. "Posey's Points," *Pittsburgh Courier*, August 15, 1942.

40. *Pittsburgh Courier*, July 8, 1933.

41. *Pittsburgh Courier*, August 12, 1933.

42. Ibid.

43. *Pittsburgh Courier*, July 22, 1933.

44. Ibid.

45. *Pittsburgh Courier*, January 29, 1938. The Courier column discusses how divisive and disordered the 1937 NNL was and says that the league needs a "'dictator'… a man who will set a course and follow it…regardless!" and ends with the statement that what Negro baseball" needs most at PRESENT is a revival of the Rube Foster method!" See also *Chicago Defender*, February 15, 1936. The *Defender* column, written by Candy Jim Taylor, indicates that the owners are at fault for various problems in the NNL and says that the greatest success and best men in baseball were in the original NNL in the 1920's.

46. Larry Lester, *Black Baseball's National Showcase* (Lincoln: University of Nebraska Press, 2001), 37 citing *Kansas City Call*, September 14, 1933 (19,568); Lanctot, *Negro League Baseball*, 23 (12,000).

47. Heaphy, *The Negro Leagues*, 108.

48. *New York Amsterdam News*, September 27, 1933.

49. *Pittsburgh Courier*, August 12, 1933.

50 *Pittsburgh Courier*, September 16, 1933.

51 *Pittsburgh Courier*, January 6, 1934.

52 Ibid.

53 *Pittsburgh Courier*, January 5, 1935. John Clark, the secretary of the NNL, stated that notices were sent to "all prospective club owners, Cum Posey and Prentice Byrd were the only men to respond" in his comprehensive description of 1934 meetings published at the beginning of 1935. In contrast, Cum Posey's version was that he attended along with representatives of Pittsburgh and Nashville. *Pittsburgh Courier*, January 20, 1934.

54 *Pittsburgh Courier*, January 5, 1935.

55 *Pittsburgh Courier*, January 6, 1934.

56 *Pittsburgh Courier*, February 17, 1934; January 5, 1935.

57 *Pittsburgh Courier*, January 5, 1935.

58 *New York Amsterdam News*, March 17, 1934.

59 Lanctot, *Negro League Baseball*, 33-34.

60 *Pittsburgh Courier*, January 5, 1935.

61 Rebecca Alpert, *Out Of Left Field: Jews And Black Baseball* (New York: Oxford University Press, 2011), 51-52.

62 *Pittsburgh Courier*, June 2, 1934.

63 Ibid.

64 *Atlanta Daily World*, July 9, 1934.

65 *Pittsburgh Courier*, June 16, 1934.

66 *Pittsburgh Courier*, June 30, 1934.

67 *Pittsburgh Courier*, July 14, 1934.

68 *Atlanta Daily World*, July 9, 1934.

69 *Chicago Defender*, July 14, 1934.

70 Once again, different sources provide different attendance figures. Lester reports an attendance of 30,000, while Lanctot has it as above 25,000. Lester, *Black Baseball's National Showcase*, 61; Lanctot, *Negro League Baseball*. 38.

71 DeBono, *The Chicago American Giants*, 137.

72 Lanctot, *Negro League Baseball*, 37.

73 *Philadelphia Tribune*, September 13, 1934.

74 *New York Amsterdam News*, October 20, 1934.

75 *New York Amsterdam News*, November 10, 1934; DeBono, *The Chicago American Giants*, 137.

76 *Pittsburgh Courier*, September 15, 1934 as quoted in Lanctot, *Negro League Baseball*, 38; *Baltimore Afro-American*, January 19, 1935 as quoted in Lanctot, *Negro League Baseball*, 39.

77 In his history of the Chicago American Giants, Paul DeBono pointed out that "the supposed World Series between the Chicago American Giants and Philadelphia Stars would not generate anything near the amount of fan interest, so it made sense from a business standpoint to schedule the games at Yankee stadium" even though they disrupted the league championship playoff. DeBono, *The Chicago American Giants*, 137.

78 Lanctot, *Negro League Baseball*, 40.

79 *Atlanta Daily World*, January 4, 1935.

80 Burgos, *Cuban Star*, 84; Lanctot, *Negro League Baseball*, 24.

81 Lanctot, *Negro League Baseball*, 41.

82 The Bacharach Giants also sent a representative to the conference but were refused admission to the league, as was a team from Boston. *Atlanta Daily World*, January 23, 1935; see also *Chicago Defender*, January 19, 1935.

83 *Chicago Defender*, January 19, 1935.

84 *Atlanta Daily World*, January 23, 1935; *Chicago Defender*, January 19, 1935.

85 *Pittsburgh Courier*, March 16, 1935.

86 Ibid.; *New York Amsterdam News*, March 16, 1935.

87 Lanctot, *Negro League Baseball*, 44.

88 *New York Amsterdam News*, March 16, 1935.

89 Lanctot, *Negro League Baseball*, 46.

90 *New York Amsterdam News*, August 31, 1935.

91 *Pittsburgh Courier*, November 16, 1935.

92 Lanctot, *Negro League Baseball*, 48-50.

93 Heaphy, *The Negro Leagues*, Appendix D, 241.

94 Courtney Smith, "A Fine Line Between Admiration and Animosity: Ed Bolden's Philadelphia Stars, the Negro National League, and the Philadelphia Tribune, 1933-1938," *Black Ball* Vol.6 (Fall 2013), 45-46 citing *Philadelphia Tribune*, January 16, 30 1936

95 *Chicago Defender*, January 18, 1936.

96 *Chicago Defender*, February 15, 1936.

97 Ibid.

98 *Chicago Defender*, February 29, 1936.

99 *New York Amsterdam News*, March 14, 1936.

100 *Chicago Defender*, June 27, 1936.

101 Heaphy, *The Negro Leagues*, 110.

102 Lanctot, *Negro League Baseball*, 53.

103 *Chicago Defender*, October 24, 1936; *see also* Lanctot, *Negro League Baseball*, 54-55.

104 *Chicago Defender*, October 24, 1936.

105 *Philadelphia Tribune*, July 30, 1936 as quoted in Lanctot, *Negro League Baseball*, 55.

106 *Pittsburgh Courier*, August 29, 1936 as quoted in Lanctot, *Negro League Baseball*, 55.

107 *Chicago Defender*, October 17, 1936.

108 *Chicago Defender*, December 19, 1936.

109 *New York Amsterdam News*, January 2, 1937.

110 *New York Amsterdam News*, January 16, 1937.

111 Ibid.

112 *Pittsburgh Courier*, January 30, 1937.

113 *Pittsburgh Courier*, March 27, 1937.

114 Lanctot, *Negro League Baseball*, 58.

115 Burgos, *Cuban Star*, 101.

116 Burgos, *Cuban Star*, 100; Lanctot, *Negro League Baseball*, 59-62.

117 *New York Amsterdam News*, June 19, 1937.

118 Lanctot, *Negro League Baseball*, 65-66.

119 *Chicago Defender*, February 27, 1937.

120 Ibid.

121 DeBono, *The Chicago American Giants*, 144-45.

122 Lanctot, *Negro League Baseball*, 59.

123 Heaphy, *The Negro Leagues*, 111.

124 *Chicago Defender*, September 25, 1937 as quoted in DeBono, *The Chicago American Giants*, 144.

125 *Pittsburgh Courier*, September 18, 1937.

126 *Chicago Defender*, October 9, 1937.

127 Lanctot, *Negro League Baseball*, 67.

128 *Pittsburgh Courier*, January 29, 1938.

129 Document titled "League Meeting," 1938 Newark Eagles Records, Newark Public Library. Documents from this set of files will be referred to as "Manley Files" hereinafter.

130 Ibid.

131 *Chicago Defender*, February 26, 1938.

132 *Pittsburgh Courier*, January 29, 1938.

133 *Pittsburgh Courier*, February 5, 1938.

134 Lanctot, *Negro League Baseball*, 75.

135 *Pittsburgh Courier*, February 5, 1938 (states upcoming meeting will be on February 19); *Pittsburgh Courier*, March 19, 1938.

136 *Pittsburgh Courier*, March 12, 1938.

137 *Chicago Defender*, March 19, 1938.

138 Lanctot, *Negro League Baseball*, 74.

139 Ibid., 76.

140 Heaphy, *The Negro Leagues*, 112.

141 *Chicago Defender*, December 18, 1937.

142 *Pittsburgh Courier*, February 26, 1938; *Chicago Defender*, February 26, 1938.

143 *Chicago Defender*, February 26, 1938.

144 Heaphy, *The Negro Leagues*, Appendix D, 241.

145 *Chicago Defender*, July 2, 1938.

146 *Pittsburgh Courier*, December 17, 1938.

147 Ibid.

148 *Chicago Defender*, January 14, 1939.

149 Lanctot, *Negro League Baseball*, 78-79.

150 *Pittsburgh Courier*, February 25, 1939.

151 Summary of 1939 NNL meeting by Cum Posey, Manley Files. Although this meeting description does not specify the meeting date, the matters covered accord with the description of the February NNL meeting discussed in the February 25, 1939 edition of the *Pittsburgh Courier*.

152 *Pittsburgh Courier*, February 25, 1939.

153 Document titled "Notes/Memo by Cum Posey," which describes spring 1939 NNL business, Manley Files.

154 *Chicago Defender*, February 18, 1939.

155 Letter, Cum Posey to Effa Manley, April 14, 1939, Manley Files.

156 Lanctot, *Negro League Baseball*, 83; Minutes, Meeting of Negro National League, June 20, 1939, Manley Papers.

157 *Atlanta Daily World*, July 1, 1939

158 Agreement Between The Negro National League and the Negro American League, Joint Meeting June 20, 1939, Manley Papers.

159 Minutes, Combined Meeting of the Negro National League and the Negro American League, June 20, 1939, Manley Papers.

160 Minutes, Joint Meeting of Negro National and Negro American League, August 27, 1939, Manley Papers.

161 Lanctot, *Negro League Baseball*, 84.

162 Minutes, Meeting of Negro National League, August 28, 1939, Manley Papers.

163 Heaphy, *The Negro Leagues*, Appendix D, 241.

164 Letter, Cum Posey to Abe Manley, October 17, 1939, Manley Papers; Lanctot, *Negro League Baseball*, 84-85.

165 Draft of Statement of Abe Manley to NAL Owners, December 9, 1939, Manley Papers. The statement, which has handwritten notations, does not explicitly state who it is intended for but its date and subject matter clearly reference an NAL meeting on December 9 at which Abe's wife Effa would attend and present his thoughts.

166 Lanctot, *Negro League Baseball*, 86.

167 Ibid., 87.

168 Report on annual meeting of Negro American League, December 9 and 10, 1939, Manley Papers. After Effa Manley's failed attempt to nominate Judge Hastie, the Judge wrote to tell her that he would not be able to handle the "larger job of guidance, direction and publicity" because of his current commitments, which included being Chairman of the National Legal Committee of the NAACP. Letter, William Hastie to Effa Manley, February 1, 1940, Manley Papers.

169 Ibid; *Chicago Defender*, December 16, 1939 as quoted in Lanctot, *Negro League Baseball*, 87.

170 *Chicago Defender*, February 10, 1940.

171 *Pittsburgh Courier*, February 3, 1940

172 See, e.g. *Pittsburgh Courier*, May 11, 1940

173 *Baltimore Afro-American*, February 10, 1940; Letter, Effa Manley to Art Carter, February 7, 1940, Manley Papers. Since the black press published on a weekly basis, one would presume that the Feb. 10 edition came out several days earlier, otherwise Effa would not have been able to date her letter February 7 and criticize Carter for his "column of Feb. 10 in the Afro" unless she was either clairvoyant or she erroneously dated the letter!

174 Letter, Effa Manley to Art Carter, February 7, 1940, Manley Papers.

175 *Baltimore Afro-American*, February 10, 1940; *Chicago Defender*, February 10, 24, 1940; *Pittsburgh Courier*, February 10, 1940. Both the *Afro-American* and *Defender* accounts contain vivid accounts of the Posey/Manley confrontation. The *Courier* account described the deadlock in more neutral terms. On February 24, two weeks after the original reportage of this meeting, the *Defender* quoted Effa as saying that "the league ought to be run for colored by colored." Recent evidence suggesting that Effa could have been white places statements like these and others by Effa Manley in a different light.

176 *Baltimore Afro-American*, March 2, 1940; Adrian Burgos, *Cuban Star*, 152 citing *New York Age*, March 9, 1940.

177 Minutes, Joint Meeting Negro National and Negro American Leagues, February 24, 1940, Manley Papers.

178 *Chicago Defender*, June 29, 1940.

179 Letter, Effa Manley to B.B. Martin and Thomas Wilson, June 2, 1940, Manley Papers; Lanctot, *Negro League Baseball*, 91.

180 *Chicago Defender*, June 29, 1940.

181 Heaphy, *Negro League Baseball*, 116; *Chicago Defender*, June 29, 1940.

182 *Pittsburgh Courier*, November 9, 1940.

183 *Pittsburgh Courier*, May 11, 1940.

184 *Chicago Defender*, January 4, 1941.

185 Ibid.

186 *Baltimore Afro-American*, January 11, 1941.

187 *Baltimore Afro-American*, January 11, 1941; *Pittsburgh Courier*, January 11, 1941.

188 Ibid.

189 Ibid.

190 *New York Amsterdam News*, January 11, 1941; *see also* Burgos, *Cuban Star*, 152.

191 *Baltimore Afro-American*, January 11, 1941.

192 *Chicago Defender*, January 18, 1941.

193 *Chicago Defender*, March 1, 1941.

194 *New York Amsterdam News*, March 8, 1941.

195 *Pittsburgh Courier*, March 29, 1941; Alpert, *Out of Left Field*, 72-74.

196 *Chicago Defender*, May 24, 1941.

197 Lanctot, *Negro League Baseball*, 105.

198 *Pittsburgh Courier*, June 28, 1941.

199 Ibid.

200 *Cleveland Call and Post*, August 13, 1941.

201 *Cleveland Call and Post*, August 13, 1941.

202 Resolutions passed at NNL Fall Meeting, September 15, 1941, Manley Papers; *Pittsburgh Courier*, December 27, 1941.

203 *Chicago Defender*, October 25, 1941.

204 Ibid.

205 Lanctot, *Negro League Baseball*, 110.

206 Letter, Effa Manley to Cum Posey, October 13, 1941, Manley Papers.

207 Heaphy, *The Negro Leagues*, Appendix D., 241.

208 *Pittsburgh Courier*, December 27, 1941.

209 *Pittsburgh Courier*, January 3, 1942.

210 *Atlanta Daily World*, December 31, 1941.

211 Letter, Effa Manley to Rufus "Sonnyman" Jackson, January 2, 1942, Manley Papers; Letter, Effa Manley to Joseph Rainey, January 26, 1942, Manley Papers.

212 Letter, Effa Manley to Joseph Rainey, January 26, 1942, Manley Papers.

213 Duke Goldman, "The Double Victory Campaign and the Campaign to Integrate Baseball," *Who's on First: Replacement Players in World War II* (Phoenix, Arizona: Society for American Baseball Research, 2015), 405-06; Patrick Washburn, "The Pittsburgh Courier's Double V Campaign in 1942," *American Journalism* (Vol. 74, No. 2 1986), 73-74.

214 *Pittsburgh Courier*, February 14, 1942.

215 *New York Amsterdam News*, February 21, 1942.

216 *Baltimore Afro-American*, February 21, 1942.

217 *New York Amsterdam News*, February 21, 1942.

218 *Baltimore Afro-American*, February 21, 1942; *New York Amsterdam News*, February 21, 1942.

219 *New York Amsterdam News*, February 21, 1942.

220 Alpert, *Out Of Left Field*, 78; *Pittsburgh Courier*, March 7, 1942.

221 Letter, Gus Greenlee to Abe Manley, February 21, 1942, Manley Papers.

222 *New York Amsterdam News*, March 7, 1942.

223 *Atlanta Daily World*, March 11, 1942.

224 *Baltimore Afro-American*, May 9, 1942 as quoted in Lanctot, *Negro League Baseball*, 119.

225 Lanctot, *Negro League Baseball*, 127-28.

226 Minutes, Joint Meeting Negro American and Negro National Leagues, June 10, 1942, Manley Papers; *Pittsburgh Courier*, June 20, 1942.

227 *Pittsburgh Courier*, October 31, 1942 as quoted in Alpert, *Out Of Left Field*, 81.

228 *Chicago Defender, December 12, 1942.*

229 Heaphy, *Negro League Baseball*, Appendix D., 241.

230 *Chicago Defender*, December 27, 1942.

231 *Chicago Defender*, December 12, 1942.

232 Ibid.

233 DeBono, *The Chicago American Giants*, 160.

234 *Chicago Defender*, December 19, 1942.

235 *New York Amsterdam News*, January 30, 1943. Although the *Amsterdam News* stated that Wilson's "entire cabinet was reelected for another term," in actuality Abe Manley was restored to the treasurer post after two years of Posey serving as both secretary and treasurer of the NNL. In light of the ongoing power plays and the reality of shifting alliances between owners, Abe Manley's being voted back into his previous league office is worth nothing.

236 *Pittsburgh Courier*, January 23, 1943.

237 Lanctot, *Negro League Baseball*, 129.

238 Ibid, 132.

239 Ibid., 131-32.

240 *Baltimore Afro-American*, April 3, 1943; *Chicago Defender*, April 3, 1943.

241 *Baltimore Afro-American*, April 3, 1943.

242 *Chicago Defender*, April 3, 1943.

243 *New York Amsterdam News*, April 3, 1943.

244 *Pittsburgh Courier*, April 10, 1943 (sell buses and train travel); *Baltimore Afro-American*, April 17, 1943 (carry on and try for special considerations); *Chicago Defender*, April 17, 1943 (trains and commercial buses).

245 *Chicago* Defender, April 17, 1943.

246 *Baltimore Afro-American*, April 17, 1943.

247 Lanctot, *Negro League Baseball*, 133-134.

248 Press Release, May 2, 1943, Manley Papers.

249 *Chicago Defender*, June 12, 1943.

250 Minutes, Meeting of Negro National League, June 1, 1943, Manley Papers.

251 Ibid. The original vote on the resolution to return the 10 players had Newark not voting and Homestead and Cleveland voting no. But Homestead and Cleveland objected to any ruling on the vote, which led to extensive rearguing of the issue. After another vote with the same result, Presidents and Martin and Wilson signed the order.

252 Lanctot, *Negro League Baseball*, 138.

253 Brian Carroll, *When to Stop the Cheering? The Black Press, the Black Community, and the Integration of Professional Baseball* (New York: Routledge, 2007), 129.

254 Minutes, Joint Meeting of the Negro American and Negro National Leagues, August 2, 1943, Manley Papers.

255 Ibid.

256 Alpert, *Out Of Left Field*, 84.

257 Carroll, *When to Stop the Cheering?*, 129.

258 J.B. Martin was reported as saying that 1943 had been the most profitable year in league history and that he expected an even better year in 1944. *Pittsburgh Courier*, December 18, 1943. The *Courier* also reported that the NAL would resist efforts by some NNL owners to form a one-league structure. In addition, there was to be discussion of disputes over NAL players being used without permission by NNL teams, in one instance by the Homestead Grays during the Negro World Series. *Chicago Defender*, December 18, 1943.

259 *Pittsburgh Courier*, December 18, 1943.

260 Ibid. See also Carroll, *When to Stop the Cheering?*, 131-132. According to Carroll, Smith's column, however inadvertently, provided cover for major-league owners to question Negro League legitimacy. Carroll goes on to characterize Smith's columns on Negro League operations as "patronizing" and delivering "unvarnished criticism" of Negro League owners, likely leading to both leagues rejecting his offer to compile statistics for league games for a fee.

261 Ibid. *See also,* Lester, *Black Baseball's National Showcase*, 208-210; Lanctot, *Negro League Baseball*, 245.

262 Lanctot, *Negro League Baseball*, 245; *Pittsburgh Courier*, December 11, 1943 as quoted in Lester, *Black Baseball's National Showcase*, 209.

263 Carroll, When to Stop the Cheering?, 129.

264 *New York Amsterdam News*, January 1, 1944.

265 *Atlanta Daily World*, December 29, 1943.

266 Lanctot, *Negro League Baseball*, 247 citing *Philadelphia Independent*, January 2, 1944.

267 *Atlanta Daily World*, December 29, 1943.

268 *New York Amsterdam News*, January 15, 1944; *Pittsburgh Courier*, January 1, 1944. Wilson's statement on baseball integration appeared in a printed brochure whereas Martin's was an oral response.

269 *Chicago Defender*, December 25, 1943. Traveling secretary Simmons was reelected even though some NAL owners had

concerns about a team's road secretary doubling as the league's secretary. *Chicago Defender*, December 18, 1943.

270 *Chicago Defender*, December 25, 1943.

271 *Norfolk Journal and Guide*, January 1, 1944.

272 *Pittsburgh Courier*, January 1, 1944.

273 *Chicago Defender*, January 15, 1944.

274 *New York Amsterdam News*, January 15, 1944.

275 Ibid.

276 Ibid.; Lanctot, *Negro League Baseball*, 134; *Pittsburgh Courier*, March 11, 1944. Although Lanctot states that the NNL "would not receive relief until February 1944 when the ODT accepted the league's somewhat dubious claim that it also operated in the south," the March 11 edition of the *Courier* states that no definitive word from ODT had yet to be received although it was assumed that approval of the 2,000 mile allowance was imminent. This author has found no evidence that the NNL did not end up receiving the allowance.

277 *Chicago Defender*, March 11, 1944; Alpert, *Out Of Left Field*, 86.

278 *Baltimore Afro-American*, March 18, 1944.

279 *Pittsburgh Courier*, March 11, 1944.

280 Lanctot, *Negro League Baseball*, 141.

281 Letter, Effa Manley to Wendell Smith, February 7, 1944, Manley Papers.

282 Lanctot, *Negro League Baseball*, 141-42.

283 *Atlanta Daily World*, March 14, 1944.

284 *Cleveland Call and Post*, March 25, 1944. The "all in caps" is reproduced here as it appears in the column by Bob Williams.

285 Ibid.

286 Ibid.

287 *Pittsburgh Courier*, March 11, 1944. The *Courier* column mentioned "a rumor circling the lobby" that owner Semler of the Black Yankees would trade Hopgood and Stone to the Philadelphia Stars for pitcher Terris McDuffie. Hopgood and Stone did end up on the Stars, but McDuffie would pitch for Newark in 1944.

288 *New York Amsterdam News*, May 20, 1944.

289 Lanctot, *Negro League Baseball*, 147; *Philadelphia Tribune*, January 6, 1945 as quoted in Lanctot, 147.

290 *Baltimore Afro-American*, June 24, 1944; *Pittsburgh Courier*, June 17, 1944. The *Afro-American* reported that the meeting's big news was that the press was admitted to the sessions, with the "bigwigs of the NNL finally agreeing to call off their series of 'executive sessions…'" Unfortunately, deciding to finally provide full access to the press in 1944 turned out to be too late given the soon-to-be integration of major league baseball and attendant dramatic shift in the coverage of the black press away from the Negro Leagues.

291 *Baltimore Afro-American*, June 24, 1944; *Philadelphia Tribune*, July 1, 1944.

292 Lanctot, *Negro League Baseball*, 147.

293 Ibid, 145; *Baltimore Afro-American*, July 1, 1944.

294 *Norfolk Journal and Guide*, July 29, 1944.

295 Letter, Wendell Smith to Effa Manley, May 19, 1944, Manley Papers.

296 *Chicago Defender*, June 24, 1944.

297 Heaphy, *The Negro Leagues*, Appendix D, 241; Lanctot, *Negro League Baseball*, 143.

298 *Philadelphia Tribune*, September 16, 1944 as quoted in Lanctot, *Negro League Baseball*, 143.

299 Letter reading as a press release, December 6, 1944, probably written by Cum Posey for league presidents Tom Wilson and J.B. Martin, Manley Papers; *New York Amsterdam News*, December 16, 1944.

300 Letter reading as a press release, December 6, 1944, Manley Papers.

301 *New York Amsterdam News*, December 16, 1944. The article criticized Landis for failing to encourage steps towards integration but noted that he did not interfere in rental arrangements between major-league clubs and Negro League owners.

302 *Pittsburgh Courier*, December 23, 1944. According to the *Amsterdam News*, after the media was barred from Friday's league meetings, some "went home in a huff. Others got some minor details from the joint session…"*New York Amsterdam News*, December 23, 1944.

303 Ibid.; *Chicago Defender*, December 23, 1944.

304 *Pittsburgh Courier*, December 23, 1944.

305 *Chicago Defender*, December 23, 1944.

306 *New York Amsterdam News*, December 23, 1944.

307 *Pittsburgh Courier*, December 23, 1944.

308 Ibid.

309 *Pittsburgh Courier*, December 23, 1944.

310 *Chicago Defender*, January 6, 1945.

311 See, e.g., Lanctot, *Negro League Baseball*, 263-271; Heaphy, *The Negro Leagues*, 198-200. There were several apparent shifts in ownership and location of United States League (USL) franchises in 1945, along with the sudden involvement of Branch Rickey in May of 1945. This article will only cover the USL as it pertains to the ongoing issues of the NNL and NAL.

312 *Pittsburgh Courier*, January 6, 1945.

313 Ibid.

314 *New York Amsterdam News*, March 3, 1945. The article mentioned that Saperstein was involved in the operations of the Indianapolis-Cincinnati Clowns and the Birmingham Black Barons of the NAL, along with his financial interest in the

315 Ibid.

316 *Pittsburgh Courier*, March 17, 1945. NNL and NAL owners had attended each other's meetings in the past, but the cooperative involvement in each other's affairs represented by a) supporting each other in the rejection of a new Indianapolis franchise and b) essentially keeping Saperstein "off limits" to USL operations seems to this author a departure from largely acrimonious dealings between the two leagues in the past.

317 Ibid.

318 Ibid; Arnold Rampersad, *Jackie Robinson* (New York: Alfred A. Knopf, 1997), 74.

319 *Pittsburgh Courier*, March 17, 1945.

320 Lanctot, *Negro League Baseball*, 252.

321 Letter, J.B. Martin to V.T. Corbett, April 5, 1945, Records of the Office of Defense Transportation, National Archives at College Park, College Park, Maryland as quoted in Lanctot, *Negro League Baseball*, 253. It is interesting to note that the final line of "Posey's Points" in the June 23, 1945 *Pittsburgh Courier* stated that East-West Game attendance in 1945 would be "limited almost entirely to Chicago fans," thereby bolstering J.B. Martin's claim. *Pittsburgh Courier*, June 23, 1945.

322 Letter, William Nunn to Abe Manley, March 22, 1945, Manley Papers.

323 Letter, Abe Manley to William Nunn, April 7, 1945, Manley Papers.

324 Letter, William Nunn to Tom Baird, May 9, 1945, Manley Papers.

325 *Norfolk Journal and Guide*, May 5, 1945.

326 Lanctot, *Negro League Baseball*, 259-262; *Baltimore Afro-American*, July 14, 1945.

327 *Baltimore Afro-American*, May 19, 1945 as quoted in Lanctot, *Negro League Baseball*, 266.

328 Lanctot, *Negro League Baseball*, 272.

329 Minutes of Joint Session, June 12, 1945, Manley Papers.

330 Ibid.

331 Lanctot, *Negro League Baseball*, 273.

332 Minutes of Joint Session, June 12, 1945, Manley Papers.

333 *Philadelphia Tribune*, June 23, 1945.

334 Minutes of Joint Session, June 12, 1945, Manley Papers.

335 *Baltimore Afro-American*, July 14, 1945.

336 *Baltimore Afro-American*, July 14, 1945. Lacy's column appeared on July 14, the same date the *Afro-American* published a separate piece reporting the fine on the Black Yankees and a week after the *Norfolk Journal and Guide* published their article reporting the fine. One can only speculate that Lacy's piece was written before the announced punishment or that he did not believe it would be enforced. *Norfolk Journal and Guide*, July 7, 1945.

337 Lanctot, *Negro League Baseball*, 274.

338 Heaphy, *The Negro Leagues*, Appendix D, 241. After V-J day, the *Pittsburgh Courier* stopped putting a "vv" between printed articles as a symbol of 1942's Double Victory campaign, presumably because victory in the war had been achieved. There is no evidence that the *Courier* knew that victory in the campaign for baseball integration had also been achieved, as Jackie Robinson's August 28, 1945 agreement with the Dodgers was a secret, not being announced until October 23. Duke Goldman, *The Double Victory Campaign*, 407.

339 *Pittsburgh Courier*, December 23, 1944.

340 Rampersad, *Jackie Robinson*, 129.

341 *New York Times*, October 27, 1945.

342 *Chicago Defender*, November 3, 1945.

343 *Kansas City Call*, October 26, 1945 as quoted in Lanctot, *Negro League Baseball*, 280 ("we have been out"); *Pittsburgh Courier*, November 3, 1945 as quoted in Lanctot, *Negro League Baseball*, 280 ("something should be done").

344 *Baltimore Afro-American*, November 3, 1945.

345 Ibid.

346 Letter, Effa Manley to J.B. Martin, October 26, 1945, Manley Papers. Johnson would be elected NNL president in 1947.

347 Letter, J.B. Martin to Effa Manley, October 29, 1945, Manley Papers.

348 Statement of J.B. Martin from the Office of the Negro American League, November 1945 (undated specifically but referred to in early November newspaper articles), Manley Papers.

349 *Cleveland Call and Post*, November 3, 1945.

350 *Cleveland Call and Post*, November 3, 1945.

351 Letter, Cum Posey to Albert B. Chandler, November 1, 1945, Manley Papers.

352 Ibid.

353 Letter, Clark Griffith to Cum Posey, November 5, 1945, Manley Papers.

354 Robert McGregor, *A Calculus of Color: The Integration of Baseball's American League* (Jefferson, North Carolina: McFarland, 2015), 149.

355 *New York Amsterdam News*, November 17, 1945.

356 Ibid.

357 Ibid.

358 Ibid.; *Chicago Defender*, November 17, 1945.

359 *Pittsburgh Courier*, December 22, 1945.

360 Ibid.; *Chicago Defender*, December 22, 1945.

361 *Atlanta Daily World*, December 22, 1945.

362 Undated resolution, likely in late 1945 or early 1946, Manley Papers.

363 *New York Times*, January 21, 1946.

364 *Hartford Courant*, January 22, 1946.

365 Lanctot, *Negro League Baseball*, 285.

366 *Pittsburgh Courier*, February 16, 1946.

367 Lanctot, *Negro League Baseball*, 284-85.

368 *Pittsburgh Courier*, January 5, 1946.

369 Minutes of regular meeting, Negro National League, February 20, 1946, Manley Papers.

370 Ibid.

371 Ibid. Wilson also claimed that Chandler "said nothing against owners being officers of the league." While Chandler may not have specifically raised such an objection when meeting Wilson, his objection to club owners holding the office of President had been reported in the media, as previously noted. *Pittsburgh Courier*, February 16, 1946

372 Minutes of regular meeting, Negro National League, second day, February 21, 1946, Manley Papers.

373 *Pittsburgh Courier*, February 16, 1946.

374 Ibid. Crossed out was a statement that "legally they were not obligated to him or anyone else."

375 *Philadelphia Tribune*, March 9, 1946.

376 Minutes of special meeting, Negro National League, March 12, 1946, Manley Papers.

377 Heaphy, *The Negro Leagues*, 200.

378 *Pittsburgh Courier*, March 23, 1946.

379 *Pittsburgh Courier*, December 22, 1945.

380 Minutes of special meeting, Negro National League, March 12, 1946, Manley Papers.

381 *Pittsburgh Courier*, March 23, 1946.

382 *Philadelphia Tribune*, May 11, 1946.

383 *Chicago Defender*, June 29, 1946.

384 Minutes of Joint meeting, Negro American League and Negro National League, June 19, 1946, Manley Papers.

385 *Norfolk Journal and Guide*, July 27, 1946.

386 *Newark Star-Ledger*, May 19, 1996

387 Effa Manley and Leon Hardwick, *Negro Baseball Before Integration* (Chicago: Adams Press, 1976), 96.

388 Doron "Duke" Goldman, "Monte's Missions: Mastering Mexico, Military Service, Defeating Monarchs and Minor League Magic," *Black Ball* Vol 9 (2017), 54-55.

389 Brian Carroll, "The Black Press and the Integration of Baseball: A content analysis of changes in coverage," *Cooperstown Symposium on Baseball and American Culture* (Jefferson, North Carolina: McFarland, 2003), 216-231 as quoted in Carroll, *When to Stop the Cheering*, 150,152.

390 Report of Meeting With Louis Carroll, Lawyer For The National League, September 26, 1946, Manley Papers.

391 *Pittsburgh Courier*, May 3, 1947.

392 Lanctot, *The Negro Leagues*, 306.

393 Ibid.

394 *Chicago Defender*, January 4, 1947; *Chicago Defender*, December 21, 1946.

395 *Chicago Defender*, January 11, 1947. The *Defender* claimed that in 1946 Wilson had tried to "relinquish the office but the owners insisted that he serve another year."

396 Lanctot, *Negro League Baseball*, 307-309. Lanctot's sources indicate that despite Wilson's ill health, he was still supported by Baltimore and Philadelphia for another term. Manley championed Johnson and was supported by the Grays and Cubans owner Alex Pompez. A deadlock was averted when Black Yankees owner Semler voted for Johnson despite having supported Wilson in previous years. Lanctot speculates that Semler's support was won over by an offer to be the exclusive promoter at Yankee stadium as Cum Posey had once suggested that "Semler will do anything if money is shoved him." Letter, Cum Posey to Abe Manley, October 25, 1942, Manley Papers, as quoted in Lanctot, *Negro League Baseball*, 301 n.13. See also James A. Riley, *The Biographical Encyclopedia of the Negro Leagues* (New York: Carroll & Graf, paperback edition, 2002), 287,400 (biographical information on Forbes and Hueston).

397 *Pittsburgh Courier*, January 11, 1947.

398 *New York Amsterdam News*, January 11, 1947.

399 Ibid.; *People's Voice*, February 1, 1947 as quoted in Lanctot, *Negro League Baseball*, 309.

400 *New York Amsterdam News*, January 11, 1947.

401 *Pittsburgh Courier*, December 22, 1945.

402 *Atlanta Daily World*, March 5, 1947.

403 *Chicago Defender*, February 22, 1947.

404 *Atlanta Daily World*, March 5, 1947.

405 *New York Times*, March 1, 1947.

406 *Atlanta Daily World*, March 5, 1947.

407 *Cleveland Call and Post*, March 1, 1947.

408 *Atlanta Daily World*, March 1, 1947.

409 *New York Times*, March 1, 1947.

410 *Atlanta Daily World, March 1, 1947*. The *Daily World* also reported that Ed Gottlieb would no longer have to be involved in booking Yankee Stadium games. This decision gives credence to the conjecture by Lanctot mentioned in footnote 396 above that

Semler may have been "bought off" by opportunities to promote his own games at Yankee Stadium.

411 See Adrian Burgos, *Cuban Star*, 179, citing *Baltimore Afro-American*, April 20, 1946.

412 *Pittsburgh Courier*, June 14, 1947.

413 Carroll, *When to Stop the Cheering?*, 156-57. Carroll gives the example of the *Chicago Defender* giving extensive coverage to Jackie Robinson's game-winning home run in the 1947 major-league World Series and minor coverage of the New York Cubans winning the 1947 Negro World Series.

414 Lanctot, *Negro League Baseball*, 312-13.

415 *Baltimore Afro-American*, June 21, 1947. For a discussion of the Duany case, see Burgos, *Cuban Star*, 171-72.

416 *Norfolk Journal and Guide*, June 21, 1947. Note that other sources say that the league was willing to consider playing yearly benefit games to raise money for a pension fund. See *Baltimore Afro-American*, June 21, 1947; Heaphy, *The Negro Leagues*, 215 citing Joint Meeting minutes, June 10, 1947, Tom Baird Papers, University of Kansas Libraries, Lawrence Kansas (rescinding visiting passes).

417 Burgos, *Cuban Star*, 175-76; *Cleveland Call and Post*, October 11, 1947.

418 Lanctot, *Negro League Baseball*, 317.

419 Carroll, *When to Stop the Cheering?*, 156; *Cleveland Call and Post*, October 11, 1946. Columnist and noted early black baseball historian A.S. "Doc" Young, who reported the $20,000 loss figure in the *Call and Post*, stated that he considered Pompez's claim to be exaggerated, but author Roberto Echevarria also reported that Pompez claimed to have lost money in 1947. Roberto Echevarria, *The Pride of Havana: A History of Cuban Baseball* (New York: Oxford Press, 1999), 207.

420 Joseph A. Pierce, *Negro Business and Business Education* (Boston: Springer Science + Business Media, 1995 reprint), 219.

421 Lanctot, *Negro League Baseball*, 318.

422 *The Sporting News*, March 17, 1948 as quoted in Lanctot, *Negro League Baseball*, 336.

423 *Hartford Courant*, December 3, 1947.

424 Ibid.; *New York Times*, December 6, 1947.

425 *Washington Post*, February 6, 1948.

426 Ibid.

427 *Chicago Defender*, January 3, 1948.

428 *Philadelphia Tribune*, January 3, 1948.

429 Ibid.

430 *Atlanta Daily World*, January 13, 1948.

431 *Pittsburgh Courier*, January 24, 1948 as quoted in Lanctot, *Negro League Baseball*, 325.

432 *Atlanta Daily World*, January 24, 1948.

433 *New York Amsterdam News*, January 3, 1948.

434 *Atlanta Daily World*, January 24, 1948.

435 See, e.g., 1941 contract of Monte Irvin, Manley Papers. The Eagles ultimately received $5,000 for Monte Irvin's contract in 1948 after successfully fighting off the Dodgers' overtures. The level of compensation for Irvin may have been a more realistic standard for future signings than that for Doby.

436 *New York Amsterdam News*, January 24, 1948. Richmond and Asheville joined another new Negro League, the Negro American Association.

437 Dan Burley, "Confidentially Yours," *New York Amsterdam News*, January 24, 1948, 13; *New York Amsterdam News*, January 24, 1948, 12.

438 *New York Amsterdam News*, September 22, 1945 (MacPhail statement); *Boston Globe*, February 24, 1948 (Johnson statement).

439 *Boston Globe*, February 24, 1948.

440 It deserves mention that at about the same time Johnson announced his bitter disappointment at being betrayed by organized baseball, Commissioner Chandler was reportedly having an official meeting with representatives of the Mexican league. It was to be the first official meeting between the organizations since the Mexican leagues raided the major leagues in 1946 and signed several of their players, and Chandler suspended those players for five years in response. The meeting was to include a discussion of a future affiliation of the Mexican league with organized baseball. *New York Times*, February 21, 22, 1948.

441 *Chicago Defender*, February 21, 1948.

442 *Baltimore Afro-American*, March 6, 1948; *New York Amsterdam News*, March 6, 1948; *Atlanta Daily World*, March 11, 1948.

443 Lanctot, *Negro League Baseball*, 328; *Atlanta Daily World*, June 29, 1948.

444 *Atlanta Daily World*, June 29, 1948.

445 Ibid. Although the Pacific Coast League never succeeded in their attempt to become the third major league, they successfully petitioned to become an "open" classification, which exempted their players from the annual draft of minor-league players under certain conditions, and gave the Pacific Coast League a status between Triple A and major league. *New York Times*, January 1, 1952. Such a status may well have been appropriate for the Negro Leagues given the level of talent they featured during the two-year period between Jackie Robinson's signing and the rejection of their application to affiliate with organized baseball. As previously mentioned, at the Feb. 20 and 21, 1946 NNL meetings, NNL President Wilson had assessed black major-league baseball as being below major league but above the Triple-A International League in caliber.

446 Richard Puerzer, "The 1948 Negro League World Series," *Bittersweet Goodbye: The Black Barons, The Grays, And The 1948 Negro League World Series* (Phoenix, Arizona: Society for American Baseball Research 2017), Frederick Bush and Bill Nowlin, eds., 386, 388.

447 *Philadelphia Tribune*, February 14, 1948 as quoted in Lanctot, *Negro League Baseball*, 332 (outlined); Jackie Robinson, "What's Wrong with Negro Baseball?" *Ebony*, June 1948 as quoted in Lanctot, *Negro League Baseball*, 332; Effa Manley, "Negro Baseball Isn't Dead," *Our World*, August 1948, as quoted in Lanctot, *Negro League Baseball*, 334.

448 Thomas Kern, "The 1948 East-West All-Star Games." *Bittersweet Goodbye*, Frederick Bush and Bill Nowlin, eds., 369, 371; *New York Amsterdam News*, August 21, 1948.

449 *Baltimore Afro-American*, December 11, 1948.

450 *Baltimore Afro-American*, September 4, 11, 1948, as quoted in Lanctot, *Negro League Baseball*, 337.

451 Lanctot, *Negro League Baseball*.

452 *Pittsburgh Courier*, December 11, 1948. Whether or not Effa Manley meant that her team lost $100,000 from 1946 through 1948, it is worth noting that 1946 was the year that her Newark Eagles won their only Negro League World Series.

453 *Atlanta Daily World*, November 24, 1948.

454 *Chicago Defender*, December 11, 1948.

455 *Cleveland Call and Post*, December 4, 1948.

456 *Chicago Defender*, December 11, 1948; *Baltimore Afro-American*, December 11, 1948.

457 *Pittsburgh Courier*, December 11, 1948.

458 John Holway, *Blackball Stars* (Westport, Connecticut: Meckler Books 1988), 21.

459 *Pittsburgh Courier*, December 11, 1948.

460 Ibid.

461 It is possible that Effa Manley was including other leagues like the Negro American Association and the Negro Southern League (NSL) when she came up with the figure of 400 remaining black ballplayers. As of 1950, those two leagues still existed, and they apparently reformulated into one Negro Southern Association in 1951. See *Atlanta Daily World*, June 15, 1950 and *Atlanta Daily World*, March 27, 1951.

462 *Pittsburgh Courier*, August 25, 1962.

463 Minutes, Schedule Meeting of the Negro American League, February 7 and 8, 1949. Minutes provided by SABR's Negro Leagues Committee Chair Larry Lester, August 2017.

464 Ibid.

465 Ibid. The offered justification for approving the move of the Buckeyes to Louisville was that "the appearance of Larry Doby and Satchel Paige with the major league Cleveland Indians had attracted most of the Buckeye fans." *Atlanta Daily World*, February 15, 1949. The team was sold by Wright to former Cleveland Buckeyes business manager Wilbur Hayes, who brought the team back to Cleveland for the 1950 NAL season. See *Pittsburgh Courier*, February 18, 1950.

466 *Atlanta Daily World*, February 15, 1949.

467 Minutes, Schedule Meeting of the Negro American League, February 7 and 8, 1949.

468 Schedule Meeting of the Negro American League, June 22 and 23, 1949. Minutes provided by Larry Lester, August 2017.

469 Ibid.

470 Heaphy, *The Negro Leagues*, Appendix D, 241.

471 Dick Clark and Larry Lester, editors, *The Negro Leagues Book* (Cleveland, Ohio: Society for American Baseball Research, 1994), 163.

472 Ibid.

473 Ibid.; *Norfolk Journal and Guide*, January 20, 1951.

474 Ibid. This researcher found conflicting information on the number of teams who played in the 1954 NAL. In *The Negro Leagues Book*, only four teams — the Indianapolis Stars, Memphis Red Sox, Birmingham Black Barons, and Detroit Stars — appear in the standings. But the March 27, 1954 *Baltimore Afro-American* stated that six teams, including the perennial NAL entry the Kansas City Monarchs, who were not in the 1954 standings in the *Negro Leagues Book*, and two new teams, in Louisville and Detroit, would play the 1954 season. The February 5, 1955 *Chicago Defender* stated that two teams — the Indianapolis Clowns and Louisville — were dropped from the league to again make it a four-team circuit. *Baltimore Afro-American*, March 27, 1954; *Chicago Defender*, February 5, 1955. Additional research or perhaps other existing resources may resolve this difference.

475 *Atlanta Daily World*, January 4, 1950.

476 *Atlanta Daily World*, January 5, 1950.

477 Wendell Smith, *Pittsburgh Courier*, January 18, 1950; *Pittsburgh Courier*, January 18, 1950 (roughest days).

478 *Chicago Defender*, June 17, 1950; *Norfolk Journal and Guide*, June 24, 1950.

479 *Baltimore Afro-American*, January 13, 1951.

480 *Pittsburgh Courier*, June 23, 1951. Apparently, the sale did not go through, and Baltimore operated as a traveling team through much of 1951, and was dropped from the league at the January 1952 meeting. *Chicago Defender*, January 5, 1952.

481 *Norfolk Journal and Guide*, May 17, 1951.

482 *Chicago Defender*, January 5, 1952.

483 *Atlanta Daily World*, January 10, 1952.

484 *Chicago Defender*, January 5, 1952; *Pittsburgh Courier*, February 23, 1952.

485 *Pittsburgh Courier*, February 7, 1953.

486 *Pittsburgh Courier*, February 13, 1954; *Baltimore Afro-American*, March 27, 1954.

487 *Chicago Defender*, February 6, 1954.

488 *Chicago Defender*, February 5, 1955.

489 Ibid. One can speculate that moving the game to Kansas City may have been related to keeping Tom Baird happy and his Kansas City Monarchs in the rapidly shrinking NAL, after his dalliance with independent play in 1954.

490 *Pittsburgh Courier*, June 11, 1955.

491 Letter, Tom Baird to Oscar Rico, May 21, 1955, Tom Baird Collection, box 3, correspondence about Cuban Giants, 1954 as quoted in Lanctot, *Negro League Baseball*, 385.

492 Lanctot, *Negro League Baseball*, 385-386.

493 *Pittsburgh Courier*, February 18, 1956.

494 *Chicago Defender*, March 3, 1956.

495 The *Pittsburgh Courier* reported that new owner Ross changed the name because previous owner Floyd Meshack had the "Black Barons" name copyrighted, but also noted that the "old name of the club had long been offensive to a large segment of the baseball fans." *Pittsburgh Courier*, March 24, 1956.

496 *Chicago Defender*, February 23, 1957.

497 *Norfolk Journal and Guide*, May 4, 1957.

498 *Chicago Defender*, March 29, 1958.

499 *Chicago Defender*, April 12, 1958.

500 *New York Times*, May 7, 1958. This author does not know anything about the Detroit Clowns.

501 *Pittsburgh Courier*, June 7, 1958 (Clowns vs. Red Sox); *New York Times*, June 30, 1958 (Monarchs vs. Red Sox).

502 *Atlanta Daily World*, January 6, 1959.

503 *Atlanta Daily World*, December 11, 1959.

504 www.cnlbr.org/Portals/0/RL/Demise%20of%20the%20 Negro%20Leagues.pdf , accessed 3/15/17. Some of the facts from the 1960-1962 period are drawn from this website. Here, the Birmingham team is called the "Black Barons" and is now owned by Arthur Dove. Perhaps Dove changed the name back to its original when he acquired the club. This source and others continues to include the Kansas City Monarchs as a league team although Neil Lanctot has indicated that the team rarely played in Kansas City.

505 Ibid.

506 *Atlanta Daily World*, May 27, 1960.

507 Ibid.

508 Ibid.

509 *Chicago Defender*, August 23, 1960.

510 Ibid.

511 *Cleveland Call and Post*, March 11, 1961.

512 *Atlanta Daily World*, April 18, 1961.

513 *Norfolk Journal and Guide*, August 12, 1961.

514 Ibid.

515 *Philadelphia Tribune*, August 22, 1961.

516 *Chicago Defender*, August 20, 1961.

517 www.cnlbr.org/Portals/0/RL/Demise%20of%20the%20 Negro%20Leagues.pdf

518 Ibid. The report was a self-report.

519 Ibid.

520 *Chicago Defender*, August 28, 1962.

521 www.cnlbr.org/Portals/0/RL/Demise%20of%20the%20 Negro%20Leagues.pdf

522 *Tri-State Defender*, January 27, 1961.

523 *Chicago Defender*, January 4, 1947; Riley, *Biographical Encyclopedia*, 339 (Greenlee Field).

524 *Tri-State Defender*, January 27, 1961.

525 Ibid.

CONTRIBUTORS

MARSHALL ADESMAN has been a member of SABR for some 40 years. A former minor league General Manager and Business Manager, he also spent twenty years working at Duke University, and is the co-author (with Chris Holaday) of *The 25 Greatest Baseball Teams of the 20th Century (Ranked)*, published by McFarland and Company in 2009. Now retired, he is devoting much of his time to writing about baseball, which includes serving as an Associate Editor for this book, and to catching up on all the reading he couldn't do while he was a working stiff.

MARK ARMOUR is the founder and Director of the Baseball Biography Project, and the author of several books on baseball. He writes from his home in Oregon.

JEFF BARTO left his native Pittsburgh in 1992 to teach at UNC Charlotte. He also joined SABR that same year. In 2005 he created a History of Baseball class for his Kinesiology department at UNCC. This course sparked his interest in baseball research. First, he indexed all 18.5 hours of Ken Burns' *Baseball* documentary. This project cataloged every spoken word, as well as descriptions of all photos and videos. It then time-stamped every item so that each could be located within any of the nine-inning discs. Jeff continues to use the index to access clips relevant to his course discussions. More recently he wrote his first piece for SABR's BioProject, covering Doug DeCinces. An avid Pittsburgh Pirates fan, he plans to expand his writing towards several Pittsburgh projects. He is currently writing Richie Hebner's BioProject. He will also contribute a chapter to an upcoming SABR Games Project book about the greatest games in Pirates history. He is assigned the last two games at Forbes Field, a doubleheader, which he attended and is the highlight of his adolescent years.

JOHN BAUER resides with his wife and two children in Parkville, Missouri, just outside of Kansas City. By day, he is an attorney specializing in insurance regulatory law and corporate law. By night, he spends many spring and summer evenings cheering for the San Francisco Giants and many fall and winter evenings reading history. He is a past and ongoing contributor to other SABR projects.

ANDY BOKSER has been a member of SABR since 1983. When he is not spending time with his wife and three children or watching baseball games, he runs his solo law practice in Brooklyn, New York.

PAUL BROWN holds a DPA from the University of Southern California. He retired from the federal government after a 30-year career with the Department of Army. He is currently a part-time consultant providing executive level education to the Army National Guard.

DR. JOHN J. BURBRIDGE, JR. is currently Professor Emeritus at Elon University where he was both a dean and professor. While at Elon he introduced and taught Baseball and Statistics. A native of Jersey City, he authored "The Brooklyn Dodgers in Jersey City" which appeared in *The Baseball Research Journal*. John has also presented at SABR conventions and the Seymour meetings. He is a lifelong New York Giants baseball fan (he does acknowledge they moved to San Francisco). The greatest Giants-Dodgers game he attended was a 1-0 Giants victory in Jersey City in 1956. Yes, the Dodgers did play in Jersey City in 1956 and 1957 as did the Havana Sugar Kings in 1960 and 1961.

STEVE CARDULLO is retired and lives in Northern California with his wife Robin. He was a contributor to the SABR publication, *Scandal on the South Side; The 1919 Chicago White Sox*. He is a proud lifelong Yankee fan.

TOM CUGGINO is a native of Bronxville, New York but currently lives in Wheaton, Illinois where he works as a financial controller for Cisco Systems and enjoys an active family life with his wife and three daughters. He is interested in all things Yankees and

Cubs, rivalries, ballparks and their influence on cities, rituals and traditions, the Pacific Coast League, and Latin America's influence on baseball.

ROSS E. DAVIES is a professor of law at George Mason University and editor of *The Green Bag* (www.greenbag.org).

HAWKINS DUBOIS is a young writer from Los Angeles, and a die-hard Dodgers fan. He played his first baseball game in jeans, dressed up as Vin Scully when asked to do a biography book report as an elementary school student, and eventually became a submarine pitcher. His playing career has since come to an end, and he now spends his time coaching, watching, learning, and writing about the game.

DONALD G. FRANK is Professor Emeritus at Portland State University. A member of the Society of American Baseball Research (SABR), his research includes baseball as social history, with a focus on leadership in baseball. He has taught at Texas Tech University, the University of Arizona, Harvard University, the Georgia Institute of Technology, and Portland State University. He has been the recipient of one regional scholarly award as well as the Reference Service Press Award, a national scholarly award.

JESSICA FRANK works alongside her father in his New York City studio, *Whirlwind Pictures*, assisting in the production of a wide range of photography, film, and mixed-media projects.

DUKE GOLDMAN is a longtime SABR member who specializes in researching the Negro Leagues, the career of Monte Irvin, and the process of baseball integration. A resident of Northampton, Mass. but born in the Bronx, he nevertheless roots avidly for the Yankees to lose every day, as well as for the Mets and the Red Sox. He is a 2016 recipient of the SABR-McFarland award for his article entitled "the Double Victory Campaign and the Campaign to Integrate Baseball" which was included in the 2015 SABR publication *Who's on First? Replacement Players in World War II*. In 2017 Duke received the Robert Peterson Recognition Award for bodies of work that increase public awareness about the Negro Leagues. The award acknowledges his *Black Ball* articles and other SABR publications.

CHIP GREENE joined SABR in 2006, 81 years after his grandfather, Nelson Greene, surrendered 18 hits and 14 runs in 6 2/3 innings pitched against the Pirates at Forbes Field. As Chip always reasons, though, yes, Nelson got bombed that day, but, hey, he made it to the major leagues, didn't he? In 2015, Chip edited the SABR book, *Mustaches and Mayhem: Charlie O's Three-Time Champions: The Oakland Athletics 1972-1974*. Chip lives with his wife, Elaine, and daughters, Anna and Haley, in Waynesboro, Pennsylvania.

CHAD HAGAN is a data-driven investment analyst and author. He is the CEO of Hagan Capital Group and a partner with venture capital firm Arcadia Blackwood. His statistical research can be found at www.zermattresearch.com and his blog is www.chaganomics.com; both have baseball statistics charts and postings. He is a lifelong Atlanta Braves and Boston Red Sox fan.

KENT HENDERSON works for the Dallas/Fort Worth International Airport in Corporate Aviation. He has been at DFW since 1984 in varying capacities all having to do with management of either a building or service at DFW. He is currently editor for SABR's Collegiate Baseball Committee Newsletter.

ALAN P. HENRY is a *New York Times* bestselling author, national fiction contest winner, and 40-year newspaper veteran in Chicago and Boston whose formative baseball years were spent at Griffith Stadium in Washington D.C. watching the Nats battle the Athletics for last place in the American League.

PAUL HENSLER received his Master's degree in History from Trinity College in Hartford, Connecticut, and is a member of the Society for American Baseball Research, as well as the Phi Alpha Theta National History Honor Society. The author of *The American League in Transition, 1965-1975: How Competition Thrived When the Yankees Didn't* (McFarland, 2013) as well as several essays on baseball published by SABR and *NINE: A Journal of Baseball History and Culture,* he has also lectured on baseball in the 1960s and made presentations at the Cooperstown Symposium on Baseball and American Culture. For more information, please visit www.paulhensler.com.

SABR member **MICHAEL HUBER** is Dean of Academic Life and Professor of Mathematics at Muhlenberg College in Allentown, Pennsylvania, where he teaches an undergraduate course titled "Reasoning With Sabermetrics." He has published his sabermetrics research in several books and journals, including *The Baseball Research Journal, Chance, Base Ball, Annals of Applied Statistics,* and *The Journal of Statistics Education,* and he frequently contributes to SABR's Baseball Games Project. He has been rooting for the Baltimore Orioles for more than 45 years.

CHRIS JONES is an attorney at Anthony & Middlebrook, P.C., where his practice focuses on church and nonprofit law. He is a lifelong baseball fan and a member of SABR since 2015. The highlight of his playing days was being drafted by the Toronto Blue Jays in the 2001 amateur draft. He resides in the Dallas/Fort Worth area with his wife and four children.

DAVID M. KRITZLER was born and bred in Chicago and is one of the rare fans of both the Cubs and the White Sox. He spent 40 years in the leather tanning industry and 14 years as a coach, manager, director, and league president of the Wilmette Baseball Association. He has served the SABR BioProject for three years.

LEN LEVIN, a SABR member since 1977, has been the copyeditor for many SABR publications. A resident of Providence, Rhode Island, he is a retired newspaper editor and adjunct journalism instructor. When he isn't busy editing for SABR, he works part-time editing the opinions of the Rhode Island Supreme Court.

DAN LEVITT is the author of numerous baseball books and essays. He is a long time SABR member, and in 2015 Dan won the Bob Davids Award. His books have won the Larry Ritter Book Award, the *Sporting News*-SABR Baseball Research Award, and twice been finalists for the Seymour Medal.

JASON C. LONG is a tax and real estate attorney with Steinhardt Pesick & Cohen, P.C., in Birmingham, Michigan. A former judicial clerk at the Michigan Supreme Court, he is an honors graduate of Oakland University and the University of Detroit Mercy School of Law, and attended the University of Michigan Ross School of Business. Mr. Long has published articles and chapters concerning tax and real estate legal topics, but this is his first foray into writing about baseball. A lifelong Detroit Tigers fan, Mr. Long finds the business of baseball almost as fascinating as the play on the field.

MIKE LYNCH was born in Boston in the year of Yastrzemski and has been a diehard Red Sox fan ever since. A member of SABR since 2004, he lives in West Roxbury, Massachusetts. His first book, *Harry Frazee, Ban Johnson and the Feud That Nearly Destroyed the American League,* was published in 2008 and was named a finalist for the 2009 Larry Ritter Award in addition to being nominated for the Seymour Medal. He's also written, *It Ain't So: A Might-Have-Been History of the White Sox in 1919 and Beyond* and *Baseball's Untold History: Volume I — The People,* and his work has been featured in SABR books about the 1912 Boston Red Sox and 1914 Boston Braves.

CHARLES H. MARTIN is a contracts and business lawyer, a former law school professor, and the author of *Lawyerball, The Courtroom Battle of the Orioles Against the Nationals and MLB for the Future of Baseball.* His reporting on this endless cable television litigation by Peter Angelos, the owner of the Baltimore Orioles, severely reduces the time he has available for his other writing projects. Mr. Martin joined SABR in 2016. He was a committed expansion Washington Senators fan until 1971, when they were moved to Texas. His grandfather worked from the 1920s until 1960 as a vendor at Griffith Stadium, the home of the American League Washington Senators, and the part-time home of the Negro National League Homestead Grays. He believes in third-time charms and in the eventual championship of the Washington Nationals, but he is not making any deals on this with anyone named Mr. Applegate.

CHRIS MATTHEWS is a writer for *Fortune Magazine*, where he covers real estate, macroeconomics, and public policy.

WAYNE G. MCDONNELL, JR., B.B.A., M.B.A. is the Academic Chair and Clinical Associate Professor of Sports Management, NYU School of Professional Studies (NYU-SPS) Tisch Institute for Sports Management, Media, and Business. Professor McDonnell is also a Co-Director, Program Development and Special Initiatives for New York University's Sports and Society Program. He is a highly sought-after commentator and analyst on the game of baseball. McDonnell regularly appears on various television and radio programs; coaches athletes as a private hitting and pitching instructor; and shares timely insights via the Twitter handle @wmcdonn25.

ABIGAIL MISKOWIEC holds a BFA in Acting and a BA in Journalism from New York University, as well as an MA in Theatre Education from Emerson College. She currently teaches English in her hometown of Charleston, West Virginia.

DARREN MUNK is the Director of Web Application Development for the Common Grant Application. He resides in Concord, California with his wife Cailin Daley. He has a BA in Economics and Political Science from the University of California, San Diego, and an MBA from San Diego State University. Darren is an avid San Francisco Giants fan and an Oakland Athletics well-wisher. He has been a SABR member since 2000, and has served as the organization's webmaster (2001-2004) and as a member of the steering committee for the San Diego (Ted Williams) chapter. This is Darren's first appearance as an author in a SABR publication.

JASON MYERS has not yet figured out how to retire based on his love of baseball, so he makes his living an in-house finance attorney. His baseball-related works include "Shaking Up the Line-Up: Generating Principles for an Electrifying Economic Structure for Major League Baseball" in *Marquette Sports Law Review* and "The Day Mick Kelleher Hit Two Home Runs" in *Growing Up with Baseball: How We Loved and Played the Game* (University of Nebraska Press). He lives in Arlington, Texas with his wife and son, and will occasionally reminisce about his days as a batboy for the 1975 Asheville Orioles (AA—Southern League).

BILL NOWLIN found out he had an aptitude for business when he and two friends founded the Rounder Records music label. Though totally unaware of the meaning of the word "invoice" at the time (despite being a college professor), he and his partners somehow built a very successful company that has lasted over four decades. In the middle 1990s, he began to devote time again to his childhood passion of baseball, and with Jim Prime wrote *Ted Williams: A Tribute*. That was so much fun, he hasn't stopped since, now having written or edited, usually in collaboration with others, more than 60 books, mostly on baseball but also on music and history.

RODGER A. PAYNE is professor and chair of the department of political science at the University of Louisville. He has been a SABR member since 1997 and has long been interested in the business of baseball.

TIM RASK, of Iowa City, Iowa, has been a member of SABR since 1992. He serves as the "Umpire-in-Chief" of the Field of Dreams (Iowa) Regional Chapter. He is the author of *Baseball at Davenport's John O'Donnell Stadium* (Arcadia, 2004) and is a contributing writer to *Edible Iowa* magazine.

LUCA ROSSI is an Industrial Economist living in Bologna, Italy and a baseball fan since the early 80's. A SABR member since 2004, he is a lifelong Cubs fan.

MARK S. STERNMAN serves as Director of Marketing and Communications for MassDevelopment, the quasi-governmental economic-development authority of Massachusetts. He has worked on economic development for twenty years for U.S. Sen. Kerry, U.S. Rep. Meehan, the Greater Boston Chamber of Commerce, and the Massachusetts Taxpayers Foundation. A SABR member since 1990, he wrote about Chicago's three 1915 teams for the 2015 edition of *The National Pastime*. He spends his winters following the Harvard women's hockey team.

JERRY SWENSON has been a long-time SABR member. Jerry was interested in contributing to this book as he enjoys reading and thinking about the value that teams receive in player transactions. The winter meetings were always a source of excitement to him as he was growing up and he was interested to learn more about other baseball activities that took place during the winter meetings. He also desired to make a contribution to the work of the Society for American Baseball Research.

CLAYTON TRUTOR is a PhD candidate in US History at Boston College. He teaches US History in the Global Pathways Program at Northeastern University. His dissertation analyzes the political, economic, and cultural impact of professional sports' arrival in Atlanta during the 1960s and 1970s. He has been a SABR member since 2009. His research for SABR has been focused on the business of baseball and the biography project. He also writes about college football for SB Nation and AACFootballFever.com.

STEVE WEINGARDEN has co-led the SABR Business of Baseball Committee since late 2009. He is an industrial-organizational psychologist. His work involves the fields of learning, talent management, organizational culture, and organizational development. He also has studied the effects of executive leadership and succession on MLB team performance. Previously, Steve worked in the radio industry as a newscaster, producer, and sports talk show host. Once, on the Tiger Stadium infield, Ernie Harwell invited Steve to call him on his home phone number. Steve has received communications awards, published in academic outlets and with professional associations. He learns something new every day.

STEVE WEST's love of math attracted him to baseball when it arrived in his native New Zealand via ESPN in 1990. He married a Texan and moved to Dallas in 1998, and did not miss an Opening Day until 2015, when he volunteered to go on his son's school field trip, and to his dismay the school scheduled it for Opening Day. Steve (a SABR member since 2006), his wife Marian, and son Joshua are diehard Rangers fans, which is one reason why Steve is now editor of a BioProject book on the 1972 Texas Rangers.

ROBERT K. WHELAN is retired as a professor of Public Affairs at the University of Texas-Dallas. He has co-authored two book chapters on baseball and economic development, among many publications. He is a lifelong fan of the New York and San Francisco Giants.

A lifelong Pirates fan, **GREGORY H. WOLF** was born in Pittsburgh, but now resides in the Chicagoland area with his wife, Margaret, and daughter, Gabriela. A Professor of German Studies and holder of the Dennis and Jean Bauman Endowed Chair in the Humanities at North Central College in Naperville, Illinois, he edited the following SABR books: *Thar's Joy in Braveland. The 1957 Milwaukee Braves* (2014), *Winning on the North Side: The 1929 Chicago Cubs* (2015), and *A Pennant for the Twins Cities: The 1965 Minnesota Twins* (2015). He is currently working on a project about the Houston Astrodome and co-editing a book with Bill Nowlin on the 1979 Pittsburgh Pirates.

SABR BioProject Team Books

In 2002, the Society for American Baseball Research launched an effort to write and publish biographies of every player, manager, and individual who has made a contribution to baseball. Over the past decade, the BioProject Committee has produced over 6,000 biographical articles. Many have been part of efforts to create theme- or team-oriented books, spearheaded by chapters or other committees of SABR.

THE 1986 BOSTON RED SOX: THERE WAS MORE THAN GAME SIX
One of a two-book series on the rivals that met in the 1986 World Series, the Boston Red Sox and the New York Mets, including biographies of every player, coach, broadcaster, and other important figures in the top organizations in baseball that year. .
Edited by Leslie Heaphy and Bill Nowlin
$19.95 paperback (ISBN 978-1-943816-19-4)
$9.99 ebook (ISBN 978-1-943816-18-7)
8.5"X11", 420 pages, over 200 photos

THE 1986 NEW YORK METS: THERE WAS MORE THAN GAME SIX
The other book in the "rivalry" set from the 1986 World Series. This book re-tells the story of that year's classic World Series and this is the story of each of the players, coaches, managers, and broadcasters, their lives in baseball and the way the 1986 season fit into their lives.
Edited by Leslie Heaphy and Bill Nowlin
$19.95 paperback (ISBN 978-1-943816-13-2)
$9.99 ebook (ISBN 978-1-943816-12-5)
8.5"X11", 392 pages, over 100 photos

SCANDAL ON THE SOUTH SIDE: THE 1919 CHICAGO WHITE SOX
The Black Sox Scandal isn't the only story worth telling about the 1919 Chicago White Sox. The team roster included three future Hall of Famers, a 20-year-old spitballer who would win 300 games in the minors, and even a batboy who later became a celebrity with the "Murderers' Row" New York Yankees. All of their stories are included in Scandal on the South Side with a timeline of the 1919 season.
Edited by Jacob Pomrenke
$19.95 paperback (ISBN 978-1-933599-95-3)
$9.99 ebook (ISBN 978-1-933599-94-6)
8.5"x11", 324 pages, 55 historic photos

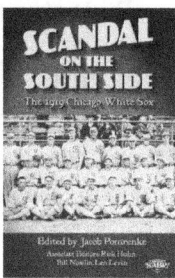

WINNING ON THE NORTH SIDE: THE 1929 CHICAGO CUBS
Celebrate the 1929 Chicago Cubs, one of the most exciting teams in baseball history. Future Hall of Famers Hack Wilson, '29 NL MVP Rogers Hornsby, and Kiki Cuyler, along with Riggs Stephenson formed one of the most potent quartets in baseball history. The magical season came to an ignominious end in the World Series and helped craft the future "lovable loser" image of the team.
Edited by Gregory H. Wolf
$19.95 paperback (ISBN 978-1-933599-89-2)
$9.99 ebook (ISBN 978-1-933599-88-5)
8.5"x11", 314 pages, 59 photos

DETROIT THE UNCONQUERABLE: THE 1935 WORLD CHAMPION TIGERS
Biographies of every player, coach, and broadcaster involved with the 1935 World Champion Detroit Tigers baseball team, written by members of the Society for American Baseball Research. Also includes a season in review and other articles about the 1935 team. Hank Greenberg, Mickey Cochrane, Charlie Gehringer, Schoolboy Rowe, and more.
Edited by Scott Ferkovich
$19.95 paperback (ISBN 9978-1-933599-78-6)
$9.99 ebook (ISBN 978-1-933599-79-3)
8.5"X11", 230 pages, 52 photos

THE TEAM THAT TIME WON'T FORGET: THE 1951 NEW YORK GIANTS
Because of Bobby Thomson's dramatic "Shot Heard 'Round the World" in the bottom of the ninth of the decisive playoff game against the Brooklyn Dodgers, the team will forever be in baseball public's consciousness. Includes a foreword by Giants outfielder Monte Irvin.
Edited by Bill Nowlin and C. Paul Rogers III
$19.95 paperback (ISBN 978-1-933599-99-1)
$9.99 ebook (ISBN 978-1-933599-98-4)
8.5"X11", 282 pages, 47 photos

A PENNANT FOR THE TWIN CITIES: THE 1965 MINNESOTA TWINS
This volume celebrates the 1965 Minnesota Twins, who captured the American League pennant in just their fifth season in the Twin Cities. Led by an All-Star cast, from Harmon Killebrew, Tony Oliva, Zoilo Versalles, and Mudcat Grant to Bob Allison, Jim Kaat, Earl Battey, and Jim Perry, the Twins won 102 games, but bowed to the Los Angeles Dodgers and Sandy Koufax in Game Seven
Edited by Gregory H. Wolf
$19.95 paperback (ISBN 978-1-943816-09-5)
$9.99 ebook (ISBN 978-1-943816-08-8)
8.5"X11", 405 pages, over 80 photos

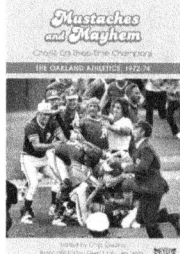

MUSTACHES AND MAYHEM: CHARLIE O'S THREE TIME CHAMPIONS: THE OAKLAND ATHLETICS: 1972-74
The Oakland Athletics captured major league baseball's crown each year from 1972 through 1974. Led by future Hall of Famers Reggie Jackson, Catfish Hunter and Rollie Fingers, the Athletics were a largely homegrown group who came of age together. Biographies of every player, coach, manager, and broadcaster (and mascot) from 1972 through 1974 are included, along with season recaps.
Edited by Chip Greene
$29.95 paperback (ISBN 978-1-943816-07-1)
$9.99 ebook (ISBN 978-1-943816-06-4)
8.5"X11", 600 pages, almost 100 photos

SABR Members can purchase each book at a significant discount (often 50% off) and receive the ebook edtions free as a member benefit. Each book is available in a trade paperback edition as well as ebooks suitable for reading on a home computer or Nook, Kindle, or iPad/tablet.
To learn more about becoming a member of SABR, visit the website: sabr.org/join

The SABR Digital Library

The Society for American Baseball Research, the top baseball research organization in the world, disseminates some of the best in baseball history, analysis, and biography through our publishing programs. The SABR Digital Library contains a mix of books old and new, and focuses on a tandem program of paperback and ebook publication, making these materials widely available for both on digital devices and as traditional printed books.

Greatest Games Books

TIGERS BY THE TALE:
GREAT GAMES AT MICHIGAN AND TRUMBULL
For over 100 years, Michigan and Trumbull was the scene of some of the most exciting baseball ever. This book portrays 50 classic games at the corner, spanning the earliest days of Bennett Park until Tiger Stadium's final closing act. From Ty Cobb to Mickey Cochrane, Hank Greenberg to Al Kaline, and Willie Horton to Alan Trammell.
Edited by Scott Ferkovich
$12.95 paperback (ISBN 978-1-943816-21-7)
$6.99 ebook (ISBN 978-1-943816-20-0)
8.5"x11", 160 pages, 22 photos

FROM THE BRAVES TO THE BREWERS: GREAT GAMES AND HISTORY AT MILWAUKEE'S COUNTY STADIUM
The National Pastime provides in-depth articles focused on the geographic region where the national SABR convention is taking place annually. The SABR 45 convention took place in Chicago, and here are 45 articles on baseball in and around the bat-and-ball crazed Windy City: 25 that appeared in the souvenir book of the convention plus another 20 articles available in ebook only.
Edited by Gregory H. Wolf
$19.95 paperback (ISBN 978-1-943816-23-1)
$9.99 ebook (ISBN 978-1-943816-22-4)
8.5"X11", 290 pages, 58 photos

BRAVES FIELD:
MEMORABLE MOMENTS AT BOSTON'S LOST DIAMOND
From its opening on August 18, 1915, to the sudden departure of the Boston Braves to Milwaukee before the 1953 baseball season, Braves Field was home to Boston's National League baseball club and also hosted many other events: from NFL football to championship boxing. The most memorable moments to occur in Braves Field history are portrayed here.
Edited by Bill Nowlin and Bob Brady
$19.95 paperback (ISBN 978-1-933599-93-9)
$9.99 ebook (ISBN 978-1-933599-92-2)
8.5"X11", 282 pages, 182 photos

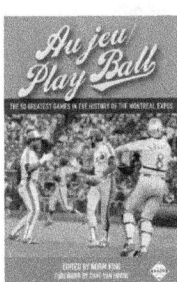

AU JEU/PLAY BALL: THE 50 GREATEST GAMES IN THE HISTORY OF THE MONTREAL EXPOS
The 50 greatest games in Montreal Expos history. The games described here recount the exploits of the many great players who wore Expos uniforms over the years—Bill Stoneman, Gary Carter, Andre Dawson, Steve Rogers, Pedro Martinez, from the earliest days of the franchise, to the glory years of 1979-1981, the what-might-have-been years of the early 1990s, and the sad, final days.and others.
Edited by Norm King
$12.95 paperback (ISBN 978-1-943816-15-6)
$5.99 ebook (ISBN978-1-943816-14-9)
8.5"x11", 162 pages, 50 photos

Original SABR Research

CALLING THE GAME:
BASEBALL BROADCASTING FROM 1920 TO THE PRESENT
An exhaustive, meticulously researched history of bringing the national pastime out of the ballparks and into living rooms via the airwaves. Every play-by-play announcer, color commentator, and ex-ballplayer, every broadcast deal, radio station, and TV network. Plus a foreword by "Voice of the Chicago Cubs" Pat Hughes, and an afterword by Jacques Doucet, the "Voice of the Montreal Expos" 1972-2004.
by Stuart Shea
$24.95 paperback (ISBN 978-1-933599-40-3)
$9.99 ebook (ISBN 978-1-933599-41-0)
7"X10", 712 pages, 40 photos

BioProject Books

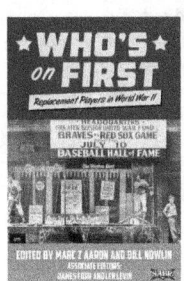

WHO'S ON FIRST:
REPLACEMENT PLAYERS IN WORLD WAR II
During World War II, 533 players made the major league debuts. More than 60% of the players in the 1941 Opening Day lineups departed for the service and were replaced by first-times and oldsters. Hod Lisenbee was 46. POW Bert Shepard had an artificial leg, and Pete Gray had only one arm. The 1944 St. Louis Browns had 13 players classified 4-F. These are their stories.
Edited by Marc Z Aaron and Bill Nowlin
$19.95 paperback (ISBN 978-1-933599-91-5)
$9.99 ebook (ISBN 978-1-933599-90-8)
8.5"X11", 422 pages, 67 photos

VAN LINGLE MUNGO:
THE MAN, THE SONG, THE PLAYERS
40 baseball players with intriguing names have been named in renditions of Dave Frishberg's classic 1969 song, Van Lingle Mungo. This book presents biographies of all 40 players and additional information about one of the greatest baseball novelty songs of all time.
Edited by Bill Nowlin
$19.95 paperback (ISBN 978-1-933599-76-2)
$9.99 ebook (ISBN 978-1-933599-77-9)
8.5"X11", 278 pages, 46 photos

NUCLEAR POWERED BASEBALL
Nuclear Powered Baseball tells the stories of each player—past and present—featured in the classic Simpsons episode "Homer at the Bat." Wade Boggs, Ken Griffey Jr., Ozzie Smith, Nap Lajoie, Don Mattingly, and many more. We've also included a few very entertaining takes on the now-famous episode from prominent baseball writers Jonah Keri, Joe Posnanski, Erik Malinowski, and Bradley Woodrum.
Edited by Emily Hawks and Bill Nowlin
$19.95 paperback (ISBN 978-1-943816-11-8)
$9.99 ebook (ISBN 978-1-943816-10-1)
8.5"X11", 250 pages

SABR Members can purchase each book at a significant discount (often 50% off) and receive the ebook edtions free as a member benefit. Each book is available in a trade paperback edition as well as ebooks suitable for reading on a home computer or Nook, Kindle, or iPad/tablet.
To learn more about becoming a member of SABR, visit the website: sabr.org/join

SABR BioProject Books

In 2002, the Society for American Baseball Research launched an effort to write and publish biographies of every player, manager, and individual who has made a contribution to baseball. Over the past decade, the BioProject Committee has produced over 2,200 biographical articles. Many have been part of efforts to create theme- or team-oriented books, spearheaded by chapters or other committees of SABR.

THE YEAR OF THE BLUE SNOW:
THE 1964 PHILADELPHIA PHILLIES
Catcher Gus Triandos dubbed the Philadelphia Phillies' 1964 season "the year of the blue snow," a rare thing that happens once in a great while. This book sheds light on lingering questions about the 1964 season—but any book about a team is really about the players. This work offers life stories of all the players and others (managers, coaches, owners, and broadcasters) associated with this star-crossed team, as well as essays of analysis and history.
Edited by Mel Marmer and Bill Nowlin
$19.95 paperback (ISBN 978-1-933599-51-9)
$9.99 ebook (ISBN 978-1-933599-52-6)
8.5"X11", 356 PAGES, over 70 photos

THE MIRACLE BRAVES OF 1914
BOSTON'S ORIGINAL WORST-TO-FIRST CHAMPIONS
Long before the Red Sox "Impossible Dream" season, Boston's now nearly forgotten "other" team, the 1914 Boston Braves, performed a baseball "miracle" that resounds to this very day. The "Miracle Braves" were Boston's first "worst-to-first" winners of the World Series. Refusing to throw in the towel at the midseason mark, George Stallings engineered a remarkable second-half climb in the standings all the way to first place.
Edited by Bill Nowlin
$19.95 paperback (ISBN 978-1-933599-69-4)
$9.99 ebook (ISBN 978-1-933599-70-0)
8.5"X11", 392 PAGES, over 100 photos

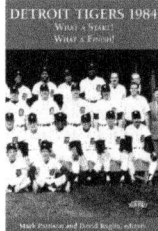

DETROIT TIGERS 1984:
WHAT A START! WHAT A FINISH!
The 1984 Detroit tigers roared out of the gate, winning their first nine games of the season and compiling an eye-popping 35-5 record after the campaign's first 40 games—still the best start ever for any team in major league history. This book brings together biographical profiles of every Tiger from that magical season, plus those of field management, top executives, the broadcasters—even venerable Tiger Stadium and the city itself.
Edited by Mark Pattison and David Raglin
$19.95 paperback (ISBN 978-1-933599-44-1)
$9.99 ebook (ISBN 978-1-933599-45-8)
8.5"x11", 250 pages (Over 230,000 words!)

THAR'S JOY IN BRAVELAND!
THE 1957 MILWAUKEE BRAVES
Few teams in baseball history have captured the hearts of their fans like the Milwaukee Braves of the 1950S. During the Braves' 13-year tenure in Milwaukee (1953-1965), they had a winning record every season, won two consecutive NL pennants (1957 and 1958), lost two more in the final week of the season (1956 and 1959), and set big-league attendance records along the way.
Edited by Gregory H. Wolf
$19.95 paperback (ISBN 978-1-933599-71-7)
$9.99 ebook (ISBN 978-1-933599-72-4)
8.5"x11", 330 pages, over 60 photos

SWEET '60: THE 1960 PITTSBURGH PIRATES
A portrait of the 1960 team which pulled off one of the biggest upsets of the last 60 years. When Bill Mazeroski's home run left the park to win in Game Seven of the World Series, beating the New York Yankees, David had toppled Goliath. It was a blow that awakened a generation, one that millions of people saw on television, one of TV's first iconic World Series moments.
Edited by Clifton Blue Parker and Bill Nowlin
$19.95 paperback (ISBN 978-1-933599-48-9)
$9.99 ebook (ISBN 978-1-933599-49-6)
8.5"X11", 340 pages, 75 photos

NEW CENTURY, NEW TEAM:
THE 1901 BOSTON AMERICANS
The team now known as the Boston Red Sox played its first season in 1901. Boston had a well-established National League team, but the American League went head-to-head with the N.L. in Chicago, Philadelphia, and Boston. Chicago won the American League pennant and Boston finished second, only four games behind.
Edited by Bill Nowlin
$19.95 paperback (ISBN 978-1-933599-58-8)
$9.99 ebook (ISBN 978-1-933599-59-5)
8.5"X11", 268 pages, over 125 photos

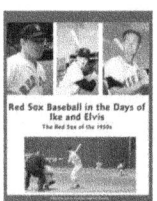

RED SOX BASEBALL IN THE DAYS OF IKE AND ELVIS: THE RED SOX OF THE 1950S
Although the Red Sox spent most of the 1950s far out of contention, the team was filled with fascinating players who captured the heart of their fans. In *Red Sox Baseball*, members of SABR present 46 biographies on players such as Ted Williams and Pumpsie Green as well as season-by-season recaps.
Edited by Mark Armour and Bill Nowlin
$19.95 paperback (ISBN 978-1-933599-24-3)
$9.99 ebook (ISBN 978-1-933599-34-2)
8.5"X11", 372 PAGES, over 100 photos

CAN HE PLAY?
A LOOK AT BASEBALL SCOUTS AND THEIR PROFESSION
They dig through tons of coal to find a single diamond. Here in the world of scouts, we meet the "King of Weeds," a Ph.D. we call "Baseball's Renaissance Man," a husband-and-wife team, pioneering Latin scouts, and a Japanese-American interned during World War II who became a successful scout—and many, many more.
Edited by Jim Sandoval and Bill Nowlin
$19.95 paperback (ISBN 978-1-933599-23-6)
$9.99 ebook (ISBN 978-1-933599-25-0)
8.5"X11", 200 PAGES, over 100 photos

SABR Members can purchase each book at a significant discount (often 50% off) and receive the ebook editions free as a member benefit. Each book is available in a trade paperback edition as well as ebooks suitable for reading on a home computer or Nook, Kindle, or iPad/tablet.
To learn more about becoming a member of SABR, visit the website: sabr.org/join

THE SABR DIGITAL LIBRARY

The Society for American Baseball Research, the top baseball research organization in the world, disseminates some of the best in baseball history, analysis, and biography through our publishing programs. The SABR Digital Library contains a mix of books old and new, and focuses on a tandem program of paperback and ebook publication, making these materials widely available for both on digital devices and as traditional printed books.

CLASSIC REPRINTS

BASE-BALL: HOW TO BECOME A PLAYER
by John Montgomery Ward
John Montgomery Ward (1860-1925) tossed the second perfect game in major league history and later became the game's best shortstop and a great, inventive manager. His classic handbook on baseball skills and strategy was published in 1888. Illustrated with woodcuts, the book is divided into chapters for each position on the field as well as chapters on the origin of the game, theory and strategy, training, base-running, and batting.
$4.99 ebook (ISBN 978-1-933599-47-2)
$9.95 paperback (ISBN 978-0910137539)
156 PAGES, 4.5"X7" replica edition

BATTING by F. C. Lane
First published in 1925, *Batting* collects the wisdom and insights of over 250 hitters and baseball figures. Lane interviewed extensively and compiled tips and advice on everything from batting stances to beanballs. Legendary baseball figures such as Ty Cobb, Casey Stengel, Cy Young, Walter Johnson, Rogers Hornsby, and Babe Ruth reveal the secrets of such integral and interesting parts of the game as how to choose a bat, the ways to beat a slump, and how to outguess the pitcher.
$14.95 paperback (ISBN 978-0-910137-86-7)
$7.99 ebook (ISBN 978-1-933599-46-5)
240 PAGES, 5"X7"

RUN, RABBIT, RUN
by Walter "Rabbit" Maranville
"Rabbit" Maranville was the Joe Garagiola of Grandpa's day, the baseball comedian of the times. In a twenty-four-year career that began in 1912, Rabbit found a lot of funny situations to laugh at, and no wonder: he caused most of them! The book also includes an introduction by the late Harold Seymour and a historical account of Maranville's life and Hall-of-Fame career by Bob Carroll.
$9.95 paperback (ISBN 978-1-933599-26-7)
$5.99 ebook (ISBN 978-1-933599-27-4)
100 PAGES, 5.5"X8.5", 15 rare photos

MEMORIES OF A BALLPLAYER
by Bill Werber and C. Paul Rogers III
Bill Werber's claim to fame is unique: he was the last living person to have a direct connection to the 1927 Yankees, "Murderers' Row," a team hailed by many as the best of all time. Rich in anecdotes and humor, Memories of a Ballplayer is a clear-eyed memoir of the world of big-league baseball in the 1930s. Werber played with or against some of the most productive hitters of all time, including Babe Ruth, Ted Williams, Lou Gehrig, and Joe DiMaggio.
$14.95 paperback (ISNB 978-0-910137-84-3)
$6.99 ebook (ISBN 978-1-933599-47-2)
250 PAGES, 6"X9"

ORIGINAL SABR RESEARCH

INVENTING BASEBALL: THE 100 GREATEST GAMES OF THE NINETEENTH CENTURY
SABR's Nineteenth Century Committee brings to life the greatest games from the game's early years. From the "prisoner of war" game that took place among captive Union soldiers during the Civil War (immortalized in a famous lithograph), to the first intercollegiate game (Amherst versus Williams), to the first professional no-hitter, the games in this volume span 1833–1900 and detail the athletic exploits of such players as Cap Anson, Moses "Fleetwood" Walker, Charlie Comiskey, and Mike "King" Kelly.
Edited by Bill Felber
$19.95 paperback (ISBN 978-1-933599-42-7)
$9.99 ebook (ISBN 978-1-933599-43-4)
302 PAGES, 8"x10", 200 photos

NINETEENTH CENTURY STARS: 2012 EDITION
First published in 1989, *Nineteenth Century Stars* was SABR's initial attempt to capture the stories of baseball players from before 1900. With a collection of 136 fascinating biographies, SABR has re-released *Nineteenth Century Stars* for 2012 with revised statistics and new form. The 2012 version also includes a preface by **John Thorn**.
Edited by Robert L. Tiemann and Mark Rucker
$19.95 paperback (ISBN 978-1-933599-28-1)
$9.99 ebook (ISBN 978-1-933599-29-8)
300 PAGES, 6"X9"

GREAT HITTING PITCHERS
Published in 1979, *Great Hitting Pitchers* was one of SABR's early publications. Edited by SABR founder Bob Davids, the book compiles stories and records about pitchers excelling in the batter's box. Newly updated in 2012 by Mike Cook, *Great Hitting Pitchers* contain tables including data from 1979-2011, corrections to reflect recent records, and a new chapter on recent new members in the club of "great hitting pitchers" like Tom Glavine and Mike Hampton.
Edited by L. Robert Davids
$9.95 paperback (ISBN 978-1-933599-30-4)
$5.99 ebook (ISBN 978-1-933599-31-1)
102 PAGES, 5.5"x8.5"

THE FENWAY PROJECT
Sixty-four SABR members—avid fans, historians, statisticians, and game enthusiasts—recorded their experiences of a single game. Some wrote from inside the Green Monster's manual scoreboard, the Braves clubhouse, or the broadcast booth, while others took in the essence of Fenway from the grandstand or bleachers. The result is a fascinating look at the charms and challenges of Fenway Park, and the allure of being a baseball fan.
Edited by Bill Nowlin and Cecilia Tan
$9.99 ebook (ISBN 978-1-933599-50-2)
175 pages, 100 photos

SABR Members can purchase each book at a significant discount (often 50% off) and receive the ebook editions free as a member benefit. Each book is available in a trade paperback edition as well as ebooks suitable for reading on a home computer or Nook, Kindle, or iPad/tablet.
To learn more about becoming a member of SABR, visit the website: sabr.org/join

Society for American Baseball Research
Cronkite School at ASU
555 N. Central Ave. #416, Phoenix, AZ 85004
602.496.1460 (phone)
SABR.org

Become a SABR member today!

If you're interested in baseball — writing about it, reading about it, talking about it — there's a place for you in the Society for American Baseball Research. Our members include everyone from academics to professional sportswriters to amateur historians and statisticians to students and casual fans who enjoy reading about baseball and occasionally gathering with other members to talk baseball. What unites all SABR members is an interest in the game and joy in learning more about it.

SABR membership is open to any baseball fan; we offer 1-year and 3-year memberships. Here's a list of some of the key benefits you'll receive as a SABR member:

- Receive two editions (spring and fall) of the *Baseball Research Journal*, our flagship publication
- Receive expanded e-book edition of *The National Pastime*, our annual convention journal
- 8-10 new e-books published by the SABR Digital Library, all FREE to members
- "This Week in SABR" e-newsletter, sent to members every Friday
- Join dozens of research committees, from Statistical Analysis to Women in Baseball.
- Join one of 70+ regional chapters in the U.S., Canada, Latin America, and abroad
- Participate in online discussion groups
- Ask and answer baseball research questions on the SABR-L e-mail listserv
- Complete archives of *The Sporting News* dating back to 1886 and other research resources
- Promote your research in "This Week in SABR"
- Diamond Dollars Case Competition
- Yoseloff Scholarships
- Discounts on SABR national conferences, including the SABR National Convention, the SABR Analytics Conference, Jerry Malloy Negro League Conference, Frederick Ivor-Campbell 19th Century Conference, and the Arizona Fall League Experience
- Publish your research in peer-reviewed SABR journals
- Collaborate with SABR researchers and experts
- Contribute to Baseball Biography Project or the SABR Games Project
- List your new book in the SABR Bookshelf
- Lead a SABR research committee or chapter
- Networking opportunities at SABR Analytics Conference
- Meet baseball authors and historians at SABR events and chapter meetings
- 50% discounts on paperback versions of SABR e-books
- Discounts with other partners in the baseball community
- SABR research awards

We hope you'll join the most passionate international community of baseball fans at SABR! Check us out online at SABR.org/join.

SABR MEMBERSHIP FORM

	Annual	3-year	Senior	3-yr Sr.	Under 30
Standard:	❏ $65	❏ $175	❏ $45	❏ $129	❏ $45
Canada/Mexico:	❏ $75	❏ $205	❏ $55	❏ $159	❏ $55
Overseas:	❏ $84	❏ $232	❏ $64	❏ $186	❏ $55

(International members wishing to be mailed the Baseball Research Journal should add $10/yr for Canada/Mexico or $19/yr for overseas locations.)

Senior = 65 or older before Dec. 31 of the current year

Participate in Our Donor Program!
Support the preservation of baseball research. Designate your gift toward:
❏ General Fund ❏ Endowment Fund ❏ Research Resources ❏ _____
❏ I want to maximize the impact of my gift; do not send any donor premiums
❏ I would like this gift to remain anonymous.

Note: Any donation not designated will be placed in the General Fund.
SABR is a 501 (c) (3) not-for-profit organization & donations are tax-deductible to the extent allowed by law.

Name _____

E-mail* _____

Address _____

City _____ ST ____ ZIP _____

Phone _____ Birthday _____

* Your e-mail address on file ensures you will receive the most recent SABR news.

Dues $_____
Donation $_____
Amount Enclosed $_____

Do you work for a matching grant corporation? Call (602) 496-1460 for details.

If you wish to pay by credit card, please contact the SABR office at (602) 496-1460 or sign up securely online at SABR.org/join. We accept Visa, Mastercard & Discover.

Do you wish to receive the *Baseball Research Journal* electronically? ❏ Yes ❏ No
Our e-books are available in PDF, Kindle, or EPUB (iBooks, iPad, Nook) formats.

Mail to: SABR, Cronkite School at ASU, 555 N. Central Ave. #416, Phoenix, AZ 85004